SUMMER, 2016

Functional Clothing Design

From Sportswear to Spacesuits

Functional Clothing Design

From Sportswear to Spacesuits

SUSAN M. WATKINS

LUCY E. DUNNE

Fairchild Books

an Imprint of Bloomsbury Publishing, Inc.

BLOOMSBURY

NEW YORK · LONDON · NEW DELHI · SYDNEY

Fairchild Books

An imprint of Bloomsbury Publishing Inc

1385 Broadway	50 Bedford Square
New York	London
NY 10018	WC1B 3DP
USA	UK

www.bloomsbury.com

FAIRCHILD BOOKS, BLOOMSBURY and the Diana logo
are trademarks of Bloomsbury Publishing Plc

First edition published in hardback and paperback by Iowa State University Press (February 1984)
Second edition published in hardback and paperback by Iowa State University Press (September 1995)
This edition published by Fairchild Books, an imprint of Bloomsbury Publishing, Inc. 2015

Library of Congress Cataloging-in-Publication Data
Watkins, Susan M., 1943-
[Clothing]
Functional clothing design : from sportswear to spacesuits / Susan M. Watkins, Lucy E. Dunne.
pages cm
Revised edition of: Clothing.
Includes bibliographical references and index.
ISBN 978-0-85785-467-4 (alk. paper)
1. Clothing and dress. 2. Fashion design. I. Dunne, Lucy E. II. Title.
TT649.W37 2015
746.9'2–dc23
2014027461

ISBN: 9780857854674

Typeset by Lachina
Cover Design Rawshock Design
Cover Art Courtesy of NASA
Printed and bound in the United States of America

CONTENTS

EXTENDED CONTENTS

PREFACE

This book began as the third edition of *Clothing: The Portable Environment* but has evolved into something much more than that. A colleague once described his attempt to create a second edition of a text as "less like adding a tier of seats at the top of a stadium than it was like raising the entire stadium and building a new base under it." Our experience has been something like that. The base has changed in terms of the expansion of the field, the projected audience, and our approach to organizing the subject matter. The original text, published by Iowa State University Press in 1984, with a second edition in 1995, was aimed at clothing design students in a university setting. We hope that this edition will be useful to a much broader group, including those in a variety of clothing-related fields and industries.

We are deeply indebted to Albert Podell for his generosity in providing a grant to fund new artwork for this text through the Cornell Association of Professors Emeriti's Podell Research and Scholarship Grant Program. The new art has significantly enriched the text and will greatly enhance understanding for many future students and those employed in protective clothing industries. We are also grateful to the University of Minnesota Imagine Fund for providing funds to support travel, graphic editing by Katie Mueller, and illustrations by Mary Ellen Berglund.

We are also indebted to students in the Fall 2013 directed study group on functional clothing design at the University of Minnesota who reviewed drafts of the text and made many excellent suggestions for improvements: Mary Ellen Berglund, Crystal Compton, Kira Erickson, Karen Fiegen, Guido Gioberto, Linsey Gordon, Harini Ramaswamy, and Jordyn Reich.

We are especially grateful to Suzanne Reeps, US Navy Clothing and Textile Research, and Carol J. Fitzgerald, US Department of the Army, for their extensive review of the entire manuscript. We are also very grateful to Stephanie Tew for her insight and suggestions for chemical/biological protective clothing and for her review of Chapter 7. Many other people contributed helpful suggestions and reviewed sections of the manuscript. We would especially like to thank Susan and William McKinney, Mark Mordecai at Globe Firesuits, Dale Strauf, Ben Rich, the Snyder family and the Presque Isle Yacht Club, Dr. Claire Fraser, and Mikko Malmivaara.

We are extremely happy that Dr. Susan P. Ashdown at Cornell University was again willing to contribute her wealth of knowledge about sizing and fit to Chapter 2.

The publisher would also like to thank the reviewers for their insights and guidance: Debbie Christel, West Virginia University; Lisa Hayes, Drexel University; Su Hwang, Texas Tech University; Karen L. LaBat, University of Minnesota; Ameersing Luximon, Hong Kong Polytechnic University; Jane McCann, University of Wales; Rachel Obbard, Dartmouth University; Huiju Park, Cornell University; Kelly Reddy-Best, San Francisco State; Sandra Tullio-Pow, Ryerson

University; and Paola Zellner, Virginia Tech University.

This text begins with three chapters of foundation material with which some members of our interdisciplinary audience may have extensive background. We believe that design methodology, mobility, and textiles are critical areas for a designer to understand in order to design functional clothing. However, we recognize that those who have extensive background in textile science, for example, may not want or need to study the information in Chapter 3. At the same time, individuals with no background in this area may need a primer on this topic before attempting to read the material in succeeding chapters. Thus, we have pulled basic information about the first three topics out of the rest of the chapters so it could be studied as needed. We have also created a glossary for all chapters, with glossary words in **boldface** at the time of first use, so that there is a reference for terminology in succeeding chapters. In addition, we created sidebars in each of the chapters that pull specific concepts out of the main text. Some of these expand on specialized areas of knowledge, such as basic physics principles, and some highlight innovative designs. Others show the critical interaction between anatomy and physiology and clothing design or demonstrate ways design methodology can be applied.

In the years since the last edition was published, there have been huge strides made in the development of technology. The addition of a coauthor whose field of expertise is wearable technology has added an even greater technology dimension to the text. Both old and new technology are represented by the designs presented throughout the text. Some of the designs illustrated are no longer produced but are included because they provide seeds of a design idea that can be used as inspiration for new designs. Even when the technology and materials may be old, it is often the approach to a problem that leads a designer to new ideas.

Both authors are extremely grateful to colleagues and students past and present, who have enriched our lives and added greatly to our knowledge in this field. As always, we are grateful to have had the support and good humor (and the comic relief!) of our families and friends as we worked on this text.

ABOUT THE ILLUSTRATIONS

Heidi Specht has provided the vast majority of the illustrations for this text. Many of these were produced for the 1984 edition of *Clothing: The Portable Environment*, when she was an undergraduate student at Cornell University. She contributed additional illustrations to a 1995 edition of that text, and we are grateful to her for continuing to create art for this text while in a demanding position as Marketing Director for West Virginia Healthcare.

Frances Fawcett is a scientific illustrator and painter. We are delighted with her venture into the field of functional clothing. She contributed Figures 2.1, 2.4, 2.6, Anatomy and Design 2.1 Figure A, 4.11, 4.20, 5.1, Anatomy and Design 5.1 Figure A, 8.5, 8.9, 8.15, and 9.28.

Mary Ellen Berglund was an undergraduate student at the University of Minnesota taking a course in functional clothing as the text was being developed. She contributed Figures 1.12, 2.23, 2.26, 4.7, 4.8, 4.12, 4.16, Anatomy and Design 9.1 Figures A–E, 9.24, 9.38, 9.39, and 9.46.

Globe Firesuits® permitted us to use their illustrations for Case Study 5.1 Figures A–H.

Except for Figure 1.2 and 1.12, the authors created all of the figures for Chapter 1. Dr. Dunne created all of the illustrations featured in Chapter 4 with the exception of those listed above and Figures 4.19 and 4.21 (drawn by Heidi Specht). She also created Figures 2.2, 2.48, Energy Basics 3.1 Figure A, 3.2, 3.3, 3.11, 3.18, 3.20, 3.24, 6.1, 6.17, 7.36, 8.1, 8.3, and 9.37.

INTRODUCTION

This is a book about how and why clothing works. Its purpose is to introduce some new ways to look at the human body, the environment, and clothing and to explore the relationships among them. Clothing can form a barrier between the body and the environment, it can mediate the interaction between the body and the environment, and it can increase the ability of the body to function in a variety of environments. Although all clothing is functional, the functional clothing design approach focuses on what clothing does before considering how it looks.

Functional clothing design is, above all, an interdisciplinary endeavor. Renbourn's description of what he called "the science of clothing" could also serve as an excellent description of the field of functional clothing:

. . . an integration of the disciplines of the textiles and materials technologist, the textiles and materials biophysicist, the clothing physiologist and hygienist, the master tailor, the clothing and footwear designer, and the fashion student and artist in the widest sense. As such clothing science represents an important aspect of man's cultural activity; a link between the technical and biological sciences and the social humanities.

(Renbourn and Rees 1972, 249)

The theories on which this book is based are built on physics, physiology, and other scientific disciplines, but it contains no mathematical formulas. Designers and others seeking clothing solutions to problems in many fields should find in it a common language linking a number of disciplines through which they can explore both problems and solutions. Engineers and scientists will find an accessible introduction to the application of science to clothing design.

Many of the items discussed in this work would not traditionally be called clothing. We view clothing as a portable environment, defining it based on just two criteria: that it is attached to or supported by the body and that it moves with it. Thus, since they are based on clothing design principles, body-related products from helmets to watches and body-related environments from space suits to isolation garments can be viewed as part of the province of clothing designers.

The figures on the next few pages illustrate items that represent this definition of clothing as a portable environment. Figure i.1 shows a 1960s vision of future clothing: a floating, automated comfort pod. In the totally encapsulating shroud, a wearer is completely free from stress points, can control the temperature inside and can activate a tension-relieving vibrator. A minicomputer warns the wearer of approaching hazards (including people with whom the wearer would not enjoy interacting!) and floats the body clear of them.

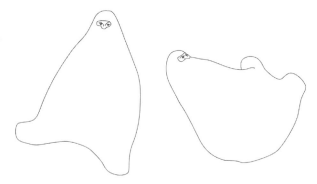

FIGURE I.1 A proposal for a totally encapsulating portable environment. (Based on a design in *Body Covering* 1968: 41)

The tunnel suit, or "pseudopod," shown in Figure i.2 was designed for use in a germ-free isolation ward. This type of garment is used to protect those *outside* the garment rather than the wearer *inside*. This tunnel suit was part of the wall of an isolation chamber for leukemia patients. While wearing it, a nurse or doctor could move into the room and care for a patient without introducing any foreign particles to the chamber.

Are the shroud and tunnel suit clothing, equipment or housing? While the terms *apparel designer, product/equipment designer* and *housing designer* are meant to connote different specialists, the lines between traditional clothing and accessories and other products that are worn often

cannot be clearly drawn. Under the definition of clothing stated above, both of the items illustrated here could be called *functional clothing*.

This text on functional clothing looks at the ways clothing achieves goals such as protecting the body, increasing health and safety, improving a worker's efficiency on the job, or increasing body function. Much of its emphasis is on achieving both protection and portability in a functional clothing item. This becomes increasingly challenging as new technological developments create new hazards and allow the exploration of new frontiers. At the same time, new technological developments, including the many advances in e-textiles and wearable technology, make it possible to create garments never before imagined. They not only protect and preserve normal body function but also make it possible for individuals to accomplish "superhuman" things.

Ultimately, this is a book for people who find clothing—in all its forms—a fascinating subject. The authors hope that those who read it will be inspired to create functional clothing that will meet the challenges of life in the future.

FIGURE I.2 A tunnel suit or pseudopod for use in a germ-free isolation ward. (Design formerly produced by AMSCO American Sterilizer)

1   User-Centered Design

The design of functional clothing ties together science and art. The evidence-based methods and processes of engineering are combined with the creative, intuitive methods and processes of art and fashion. Most important, because all functional clothing is worn by humans, the human user is at the very center of all functional clothing design activities. This chapter will discuss the *process* of design (i.e., the nature of design and the thought processes and methods designers use to develop effective design solutions).

What Is Design?

There are as many definitions of design as there are authors to write about it. Design is used as a noun, verb, or adjective that can be applied to products as diverse as apparel, space vehicles, graphics, architecture, and cities. The wide variation in end products that are the result of design makes it difficult for many people to pinpoint the common elements that bind together the various design professions. Is design artistic or mathematical? Rational or imaginative? Systematic or chaotic? Among the many attempts to define design are the following:

Design is a highly complex and sophisticated skill. It is not a mystical ability given only to those with recondite powers but a skill which, for many, must be learnt and practised rather like the playing of a sport or a musical instrument.

(Lawson 1983, 6)

Design is converting the actual to the preferred. It is a conversation with the materials of a situation.

(Schon 1983, 77)

Design can be defined as the process of creative problem-solving; a process of creative, constructive behavior.

(Koberg and Bagnall 1981, 16)

[Design] ... involves a highly organised mental process capable of manipulating many kinds of information, blending them all into a coherent set of ideas and finally generating some realisation of those ideas.

(Lawson 1983, 6)

Designers need the same skills that are those used by people in other professions to solve problems. In general, however, people who label themselves designers have been trained to trigger more quickly the process that generates creative approaches to solutions and bring them to reality.

A designer must be familiar with both content and process. Many in the design professions believe that a good designer can design anything. To the extent that one can process information in a creative way to generate design solutions, this is true. However, the *content* of the various design professions may be quite different, and this is primarily what creates design specialists. Consider, for example, the materials, scale, and use of products such as apparel and architecture. Even though an apparel designer might generate ideas for an innovative building and an architect might develop an innovative garment on paper, most individuals in these respective fields are not trained to use the materials (soft versus hard); work in the scale (apparel must move on the person; people move within buildings); or provide the functions needed to use the other product. Designers who have trained in one specialty simply have greater facility in moving through the process of product development because they have a stored bank of knowledge about specifics in that field. They are called upon because they can take a project from the request for a solution through idea generation to production of the final product.

One cannot minimize the value of designers who move across to fields with which they have had less experience. Their lack of knowledge of specifics may actually help them to develop exciting new, untried approaches because they have no preconceptions about what cannot be done. In many instances, projects have moved along at a faster pace when both generalist and specialist designers work together. Both generalists and specialists are helped by having a process with which to attack new design problems.

The Design Process

The creative problem-solving (design) process is most easily understood as a sequence of stages or stopovers on a journey to a given destination . . . (it) involves the conscious application of incentives, intentions, decisions, actions and evaluations.

(Koberg and Bagnall 2003, 16)

Designers work out problems in a variety of ways. When they talk about *process*, they generally mean a step-by-step sequence of methods they use to develop design concepts. For many practicing designers, the process they use to solve problems is so much a part of their work style that they would be unable to identify what was taking place or delineate their processes into steps. Many scholars who have studied design have attempted to identify and name the steps in a design process; consequently there are a multitude of systems and sets of terminology.

Many of the activities attributed to typical design processes are divided into a series of alternating periods of "opposite" forms of behavior. Thus, the designer is said to move between two forms of thinking: *divergent* (spreading out to explore a wide range of ideas and information) and *convergent* (narrowing in or focus attention on the most pertinent ideas and concepts). Alternatively, they may be said to move back and forth between decision making that is *explicit* (conscious thinking; based on logic) and decisions that are *intuitive* (feeling; based on instinct). A similar analogy is drawn between so-called *rational* periods of thought and *imaginative* periods that might be identified as creative thinking. (These have sometimes been referred to as *left brain* and *right brain* modes of thinking.) Effective problem solving involves both of these approaches, with designers often shutting down one approach at a time to focus on the other.

Most analysts of design behavior, if asked to pare the design process down to its most essential elements, would focus on a similar set of opposite forms of behavior: analysis and synthesis. Designers alternate between *analysis* (breaking down a problem into its essential elements) and *synthesis* (building up a design concept by linking ideas) to develop effective designs. This does not mean that the design process is one that contains only two steps. Analysis and synthesis may be applied to a single problem many times, until a designer reaches what philosophers call *reflective equilibrium* (i.e., the design solution reaches a balance in the designer's mind between what can be defended by rational means or 'proved' and what feels right).

Regardless of the number of steps in the design process or the names given to them, designers rarely progress through them in a simple sequence. Since each step builds on those that precede it, designers are continually uncovering more information and gaining new insights into problems. Often, during this process, misconceptions are uncovered or new ideas cause a designer to want to return to earlier steps, plug in this new information and rework the process in order to develop an improved design. Koberg and Bagnall (1981) provide a number of views of the ways in which their design process steps can be configured (See Figure 1.1). The process chosen may vary with the designer or may change for each designer due to the nature of the problem being solved.

The following sections of the chapter detail each of the activities in the design process that appear in one form or another, often under different labels, in most designers' versions of how they go about designing. These are the critical tasks that cannot be ignored in the development of effective functional clothing.

CONDUCTING RESEARCH

Men give me credit for some genius. All the genius I have lies in this; when I have a subject in hand, I study it profoundly. Day and night it is before me. My mind becomes pervaded with it. Then the effort which I have made is what people are pleased to call the fruit of genius. It is the fruit of labor and thought.

(Alexander Hamilton)

Genius is 1% inspiration and 99% perspiration.

(Thomas Edison)

These two quotes help dispel a popular misconception about designers—that they simply lie back and wait for inspiration to strike. Most laypeople assume designers are primarily involved in idea generation; however, analysis of the design problem probably occupies the vast majority of an effective designer's efforts. In fact, the research stage of the design process is generally responsible for design inspiration. Good design is often the result of hours, weeks, or even years of disciplined study of factors related to a problem, not just a stroke of brilliant thought. Skilled designers have what might be called *design insight*. This is the unique ability to extract from what is sometimes

FIGURE 1.1 The design process. The design process may (A) proceed in a linear fashion; (B) be continually repeated in a circular fashion; or (C) return at any stage to refine prior steps.

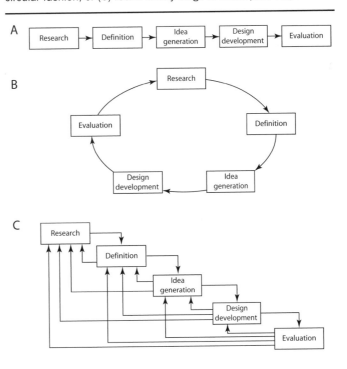

a very large body of information the important details that will lead to an innovative (and sometimes transformative) approach to a solution. Design insight is developed through many years of learning to listen and to uncover critical factors during the research process.

A large part of designers' research is exploratory. Exploratory research helps designers analyze and become familiar with problems. Koberg and Bagnall describe what they call the analysis phase of the design process with such phrases as "gathering facts and opinions" and "dissecting or decomposing the problem" (2003, 47).

When designers begin with thorough research, all subsequent stages of the design process should be more productive. Research exposes designers to the subtle variables of the specific problem at hand so that they can be effectively addressed and manipulated when design solutions are being generated. When design criteria are based on research, they form the basis for a more effective evaluation of the end product in the later stages of the design process.

In the research phase, the designer's objective is to learn as much as possible about (1) the user, (2) the task, and (3) the environment. In addition to these major areas, the designer must also learn as much as possible about peripheral areas that influence the user, task, and environment as well as the life cycle of the design. Peripheral areas include other stakeholders (employers, manufacturers, individuals related to the user), methods and processes of manufacture, sales channels, and many other elements in the ecosystem of the design. Together, these elements and the relationships between them form the problem, or landscape of the design challenge. A deep understanding of the problem is fundamental to designing a good solution.

There are a variety of research methods that can provide analytical tools for designers. The following subsections will outline some of the more prevalent methods used by designers to gather information to inform a design. A designer's skill in administering any research method has a direct impact on the usefulness of the information obtained, so in many cases it is in the best interests of the designer to seek training in these methods outside of the scope of this text.

Literature Review

In any design challenge there is, of course, a tremendous amount to be learned by conducting a literature review of areas related to the design problem. Two of the key reasons for conducting a literature review are to learn the language of the field and to understand and evaluate what other researchers and designers have already done. Understanding and being able to use the language of the field allows a designer to have more productive interviews with specialists and to read the literature of the field to generate a more complete analysis. Literature review should be used to learn more about user needs and to understand hazards in the environment. It also should reveal information about other individuals who have a stake in the outcome of the design efforts for a particular activity.

Markus suggests that designers look at research in terms of the *sources* of information available in a design decision-making situation: the designer's own experience, others' experience, existing research and new research (Lawson 1983, 97). Lawson states that "It is perhaps the inevitable mixing of these sources which contributes to designers' seemingly random behaviour, sometimes apparently intuitively leaping to conclusions whilst at other times making very slow progress." As the research process unfolds, designers learn more and more about where to look and what to look for. They then need to determine if there are unexplored aspects of the design situation that demand original research (i.e., observation, data gathering, etc.) before a problem can be truly understood.

Market Survey

The current marketplace can also be helpful to designers in early stages of the design process. A market review that comprehensively assesses the existing commercially available solutions to the design problem can help the designer to avoid redesigning solutions that already exist and to find trends in product solutions. Product trends, however, are not always evidence of an optimal (or even successful!) solution. Persuasive marketing can sometimes promote a solution that is not actually effective in meeting user needs.

In addition to direct competitor products and solutions, peripheral products and products for users with similar needs can lend insight from a slightly different perspective. For example, a designer researching protection of scuba divers from sharks might also research the market for cut-resistant butcher's gloves. Other products and tools used by the user group can highlight user needs that may not have been met by a wearable solution. For example, researching the features of ski poles can generate ideas about ski glove design.

Insight gained from reviewing literature is often a powerful guide for planning a market survey. Using themes and concepts discovered in literature review, a quantitative, directed survey of the market can be conducted to determine which are the most popular strategies for existing design solutions, and whether or not specific strategies have been explored. Themes exposed in the market survey can also alert a designer to topics that need further literature review. Collecting product examples and classifying similar characteristics can help in identifying areas where new research is needed.

Direct Observation

Direct observation involves going to the site of work or recreation where protective apparel is needed and watching both people and the environment to obtain relevant information. It is an effective way of becoming familiar with the range of problems a designer must resolve and may be used to acquaint designers with specific design situations. The information gathered may then be used to identify specific areas in which data should be collected, for example, on a specific portion of the activity, a specific body part, or a certain cycle of events.

Direct observation requires that the designer use the same types of opposite behaviors discussed earlier in this chapter. An explicit, rational approach applies information gained during the research process to generate *hypotheses* or open questions that are best answered through observation. By having predetermined questions to ask, designers are better prepared to gather useful information. With them, a designer is more likely to uncover useful insights, whether they confirm a preset hypothesis or not.

At the same time, intuition also plays a critical role during observation. It is important to be open to random factors not previously considered in setting up tools for observation. Therefore, in addition to formal methods of collecting data, it is helpful to have recording tools that allow for the noting of random thoughts and observations.

There are many ways to prepare for observation, from identifying the most important areas to observe and important questions to ask to developing data-collection charts, checklists, and tools. The section "Identifying User Needs for Movement" in Chapter 2 will outline some approaches used in observing and recording body movement that may be useful for conducting observations for other areas.

Well-planned direct observation can be an effective method of *task analysis* (i.e., analyzing the activities of the user). In a physical task, this might involve noting what a construction worker does on a particular type of job site (hammering by hand, using a nail gun, using a jackhammer, etc.). For the user of a wearable technology, this might involve noting what the user expects to get from the technology (looking up directions, taking a picture, sending a message, etc.). For some activities, direct observation can be more effective than asking the user because users are not always aware of the things they are actually doing. Task analysis is important to the design process because it may help the designer to analyze which tasks are more important to the activity and which are less important, as well as which tasks are currently causing difficulty.

The nature of a task may help determine the tools that can be used for direct observation. For most sports, a great deal of information useful to the protective equipment designer can be gathered at the site. For activities such as asbestos removal, where law prohibits persons other than the work crew from entering the workplace, films or videotapes of the activity may provide an alternate form of direct observation. Regardless of the tools designers employ to observe users as they participate in their activities, direct observation is a critical part of research.

Participant Observation

One variation of direct observation that provides unique insight for a designer is **participant observation**. When designers physically engage themselves in the activity, additional senses can be brought to bear on observation, and the psychological factors can be personally felt. Playing a sport in protective gear, trying to use equipment while wearing a totally enclosed chemical suit, and trying to operate instruments in bulky gloves or mittens in below freezing conditions all give a designer a different perspective than simply hearing about others doing it. In some instances, designers may participate simply by becoming an accepted part of the environment. For example, designers who develop clothing for individuals in nursing homes cannot suddenly will themselves to be old. They can, however, participate regularly in the activities at the nursing home through volunteer work or by adopting a "grandparent" so that they have a first hand view of the design situation in many aspects of an older person's life. This type of direct observation nets far more useful information for a designer than can be obtained through one or two observation sessions with no direct interaction with users.

There are, of course, limits to participant observation. In police work, for example, where direct observation of the behavior of ballistics vests would be dangerous, this method is not feasible. And although it is possible to restrict mobility to simulate handicaps (see Chapter 2, Design Strategies 2.1) or don thick mittens to simulate the effects of arthritis on manipulating fasteners, it is often not possible to fully replicate the situations of users.

Another danger of participant observation may be initially less obvious. Designers who already participate in the activities of a user group may assume that their experience can be leveraged in the design process. Designer-users sometimes suffer from inflating the relevance of their particular experiences and preferences. It can be too easy to want to design a solution that is ideal for the designer, but perhaps not for others. These individuals have the additional challenge of remaining objective and subjecting their own experience to extra scrutiny in the research process.

Indirect Observation

When direct observation is not feasible, **indirect observation** may provide another useful tool. Where conditions such as those in the Arctic or outer space are not available to a designer, the needs of a design situation can be indirectly observed by examining changes in apparel or equipment that has been used in those environments. Apparel specialists often examine wear patterns on clothing items or test their durability following a specific wear cycle. Heat-damaged yarns from a firefighter's coat or broken yarns in a ballistics vest may be examined under a microscope; or rips in disposable protective coveralls may be measured and catalogued to provide a record of areas where problems with garment design exist.

For impact-protective equipment, injury data can provide a basis for design criteria. It is important to explore existing information both in the literature and in data banks of concerned organizations. Various government agencies, sports research groups, and standards groups have collected injury data for specific activities. Many of their surveys provide information on the number and severity of accidents related to products such as protective equipment and clothing, often with a breakdown of the data by age and sex. Many of these groups, as well as a variety of library bibliographic search services, compile lists of impact and injury studies that have been performed independently throughout the country.

Direct Communication

Design criteria may also be based on information from direct communication techniques. *Interviews* with people involved in an activity will not only yield a wealth of information about the problems involved but can expand a designer's knowledge of the many environmental factors that affect a design situation. These can be helpful in setting up a realistic program of direct observation.

It is important to remember to interview other stakeholders as well as users. (See Design Strategies 1.1.) Subjective information from those being interviewed can reveal the attitudes of participants and others connected with an activity. Manufacturers have a great deal of insight to offer with regard to production costs, time to produce, methods of production, and sales potential (LaBat and Sokolowski 1999). Retailers can offer insight about their customers, customer complaints about designs currently on the market, and potential markets. A designer with a solid understanding of how current products are produced and sold can work more effectively within existing structures as well as be better able to propose viable changes or deviations from current practice.

It should be noted that many researchers believe that interviews do not provide altogether accurate information about behavior since what people *do* and what they *say* they do are often at odds. It is easy for novice interviewers to lead interviewees and thus prejudice their responses. Designers need to become familiar with the literature on interviewing, or they need to team up with social scientists skilled in interview techniques.

Another form of direct communication involves the use of questionnaires. Questionnaires allow a designer to reach a much greater number of individuals in a much shorter period of time. Often, direct observation and selected interviews may be used to frame the questions asked by a questionnaire. Like the structuring of interviews, questionnaire development is not for the inexperienced. A designer should either become familiar with appropriate techniques or team up with a specialist in that area.

Design Strategies 1.1: Who Is the Client?

One factor that is often ignored by designers as they begin the research process is the need to explore not just users but also other people who are associated with a product. Many people are actually "clients" who need to give their stamp of approval to a design for it to even get to the market, let alone be successful. For example, the primary client for football shoulder pads would appear to be a player, who in addition to desiring protection, wants to achieve a certain appearance on the field and wants be comfortable and able to move without restriction. However, for younger players, parents are often the ones who purchase the pads, and they are primarily concerned with cost and injury prevention. In later years, coaches may be the selectors of equipment, and they want maximum player performance and injury prevention. At the college and professional level, equipment managers may be the purchasers, and they add ease of care and cleanability to this list. Trainers and team physicians may dictate what can and cannot be worn by specific players based on the injuries they see, and this can affect future purchases for a team.

In addition to users and buyers, there are often governing boards for sports that have specific standards that an item of protective clothing must meet if it is to be used in an officially sanctioned game. Safety rules and regulations exist for many protective apparel items. Garments such as firefighting apparel, for example, must meet strict federal regulations. Government regulations may force nursing home administrators to mandate that specific garments must be used or must be banned from their facilities. Factory owners must continually be aware of changes in materials and processes in their plants that affect the safety of their employees and necessitate new protective apparel. The rise of lawsuits involving protective apparel has placed an even greater emphasis on meeting both voluntary standards and government regulations for many design situations.

Manufacturers need to consider production costs and the cost of retooling to produce new designs as well as the cost of testing and going through a rigorous certification process for new design features if regulations exist for their products. They may be able to contribute valuable insight about potential customers and sales potential. Even when good design ideas come along, it may be difficult for designers to find a manufacturer willing to take on the expense of putting a new product on the market.

Users, purchasers, administrators, medical personnel, governing bodies, and manufacturers should all be considered a designer's clients and each group has important contributions to make to the list of important criteria for a design.

Laboratory Simulation and Experimentation

Laboratory simulation may be needed when the actual design situation is not available or is too dangerous or infrequently occurring in the real world for the designer to study directly. Laboratory simulation also allows designers to generate research data in areas where none exists. Exploring design variables uncovered in the literature review in a setting where they can be controlled and human responses can be measured can add an even greater understanding of a design situation.

When laboratory simulation is simply used for convenience (i.e., simulating winter conditions in the summer rather than moving to the Arctic or Antarctic to do research), many excellent results can be obtained. There are a number of facilities that can accurately re-create climatic conditions, and protective apparel can be tested on live, active subjects inside these climatic chambers. However, laboratory simulations are most often employed when the potential for injury does not make it feasible to use live human subjects. In these situations, each substitution for a human component becomes a potential weak point in the procedure. Research results in the laboratory that reflect behavior in a field setting must involve simulated body parts that have a physical composition and/or a reaction time as close as possible to that of a live human. Because no universally accepted reproduction of the human body exists, many laboratory simulations simply identify at the outset the way in which the simulated models (and thus the outcome of the experiments) will differ from the actual end-use conditions. Where many variables exist, mathematical models or finite element analysis may be used to predict the effect each change in a variable will have on a design situation.

Laboratory tests are often used to test materials alone. It should be noted, however, that the behavior of materials may be quite different in a laboratory than when they are contoured to the body and backed by human flesh and bones.

Each of the methods just described—direct observation of behavior, indirect observation, direct communication, and laboratory simulations—provides a different type of useful information. In order to define a problem (i.e., to set design criteria), more than one, or perhaps all four, of these methods may need to be used in studying a specific activity. In that way, a designer can draw on the strengths and overcome the weaknesses inherent in each method of gathering information.

One difficulty that designers face with research is that it can never be complete. There is always more one can learn about any subject. In addition, even though one would assume that designers who are experienced in research would be able

to undertake it more quickly, this is not always the case. Experienced designers are often able to identify and access resources more quickly, but as Lawson points out, they may also be able to identify more critical areas that *need* research. He likens the situation to a chess master who can manage many games at a time because his experience allows him to identify patterns and react quickly to situations (1983, 96). However, sometimes a chess master may actually take longer to make decisions because he can see more possibilities and recognize potential problems further ahead than can the average player.

Perhaps the most difficult decision for a designer to make with regard to research and analysis is when to stop the process and move on. Often, either time or financial limitations dictate the termination of any phase of the process. However, keep in mind that research continues to occur throughout every stage of the design process. One may frequently circle back to collect information needed to move design development forward.

DEFINING THE PROBLEM

One of the many ways in which our mind attempts to make our life easier is to solve the first impression of the problem that it encounters . . .

We pick the most obvious (to us) shortcoming and set to work on it. In doing so, we are embarrassingly casual about the directions implicit in the wording of the problem.

Adams (1986, 114)

The research phase of the design process may result in a messy array of information that can be overwhelming to a designer. The goal of the definition phase of the design process is to create a new structure or understanding out of all of the information acquired through research. It is one of the most critical tasks of designing.

There are as many approaches to sorting through research and defining a problem as there are designers. The steps detailed here are simply one suggested pathway. Regardless of the method a designer chooses, in order to define a functional apparel design problem, it is important to clarify three important factors: (1) Who are the users? (2) What is the activity? and (3) What are the environmental conditions under which apparel will be used? In addition, it is important to determine and state specific goals for the apparel being developed (e.g., thermal protection, mobility).

Among the activities helpful to developing a definition are creating personas, identifying problem variables and constraints, developing frameworks, and developing a list of specific design requirements. The next section will provide information on how to approach each of these activities.

Creating Personas

Personas are characters that represent potential users or groups of users. One of the important outcomes of design research activities is a more in-depth understanding of who the users are. This is often a nuanced, detailed impression that is difficult to exhaustively record. Building **personas** is a technique that can help the designer to wrap up all of the nuanced detail they have come to understand about their user group.

Personas capture the aspects of research observations that deal with the personality of the user rather than the concrete variables like body dimensions and range of motion. They help a designer address the emotional, psychological, and social elements of a design. These factors cannot be ignored because they often determine whether even the most functional design will be worn. For example, if users do not like the way the design looks or feels, they may refuse to wear it. Identifying

potential downfalls of a design solution early in the process is crucial, and it is hazardous to rely on the designer's intuition to discover these variables.

Personas are usually an *archetype* of a user group. That is to say, they are not extreme stereotypes or caricatures of the ends of the user spectrum, but rather they represent the "average Joe" of a user type. They are given proper names to further humanize the characters and are usually fleshed-out into something that would resemble a movie character. The designer uses observations of multiple users rather than the specifics of one individual person's life. Characteristics such as age, occupation, likes, dislikes, and habits are specified to communicate the identity of this hypothetical user.

Personas must be specific to be useful. Designers need to be able to imagine seeing and talking to the person described. Because of this, multiple personas are often needed to fully capture the scope of users. In developing garments for rock climbers, for example, a designer may have identified a few groups of potential users: the novice enthusiast, the nature-loving voyager, and the expert athlete. Personas developed based on these three groups are illustrated in Figure 1.2. These are distinct groups of users with differing needs, goals, experiences, and skills, but none is an extreme stereotype.

Personas are used during several stages of the design process. They help a designer synthesize information collected about the personalities, experiences, and feelings of the people who will be using the design solution in order to set design requirements. They are also used in assessing potential design solutions during the later phases of the design process as a quick and easy way to illuminate important user experience variables. As design alternatives are developed and decisions are made, the designer can conduct imaginary consultations with each persona, imagining what Joe would do in

FIGURE 1.2 Examples of personas.

Karen, the novice enthusiast

Age: 23
Job: College admissions counselor
Climbing for: 4 months

-Decided to take a class at a local climbing gym to meet people in a new city.
-Got hooked right away!
-Wants to make sure she 'looks the part' and doesn't seem like a complete newbie.
-Still a little nervous about heights.

Joe, the nature-loving voyager

Age: 28
Job: Takes odd jobs as he travels
Climbing for: 8 years

-Took a 'summer trip' to Europe after grad school and has been on the road for 3 years.
-Loves sleeping outside and not needing to pay for hotels.
-Climbs whenever he gets the chance -- finds it a great way to meet like-minded people.
-Wants to feel as close as possible to nature as he climbs.
-Doesn't like fancy tools or equipment, climbs barefoot.

Helen, the expert athlete

Age: 35
Job: Project manager
Climbing for: 5 years

-Was a nationally-ranked athlete in college, but has had too many injuries to sustain high-impact sports.
-Climbs competitively -- wants to be the best female climber in her state.
-Doesn't believe in 'cheating' through technology, but wants to help her body perform at its highest level.

this situation, or how Karen might like the aesthetics of this option, or how Helen would feel about using a high-tech solution. Personas can also be created for other stakeholders who will not actually be using or wearing the solution. (For more on other stakeholders, see Design Strategies 1.1.)

Identifying Design Variables

Design variables are elements related to the user, the context, the design objective, or the problem itself that influence how effective a particular design solution will be. They are usually identified through research as a designer explores the problem. Variables might include things like the user's body temperature, the amount of moisture in the air, or the range of movement needed by the user.

In the course of the research process, many facts, figures, ideas, concepts, and bodies of knowledge will be uncovered.

Not all of these pieces of information are truly *variables* of the design challenge; they may instead be examples or values of a variable. The designer's task is to identify the root variable. (See Figure 1.3.) For example, a designer may have recorded during the research phase that rock climbers often report being "too hot." Too hot, however, is not the root variable; the underlying variable is

FIGURE 1.3. Identifying a root design variable from information gathered in the research process.

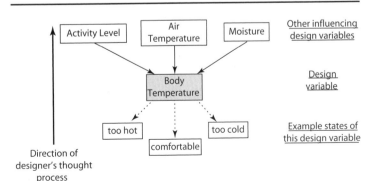

probably *body temperature*, and too hot is a possible value or state of body temperature. Defining the variable as *body temperature* may allow the designer to study all of the influences that create thermal balance, such as ambient air temperature, amount of moisture, and activity level of the climber. It may also help the designer to think about other states of the variable *body temperature*. For example, looking at factors that make the body too cold may offer insight that leads to innovative problem solutions.

It is tempting to think of design variables in terms of the materials and tools a designer can use, things like textiles, fasteners, and design features. However, these elements are more likely to be alternative *solutions* to the problem rather than more fundamental variables that influence the problem. For example, defining *insulation type* as a design variable when designing a winter coat could cause designers to think only in terms of insulation as a means of providing thermal comfort. Using *thermal comfort* as the design variable instead, allows consideration of a range of other design solutions such as chemical or electrical heating. It is extremely important that the design variables identified are phrased in terms of problems, *not* solutions.

Identifying Design Constraints

Design constraints are another kind of variable influencing a design problem. Constraints differ from other problem variables in that they are not directly under the control of a designer. They are commonly part of the environment or the task; for example, the requirement that the garment attach to a specific structure (a component of a building or vehicle, or an accessory like a glove or shoe) or the need to wear a pack on top of the garment. In the example of designing clothing for rock climbers mentioned earlier, a design constraint might

be the safety harness that is worn on top of the climber's clothing. The harness will exert pressure on the body in specific places, and the wearer must be able to reach and interact with the harness at times during his or her climb. Depending on the scope of a designer's influence, the harness may or may not be changeable. Indeed, a designer may not have control over even what specific harness type is worn. A designer with holistic control over an entire ensemble might have the option of designing a harness built into the garment. However, designers must establish with a client at the outset the factors in the design situation that they will be permitted to manipulate. There may be federal safety standards or other regulations that cannot be ignored for many items of functional clothing.

Not every design problem has constraints significant enough to articulate separately. However, in cases where the peripheral needs of the system have a strong impact on the designer's decisions, it can be helpful to outline and specify the constraints on the design in the same way that the variables of the problem are described.

It is important that designers use critical thinking to assess whether any articulated constraints are fundamental parts of the problem, or whether they are simply a narrow or mistaken view of the real problem. Like design variables, design constraints can be disguised solutions, and designers must explore the problem deeply enough to determine which constraints are permanent and which can be resolved through a clever design solution.

Developing Frameworks

Frameworks are graphic illustrations of two important things: the most important variables of the design problem and the relationship between these variables.

Figure 1.4 shows a framework for the problem of designing clothing for rock climbing. One

FIGURE 1.4 A framework of variables related to rock climbing.

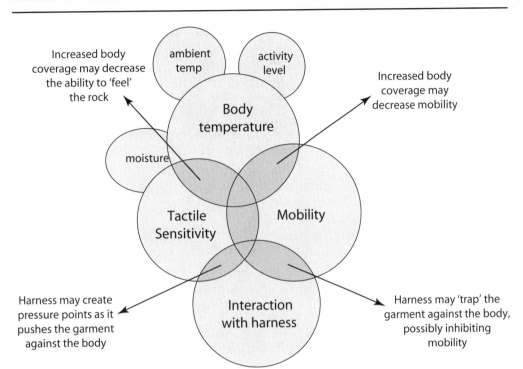

simple method of creating a framework is to begin by writing each idea, concept, or observation that emerges from the research and analysis process on an individual index card or adhesive note. This allows each thought to be mobile and malleable as a designer attempts to sort the variables into groups.

Once this sorting has been done, the next step is to label each group of notes or cards with a heading or title. Then, thoughts can easily be arranged and rearranged according to new groupings and variables as the inductive process of identifying design variables continues. In the rock climbing example, this sorting and labeling process yielded design variables such as body temperature, air temperature, activity level, mobility of the wearer, tactile sensitivity (the need to "feel" the rock), and interaction with the safety harness. Significantly more detail about each of these variables is known

by a designer, but at this stage detailed information is represented only by the *categories* or variables shown in each circle.

Once this step is completed, it is important to explore the relationships between variables to understand the ways in which variables interact and influence one another. Figure 1.4 shows just one of a number of possible framework formats based on the previously listed variables. In practice, this framework would be far more complex and include many more variables.

In many ways, this step of framework-building is one of the most difficult parts of the design process because there is no one typical example of what a framework should be. Figure 1.5 shows some common forms that frameworks can take. It is important to note that many frameworks do not fit neatly into one of these categories, and designers very commonly need to create a new type of

FIGURE 1.5 Common graphic representations of frameworks.

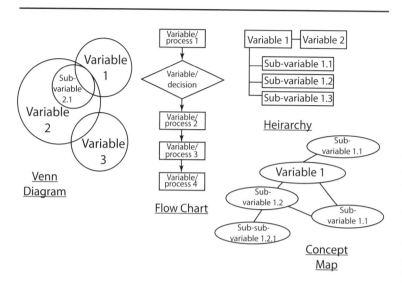

clothing with other accessories such as gloves, boots, and helmets. Other accessories were not represented in the original framework, but adding them could provide a designer with new perspectives on the problem. It could also inspire a designer to seek out more information, such as how continuous coverage between clothing and other accessories has been provided for other types of clothing.

Identifying Design Requirements

Design requirements are the most concrete result of the research

illustration of the problem or combine multiple approaches to effectively describe their insight.

One of the benefits of building a framework is that by forcing designers to think around the problem and into its corners, the framework-building process can help identify possible gaps in the research and analysis process and identify new design variables that may have been overlooked. It can help a designer discover new categories and relationships within a problem. For example, simply exploring the variable *interaction with harness* could lead to concerns about the interaction of

and definition phases of the design process: They translate abstract concepts from the framework and problem definition into itemized, specific details about what the design should or must do. Table 1.1 shows some examples of design requirements derived from the framework in Figure 1.4. As the table shows, specific values have been assigned to variables and subvariables identified as influential in the design problem.

Abstract frameworks allow a designer to fully describe and discuss the problem itself, before even beginning to think about solutions. Moving from a

TABLE 1.1 Examples of Design Requirements for Rock Climbing

VARIABLE	SUBVARIABLE	REQUIREMENT
Mobility	Shoulder mobility	Allows unimpeded shoulder flexion to 180°
Mobility	Spinal mobility	Allows unimpeded spinal flexion to 90°
Tactile sensitivity	Pressure sensitivity	Prevents localized pressure of greater than 100 kPa
Body temperature	Surface temperature	Maintains body surface temperature within the range of 32–37 °C

framework to a list of design requirements allows the qualities that would make up an effective solution to be described *specifically* before a solution is designed. Sometimes this is because of the need to communicate between groups of people (e.g., designer with client; design team with engineering team, etc.), and sometimes it is used as an internal checkpoint for the designer to help make sure the research leading up to this point has been thorough enough to be articulated in terms of requirements. In many cases, there are specific government regulations that set concrete design requirements that designers and manufacturers cannot ignore if their products are to reach the market.

The final list of design requirements can be very short or very long, depending on the level of detail required by the design challenge. In some cases, design requirements are nearly all quantitative, expressed in terms of the temperature or force or weight that the solution must withstand or have. In other cases, design requirements are much more descriptive and expressed in terms of the user needs that must be met.

For example, Table 1.1 shows how the designer's specific knowledge that is wrapped up in each of these variables is unpacked into explicit requirements. To begin, look for root variables. During the research phase, a designer has probably listed all of the movements that the climber will need to be able to comfortably do in the garment. The root variable that movements needed have in common is the range of motion of each body joint involved. Instead of listing every movement that involves bending the elbow, for example, it makes more sense to list as a design requirement a single value for the minimum range of motion of the elbow. By specifying that the spine needs to be able to flex easily to a 90° angle, or the shoulder needs to flex to a minimum of 180°, the designer need not list all of the possible activities that would require flexion of those joints.

In creating design requirements, it is important that designers continue to refrain from forming requirements that limit the range of possible design solutions. For example, a design requirement that states that "the skin surface must be kept between 32 and 37 degrees C" is quite a different from a criterion that says that one should design "a vest for the rock climbers that will keep the skin surface between 32 and 37 degrees C." The first statement gives the parameters of the problem; the second limits the solutions to a vest. Thus, the designer is effectively prevented from using a whole arsenal of other design configurations—from jackets to shirts to electrically heated wrist bands to a rock-mounted radiator blowing hot air at the climber. The language used to define design problems can significantly affect the creativity with which a designer can tackle problems. (See Design Strategies 1.2)

Creating a Concise Problem Definition

Design requirements comprise a specific, detailed definition of a design project. However, it is helpful to be able to communicate overall design goals with a one- or two-sentence definition. This concise, overarching definition is useful for communicating the nature of a project to others, but it also helps to focus and clarify a designer's efforts.

For example, in the rock-climbing project described throughout this chapter, a project definition might be "Provide a means by which female rock-climbers of average ability may climb unimpeded in 40–100 degree F weather under any conditions of precipitation while maintaining thermal and tactile comfort." Each factor in this definition may be backed up by several design requirements. Some design requirements may contain numerical values for specific physical tests a design needs to pass or percentages of test subjects that need to approve of a design. Designers are wise to return to the concise

Design Strategies 1.2: The Importance of a Good Definition

One drawback of designing with an ill-conceived definition: the designer may ultimately work to solve the wrong problem. Ashdown and Watkins (1993), in describing an industry-sponsored project aimed at improving the fit of a totally encompassing chemical suit, state that one of the design criteria set by the client was "make the bootie smaller." The researchers' analysis of the garment pattern and anthropometric data revealed that the uncomfortable wrinkling and excess bootie material around the foot was due *not* to the bootie being too large, but to it being considerably too small, forcing wearers to step on part of the lower leg of the garment, pulling it down under the heels of the wearer's foot. This created the appearance of excess bulk and a bootie that was, in the words of the client, "too large." A good criterion in this case—one that would allow designers to form a clearer and more accurate problem definition—might have been, "Reduce the wrinkling around the bootie of the suit."

---

problem definition often to be certain they are focusing on the problem they set out to solve.

Framing a concise definition at this stage of the process may allow a designer to add a direction for the research that was uncovered during the process of forming design requirements. For example, for the preceding definition, one might add the criterion that the design should allow a climber to feel as "natural" and "unencumbered" as possible while being protected and comfortable.

A good definition can form both the guidelines for selecting the best design ideas and the basis for evaluating the final product. By articulating the definition to clients and checking it throughout the design process, a designer can ensure that the goals of a project are being met.

GENERATING IDEAS

There have been many great discoveries, both in science and in art, in which the critical link has been met by chance . . .

It is the highly inquiring mind which at that moment seizes the chance and turns what was an accident into something providential.

(Jacob Bronowski)

You see things; and you say, "Why?" But I dream things that never were; and I say, "Why not?"

(George Bernard Shaw)

Chance favors the prepared mind.

(Louis Pasteur)

Idea generation (sometimes called **ideation**) is considered by the layperson to be the work that designers are really equipped to do. It is the creative, idea-generating part of the design process that most designers find to be great fun. If the problem has been thoroughly analyzed and a clear definition has been developed, good ideas may simply flow naturally out of a designer's brain.

The ability to generate creative ideas evolves in part from experience and in part from the way individuals process and use information. One might think of the brain as a sort of file cabinet in which one can deposit ideas and observations and then open it to retrieve them when they are needed. It is clear that the more experiences one has, the more files there are to retrieve and thus the more ideas one can contribute to a problem. At the same time, two people who share the same experience may draw out of it quite different qualities and quantities of ideas to store in their files. This is one of the reasons why it is often valuable to have teams of designers from different backgrounds working together to solve a problem. The ability to maintain an active curiosity about the world—to keenly observe, question, and perceive unusual configurations and situations—all increase the material one draws from a single experience.

Two attributes that are vital to creative problem solving are fluency and flexibility. Individuals who possess these attributes are able to "scan more alternative thoughts, ride the wave of different associative currents, and think of more ideas in a given span of time than can people who are less creative" (Raudsepp 1983, 173).

Fluency is the ability to come up with many ideas in a single category, whereas *flexibility* is the ability to come up with many categories of design requirements or approaches. Fluency has no judgment component. It simply allows the idea generator to come up with as many ideas as possible regardless of their feasibility. Flexibility allows the creative person to "choose and explore a wide variety of approaches to a problem without losing sight of the overall goal or purpose" (Ibid. 174). It allows one to free associate (i.e., to move in random directions from an original idea without any apparent pattern). One idea triggers another even though it may be only tangentially related.

For example, one might ask people to come up with as many uses as they can for a toothbrush. If one person lists many uses for personal grooming, that person demonstrates fluency. If another proposes a use in art, one in gardening, one in auto repair, one in cooking, one in home construction, one in poetry, one in interior decoration, and so on, this demonstrates flexibility. When an individual

possesses both fluency and flexibility, the number and variety of ideas increases exponentially.

Both of these qualities are important to all stages of the design process. Even in research, a fluent designer is more easily able to think of additional subtopics within a topic at hand that may need investigating. A flexible designer is better able to think around the problem and discover peripheral areas relevant to the problem. Having both fluency and flexibility often allows designers to illuminate additional design requirements, personas, and the like at this stage of the design process.

It is important to allow creative design ideas to flow freely without censoring them. Adams (1986b, 46) states, "if you analyze or judge too early in the problem-solving process, you will reject many ideas. This is detrimental for two reasons." The first is that newly formed ideas are fragile and need detail and maturity. The second is that many ideation techniques depend on unreasonable, "way out" ideas (Ibid., 47). Even insignificant or apparently absurd ideas can serve as links to truly creative solutions.

When problem solving, one can never have enough ideas. It is important not to reject any ideas during the idea generation process, and it is equally important to note ideas as they come along, in words, sketches, or both. Designers always need to keep recording tools handy because the freest flow of ideas often occurs when the brain is relaxed and not working directly on a problem.

There are many approaches to the improvement of creative thinking skills and many excellent methods that have been established to help designers who have difficulty generating new ideas and design concepts. It is impossible to describe each of the methods in enough detail here for the reader to fully implement them. The methods and their authors are mentioned and included in the reference list in the hope that the reader will explore full texts on many of them as they approach various design problems.

Idea Generation Techniques

One of the most often used techniques for generating ideas is **brainstorming** (Osborn 1957). Brainstorming can be used in any stage of the design process. It is especially helpful in generating large numbers of ideas in a short period of time. It is intended as a group technique that seeks quantity of ideas without concern for quality, encourages "tagging on" to an idea that originated with another group member, and forbids criticism of ideas.

Lateral thinking is an approach to creative thinking that is different from traditional methods of thinking in that it may deliberately seek out irrelevant information, use information only for its effect on stimulating creative thinking, and use incorrect assumptions to achieve a correct solution. In contrast, with traditional thinking (i.e., *vertical thinking*), "one moves forward by sequential steps each of which must be justified" (de Bono 1985, 11). In vertical thinking, incorrect information is discarded, and only relevant information is sought. Lateral thinking generates insight and produces new connections. It is a way of cutting across established patterns to find new ones. The difference between lateral and vertical thinking may remind one of the divergent and convergent thought processes discussed earlier in this chapter.

The concept of the "six thinking hats" is a form of lateral thinking that asks designers to challenge the ways their brains work by temporarily donning different colored hats, becoming individuals who think in different ways (de Bono 1999).

Synectics is a method of joining together different and apparently irrelevant elements as a stimulus to generating creative solutions to problems

(Gordon 1961). Synectics theory holds that the emotional component is as important as the intellectual component in problem solving and that individuals who understand these emotional, irrational components have an increased probability of success in a problem-solving situation. In a synectics session (which in itself is a complete design process), the group first attempts to become familiar with the problem and the goals or wishes of the client. Then, the group takes an *excursion*, that is, it leaves the problem for a while and examines how other problems with similar wishes have been solved. Finally, it returns to the original problem with fresh insights and attempts to apply that new energy to the problem.

Another method involves using *manipulative verbs* to view problems in unique ways. Verbs such as *magnify*, *minify*, *rearrange*, *combine*, *reverse*, and *substitute* are used to suggest ways to manipulate a subject by, among other things, altering its size or changing its position or function (Koberg and Bagnall 2003, 69). This has much the same effect as an excursion in synectics in that it moves a designer out of the specific problem and focuses instead on stimulating new insights that may later be applied to the problem.

Mind mapping seeks to stimulate both flexibility and fluency by recording ideas in a way that is much more like natural thought processes than are the outlining, note-taking methods taught in most schools (Buzan 1984). It encourages the person seeking ideas to explore a central topic by letting the mind wander in any direction and recording the thoughts in the order they come, in a pattern that branches out from the central idea. (See Figure 1.6.) The nature and number of ideas nearest the center subject demonstrate the flexibility of the designer, and the number of ideas on the outer edges of the map demonstrates fluency.

FIGURE 1.6 A mind map.

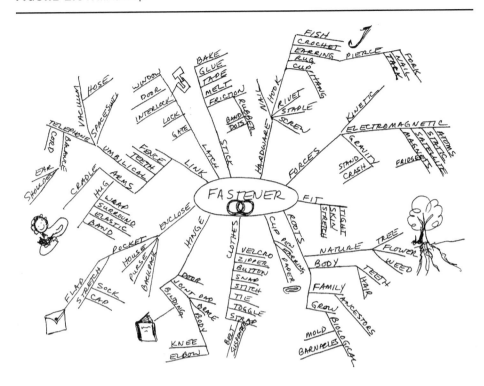

Small sketches and symbols may be used rather than words to record ideas. The purpose of mind mapping is to generate an individual brainstorming process without having to worry about fitting ideas into categories. As the ideas are generated, they become a stimulus for additional ideas and categories of thought. The branching out of the mind map is a form of lateral thinking and reflects the type of excursion taken in synectics. Therefore, the process can serve as a route to innovative design ideas.

Ideas generated through brainstorming often need incubation time. This is undoubtedly true for other idea-generating techniques as well. One creativity expert established the practice of contacting the members of a brainstorming group the following day when they had had a chance to sleep on their ideas. He often found that the afterthoughts were better than the ideas generating in the original session (Osborn 1957, 250). Similarly, an individual designer would be wise to revisit an idea-generating session a day after it takes place.

Interaction matrixes are another tool. They use design variables themselves to generate new design ideas. In this technique, design variables are listed on both the horizontal and vertical axes of a matrix grid. (Figure 1.7). Then a designer selects a variable from each axis and uses the combination of those two design variables to stimulate new design ideas that address those two variables simultaneously. Figure 1.7 illustrates several design ideas that result from exploring the intersection between variables.

FIGURE 1.7 Using an interaction matrix to generate design ideas.

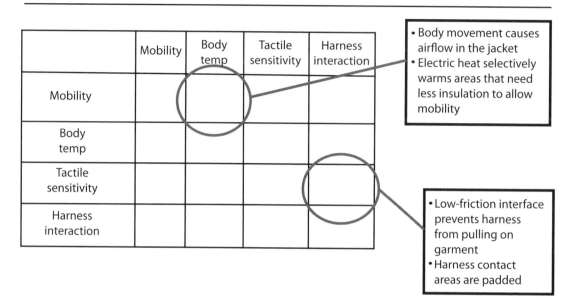

Some designers find a three-dimensional box-like matrix to be more helpful than a two-dimensional one. The shaded box on the 3-D matrix in Figure 1.8 shows the intersection of three variables relating to a rock-climbing ensemble—*hip*, *harness*, and *moisture*. One idea that might come out of the consideration of these three variables together might be to use a spacer fabric around the hips to prevent moisture buildup under a rock-climbing harness.

As with analysis, designers find it difficult to ever consider the process of idea generation completed. There is never only one correct answer; a better design can always be developed. Lawson concluded that "The designer identifies the end of his process as a matter of judgment. It no longer seems worth the effort of going further because the chances of significantly improving on the solution seem small" (1983, 88). Conversely, however, when generating ideas, it is tempting to consider the task finished when the end of the first, easily retrieved set of ideas is reached. Since early ideas

can tend to be more obvious and commonplace, it is vitally important that designers continue to pursue additional ideas beyond those that come easily to mind. This is where ideation tools and techniques are most useful; even experienced designers can come up with more ideas and better ideas using ideation tools than those relying only on what comes to mind.

Sketching

Sketching and drawing may be the most stereotypical designer activities, even though the bulk of the design process arguably happens while doing other activities. Sketching is more than the process of recording an idea that passes through the brain of a designer; it is actually a way of developing ideas. Because the connection between the brain and the hand is not perfect (the sketch is never 100 percent what the designer intended), the process of drawing is only an interpretation of the original idea. Goldschmidt (1991) describes this process as a "dialog" between the designer and the sketch, or

FIGURE 1.8 Using a three-dimensional interaction matrix to generate design ideas.

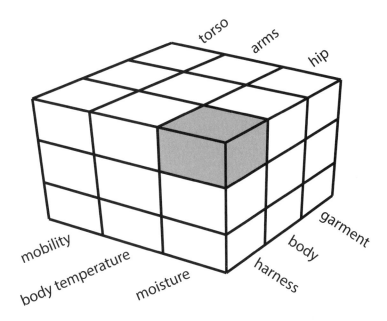

even between the designer's conscious and subconscious mind. She differentiates between drawings (renderings of fully formed ideas, aimed at recording detail as accurately as possible) and sketches (components of a developmental process, aimed at helping to discover or develop an idea). In the sketching process, a designer may not have fully realized the objective being pursued. The sketch may actually result in a design direction that was not explicitly intended when the sketch was begun. An idea held in the mind is inherently less explicit than an instance of that idea put on paper. By making the idea explicit, a designer can raise questions or flesh out critiques of the idea that are not possible when the idea is still implicit in the mind.

Many beginning designers can be hesitant to engage in a sketching process because they perceive that they are not good at drawing. Although skill in drawing can certainly be helpful, it is by no means essential to a sketching process. Because the benefit of sketching is the transition back and forth between a vague idea and a concrete expression of that idea, accuracy is not necessarily required for the dialog to take place.

DEVELOPING DESIGNS

No one deserves either praise or blame for the ideas that come to him, but only for the actions resulting therefrom.

(A. R. Wallace, qtd. in Madigan and Ellwood 1983, 284)

The creative process does not end with an idea—it only starts with an idea.

(John Arnold, qtd. in Osborn 1957, 249)

Many designers believe that the point at which the most creative design behavior takes place is not during idea generation, but in the *shaping* and *selection* of the design ideas that best solve a problem. Often the best design cannot be found among a series of design ideas presented during idea generation. Instead, it may evolve from recombining aspects of several of the original design proposals. The shaping and recombining of ideas may also uncover new design variables or constraints. At this stage moving between concrete examples and abstractions or categories in a process similar to creating a framework of the problem can greatly expand the number and quality of design concepts available to solve a problem.

One designer recommends selecting the most promising design ideas by following brainstorming with a *screening session* done by individuals *not* involved in the brainstorming session. This is to avoid the tendency for brainstorming to be like "a beauty contest being judged by the mothers of the would-be Miss Americas" (Osborne 1957, 251). Others believe that this screening committee should be charged with more than just "judge and select. One of its prescribed functions is creatively to reprocess the ideas through combination, elaboration, and other means" (Ibid., 252).

Ranking and Weighting Criteria

Not all criteria (variables) are equally important to the success of a design. At some point in the design process, it is important to prioritize criteria so that the relative importance of each plays a part in the selection of the final design. This is generally done by ranking and weighting them. *Ranking* criteria involves listing them in order of importance while *weighting* involves assigning a relative value to them. Ranking and weighting design criteria can be difficult processes that are further complicated by the presence of multiple clients, each of whom has his or her own set of priorities. Both need to evolve from the initial problem statement in combination with a thorough analysis. Even assigning

a weight to each criterion, something often thought to be particularly difficult, can be greatly simplified if a thorough analysis of the problem has been completed. Because ranking and weighting of criteria is so intimately connected with idea selection, a discussion of some of the methods that can be used for these processes will be presented here.

Using Forced Connections

Koberg and Bagnall have suggested a technique they call "forced connections morphology" to help a designer connect some alternative ideas generated in the ideation process (2003, 72). Figure 1.9 shows an example of an attribute chart prepared for this method. The problem for which a solution is being sought is that of developing a postural support for elderly persons with deteriorating posture. Across the top of the chart are some attributes of the problem and under each attribute is a list of alternatives generated during analysis and ideation. The breadth of the list of attributes shows the flexibility of the designer; the alternatives below each heading demonstrate fluency. Note that, unlike an interaction matrix, this method allows more than two attributes to be explored at once. When the lists are as complete as possible, a designer can make random passes through them. An alternative to random passes might be to cut up the lists, place each of the alternatives in attribute piles and draw one alternative out of each pile. Then, attempts to flesh out the details of a design can be based on those characteristics.

For example, based on the list in Figure 1.9, one might develop an inflatable backpack secured on the body with D-rings that had shoulder straps that pulled back on the shoulders. An alternative pass through the lists might suggest a zippered vest made of woven, nonstretch fabric in front and stretch fabric in back that incorporated semirigid supports at intervals all the way across the front to *push* the body upright.

FIGURE 1.9 Forced connections morphology. Random passes through the lists provide alternative design concepts. *(Koberg and Bagnall 2003, 72)*

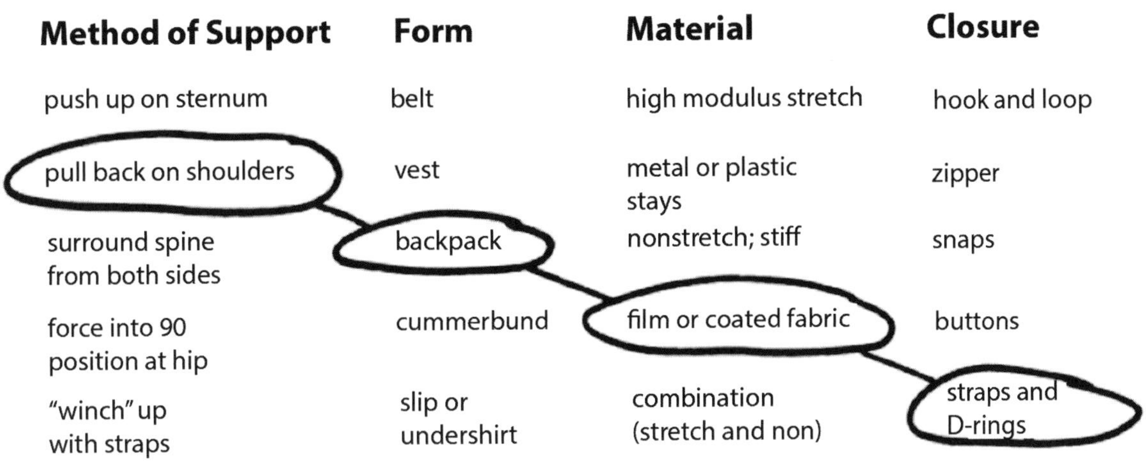

Method of Support	Form	Material	Closure
push up on sternum	belt	high modulus stretch	hook and loop
pull back on shoulders	vest	metal or plastic stays	zipper
surround spine from both sides	backpack	nonstretch; stiff	snaps
force into 90 position at hip	cummerbund	film or coated fabric	buttons
"winch" up with straps	slip or undershirt	combination (stretch and non)	straps and D-rings

Using Decision Matrixes

A **decision matrix** (also sometimes called a Pugh chart) is a visual representation of design criteria in rows and columns that helps a designer to understand and investigate the influence of their design decisions on the success of the resulting design. The matrix format helps designers to understand and assess the influence of individual criteria and the relative success of different design solutions. Table 1.2 shows a decision matrix for four criteria applied to three design concepts. In the table, design criteria are listed individually in the left-hand column. In the next column, each criterion is assigned a weight (from 1 to 5 in this table) that reflects its relative importance to the success of the design solution. Appropriate weights may be determined by soliciting input from users and other stakeholders. A useful tool is a pairwise

TABLE 1.2 A Decision Matrix

CRITERION	WEIGHT	CONCEPT 1 SCORE	CONCEPT 1 WEIGHTED SCORE	CONCEPT 2 SCORE	CONCEPT 2 WEIGHTED SCORE	CONCEPT 3 SCORE	CONCEPT 3 WEIGHTED SCORE
MOBILITY	5	5	$5 \times 5 = 25$	4	$5 \times 4 = 20$	2	$5 \times 2 = 10$
BODY TEMPERATURE	4	2	$4 \times 2 = 8$	4	$4 \times 4 = 16$	5	$4 \times 5 = 20$
TACTILE SENSATION	4	3	$4 \times 3 = 12$	2	$4 \times 2 = 8$	5	$5 \times 2 = 10$
AESTHETICS	3	5	$3 \times 5 = 15$	1	$3 \times 1 = 3$	3	$3 \times 3 = 9$
TOTAL SCORE			60		47		49

comparison that allows people to compare two characteristics at a time and identify which is more important. Respondents can also be asked the relative importance of each (i.e., is one "slightly more important" or "a lot more important" than the other?). Then, these comparisons can be put into a decision model that can determine the overall weightings of the criteria.

Next, each design concept is scored on each criterion (also with a score from 1 to 5 in this example). The score is multiplied by the weight in order to arrive at a weighted score for each criterion. Finally, all of the weighted scores for each concept are summed to form a total score for the concept, which can be compared to the total scores for other concepts.

A tool like this matrix can be helpful in illuminating some of the implicit values or assumptions that may have influenced the designer's decision making, by substituting a very explicit decision-making process. In the example in Table 1.2, for instance, a designer may have been surprised to find out that Concept 1 was the winner. This might help the designer to reflect more objectively on why that concept was not previously thought to be as strong as other concepts or to stop and ask why the objective evidence does not line up with the intuitive choice made. This could help the designer to understand which factors might have been overlooked in previous analyses.

Resolving Conflicts

Regardless of how carefully a matrix is set up, it cannot really serve as an ultimate decision maker. It simply helps designers to explore combinations of ideas that may have fallen between the cracks. Sometimes the combination that yields the highest total simply feels wrong. A designer needs to use both intuitive and explicit means to select the best ideas and develop the final design.

In addition to setting ranked and weighted design criteria, it is often helpful to identify the criteria that are likely to be in conflict with one another. When the best solution to one criterion exacerbates the problem expressed by another, a designer has to determine the relative importance of each criterion and work to develop a design solution that maximizes the benefits for both. DeJonge discusses what she calls an "interaction matrix and net" (Watkins 1995, 351) that identifies the interactions between design criteria for a sleeping ensemble (Figure 1.10). The nets at the bottom of the figure were developed on the basis of the matrix. They show areas that "need additional work if they are to be incorporated into the design."

Working on a design for a total enclosure such as a space suit, a chemical protective suit, or a military protective ensemble that has multiple and often conflicting requirements presents one of the most challenging tasks in design development. The selection process becomes chicken-or-egg decision making, in which each decision made for one part of an ensemble is linked to each decision made for every other part of the ensemble. One of the most interesting approaches can be found in a concept plan for an integrated protective clothing and equipment ensemble for the Canadian soldier, which was projected for the year 2005 (Knapp 1988). This project involved the design of an ensemble to protect soldiers from a wide range of threats: weather (temperature, precipitation), ballistic, chemical, biological, nuclear, flame, directed energy (lasers, microwaves), detection, impact, sensory, insects, and so on.

Knapp developed what he called a *concept generator* and established *levels of decision* that he used to sequence his idea selection. The purpose of the concept generator was to move from a

FIGURE 1.10 An interaction matrix and net for a sleeping ensemble.

	1 2 3 4 5 6 7 8 9 10
1. Cover torso completely	2 2 2 1 2 2 2 2 2
2. Cover limbs completely	2 2 1 2 2 2 2 2
3. Cover feet completely	2 2 2 1 0 2 2
4. Provide head covering	1 1 1 0 2 2
5. Secure garment openings at sleeves and neckline	1 1 1 2 2
6. Provide adjustable closures for easy on/off operation	2 1 2 2
7. Garment should be comfortable	1 2 2
8. Garment should be aesthetically pleasing	2 2
9. Garment should be machine wash and dry	2
10. Garment should be capable of mass production	

Accommodation interaction net   Conflict interaction net

0=Conflict
1=Accommodation
2=No conflict

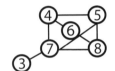

specific requirement or criterion to a list of all of the possible technologies that could meet that criterion. This is analogous to the definition and idea generation phases of the design process discussed earlier in this chapter. Knapp kept these lists of requirements and possible solutions in front of him as he began the selection process so that none of them could be forgotten, but new ideas could be inserted as they evolved in the process of idea selection. Knapp applied this concept generator to the development of his protective ensemble for the Canadian soldier. If his lists were made into a morphological box, Knapp estimated that 146,750 different designs would have been possible.

Determining levels of decision involves studying the design problem to determine which decisions need to be made first. Figure 1.11 shows the decision path through which Knapp's ensemble was created. Knapp decided that the most basic decision that needed to be made was whether the ensemble would be permeable or impermeable to air. Many other decisions, such as how to achieve thermal balance (including power requirements to do so), whether to use a soft or hard material shell, and how to support the weight of the system, rested on that initial decision. The pros and cons of permeable and impermeable systems were considered, and it was decided that a hybrid system would best satisfy the needs of the soldier. (The hybrid system included a permeable garment with an impermeable overgarment to be worn at specific times.) After this decision was made, he moved

FIGURE 1.11 Concept generator for an infantry soldier's protective ensemble. *(Knapp 1988)*

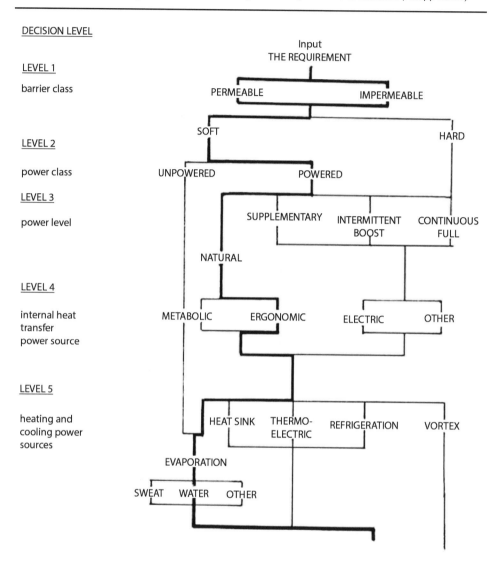

on to the issue of whether a hard or soft shell approach should be chosen.

Knapp's decision path looks fairly simplistic, so it is important to emphasize again the importance of thorough research and analysis, a clear definition of the problem, and a free and open idea generation process. Knapp used nine levels of decision, each of which involved analysis of many factors, from the threats and hazards confronting a soldier to the tasks that needed to be accomplished to the costs involved in production. Having well-outlined requirements and many approaches to meeting them are critical to this phase of the decision-making process.

Using Interaction Narratives

After an idea has been selected for further development, the designer's next task is to 'flesh out' the concept into the full detail required of an actual garment solution. The designer must make many small decisions during this process. It can be tempting to make these smaller decisions based on more direct influences such as cost or the designer's intuition. However, even small variables can have a significant effect on the overall success of the design. Things like closures, seam placement, and even color can determine whether or not a design will be effective and usable.

One method of working through the development of detail in a design concept is to bring personas back into play in the form of **interaction narratives**. Interaction narratives are short storytelling exercises that allow a designer to imagine in some detail how the user will interact with the design solution. The process of storytelling encourages the designer to consider *how* something will happen, which can illuminate some of the overlooked variables of the design. For example, Figure 1.12 shows a storyboard style of interaction narrative for one of the personas illustrated in Figure 1.2. It is annotated with design sketches showing the details of the design. To fully describe *how* the user will interact with the design, the details of the interaction must be thought through.

At this point, it is crucial that the designer fully understand the person who will be engaged in the activity. This is where the personas described earlier in this chapter become very useful as developmental tools. Because personas encapsulate the rich understanding that the designer has of various users, those personas can now be consulted by hypothetically testing out a design solution. Storyboards based on personas help the designer take into account a user's personality, knowledge, abilities, and needs rather than making assumptions or thinking based on their own subjectivity.

Low-Fidelity Prototyping

As the details of a design are developed, it is crucially important that the evolving design be tested by users as early and as often as possible. This feedback is important for two reasons: so that the user's perspective is integrated throughout the design process, allowing inaccurate assumptions to be caught before they become poor design decisions, and so that design alternatives can be evaluated by an objective outsider early in the process, before the designer becomes too attached to a pet idea whose conceptualization and actualization are quite disparate.

Testing ideas is much more effective when they can be tested in physical form. Discussing ideas verbally is somewhat helpful but requires all of the parties in the discussion to make assumptions, which can lead to misinterpretations. Physical form brings a design concept into reality and gives the designer and user something concrete to discuss.

It is important that emerging concepts be evaluated in physical form, but it is *not* important that the physical form be refined or polished in any way. In fact, it is often *more* effective for designs to be evaluated in very obviously unfinished or **low-fidelity** form. This helps the designer communicate to the user that the design is not finished and that it is still acceptable to implement changes.

Conducting User Feedback Sessions

Conducting an effective feedback session with low-fidelity prototypes requires experience and skill in much the same way that effective interviewing does. Two of the important elements of a feedback session are *enacting use scenarios* and *gathering*

FIGURE 1.12 A storyboard illustrates the rock-climbing experience of one design persona.

Karen arrives at the gym for her weekly class. She's wearing her new vest and excited to see her new friends and impress the coach.

She drops her bag and shoes and straps in to her harness.

She chalks up, clips in, and starts an easy climb.

Now that she's warmed up, she tries something harder on her next turn.

This one is pretty tough! She's getting nervous, and her hands are sweating. Where's that chalk bag??

She can see the ground out of the corner of her eye and is starting to get a bit scared. She hopes that coach can't tell!

Success! She reaches the top and tries for a victory gesture!

Getting down is easier: she belays expertly down.

concrete feedback. In the first case, it is important that users actually physically interact with the design concept as if they were using it in real life. They should put it on and engage in, or pretend to engage in, tasks and activities that they would need to undertake in the field. It is important to include accessories normally worn over or under garments for these sessions. Feedback sessions illuminate specific drawbacks, such as not being able to move in a certain way or not having the appropriate contour in a given area.

Second, as users enact these use scenarios, it is important to capture their feedback in a very concrete way, by actually reshaping or drawing on the low-fidelity prototype itself. For this reason, it can be very helpful to arrive at a feedback session with multiple versions of a low-fidelity prototype! Capturing concrete feedback again helps minimize misinterpretations in the feedback process. Rather than assume that "too tight right here" means a 0.5 inch (1.27 cm) increase in diameter at the knee, the designer can actually capture that what the user really needed was a 0.75 inch (1.9 cm) increase in diameter 2 inches (5.08 cm) above the knee.

EVALUATING DESIGNS

Evaluation (is) a form of accounting. It involves the comparing of actions with consequences; detecting flaws and making improvements; planting the seeds of future challenge.

(Koberg and Bagnall 2003, 94)

Evaluation involves taking a critical look at the decisions made in the design process. It may involve numerical ratings based on tests with many subjects or simply the informal, subjective opinion of a designer. In the field of functional clothing design, evaluation tends to lean toward the former. If evaluation is seen as a stopping point along the way—a time for assessment before moving ahead—it makes sense to achieve the most objective assessment possible and use it as a guide to further design development.

It is preferable to set up evaluation procedures prior to ideation in order to be certain that the choice of evaluation technique is not prejudiced by the final design selected. Evaluation techniques may take many forms, including observation,

interview, questionnaires, laboratory testing, and field testing. Many types of laboratory and field tests specific to various clothing problems are discussed throughout this text.

In many fields, evaluation is undertaken *before* a full-scale design is begun. The more complex and expensive the construction process is, the more likely it is that this will occur. Because many items of apparel are relatively inexpensive, full-scale garments in final materials are frequently constructed and evaluated on users. Prototypes or parts of models may also be constructed and evaluated throughout all phases of the process as the decision-making process proceeds.

Regardless of the stage at which evaluation is performed, this part of the design process is made considerably simpler by the establishment of clear design criteria at the definition stage of the design process. As Koberg and Bagnall state, "If you can't explain where you're headed, you'll never know when you've arrived" (2003, 23). If the goals of a design problem are clearly defined, evaluation can often be almost a checklist process of assessing whether or not goals have been met. For some projects, the physical aspects of an acceptable product can be precisely defined. For example, survival handwear designed for pilots may be required to take no more than 10 cubic inches (163.87 cu cm) of storage space on an ejection seat. Other criteria may be defined by more subjective means such as "the appearance of the handwear must be acceptable to the pilot community." If precise acceptance levels are set in the definition phase of the design process, evaluation becomes a matter of providing an appropriate test to determine how effectively the designer's goals were met. For example, the above definition may be further narrowed so that it specified that "the appearance of the handwear must be acceptable to seventy percent of a random sample of one hundred pilots."

All evaluations should end with a look toward the future. Aspects of designs that did not meet the goals set by the design criteria can be explored again. Like test grades, the evaluation provided by an objective assessment of a product should not be considered a catalog of its failures but rather a guide to areas that need attention in future efforts.

Conclusion

A few people may pick up a golf club and swing it naturally or easily sound a flute . . . but for the vast majority the skills must be acquired initially by attention to detail. It is in the very nature of highly developed skills that we can perform them unconsciously. . . . So it is with design. We probably work best when we think least about our technique. The beginner however must first analyse and practise all the elements of his skill.

(Lawson 1983, 6–7)

The great cutting edge of economic change in this country is not technology but design.

(John Kenneth Galbraith)

Graduates have been well equipped to think analytically about a clearly defined deterministic problem, but they have been poorly prepared to solve complex, ill-defined problems in the presence of uncertainties.

(Haupt 1978, 55)

The profession with the brightest future is that of creative problem-solving. The statute of limitations on problem-solutions is short.

(Koberg and Bagnall 2003, 25)

In this highly technological age, where virtually anything is possible, more and more problems—both nationally and internationally—are complex ones that involve endless numbers of factors. Problems that involve human beings and/or changing environmental conditions will remain, as Haupt states, "ill-defined." The capacity to deal with those problems—to design—is, and will continue to be, a highly prized skill.

Each of the following chapters in this book is intended to help designers become familiar with the content of a specific problem area in functional apparel. Every designer needs to develop a personal process that can help convert knowledge of this content into innovative functional apparel.

2 Providing Mobility in Clothing

Protective clothing may be enhanced or defeated by its mobility features. Movement is critical to function in virtually every activity. Protective sports equipment that moves with the body is highly prized by athletes whose livelihoods depend on their ability to move quickly and precisely. The space industry has invested millions of dollars and many hours developing pressurized suits that move with the astronauts so they can accomplish a variety of tasks in outer space. Clothing for individuals such as firefighters needs to be as easily mobile as possible in order not to increase the energy needed for their physically demanding work. Many people have jobs that require them to wear clothing that allows them to move quickly to avert danger.

Before designers can create garments that provide ease of movement, they need to understand how movement occurs and know what kinds of body movements take place in a particular activity. Obviously, movement patterns for different activities vary greatly. Therefore, it is important to find ways to determine the movements of the particular group for which clothing is being created. This chapter provides a framework for studying and recording movement and applying this information to clothing design.

Human Body Movement

Since clothing is intended to be a *second skin*, there is no better way to begin a study of mobility needs in clothing than by looking at the mobility of the body itself. Put most simply, movement

is the result of the following chain of events: (1) the brain sends signals to the appropriate nerve fibers or **motor neurons**; (2) they in turn send out impulses, via nerve fibers, which extend from the spinal cord to muscle fibers all over the body; (3) these impulses stimulate the appropriate muscle fibers so that they contract (i.e., shorten in length); and (4) they then exert their contracting force on bones in the area around a joint to produce movements.

SENSORY ASPECTS OF MOVEMENT

The brain uses input from the body's sensory organs to perceive the position of the body and body parts and to control movements of the body. This happens in two important domains. The **vestibular sense**, or sense of balance, relies primarily on the eyes and inner ear to sense the position and acceleration of the head relative to gravity. The **kinesthetic sense** (sometimes called **proprioception** or the proprioceptive sense) is active during movement. It gathers information from sensory receptors in the skin and muscles to help the brain determine the position of a joint and the type and amount of joint movement. Both of these domains use similar sets of sensory or neurological inputs to understand and control body movements.

The brain is the body's nerve center, where pathways and connections between neurons are used to remember and recall information and to process sensory inputs. The brainstem and spinal cord emerge from the base of the brain. The brain-stem forms the connection between the brain and the rest of the nervous system and controls many basic functions that are essential for survival, like regulating the heart. The spinal cord is a bundle of nerve pathways that passes through the middle of the spine, protected by the bony vertebrae, which form a cage around the spinal cord. At each vertebra, a subsection of the bundle of nerves that compose the spinal cord exits the spinal column to enervate peripheral body areas. Figure 2.1 shows a basic map called a *dermatomic map* that shows where these bundles go (i.e., which body areas are innervated by bundles exiting at each vertebral level).

Two important types of nerves that are essential to movement and to the brain's understanding of movement are **sensory neurons** and **motor neurons**. Sensory neurons take signals from the muscles and from the sensory organs to the brain, where the brain translates these signals into an understanding of position and movement. Motor neurons send messages in the other direction: from the brain to the muscles, telling them when to contract and when to release. Some motor neurons are directed mainly by conscious thought (e.g., the decision to reach and pick something up), and others (e.g., the beating of the heart) are directed automatically by the brain.

Sensory neurons are often attached to specialized structures or organs that serve as **transducers**, transforming a stimulus (e.g., light, touch, sound) into electrical signals carried by the sensory neuron back to the brain. The skin, for example, contains many types of **mechanoreceptors**, which are specialized structures that respond to specific types of touch, such as vibration, pressure, or stroking.

The brain uses many different sensory organs and sensory neurons as transducers to convert a stimulus into a neurological impulse that can be used to understand the position and movement of the body. Vestibular sensing uses the eyes and the sensory neurons of the muscles in coordination with the inner ear to determine body orientation and acceleration. The body is not able to detect constant velocity (movement at a steady pace in a given direction), only **acceleration**

FIGURE 2.1 Body areas innervated by bundles exiting at the level of each vertebra. *(Keegan and Garrett 1948, 409)*

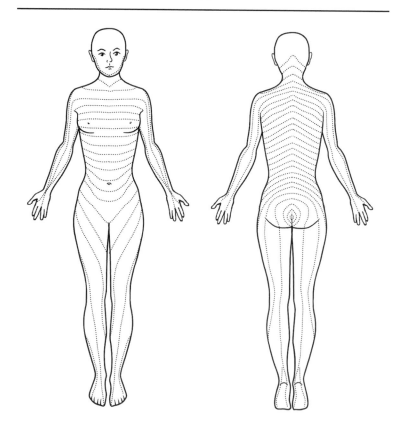

(acceleration is the rate of change of velocity, the speeding up or slowing down of movement). In fact, many of the body's sensory organs, especially those related to the sense of touch, are best able to sense things that are changing and often unable to sense a stimulus that is constant, such as constant pressure.

For example, the inner ear is a system of fluid-filled cavities. The fluid within these cavities moves around due to gravitational forces when the head is moved. Nerves within the walls of these cavities detect the fluid movement and transfer that information to the brain. The brain then compares these signals with other sensory signals to interpret the position and acceleration of the body. When the signals of the inner ear do not match with the signals of another sensory organ, the result can be motion sickness. This often happens when riding in a car or plane because the inner ear is detecting accelerations but the eyes see a constant, unmoving environment.

Kinesthetic (or proprioceptive) sensing uses inputs like vision, sensory neurons in the muscles, and tactile feedback from the skin to understand the orientation and relative position of joints and body parts (e.g., whether or not the elbow is bent). This information is used to navigate body parts through space.

Over time, the brain builds an unconscious representation of the body that allows it to move the body through space without consciously controlling each movement. This representation is called the **body schema**. The body schema (Figure 2.2) was first identified by neurologists Sir Henry Head and Gordon Morgan Holmes in 1912 (Head and Holmes 1912). Legend has it that Head and Holmes were inspired by watching ladies of that era navigate through doorways in hats with extravagant plumes. They noted that these women ducked just enough to clear the top of a feather or ornament,

and no further, and theorized that the hat had actually become part of the wearer's implicit understanding of body space.

By definition, the body schema is unconscious and nonemotional (as opposed to the **body image**, which is an emotional representation of the body). The body schema is the brain's understanding of what is and is not part of the body, or where the body starts and ends in space. Interestingly, the body schema is not always the same as the actual physical body. Held or worn items can also be incorporated into the body schema, and many studies have shown that things like hand tools or even cars can actually become part of what the brain sees as body space.

Outside of the body schema is an area known as **peripersonal space**. Peripersonal space is generally

FIGURE 2.2 The body schema, peripersonal space, and extrapersonal space.

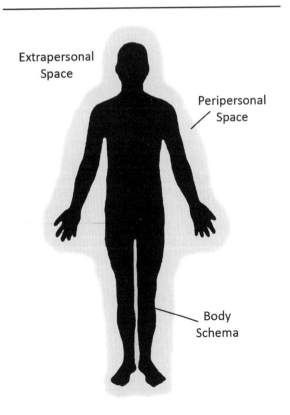

described as space that is within reaching distance and is a highly sensitized area. Quick movements or unexpected objects within peripersonal space demand attention and are hard to ignore. The space around the body outside of the limits of reach is **extrapersonal space**.

MECHANICAL ASPECTS OF MOVEMENT

Bones and muscles working together form a system of levers and forces that produce movement in much the same way that other mechanical devices or machinery do. The axes around which the motions of these body levers take place are the joints. The joints discussed in this chapter are the freely movable joints, called *diarthroses*. Some body joints are only slightly movable; others, such as those joining the sections of the skull are essentially immovable, performing more like seams.

A diarthrosis is generally classified into one of six types, which differ in their articulating surfaces (the shapes of the bony surfaces that come together) and in the movements that they allow. The two most common types of diarthroses are the **ball-and-socket joint** and the **hinge joint** (Figure 2.3). The ball-and-socket joint, which is found at

the hip and the shoulder, consists of a spherical shape at the end of one bone that fits into a cavity on the articulating bone. It permits a wide range of movement and is the most freely movable type of joint. The hinge joint can be found at the elbow or knee. It permits extensive movement only in one plane (i.e., it allows primarily bending and unbending).

An important part of the complex system of levers formed by the various bones and joints are the ligaments and tendons. **Ligaments** are strong cords of fibrous tissue that support and hold articulating surfaces together at the joints. **Tendons** are tough, fibrous bands of tissue that join muscles to bones. These connective elements are critical to movement. For example, Ashdown states that

One area where the connective system is particularly extensive is the series of muscles and tendons that stabilize and allow movement in the area of the shoulder. There is not a direct bony joint connecting the shoulder blade, and through it the arm, directly to the axial skeleton. Instead, wide arrays of muscles are attached to the shoulder blade through tendons. This muscle structure connects the shoulder blade to the vertebrae, allowing the whole shoulder blade to shift over the back of the ribcage. The combination of this structure and the ball-and-socket joint at the shoulder results in an extensive range of movement for the arms and shoulders in all directions. This area is particularly critical in terms of clothing fit and movement, as many articles of clothing are suspended from the shoulder, yet the movements required from the shoulders, arms, and hands in our lives are varied and constant. (2011, 280)

FIGURE 2.3 (A) a ball-and-socket joint (hip joint); (B) a hinge joint (elbow joint).

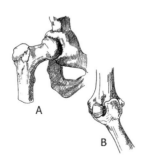

Movement occurs because muscles contract and pull on tendons, which exert a tensile stress on bones. Figure 2.4 shows this happening in the upper arm. The active muscle, in this case, the biceps, is contracting and exerting tension on the tendons connecting it to the lower arm, so the elbow is flexing. To straighten the elbow, the muscle at the back of the arm, the triceps, contracts and exerts tension on tendons at the back of the elbow, and the arm extends.

Another connective tissue, *cartilage*, exists in the body in several forms. One form, hyaline cartilage, lines the articulating surfaces of bones so that joints are cushioned and move over one another smoothly. Some hyaline cartilage provides a connection between bones, as it does for the ribs, allowing the rib cage to be flexible. Most of the human embryonic skeleton is made up of cartilage, which is converted to bone as a fetus grows. Hyaline cartilage is also present in the growth plates of bones in childhood, which gradually grow and convert into bone.

Cartilage has some stiffness but is flexible. It is not as rigid as bone, but it provides structure for parts of the body such as the outer ear and the nose. Cartilage has no blood vessels, and because it does not receive blood supply, it grows and heals more slowly than other body tissues.

The range of motion in a joint varies considerably from individual to individual and from time to time for each individual. Age, sex, race, health, conditioning, fatigue, body build, and other factors may affect the way an individual moves. The position of a neighboring body part may alter a particular movement, and psychological factors such as motivation and external factors such as weather may also influence the degree of movement that takes place. Injuries to any body part involved in the movement sequence—from the brain and motor neurons to the muscles, bones, tendons, and ligaments—will result in impaired movement or paralysis.

Describing Body Movement

The study of human movement is called **kinesiology**. Kinesiology is a broad field that encompasses information about the origins of movement in the brain and in other parts of the central nervous system, the chemical and biological processes that cause responses of the nervous system to be translated into motion, and the actual mechanics of motion. Kinesiology is closely allied with anatomy, physiology, and **biomechanics** (the study of the effects of force on motion in living bodies) and is based on knowledge in those fields. One branch of kinesiology that provides a useful background for clothing design is a type of mechanical kinesiology called *kinematics*. In kinematics, motion is described without concern for the forces involved

FIGURE 2.4 Flexing the elbow. Contracting the biceps muscle pulls on the tendon connecting it to the lower arm at the elbow and the arm bends.

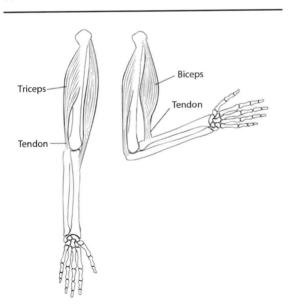

or the causes of motion. Kinematic analysis simply provides a description of the movement variables, not the factors that cause movement.

Body movement is not easy to describe. The human body is a complex anatomical system capable of hundreds of subtleties in type and direction of movement. Much of what a clothing designer needs to know about movement relates not only to the type and direction of movement that takes place at a specific joint, but to the degree of movement as well. One language for describing all three aspects of movement can be found in kinesiological literature.

In kinesiology, movement is defined in relation to a basic position called the **anatomical position**. The anatomical position (Figure 2.5A) is one in which the individual stands in an erect position with legs straight, feet flat on the floor, head erect, and the arms hanging straight down beside the body with the palms forward. The body can be thought of as a series of segments or links (the areas between

major joint centers) and the anatomical position defines a particular relationship of those segments to each other. Since movement is described in terms of the relationships of the body segments when they are in the anatomical position, the name given to a joint motion remains the same whether an individual is lying down, doing a handstand, or floating in the weightless environment of outer space where gravity does not define *up* and *down*.

Movement may also be described in terms of three bisecting planes and the axes of rotation for each of them. These planes and axes are shown in Figure 2.5B. The planes divide the body into the following sections: left and right; front and back; and upper and lower. Movement on any of the three planes takes place parallel to the plane.

The axes are the lines around which motion occurs. It may be easiest to think of them as pins or rods passing through a body joint in a specific direction. Rotation around an axis might be more easily understood by trying to identify the axes of some everyday items. In a book, for example, the axis around which the pages turn is the line along the area of the spine that holds the pages together. If you laid a pencil along the book spine, the pencil could represent the axis. An axis is not just a single point but a line, which in this case runs the entire length of the spine of the book.

The **sagittal plane** divides the body into right and left halves. Movement on the sagittal plane takes place parallel to it. When the head nods up and down as if to say, *yes*, this movement takes place on the sagittal plane. In order for this nodding movement to rotate around an axis, the axis must pass through the neck area horizontally from side to side. The axis around which head nodding takes place runs perpendicular to the sagittal plane and is called the **transverse axis** or sometimes the *y axis*.

The **frontal plane** divides the body into a front and a back. Some texts may refer to this plane as

FIGURE 2.5 (A) The anatomical position; (B) the planes and axes of motion of the body.

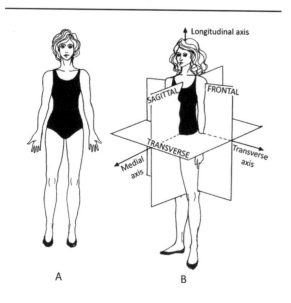

A   B

the coronal plane. The axis that runs perpendicular to this plane is called the **medial axis** or sometimes the *x axis*. When someone moves his or her head from side to side trying to touch the left ear to the left shoulder and then the right ear to the right shoulder, this movement takes place on the frontal plane around the medial axis.

The **transverse plane** divides the body into upper and lower sections. The axis perpendicular to it is the **longitudinal axis** or sometimes the *z axis*. The movement in shaking the head to say, *no*, takes place in the transverse plane around the longitudinal axis.

It is important to note that different fields may use completely different terminology to describe

the planes and axes. Todd notes, for example, that engineering terms are sometimes used in research studies so that "the term, sagittal plane, is sometimes replaced with the term, 'xz plane,' or lateral plane or horizontal plane" (1991, 16).

Body segment movements that occur at the joints are described in terms of their beginning from or returning to the anatomical position. Table 2.1 illustrates some of the terms, taken from the field of kinesiology, that are commonly used to describe basic body movements.

Flexion and extension are forward and backward movements that take place on the sagittal plane. **Flexion** is bending; **extension** is straightening (Table 2.1A and B). When the knee bends,

TABLE 2.1. Basic Kinesiology Terms Used to Describe Body Movement

---

MOVEMENTS ON THE SAGITTAL PLANE

A. Flexion: bending

B. Extension: straightening; returning to the anatomical position

---

MOVEMENTS ON THE FRONTAL PLANE

C. Abduction: movement to the side, away from the body's midline

D. Adduction: movement toward the body's midline

MOVEMENT AROUND AN AXIS

E. Rotation: movement of a body part around its own longitudinal axis

F. Pronation: rotation of the forearm so that thumb points toward the midline of the body

G. Supination: rotation of the forearm so that the thumb points away from the midline of the body

---

MOVEMENT ON SEVERAL PLANES

H. Circumduction: conical movement around a joint; a sequence of flexion, abduction extension and adduction

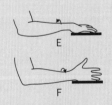

it is being flexed; when it straightens, it is being extended. The body segments in the anatomical position are fully extended.

Abduction is movement away from the midline of the body; **adduction** is movement toward it. Both movements take place on the frontal plane around the medial axis (Table 2.1C and D). These two terms are only used to describe movements of the limbs, hands, and feet since any sideward movement of the trunk or head distorts the midline of the body so that it can no longer be used as a reference point. When the neck or trunk is bent to the side, this is referred to as **lateral flexion**.

Rotation is the movement of a body part around its own longitudinal axis. Movement during rotation takes place parallel to the transverse plane. The model in Table 2.1F is rotating her hand from the anatomical position toward the midline of the body. This is called medial rotation or **pronation**. In Table 2.1G, she is turning her hand back toward the anatomical position (the thumb moving away from the midline of the body). This is referred to as

lateral rotation or **supination**. These terms are also used to describe similar motions of the feet.

Circumduction (Table 2.1H) is a combination of flexion, abduction, extension, and adduction. In circumduction, a body segment makes a cone shape, the point of which is at the joint center. The movement of an arm or leg swinging in a circle would be termed circumduction.

Figure 2.6 shows the whole body in flexion and in extension in comparison with the anatomical position. Many modifying terms are used in combination with these basic kinesiology terms. Table 2.2 contains a list of the most common terms.

FIGURE 2.6 Flexion (left) anatomical position (center) and extension (right) of all body joints.

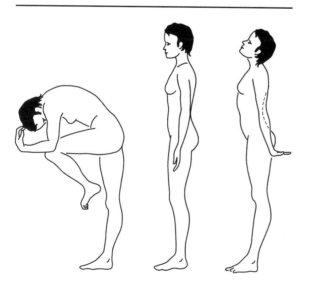

TABLE 2.2 Common Modifying Terms for Describing Body Movement

Hyper	A prefix denoting movement beyond the anatomical position or the body's normal range of motion
Lateral	Toward the side of the body, away from the body's midline
Medial	Toward the middle of the body
Proximal	Nearer to the center of the body or the point of attachment
Distal	Farther from the center of the body or the point of attachment
Anterior (ventral)	Toward the front of the body
Posterior (dorsal)	Toward the back of the body
Superior	Nearer to the top of the body (the head)
Inferior	Nearer to the bottom of the body (the feet)

The prefix **hyper** may be used in combination with extension or adduction. Webster's defines hyper as "beyond the ordinary." It is used in kinesiology to indicate movement in which a body segment is moved beyond the anatomical position. The term *hyperextended knees*, for example, is used to indicate a condition where the knee joint may extend beyond the anatomical position and actually take an angle the reverse of the one it assumes during flexion. When the arm is extended past the side of the body toward the rear, this movement would be called hyperextension of the arm.

The modifiers medial and lateral were mentioned earlier with regard to rotation and flexion. The **lateral** in lateral flexion simply indicates that the movement is toward the side or away from the midline of the body. The term **medial** is used to indicate movement toward the midline of the body. Medial and lateral are often used in anatomy to indicate the position of a body part or the side of a particular bone toward the middle or the side of the body. When referring to the inside of the thighbone, for example, it would be called the *medial aspect* of the bone.

Proximal and distal are terms that serve to identify a reference point in relation to the attachment of a body segment. **Proximal** means closer to the attachment point, whereas **distal** means farther from the attachment point or the midline of the body. With reference to the arm, then, the shoulder would be the proximal joint, while the wrist would be the distal one.

The terms **superior** and **inferior** are also used to describe the position of one body part relative to another. Superior parts are located closer to the head, or higher than inferior parts, which are located closer to the feet. When a body part moves to a superior position, it is moving closer to the head.

Some complex movements involve either a series of related motions or a motion that takes place on more than one plane. These require additional terminology. For example, two special terms are used for movement involving the shoulder joint, which has three planes of movement. When the arm is flexed to the shoulder level and then abducted, this movement is termed **horizontal abduction** (Figure 2.7A). When the arm is abducted to shoulder level and then moved horizontally (adducted) to a forward flexed position, this is termed **horizontal adduction** (Figure 2.7B).

Because the shoulder is capable of such free and varied motion, a number of terms are used to refer specifically to shoulder movement. Two of the most common ones are elevation and depression. The upward or shrugging movement of the shoulders is referred to as *elevation*. The opposite or downward movement of the body part is referred to as *depression*.

Abduction and adduction of the fingers and toes are described in reference to the longitudinal

FIGURE 2.7 Combined movements. (A) Horizontal abduction of the arm; (B) horizontal adduction of the arm.

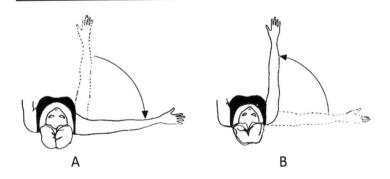

A   B

midline of the hand or foot rather than the midline of the trunk (Figure 2.8). The specialized function of the thumb also has resulted in a distinctly different application of standard terminology to describe its movement.

Additional prefixes aid in the precise description of movement. Some indicate the relative positions of the body parts or movements. Anterior means "*toward the front*"; posterior means "*toward the rear*." The prefixes **antero** and **postero** are derived from these terms. When something moves **anteroposteriorly**, it is moving from front to back along the sagittal plane. Often, the abbreviation AP is used for anteroposterior.

A specific numerical value can be assigned to flexion, extension, abduction, and adduction by measuring how far a body part moves from the original anatomical position. For example, when the arm is in the anatomical position, fully extended, the upper and lower arm form almost a 180° angle at the elbow joint. When the elbow is bent (Figure 2.9), it may move as much as 130° from its original position; that is, it may be in 130°

of flexion. This combination of terms and numbers forms the basis for several more complex and specific systems of classifying movements that are discussed later in this chapter.

It is important to note that some systems of recording joint motion express the *actual angle* between body segments rather than the *change* from the basic position. Under these systems, flexion at the elbow joint depicted in Figure 2.9, for example, would be reported as 50° flexion. A designer must be aware of the system in use when reading literature concerning body movement.

Kinesiological terms are useful in discussing basic movements. However, in clothing design, as in many other fields, it is important for a designer to study the joints, muscles, and connective tissues in the areas involved in movement and develop clothing or items of protective equipment that will meet movement needs. The basic summary of terminology and concepts presented in this chapter are designed to serve only as a framework for further in-depth study as more specific movement problems are addressed. Learning the anatomy and

FIGURE 2.8 (A) Abduction and (B) adduction of the fingers.

FIGURE 2.9 Describing joint movement. The measurement of elbow flexion based on the degrees it moves away from the anatomical position.

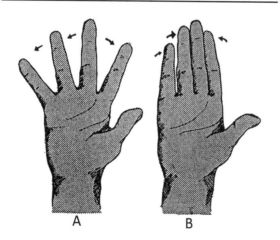

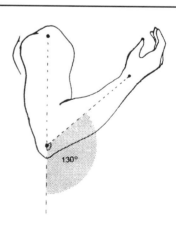

physiology of the areas of the body for which an item of functional or protective clothing is being designed is critical to its success. Understanding how the knee moves, for example, not only can help set design goals for a knee protector but also may provide designers with inspiration for design.

When protecting a body part, it is also very advantageous to know the names of bones, muscles, and connective tissue in areas being protected so that medical experts can be consulted and discussions with them can be understood. Anatomy and Design 2.1 provides one example of how knowledge about a body part can be used to inspire unique approaches to protective clothing design.

The innovative design shown in Anatomy and Design 2.1 Figures D and E was achieved by looking at only one aspect of the structure of the hand. It provides an illustration of how unique, effective design can evolve if designers understand the workings of the human body. When designing a glove for temperature extremes, it is important to understand where the major blood vessels of the hands are and how capillaries function. When designing a glove that needs a high degree of tactility, it is critical to understand how nerves and skin structure allows touch to be registered in the brain. Human anatomy is far too complex to discuss in detail in this text, but the example in Anatomy and Design 2.1 illustrates the significant influence that anatomy has on garment design. Every protective apparel designer should own good anatomy and physiology texts and a good medical dictionary.

Identifying User Needs for Movement

It is critical that clothing designers understand the movement needs of individuals who will be wearing their garments. Movement involves time, energy, and space. Designers need first to determine which aspects of movement are most critical to users and then to determine how to realistically gather information about them.

Although most of the information an apparel designer requires may seem to be concerned with the spatial aspects of movement, certain aspects of all three factors are involved in most design problems. Clearly, it is of primary importance to know the precise positions of the arm as it swings a tennis racquet in order to design a tennis garment with just the right shape of **armscye** (armhole). However, it may be just as critical in some situations to study movement frequency or the energy needed to complete a particular movement. If a factory worker strains a glove very slightly every time he places a new part on a machine, and he handles 300 parts a day, the glove may cause considerably more discomfort, muscle strain, and energy drain than his shirt, which strains greatly the once or twice he bends to retrieve an item from the floor. The designer should consider that the glove itself needs to be designed to withstand this continuous slight strain (with reinforced seams or special thread for example) so that it does not experience the garment equivalent of fatigue failure.

Many of the methods discussed in Chapter 1 under "Conducting Research" can be employed to uncover critical information. One of the best ways to gather information is for designers to become *participant-observers* (i.e., to engage in a client's activities themselves). One unique example of an attempt to become a participant-observer can be found in research on aging. (See Design Strategies 2.1.)

If participation in an activity is not an option, direct observation may need to be employed. In very specific cases, it may be beneficial to directly film the user at work and analyze the recording

Anatomy and Design 2.1: Skeletal Structure and Glove Mobility

The hand is a complex anatomical structure capable of a wide range of movements. If the focus of glove design is on mobility, it makes sense to begin by examining the joints of the hand. The bone structure of the hand (Figure A) consists of

1. Fourteen phalanges (finger bones). The thumb has two phalanges: a distal phalanx and a proximal phalanx. The four fingers each have three phalanges: a distal phalanx, a middle phalanx, and a proximal phalanx.
2. Five metacarpals (the middle bones of the hand in the area of the palm).
3. Eight carpals (wrist bones). These bones form joints with one another. In addition, some form joints with the radius and ulna (the bones of the lower arm), and others form joints with the metacarpals.

The joints between the phalanges are capable only of flexion and extension. The joints between the fingers and the hand (the metacarpo-phalangeal or MP joints) and those between the wrist and the hand (carpometacarpal or CM joints) allow flexion, extension, abduction, and adduction. The joint between the thumb and the wrist is a saddle joint that allows circumduction. Each of the joints of the hand has a different capacity for movement and each individual may have joints that have different capacities as well.

If one looks at the hand in a relaxed position, it is easy to see that its particular arrangement of muscles and ligaments pull the hand naturally into a partially flexed position. So the neutral position of the hand is not flat, and almost every work situation requires the hand to increase flexion. The goal for glove designers, then, is to create a design that achieves the maximum flexion so that the most mobile hand can fully bend without straining the glove.

One of the easiest solutions to the problem is to use comfort stretch materials to form the glove. In many hazardous situations, however, the most easily stretchable materials do not provide sufficient

FIGURE A The bones of the hand.

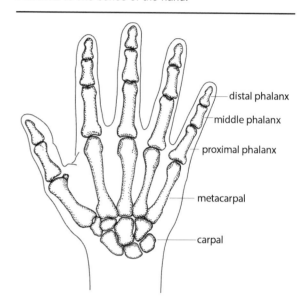

distal phalanx
middle phalanx
proximal phalanx
metacarpal
carpal

protection. If one examines the appearance of a flat, nonstretch glove on the hand as it bends, it is easy to see the strain over the top of each knuckle and the bunching of fabric on the underside of each. So more length is needed in the fingers on the back of the glove fingers and less length is needed on the palmar side of the fingers. Many dress gloves are cut with a handprint shape for the palmar side of the hand and another for the back of the hand. The sides of the fingers are then covered with strips called **fourchettes** (Figure B). The fingers on the back or dorsal pattern can be cut slightly longer than those on the palmar side to allow more length over the knuckles and contouring of the fourchettes allows the two to be joined. This gives the fingers of a glove a slight curve, but not enough to fully flex the fingers.

One solution to adding length over the back of each finger would be to add a pleat over each knuckle. The difficulty with this approach can be seen immediately if one studies the joints of the hand. With a hinge joint,

FIGURE B A shaped, fitted glove with the fourchettes (in black).

FIGURES D AND E The *daisy-wheel* pattern for the fingers allows seaming to be placed along the side of each finger; pleats over the back of the hand and shorter fingers on the palm than the back of the glove allow it to take a contoured, working position. *(Design by Dixie Rhinehart)*

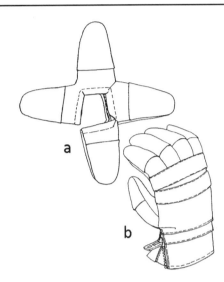

there is an area that expands in length, an area that contracts and shortens in length and a line down the side of the joint that does not change length at all. In this case, a line down the center of the sides of the fingers does not change length as the fingers bend (Figure C). If pleats are added to the back of the fingers to give them extra length at the knuckles, ideally they should extend from this line. With fourchettes, they cannot achieve this.

One creative designer looked at the way that fingers flexed and developed a way to place a seam directly along this nonextending line. He cut away all of the fingers of the glove at a line along the MP joints. He then made the fingers the width required by the end use and set them in a *daisy-wheel* pattern (Rhinehart

FIGURE C The axes of bending (dotted lines) of the fingers. *(Design by Dixie Rhinehart)*

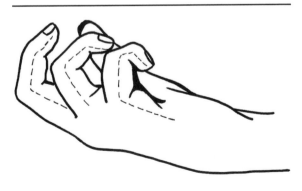

1987) (Figure D). The fingers on the back of the hand could then be given a pleat that had maximum extension over the knuckle with no extra length at the seamline. The seamline joining the back to the palmar side of the fingers then ran directly over the axis of bending allowing the pleat to expand exactly where extra length was needed.

This design allows the glove to move into a working position without strain. (See Figure 2.39 for other examples of the working position.) It provides length over the knuckles and eliminates bunching of material in the knuckle creases on the palmar side of the hand. It also allows free adduction of the fingers. The seam at the base of the fingers makes it possible to shorten the palmar side of the fingers to add even more contour to the glove shape. Similar approaches can be taken at the MP and CM joints of the hand and the concept can often be applied to other hinge joint coverings.

Design Strategies 2.1: Participant Observation: the AGNES

Whenever possible, it is helpful for designers to put themselves in their clients' shoes. One tool that has been used to help designers understand the physical problems of aging was developed by researchers at the Massachusetts Institute of Technology (MIT) with their AGNES (Age Gain Now Empathy System).

The system is composed of a suit (Figure A) that incorporates features that interfere with a wearer's joint flexibility, balance, vision, and hearing. Braces and straps on the arms and legs limit elbow and knee flexion and make movement more difficult so that muscles fatigue more quickly. A neck brace makes it difficult to turn the head. Yellow-lensed eyeglasses reduce contrast and make it difficult to see in dim light. Earplugs limit the hearing of high-pitched sounds such as those that form consonants and make it difficult to hear soft tones. Special shoes help create balance problems. Gloves reduce tactile sensations, and braces at the wrist decrease both its strength and mobility.

MIT engineers believe that the suit will help individuals in many fields better understand the problems of aging. A number of companies have produced garments to simulate other user conditions such as hemiplegia (Sakamoto) or obesity (Sim U Suit). Designers, architects, city planners, nursing home

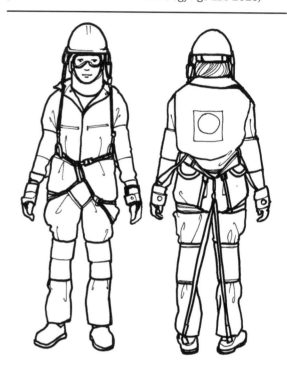

FIGURE A The AGNES (Age Gain Now Empathy System). *(Massachusetts Institute of Technology Age Lab 2013)*

staff members, and many others can gain design inspiration and test their design ideas while wearing these suits.

frame by frame. A designer might attend a karate exhibition, for example, and film and make notes on the types of movements participants use while executing their moves. Data may also be gathered by observing strains on a garment during movement or by looking at used garments to see where strain has caused seams to tear out or fabric to stretch.

Designers must be constantly aware that athletes, workers, and others they are observing may have their optimal movement restricted by their current clothing and equipment. In many sports and occupations, training films can be observed or interviews can be conducted with coaches and players or training personnel to help determine *optimal* movement patterns. Some restrictions posed by clothing can be studied in laboratory simulation of an activity. In a sport like fencing, for example, fencers might wear stretch leotards and use noninjurious weapons so that their unrestricted movement patterns can be clearly noted.

Notating Movement

Many movement studies collect data by notating or recording body movement so that movement data from many participants can be compared and a complete cycle of movements can be charted. Even though much of this task has been taken over by electronic recording devices, there are still situations in which information needs to be gathered by manual notation. Because of privacy concerns, electronic equipment may not be allowed in nursing homes and hospitals, for example. In addition, during the early stages of research, it may be desirable to take quick notes in order to establish what is needed to set up electronic recording equipment.

Movement notation requires a language, whether it be one of words, numbers, or other symbols. Researchers sometimes develop their own notation systems for a specific research projects and train their staff to use them. Others adopt or adapt language that is already established. Movement studies have been undertaken in fields as diverse as anthropology, aerospace science, dance, industrial safety, medicine, physical education, physical therapy, and psychology. For each, the focus on movement is slightly different, and the terms used may be specific to the field. Whatever language a clothing designer uses, it is important to keep in mind from the beginning that the data collected with it must be able to be translated into information that can be applied to clothing design.

One of the simplest methods of movement notation is called symbol substitution, in which a single letter or number stands for a specific movement.

One of the most familiar examples of symbol substitution occurs in ballet where the basic positions of the feet are described by number (Figure 2.10). Square dancing calls are an expanded form of symbol substitution as are phrases that identify movement cycles in various sports, such as the "triple toe loop" in figure skating.

A great deal of work on more complex forms of movement notation has taken place in the field of dance. These notation systems arose in order for choreographers to have a way to record dance in much the same way that composers write music scores. Among the most well known of the systems are Labanotation (Hutchinson 1970); Benesh notation (Benesh 1956); and the Eshkol-Wachman movement notation (EWMN) system, which is based largely on a stick figure format.

In many situations, it will be important to be able to *quantify* the degree of individual body segment movements. Roebuck developed a precise and comprehensive system of movement notation for the space industry during the Apollo program of the U.S. National Aeronautics and Space Administration (NASA). His system was developed so that all of the contractors involved in developing the Apollo space suits would have a very precise common language to describe suit

FIGURE 2.10. Symbol substitution in ballet for basic position of the feet. (A) Position one; (B) position two; (C) position three; (D) position four.

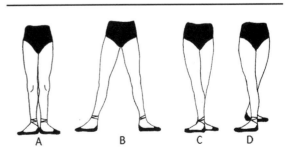

mobility requirements (Roebuck 1968, 79). He developed the system after looking at work on movement notation in dance, occupational therapy, industrial engineering, prosthesis design, anthropology, mathematics, and kinesiology.

The system Roebuck describes is based on the concept that the human body is "a collection of mechanical linkages" (1968, 81). The first portion of his system is a classification method used to identify each link or body segment with a number. This number is then used to identify the body part involved in a specific motion. Figure 2.11 shows the overall numerical classification system. Each major body segment (head, arm, torso, leg) is given a two-digit classification such as 10, 20,

30, or 40. In general, numbers beginning with an even digit (20, 40, 60) are assigned to the right side of the body and numbers beginning with an odd digit (30, 50, 70) are assigned to the left side of the body. As each body part is divided into smaller segments, each of them is given a number that relates to the original two-digit number used for the body part. For example, the whole right arm is indicated by the number 20. The upper arm, from shoulder to elbow, is designated 21. The lower arm is designated 22, and the hand, 23. Further subdivisions may be made by expanding the two-digit number to as many as four digits, as has been done on the hand in Figure 2.12. The thumb takes its number from its position on the hand and, therefore, is designated 231. The links on the thumb

FIGURE 2.11 A link diagram and numerical notation system for the Roebuck study on mobility notation. Each major body 'link' or segment is given a two-digit number. *(Roebuck 1968)*

FIGURE 2.12 A numbering system for link subdivisions of the hand in the Roebuck study. *(Roebuck 1968)*

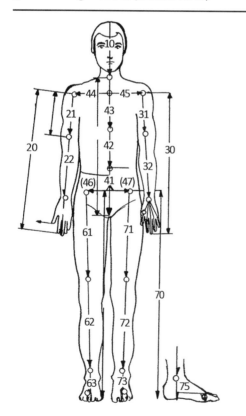

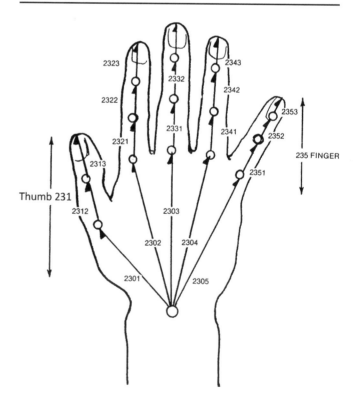

are numbered in relationship to the thumb. The area from the tip of the thumb to the first knuckle is assigned the number 2313. Each body link then can be numerically identified. In order to use the system for clothing research, a postscript, B or S, may be added to each number to make clear whether the link being described is part of the body (B) or part of the suit (S).

The second portion of Roebuck's system involves a method of describing the position of each body link in relation to the three planes of motion (see Figure 2.5). Each plane is given a shorthand symbol: F for frontal, S for sagittal, and T for transveral. An individual joint is considered to be at the center of a sphere. The position of a link is then described in standard kinesiological fashion, as the degree of motion from the anatomical position. Figure 2.13 shows a figure with his arm abducted 126°. The position of the arm is notated as 20B F:126, S:173, T:75. The number 20 indicates the whole arm. The postscript B means that body movement is being described. F:126 indicates a position 126° from the anatomical position on the frontal plane. The remaining numbers indicate positions of 173° on the sagittal plane and 75° on the transverse plane.

In addition to precisely describing limb position, Roebuck's work also included a proposed system of terminology to describe limb motion (Table 2.3). Not only could the endpoints of a movement be precisely described alphanumerically, but the entire progress of the motion could be

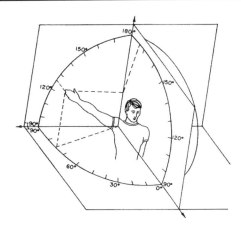

FIGURE 2.13 Notating body link position in the Roebuck study. *(Roebuck 1968)*

given a name such as frontinvection or sagerotation. This system is extremely complex, but at the same time it permits precise, unambiguous communication about body position and movement.

Analyzing Movement

When notation systems involve data collection and analysis, they can be of great value to the clothing designer in planning garment shapes and sizes. Systems that precisely note human body movement generally have several components: a measuring tool, a recording system, and a system of data analysis. The measurement tool and recording system are often found in one unit and are identified together as the *data acquisition* instrument or phase of a movement study.

TABLE 2.3 Terminology Used to Describe Limb Motion *(Roebuck 1968)*

PLANE	DIRECTION	TYPE
Frontal	Outward (e)	Pivotal (vection)
Sagittal (sag)	Inward (in)	Around axis (rotation)
Transversal (trans)	Downward (negi)	Twisting (torsion)

GONIOMETRY

There are a variety of ways to collect data on body movement. The most common tool used to measure movement is the goniometer. (See Figure 2.14A.) A **goniometer** (from the Greek, gonia, meaning "angle") is a simple, two-armed tool used by physicians and physical therapists to measure both active movement (the extent to which a patient's muscles can move a body part unassisted) and passive joint motion (the extent to which a therapist can bend a joint without any muscle contraction on the part of a patient). The central pivot point of the goniometer is placed at the center of the joint axis. Then, each arm is lined up along the long bones on either side of the joint and held there. For example, the pivot point might be placed on the side of the leg at the center of the knee joint, one arm would then be lined up along the femur (thighbone), and the other arm lined up along the tibia (calf bone) (Figure 2.14B). As the knee is flexed (i.e., as the calf is brought closer to the thigh), an indicator on one arm of the goniometer points to a scale on the instrument that tells the number of degrees the knee joint has flexed. Goniometers come in many sizes with even tiny versions being available to measure the joint motion of the fingers.

The reliability of data collected with a goniometer is largely dependent on the skill of the researcher or therapist in placing it accurately on the joint and bone axes. The major difficulty in using a goniometer is the accurate placement of the center of the instrument (Norkin and White 2003). Riddle, Rothstein, and Lamb (1987), who studied the reliability of goniometric data, found that data appeared to have a high reliability when a single therapist directly measured movement, but results could not be as easily compared between therapists. Adams and Keyserling (1993) also found that data gathered by different types of goniometers often could not be compared. Despite these limitations, goniometers are standard clinical and research tools because they are inexpensive and easy to use.

Some of the goniometers used in physical therapy may have digital readouts and the capacity for data storage. Many goniometers, such as the type shown in Figure 2.15, may be connected through an interface to a computer for digital data storage and processing.

Some joint angles are more easily measured by a **gravity-dependent goniometer**, sometimes called an inclinometer. An example of an inclinometer is shown in Figure 2.16. The inclinometer operates on gravity using a counterweighted needle so it

FIGURE 2.14 (A) A goniometer; (B) placement of a goniometer to measure flexion of the knee.

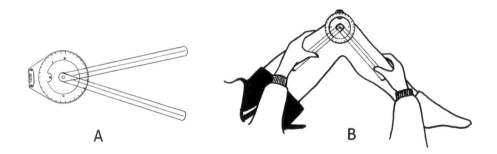

FIGURE 2.15 A digital goniometer that has the capacity to store data and interface with a computer.

FIGURE 2.16 A gravity-dependent goniometer measuring hip flexion.

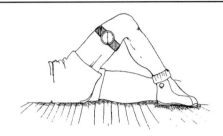

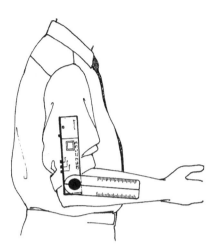

can be noted on its dial. Inclinometers may also be mounted on a base and held against a moving body surface. Several units can be used simultaneously to measure compound motion in areas such as the spine. Care must be taken not to strap the inclinometer over clothing in a way that causes it to bind and limit movement.

ELECTROGONIOMETRY

Measurement of joint movement may also be made electronically with the aid of a continuous-measurement goniometer called an **electrogoniometer** or **elgon** (Figure 2.17). The elgon is designed to be centered on the joint axis,

also can only be used to measure movement in a vertical plane. One of its advantages is that it does not have to be placed directly on the center of the joint but can be strapped on any body part as long as it is parallel to the plane in which the angle of movement is to be measured. Working much like a compass, the device can be zeroed at any beginning position, and movement from that position

FIGURE 2.17 An electrogoniometry system with a close-up of the electronic device (the elgon) placed at the center of the elbow joint.

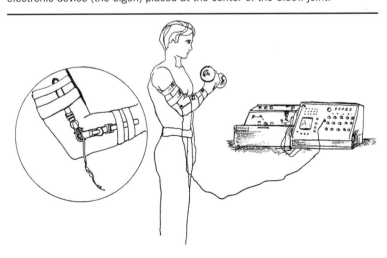

where it converts physical motion to an electrical signal so that it can be stored, processed, and transmitted electronically. Like a nonelectronic goniometer, the elgon does not provide information about where a body part is in space; it simply indicates the relationship between two body parts (i.e., the joint angle). One of its advantages over other types of goniometry is that data can be collected continuously throughout an entire movement and subjects can wear clothing over the instrument. If worn with clothing, care must be taken, however, that the sensors and wires used in the electrogoniometer do not have an effect on the ability of the garment to move as completely as it would under normal wear conditions.

MOTION CAPTURE: CAMERA-BASED METHODS

One of the most popular methods of data acquisition is motion capture that takes place by recording the movements of points or surfaces using still cameras or video cameras. Camera-based motion capture methods either involve placing extensions on the body so that the position of body segments can be more easily seen (Figure 2.18) or marking the

FIGURE 2.18 Fins used to provide a clearer picture of the relationships of body segments.

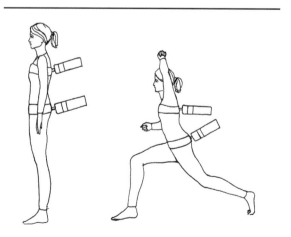

body in some way so the camera picks up visual reference points. With motion capture, movements can take place in the context of an activity (there is no need to stop mid-movement to take a measurement) and the movement can be broken down into its components and analyzed frame by frame. Movements can be repeatedly viewed and analyzed by different researchers and/or a variety of analysis tools using the same record. Both still images and video have high-speed recording capacity so that movements can be replayed in slow motion.

Using and Placing Markers

Marking pens, adhesive dots, reflective material, small lights or any materials that stay in place and provide a clear contrast with the skin may be used as markers. Because most of these markers are passive (not powered) or use wireless communication, there is no impediment to movement due to cables or wires. Markers that do not need power are often nearly weightless, further reducing any effects on the movement of the body or clothing. Many camera-based systems offer the potential to adjust the captured image contrast so that only the light reflected or produced by the markers is visible during analysis (Figure 2.20). For approaches that use video recording, bodies may be recorded against a specific color background that can later be dropped out of the picture. Then, the body may be superimposed on other backgrounds that contain grids or against more contrasting backgrounds to make measurement easier.

A major problem confronting those who do motion analysis is the ability to locate markers accurately and to secure them to the body in ways that do not interfere with movement or measurement. Skin movement introduces a kind of slippage between the joint center and a marker that can lead to measurement error. Most reflective markers are taped in place on the body (Figure 2.19), but the tape used must not obscure the marker or loosen during movement. If it does, error of another sort will be introduced.

FIGURE 2.19 Marking joint centers for photographic analysis using black adhesive patches with white reflective dots at the center.

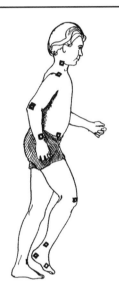

FIGURE 2.20 Motion analysis using markers on joint centers. (A) Markers placed on a walking girl; (B) a stick figure superimposed on the dots for viewing.

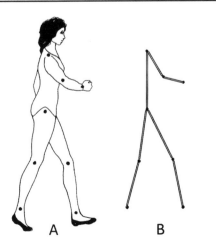

Using Reflective Markers for 3-D Motion Capture

The most common type of camera-based motion capture uses small markers to reflect infrared light back to an array of cameras. Each camera is surrounded by a ring of infrared light sources, and the reflective markers send this light directly back to the camera when illuminated. Infrared light is commonly used because the camera can be tuned to see only infrared light. This helps the light reflected by the markers to be more easily distinguished from the visible light in the room, which will also be reflected by the markers. The cameras then use 2-D image processing to triangulate the position of a marker that is seen by more than one camera. In this way, the 3-D coordinates in space of each marker are recorded for each frame of video. Markers can be placed anywhere on the body and used to measure speed and quality of movement, joint angles, and relationships between body parts. An array of many reflective markers can be applied to the skin in an evenly spaced grid or mesh layout to capture the movement of an entire surface like the face, rather than a point like the elbow.

Capturing Motion with Laser Scanning

Unlike systems that track the position of individual points or markers, laser scanners have the ability to capture the topology of a surface. Three-dimensional laser scanning can be used to generate a video capture of a very large number of points on a surface as it moves. The points are then connected into a mesh surface topology. This kind of scanning uses a set of cameras that capture reflected laser light to reproduce a surface in fine detail.

3-D SENSOR-BASED MOTION CAPTURE

A drawback to marker-based 3-D motion capture is that to capture the marker, the camera must be able to see it. Markers that are occluded by moving limbs or pieces of clothing are lost, and no data is then recorded. Sensor-based motion capture systems use sensors mounted directly on the body surface to detect the positions, dimensions, and movements of the body. This information is then either processed on the body itself (in a self-contained or mobile system) or sent to a central computer for processing (in a tethered system). One drawback is that sensors (and even more so batteries and processing units) are usually bulkier and heavier than reflective markers.

Sensing Bend and Stretch

One method of continuously gathering information about body dimensions, positions, and movements is through sensors that detect bend and stretch. Even though sensors can be strapped or adhered to the body, using a sensing *garment* rather than individual sensors or devices is helpful in cases where there are many sensors to affix to the body. The garment keeps sensors in a fixed configuration and allows all of the sensors to be put on the body at once. There are many ways to detect stretch and bend (some of which will be discussed in Chapter 4 under the heading "Sensors"). Here, it is important to understand how these signals can be used to understand changes in the dimensions and movement of the body.

Stretch sensing can be used to sense joint movements or positions by detecting changes in the length of the outside of the joint. As a joint bends, the inner surface gets shorter while the outer surface gets longer. Placing a stretch sensor on the inside or outside of a joint allows that change in length to be detected as the sensor extends or contracts. Stretch sensors can also be used to detect body dimensions. An elastic garment that can sense stretch in many directions will register a baseline length when relaxed (e.g., on the table). After a specific person

dons a garment, sensors will expand to accommodate the wearer's body, and the new sensor lengths can be used to measure the dimensions of each individual body area.

Bend sensors can also be used to detect joint movements and positions. The DataGlove (Figure 2.21) uses bend sensors to detect flexion of the fingers. It also uses a combination of ultrasonic and magnetic sensors to detect the position of the hand relative to the body (Greenleaf 2001). The position sensor unit is located on the back of the glove, and optical fiber bend sensors run down each digit. The sensors and cables are mounted on a stretchable, spandex and nylon glove allowing the wearer to have full flexibility of the hand. When each finger joint is bent, the sensor detects these bends and sends a signal to a processor. The transmitted signal describes the direction and amount of flexion of each joint.

This system tracks both the position of the hand and fingers in space and the relationship of body segments to one another (the flexion and extension

FIGURE 2.21 The Data Glove®, a glove that contains fiber optic cables that measure hand movement. *(Greenleaf 2001)*

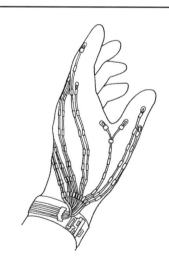

of the joints). Although originally of primary interest as a part of virtual reality entertainment systems, it was also one of the first sensor-based methods of measuring range of motion at each joint. The capacity for the system to convert joint movements, hand gestures, and hand positions into data that could be electronically processed led to a variety of other end uses. For example, the movements of a gloved person using sign language might be tracked and translated by a computer into a written document. A virtuoso pianist might have a performance analyzed and recreated on a piano. Many sensor-based motion capture garments use a similar approach to provide the same information for other major joints of the body. Both gloves and suits can be donned under garments to be tested so that movement capabilities for clothed individuals can be precisely measured and depicted.

Sensing with Inertial Measurement Units

Another form of sensor-based motion capture uses sensor packs made up of *inertial measurement units* (IMUs). IMUs usually contain an assortment of inertial sensors that sense acceleration and orientation (for more about sensing, see Chapter 4, under the heading "Sensors"). IMU packs are placed on various body segments and transmit data either wirelessly or through cables to a central processor. The processor takes orientation and acceleration information from the IMUs and uses that information to deduce things like direction and degree of movement, and even body position in space. Because IMU-based motion capture does not rely on cameras, it is easy to use outside of the laboratory and easy to set up. However, because the packs are relatively large, it is usually not possible to capture fine-grained movements like facial expressions.

ANALYZING HOW VOLUME AND SHAPE AFFECT MOVEMENT

For many kinds of protective clothing and equipment, such as athletic pads, mobility is affected by the volume of the items placed on a body surface. Placing a bulky pad near a joint can shorten the range of motion and can interfere with navigating through the environment, particularly in tight spaces. As electronic technologies become more wearable, it is becoming increasingly important for designers to understand the relationship between the size and shape of a hard component and its placement on the body.

Researchers at the Natick Soldier Systems Center investigated this relationship as it related to soldiers on the battlefield. In their Bubbleman study, designers created an envelope or bubble of rigid polystyrene foam around a soldier's body (Pensotti et al. 1997). Horizontal cross sections of foam were cut shaped to the wearer's body, starting as very thick, bulky shapes. Wearing the foam bubble, soldiers attempted to perform job-related tasks such as crawling, running, and firing weapons. If the soldier was unable to successfully perform a task, parts of the foam sections were cut away (Figure 2.22). This cycle continued until the soldier could successfully perform all tasks, and the resulting size and shape of the maximum feasible volume was recorded.

In a similar project, researchers at Carnegie Mellon University focused on developing comfortable volumes for everyday users of technology, such as a runner who may want to wear a phone or music player mounted on his arm. They began with smaller, blocky shapes, which were then gradually curved and shaped to the body (Figure 2.23). Participants wore these volumes and evaluated their comfort and wearability, and the shapes were gradually refined to allow mobility and physical comfort (Gemperle et al. 1998).

FIGURE 2.22 The Bubbleman study. *(Pensotti et al. 1997)*

accommodates that expansion and contraction best if it follows the same patterns. When the knee is bent, for example, the leg increases in length over the kneecap and correspondingly decreases in length along the back of the knee. The circumference of the leg in the bent area may also increase as muscle tissues and fat move into different positions. Thus, if tight, nonstretch pants styled for the body in the anatomical position are worn, it may be difficult to bend at the knee. Not only is the length over the kneecap inadequate to accommodate the changes there, but the excess fabric at the back of the knee bunches up and adds to the difficulty of bending the leg.

It should be noted here that data on the frequency of specific movements and/or the forces involved in movements may also provide significant information for the designer.

EXAMINING THE BEHAVIOR OF THE SKIN DURING MOVEMENT

One method of exploring body expansion and contraction is to look at skin stretch or *local skin*

FIGURE 2.23 Determining comfortable volumes for electronic devices worn on the body. *(Gemperle et al. 1998)*

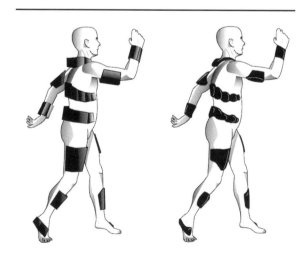

Applying Data on Body Movement to Clothing Design

Moving from what is known about body movement into the process of designing clothing for mobility can be achieved in a variety of ways. One of the best ways to precisely identify the areas in which ease is needed is to look at the elongation and contraction of a specific body area and relate it to the elongation and contraction of clothing placed over it. During movement, the body expands and contracts in the area surrounding its joints and clothing *strain.* Research on **skin strain** is based on the premise that the most freely moving clothing would act like a second skin, adjusting without strain as the body moves (Figure 2.24).

In a pioneering study, Kirk and Ibrahim (1966) developed a method of measuring the expansion and contraction of the body over joint areas that they called *anthropometric kinematics.* They took a series of measurements to determine precisely where skin strain actually occurred. Figure 2.25 shows what this process looked like when it was used at the knee. Measurements were taken outward from the center of the knee joint, for example, until the *difference* between the flexed knee and extended knee measurements no longer changed. Their research indicated to them that there was a local skin strain of approximately 42 percent in an isolated area from 2.5 inches (6.35 centimeters) above the kneecap to 2.5 inches (6.35 centimeters) below the kneecap. Since the major portion of the lengths of the thigh and calf do not change during movement, earlier research that reported the percentage of change from hip to ankle was fairly misleading. It is not a gradual expansion over the entire length of a pant leg that will best solve the problem but rather a 0 percent length expansion throughout most of the calf and thigh and a 42 percent expansion in a 5 inch (12.70 centimeter) area centered

FIGURE 2.24 Skin strain as an indicator of expansion needs in clothing. (A) Precisely measured square blocks drawn on the body at rest; (B) changes in the shape and size of blocks when the body moves from the anatomical position.

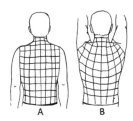

A   B

FIGURE 2.25 Anthropometric kinematics. (A) Guidelines marked on extended knee; (B) the amount and areas of skin stretch are determined by measuring the distance between lines when the knee is bent. *(Kirk and Ibrahim 1966)*

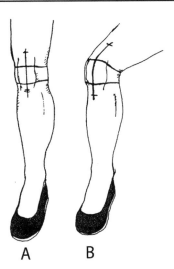

A   B

on the knee. The authors found that, for many of the measurements of expansion during body movement, some of the local skin strain measurements were many times those previously published.

Motion capture technologies and sensors can also be used to precisely measure local skin strain and changes in body dimensions during movement. Placing markers or sensors to form a grid over a body surface allows the amount and direction of stretch to be measured in three dimensions. There are many garments for which design could be greatly improved with this approach to planning mobility, concentrating on adding maximum ease or fabrics with appropriate stretch capacity directly in areas where the body expands rather than adding ease in every garment area.

Several bodies of research have explored skin strain from another perspective. In the 1860s, Austrian anatomist Karl Langer used an idea given to him by a local surgeon to map "cleavage lines" over the body surface (Langer 1861). These lines correspond to the direction of collagen fibers in the skin and were used by surgeons to place incisions such that the incision would experience stresses that would pull the sides of the wound together (rather than apart) as the wound healed. In the 1960s, Iberall mapped what he called **lines of nonextension**, lines on the body surface that indicate the direction in which the skin does not elongate during body movement. To determine the location and direction of these lines, Iberall stamped perfect circles on a subject's skin in the anatomical position (in Langer's case, circular holes were cut in the skin of cadavers). The subject then moved specific body parts in specific ways, and the stamped circles were photographed and measured. Stretching of the skin deformed the circles into ellipses. Diameters could then be measured from the ellipses. Unchanged diameters could be assumed to have not extended, and connecting these diameters produced lines that did not experience stretch during that movement. Iberall's lines were used by the U.S. space program in the development of pressurized space suits (Iberall 1964). An exploration of Iberall's and Langer's maps (see Figure 2.26) is extremely useful to a designer in terms of placing seamlines and other garment features.

EXAMINING THE EXPANSION OF CLOTHING DURING MOVEMENT

Stretch clothing can also be used to give the designer information about the expansion of specific body areas as the body moves. One method used in a number of studies has been to make a garment out of stretch fabric and then draw a grid pattern or circles on it (Figure 2.27). The changes in dimensions of the squares or circles when the body moves can be observed and measured.

It is also possible to use nonstretch garments with slits or openings to measure expansion. This can be done by opening seams between garment

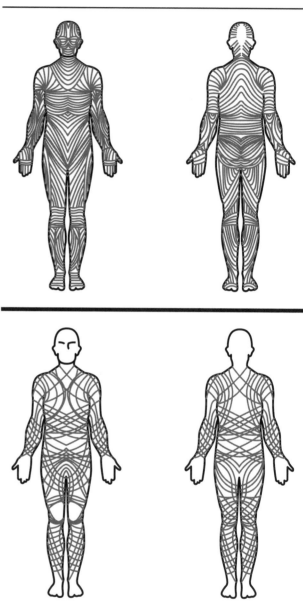

FIGURE 2.26 Cleavage lines (top) and lines of nonextension (bottom). *(Top, derived from Langer (1978); bottom, derived from Iberall, (1964))*

segments at areas of strain (See Figure 2.28) or by slitting fabrics to observe the openings that occur when various movements take place. Ashdown (1989) adapted a slitted-fabric research method developed by Crow and Dewar (1986) to study the stresses placed on disposable coveralls by asbestos

FIGURE 2.27 Studying body expansion by observing fabric strain. (A) Circles drawn on garment fabric; (B) changes in circle dimensions and shape during movement can be checked to determine strain.

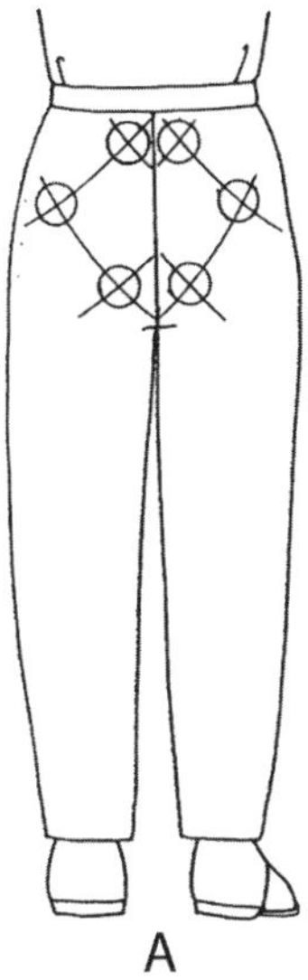

FIGURE 2.28 Detached garment segments help determine body expansion needs during movement. (A) Opening at armscye seam during abduction; (B) tracings of the same opening at varying degrees of abduction. *(Atkin 1980)*

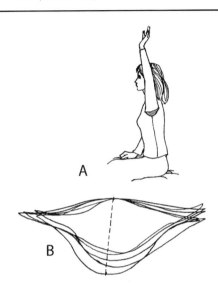

abatement crews. The coveralls involved in laboratory testing were slit in a honeycomb pattern (Figure 2.29A). Subjects then donned the slit coveralls over contrasting stretch bodysuits and replicated movements typically used in asbestos removal. Video cameras recorded the stresses placed on the garments as the slits opened during movement (Figure 2.29B). Ashdown used this method both to analyze problems that needed to be solved by redesign and to evaluate the success of redesigned coveralls. Her evaluation involved the use of independent observers who rated the designs visually; however, subsequent developments in computer analysis have allowed video frames of a garment area

to be fed directly into the computer where the areas of light garment and dark body suit could be precisely quantified (Ashdown 1994, personal communication).

FIGURE 2.29 (A) Alternative honeycomb slashing configurations for test garments; (B) resulting openings on the side torso and elbow of garment as wearer raises an arm. *(Ashdown 1989)*

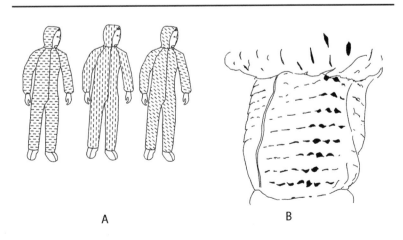

A   B

ANALYZING WRINKLES

Wrinkle analysis is a long-established method of collecting informal data on the fit of clothing (Figure 2.30). In fitting and flat pattern theory, the basic information provided by wrinkles generally includes the following:

1. Horizontal wrinkles indicate that a garment segment is too long or too tight around the body. If the wrinkles are full and loose, the garment segment is too long; if they are tight and strained, the garment is too tight around the body.

2. Vertical wrinkles indicate that a garment segment is either too short or too loose. If the wrinkles are tight and strained, the garment segment is too short; if they are full and loose, the garment is too big around the body. Although gravity may affect the location of horizontal wrinkles, vertical wrinkles generally point directly to the areas where tightness or looseness occurs.

3. If diagonal wrinkles are tight and strained, they point to the areas where insufficient ease is located. If they are full and loose, it generally means that there is excess length above the lowest point of the wrinkle.

It should be noted that folds and fullness in garments may be desired design features for both function and fashion, so not all wrinkles indicate potential movement problems. Some garments appear to contain excess fabric in the anatomical position, but they fit perfectly when the body is in a specific desired position. An example of this is shown in Figure 2.31A. The skirt shown has been planned for the seated figure, in this case, a paraplegic woman confined to a wheelchair. It fits smoothly in the seated position, eliminating excess folds in the lap and allowing extra length needed over the hips in their flexed position. On a standing figure, the skirt would appear as it does in Figure 2.31B. Loose, horizontal folds indicate that there is extra length in the back hip area. This extra material, while allowing proper fit for the seated figure, makes this skirt design inappropriate for the upright figure. Identifying the wrinkles and folds in garments while wearers are in active positions can provide the designer with a great deal of information about desirable garment forms for specific end uses.

FIGURE 2.31 A skirt designed for a woman in a wheelchair shown from the side. (A) The skirt fits smoothly in the seated position; (B) the same skirt on an upright figure. Extra length needed at the skirt back for the seated position bunches unattractively on the upright figure.

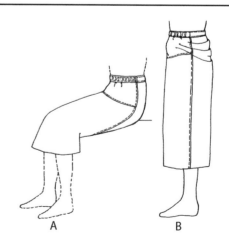

A   B

FIGURE 2.30 Wrinkle analysis. Tight diagonal wrinkles indicate areas where more garment ease is needed for a particular movement.

In some instances, movement can be prohibited by *excess* material as well as too little ease in a garment. The bunching up of a fabric that occurs behind the knee as it bends can limit knee flexion as much as tightness over the kneecap. The areas where excess fabric gathers can be as important for a designer to note as those where there is strain. Excess that appears in folds can actually be pinned out and measured to determine where and how much a garment needs to be changed to better accommodate movement.

Increased Mobility in Clothing

There are two basic approaches to increasing mobility in clothing: selecting a fabric that will move easily with the body and developing a garment design that promotes mobility. Ideally, both approaches should be used so that fabric and design work together to allow the maximum possible freedom of movement for the wearer. This takes careful planning in the early stages of designing.

FABRICS

The ideal fabric for clothing that moves easily with the body would be stretchy, flexible, light in weight, thin, and slippery. Frequently, however, these characteristics cannot be found in materials that provide other protective functions for a specific situation. For example, it is obvious that the easiest way to achieve mobility in a design is to use stretch fabric. The actionwear market is filled with second skins that move perfectly with the body. Typical stretch fabrics that are in use for exercise clothing are knits that have spaces between the yarns that expand every time the body moves. This means that they cannot serve as an effective barrier—or even as a filter—and these are important functions for many items of protective apparel. At the same time, many improvements have been made to impart stretch characteristics to a number of types of protective materials.

Stretch has been incorporated to some degree in many specialty fabrics that have achieved wide acceptance in the market in nonstretch forms. Microporous materials and microfiber insulation have had stretch capacities added to them. These developments were largely in response to the growing actionwear market in leisure activities such as skiing where consumers had grown attached to nonstretch versions of these high-performance materials and wanted more mobility in their apparel. A number of expandable solid membranes have entered the market, and these can often be laminated to stretchable fabrics to form a stretchable barrier fabric. Many of these are as thin as a surgeon's glove, so the finished fabric retains a great deal of flexibility and remains thin and lightweight. Rubber and synthetic rubber materials have usable stretch, and they function well for many types of protective garments.

It is just as important for a designer to know how well a material *recovers* from being stretched as it is to know the degree of elongation or extensibility of a material. When fabrics do not return to their original form after being stretched (i.e., they "bag out"), this can create bulk that itself may interfere with movement. Both the percent of recovery and the time needed for recovery are important to the performance of protective clothing.

If the material needed for a specific garment cannot stretch, the next most important thing is that it be *flexible*. One of the biggest problems for protective clothing designers is that the fabrics needed to provide adequate protection are often relatively stiff. Stiffness poses different design problems for a functional apparel designer than are normally faced by fashion designers whose creations generally involve more drapable materials. It is important to note that flexibility changes in different environments, particularly in relationship to temperature. The temperature extremes of an environment must be identified before a material can be considered appropriate for use.

Close behind flexibility in importance are *bulk* and *weight*. Often the protective capacities needed dictate that fabrics or layered systems of fabrics be thick or be given treatments that stiffen and weigh down clothing. These qualities make it difficult to use these fabrics in clothing that will move without a lot of effort. Bulk is particularly characteristic of protective clothing for high-temperature extremes. Thick materials can make a designer's ability to provide adequate mobility much more difficult (Figure 2.32).

One major factor that can often be varied without affecting the function of protective fabrics is the *friction* they present in relation to other clothing layers. The effect of friction drag in clothing layers is perhaps the least appreciated factor in movement restriction. In a study of the effects of clothing on energy expenditures, Teitlebaum and Goldman (1972) tested soldiers who dressed in typical

extreme cold weather gear worn over their fatigues, having them walk on a treadmill at a specified rate for a specified length of time. Then they took the weight of the extreme cold weather gear and placed the equivalent of that weight in a belt the soldiers wore over their fatigues alone. Since the belts did not affect their body movements as did the gear, it was presumed that any difference in metabolic rate would be due to the energy needed to work against clothing. The researchers found that the subjects wearing the extreme cold weather gear experienced 16 percent greater metabolic costs than those who carried the equivalent weight in a weight belt. They attributed the increased metabolic costs to "the friction drag between layers, i.e., the frictional resistance as one layer of material slides over another during movement, and/or a 'hobbling' effect of the clothing, i.e., interference with movement at the body's joints, produced by the bulk of the clothing" (Teitlebaum and Goldman 1972, 744). Even though most people are not aware of this in everyday clothing, almost everyone has had the experience of trying to slip on an unlined jacket over a flannel shirt or having various items of underclothing *hike up* uncomfortably as they rubbed against textured clothing worn over them. Many of the materials used in protective clothing considerably magnify this effect. Rubberized surfaces and plastic coatings can be extremely resistant to sliding over one another.

It is sometimes possible to smooth the surface of a material or to laminate a smooth material to the inner surface of a protective fabric to decrease the effects of friction. Wet suits for scuba diving, for example, generally have a nylon knit laminated to their inner surfaces to make them easier to slide on and off the body. It is also possible to laminate (adhere) several protective layers in a garment to one another so that they all move together and cannot catch or snag on each other. One caution

FIGURE 2.32 An entry suit for firefighting. The bulk needed to provide protection from the high temperature of the fire can interfere with mobility.

when using this method, however, is that lamination and other methods of joining multiple layers can create more stiffness in the final fabric system (because it prevents shear between the layers), so the trade-offs between the two need to be weighed. In choosing or developing the best fabric combination for a particular end use, designers often need to experiment with several different approaches to see what yields the best end results. Often, however, the reduction of frictional drag between garment layers can add significant mobility without posing a potential loss in other functional properties of a clothing system.

CLOTHING DESIGN

Despite the constant improvement of materials in terms of their mobility characteristics, it is likely that protective garment designers will have to continue to deal with fabrics that are less stretchy, heavier, stiffer, and thicker than their counterparts in the ready-to-wear fashion industry. Therefore, it is important to look at the ways in which designers can take a given protective fabric and create designs that relate them effectively to the human body.

A basic list of desirable characteristics can be presented for fabrics, but it is not as simple to provide a similar list of characteristics for design. There are, however, some important factors for a designer to explore when planning movement capacity in a garment. These include *ease* (the difference between garment measurement and body measurement in each garment area); **cut** or *contour* (the shape of pattern pieces and the relationship of garment segments to one another); and the way ease and cut affect the *fit* of a garment on different body shapes and sizes.

One reason why it is difficult to set forth a precise list of desirable characteristics for mobile clothing designs is that movement needs are different for every activity; thus, optimum design forms for each activity may be different. Before appropriate decisions can be made concerning the ease, cut, and fit of a garment, a designer must know as much as possible about the environment and activity of the intended wearer. A sleeve that is going to work well for a gardener who spends most of the time reaching forward and down toward the ground may not work well for an airline mechanic who spends a good deal of time reaching upward. Every movement made by an individual affects the set of clothing on the body and necessitates different amounts and placements of ease or different garment contours. Thus, the specific design mechanisms used to add mobility to a garment must be carefully chosen to relate to user needs.

There are a number of ways that **ease** can be added to increase mobility in a protective ensemble. The most common way is to add extra inches to either the width or length of a garment segment to allow for the change in body dimensions during movement. Because the extra bulk of ease can get in the way of movement, sometimes these additions are pleated or elasticized inside the garment so that they move back into their original position when the body relaxes. An example of this can be seen in the series of pleats planned for the astronaut's intravehicular activity (IVA) suit for NASA's Space Station (Figure 2.33). The need for these pleats was established during the first Skylab mission when designers discovered how body fluid distribution and other body changes occurred when astronauts lived in zero gravity for longer periods of time. The expanding/retracting pleats allow a jacket to fit closely at the beginning of a mission, but expand easily to accommodate both shoulder movement and an increased chest size when fluids migrate upward in the body in response to microgravity.

Ease is sometimes added to garments through the use of extra panels or **gussets** that allow

FIGURE 2.33 Expansion pleats built into the front shoulders and down the back of an IVA jacket planned for the Space Station. *(ILC Systems 1984, 4–11)*

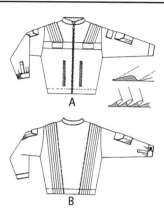

A

B

FIGURE 2.34 A special design for pants using a gusset to provide separate movement for the legs for activities such as climbing and sitting cross-legged. *(Design: Chi Pants)*

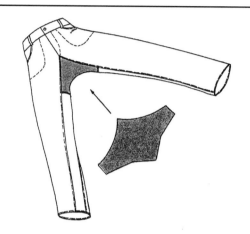

specific kinds of movement. Activities, such as reaching, climbing, and straddling, that are common to many types of workplace extra strain on two areas in particular: the underarm and the crotch. The pants illustrated in Figure 2.34 show the use of a gusset to allow increased separate leg movement and sitting cross-legged without strain in the crotch area.

As discussed earlier in this chapter, one aspect of body movement needs to be recognized regardless of the method used to solve ease problems: For many body movements, the need for ease is relatively isolated, occurring in areas immediately surrounding each joint center. One method of using this information to design mobile garments is simply to leave areas around joint centers open. This is the approach taken with items like the protective ensemble for the pesticide worker shown in Figure 2.35A and other activities where a garment needs only provide protection from a specific direction. Since the hazard in this particular situation comes during the pouring operation, the apron and long gloves protect the front torso, arms, and hands from chemical spills while allowing the upper arms and back freedom to reach forward. This is also the approach used for many items of active sportswear.

(See Design Solutions 2.1.) A variation of this open area approach can also be found in garments that support protective padding. Pads are placed in the most critical areas, leaving other body areas open for movement and ventilation (Figure 2.35B). Chapter 6 contains information on a number of

FIGURE 2.35 Using open areas in an ensemble to provide mobility.

Design Solutions 2.1: Sports Bras

There are two aspects of body movement that are important for the design of effective sports bras: the movement or bouncing of the breasts themselves and the ease of movement of the arms and shoulders while wearing the bra. The purpose of regular bras is to resist gravity (i.e., to keep the breasts lifted upward). In active sports, the body can be in a variety of positions, and in activities such as running, there is upward movement of the breasts as well. Therefore, a sports bra needs to protect the breasts from movement in all directions.

There are two approaches to keeping the breasts from moving on the chest wall. One is to closely encapsulate each breast separately and the other is to flatten both breasts against the chest. While research has shown that encapsulation allows the least breast movement regardless of breast size, some women with smaller breasts feel more comfortable in a bra that flattens and compresses the breasts.

Two additional goals for a sports bra design are to reduce chafing (so that movement does not rub skin raw) and to reduce localized pressure during movement. Continuous chafing and pressure may eventually lead to pain and cause an athlete to avoid certain movements.

The reduction of chafing is accomplished in a variety of ways: by using fabrics that do not allow perspiration to build up on the skin surface; by using smooth fabrics and molded bra cups that do not contain seams (or by turning seams to the outside to reduce skin contact with the ridges caused by seam allowances); and by using fitting techniques that prevent breasts from moving within the fabric.

One of the most significant ways to reduce pressure is to pay attention to strap construction, size, and arrangement. Wider straps provide more comfort and more contact with the trapezius muscle at the top of the shoulders so they may be better able to stay in place during movement. However, if maximum abduction and/or flexion of the arms is critical to performance, strap placement may be the most critical issue. Figure A shows a bra with a halter type of strap that passes close to the neck so that arm and shoulder movement have little effect on it. Much attention has also been paid to the arrangement of straps at the back of a sports bra, so that unlike a regular bra, they avoid the shoulder blade area. Y-straps (sometimes called T-straps) or crossed straps (Figures B and C) at the back allow complete freedom of movement for the shoulder blade. At the same time, these straps lie close to the neck, on a sensitive body area. When this strap arrangement is used, it is important to engineer the construction of the bra so that Y-straps do not dig into the neck. It should also be noted that, like bra cups, many straps are lined with comfortable, moisture transporting materials and have any seams turned to the outside to reduce chafing.

FIGURES A, B, AND C Bra designs that allow freer shoulder movement. (A) A halter bra; (B) a T-back (sometimes called a Y-back or racer-back) bra; (C) a sports bra with straps crossed in back.

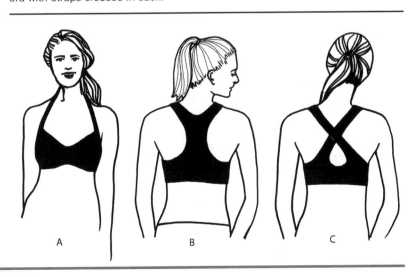

A   B   C

methods used to relate rigid pads to one another in ways that promote movement.

Figure 2.36 shows one method that has much the same effect as leaving the areas between rigid pads open. The designer has used a *second skin*, a stretchy bodysuit, and located pads in pockets on the suit. This allows protective padding to stay in place over specific body areas while movement takes place easily with the stretch material in adjacent areas.

If it is not practical to leave any area of the body uncovered, another way to allow ease is to use separates rather than a one-piece outfit. In general, every part that can be linked together in a continuous protective envelope increases the protection. The downside of this, however, is that all-in-one ensembles often have fit problems that interfere with mobility. The disposable suit shown in Figure 2.37A covers the body continuously

FIGURE 2.37 Suits designed for trawler fishermen. (A) A one-piece disposable coverall; (B) separate components that provide the same coverage. (B: Crockford 1977)

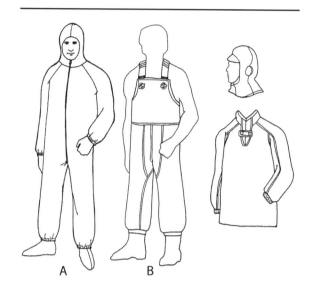

from top of the head to the ends of the extremities. A facemask and gloves seal off the entire system. The problem with this approach is that it does not allow for variations in body segment lengths unless the garment segments are produced in different lengths for individual fitting. These individual segments would then need to be joined together by fastening systems that continue the type of protection offered by the suit and do not interfere with movement themselves. Without individual fitting, if a person had a short torso, the crotch of the garment shown in Figure 2.37A would drop down between the legs. If other individuals were very long from shoulders to crotch, their bodies might not be accommodated by this garment unless larger sizes were provided. That is why, unless total encapsulation is absolutely vital to life, many designers prefer to provide separate components like those shown in Figure 2.37B. The overalls on this ensemble can be adjusted with shoulder

FIGURE 2.36 A stretch bodysuit with pockets that incorporate hockey padding.

FIGURE 2.38 Configurations for firefighting apparel. (A) A typical turnout coat and bunker pants with overlap from waist to mid thighs; (B) a contemporary uniform with overlap from high on the chest to just above the waist. *(Design: Mary Valla Ippolito and Laurie Rosen Cohen)*

A   B

straps to accommodate different lengths of torsos. The separate hood allows for different head sizes and shapes as well as free turning of the head. The separate jacket is free to extend comfortably over the pants to accommodate any shoulder-to-crotch length. Separate garments allow the system to fit more workers with different combinations of body segment lengths than is possible with one continuous garment.

It should be mentioned that if separates are the only solution, all parts of the ensemble need to have well-designed overlaps. An overlap needs to provide sufficient enough coverage so that the parts of an ensemble do not to separate during movement. Overlaps on one garment part may need to be fastened securely to the garment beneath it, and the fasteners should be placed in an area where it will be most advantageous for movement. Overlaps also need to be planned in relation to the hazard presented to the garment. (See, for example, the

recommendations for overlaps used in X-ray protective garments in Chapter 7.)

Sometimes, the *location* of an overlap can provide the solution to problems of both protection and mobility. For example, traditional turnout coats and bunker pants used for firefighting (Figure 2.38A) have an overlap of protective materials that begins at the waist and extends to the hem of the coat just below the hipline. Figure 2.38B shows an alternative system that changes the location of that overlap. With the shorter jacket and overalls, the overlap occurs from slightly above the waist to the top of the bib overalls at the mid chest. The same amount of overlap might result in both ensembles, but in the longer turnout coat version, the waist strap of the backpack a firefighter wears cinches the coat at the waist, making arm movement very difficult. In the shorter coat version, the backpack waist strap falls below the level of the coat so that it does not interfere with upper body movement. This example points out the importance of considering all of the garments and equipment that will be worn in a particular situation. If appropriate design decisions are made, the designer can avoid problems with fit and ease of garments caused by equipment strapped on over them.

One of the most important aspects of mobility lies in the **cut** or contour of garments. Subtleties in contour can often make a much more important contribution to success in garment mobility than changes in ease or size. Contouring involves planning a design so that when a worker is in his or her most frequently taken position, the garment fits without strain. Garments designed in this way are generally referred to as being in the **working position**. Probably the most familiar working position garment is a rubber glove (Figure 2.39A). Rubber gloves are generally molded with the

FIGURE 2.39 Working positions. (A) A thick foam glove for protection from extreme cold formed in the working position; (B) a scuba suit with the knee curved in the swim position; (C) the sleeve of a motocross jacket curved in the riding position.

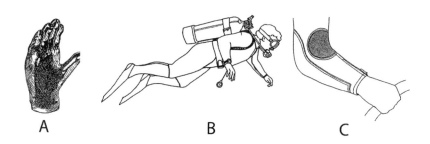

A   B   C

fingers in a curved position. This allows the wearer to take hold of an item without having to first work against the glove to get into the grasping position. Knees and elbows are the other areas of garments most likely to be formed in the working position. For example, the knees of wetsuits for scuba diving are formed in a bent position because this is the natural position of the legs when suspended in water (Figure 2.39B). A sleeve for a motocross racer may be formed in the riding position, allowing the rider to easily grip the handlebars (Figure 2.39C).

The working position becomes extremely important when designing clothing to be worn in microgravity in outer space because, as is true under water (Figure 2.39B), the body takes a more neutral position when in essence "floating" in this environment. Items of clothing worn by astronauts within the spacecraft (see Chapter 8) have been designed to contour to their weightless bodies.

Some garments are even designed beyond the normal working position so that a full range of motion is easier. For example, some positive pressure (slightly inflated) suits, such as the chemical suit shown in Figure 2.40, have the sleeves attached at an angle that allows full range of motion of the arm. The weight of the arm allows the wearer to stand easily in the anatomical

position, but this contour allows the arm to be more easily raised, even when the suit is inflated.

To design garments in the working position, the contour of the garments sections must be carefully planned in the pattern or draping stage. In traditional flat pattern methods, the shapes needed to cut a garment in the working position are incorporated into garments by *slashing and spreading* a pattern (i.e., cutting across a pattern and spreading it open so that garment segments are related to one another in a shape that allows freer

FIGURE 2.40 A fully inflated positive pressure suit. The sleeves are cut in an extreme position to make it easier for the wearer to raise an arm and to prevent strain on the material when an arm is raised.

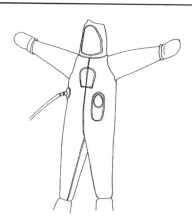

movement). As was shown earlier in this chapter with the skirt for a woman in a wheelchair (Figure 2.31), working position garments appear to contain excess fabric in the anatomical position, but they fit perfectly when the body is in a specific desired position. Implementing the motion analysis methods described earlier in this chapter can allow the designer to extract the precise amount of additional length or shortening needed in a specific area of a garment by measuring the changes in dimensions on the body surface.

Another method of achieving a working position involves laying pattern pieces next to one another in a way that results in the position of body segments desired. For example, Figure 2.41A and B show two of the many shapes a kimono sleeve pattern can take depending on the degree of desired abduction of the arm. These result in varying degrees of comfortable movement. Patternmaking can be built on kinesiological data (e.g., a sleeve pattern can be laid against a bodice pattern and the sleeve pivoted upward until the desired arm angle is achieved). The pivoting process is shown in Figure 2.41C. Differences in the length of the underarm seam that result from different "truing up" processes are shown in Figure 2.41D and E. These also affect the degree of freedom movement allowed.

The so-called *action sleeve* of men's shirts and many sportswear items is the result of placing a sleeve pattern on a torso or bodice pattern so that the sleeve is in an abducted position. Then, part of the height of the cap is cut away. (See a similar effect in the overlap of the sleeve cap on the bodice in Figure 2.41B.) The resulting sleeve allows free abduction for the arm but contains wrinkles when the arm is in the anatomical position—an indication that it was not planned specifically for the arm at rest.

Similar methods may be used for any garment segments. Jodhpurs for horseback riding have been designed using a similar method to relate the left and right pants patterns, in order to allow for the leg abduction needed for the riding position. In Figure 2.42, for example, the left and right front patterns are placed together at the center-front waist and crotch points. Then, the entire pants front is cut in one piece without a center seam. Note that this changes the angle of the legs from the midline of the body to more appropriately relate them to the position in which the rider will be while on horseback. The extra width and length adds ease that appears as folds in the lap of the rider. The waistline edge of the jodhpur pattern in Figure 2.42 has been gently curved in order to add excess length, but often the edge of a pattern that has *not*

FIGURE 2.42 One method of developing a pattern for riding breeches that allow abduction of the legs.

FIGURE 2.41 Patternmaking to achieve a working position. (A) and (B) the relationship of the sleeve to the bodice is varied; (C) pivoting the sleeve from the center of the shoulder joint; (D) and (E) two methods of truing up the slashed edges of (C).

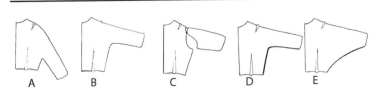

A   B   C   D   E

been opened and spread is left exactly in the curved shape that results. This helps direct fabric excess exactly to the position where it has been planned. This is what has been done on the side seam of the skirt in Figure 2.31 so that the fullness of the skirt needed for sitting is placed directly in the area of the hips where it is needed.

Draping methods increase freedom of movement similarly by adding length and width in appropriate garment areas. The simplest way to develop a mobile garment with draping is to drape fabric on a live figure that is in the most extreme body position needed for an activity. One noted couturier, in order to achieve a comfortable sleeve, kneels beside his clients and asks them to place their hand on his head. Fitting of the underarm area then proceeds with the arm in this abducted position (Kleibacker 1981). When activities call for extremes of movement, a garment designed in this manner may not be as attractive or comfortable when the body is at rest. In this event, choices or compromises must be made. When performance is critical to livelihood or safety, the appearance at rest may simply have to be accepted. The alternative, if appropriate protective materials can be found, is to use stretch fabric, stretch inserts, slits, pleats, tucks, or other retractable design features to preserve an attractive appearance both at rest and during movement.

The most effective way to create more mobile garments is often not just to add ease, but to change the *contour* or cut of a garment so that it can easily follow the body movement during specific activities. Research by Ashdown (1989) provides an example of how contour changes can affect garment performance and acceptance. She translated the data gathered from initial studies on the activities of asbestos abatement workers into recommendations for contour changes in typical disposable coveralls. Dotted areas on Figure 2.43A indicate the

FIGURE 2.43 Contouring a coverall pattern to accommodate working positions. (A) Dotted areas show areas of expansion (spread) of pattern; striped areas show areas of contraction (lap). (B) The final pattern. Dotted line indicates original pattern; solid line indicates contoured pattern. Note that little if any increase in pattern size is involved; mobility is achieved by forming the coverall in the working position. *(Ashdown 1989)*

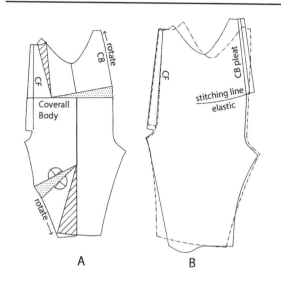

A   B

areas in which the coverall pattern was slashed and spread (i.e., length and/or width was added). These occurred over the back of the garment, to allow bending forward, and at the knee, to allow length for knee flexion. Striped areas indicate portions of the garment that were slashed and lapped to remove excess length and/or width. For example, when the body is leaning forward, excess folds appeared at the front neckline area indicating too much fullness there. Figure 2.43B shows the shape of the original design (dotted line) in relation to her proposed improved design (solid line). It is clear that the design changes made do not involve a significant increase in size. They simply change the contour of the garment so that it accommodates the shape of a *working* body inside.

Hobbling can occur when any two body segments are tied together in some way or when the bulk of clothing makes separate limb movement difficult. People who have worn capes will understand the movement restrictions that can occur. Despite adequate length for movement of the shoulder joint, movement may be difficult since the arm and shoulder coverings are not separated. Whenever clothing styles have returned to shapes that restrict body movement, such as the long, slim pencil skirt, slits have become popular. These allow a certain silhouette to be maintained, yet make possible the freedom of movement many individuals desire in clothing. In exploring how and why a garment might restrict movement, a designer should analyze the activity, the design itself, and the weight and flexibility of the fabric chosen for the garment to make certain there will be no hobbling effect on the wearer. (See Design Strategies 2.2.)

The next section of this chapter will deal with garment fit in detail. Since fit is simply the relationship of ease and contour of a garment to the body, many of the same techniques recommended thus far will apply to fit as well. One design technique developed by Ashdown and Watkins that takes all three—fit, ease, and contour—into account is the *zone method*. Although developed for a complex chemical protective garment, it could be applied to any design. The researchers divided an existing chemical suit into zones, each anchored to the body with its own suspension mechanism. Then, it was possible for each area of the suit to be analyzed independently of other portions of the suit. Changes in the fit and/or design of one area would not affect other areas of the garment. This process also allowed members of a design team each to focus concurrently on refinements in specific areas and meant that any last minute changes in equipment items would only necessitate changes in the zones they covered, not the entire garment. Figure 2.44 shows the zones established for a specific chemical suit. These were maintained with a variety of straps, tethers, and elastic threaded through carriers on the inside of the suit and suspended from shoulders, a waist belt, etc. Although this project involved redesign

FIGURE 2.44 Fit/function zones of a chemical protective suit. Schematics of the interior anchoring devices are shown. Boots and gloves also serve as anchoring points because of flanges on the outside of the suit. *(Ashdown and Watkins 1996)*

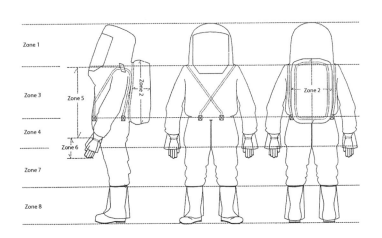

Design Strategies 2.2: Adjusting Armscye and Crotch Curves

When exploring the ways in which length and width can be added in the armhole and crotch area of garments to allow more freedom of movement, it is important not to fall into the "just make it bigger" trap. Adding length or width to these areas can often *increase* restrictions on movement. When arm movement is restricted, for example, the temptation is to simply cut a deeper armhole. Because the armscye curve lies in two different planes, this lowered armhole may result in even greater movement restriction. (See Figures A and B.) Although it might free up a sleeveless garment, for a long sleeved garment, the length of the seam from waist to wrist shortens considerably. A similar effect occurs at the crotch. This type of pattern adjustment on pants will drop the crotch of pants closer to the knees, making separate leg movement for walking difficult. The effect can be observed again in the kimono sleeve pattern shown in Figure 2.41D and E. Even though the angles of the sleeves to the bodice are the same, the difference in the shape of the underarm seam radically changes the mobility offered by the sleeve. A relatively straight line between the waistline and wrist (Figure 2.41E) creates a short underarm seam that can hobble the

arm (tie it too closely to the bodice area). A seam that comes up high into the armpit and returns down the full length of the arm (Figure 2.41D and Figure A below) provides the greatest underarm seam length and allows greater abduction of the arm.

FIGURES A AND B Cutting an armhole larger actually reduces the freedom to abduct the arm. (A) The dark line shows the length of the underarm seam in the original garment; (B) the dark line shows the length of the underarm seam in the same garment with a lowered armhole.

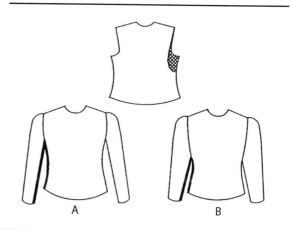

A   B

of an existing garment, the zone method could be used to develop new designs as well, with zones being established for each body area to be covered.

Fit and Movement

Contributed by Susan P. Ashdown

One key issue in providing movement in functional clothing is in providing appropriate fit. Most people have experienced the constriction encountered when clothing is too tight, or the entangling

effect of garments that are too long or too loose. A crotch that is too low in a bifurcated garment can impede walking stride and a garment that is too large can be a hazard around certain types of machinery. When fit is not optimized, the energy required to move in clothing to perform tasks can be substantial and can add significantly to metabolic heat gain. Some design features that improve movement in clothing also require precise fit. For example, a pleated insert in a garment will not improve movement if the garment does not fit well enough so that this design feature is centered over the joint. Overall fit issues are therefore important both in the relationship of the garment to the body and in specific areas of concern.

Creating optimal fit can be complicated when the function of specific garments is factored in. For example, the air layer captured in garments is an important protective barrier in environments with extreme thermal challenges; compression garments have been thought to optimize muscle performance for athletes; and a glove used to handle very hot materials may need to be loose enough to shed in a fraction of a second. However for any clothing ensemble, within its functional purpose, good fit (defined as the optimal relationship of the garment to the body for function, comfort, and aesthetic needs) does exist. Providing optimal fit for every user is a challenge. Of course, garments could be individually constructed to give a custom fit, as was done in the early days of spacesuit design; using this method, good fit could be ensured for everyone. However, other strategies are generally needed to keep cost and effort within reasonable limits.

SIZING SYSTEMS AND FIT

The most common solution to providing good fit for every wearer of clothing is to create a set of discrete sizes, dividing the population into groups such that each individual can be fitted reasonably well with one size in this discrete set of sizes. Adjustable design features within garments can also contribute greatly to good fit. A simple feature, such as an adjustable hook-and-loop fastening on a cuff, is an elegant solution to fit issues that does not add a lot of complexity or cost to the garment. It allows the sleeve to have excess length to provide movement but keeps the cuff precisely aligned with the wrist. In this case, a slightly

longer sleeve can provide good fit for many users with different arm lengths. Materials provide more or less flexibility depending on their properties (e.g., think of Lycra® bike shorts compared to denim shorts). Fabric stretch or stability, compression, amount of slip over the body, and/or qualities of softness or stiffness can have a large impact on movement capability, comfort, and fit. Therefore, variations in desired function, material properties, and design features all play a part in creating sizing systems.

The goal of a sizing system is to provide good fit for everyone in the intended user group with the fewest number of sizes, identified in such a way that users can easily find the size that fits them best. The sizes in the system are kept to a limited number both to save cost and to avoid complexity in size selection.

Collection and Use of Anthropometric Data

When designing a sizing system, it is necessary to know the population of users to be fitted. Anthropometric studies are the mechanism by which information about body sizes and proportions of a population are acquired for the purpose of creating or validating a sizing system. Such studies can be conducted on the population as a whole (e.g., national sizing surveys conducted in 2004 and 2005 dubbed SizeUSA, SizeUK, and SizeKorea, measured thousands of subjects using 3-D whole-body scanning technology) (Zernike 2004) or can be conducted on some targeted group within the population. Gathering demographic information increases the value of a study as differences in body size and proportion based on age, ethnicity, body condition, and occupation can then be determined.

The most effective sizing systems are generated based on data that is collected specifically on the portion of the population to be fitted (e.g., firefighters or naval airmen). Military organizations conduct frequent anthropometric studies in order to create effective sizing systems; they understand that providing good fit depends on an accurate assessment of the users in the population. Understanding the range of variation in a population is also important. For example, a sizing system designed for firefighters will need to provide good fit for both career firefighters (who generally have the resources to stay in shape) and also for volunteer firefighters (who may have an office job resulting in a very different body shape).

If resources do not allow one to conduct an anthropometric study of the specific user group to be fitted, sometimes data from a well-conducted population study with enough demographic information can be useful. If ethnicity, age, and occupational data are collected for each participant in the study, then the population can be sorted to target a specific portion of the population. For example, one could match the percentage of specific ethnicities in the population to be studied, the range of ages, and the general level of activity (e.g., office work versus more active occupations) and derive a subset of the SizeUSA database appropriate to the task in hand.

SizeUSA is an example of a study in which data was gathered using 3-D body scanners (Figure 2.45) instead of traditional anthropometric tools of tape measures, anthropometers, and calipers. In a traditional study, landmarks (generally identifying joint centers) are placed on the body and measurements are taken manually in a process that can take up to an hour or more per participant. A 3-D body scanner is an image capture device that in about twelve seconds or less can capture the topology of a surface using a set of cameras in the same manner as the laser scanning technique described earlier in this chapter. These points can then be

merged and visualized on the computer screen, providing a high-resolution three-dimensional virtual image of the participant that can be measured on the screen. Automated measurements can also be taken using computer software designed to identify landmarks from surface geometry. The advantage of collecting a digital scan image of each participant in an anthropometric study is that additional measurements can be taken from the scans at any time. Measurements related to designs providing special functional features can be generated from a set of scans taken for general use that might not

FIGURE 2.45 A body scanner.

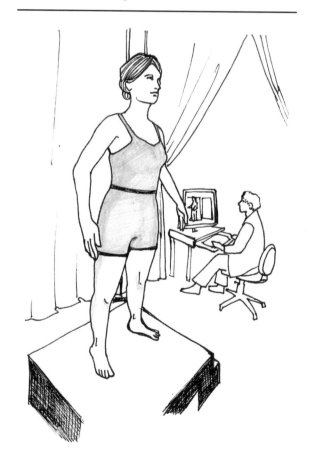

have included such measurements initially. Scan studies are also an efficient and inexpensive option due to the limited time needed with each participant and the automated data generation. Though the initial cost of a scanner can be high, the cost of incentives to recruit participants for time-consuming and intrusive manual measurements, and the cost of locating, training, and retaining good operators to take reliable manual measurements will cost even more for a large population study.

To design a valid anthropometric study of the general population, it is necessary to consider the range of variation and to measure enough participants to represent the population as a whole. Gender, geographic range, and the range of sizes, ethnicities, and socioeconomic situations may be considered as each of these factors can impact body size and shape. It is sometimes necessary to recruit from specific categories of participants who are less likely to participate in such a study (e.g., men, certain ethnicities, or people who are overweight).

Studies of User Groups

Recruiting participants of a specific user group for an anthropometric study can be easier if researchers can contact them through union groups, agency organizations, or at their places of work. Military groups are the easiest population to recruit, as a random selection of the population as a whole can be identified and measured. In some cases, where the user group is expected to change, it may be useful to increase participation in the study of a subgroup (e.g., measuring more female firefighters to get a representative sample that might reflect the proportion of the population in the next 10 years). It is important to conduct new studies when necessary. For example, the increase in obesity in recent decades warrants a new look at many user groups of functional clothing.

Understanding Variation within Populations

It is important to understand the range of variation in a population in order to understand the decisions that must be made to provide the best fit possible for a user group. The basic range of overall size is easy to visualize and understand. For example, the difference between the shortest and tallest person or between those with the largest and smallest hip circumferences in the population can be easily seen and represented in a graph (Figure 2.46A). Adding a second dimension adds a level of complexity. For example, if you look at the number of people who have a specific hip circumference and crotch length together you begin to get a range of body types from thin and short, to thin and tall, and from stout and short, to stout and tall (Figure 2.46B). Adding new variables, such as crotch height (a body measurement related to inseam length) further complicates the picture (Figure 2.46C). A sizing system that must provide fit for variations in many different variables can quickly become highly complex. Adding shape factors, such as waist to hip ratio, increases the complexity further.

There are also variations in a population that can be measured related to ethnicity, age, or other demographic variables. For example, northern Europeans are generally taller than southern Europeans. However, it is important to note that these differences are based on averages and do not say anything about the actual distribution of heights in either population. It is not at all useful to think in terms of averages when developing a sizing system, as it is the range of variation that must be accommodated. Actual distributions of the different sizes and shapes of people in the population under study are more useful in determining the number of people in different size groups. If average values are calculated and compiled for a set of measurements, they very quickly (within about 8 to 11 values) begin to describe a set of body

FIGURE 2.46 (A) A histogram that divides people in a population into groups with specific hip sizes; (B) a bivariate plot showing the relationship between hip size and crotch length; and (C) a 3-D graph showing crotch height versus crotch length versus hip circumference. *(Susan Ashdown)*

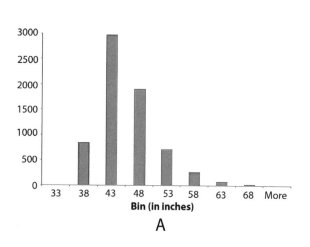

A

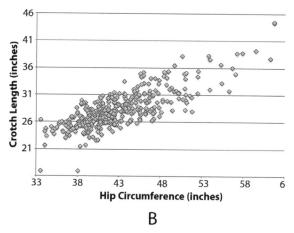

B

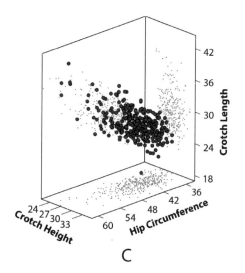

C

proportions that do not exist in the population (Daniels 1952). (See Figure 2.47.)

SIZING STANDARDS

The development and implementation of standards can be a useful endeavor, as it can guide manufacturing and regularize size selection. Clothing manufactured to meet a size standard can, within certain limitations, provide a known quality of fit. However, small variations in textile properties can quickly change the fit characteristics of two garments manufactured to meet the same size standards. Variation in design also has a large impact on fit, and therefore on sizing. A size standard that is too limited in scope can have a dampening effect of innovative design development.

METHODS OF CREATING SIZING SYSTEMS AND PATTERN GRADING

Traditional methods of creating sizing systems based on anthropometric data are generally well established. The first step in developing a sizing system is to choose the key dimensions for the system from those body measurements relevant for the garment type for which the system is designed. These dimensions are used to determine the structure of the sizing system, and they are also the measurements needed for size selection once the system is developed. Principal component analysis, a statistical method of sorting measurements into groups that tend to be correlated with one another, is generally used to identify key dimensions. Typically, a length measurement and a circumferential measurement are used, as a fairly high correlation with the rest of the body measurements can commonly be found with one or the other.

Sometimes the measurement that accounts for the greatest variation in the population is not suitable as a key dimension because it does not lend itself to the size selection process by the user. For example, a cervical (the protruding bone at the nape of the neck) to floor length may be a better

FIGURE 2.47 What the female body would look like if average data were used to create it.

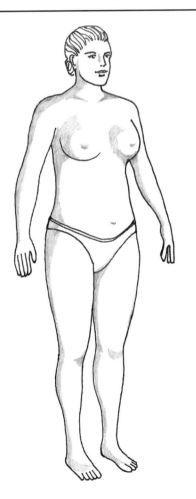

measurement statistically as a key measurement than height, but it is not a measurement that people generally know about themselves so it would not be a good choice for a user to use to select his or her best fitting size.

The next step is to use the key dimensions to determine the range and intervals of the sizing system. The range of the intervals determines how many sizes are in the system. If everyone in the population is to be fitted, more sizes will be needed. On the other hand, if the system is designed to provide good fit to 90 percent of the population, although the smallest and largest 5 percent will not have the best fit, the number of sizes can be reduced. The intervals between sizes also determine both fit and the number of sizes. Garments that must be closely fitted to the body and that do not allow much ease for good fit would require smaller ranges of body sizes in each size category, and therefore more sizes, than garments that can have more ease, and thus fit a wider range of body sizes acceptably.

Once the key measurements and the size intervals are set, the other important body measurements are calculated for each size using multiple regression analysis of the key dimensions in order to determine the most common associated measurements with these dimensions. This calculation determines the set of body measurements for each size that can then be expressed in a table. This table is the basis for grading the garment pattern, a process used to develop the pattern dimensions for each size in the range. Generally, a garment pattern will first be developed and perfected for one size, usually a size in the middle of the range (for purposes of marketing, a smaller size is often used for the initial pattern development because this pattern is also used to create sample garments for marketing). This pattern is then scaled up and down, for the larger and smaller sizes, based on the intervals between each of the body measurements in the body measurement table.

One of the issues with sizing systems developed in the traditional manner is that as the body chart and the sizes are graded proportionally through the size range, they reflect the proportions of the base size individual. If different proportions are desired to fit people with different body shapes, then a new sizing system and body chart must be developed. Figure 2.48 shows five sizes (solid squares) calculated based on the relationship between waist and hip measurements in a population. Each solid square represents 2 inches (5 centimeters) in each dimension, which might be the amount of variability in body measurements that can comfortably fit into each size. The dotted squares show the amount of body variability that might actually need to fit into each size if the entire population had only these sizes to choose from.

Stockkeeping Units and Tariffs

After a sizing system is developed, the next task is to have the correct number of garments produced and made available for the ready-to-wear market. For the ready-to-wear retailer, this means ordering the correct size mix of stockkeeping units (SKUs) (i.e., the range and number of each size that they can sell). A style that looks good on only smaller sizes may only be ordered in a limited size range, and fashion forward styles may be purchased in smaller numbers than more classic styles. Generally more of the sizes in the middle of the range are ordered, as they are more common.

In cases in which all users must be accommodated, the number and range of sizes provided is based on size data from the user group. For example, the armed forces uses a system of what they call tariffs to ensure that the appropriate sizes are sent to the deployment area. Tariffs are calculations of the numbers of garments in various sizes that will be needed to cover the population to be accommodated.

Calculating tariffs to determine the correct number of sizes is a simple process of calculating key measurements for the population and finding how many people are in each size category. However, this will not necessarily provide the sizes needed, as key measurements alone do not predict the size of best fit. Due to the complexity of fit for those garments that need to fit well in several dimensions and variations in fit preference, it can be very difficult to predict fit.

FIGURE 2.48 A sizing system of five sizes based on only two variables, waist and hip circumference, plotted on a bivariate graph.

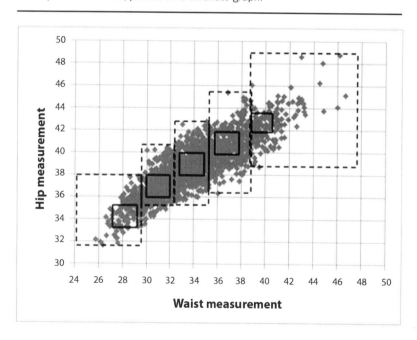

Assigning the correct size to any one user can also be complicated for the same reason. People vary in body dimensions continuously, yet sizes are categorical. Finding the correct size for any one person may require a decision about which of two or more choices provides the least misfit if a person is between sizes. Fit preferences of individuals can also impact which size they prefer. Sometimes the person choosing sizes is not the person who will wear the garment, particularly when some types of protective gear may be provided for workers. In this case, it may be important to help procurement personnel understand why ordering the largest size for everyone may compromise safety.

FIT TESTING

Fit testing of garments is a necessary part of the process of developing garment pattern shapes and garment features in the original prototype development, to ensure that the garment relates to the body in a way that provides both comfort and needed functionality. The choice of a fit model or fit models for this process should be carefully done. It is generally better to find users of the clothing or equipment to test the fit of prototypes, both because they are more likely to have an appropriate body shape for the population being fitted and because they may have insights that will help guide the development process. They will also be experts at the tasks or movements required in the clothing. A person in the middle of the size range, with body proportions that match the majority of the population to be fitted is preferable.

Once a sizing system is developed, it is also preferable to fit test garments throughout the size range to validate the sizing system. This is a complicated process and is seldom done, but it is the only way to ensure that both the garment design and the sizing system are performing as desired. The reason that it is difficult to actually test the effectiveness of a sizing system is that it is difficult to recruit fit testers from the full range of sizes and body proportions in the population of users.

After fit testers are found, the next step is to design a study that will result in good information on the fit of the garment or equipment being tested. Fit can be assessed by using objective measures of the relationship of the garment to the body, by having the fit tester rate fit, by having an expert judge or a panel of judges rate fit, or indirectly by conducting tests of the ability of the fit tester to perform functional activities. Each method has its own drawbacks and advantages.

Objective Measures of Garment Fit

Understanding fit holistically is a complex process. The relationship of the whole garment to the surface of the body, in both static positions and in motion, must be understood in order to assess fit. Some measuring processes have been developed to gather data, but they are often difficult and expensive to implement. Pressure sensors have been used to measure the actual pressure of the garment in the body, but they can only provide data at specific locations and are generally useful only in cases where a snug fit overall is desired. If a fit tester is body scanned first without a garment and then in the same position with the garment, scanning can also provide information about the garment/body relationship. These scans can then be merged, and the distance from the body surface to the garment surface can be derived by extracting cross sections from the scans. However, analysis is a time-consuming process, and it is difficult to collect reliable data due to the difficulty of repeating a body posture exactly for the two scans. This analysis is also less useful when the clothing or equipment has variable thickness, as the scan only captures the outer surface, not the inner surface that is against the body. Virtual fit tools are being developed and may someday provide another tool for fit assessment.

Assessment by Fit Testers

A fit tester will generally perform a series of movements to see the range of movement possible in a garment. Sometimes specific tests are developed, such as the Purdue Pegboard Test for glove dexterity. (See Figure 2.49.) This device was first developed by an industrial psychologist in the late 1940s. It is a manual dexterity test that consists of a board with a series of slots into which pins can be inserted. Additional small parts are provided to test a subject's dexterity for assembling parts.

ASTM F2669, "Standard Performance Specification for Protective Clothing Worn by Operators Applying Pesticides" is a performance standard for protective clothing. It specifies a series of tasks such as kneeling, climbing, bending, and crawling (ASTM 2013). When choosing these tests, it is important to decide if they reflect the types of movements that the wearer of the garment will perform. Generally, information about a fit tester's response to the fit of the garment is collected using a Likert scale (a scale commonly involved in research that employs questionnaires).

FIGURE 2.49 The Purdue Pegboard. *(Lafayette Instruments)*

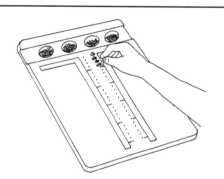

Other aspects of the garment performance such as ease of donning and doffing can also be assessed. The advantage of collecting the responses of the fit tester is that the person wearing the garment can feel garment/body interactions that cannot be seen. The disadvantage is that individual fit preferences can introduce variability into the data.

Expert fit analysis can provide more reliable data, particularly if a trained panel of judges is recruited to look for specific fit issues. However, this can be a time-consuming process and does not capture all the information that a wearer can provide. Generally a combination of a fit tester's and expert fitter's analysis is used, but in this case there may be some disagreement in the data that must be resolved.

CREATION OF A SIZING SYSTEM

Once a sizing system has been developed from anthropometric data and validated in a series of fit tests, it is still important to continue to monitor fit by testing the fit and performance of new styles as they are developed. Even though it is a complex process to address variation in the population, the properties of materials used, and different tasks and work environments, continual improvement of appropriate sizing algorithms can result in better clothing function, comfort, and appearance.

Given the difficulties of creating successful ready-to-wear sizing, other options are sometimes developed when it is important to provide good fit for a wide range of body types and when the cost of these systems can be justified. Two examples of this are the development of modules for space suits (Case Study 2.1 Figure I) and the customization of firefighter uniforms. (See Design Strategies 2.3.)

Design Strategies 2.3: Mass Customization and Sizing

The idea of mass production and custom fitting are not usually thought of as compatible. A number of companies have, however, provided ways to produce relatively custom-fitted garments in a cost-effective way. One excellent example of this is the system used by Globe Firesuits. Their process involves the development of style and fitting options, detailed measurement instructions, patterns and markers developed by computer for individual customers, and a computerized cutting system.

First, Globe has developed different patterns for male and female firefighters to provide for typical gender differences in proportion such as the waist to hip ratio. To custom fit pants for each gender, firefighters can select a relaxed or "regular" (straighter leg) shape and provide individual body measurements for the waist and inseam. For the jacket, they may choose a straight or tapered jacket shape and provide girth measurements for the chest and length measurements for the torso and sleeve. The shape choices allow firefighters who have a trimmer, more athletic build to avoid the bulk needed to fit those with, for example, a larger waistline. At the same time, the shaping of more relaxed, less tapered garments allow those with a more pear-shaped body to avoid ordering garments several sizes larger that might then have too much bulk in the shoulders and arms.

The first step in making a mass customization system work is to gather accurate measurement data from customers. Globe provides its customers with measurement instructions that include cautions about having someone else take the measurements; instructions and illustrations about stance and body position and the advice that they should wear the garments they typically wear under their protective clothing when having the measurements taken. The measurement form also includes diagrams and specific landmarks for each of the measurements. Many thoughtful insights about good fit appear in the measurement instructions. Customers are advised to take a deep breath and hold it before taking the chest or bust measurement and to wear any tools or instruments such as beepers that are typically worn when taking the waist measurement.

The style preferences and measurements provided by a customer can be entered into a computer program that will create a custom pattern for an individual. A combination of standard patterns and the individually created pattern pieces for the orders in process are fed into a marker-making program. This program arranges the pattern pieces on markers in order to achieve the highest percentage of fabric usage. The markers are then sent to a computerized cutting machine. In the cutting room, from one to 12 layers of fabrics chosen by the customers are spread on the cutting table so that like parts in the same size and shape can be cut together. After the marker has been cut, each stack of like pieces is removed from the cutting table, labeled with the marker and work order number, and placed on a labeled rack. The bundling and delivery of the pieces for each separate work order to sewers proceeds in much the same way as in other garment manufacturing.

There is another step in the customization plan for Globe, and that is the provision of sample garments by company representatives. Each person may have a different idea about what constitutes a good fit. So, company reps take a series of garments (usually every other size) with them when they visit fire stations so that firefighters can actually try on clothing. This step adds to Globe's ability to satisfy their customers with the best possible fit.

Analyzing the Effects of Clothing on Movement

After clothing has been designed, various tests can be used to evaluate its success in allowing free mobility. Postdesign tests are probably the most common way of approaching clothing movement problems today. If they are used early enough in the design process—*at the prototype stage* rather than as a postproduction evaluation—they can be extremely useful tools for the designer. It should be noted that there is a great deal of overlap between the methods described earlier in this chapter under "Applying Data on Body Movement to Clothing Design" and the methods described here. The previously described methods provide more direct data for the designer to use in *developing* a design that will meet user needs. The methods described here are used to indicate to the designer how well those design efforts have succeeded. These evaluative tests are usually performed to compare several designs, generally including the garment typically worn prior to new development efforts. The basic methods used to evaluate the effects of clothing on mobility fall into four categories: simple motor tests, time/motion studies, work/energy studies, and pressure/load analysis.

Simple motor tests involve some measurement of performance on a specific task. Range of motion (ROM) tests fit in this category. A wide variety of test devices are commercially available and researchers have developed unique tests for individual projects. Figure 2.50 shows a range of motion test for hip and back flexibility. Subjects sit on the floor with feet against the box and reach forward to move a sliding bar as far as possible. Ruled markings on the bar indicate the amount of reach attained. *Functional reach tests* have been widely used in the automotive and aerospace industries to test the layout of instrument panels

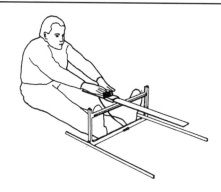

FIGURE 2.50 A test for lower back and hip flexibility.

and by human factors specialists to determine proper chair height, keyboard level, and so on, in office design.

It should be noted that the devices used to measure joint angles can also be used to measure performance in a simple motor test. For example, a goniometer might be used to measure the joint angles achieved during a specific task while wearing different garments.

Time/motion studies are similar to simple motion studies, except that the data collected concerns the *time* it takes to accomplish a specific task *or* the tasks accomplished in a specific time period rather than the degree to which a movement can be accomplished. Many industrial studies prefer to use time/motion studies rather than a more direct measure of mobility because it tells an employer not just how mobility has been restricted but whether that restriction makes a difference in what an employee can accomplish in a work cycle. Among the many instruments available for time/motion studies, perhaps the most well-known is the Purdue Pegboard, mentioned earlier. (See Figure 2.49.) Subjects are rated on their ability to accomplish various tasks with their left, right, and both hands under time limitations. Pegboard and other time/motion studies can be undertaken with gloves or other clothing items in place in order to determine the detriment specific clothing places on task completion.

Work/energy studies focus on the amount of energy an individual needs to accomplish a specific task while wearing specific clothing items. The Teitlebaum and Goldman study on friction drag in clothing reported earlier in this chapter is an example of a study that measured energy output for subjects wearing varying ensembles in identical work conditions. A variety of clothing ensembles, tasks, and environmental variables may be used in work/energy testing. Among the typical physiological responses that are monitored during tests are an individual's blood pressure, oxygen consumption, rectal and skin temperature, perspiration rate, and the chemical composition of the urine and blood. Muscles and muscle groups may also be tested to determine the force needed to complete an activity while an individual is dressed in a specific garment.

In *load or pressure analysis*, the pressure placed on various body areas by clothing is monitored. Various devices and materials can be used in pressure studies. Most incorporate some sort of sensor or pressure-sensitive material that is connected electrically to a readout unit or display chart. The sensors are then placed between the garment to be tested and the body. As the subject moves, the amount of pressure on each sensor can be determined. Increased levels of pressure indicate the areas in which the garment is putting the most pressure on the body as it moves. This is often a good indicator of movement restriction.

Early pressure testing research was undertaken by the U.S. Army during the 1970s with its development of the Load Profile Analyzer (LPA). Although the LPA was conceived in large part as a device to communicate technical information to the layperson, it also functioned as both a design and evaluation tool. Because their work was concerned with protective armor for the upper body, this particular research group developed a vest embedded with sensors and a console that displayed, in manikin form, a front and back torso (Figure 2.51). Sensors were placed in small pockets over the entire inner surface of the garment.

The LPA vest was put on a subject, and a garment to be tested was placed over it. When pressure was placed on the vest and a sensor compressed, contact took place between two components inside the sensor and an electrical circuit was completed. Wires leading from all of the sensors were joined into a single cable that connected the vest to the display panel. The lights on the display panel changed color as greater amounts of pressure were placed on the sensors, so that both the amount and the location of the pressure could be observed. The unit showed a designer instantly where points of stress occurred during movement. At the same time, the analyzer could be connected to a computer so that precise data could be collected and reviewed. By using the analyzer *during*

FIGURE 2.51 The Load Profile Analyzer. *(Barron 1975)*

the design process, Army designers were able to identify problem areas and develop a ballistics vest that achieved 100 percent troop acceptance in its first field tests (Barron 1975).

One aspect of load analysis to consider is that even though these tests provide data on pressure levels, not all individuals nor all areas of the body respond in the same way to pressure. Age, sex, medical conditions, and other factors may affect the way in which pressure affects mobility. Figure 2.52 shows the results of a test done by the U.S. Army on torso sensitivity of a male adult. In general, the Army found that the fleshy areas of

the body were more able to tolerate pressure than the bony ones, and that pressure on major nerves, arteries, and veins, particularly those that supply the brain, can affect coordination and produce fatigue (Scribano et al. 1970). Since specific body areas seem less able to tolerate loads, designs that place even small amounts of pressure there may cause muscle fatigue, which may make movement more difficult.

Conclusion

Movement is so critical to the function of clothing that you will see references to its importance in each of the remaining chapters. The thick layers of fabrics needed for protection from extreme cold or heat may greatly interfere with movement. The rigid materials and foams used in many items of impact-protective sports equipment may also limit movement. Many of the activities for which protective clothing is worn involve exertion and whenever work must be accomplished by straining to move against restrictive clothing, energy that could be used to accomplish a task is being wasted, and wearers fatigue more quickly. There will be many opportunities to use the material in this chapter to develop more effective items of functional apparel.

FIGURE 2.52 Variations in torso sensitivity. *(Scribano et al. 1970)*

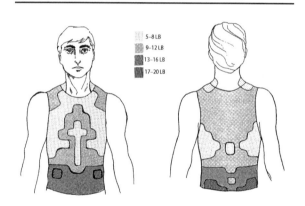

CASE STUDY 2.1 Movement in Pressurized and Positive-Pressure Garments

Some of the most fascinating provisions for movement can be found in the pressurized garments worn for space exploration or high-altitude flight. Although the physical pressure of the air around the body is not really perceived, the Earth's atmospheric pressure of 14.7 lb/in^2 (1.03 kg/cm^2) helps to hold the body's tissues and gases in place.

Since there is a lack of atmospheric pressure in outer space, space suits must provide it for the astronaut. Otherwise, internal gases would migrate out of the astronaut's body into the relatively less pressurized atmosphere of space, and the body would actually fly apart. The space suit, then, must be a sealed system—either a rigid container such as a deep-sea diving bell or a flexible system that can be blown up like a balloon until enough pressure is put on the body to sufficiently pressurize the gases and liquids within it. The provision for this in space suits made of fabrics and films is what is called a *bladder* layer. The bladder is made of a strong fabric such as rip-stop nylon and rubberized to form a totally impermeable portion of the suit.

The problems of a pressurized suit designer can be better appreciated if each section of the suit is thought of as a long balloon. If each balloon is blown up completely, the balloon is virtually impossible to bend. Similarly, a fully inflated space suit that had no provisions for mobility would become so rigid that the astronaut inside would not be able to bend an arm, leg, or torso. Anyone who has ever tried to make animal shapes out of balloons knows that there are two ways to make balloons easier to bend. The first is not to blow them up completely. The second is to use long, thin balloons with smaller diameters. Since the pressure in a space suit cannot be decreased—it must be kept at a minimum constant pressure of 3.5 lb/in^2 (0.253 kg/cm^2)—blowing it up less fully does not solve the problem. However,

it is possible to increase mobility somewhat by decreasing the diameter of the cylinders that make up the suit, so that they conform to the body more closely.

The history of pressurized suit development illustrates a variety of approaches to designing for mobility. Wiley Post, who developed the first pressurized suit for high-altitude flying, tried to overcome the problem of bending to sit in an inflated suit by designing the rubberized fabric suit shown in Figure A. Since the suit was pressurized only when he was seated in the cockpit of his plane, he was able to permanently mold it in his seated (working) position. Astronauts today, however, must accomplish many tasks in pressure suits. Methods of providing mobility for them must allow for standing, walking, bending, and sitting. Two general approaches have been taken to providing mobility. One has been to provide flexibility for the entire body, and the other has been to provide flexibility just in the area of the joints. Both methods

FIGURE A An early pressure suit restraint system for mobility. *(Radnofsky 1967)*

involve some type of restraint that decreases the circumference of each segment of the suit and keeps it from ballooning.

Some early restraining devices consisted simply of nonstretch straps, such as those used for parachute harnesses, placed in a latticed network over the pressurized suit. In the Mercury program space suit, for example, restraints were sewn around the elbows and knees of the suit (Figure B). These restraints were then tied together along the side of the arm or leg (the line of nonextension) so that the areas between the straps provided length and width to accommodate a bending elbow or knee. The overall effect resembled a type of smocking. Although this technique did not allow the degree of flexion the joints were capable of, the arm and leg coverings could bend enough to allow some mobility.

Another approach that yielded a subtle shaping involved placing a link net fabric over the pressurized suit (Figure C). In this special fabric formation, called a *slip-knit*, the yarns were free to slide over one another, allowing the fabric to give in all directions. This allowed a gentle curve to form in each suit segment. This approach, however, is subject to some of the ballooning effect that creates mobility problems.

Several space suit models have used features like the torso strap shown in Figure D to help an astronaut to bend. When the strap is pulled, the front length of the suit becomes

FIGURE B An early pressure suit restraint for mobility. *(Radnofsky 1967)*

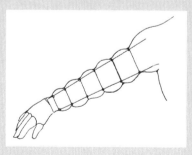

FIGURE C A link-net (slip-knit) overlay for space suit mobility. *(Radnofsky 1967)*

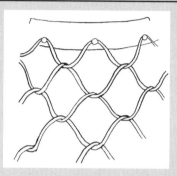

shorter and the astronaut is held in a bent position. When the strap is released, the body can straighten again. For more complete movement at the joints, the rubberized fabric in the impermeable bladder layer can be shaped just

FIGURE D A torso-adjusting strap for a space suit. *(NASA)*

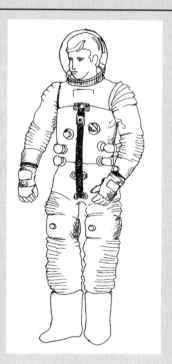

in the joint areas by stiffening it with metal rings or cables. Figure E shows a section of a suit that has the ridged joints called *constant volume bellows*. Metal restraints in the valleys of the ridged surface prevent the entire joint from ballooning. Along the sides of the joint, perpendicular to the body joint's axis of movement, are lengthwise restraints that gather up the material and thereby create the hills or ridges seen on the outer surface. As the ridges on one side bunch up, the ridges along the opposite side expand and flatten out, so that when a limb is bent, the joint maintains the same circumference and the same volume inside. This joint provides a considerable increase in mobility over the methods previously discussed.

Several types of constant-volume joint constructions are possible. Some involve the use of multiple cables or movable side cables that allow greater variation in the hills and valleys of the bellows and can thus accommodate the complex movements of joints like the shoulder. After suits began to be made of rigid materials such as Fiberglas®, a number of other interesting constant-volume joints were developed. Radnofsky (1967, 38) describes one that

FIGURE E A constant volume bellows that keeps a pressurized suit from ballooning. *(Radnofsky 1967)*

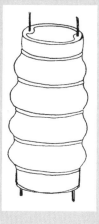

involves both rigid and flexible materials that he calls a "nest of metal hoops interconnected by rubberized fabric." A movable cable running along the side of the joint restrains the hoops and allows them to pivot alternately against and away from one another as the joint flexes and extends (Figure F). Another way of increasing flexibility is to create a series of pleats and shaped seams to allow the suit to conform to the action lines of the body. Such suits often involve a network of cables inserted through guides on the suit, which help distribute the forces placed on various limbs by pressurization (Figure G).

Suits made entirely of rigid materials employ different methods to achieve joint mobility. Rigid suit segments allow the body to move inside them by rolling, sliding, rotating, twisting, or even circumvolving much like the shoulder or hip joint. Even though rigid joints are relatively simple to achieve in many hardware items, they are more difficult to design into clothing precisely because clothing is a *covering*. Rigid joints typically revolve around a pin or axis that passes through their center. Such a system in clothing would be decidedly uncomfortable! Most rigid clothing joints, such as those in many space suits or chemical/biological protective suits, involve rotation and use a freely moving bearing joint of some kind. The *stovepipe joint* shown in Figure H shows the basic

FIGURE F A constant-volume joint that uses rigid and flexible materials. *(Radnofsky 1967)*

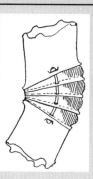

FIGURE G Shaped seaming for increased mobility of a space suit sleeve. *(NASA)*

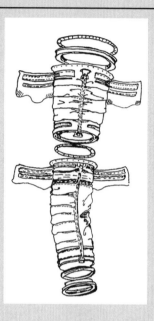

FIGURE H Stovepipe joints for rigid materials. Rigid sections are joined with ring bearings and rotated by body movement. *(Radnofsky 1967)*

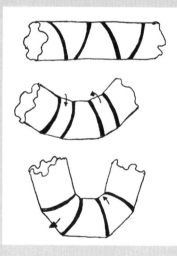

principle on which they operate. It is created by taking a cylinder of rigid material, making angled cuts through the area where the body joint will lie, and joining the sections back together again with ring bearings. In order for an elbow to bend in such a cylinder, the bending movement must force the wider portions of each section to rotate around the arm until they lie next to the point of the elbow where the expansion created by bending the arm has taken place. Figure I shows a hard suit that contains this type of ring-bearing joints. These unusual configurations, which resemble science-fiction creations, are often quite bulky, but movement in them is considerably easier than in soft suits because there is no ballooning effect and body movement does not take place against alternately expanding and compressing materials. The suit's constant volume, which results in its remaining a constant distance from the skin surface, holds advantages for ventilation as well as mobility. Sealed ball-bearing joints are used to attach gloves, and sometimes the helmet, to a suit. These allow the wrist and head to rotate completely without straining against the garment. An alternative method of providing head movement is shown in the helmet in Figure I. The neck-to-helmet joint is fixed and stationary, but it stands away from the head and the helmet is completely clear so that the head is free to move within it without shifting the helmet.

FIGURE I A hard suit for outer space that uses stovepipe joints.

CASE STUDY 2.2 Movement after Injury

Even though this chapter has been primarily about studying movement to create clothing that moves freely with the body, it should also be noted that much of this information could also be used to create clothing that can teach the body how to move. Movement data can be used to program exoskeletons and prosthetic devices. It can also be very useful in developing items for physical therapy that can either promote or restrict movement.

There are a number of rehabilitative garments and braces on the market that restrict movement in order to allow an injured body part to heal. Some include provisions that vary the amount of movement that is possible, so that as a patient recovers, full movement can be

gradually restored. Some rehabilitative items may have an additional function, however, and that is to passively stretch the muscles in the area of the injury so that a contracture (a permanent shortening of a muscle) does not occur. When a body part is encased in a cast or a brace for a long period of time, muscles and tendons can permanently shorten, making normal movement difficult or impossible once the cast is removed.

Figures J and K show a proposal for an elbow brace that has been designed to help prevent contractures of the elbow. Many experts recommend both active motion and limited passive stretching of the elbow almost immediately after trauma or surgery. Then once the

FIGURES J AND K Elbow brace with provision for passive stretching. (A) The brace with inflatable tubes in place; (B) the rigid brace mounted on arm bands. *(Design: Nathan Demarest)*

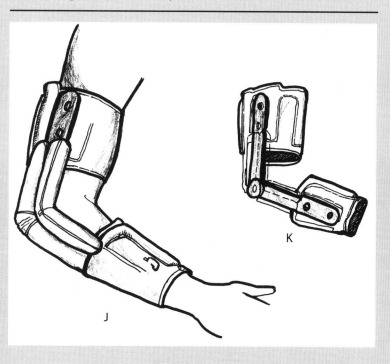

joint has healed, most rehabilitation follows "a more aggressive and prolonged stretching of involved muscles." (Demarest 2000, 26)

The brace is composed of two bands—one that fits closely around the upper arm and another that encircles the forearm. Between these two bands is a metal support attached to the bands on the lateral aspect of the elbow (Figure K). This support includes a metal hinge joint that is positioned at the center of the elbow joint. This type of metal joint normally includes a range-of-motion block that can be varied so that flexion and extension can be limited and then gradually restored. This particular brace contains an additional feature—it not only *allows* gradual increases in elbow flexion and extension but also provides for increases in passive stretching.

A pair of inflatable fabric mobilizing cylinders lies overtop, along the length of the metal hinged joint (Figures J and K). One cylinder is a straight form, and the other is curved. When the straight cylinder is inflated, it becomes more rigid and will not bend, forcing elbow extension. When it is deflated and the curved cylinder is inflated, the curved cylinder becomes rigid and will not allow the elbow to straighten. Flexion and extension can be controlled by regulating the inflation of each cylinder, allowing gradual increases throughout the rehabilitation process.

Thus, inflation, which interferes with movement in positive pressure suits, can be used to great advantage in another application.

3 Materials

Functional clothing is made from many of the same materials as fashion apparel, but it often incorporates other materials less familiar to a clothing designer. This chapter will introduce the basics of some of the materials most frequently used to make protective clothing. The formation of textiles, foams, films, and rigid materials such as metal and plastics used for functional apparel items and accessories will be presented, and treatments that add properties needed to make them more protective will be discussed. The properties that allow materials to respond dynamically to changes in the environment will also be explored.

Textiles

A **textile** is defined as "any flexible material that is composed of thin films of polymers or of fibers, yarns, or fabrics or products made of films, fibers, yarns, or fabrics." (Kadolph 2010, 6) The flexible nature of textiles is of great importance to apparel, which needs to move with the human body. Protective clothing systems are often based on textiles and augmented with other types of materials like foams and rigid materials.

There are a number of different types of textiles: textiles for apparel and interior design, textiles for industry, and materials in the emerging field of smart textiles. Because of the nature of protective clothing, all of these types of textiles may be applied to functional clothing designs.

It is important for a functional clothing designer to understand the many stages at which properties can be built into a material and how these affect the final garment. Figure 3.1 provides an illustration of the stages of textile development that will be covered in this chapter: the formation of a fiber (Figure 3.1A); yarn structure (Figure 3.1B); fabric structure (Figure 3.1C), and fabric finishing/dyeing treatments (Figure 3.1D). Many functional properties of materials can be applied at any of these stages and will be discussed as they relate to each stage of development.

FIBERS

Fibers are the smallest visible units of a textile. A fiber has an extremely long length in relation to its diameter. At a minimum this ratio is 100 to 1, although most fibers have ratios of several

FIGURE 3.1 Stages of textile development: (A) fibers; (B) yarns; (C) fabric formation; (D) fabric finish.

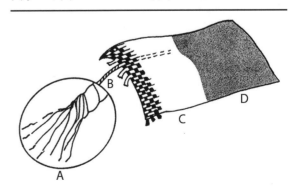

thousand to 1 (Hatch 1993, 85). Both their length and diameter may be used to describe fibers. Diameter is expressed in micrometers, or in terms of **denier**, with one denier being the weight in grams of 9,000 meters (9,842.5 yards) of fiber. Thus, the smaller the denier number, the finer the fiber.

Fiber Classification

Textile fibers are generally divided into two major classes: **natural fibers** and **manufactured fibers**. Natural fibers are those found in fibrous form in nature, such as wool, silk, and asbestos. Manufactured fibers are those that do not occur as fibers in nature but instead are created through a manufacturing process.

There are several dozen generic manufactured fibers, and they are often confusing to consumers. Table 3.1 provides some examples of both natural and manufactured fiber classifications. The names of manufactured fibers in this table are generic polymer names or family names. In many but not all product descriptions, these generic names begin with a lowercase letter, as for example, nylon or polyester. Many fiber manufacturers produce fibers of the same basic polymer but with different additives (plasticizers, lubricating agents, antimicrobials, antistatic agents, and so on) to form it into a different physical structure, treat it with different finishes, and give it their own trade or brand names. Trade names are capitalized, followed by the registered trademark symbol (®) and placed before the generic name. Thus, there is, for example, Dacron® polyester, Fortrel® polyester, and Kodel® polyester.

The U.S. Textile Fiber Products Identification Act, passed in 1960, requires that, at a minimum, the generic name of a fiber be listed on all product labels (Reg.303.6) and the same requirement exists in EU directives (2008/121/EC). Trade names may also be listed, but they cannot replace the generic names. Thus, you may see "Dacron® polyester" or simply "polyester" listed on the hangtag of a garment.

There are many textbooks on textiles that can provide detailed information on the strengths and weaknesses of fibers. Many fiber properties affect apparel performance: their relative strength, stiffness, absorbency, density, elongation, and elastic recovery, for example. Tables 3.2 and 3.3 provide just a few examples of fiber property comparisons.

TABLE 3.1 Examples of Some Fiber Classifications (*Hatch 199, 84*)

NATURAL FIBERS	
PROTEIN	Fur
	Hair (alpaca; mohair)
	Silk
	Wool
CELLULOSIC	Cotton
	Flax
	Jute
	Hemp
	Ramie
MINERAL	Asbestos
MANUFACTURED FIBERS	
CELLULOSIC	Acetate
	Rayon (Viscose; Lyocell; Bamboo)
	Triacetate
SYNTHETIC	Acrylic
	Modacrylic
	Nylon
	Olefin
	Polyester
	Polyvinyl Alcohol (PVA or Vinal)
	Polyvinyl Chloride (PVC or Vinyl)
	Saran
	Spandex
INORGANIC	Carbon
	Ceramic
	Glass
	Metallic

Other fiber properties may be more critical for a specialized end use of apparel and must be carefully explored. Many of the fibers appropriate for specific types of protection will be discussed in more detail in later chapters that deal with specific design situations. For example, metal, glass, and carbon fibers, while introduced later in this chapter, will also be discussed in the section on flame resistant clothing and when there are examples of specific military and industrial applications.

Fiber Formation

Manufactured fibers are made by converting a solid substance to a liquid, generally referred to as **dope**, and then forcing the dope through a **spinneret**, a device that looks somewhat like a showerhead (See Figure 3.2). The resulting strands, which look much like very thin spaghetti, are then quickly returned to a solid state.

FIGURE 3.2 A spinneret.

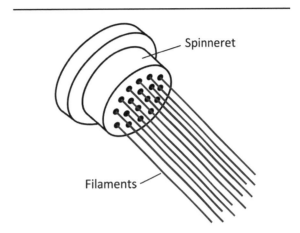

TABLE 3.2 Comparisons of the Absorbency, Abrasion Resistance, and Resiliency of Textile Fibers. (Price, Cohen and Johnson 2003: 52)

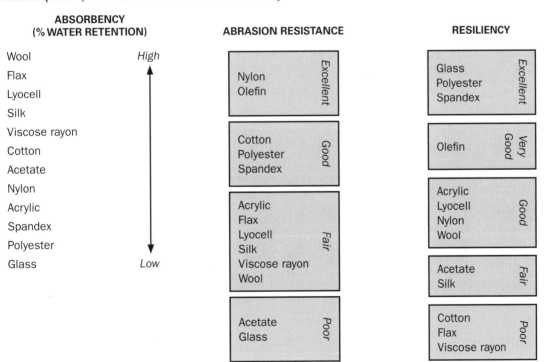

TABLE 3.3 A Comparison of Fibers with Regard to Strength and Melt or Burn Temperatures

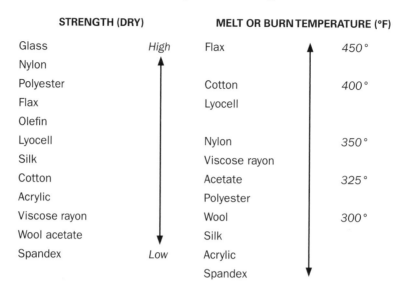

STRENGTH (DRY)		MELT OR BURN TEMPERATURE (°F)	
Glass	*High*	Flax	*450°*
Nylon			
Polyester		Cotton	*400°*
Flax		Lyocell	
Olefin			
Lyocell		Nylon	*350°*
Silk		Viscose rayon	
Cotton		Acetate	*325°*
Acrylic		Polyester	
Viscose rayon		Wool	*300°*
Wool acetate		Silk	
Spandex	*Low*	Acrylic	
		Spandex	

Sometimes natural materials are chopped finely and converted to a liquid using chemicals. This is the case, for example, with wood pulp. When the cellulose in wood pulp is merely softened using chemicals, it forms a dope that may be forced through spinnerets and result in some type of rayon. When the chemicals actually change the chemical structure of the wood pulp in the process of softening it, the resulting fibers are labeled as acetate. You might think of this difference as similar to that of forming different liquids out of grapes. When grapes are chopped up and squeezed, they form grape juice. When they undergo the chemical reaction of fermentation, they form wine. Because it is not altered chemically, rayon is often marketed as a "natural fiber," even though it is essentially a manufactured fiber.

Other manufactured fibers are made from polymers. **Polymers** are large molecules made up of a chain of repeating smaller units called monomers.

Monomers are made up of individual atoms. (For more about the structure of atoms and molecules, see Energy Basics 3.1.) Polymeric materials (i.e., those made of polymers) include a broad range of fibers, plastics, and rubbers. The polymers used to make manufactured fibers are **thermoplastic** (i.e., they are solid at room temperature but can be changed into liquids by heating them). After the heated polymers pass through the spinneret, they are quickly cooled either in water or air so that they return to solid forms. The thermoplastic nature of these polymers means that materials made of them can be reheated and reshaped. This is important to many finishing processes for both fibers and fabrics.

Bicomponent Fibers

Some fibers are made of more than one polymer. The polymers may be different chemically or physically. The resulting fiber, which is called a

Energy Basics 3.1: Atoms, Molecules, and Energy

All matter in the universe is composed of *atoms*, which can be described as the smallest unit of a chemical element. There are currently 118 known chemical elements existing in nature. An atom is the smallest unit that retains all of the properties of each of these chemical elements. The particles that make up an atom, especially those of the nucleus, are difficult to separate due to the very strong forces that hold them together.

Atoms are composed of three types of particles: *protons*, *electrons*, and *neutrons*. Electrons, which have a negative electrical charge, exist in a cloud around the nucleus of an atom, which is composed of positively charged protons and neutral neutrons (see Figure A). Each atom carries a positive, negative, or neutral charge that is based on the balance of protons and electrons within the atom. The number of protons in an atom of a given element is always the same, but the number of electrons can change.

An equal number of protons and electrons would result in an overall neutral charge for the atom (the positive and negative charges of the particle balance each other). When an atom loses or gains electrons this creates what is called an **ion** of that element. More electrons than protons would result in an ion with an overall negative charge, and more protons than electrons would result in an overall positive charge.

When two or more atoms are joined together by a bonding force, they form a structure such as a molecule. Hewitt defines a molecule as "the smallest unit of a particular substance; a specific cluster of atoms with different properties from the separate atoms themselves" (1989, 714). Molecules may contain as few as two or as many as several million atoms joined by a chemical bond. Because negative and positive charges in a molecule may group together, molecules

FIGURE A The structure of an atom.

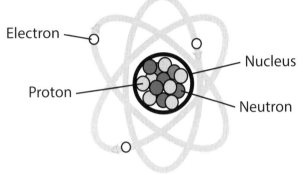

may have negative or positive sites that strongly attract other molecules.

Groupings of atoms or molecules form *matter*, which exists in three states: solid, liquid, or gaseous. The atoms and molecules of solid matter possess the lowest kinetic energy (the energy of motion) and have the highest strength of the intermolecular attractions between them; those in gases have the highest kinetic energy and lowest strength of attraction to one another.

Electrostatic energy or *electric potential energy* comes from the forces between charged ions. Ions with opposite charges attract each other, while ions with the same charge repel each other. When these forces occur between molecules, they are described as *chemical energy*, a form of potential (stored, nonmoving) energy. When these forces are within the nucleus of a single atom, they are described as *nuclear energy*, a very strong form of potential energy. Electrostatic energy can be converted from potential energy into another form of energy, such as mechanical energy or electromagnetic radiation. (For more information about conversion of energy, see Energy Basics 3.2.)

bicomponent fiber, contains two different materials selected so that the best qualities of each can be exploited. If the polymers used come from two different generic classes, the fiber may be labeled *bicomponent-bigeneric*.

Some bicomponent fibers are made by forcing more than one liquid polymer through each spinneret hole. (See Figure 3.3.) This is similar to the method used to create a striped toothpaste or one that squirts out two different types of paste when you squeeze the tube.

Other bicomponent fibers are made by embedding *fibrils* (tiny pieces) of one fiber in a matrix of another fiber. When these fibrils or other particles of the embedded fiber are at a nanoscale, these fibers are labeled **composite fibers**.

The chemical and/or physical differences between the polymers in a bicomponent fiber can create a variety of unusual attributes in the resulting fabric. For example, if a fiber contains two materials that shrink at different rates when exposed to liquid, the use of this bicomponent fiber can add built-in texture to materials when they are dyed. A bicomponent fiber that contains a strong,

thermoplastic polymer and a polymer treated with an anti-static agent (such as a nylon dope impregnated with carbon) allows the strong nylon fiber to be used in industrial settings where nylon's static-generating properties might otherwise prove to be a hazard.

Fiber Cross Section Variations

Many manufacturers change the basic size and cylindrical shape of a thermoplastic fiber in order to change a variety of fiber characteristics from luster to thermal insulation. The cross sections of the fibers shown in Figure 3.4B, C, and D, for example, are planned so that air spaces will naturally occur as the fibers are formed into fabrics. The spaces left by these fiber configurations may

FIGURE 3.4 Cross sections of fibers. (A) A basic cylindrical filament, (B) a trilobal fiber, (C) an oval filament, and (D) a dogbone fiber.

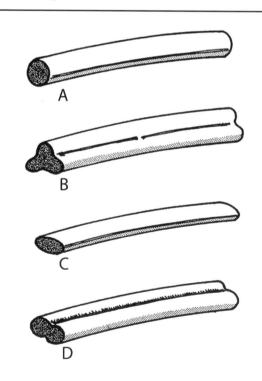

FIGURE 3.3 Three methods of creating bicomponent fibers. (A) Side by side; (B) core-sheath; and (C) embedded fibril.

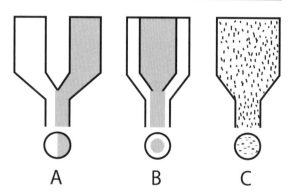

also play a part in the way the fiber handles water or reflects light.

Manufacturers may also imitate other qualities of natural fibers, such as the hollow core found in wool. Some hollow core polyesters used in thermal insulation contain single or multiple hollow channels down the length of each fiber (Figure 3.5). These fibers incorporate more air and are lighter in weight than a solid fiber of the same substance.

One method of varying fiber cross section that has had a major impact on the appearance and function of many manufactured items can be found in the development of **microfibers** (Figure 3.6), ultrafine microfibers, and nanofibers. Microfibers are many times finer than human hair. Microfibers are those that have deniers of less than 1, with most falling in the range from 0.5 to 0.8 denier per filament (dpf). Ultrafine fibers have a denier per filament of less than 0.3 (Kadolph 2010, 117). Extremely fine fibers with diameters of less than 100 nanometers are called nanofibers.

Microfibers may be formed using spinnerets with finer holes, by stretching the fibers after they emerge from the spinneret, or by splitting or separating the filaments after they are formed. Nanofibers are made by different processes. The most common process is called *electrospinning*. It involves the same polymers used to make other fibers, but a high electrical voltage is used in production. Hatch, discussing polyester microfibers, states that fabrics structured of them may contain as many as "6200 fibers per square inch" (1993, 222). The fineness of microfibers and nanofibers leads to many potential improvements in the qualities of fabrics made from them. Microfibers can enhance the smoothness, drape, luster, and thermal insulation of a textile material. Nanofibers can be used in many medical applications such as the creation of artificial body parts and the removal of viruses and bacteria from air and water.

Flameproof and Flame-Resistant Fibers

Although the properties of flame resistance or ignition resistance can be built into the fabric at several stages—in the fiber, fabric formation, or finish—many items of clothing for hazardous environments are made of inherently flameproof or flame-resistant fabrics. That is, flame and ignition

FIGURE 3.5 Hollow core fibers.

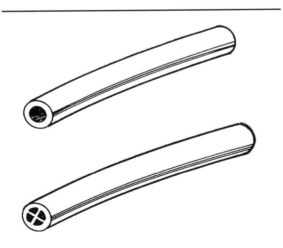

FIGURE 3.6 Thinsulate® microfibers and typical Dacron fiberfill fibers under the same magnification. *(The 3M Company)*

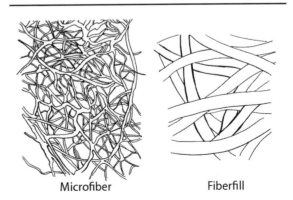

Microfiber   Fiberfill

resistance are due to the chemical nature of the fiber rather than the way it is treated in production. This inherent resistance prevents a breakdown in the finish, for example, from affecting the protection available at a critical moment.

When a fiber is labeled as **fireproof** or **flameproof**, it means that it will not burn when exposed to fire. The only flameproof fibers are inorganic ones such as glass, metal, carbon, and asbestos. Glass and metal conduct heat readily and thus have to be carefully applied to clothing end uses. Glass fibers have a low flex resistance and break easily, breaking down both the material structure and the surface of anything next to it. Many metal fibers are very dense and thus can add significant weight to an ensemble. Carbon fibers have a high strength but a low flexibility. Asbestos fibers are no longer used because they constitute a health hazard if bits of fiber are inhaled. Although, except for asbestos, these fibers can all be used in clothing, their characteristics must be carefully considered and dealt with.

When a fiber is labeled as **flame resistant (FR)**, it means that it will ignite with difficulty, burn slowly when touched with flame, and usually self-extinguish when the flame is removed. There are a number of flame-resistant fibers. **Aramid** fibers such as Nomex® and Kevlar® are inherently flame resistant and do not melt. Thermoplastic fibers such as polyester and nylon will resist ignition, but they do melt at relatively low temperatures, approximately 480°F (248°C) and melting fibers can cause significant burn injury. Other high temperature-resistant materials include FR cotton, FR wool and rayon; polybenzimidazole (PBI), Polytetrafluoroethylene (PTFE), best known by a trade name, Teflon; novaloid, which is marketed under the name of Kynol®; Polybenzoxazole (PBO); p-phenylene sulfide (PPS) and carbon

fibers. Many fabrics used in protective clothing are blends or composites of several of these fibers.

Another approach to flame resistance is to engineer fabrics that are self-extinguishing. For example, one company impregnates cotton fibers with FR polymer cores. These polymer cores act as catalysts to promote the charring of the cotton fibers, in essence, eliminating the source of fuel for flames (Westex FR fabric).

One term that should be mentioned here is **inflammable** because it is frequently used incorrectly. Inflammable means easily set on fire. Both **flammable** and inflammable materials burn readily.

Fiber Treatments: Finishes and Texturing

Even though finishes are generally applied to a fabric, both single fibers and yarns may be treated in a variety of ways before they are made into fabrics. They may be dyed, given more texture, or coated with a variety of substances to make them more water resistant or absorbent; more or less reflective; more stain resistant, more durable, etc. Some metal-coated fibers are produced by coating a woven or knitted fabric and then deconstructing it to retrieve the coated fibers. Many of these treatments will be covered when materials for specific end uses are discussed throughout the text.

One process that is frequently applied after a manufactured fiber is made is texturing. **Texturing** is the process by which smooth filament fibers are given a texture in the form of a loop, curl, or crimp. Texturing processes depend on the thermoplastic nature of manufactured fibers. Figure 3.7 shows the results of several of these processes. Basically, a filament fiber is distorted by twisting it, looping it, or pushing it into a confined space and then heating and cooling it while in this position. After the fiber is cooled, it retains the memory of the distorted position, and its residual stress

FIGURE 3.7. Textured thermoplastic yarns. (A) The stuffer-box method; (B) the false-twist method; (C) the air-jet or looped method. *(E. I. duPont de Nemours and Company)*

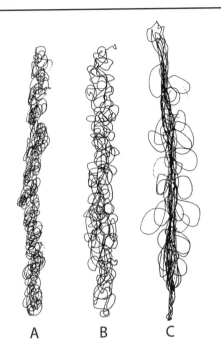

A   B   C

will tend to return it to this position after external forces are removed.

Textured fibers can be combined to form yarns or fabrics having a fuzzy, more natural fiber appearance and containing more air spaces within their structures. When textured fibers are twisted into yarns or formed into fabrics, they continue to attempt to return to their distorted position, and this causes a fabric surface to be more textured as well. Nonthermoplastic fibers may also be textured by coating them with substances that are thermoplastic first and then proceeding with the heating and cooling process.

Fiber Interactions with Moisture

There are a number of ways in which water interacts with fibers (Figure 3.8). It may be *absorbed* into the fiber so that it penetrates the surface and travels throughout the fiber structure; it may be **adsorbed** or attracted to and held on the outer surface of the fiber; it may be wicked or transported along the fiber surface; or it may be repelled by the fiber.

The physical attraction of liquids to a fiber surface plays a major role in the reaction of fabrics to water. For example, the molecules of water are sometimes more attracted to fibers than they are to each other. This results in water molecules being drawn along the surface of a fiber by a process called **wicking**. Thermoplastic, manufactured fibers are particularly suited to wicking because they are relatively non-absorbent and can be formed in thin filaments that promote this kind of mechanical movement, which is called capillary action. Not all thermoplastic fibers are equally effective in liquid transport. Some, such as polypropylene, an olefin fiber, have a chemical composition that is attractive to water, and thus it is a particularly good wicker. Of the natural fibers, silk, with its filament structure, is most likely to serve to wick water effectively.

FIGURE 3.8. Modes of interaction of water with fibers. (A) Absorption; (B) adsorption; (C) wicking; (D) being repelled.

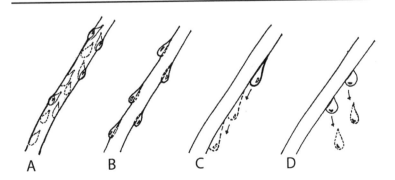

A   B   C   D

Fiber finishes and other treatments may greatly affect their reaction to water. For example, Capilene® polyester, a fiber created for cold weather undergarments, is the result of a treatment grafted into the polyester fiber that attracts water to the fiber surface, spreading it out so that it moves from wetter areas of the fiber to drier ones and eventually dissipates. This spreading action is another form of wicking.

YARNS

The American Society for Testing and Materials (ASTM) defines **yarn** as "a continuous strand of textile fibers, filaments or material in a form suitable for knitting, weaving or otherwise intertwining to form a textile fabric" (ASTM 2012, 58).

The relatively short fibers that occur in nature such as wool and cotton, are called **staple fibers**. These need to be twisted or spun into yarn before they can be formed into fabrics (Figure 3.9). The twisting process adds strength and durability to staple fibers. A single long filament created in the process of making manufactured fibers can serve as a yarn, or filaments may be chopped into short lengths and twisted to form yarns. It is important to note that the ways in which fibers are formed into yarns may be as critical or even more critical to the final characteristics of a fabric than the type of fiber used. Fabrics made of staple fibers tend to be more textured than those made of filaments, although many treatments can be used to add this quality to filament fibers.

Single yarns may be twisted or **plied** with others to form a larger yarn (Figure 3.9C). When two yarns are plied together, the result is called a two-ply yarn; when three yarns are used, a three-ply yarn results, and so on. When plies are twisted together, they result in *cord* or **cable yarns** (Figure 3.9D). Yarns and plies can also be braided,

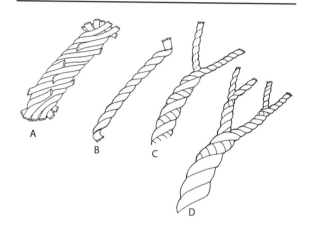

FIGURE 3.9 (A) Staple fibers twisted together to form a yarn; (B) filament fibers twisted to form a yarn; (C) several yarns twisted together to form a plied yarn; (D) plied yarns twisted together to form a cord or cable.

resulting in strong, pliable products such as shoelaces or coverings for wires and hoses.

The type and degree of twist used to form a yarn may also change the functional and aesthetic properties of fibers. For example, by tightly twisting wool fibers together into yarns, wool can be made suitable for summer weight suits and other garments that retain many of wool's other excellent properties while decreasing its air spaces and thus its thermal insulation.

FABRIC STRUCTURES

A *fabric* is generally defined as a cloth made of textile fibers by weaving, knitting, or employing a nonwoven process such as felting. The fiber filaments and yarns just discussed can be made into a wide variety of fabrics using these three methods of production. The choice of a fabric structure can significantly affect the protective capacities of fibers.

Weaves

Woven fabrics are made on looms by interlacing two sets of yarns at right angles. The yarns that are threaded onto a loom are called **warp yarns**; those that are interlaced across the warp yarns are called **weft yarns** or **filling yarns**. Weaves are classified both by the number of warp and weft yarns per square inch and the type of weave. The number of yarns per square inch is referred to as the **fabric count** or **thread count** of a fabric. For almost all fabrics, the higher the thread count, the finer the yarns will be.

Weave types are classified according to their method of interlacing the warp and weft yarns. The most basic and simplest of weaves, the **plain weave** (Figure 3.10A), is achieved by alternating the yarns in a one-over, one-under pattern. The plain weave

has many interesting variations. For example, the **rib weave** is achieved when heavier yarns or groups of yarns are used in one direction. In another variation, the **basket weave** (Figure 3.10B), two or more yarns are woven together as if they were one. In so-called **ripstop** materials, heavier, stronger threads are part of the weave at intervals. They form a grid of squares approximately ³⁄₁₆ inch (4.76 mm) wide. These threads help prevent propagation of tears when a fabric is punctured.

Another type of weave, the **twill weave** (Figure 3.11A), is characterized by stair step diagonal ridges formed by the yarns. It is made by allowing each weft yarn to float over at least two warp yarns during the interlacing process. Because there are fewer interlacings, twill weaves are very tightly packed and therefore are very durable.

Satin weaves (Figure 3.11B) are similar to twill weaves, but either the warp or the weft yarns form **floats** by passing over at least four yarns (generally as many as seven yarns) and then passing under only one. Since the basic satin weave has an

FIGURE 3.10 Plain weaves. (A) A basic plain weave; (B) the basket weave.

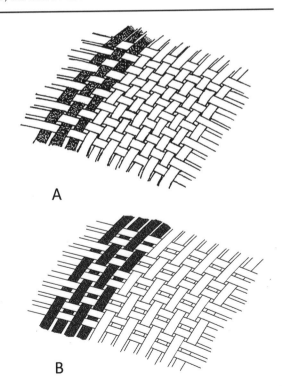

A

B

FIGURE 3.11 (A) A twill weave; (B) a satin weave. The shaded yarns are floats.

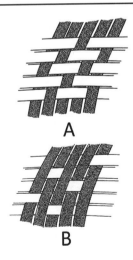

A

B

even greater potential for tightly packed yarns with fewer interlacings than the twill weave, it can possess great strength. However, satins are often very easily damaged by abrasion, since the floats can be snagged in general wear. One advantage of this weave for protective clothing is that its tight weave yields a high wind resistance.

Other more complex weaves require three or more yarns in the interlacing process. The *gauze* or **leno** weave (Figure 3.12) is achieved by having two weft yarns form figure eights around the warp yarns. This weave, which requires a special attachment on the loom, is used to make open types of fabrics, such as those used for mosquito netting, curtains, and shopping bags.

Pile weaves (Figure 3.13) such as corduroy, velvet, velveteen, and terry cloth are made by using extra warp or weft yarns. The loose floats that occur with this extra yarn form loops on the surface of the fabric. In terry cloth, the fabric used for bath towels, these loops are generally left as is. In other pile fabrics, these loops are cut and then brushed into a position perpendicular to the fabric surface. Pile fabrics may also be made by weaving two fabrics together with a fifth yarn. The two fabrics are

FIGURE 3.13 A pile weave.

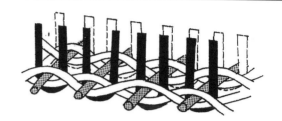

then cut apart, forming a pile. Velvet is often made using this process.

The fibers that stand out from a pile fabric are generally called its **nap**. Sometimes the nap lies in a specific direction, and this creates a directional smoothness and affects the way light is reflected off the fabric surface. This means that when designers put together a garment made of pile fabric, they need to plan to cut the various pieces of the garment so that the nap lies in one direction throughout.

Woven fabrics have what are called selvages, a straight of grain, and a bias. The **selvage** results as the fabric is woven and weft yarns wrap around the warp yarns at the edges of the loom. Selvages, which do not ravel, occur on both edges of a woven fabric. Because warp yarns have to be stretched on a loom, they are often stronger than weft yarns and they tend to hang perpendicular to the floor when allowed to drape freely from the body. A line that runs lengthwise parallel to a warp yarn is called the **straight of grain**. The **bias** direction in a fabric is one that runs at a 45° angle between the warp and weft yarns. It is the stretchiest direction of a woven fabric. Designers must be very aware of both the straight of grain and bias directions of a woven fabric as it is placed in a design because they influence drape, ease, fit, and stability of various areas of a garment.

FIGURE 3.12 The leno weave.

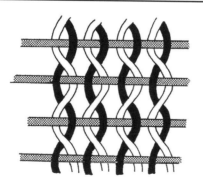

The lack of stability of basic woven fabrics in their bias direction led manufacturers to develop the **triaxial weave** (Figure 3.14). Triaxial weaves have three sets of interlacing yarns (the warp, the whug, and the weft), and the result is a structure without a bias (stretchy) direction. The most familiar triaxial weave may be the one used in caning chairs. Those formed with textile fibers are primarily used for industrial textiles where high strength and stability is required. They may be used to make stable 3-D structures as well.

Knits

Some yarns are knitted into fabrics rather than being woven. **Knit** fabrics are formed by linking loops of yarns on needles. Knitted fabrics can be made from one very long yarn, as opposed to woven fabrics, which must be made from at least two yarns. The very process of knitting naturally places more open spaces in fabrics and gives them the capacity for stretch. Knit types fall into two general categories: **weft knits** (sometimes called **filling knits**) and **warp knits** (Figure 3.15).

Weft and Warp Knits

To form weft knits, the yarn forming the fabric moves *across* the fabric as one row of loops is drawn through the previous row of loops. Hand knitting produces a weft knit. There are vertical lines called **wales** down the face side of a weft knit

FIGURE 3.15. Knits. (A) The weft knit; (B) the warp knit.

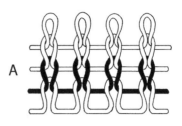
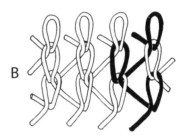

and horizontal loops called **courses** on the back. Weft knits can be made by hand or by machine, and both may suffer *runs* like those familiar to wearers of nylon stockings. The most familiar weft knits are probably those found in sweaters and women's hose. There are a number of different types of knit stitches, and several of these are illustrated in Figure 3.16.

Warp knitting is done by machine and involves the use of a latch needle that pulls yarns through succeeding loops. The yarn in warp knit moves from one vertical row of loops to the one beside it. This forms a pattern distinctly different from that of weft knit materials. It also forms a structure that does not run. The machines used to form weft knits use many needles so these knits can be produced very quickly. The most common warp knit is the *tricot* knit found in women's slips and nightgowns. (See Figure 3.15B.)

Double knits are more stable and less easily stretched than single knits. They are made with

FIGURE 3.14 A triaxial weave.

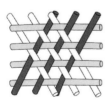

FIGURE 3.16 Knit stitches. (A) Knit stitch; (B) purl stitch; (C) float or miss stitch; (D) tuck stitch; (E) interlock knit. *(Courtesy of Fairchild Books)*

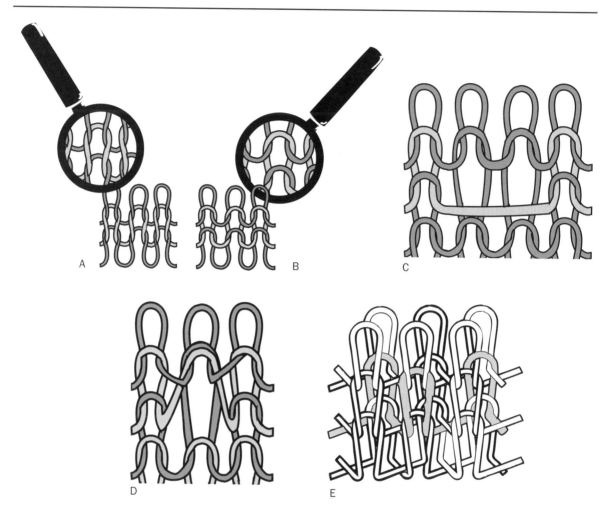

two separate layers of loops—one set on each of two machine beds—with each yarn forming patterns that appear the same on both faces of the fabric.

Circular knitting machines offer the possibility of forming garments at the same time as the fabric is being formed. This is the case with items such as tube socks and gloves, as well as the torso of undershirts, etc., that are made without side seams.

Warp knits may also have a more complex structure. For example, the **raschel knit** (Figure 3.17) contains extra yarns, which are laid into the knit, traveling from one column of loops to another creating an open, lace-like structure.

Three-Dimensional Knits

Knitting can also be used to produce three-dimensional structures. Depending on the fibers and yarns used to produce a 3-D knit, it can be stiff and strong or flexible and soft.

There are several ways to produce a 3D knitted structure. Among them are those that selectively shrink fibers so that the yarns around them buckle

FIGURE 3.17 A raschel warp knit with laid-in yarns. Both warp and filling knits may be the base for pile fabrics such as fake furs or velours. They may also be brushed to form a stretchable fleece. *(Courtesy of Fairchild Books)*

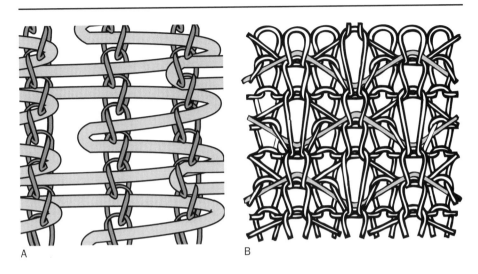

A   B

to produce a 3-D shape and those that knit fully formed 3-D cells like small boxes.

The most common type of 3-D knitted structure is called a *spacer* fabric. Spacer fabrics are produced by knitting in multiple layers, in a manner similar to producing a double knit, and connecting the layers with a stiff filament that passes between the face layer and the backing layer and holds them apart. Figure 3.18 shows the way such a structure may be formed.

Nonwovens

Some fabrics are produced without interlacing filaments or yarns. These fabrics are called **nonwovens** or **fiberweb structures**. The fibers in nonwovens are held together using chemicals, adhesives, heat and moisture, stitching or other mechanical methods (Figure 3.19). Fibers laid into a nonwoven configuration may result in a fabric structure called a **web**, presumably because of its appearance as a network of entangled fibers that sometimes look like a spider's home.

Probably the most familiar nonwoven is **felt**, a fabric used for many crafts. Felt is made by laying wool fibers out in a sheet and subjecting them to a combination of heat, moisture, and pressure. Similar felt-like fabrics may also be made with nonwool fibers by quilting fibers together with stitching or using a **needlepunch** process. In needlepunching, fibers are laid out in a sheet and entangled using the mechanical action of hundreds of hooked needles as they pass through the layers of fibers. Because of the random arrangement of fibers and the many interlockings that result from

FIGURE 3.18 3-D knitted spacer fabric.

FIGURE 3.19 A typical fiberweb structure.

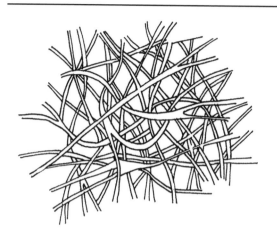

as many as 2,500 punches per square inch (388 punches per square centimeter), needlepunched fabrics contain many protected air spaces. For this reason, they are often used for insulation for winter garments or for items such as blankets.

Many insulations as well as the flatter, more compact nonwovens used for disposable garments in hospitals, scientific laboratories, and industry are made by **bonding** fibers together with adhesives or heat. Thermoplastic fibers lend themselves especially well to making bonded fiber fabrics because they soften and fuse together when heat and pressure are applied. The flexibility and comfort of a bonded material as well as the ease with which it can be incorporated into garments depends greatly on the method used to form the material. Fibers that are heavily bonded together shift less when sewn inside a garment and do not need quilting to hold them in place, but they are stiffer and conform less to the body.

Even though a loose, nonwoven configuration sold in a thickness suitable for insulation may, like other nonwovens, be called a web, it is often called a **batt**. The term **batting** originally referred to a nonwoven made of cotton fibers and used in quilting, but it is commonly used now as a descriptive term for synthetic insulations. The most commonly used batts for cold weather apparel are called **fiberfills** and are made of polyester or other polymers. Fiberfill is produced in dozens of types under a number of trademarks. Unfortunately, there seem to be no standard methods in the industry for establishing designations for these various types, so it is up to the designer to find out what individual manufacturers mean by their own names and numbers. Batts of polyester fiberfill may contain different lengths and thicknesses of fibers, different fiber finishes such as crimp and surface treatment, and they are formed using different nonwoven fabrication methods.

Stretch Fabrics

The stretchable nature of a material is termed its **elasticity**. For most end uses, it is important to know three aspects related to a material's elasticity: how *much* it stretches; how *easily* it stretches; and how well it *recovers*.

How much a textile material stretches is generally expressed in terms of percentage of its original length. Single fibers may stretch to 500 percent of their original length or more. However, the process of putting fibers and yarns into a fabric structure results in it having less elongation. A minimum of 15 percent elongation is usually required for a fabric to be thought of as stretch, but some fabrics may stretch up to 200 percent or more.

The ease of stretch is often communicated by the terms **comfort stretch** and **power stretch**. Materials designated as comfort stretch require very little effort to stretch and are thus used for exercise clothing and any end use that requires ease of body movement. In some documents, these materials may be referred to as having a low

elastic modulus. Those designated as power stretch require much more effort or tension to stretch and are thus used either in body shaping garments or in support devices such as braces or support stockings. These are sometimes referred to as *high elastic modulus* materials.

There are two aspects of a material's **elastic recovery** that are important: the *extent* to which a material's original length and width returns when tension is released and how *quickly* the material recovers. These factors may simply be important for appearance (e.g., avoiding the bagging out of knees in nylon hosiery), or they may be critical for performance (e.g., maintaining pressure on a weakened knee after extending to allow bending).

Fabrics are made more stretchable through the choice of both fiber and fabric structure. Rubber and spandex lend the greatest capacity for stretch to a material and have almost full elastic recovery, but they are not often used alone for a variety of reasons, among them: comfort against the skin and aesthetics. When they are used, they tend to be the core of a yarn that is wrapped with stretchable fibers such as nylon or polyester. Figure 3.20 shows a covered or **core-spun yarn** that has a spandex core wrapped with a textured nylon fiber. Spandex-core yarns like this one are used in both woven and knitted fabrics. Texturized yarns of manufactured fibers may also be used with or without spandex to impart the capacity for stretch in a fabric.

Knits tend to be more easily stretchable than wovens or other nonwovens. This is because the loops in a knit structure are able to flatten and slide through each other when stress is applied to the fabric. This gives knits the capacity to change shape relatively easily. Stretch wovens, by the very nature of the woven structure, stretch far less in amount. Since all of the capacity for woven stretch materials has to come from the fiber, these fabrics usually incorporate a certain amount of spandex.

Stretch knits and stretch wovens also differ in their ability to recover from being stretched and resume their original shape. When loops in a knit structure slide through each other, the friction between yarns can make it less likely that the loops will slide back into place after the stretching force is removed. A spandex core in a yarn aids elastic recovery, helping the structure to return to its original shape.

Many stretch materials have more stretch in one direction than the other. The stretch in weft knits tends to be greater in the cross direction, at 90° from the wales, but they also stretch a good deal lengthwise. Warp knits stretch less than weft knits, extending more in the crosswise direction and very little in the lengthwise one. Knits that expand primarily in one direction are usually called **two-way stretch** materials, and those that extend in both crosswise and lengthwise directions are designated as **four-way stretch**. Confusingly, however, some companies refer to knits that stretch only crosswise or lengthwise as one-way stretch, knits that stretch both crosswise and lengthwise as two-way stretch, and knits that stretch in any direction, usually due to a spandex fiber component, as four-way stretch. Most four-way stretch knits use a spandex-core yarn to allow the fabric to stretch and recover more

FIGURE 3.20 A core-spun yarn.

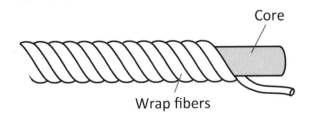

Core

Wrap fibers

easily in any direction, without relying only on the knit structure.

FABRIC TREATMENTS, FINISHES, AND COMPOSITES

The variables involved in producing fabrics are endless. The basic fabrics produced by weaving, knitting, and bonding and the like are called **greige goods** (pronounced "gray" goods). These unfinished fabrics are taken to manufacturers called **converters**, who treat them to make them more beautiful or to improve their behavior. Converters may dye, bleach, polish, stiffen, or print a fabric or add coatings and surface texture to it. Multiple materials may be merged together to combine properties. Wrinkle-resistant, flame-retardant, water-repellent, or antistatic finishes might be added. The converting industry is constantly developing new methods to treat fabrics to improve their appearance and function.

Many treatments can be applied to fabrics. Some of the more commonly used finishes involve applying a substance or material to the surface of a textile by adding a coating or laminating it to another material. Others may add texture and color treatments to a textile to change its appearance or surface properties.

Coatings

Hatch defines **coating** as "the application of a semiliquid material to one or both sides of a base fabric in such a manner that the material lies on the surface, without permeating the entire base" (1993, 376).

Coatings may be rolled onto a fabric surface, or, in the case of molded structures such as gloves, whole items may be dipped into a vat of coating material. Manufacturers are always working to improve the durability of coatings by increasing both the durability of the coating itself and the ability of coatings to adhere to various fabrics. The continual flexing of fabrics in clothing during movement, cleaning, and storage make coatings susceptible to cracking and peeling and may change the appearance of the fabric surface. In addition, because of the abrasion to which they are exposed, even when aesthetics is not an issue, many coatings are applied to the inside of a fabric where they are more protected.

The most typical coatings found on apparel are used to seal out water, chemicals, and other liquids and airborne hazards or to change a garment's radiant heat-reflective qualities. Coatings fill in the interstices between yarns or fibers and prevent water and other liquids from being absorbed by the fabric surface. They may also prevent chemical interactions with a fabric.

One substance frequently used in coatings for protective clothing is aluminum. The most familiar aluminized materials are probably those used by firefighters in high-temperature airport or industrial fires or in the blankets wrapped around marathoners at the end of a race to prevent them from losing body heat too rapidly. (See also "Aluminized Fabrics" in Chapter 5.) Depending on the end use, thin films such as Mylar® or heat-resistant materials such as Nomex® aramid may be coated with an aluminum finish that is rolled on or joined to an aluminum film.

Laminates

Lamination involves the joining of two or more materials with an adhesive, or sometimes, with a foam. Fabrics may be laminated together to add strength, stability, or more body to each other. Films may be laminated to fabrics to produce waterproof or chemically-resistant materials or add allergy control or moisture transport. The term *bonding* is often used synonymously with lamination although bonding may also describe a process by which fabrics and foams of thermoplastic materials and others such as rubber, softened or liquefied by heat, may be melted together, eliminating the need for a separate adhesive.

Foam-laminated fabrics generally consist of a layer of foam between two fabrics. Because they incorporate many tiny air spaces, they are used primarily for insulation in cold weather clothing. Since a large proportion of the fabric is air, these materials are lightweight and in most cases very flexible, although they do not drape well and tend to have a rather stiff appearance.

Texturing Processes for Fabrics

In **brushed** or **napped fabrics**, the surface yarns have been raised so that the materials have a soft, fuzzy feel and appearance. These materials are generally created by brushing the fabric with wire brushes, forming what is essentially an artificial pile. Brushed fiber surfaces, like those found on flannel shirts, are usually intended to provide softness against the skin. In heavily brushed materials such as fleeces, the many raised fibers on both sides of the fabric incorporate a lot of air and are thus lightweight for their volume and very warm.

Addition of Color to Textile Materials

Color is a key sales factor for fashion garments, and many people who wear protective garments also value its contribution to the appearance of functional clothing. However, color may be an important part of protective garments for a number of additional reasons. It is a factor in visibility and thus helps ensure the safety of people in many different occupations and activities. It is critical in the camouflage clothing of soldiers.

The methods by which textiles are given color are complex and need to be pursued in texts that focus on dyeing and printing, etc. This overview will simply present some very basic terminology in those fields and a brief outline of some of the variables involved in adding color, so that the reader can find in-depth information on these topics in additional references.

Textiles are colored either with **dyes** or **pigments**. Dyes are colored substances that are made of molecules that dissolve in water. Whatever is being dyed is immersed in a dye bath, and the dye bonds chemically to it. Dyeing can take place at any of the stages of textile development. It can be added to a thermoplastic fiber solution before it enters the spinneret. This so-called **dope dyeing** results in a more colorfast, durable color because it is essentially integrated into the fiber formation. It is also possible to dye loose fibers, yarns, and garments once they have been made.

There are a number of classes of dyes, each designed to interact chemically and physically with different fibers. So, for example, acid dyes have an affinity for protein fibers such as wool and silk; vat dyes have an affinity for cellulosics such as cotton and linen; disperse dyes have an affinity for synthetic fibers such as nylon, polyester, and acrylic. Sometimes the affinity of dyes for one material and not another can be used to advantage in producing cross-dyed materials, where one set of yarns (such as the warp yarns) of a material dye in one dye bath and another set (such as the weft yarns) made of another fiber take up another color of a different dye in a second bath.

Dyeing a fabric deeper, darker colors can result in a fabric that is slightly heavier than the same fabric dyed a light pastel color. The weight added by different shades of dye is expressed as *percent on weight of goods* (OWG) or *percent on weight of fabric* (OWF).

The ability of dyers to use computers to do color matching has greatly improved the consistency of dyeing different batches of materials. There may still be differences between materials that are dyed with the same dye in different batches or *dye lots*. In addition, it may be hard to dye two different fabrics used in the same garment so that they look to be exactly the same color, especially if their textures are different.

Unlike dyes, *pigments* are not soluble in water. Microscopic pigment particles may be either placed within the dope used to make synthetic fibers or mechanically bound to the surface of a fiber with a resin. When they are applied with a resin to a fabric in either a solid color or a print, the pigment lies on the surface of the fabric. Since the fibers do not absorb it, less pigment than dye is needed to achieve a specific color, and the pigment color does not appear on the back of the textile. However, one of the concerns with pigments is that, because they are on the surface, they can be easily abraded and rubbed off.

Pigments can be used on almost any fabric as long as an effective resin or binder can be found. The specific binder used to attach a pigment depends on the fiber content of the fabric. Many resins need to be *cured* (i.e., heated to melt the binder into the fibers of a fabric), and the resulting fabrics are often stiffer, although much effort is made to keep fabric hand soft.

Water Resistance, Water Repellency, and Waterproofing

The composition of the fibers of a fabric is one of the most important influences on its interactions with moisture. However, much of the mechanics of water transport is determined by the way that fibers are joined to form fabrics. For example, polypropylene, a fiber that absorbs virtually no water and is noted for its ability to wick, can be made into fabrics that hold a great deal of water. Early garments made of polypropylene were often composed of extremely fine fibers made into dense, thick materials. Even though one would

expect materials made of polypropylene to dry quickly, these took an inordinate amount of time to dry. Water that is wicked or repelled from a fiber or yarn surface can still become physically entrapped in the structure of a fabric or between the fibers that make up a yarn. Hatch uses the term **imbibed** (1993, 35) to describe the saturation of a fabric with liquid due to this type of physical entrapment (Figure 3.21).

Water-resistant and **water-repellent** fabrics help prevent water from penetrating from one face of a fabric to the other. Although consumers often use the terms interchangeably, *water resistance* generally means that a fabric, either because of its fiber, weave, or surface treatment, will simply shed water in a light rain. In a heavy rain, water will quickly work its way through to the other face of a fabric. A *water-repellent* fabric has been treated with a finish or coating that is not easily penetrated by water.

Water repellency depends on the attractive forces between the molecules in a drop of water and the lack of attraction the water-repellent fabric holds for water. In other words, a fabric repels water if the attractive or cohesive forces within a droplet of water are stronger than those between the water and the water-repellent fabric. This aversion of water to the fabric causes the drop of water to pull into a spherical shape rather than to spread out and be absorbed into the fabric surface.

FIGURE 3.21 Water being imbibed in (A) a yarn; (B) a fabric structure.

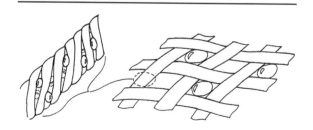

Manufacturers of water-repellent fabrics may talk about the **contact angle** of a water drop with their fabric. This is the angle that the edge of the drop of water makes with the surface of the fabric (Figure 3.22). Since drops on a water-repellent fabric tend to draw up into a spherical shape, a larger contact angle, one greater than 90°, indicates a fabric that is hydrophobic (water-hating) and is thus water-repellent.

Since the interstices between yarns of the material are still present in both water-repellent and water-resistant fabrics, it is possible to force water droplets through the fabric by adding pressure and, in some cases, squeezing them into elongated rather than spherical shapes. This is why water may pass through a water-repellent coat if, for example, an individual sits down on a wet surface. The pressure caused by the weight of the body can eventually force water through the fabric surface. Pressure may also result from the impact of water droplets in a hard, driving rain. However, for this pressure to force rain through fabric interstices, it must overcome the cohesive forces within the water molecule.

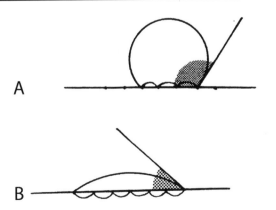

FIGURE 3.22. Water repellency. (A) Water drop repelled by a fabric draws up into a spherical shape; (B) water drop landing on an absorbent fabric spreads out, forming a smaller contact angle.

A

B

As the size of fabric interstices decreases, it takes greater and greater amounts of pressure to squeeze the water molecules through. Manufacturers measure the water resistance of a material using either two basic methods. One is a static method, where a column of water of a varying heights is placed over a test swatch of fabric (AATCC n.d.). The other is a more dynamic test where varying levels of water pressure are applied to the fabric surface (ISO n.d.; ASTM n.d.).

Waterproof fabrics are capable of excluding water during demanding conditions of pressure. A truly waterproof garment would simply not leak under any conditions. Because different tests result in different numbers, there is no real waterproof standard for fabrics. For many years, fabrics were labeled waterproof if they could withstand a minimum water pressure of 25 psi (172.37 kPa). More recent developments in technology have allowed even breathable microporous fabrics to well exceed this level. Different manufacturers use different levels of psi to declare their products waterproof. In part, this is because there is much more to waterproofing a garment than simply relying on waterproof fabrics. The activity and weight of the wearer and the body part being covered may also result in different levels of waterproofing needed. Gore provides one example: "a person weighing 165 pound exerts about sixteen pounds per square inch (or psi) on his knees when kneeling. To be waterproof, a fabric must not leak when subjected to these types of pressures." (Gore n.d.) The waterproofing needed in other areas may be quite different. Seams and closures must also be designed and manufactured properly, and openings at cuffs and hems and the like must be considered.

The interstices of weaves, knits, and other materials are made waterproof in a variety of ways: by applying a coating of a substance such as rubber or polyurethane (see "Coatings" earlier) or by laminating the material to a microporous or solid film or by forming a woven fabric with extremely fine yarns that act as micropores.

Waterproof/Breathable Laminates

The use of **microporous** laminated structures to create waterproof but breathable fabrics has mushroomed over the past several decades. Micropores are many thousand times smaller than a drop of water, but larger than water vapor. So they exclude liquids such as rain while allowing moist vapor on the surface of the skin to pass through them. In addition to making activewear more comfortable, microporous materials may be used in many protective applications, including those in the fields of medicine. For example, microporous surgeons' gowns may be worn to prevent the transfer of blood-borne pathogens in the operating field while allowing vapor from the surgeon's skin surface to escape.

The first microporous material that became popular on the consumer market was Gore-tex®. (Figure 3.23) Gore-tex® is a microporous membrane that can be laminated to various types and thicknesses of permeable fabrics to create a waterproof but breathable fabric system. Gore-tex® and other microporous membranes that have been developed are relatively fragile and therefore, are almost never used alone but always as part of a fabric system. A Gore-tex® membrane is made by heating and stretching a thin layer of Teflon (polytetrafluoroethylene, or PTFE). As it stretches, the membrane develops tiny holes or *pores*. This membrane is then in turn laminated in a layered system consisting of an outer fabric and often a thin inner lining fabric like a warp knit, which serves as abrasion protection for the Gore-tex® film (Figure 3.23A). A woven nylon/Gore-tex®/nylon knit laminate, then, 'breathes,' allowing air and water vapor to pass through, but prevents

FIGURE 3.23 (A) A microporous membrane laminated to an outer fabric and a liner; (B) comparison of the size of a drop of water to the size of a micropore of Gore-tex. *(W. L. Gore Associates)*

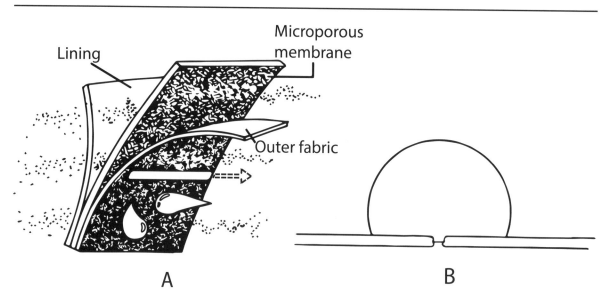

water drops from entering. Figure 3.23B shows the relative size of a water drop and a micropore in Gore-tex®.

Microporous coatings, generally of polyurethane (PU) or polyethylene (PE) may also be applied to a material. Eclipse® also uses ceramic technology in its coating. These substances cover the surface and interstices of a fabric in a way that results in the same microporous openings for vapor transport. Entrant® is an example of a microporous coating that penetrates deep into a material to become an inherent part of its structure and impart breathable but waterproof protection. Both coatings and laminates may incorporate hydrophilic (water-loving) components to attract water into a material or include a combination of hydrophilic and hydrophobic properties to move moisture through a fabric system.

Other breathable but waterproof materials may be created using a nonporous membrane. These work by blocking liquids but allowing the diffusion of molecules of moist vapor. If you have trouble with the concept of diffusion through a solid membrane, think of storing a very pungent soup in a plastic bag. Even when the bag does not appear to allow any leakage of soup, you have some evidence that air has managed to work its way between the molecules of the plastic when you open the refrigerator the following day and can smell nothing else but the soup. (See Chapter 7, Energy Basics 7.1, for an additional discussion of diffusion.)

Both membranes and coatings are used as part of a waterproof system—they are essentially a finish that can be applied to many fabrics. Therefore, it is not entirely accurate to state that, for example, "The jacket is made of Gore-tex®." A fully accurate statement would need to include details about the surface fabric and any lining that was part of

the system; for example, "The jacket is made of a nylon taffeta/Gore-tex®/nylon tricot laminate."

Each method of providing waterproofing or water repellency to a fabric has advantages and disadvantages and must be chosen after careful exploration of the end use for which the fabric is intended. For example, despite the waterproofing that microporous laminates provide, they may not be able to be used in situations where toxic liquids are present because they could allow vapors from those liquids to pass through.

Waterproof Fabric Structures

Another method of creating a breathable, waterproof fabric is by using extremely fine yarns and packing them densely into a fabric structure. Because of the fineness of the yarns, the interstices between them are so small that they act as micropores, and the dense packing prevents larger openings from being created as the fabric is flexed. One of the earliest examples of this is the natural fiber material, **Shirley cloth**, developed at the Shirley Institute in England. This material is now being manufactured under the trade name Ventile®. It is composed of long, fine cotton fibers that swell when wet and, in so doing, close the interstices between the yarns of the fabric. Therefore, the fabric breathes when dry, yet is almost waterproof when it is wet.

Because of the fineness of fibers that can be achieved with manufactured fibers, many fine yarn, densely packed, breathable, waterproof materials are now made with microdenier synthetic filament yarns. Since they do not absorb moisture, they do not swell like Shirley cloth does, but because of their extreme fineness, they can be packed more tightly. Since fine manufactured fibers promote capillary action, these fabrics are often positioned in a clothing system so that they can move moist vapor out from the skin surface to the environment.

Stretch has been added to breathable, waterproof materials in several ways. A thin microporous or nonporous membrane can be laminated to a stretch material such as a knit, while the stretch fabric is fully extended. This results in a composite in which the membrane appears wrinkled when tension on the fabric is released. Highly stretchable coatings or nonporous membranes can also be laminated to the underside of stretchy fabrics. These coatings must provide enough stretch to allow the fabric to extend fully and must be strong, resilient, and firmly adhered to the base fabric in order to be effective.

Permselective Treatments

A **permselective fabric** is a material that allows some substances to pass through while excluding others. Many permselective materials are continuous membranes that work by allowing only certain molecules to pass through by diffusion. These membranes may sort molecules by size, electrical charge, or solubility. Depending on what they exclude and the way in which they exclude certain molecules, they may be referred to as **selectively permeable membranes (SPMs)**, sorptive materials, semipermeable membranes, partially permeable membranes, or differentially permeable membranes.

Permselective materials are frequently used for protection from toxic gases and chemical/biological agents. Since gas molecules do not form drops or particles, a permeable fabric would need to have a pore size less than the diameter of a single gas molecule to exclude it. These pores would of necessity also exclude air molecules. Therefore, in order to develop a breathable material that protects from toxic gases, the material

must contain some kind of purifying substance that either excludes or attracts the toxins and holds them in such a way that they cannot pass through to the inner face of the material.

The most common substance used for attracting and binding toxic gases is active carbon. Active carbon is created by a complex process by which carbon molecules develop many types of attractive sites to which hazardous gas molecules can attach themselves. Carbon filters are used as air purifiers in cigarettes and ventilating fans. Carbon, in a powder form, can also be bound into foams or nonwoven fabrics and made into protective garments. Carbon fibers can also be produced and woven into fabrics. These fabrics offer an obvious advantage over impermeable materials in that they breathe.

Carbon powder is somewhat difficult to hold in a fabric. If it is bound in a resin, it is not free to adsorb gases. Consequently, far more carbon than is actually needed is sometimes used to ensure protection since some powder will be lost from the material during garment production and wear. Carbon fibers present other problems. They have an extremely low abrasion resistance, and the effectiveness of the carbon in them is reduced if the fibers adsorb sweat as they would from the body of a worker wearing carbon-fiber clothing.

A number of methods have been used to successfully incorporate carbon in clothing materials. Carbon powder may be surrounded by microporous materials, either in single fibers or in fabric laminates. Gore® uses its microporous PTFE membrane to protect the carbon layer in its permselective material. One material in use by the military is a charcoal powder incorporated into an open-cell foam. Others have embedded charcoal in nonwoven fabrics using needlepunching. These charcoal-impregnated materials are either bonded or laminated to a tricot backing or sandwiched between other materials. A method commonly used to make fabrics for chemically protective undergarments is to laminate microspheres filled with charcoal powder between two layers of a knit fabric base. This microsphere-filled material called *Bleucher fabric* provides enough protection while allowing laundering with very little loss of the carbon's adsorptive capacity.

The Structure of Other Materials Used in Apparel

Even though most fashion garments are made of textiles, protective clothing is often made with films or foams, and solid forms made of materials such as metals and plastics are often part of a protective clothing ensemble. These structures may be made of some of the same base materials as textiles, but they are manufactured differently and often require designers to rethink garment design.

FILMS

Films are not made with fibers, but with the synthetic dope or polymer solution before it is spun into fiber form. Liquid dope is extruded into a sheet form rather than being fed through a spinneret. **Films** are skin-like, flexible materials that are less than 0.01 inch (0.025 cm) thick, and **sheets** are similar structures that are 0.01 inch (0.025 cm) thick or greater. Films are used to make a wide variety of protective garments, such as rainwear or chemical protective clothing where a nonporous material is essential. Films may be very thin, as they are in plastic food wraps, or thick as is the vinyl used in upholstery or chemical/biological protective suits. Since air and water cannot penetrate them, they tend to be very warm to wear.

Many of the films commonly used in industrial, agricultural, and medical protective clothing are made of polyvinyl chloride (PVC). PVC is one of a number of vinyl polymers that can be extruded into sheets or films. A PVC film is tough, does not react with most chemicals and solvents, and is impervious to liquid and vapor. Because it has no pores or interstices, it can be used in a variety of anticontamination suits as well as in protective clothing for medical research or biological warfare. Fabrics or scrims can also be laminated to the inside of PVC films for added strength and comfort.

Films of other similar thermoplastic materials such as polyethylene, polyurethane, and polypropylene may also be used in clothing. These materials all have an excellent resistance to corrosive chemicals and solvents. To defeat a wider range of chemicals, several layers of different films may be laminated together into a single thin film.

FOAMS

Foams are another material formed from solution rather than from fibers or yarns. They are important to a number of types of functional clothing and protective equipment.

Foams are made by mixing a liquid polymer with a series of ingredients one of which is a **blowing agent** or **foaming agent**. This substance creates the gas bubbles that form cells in the basic material. The blowing agent chosen for a specific polymer must be capable of decomposing (changing into a gaseous state) at the same temperature at which the polymer becomes fluid or viscous, and it must generate a considerable volume of gas bubbles as it decomposes.

It should be noted that not all polymers are foamed with the use of a blowing agent. For example, natural rubber generally has added to it a substance that forms a froth when it is beaten (Rodriguez et al. 2003, 555). As anyone who has ever aerated eggs or cream with a wire whip can imagine, an important ingredient in this type of process is a stabilizer that keeps the froth from collapsing while the solid foam is being formed.

Another essential ingredient to be added to the polymer/blowing agent mix is a surfactant (surface-active agent). A **surfactant** is a chemical compound that helps strengthen the bond between two surfaces. In foams, the surfactant lowers the surface tension between the gas and polymer interface, allowing individual bubbles of gas to be formed. During the foaming process, the surfactant regulates the cell size, uniformity, and nature to a large extent, controlling the viscosity and surface tension of the cell membranes as they are stretched during foaming (Rodriguez et al. 2003, 553). Without a surfactant, smaller bubbles would dissolve in the polymer or gradually migrate into nearby larger bubbles. Impact-protective foams in particular need the presence of many small, uniform cells to provide reliable energy absorption. Being able to control cell size and the thinness of cell walls with a surfactant also allows a manufacturer to create a foam with other desirable properties such as flexibility.

The polymer, blowing agent, surfactant, and other ingredients needed to regulate the process or contribute features to the final foamed material are mixed together and heated. As the blowing agent decomposes and the foaming process takes place, the mixture can be placed in a shaped mold or poured out into a slab or sheet form. It also may be foamed in place on the surface of a rigid form or the inner face of a textile material. In any case, an important factor is whether or not this process takes place under pressure.

Open- and Closed-Cell Foams

If the foaming process takes place in an open mold, or the substance to be foamed is poured into container where it is *not* under pressure, the gas bubbles escape through the surface of the mixture and an **open-cell foam** is formed. This process is similar to what happens when a cake is baked. The gases formed by a leavening agent form bubbles around which the batter bakes, but as pressure builds up in each cell in the batter, the gases eventually break through and migrate out of the top of the cake pan. You can see interconnected cell formations when you cut a slice of cake or examine the edge of a kitchen sponge.

When the foaming process takes place in a closed mold, under pressure, a **closed-cell foam** is formed. After the foaming process is completed, a mold containing closed-cell foam is gradually cooled until the item has set. Then the mold is removed and the finished items or sheets of foam are heated slightly to force the gases in the cells (and thus the cells themselves) to expand. When the foam is returned to room temperature, each of its cells contains gas at partial pressure. The presence of these gas-filled cells in a closed-cell foam means that it can never fully collapse, as can an open-cell foam.

Open- and closed-cell foams have very different properties and need to be chosen carefully for an end use. More extensive discussions of their applications appear in Chapter 6 under "Foams as Impact Protectors" and in Chapter 8 under "Clothing for Diving and Water Safety."

Aerogels

Unlike foams, which are created by introducing gas bubbles into a fluid, **aerogels** are created by removing the liquid from a gel, leaving an empty solid matrix behind. Gels are made of liquid held in a cross-linked network, so that they behave as soft, malleable solids. Normally when the liquid is removed from a gel (e.g., when a gel is left open to the air and dries out), the gel shrinks (reducing the amount of air held in the solid network). Aerogels are made by removing the liquid using a process called *supercritical drying*, which allows the solid network to remain in its original shape, trapping a very large amount of air in the aerogel. Aerogels are among the lightest solids on earth.

A gel substance is flexible and malleable mostly because of its water content. When the water is removed, only the solid matrix remains, and the structure takes on the properties of that solid material, which is often brittle. The first aerogels were made of very brittle materials like silica (glass). Because there is so little glass in a traditional silica aerogel, it is very fragile and not suitable for clothing. However, techniques like polymer cross-linking are used to make the aerogel more flexible and strong. Similarly, for use in apparel, the aerogel can be reinforced with a fiber (like the fiber-reinforced resins described in the next section) or deposited onto a fiber batt.

RIGID MATERIALS

Three types of rigid materials may be used in protective clothing: *metals* such as steel, aluminum, and titanium; *ceramics* such as aluminum oxide or boron carbide; and rigid *plastics*, including fiber-reinforced resins, such as fiberglass. Although for some clothing accessory items rigid materials may be used alone, all three materials are most frequently used in conjunction with textile materials and/or foams.

Apparel designers do not often work with rigid materials, but it is important to become familiar with their behavior and properties and the terminology with which they are described since they are a vital part of many protective apparel items. In this way, designers will be able to choose appropriate materials and coordinate rigid and soft materials in a protective apparel item effectively.

Because they are most frequently used for garments that protect the body from impact (e.g., in

sports equipment and ballistics protection) and their use is based on principles that relate to attenuating impact, several of these materials will be discussed in more detail in Chapter 6.

Metals

There are several properties of metals that are critical for a designer to understand when choosing an appropriate metal for an item of protective clothing. The term elasticity has already been defined as the ability of a material to return to its original shape after it has been deformed. Remember, however, that materials have an elastic limit. If enough tension or compression is applied to a material so that it reaches its elastic limit and permanently deforms, it will no longer be able to return to its original shape. A metal's elastic limit is expressed in terms of the stress, expressed in pounds per square inch (kilograms per square centimeter) or megapascals (MPa) at which permanent deformation occurs. For example, the elastic limit of structural steel is approximately 250 MPa, whereas the elastic limit of human skin is approximately 12 MPa.

Another important thing to know about a metal to be used in protective apparel is whether it is ductile or brittle. **Ductile metals**, when they pass their elastic limit, become plastic. That is, they stretch or draw out until they are very thin. **Brittle metals** shatter when they reach their elastic limit. Ductile metals may become brittle under certain conditions (such as extreme temperatures), and brittle metals may become ductile. Therefore, many texts talk about metals as being in a brittle or ductile state. Each state may have advantages and disadvantages for protection from specific hazards.

Another property of concern is toughness. The **toughness** of a metal is defined as the total energy required to fracture a bar of that metal. Since metals are made up of atoms that are bonded together, fracture does not occur unless forces are great enough to break those bonds. Some materials are characteristically tougher than others. In other words, the bonds that hold them together are more difficult to break. Some materials may withstand a great deal of stress when a load is applied gradually or in a static manner, but may fracture when the same load is applied quickly as it is during a collision. Under a static load, the stresses and strains have time to be distributed over the entire piece of metal, whereas during a collision fewer bonds in the metal may be involved at the point where the hit occurs. Consequently, fracture may occur at much lower levels of force. It is not sufficient, then, to say that a metal is tough. The conditions under which it is going to be used must be known if test data are to be compared.

Several methods are used to increase the toughness of metals. Four such treatments, each of which involve heating and cooling, are called annealing, normalizing, quenching, and tempering. These processes, which differ in the rate and method of cooling metals from a highly heated state, serve to refine the *grain* or coarseness of the metal. Metals may also be combined to form *alloys*. Alloys can be likened to textile blends in that some of the best properties of each metal (fiber) are retained in the final product.

Because it was relatively lightweight and inexpensive, aluminum was the metal used for early hard hats, and for many years, U.S. Army helmets were "steel pots" that provided shrapnel protection (and doubled as a cooking pot!). Both aluminum and steel have been largely replaced in recent years by thermoplastics and composites that incorporate manufactured fibers. Titanium is the metal with the best combination of extreme strength with lightness of weight, known as specific strength (strength as a function of density). Some ballistics vests for the Army around the time of the Korean War incorporated titanium plates. Although titanium has been replaced in most military ballistics vests by thermoplastic composites, it still may appear in metallic laminates and composites in a variety of items such as protective equipment for contact sports and in orthopedic devices.

Ceramics

Ceramics have been used to make both fibers and coatings for applications where high heat and chemical resistance is needed. Because of the weight of solid ceramics, they are not widely used in clothing. They are found in some ballistics garments, primarily those worn by helicopter pilots or others who remain seated during their work, and thus do not have to carry the weight of the material, or by special forces in the police who face higher powered threats such as automatic weapons or rifles. Information about how ceramics work for ballistics protection will be covered in Chapter 6.

In order to be supple and light enough for clothing fibers, ceramics are generally spun into microfibers and combined with other more typical clothing fibers to create a fabric. They may also be used as the core in core-spun yarns. Powdered ceramics may also be imbedded in thermoplastic resins to create fibers. Ceramic fibers and those with ceramic components have been used in materials that provide sun protection (both from UV rays and heat), and they can also add anti-static properties to fabrics.

Plastics

Rigid plastics are used to form the outer shell of apparel accessories such as hard hats and helmets. They may also be used as armor plates or for the shaping of protective pads for many sports and for support in a variety of medical devices.

The most common rigid plastics used for hard hats and helmets for contact sports are polycarbonates, acrylonitrile butadiene styrene (ABS), high-density polyethylenes, and composite materials called fiber-reinforced resins. Polycarbonates, ABS, and polyethylenes are thermoplastic, so they can be softened by heating and then molded into precise shapes to form helmets and other protective items that are tremendously strong and resistant to breakage.

Fiber-reinforced resins are composed of two substances: a fiber and a resin. The basic material—the resin—can be thought of as the original solid lump of thermoplastic material before it is melted and drawn into fibers. Polyester, nylon, polypropylene, and polycarbonate are among the most common resins used in protective items. These thermoplastic resins are ductile but have a rather low elastic limit. In order to increase their elastic limit and strength, chopped fibers or woven textiles of fibers with high tensile strength such as glass or Kevlar are embedded in them. While strong under tension, these fibers can be brittle and weak when bent. Combining them with a resin allows the resulting material to have the best properties of both fibers and resins. The fibers have a very high tensile strength and they help to prevent indentation or penetration of the basic rigid form. The resin gives an item its rigid shape. Common usages include bulletproof vests, ski boots, and hockey goalie masks.

Fiber-reinforced resins have become popular for many types of protective apparel and equipment because of their lightness in weight, high specific strength, durability, corrosion resistance, resistance to electrical conduction, and the ease with which they can be molded into complex forms more related to the shape of the human body.

Most items composed of fiber-reinforced resins are made using one of the processes discussed in the "Molding and Heat Shaping" section of Chapter 9. Methods such as compression molding involve softening the resin with heat, incorporating the fibers or fabric, pressing it into a mold, and then cooling it. Resin may also be poured on a slab to make a thin sheet of rigid material that is then vacuum-formed by softening it with heat and drawing it against the surface of a perforated mold with a vacuum.

It is important to note, however, that not all resins are thermoplastic and can be molded by heating. Other materials have the opposite reaction to heat: heat cures them, or sets them into a rigid structure. These are called **thermoset** materials. The heat used to set thermoset materials is often produced by the chemical reaction that creates the polymer. For example, the components of a thermoset polymer can be poured into a mold where they react with each other as they mix, producing a thermal reaction that sets the polymer into a rigid state. Their strength is due to the chemical cross-links that form between polymer chains. Cross-linking is irreversible, and thermosets will not soften and permit reforming when heated.

Responsive Fabrics

Responsive fabrics are those that change in some way when activated by a human or in response to a change in the environment. These fabrics are often called smart. They respond to conditions such as a change in ambient temperature or exposure to radiation, a specific chemical, or an electric current.

Responsive materials are usually designed for use in specific environments. Electrically-activated smart materials, on the other hand, can be 'turned on,' either by the flip of a switch or through a more complex system of sensors and programmed responses. Chapter 4 will address electrically-activated smart materials in depth. The following sections focus on materials that are capable of responding to change without electrical activation.

INHERENT MATERIAL RESPONSES

Designing with smart materials that respond only to an environmental trigger (rather than being activated by electricity) requires the designer to specify exactly what kind of response is needed from the smart material, and then select or develop a material that responds appropriately to that stimulus. The challenge for designers is finding a way to tune a smart material's response to a specific set of circumstances so that it meets the needs of a design. Smart materials with inherent material responses often have a narrower set of capabilities than electrically activated smart materials, but they have the advantage of not needing a power source, electronics, or wiring.

Inherent material responses depend on the principle of *conservation of energy*, whereby one form of energy is transformed into another form of energy. Energy Basics 3.2 explains this principle and how it relates to smart systems.

Responding to Temperature

Most materials respond to temperature in some way (e.g., by becoming more brittle in extreme cold or by melting or burning in extreme heat). The act of melting, or changing from solid to liquid form, is a change in the **phase** of a material between one of three phases (solid, liquid, and gas) and another. This is one of the most common responses of a material to a change in temperature, but it can also be harnessed to provide a specific benefit in a clothing system. **Phase-change** materials that are used in apparel respond to temperature change by changing back and forth between liquid and solid form when they are above or below a specific temperature. The material changing phase is usually encapsulated in

a fiber or applied to the surface of a textile in the form of tiny microcapsules. This allows the material to change back and forth between liquid and solid form without evaporating or being wiped off the textile. The temperature at which phase change occurs for a specific material is called its **transition temperature**. By changing phase, materials are able to absorb or release a small amount of heat. When the wearer's body is colder than the transition temperature of the phase-change material, the material changes from liquid to solid and releases heat energy to the wearer. When the wearer's body warms up above the transition temperature, body heat is absorbed and used to melt the phase-change material.

Not all materials respond to temperature only by changing phase. Some materials, like **thermochromic** materials, respond by changing color. The HyperColor™ t-shirts that were popular in the 1980s used a form of thermochromic ink to change the color of a t-shirt when warmed by body heat.

Responding to Light

Light can act as the trigger for many responses, including chemical reactions. Plants and animals use light to perform essential chemical reactions (e.g., photosynthesis in plants and the formation of vitamin D in humans). Light energy can cause subtle changes in atoms and molecules. Many materials decay or break down as light energy breaks chemical bonds between molecules over time. This can be used for specific purposes (e.g., to allow part of a garment or material to be deconstructed or taken apart) or to release an encapsulated substance (e.g., when exposed to light or, sometimes, to a specific kind of light).

Materials described as **photochromic** respond to light by changing color. These materials usually respond to a specific kind of light such as a

Energy Basics 3.2: **Conservation of Energy**

Energy is a slippery but fundamental concept that will underlie many of the discussions in this book. Energy is not as much a tangible *thing* as it is a state of being. Most commonly, energy is described as the capacity of a system to do work. This definition evokes the idea of mechanical energy (the energy of movement or force), but it also applies to other forms of energy such as thermal energy, electrical energy, chemical energy, light energy, or sound energy. The concept of work in this definition of energy refers to the ability to exert a given amount of force over a given amount of distance. All forms of energy can be converted into a force that can be used to move an object.

Energy is often transformed between its various forms, but it is always conserved: that is to say, energy is never lost or made; it is only changed from one form into another form. Besides the forms of energy mentioned above, energy also exists in two primary states: **kinetic energy** and **potential energy**. Kinetic energy is energy directly used to create a force, and potential energy is stored energy, which could be used to create a force if it were released.

For example, consider the energy of the body. Metabolizing food breaks down the molecules in food, releasing chemical potential energy in the process.

Some of this energy is transformed by the muscles into mechanical kinetic energy by contracting muscles to move body parts, including the heart muscle, which pumps blood around the body. Not all of the energy used by the muscles is transformed directly into forces used to move body parts or objects. Some of it is converted into thermal energy. This is why exercise makes the body warmer. Thermal energy is then absorbed by the blood and transported through the blood vessels to warm the entire body. The body also transmits some thermal energy into the environment, by transforming it into radiant thermal energy. In the course of metabolizing molecules to release energy, electrons are exchanged and begin to flow through muscles and tissues. This flow of electrons is yet another transformation of the potential energy released during metabolism, this time into electrical energy.

You will see energy conversion at work in a number of chapters in this text: as you read about how protective clothing converts the mechanical energy of an impact into less harmful heat and sound energy, or electrical energy is converted to kinetic energy or heat in various items of smart clothing. As each topic is discussed, think about the ways in which energy transformation is taking place.

---

specific color or a type of light like ultraviolet or infrared. (See Figure 4.1.)

Materials that are **phosphorescent** store light energy and are able to give off light after the light source has been removed. Glow-in-the-dark items are generally made from phosphorescent materials. (See Chapter 8, "Emitted Light" for an additional discussion of phosphorescent light.)

Responding to Movement and Force

Some materials respond with a change in properties when they are moved or struck. In some cases, this response is similar to the phase change response: materials that behave like liquids can act like solids when they experience sudden forces. These materials are called **dilatant** materials or non-Newtonian materials, and they are commonly made from small particles of a solid substance suspended in a liquid. An easy dilatant to make at home is a combination of cornstarch and water. When mixed in the right ratio (roughly 2 parts cornstarch to 1 part water), it will form a liquid that can be stirred, and will flow when poured. However, if the same liquid is struck suddenly (e.g., by hand or with the back of a spoon), it stiffens and resists the force. Silly Putty and Charleston Chew candy bars are other examples. When external forces are weak, the solid particles are pushed around by the movements of the liquid. Strong external forces overcome the weaker forces between the liquid and solid particles, and the solid particles behave as a solid. Dilatant materials are very useful in impact protection, such as in bulletproof vests (see Chapter 6, "Dilatant Materials"), and the dilatant material tradenamed d3O is used in alpine ski racing suits, baseball batters' helmets, and volleyball knee pads. They allow a material to be flexible and comfortable during everyday body movements, but to stiffen into a protective shell when struck suddenly.

Most materials get thinner when they are stretched: If a rubber band is stretched, it gets narrower. However, some **auxetic** materials are made of molecules whose structures resemble collapsed boxes. When this type of auxetic material is stretched, its molecules straighten up (as if the box were being reshaped), and the material actually gets thicker. Unlike other structured polymers, they can achieve forms with double curves, such as domes. Auxetic materials are useful in impact protection, where they can offer extra padding in high-stress areas such as the elbow. Figure 3.24 shows an auxetic yarn structure.

Responding to Chemical Changes

A change in the chemical environment can have a tremendous impact on many materials. Garments that protect from chemical hazards, for instance, must be made from carefully selected materials that will not break down when exposed to harsh chemicals. Some materials, however, respond to specific changes in chemistry in other ways than breaking down. For example, *halochromic*

FIGURE 3.24 As auxetic materials are stretched, they thicken.

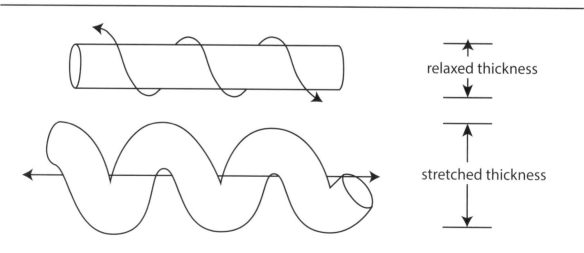

relaxed thickness

stretched thickness

materials change color in response to changes in the pH of their environment. The color of the material can be used to evaluate the acidity of the environment. In a diaper, this could be used to measure the pH of urine to monitor kidney function or urinary infections.

Other pH-sensitive materials respond to changes in the acidity of their environment by changing shape or permeability. These materials are often used in medicine. For example, by delivering medication in a shell made of a pH-sensitive material, the shell might allow a medication to be released only when it leaves the acid environment of the stomach. These materials can also be used in clothing to allow a contained substance such as a topical medication to be released by a wound

dressing or protective garment when the pH of the skin changes.

Conclusion

The many choices available at every level of material design selection result in an endless variety of textiles, films, foams, and other materials used in protective apparel. Varying even one factor in textile development or manufacturing can result in material behavior that is completely different from another made of same base fiber. Changing the yarn or extruded filament shape, the fabric structure, the finish, and the like may allow designers to develop unique solutions to protective clothing problems (See Design Solutions 3.1).

Design Solutions 3.1: Fabric Structure and Protection: Lumberjack Pants

New materials may be developed in response to specific needs, but often, by making modifications in some aspect of the original material—its fiber, yarn structure, fabric construction, or fabric finish—a designer can create innovative end uses for materials that are quite apart from the original purpose for which they were designed.

One example of this can be found in the logging industry, where there have been a variety of approaches to keeping loggers from being cut by a chain saw. Early protection involved the use of cut-resistant leather chaps just over the upper legs, where the chainsaw was most likely to fall if knocked from the hands. When aramid fibers were developed, several layers of woven Kevlar were used in chaps or added to pant linings in the thigh area. Aramids were lighter and more flexible and provided more time for

lumberjacks to take evasive action although the last layer of aramid could still be penetrated, and considerable damage done to the body before the saw fully stopped.

An innovative solution came about when a designer noted an interesting aspect of the behavior of Kevlar in a *knit* structure. In a weave, the material simply provided cut-resistance, but in a complex knitted structure, the first response of the yarns was to pull out of the structure. When touched by the chainsaw, they caught in it and wrapped around it, tangling the chain and quickly jamming it long before the saw could penetrate the whole knit structure. Thus, the saw was deactivated even if a logger still had a thumb on the switch. Placing knitted Kevlar in pants and chaps produced lighter, more flexible *and* more protective garments.

FIGURES A AND B (A) Logger's chaps made of high-strength fibers; (B) automatic protection: strong fibers pull out of pants, tangle in the chain and shut off the saw. *(Reprinted with permission from the* Berg Encyclopedia of World Dress and Fashion 3: 247–248)

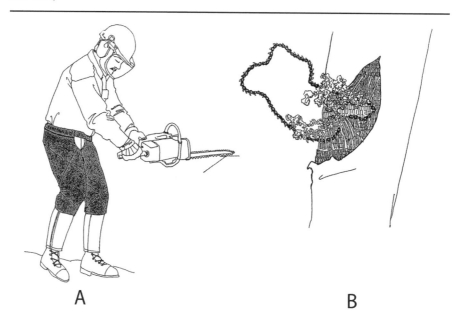

A   B

4 Smart Clothing and Wearable Technology

The term *wearable technology* encompasses a broad variety of interpretations and definitions. Basically, it refers to technology that is worn on the body. In theory, this could include any technology including the fibers and fabrics that are used in most clothing, but in practice it generally refers to electronic technology.

Some forms of wearable technology are described as *smart clothing*, using the qualifier *clothing* to distinguish garments from other worn accessories like bracelets or adhesive patches. Technology described as smart has the capability to sense something and respond appropriately without being directly controlled by a human. However, colloquially the term *smart* is often used interchangeably with *high-tech*.

Finally, some wearable technologies are described as *wearable computers*. Wearable computers typically perform functions similar to desktop or mobile computers, with a focus on information access and communication. Each of these terms encompasses some aspect that is relevant and interesting for functional clothing.

One of the most interesting functions that technology brings to clothing is the ability to continually access information and communicate with other people at a distance. Mobile technologies have the ability to provide just-in-time, instantaneous access to information. Wearability is sometimes seen as the next frontier in mobile technologies because it allows access to information to be even more seamless. To use a device carried in a pocket, the user must locate and retrieve it, activate it, navigate to the right application, and ask for information. By contrast, a wearable device can sense that need for information and display it peripherally in a manner that is both accessible and non-intrusive. Further, wearable technology can access information about the wearer that is difficult for mobile technology to achieve. For example, a wearable heart monitor can gather continuous information about the heart over a long period of time. This may make it possible for a doctor in a city to monitor a patient in a remote village, for example, or to allow a patient to be monitored from home following a surgery.

Electronically enabled functionality is applicable to most of the topics in this book, and subsequent chapters discuss the electronic technologies and approaches relevant to each topic in parallel with nonelectronic technologies and approaches. However, there are additional functions that cannot be achieved without electronics. This chapter focuses on the fundamentals that support smart clothing and wearable technology (the materials and design principles that are specific to electronically enabled systems), and on those applications, such as body sensing, in which collecting, communicating, and understanding information is the primary function enabled by a garment.

Electricity and Electrical Systems

Electricity is the medium through which information flows in a smart garment system. Changes in the flow of electrical energy through sensors are used to deduce information about the wearer or the environment. Electrically controlled displays present information to the user in the form of images, text, sound, or movement. In order to understand electrical systems, it is important to understand the basics of electricity. Energy Basics 4.1 describes some of these basic concepts.

POWER SOURCES

All electrical systems rely on a source of power in order to operate. Electrical power comes from many different sources and mechanisms. Batteries (Figure 4.1) are the most common source of DC power. A battery cell contains two materials: the *cathode* material, which has a positive charge, and the *anode* material, which has a negative charge. Inside a battery, the cathode and anode are surrounded by an *electrolyte* solution. Electrolytes are electrically conductive substances that contain free ions. The presence of these free ions causes some substances to react chemically by attracting the ions; other substances repel them. In a battery, the positively charged material, the cathode, attracts negatively charged ions freed from the electrolyte, while the anode loses electrons. Because the materials within the battery are contained, the electrons

in the negatively charged material (the anode) cannot be repelled outside of the battery, so they simply build up, and the reaction stabilizes. This stalemate situation is called an *open circuit*.

When the anode and cathode are connected by a material that conducts electricity, the electrons in the anode have a pathway or *circuit* by which they can leave the anode and flow into the cathode. This is because the circuit contains materials to which these built-up electrons can be passed. The movement of electrons creates an electrical current. Connectors may be wires or strips made of electrically conductive materials such as metals. When the switch on a flashlight is flipped, for example, it brings together two conductive metal pieces and completes an electrical pathway that runs through the batteries and the flashlight lamp. The flow of electrons through the lamp filament causes it to glow. Because the lamp filament is resistive, as the flow of electrons passes through the filament, many collisions occur between atoms. The energy from these collisions is transformed into heat and light energy. The operation of the lamp relies on the amount of resistance of the filament and the way that the filament material reacts to high current. If the filament used has very little resistance, the electrons will flow out of the anode so fast that it will quickly exhaust the battery by creating a *short circuit*. A short circuit creates heat, but not necessarily light.

Batteries are an example of a system that uses a chemical reaction to start an electrical current. However, other forms of energy can be transformed into electricity in many ways. The electrons contained in a photovoltaic material flow when they are excited by electromagnetic energy such as light. Solar cells use these materials to convert light into electricity. The word *generator* can be used to describe any method of converting another form of energy into electrical energy, but

FIGURE 4.1 Basic structure of a battery.

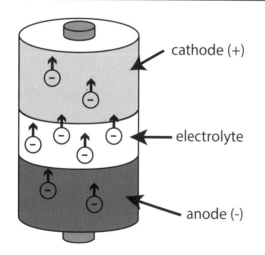

cathode (+)

electrolyte

anode (-)

Energy Basics 4.1: Electrical Energy

Many forms of energy involve atoms moving through space in some way. (For a refresher on the structure of atoms and molecules, see Energy Basics 3.1.) Sometimes, however, individual electrons can detach from an atom and move to another atom. If this process continues, with electrons moving from atom to atom, the potential energy held within the atom is translated into electrical energy, its kinetic form. Some materials allow electrons to flow freely between atoms, and others hold electrons more tightly to a specific atom. This results in some materials (like wood) being less likely than others (like metal) to transfer electrical energy.

The rate at which free electrons are flowing is called *current*. Current is measured in amperes (generally referred to as amps). A faster flow of electrons creates a higher current in the material. Whether or not the direction that these electrons are flowing is always the same determines whether or not the power source is described as direct current (DC) or alternating current (AC). In a DC power source, the current always flows in one direction and one direction only. In an AC power source, the electron flow reverses direction periodically. AC current is used to deliver power over long distances because it results in less energy loss than DC current. Because of this, AC current is the form of energy transmitted by power lines that comes out of wall outlets, but most consumer electronics operate on DC current, which is easier to store and release.

The speed of the direction of current change (the length of time between forward and backward cycles) over time is its *frequency*, which is measured in Hertz, or Hz. One Hertz is equal to one cycle per second. In the United States and North America, AC power is standardized at 60 Hz, and in Europe and most of Asia it is standardized at 50 Hz.

Electrical power sources are also characterized in terms of their *voltage*. Voltage can be described as the amount of potential energy available to propel the electrons through a conductor. Batteries and other DC sources come in many different common voltage levels: for electronics, 3.3 and 5 volts (V) are common levels, although many components are rated to accept higher common voltages such as 9 V. Car batteries are standardized at 12 V. AC sources also are characterized in terms of their voltage levels. For example, the electricity delivered by a wall outlet in the United States and Canada is standardized at 120 V, and in Europe and most of Asia it is 230 V. This value represents an average voltage over time delivered by the power source, since the exact voltage of an alternating current is always changing.

The differences in standard voltage/current levels that different countries have for AC power sources are the reason adapters are needed for plug-in devices when traveling. Sometimes a *converter* or *transformer* is needed to transform the voltage/current from one level to another, and sometimes only a *plug adapter* is needed to change the shape of the prongs on a plug to fit the standard shape of an outlet in a different country with the same voltage/current level. Confusingly, the term *adapter* is also used to describe a device that can turn AC power into DC. The charger for a mobile phone or laptop adapts AC power from a wall outlet into DC power that can recharge a battery.

As electrons flow through a material, they frequently collide with the ions of the conducting material. These collisions turn some of the electrical energy into heat, and the current slows down. The amount a given material slows current is described as its *resistance*, which is measured in ohms (Ω). Materials that slow current a specific amount can be used to control the flow of electrons. These materials are called *resistors*. Most metals have very low resistance, which is why they are commonly used as wires or other electrical conductors. However, the size of the conductor also has an effect on the resistance of the material; very thin wires have higher resistance than thicker wires. The wire is the path that the current must travel, and the narrower the path, the less room there is for electrons to spread out. When electrons are tightly packed, more collisions happen between electrons and the ions of the conductor. If a very high current with its many electrons is passed through a resistive material such as a very thin wire, the wire will heat up as electrons constantly collide with ions. Electrically heated blankets and clothing use thin wire conductors and high current to produce heat.

it is most often used to describe devices that use mechanical energy to create a magnetic field that forces electrons to flow through a conductor, transforming mechanical energy into electrical energy.

ELECTRICAL CIRCUITS

An electrical circuit is a path that electrical energy follows. In order for electricity to flow, the circuit must have a power source and a *ground*, or sink. Current generally flows from the source to the sink. Voltage is always measured as a difference between two points in the circuit and generally decreases throughout a circuit as it moves from positive to negative (from a voltage source to sink). The word *ground* is derived from earth ground, but the earth is actually rarely used as a power sink. It is more commonly used as an electrically neutral reference point from which to measure other voltages, as is the power sink (the negative terminal) on a self-contained system like a battery.

Electrical circuits are composed of components (such as sensors, processors, and actuators) that are arranged to manipulate voltage and current in specific ways or transform electricity to or from other forms of energy (e.g., light, heat, or kinetic energy). (For more discussion of energy conversion from one form to another, see Energy Basics 3.2.)

SENSORS

Sensors are the way in which a circuit detects changes in the environment—either in the surroundings of the wearer or on the wearer's body. Not all electrical circuits use sensors, but most electrically activated smart materials do. Sensor components are sometimes described as *transducers* because they often allow a stimulus like heat, light, or movement to be transformed into a change in the flow of electricity (the amount of voltage or current that flows through the circuit). Sometimes

sensors act as switches, opening or closing a connection in an electrical circuit.

It is commonly believed that the ability to sense changes in the environment and respond to those changes is what makes a material smart. Sensors transform one type of energy (the stimulus) into another type of energy (the response). They respond to a stimulus by changing the way that they conduct electricity. That change in flow of electricity must then be interpreted by a circuit, which can decide to create a response by using electricity to activate yet another material, called the *actuator*. An example of this process is illustrated in Figure 4.2.

Sensors that respond to light energy usually rely on light to excite the electrons in the sensing material, allowing them to flow more easily. One example of material that can be designed to respond to light is a *semiconductor*. Semiconductors are a class of materials that allow current (electrons) to flow, but only when the electrons are encouraged to flow. Almost any kind of energy—electricity, light, heat, force, radiation, etc.—can be used to start the flow of electrons. A light-sensitive semiconductor uses light energy as encouragement. Light energy excites the electrons in the semiconductor and allows current to flow even more freely when it is exposed to more light. Three types of semiconductor light sensors are *light-dependent resistors* (LDR), which change in resistance according to the light level; *photodiodes*, which allow current to flow when exposed to light, but only in one direction; and *phototransistors*, which use light as a gate or switch in the circuit, completely preventing current from flowing until they are exposed to a certain amount of light. Light sensors can be used by a smart system to detect that something has been covered up (by putting on an additional garment, for instance) or to detect the

FIGURE 4.2 An example of a sensor/processor/actuator circuit that detects the presence of sunlight and generates a response (heat).

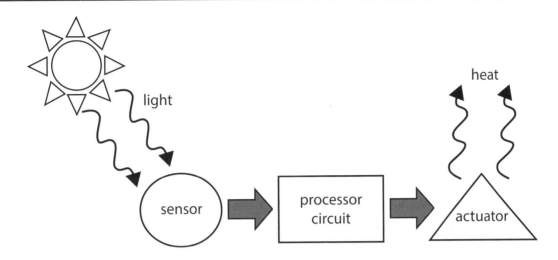

surrounding light level (turning on safety lights in the dark, for instance).

When a temperature sensor like a *thermistor* (thermally sensitive resistor) is close to a source of thermal energy such as the body, the electrons in its semiconducting material absorb the thermal energy and start to move more rapidly through its structure. In a similar manner to the LDR described earlier, this change in current flow can be measured by the system and interpreted as a change in temperature. This temperature change could then be used by a smart system to turn on a heater when the temperature gets too low.

Sensors can also respond to movement and force. Applied pressure, such as the pressing of a switch, can bring two conductors together in a circuit and allow electrical energy to flow from one point to another. *Strain gauges* respond to bending or flexing of a material. A **strain gauge** is usually made of a long strip of flexible backing, on which a zigzag path of conductive material is laid, oriented parallel to the length of the sensor, as shown in Figure 4.3. In general, conductors get more

resistant to electrical current as they get longer and thinner because electrons then have a narrower and longer path along which to move. The zigzag path on a strain gauge is like a very long, very thin wire. When the strip is bent away from the surface laid with the conductive path, the segments of the path are stretched and elongated over the top side of the gauge. This causes each individual line to get even thinner and longer, increasing the overall resistance of the whole pathway (remember that the narrower the conductive path, the harder it is for current to flow through). This type of sensor can be applied to the skin to detect joint bends, for example.

FIGURE 4.3 A strain gauge. Bending the strain gauge increases or decreases the length of the electrical pathway.

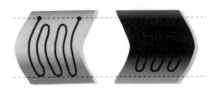

Inertial sensors are another common class of sensor/transducers that use the inertia of an object to detect changes in position and movement. Inertia is the tendency of an object at rest to stay at rest and an object in motion to continue in motion. Objects at rest have an inherent resistance to moving that requires a force to overcome. This force can be measured and used to detect acceleration or movement. In wearable systems, inertial sensors may be used to detect the movements and the orientation of body parts. Common inertial sensors are *accelerometers* and *gyroscopes*.

ACTUATORS

Actuator components make a physical change: they transform electricity into a response such as light, heat, or movement. Sensors and actuators can be compared to the body's sensory organs and physical responses: sensory organs (sensors) turn external stimuli into nerve signals that are carried to the brain, and physical responses (actuators) turn a nerve signal from the brain into a physical change like a muscle flexing.

For example, a **light-emitting diode (LED)** is an actuator that transforms electrical energy into light energy. LEDs are made of a specific kind of semiconducting material that causes electrons to drop from a higher energy level to a lower energy level as they move from one kind of conducting material to another. As the electrons fall to a lower energy level, they release the excess energy in the form of light.

A *heat-generating actuator* transforms excess current flowing through a resistive material into heat, which could be used to warm the body in smart clothing. As discussed in Energy Basics 4.1, in resistive materials, the electrons that make up an electrical current collide with the ions of the conducting material as they travel through it, and these collisions turn some of the electrical energy

into heat. Therefore, the more electrons that race through a resistive material, the more collisions happen, and more energy is released as heat.

Piezoelectric materials respond to mechanical energy, but can act as either a sensor or an actuator. The crystal structure of piezoelectric materials expands and contracts when exposed to electricity. However, unlike other materials, the reverse is also true: If the crystal structure is compressed or stretched by an outside force, it transforms this force into a tiny amount of electrical energy. Because of this, piezoelectric materials are used for both microphones (sensors) and speakers (actuators). Functioning as a microphone, a piezoelectric film generates tiny current fluctuations when sound waves deform the film. Functioning as a speaker, tiny current fluctuations cause the film to vibrate, generating sound waves.

In clothing, piezoelectric materials can be used as sensors because they generate a small current when they are bent by a joint movement and as actuators or artificial muscle because they can be made to bend when a current is applied.

PROCESSORS

Processors use complex arrays of smaller components to perform calculations and execute programs. All computers and most electronic devices contain some kind of processor, which is the brain of the device. Programmable processors allow designers to control the specific response of a system to a given input. For example, a software designer can specify that an actuator (such as a set of lights) should respond only under a specific set of sensor readings (e.g., when it gets darker than a certain threshold).

Most processors are *digital*, meaning that they understand only two voltage levels, high and low. *Analog* components respond to a range of levels. Most sensors are analog, so their responses must be converted into digital information to be understood by the processor. The reason that digital processors only understand high and low levels (sometimes described as 1s and 0s) is that they are made of huge arrays of little *transistors*, components that act as switches inside the processor. Each transistor is designed to provide a high (1) or low (0) to the next transistor, and complex arrangements of transistors allow decisions to be made and calculations to be performed. This type of processing is known as *digital logic*, and it is the language of circuits that use digital components.

INTERFACES

Sensors, processors, and actuators are the components that allow information to be collected and displayed. However, some kinds of sensors and actuators are also described as interfaces because they allow the user to directly interact with the electronic system. In desktop devices, interfaces are typically things like screens, keyboards, and pointing devices (e.g., a computer mouse). Interfaces are separated into two classes: input devices and output devices. An input device takes direction from the user and communicates it to the device, and an output device displays information to the user. A wide variety of technologies can be characterized as interface elements, including printers, cameras, speakers, microphones, switches, and sensors. In general, sensing technologies are usually input devices, and actuator technologies are usually output devices.

Information in Wearable Technology

Interacting with wearable devices is different from interacting with stationary devices for the key reason that the wearer may likely be moving around and/or doing something else while interacting

with the device. For stationary devices, it may be reasonable to assume that the user is also stationary and concentrating on the device, but this is not always true for a wearable device. The wearer may be doing something relatively simple, like walking down the street, or something more cognitively complex, like engaging in conversation or driving a car. Concurrent tasks mean that the wearer's mental and physical resources may be divided. They may not be able to look at an input device. They may have only one hand free to operate the device, or they may be distracted while trying to use the device.

Because clothing is constantly present and held close to the physical body, it is a useful platform for sensing and monitoring the movements, activities, and context of the human body. Integrating sensing technology into clothing opens a window into the needs and objectives of the human inside, as well as the surrounding context and environment in which humans find themselves. For the same reason, clothing is an effective platform for communicating information to the wearer because it is easy for actuators in clothing to be placed close to many different sensory receptors and for the user to quickly and easily access interfaces. Information processing and delivery devices can become more seamless extensions of the wearer's body and brain when they are in wearable form.

The following sections will address the ways in which information flows into and out of a wearable system. Information can enter the system explicitly (by the user issuing a command to the system) or implicitly (by the system using sensors to detect changes in the wearer or environment). Information exits the system through an output device or **display**, a device that communicates information to the user through any sensory modality.

WEARABLE INPUT

Many of the ways in which a user of a wearable technology interacts with another device have been inherited from earlier (stationary) technologies. Things like keyboards and mice, menu-based navigation, and touchscreens are all carry-overs from other forms of technology. As will be discussed later in this chapter, there are advantages to using well understood patterns of interaction, primarily that it is easier for a new user to learn how to use a system that is similar to a familiar system.

One prevalent form of input to an electronic system is through button-presses. "Buttons" are usually some form of switch, which is either closed or opened when it is pressed. The simplest way to use a button is to link it directly to an action (e.g., actions such as turn on, take a picture, or activate). In systems with relatively low complexity, such as a garment with only one electronic function, it can be feasible to create one button to control each individual function. However, as complexity increases, the system can run out of surface area for buttons and/or become so complex that it is difficult for the user to locate the appropriate button.

Switch-based interfaces can also be used to select among options. For example, the system in Figure 4.4 is a wearable telephone interface

designed for groups of skiers or snowboarders. When a mobile phone is linked to the wearable interface, the short tabs can be pulled out and snapped to a variety of positions to select specific groups or individuals. Pulling on the long tab then allows simple actions like placing a call to be performed. This type of interface may be easier and more robust to operate when dexterity is reduced such as when wearing heavy gloves. It is designed to be worn over the coat like a bag but could easily be integrated into a winter coat.

A switch need not resemble a traditional button or key. Switches can take any form that brings conductive elements into and out of contact. Traditional garment fasteners can often be used as single-function switches to control elements of a smart garment or wearable system. This also can allow normal garment interactions to trigger a smart response: for example, a zipper switch can allow the temperature in a smart garment to be turned down when the wearer unzips it (an action which is often associated with being too hot).

More complicated button-based input often takes the form of text entry. A computer keyboard is an example of a button array that can be used to create more complex commands. Text-based input can also allow the user to compose a natural-language message and send it to another user (as mobile phones do). Text-based input in wearable systems can be complicated, for many of the same reasons that complex arrays of buttons are often complicated in wearables. The surface area required for a full keyboard can be difficult to find on the body, and in many contexts the user may have only one hand free for text entry. Easily reached two-handed body locations with large surface area such as the lap can be socially problematic for button-based interfaces.

An area with potential for text-based input in wearables is the hands themselves. Figure 4.5

FIGURE 4.4 A wearable telephone interface. *(Based on Mikkonen et al. 2001.)*

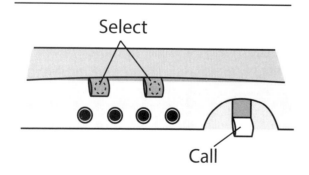

FIGURE 4.5 Two approaches to wearable text entry. (A) A handheld chording keyboard and (B) a glove-based text entry device.

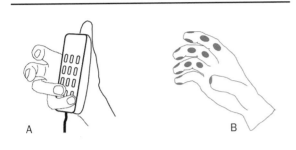

A   B

illustrates two approaches to wearable text-input devices: Figure 4.5A shows a handheld chording keyboard, in which combinations of buttons are pressed like chords in music to type each letter. This allows a greater number of individual actions to be completed with a smaller number of buttons. Figure 4.5B shows a glove-based system, in which the thumb contact is pressed to different locations on the inside and outside of the fingers. The finger contacts correspond to groups of letters and numbers, which can be selected among using multiple taps or predictive-text typing. Each of these has drawbacks: the handheld keyboard requires that the user learn a large set of chords in order to use the device effectively, and the glove-based system requires that the user wear gloves continuously. However, both accomplish the goal of wearable text entry.

Voice commands are a truly hands-free method of text entry for wearable devices. However, a voice-controlled system still needs a method for the user to activate voice control or to allow the system to distinguish between everyday speech and speech commands. A common method of accomplishing this is to embed a command trigger in the system. The trigger may be a button that is pressed, in the manner that characters on the TV show *Star Trek* tap their chest-mounted badge to

activate voice input, or it may be a vocal command that the system *listens* for, such as the "Okay, Glass" command used to activate voice input on Google Glass.

Another method of circumventing the need for a large number of buttons on an interface is to create virtual buttons on a screen. In a smartphone, for example, one screen can display many buttons, which change depending on the application that is active. In order to interact with virtual buttons, the technology must include a navigation and selection input device, like a computer mouse or touch screen. However, most current screen-type display technology is rigid and fragile, and although touch screens are increasingly common in accessories like watches and bracelets, the technology remains ill-suited for integration into garments, except in the case of very small screens. (For a discussion of designing large, bulky, and/or rigid forms to be worn on the body, see Chapter 2 under the heading "Applying Data on Body Movement to Clothing Design.") Similarly, navigating a touch screen or using a mouse while mobile can be a challenge. The Cyberia suit described in the case study at the end of Chapter 5 uses a unique yo-yo interface to allow a user to navigate a scrolling menu (by pulling on the yo-yo) while wearing heavy gloves.

Finally, navigation through gestural input can be accomplished using body-sensing techniques such as on-body sensors or camera-based methods to determine the position of the body and/or limbs. This can allow the user to physically point at an object in the field of view, for example, and select it by making a "come here" gesture. Gesture-based input can also be used to tie specific gestures to system functions. For example, swiping an arm in the air to the left could trigger a move to the next track in a music application. Most gesture-based input is facilitated by body sensors, which will be discussed in the next section.

BODY SENSING

The input methods described in the previous section rely on the user intentionally providing a command or instruction to the system. However, in smart systems, all or part of this decision making can be delegated to the system. Information gathered from sensors embedded in a garment can be used to automatically trigger appropriate responses from the system.

For most people, the term *body sensing* evokes an image of measuring vital signs, the kind of sensing that is commonly performed during a medical check-up. Vital signs are some of the most important pieces of information about the current state of the individual body (hence the term *vital* signs). They can be used to monitor medical conditions, detect context, and even deduce emotions. In a similar way, information about the movement and position of the body can be used to monitor symptoms of a developing condition, as well as provide more detailed information about movements and activities. Together, vital signs and body movements provide a very detailed picture of the physical state and activity of the individual. Taking a step beyond these two factors brings sensing into the realm of detecting or interpreting emotion and intention—a much more nuanced and complex arena. (See Design Strategies 4.1.)

Vital Signs

The most common vital signs are heart rate, blood pressure, body temperature, and respiration (breathing). Each is measured in a variety of ways, which present different requirements for wearable devices.

Heart activity is one of the most complex vital signs and is measurable with perhaps the widest array of methods. First, the heart is a specialized muscle that contracts in a consistent rhythm. Like any muscle in the body, the cells of the heart transport ions across the cell membrane during contraction and relaxation. This process creates an ebb and flow of positive charge (an electrical potential) as the cells contract and relax. This electrical potential can be measured in an electrical circuit, and is the basis of the **electrocardiogram** (also known as ECG, or EKG for the German elektrokardiogramm). This is the common heartbeat wave that is often seen in medical graphics or on hospital bedside monitors.

The ECG signal is measured using electrodes placed on the skin, shown in Figure 4.6. Electrodes are conductive patches that form an electrical connection between the skin and the electrical circuit, allowing the electrical potentials of the body to be measured by an electronic device. As few as three electrodes can measure the ECG signal (the difference between two electrodes is used to measure the potential between them, and the third is used as a reference point to calibrate the signal). In a medical environment, the 12-lead ECG (which uses ten electrodes) is used to measure smaller parts of the heart muscle more precisely.

FIGURE 4.6 Three-lead (left) and twelve-lead (right) ECG electrode configurations.

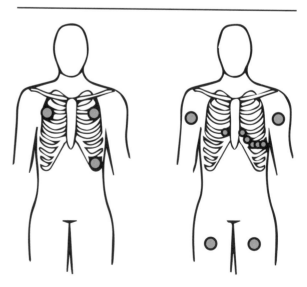

Design Strategies 4.1: Emotion and Intention

Understanding the psychological state of the wearer can be immensely helpful for a wearable system. Physiological signals discussed in the previous sections are often correlated with emotion, and interpreting them in the right way can provide insight into the wearer's mind and heart. Interpreting emotion and action can provide a basis for determining the wearer's intent or objective: in some ways, predicting the wearer's next actions.

Rosalind Picard, seminal researcher in affective computing (computing that relates to emotions) describes the process of detecting emotions from physiological signals in this way:

> With emotion, as with weather, one can build sensors for measuring the physical equivalents of temperature, pressure, humidity, etc. One can also build successful algorithms for combining patterns of such measures, and thus recognize the emotional equivalents of a tornado or a blizzard. (Picard 2003)

Signals like tone and volume of voice, speech content and pattern, heart rate and blood pressure, galvanic skin response, skin temperature, breathing rate, muscle activity, and physical gestures are good indicators of various emotional changes, and are feasibly detected through wearable systems. However, different emotions cause changes in different combinations of physical signals, and many other physiological changes that indicate emotional changes (like changes in electrical and chemical activity in the brain or chemical composition of the blood) are currently difficult to achieve in a wearable form.

Deducing intention, objective, or future actions from the combination of emotion and activity sensing is a further layer of complexity. Patterns of behavior can to some extent be used to predict future behaviors, and emotional changes may signal deviations from these patterns. However, as each person is unique, the sensing system must be designed to take into account individual variability and patterns.

Most sensing mechanisms are able to detect one specific type of change, such as temperature, color, light, movement, or distance. In many cases, there is no one sensor specifically designed to detect a given body signal; instead, one or more properties of that signal are detected by sensors capable of reacting to those specific properties. For example, there is no one heartbeat sensor. Heart activity is detected by sensors that respond to the electrical signals of the heart muscle, to the sound of the heartbeat, to the movements created by the contractions of the heart, or to the way that the ebb and flow of blood in the blood vessels absorbs or reflects light. This chapter outlines some of the methods for detecting common body signals that can be integrated into clothing and body-mounted devices.

Medical electrodes are typically made of silver coated with silver chloride (Ag/AgCl), which forms a very good electrical connection with the skin. Further, these electrodes are often wetted with a conductive gel, which coats (and is partially absorbed by) the skin to form an even stronger electrical connection. In essence, an ECG sensor is trying to detect the electrical signal of the heart through many, many other muscles (each of which generates its own electrical signal when it contracts), and through the bones, skin, and hair between the heart and the skin surface. Many techniques associated with ECG sensing are aimed at removing obstacles to that signal: such as by wetting the skin, removing dead skin, and removing hair to minimize dry insulating barriers to electrical conductivity. Because electrodes are simply conductive patches, it is feasible to integrate electrodes into textiles and garments. However, many of the additional factors that improve ECG sensing (wetting, abrasion, very close contact) are much more difficult to achieve in clothing. In addition, the exact chemical composition of the electrode has a significant impact on the quality of the electrical connection, and many materials that are more ideal for electrode sensing are difficult to integrate into textiles (Neuman 2000).

Another method of sensing heart activity is by detecting changes in the flow of blood pumped by the heart as it beats. A common method of heart rate sensing through blood flow is *pulse-oximetry* (often referred to as pulse-ox). This type of device is often seen clipped to a patient's finger or earlobe in the hospital. The pulse-oximeter shines an infrared light on the skin and monitors the amount of light that is either transmitted through the finger (Figure 4.7 top) or reflected back to a light sensor (Figure 4.7 bottom). As blood ebbs and flows in the vessels, it accumulates and disperses. During the ebb part of the heartbeat, there are more blood cells in the vessel, creating a darker area. This area will absorb more light than a lighter area with

fewer blood cells will during the flow part of the heartbeat. The changes in the amount of reflected light correspond to the ebb and flow of the blood within the vessel. Thin body areas like the fingertips and earlobes are commonly used because they have less other matter behind the surface vessels and allow the sensor to see the blood more easily.

The amount of oxygen in the blood also affects its color. Fully oxygenated blood is red, and deoxygenated blood is blue. These color changes also affect the amount of infrared light absorbed by the blood as it passes under the sensor, allowing the pulse-oximeter to also detect the amount of oxygen in the blood (the "oximeter" part of *pulse-oximeter*). Although thin parts of the body like the fingertips and earlobes are often difficult to access in clothing, an approximation of pulse-oximetry can be achieved by using a similar sensor inside a garment that directs light into the skin in almost any garment area, such as under a tightly fitted cuff or collar.

As the heart contracts and blood rushes through the vessels, it also makes a sound. The doctor's stethoscope is used to detect this sound, and changes in the quality of the sound can measure heart rate and detect cardiac irregularities. Wearable microphones can achieve the same objective, using sound-processing techniques to detect and interpret the heart sounds. As with many other wearable sensing methods, keeping the microphone from moving around and removing outside "noise" from the signal can be a challenge.

The contraction of the heart muscle also creates a physical movement that propagates through the body by way of the blood vessels. This is the signal that is detected when pulse rate is measured by feeling the wrist or side of the neck and is known as *cardioballistics*. Cardioballistic signals can be detected using inertial sensors like accelerometers.

FIGURE 4.7 A basic pulse-oximetry mechanism.

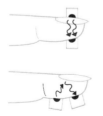

However, even though this kind of technique can be effective when the individual is sitting very still or sleeping, it can be very difficult to extract the heart signal from other movements when the individual is moving around.

As with heart activity, the movement of the blood in the blood vessels is the most common way to measure blood pressure. Blood pressure is a measure of how much resistance there is to blood flow in the vascular system. As conditions like narrowed blood vessels or a weakened heart develop, the amount of pressure in the blood vessels changes.

The most common medical device for measuring blood pressure is a *sphygmomanometer*, an inflated cuff placed on the arm to cut off the flow of blood. After blood flow is cut off, pressure is gradually released and using a stethoscope, a medical professional measures two values. The first is *systolic pressure*, the point at which a swishing noise indicates that blood flow is beginning again. The second is *dyastolic pressure*, the point at which this swishing sound ceases indicating that normal blood flow has returned. The blood pressure results are then reported as systolic/diastolic. Wearable cuff-type blood pressure monitors are available, but are generally not used for long-term or everyday monitoring of blood pressure since they require the interruption of a periodically inflated cuff.

A more wearable method of measuring blood pressure is to measure the speed at which a pulse of blood travels. This is done using a device similar to two pulse-oximeters, located in different places along a blood vessel. Each oximeter detects the pulse of blood flowing through a vessel, and the amount of time it takes for the pulse to travel from one oximeter to the next is calculated. If the vessel is narrower, it will be more difficult

(and therefore take longer) for the blood to travel through the vessel. Because oximeters work better on appendages than on the torso, cuffless blood pressure monitors often take the form of a ring and wrist- or armband, as shown in Figure 4.8. However, the arm moves around a lot and gravity can change the amount of pressure in the vessels of the arm and hand. Therefore, it is often necessary to simultaneously measure the position of the device relative to the heart, to take into account gravitational effects on blood pressure (Shaltis et al. 2008).

Detecting body temperature with wearable technology usually involves using a substance for which changes in temperature cause corresponding changes in electrical properties. Changes in thermal energy then result in changes in the flow of electricity. This can be done at specific points, through individual temperature sensors, or over a surface, through the integration of a temperature-sensing fiber.

One of the biggest challenges of sensing body temperature as a vital sign is correlating the accessible temperatures with core temperature, which is often more indicative of the medical condition of the body. Garment-integrated temperature sensors

FIGURE 4.8 A cuffless blood pressure monitor concept.

often cannot access body cavities and locations where core temperature can be measured.

When used in the context of vital signs, the term *respiration* usually refers to breathing rather than cellular respiration (which would be very difficult to sense). Breathing can be monitored clinically in a variety of ways, but many (especially those that rely on measuring airflow) are not appropriate or feasible in the wearable environment. The two aspects of breathing that are most directly sensed through garment-integrated systems are breathing sounds and the expansion and contraction of the torso during breathing.

Breathing sounds are sensed in a manner similar to sensing the sounds of heart activity—through microphones. Expansion of the chest and abdomen can be sensed directly through stretch sensors or indirectly, using a bend sensor. With a more precise sensor, breath volume can also be detected. Detecting other qualities of breathing, such as the differences between chest breathing and abdominal breathing, often requires more than one sensor on the torso to measure different points of expansion.

Body Postures and Movements

Body positions and movements can be detected by a garment system through an array of sensors that detect joint bends, orientation of body parts, and acceleration of body parts. Information about the proximity of a body part to other body parts can also be used to deduce body position.

As discussed in Chapter 2, joint bends can be detected in a variety of ways. Most directly, they can be sensed using bend sensors, such as the optical bend sensors or piezoelectric materials discussed earlier in this chapter. Slightly more indirectly, the stretch experienced by the outside surface of a joint bending can also be measured, and this measurement can then be used to deduce bend.

There are several approaches to detecting elongation or stretch. One of the more common textile-based methods is to implement a looped conductor in the textile structure. As discussed earlier in this chapter, conductive materials are generally slightly resistive per unit length; that is to say, the longer they are, the more resistive they are. If a conductive yarn or a wire is looped so that the loops touch each other at some point in the structure, the length of the electrical pathway is much shorter, since electrons can take a shortcut through the contact points rather than traveling the entire length of the conductor. If, however, the loops come out of contact, the electrical pathway becomes much longer, and the resistance of the structure increases. One way of implementing this kind of stretch sensor is to knit a conductive yarn into a knit structure. Figure 4.9A shows the shape of one type of knit structure that is conducive to stretch sensing. If the dark yarn highlighted in that image is replaced with a conductive yarn, the loops will be in contact when the knit is not stretched in the horizontal direction. If it is stretched, these loops will move away from each other, coming out of contact. Another way to implement this concept is through a stitched structure that uses looped yarns, such as an overlock or coverstitch. If the fabric that the stitch is applied to stretches, the loops of the stitch will similarly pass in and out of contact as the fabric is stretched.

Another approach to stretch sensing is to use conductive particles suspended in a stretchy medium such as rubber or latex. When the stretchy substrate is relaxed, there are many conductive particles in relatively close contact, making the whole structure fairly conductive. When the substrate is stretched, the particles move farther away from each other, increasing the resistance of the substance. (See Figure 4.9B.)

FIGURE 4.9 Three ways to sense stretch. (A) A looped conductor; (B) suspended particles; (C) adapted bend sensor.

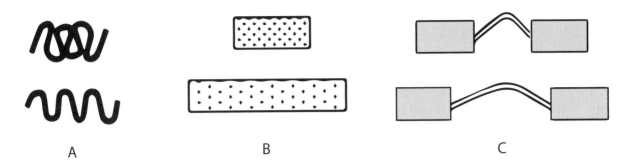

A   B   C

Finally, bend sensors can also act as stretch sensors if properly implemented. If a bend sensor such as an optical bend sensor or piezoelectric film is attached to a stretchy fabric such that it is slightly bent when the fabric is relaxed, the sensor will straighten as the fabric is stretched. In that way, the reverse response of the bend sensor can be used to interpret stretch. (See Figure 4.9 C.)

Orientation of body parts is often sensed using orientation sensors. The simplest of these is the tilt switch, which most commonly takes the form of a tiny can a little bigger than a pill capsule (but also available in other shapes and sizes). A tilt switch has two contact points at one end of the can and a conductive ball inside. (See Figure 4.10.) The switch must be affixed to the body or garment in a specific orientation, such that when a body part is moved in a specific way, gravity pulls the ball to one side or the other of the can, opening or closing the switch. Because the switch has only one contact point and relies on gravity, it is very limited in its ability to communicate information about the orientation of the body part, but it is also very simple to implement.

A more complex type of orientation sensor is the magnetic field sensor or *magnetometer*. Many different kinds of magnetic fields can be sensed,

including natural magnetic fields like the Earth's magnetic field, as well as magnetic fields generated by an electric current or a magnet. There are also many different ways to sense the strength and position of a magnetic field, some of which are quite complex. A compass is a simple magnetic field sensor that senses the position of a magnet, which aligns naturally with the magnetic field of the Earth, to determine changes in position. If a compass-type sensor is affixed to a body part, the movement of the body part relative to the Earth's magnetic field can be sensed by measuring the movement of this small magnet.

FIGURE 4.10 A tilt switch. (A) The switch is closed and able to conduct electricity; (B) the switch is open so the system no longer conducts electricity.

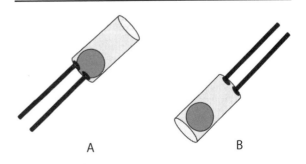

A   B

Magnetoresistive materials are normally resistant to electric current, but they become very conductive when in proximity to a magnetic field (such as a magnet). These types of sensors can be used in conjunction with magnets placed on or implanted into a body part, to detect the position of the body part relative to the sensor. For example, systems have been developed for patients who have lost the ability to speak following a tracheotomy. Magnetoresistive sensors are embedded into a frame that resembles eyeglasses and used to detect the movement of magnets attached to the lips, tongue, and teeth. Sensor signals can then be used to generate artificial speech. It is possible that a similar approach could be used with sensors embedded in the collar of a garment.

Another way to sense changes in position is using a *gyroscope*. The first gyroscopes were composed of a disc set in two concentric rings, each of which was free to spin on one axis. The disc spun on an axis attached to the first ring, which spun on a perpendicular axis attached to the second ring, which spun on a perpendicular axis attached to the frame of the gyroscope. Between these three axes, rotation in any direction was possible. (Giant gyroscopes are sometimes seen as amusement park rides, where the rider is strapped in the center of the rings and spun in different directions.) Gyroscope sensors are used to detect rotation or angular momentum. Wearable versions of gyroscope sensors usually use tiny vibrating masses suspended inside a square frame by springs. As the frame experiences angular momentum, the mass is moved within the frame, and finger-like sensors around the outside of the frame sense the movement.

Detecting the acceleration of body parts can also help in sensing or measuring body movements. Acceleration is the rate of change of velocity,

which is the rate of change of position. *Accelerometers* are the most common way to detect the acceleration of a body part. However, because they do not directly measure velocity or position, they can be prone to error. Therefore, to arrive at velocity or position from information about acceleration requires back-calculating, and tiny errors in the sensor signal can be highly magnified in the resulting information.

Although position or orientation information alone may not be enough to determine the pose of the body, position in addition to orientation information can make this possible. Successive body poses can be used to identify movements, like walking or running, as described in Chapter 2. However, in some cases it is also useful to know the distance between body parts, such as the distance from the torso to the hand. This can serve as a check on other sensors that may be prone to error (like accelerometers), or it can be used alone in some applications where distance itself is important (such as to detect a movement like standing up, where the knees move farther from the head or torso).

One method of sensing distance is similar to the mechanism that bats use to navigate in the dark: emitting a signal from a specific location and measuring the time it takes for the signal to return to that location (bouncing off an obstacle). Bats generate their own signal, a high-frequency sound that is above the range that humans can hear. In wearable sensors, this signal can also be a high-frequency sound or another wave frequency such as radio frequency or even light. Motion sensors in many security systems also work in this way. This method detects any obstacle, however, not necessarily a specific obstacle like the arm. If the device that generates the signal and the device that senses the signal are not located in the same place, the distance between them can be detected. For example, the emitting device may be located on the torso, and the detecting device may be located on the arm. The time that it takes for the signal to reach the detector can be used to determine the distance between them. Because most of these wavelengths are absorbed or reflected by solid objects, most of the time this type of sensing relies on what is called line of sight; there must be a clear path between the emitter and the detector for the sensor to function. That means sensors need to be on the outside surface of clothing and cannot be obscured by body parts or fabric folds. This can pose a serious limitation.

Information from the Physical and Social Environment

In addition to sensing information from the wearer's body, a wearable system can also gather information from the environment around the wearer. Parameters of the physical environment are more straightforward to sense than are social factors. Physical factors include variables like temperature, light level, sound level, location, or distance. They can be measured through sensors on the wearer's body (outward-facing sensors) or communicated to the wearer's systems from other systems situated in the environment. For example, the wearer could detect the temperature of a room through a wearable temperature sensor, or the room's thermostat could communicate that information to the wearer's systems. In many cases, the same sensors used to detect body signals can also be used to detect environmental signals, depending on how the sensors are designed and oriented.

Deducing more complex information from sensor data can require additional sensors, processing, or pattern recognition. For example, a wearable sensor may detect that the user has entered a dark area, but knowing that the dark area is indoors during the day may trigger a different response than knowing that the dark area is outdoors at night. It may be appropriate to activate a night-visibility lighting system outdoors at night, but it may not be appropriate to activate the same system in a dark movie theater. Further, it may be appropriate to activate the safety lights if the wearer is out for a nighttime jog but less appropriate if the wearer is out for a romantic evening stroll.

Social parameters are less straightforward to detect. A wearable microphone may easily detect the presence of another speaker, but to effectively sense social context it is probably necessary to know the identity of the speaker and even perhaps the emotional state of the speaker and the content of the speech. Physical parameters may also contain clues about social context; for example, the physical distance between the wearer and the speaker may provide contextual clues about the relationship between the two individuals or the emotional tone of the conversation.

Much of the complexity of making sense of contextual variables is handled through the information processing part of a wearable system, which is rarely the domain of the apparel designer. However, even though more sensors (and even redundant sensors) usually improve the accuracy and sensitivity of a context-sensing system, the corollary effect is an increase in the complexity and difficulty of manufacturing the system, a likely decrease in the comfort and wearability of the system, an increase in the cost of the system, and an increase in the complexity and difficulty of interpreting sensor input. Therefore, it is important that all of these trade-offs be addressed in the design of the system.

WEARABLE DISPLAY

In addition to developing ways in which information can pass into the wearable system (input), many wearable systems also must be capable of output or display (i.e., communicating information *to* the user, either from another user or from the system). As with input methods, there is both overlap and distinct difference between output methods used in stationary or mobile technologies and the methods used in wearable technologies.

Wearable displays are effective because they can comfortably be placed closer to the user's sensory organs than nonwearable displays. For example, the visual display (screen) of a mobile phone is located wherever the phone is, which is unlikely to be close to the user's eyes. The phone's auditory display is also attached to the device, and is not likely to be close to the user's ears. Peripheral devices like wireless headsets seek to alleviate this problem by putting the auditory display component close to the sensory receptor. Wearable visual display is slightly more complex, but head-mounted display technologies have seen major advances in the last decade.

Visual and auditory displays are by far the most common display modalities. In traditional (hand-held or stationary) technologies, they are quite effective in communicating information quickly and effectively. However, for the designer of functional clothing, neither is a particularly high-potential display modality. In the case of visual display, the area of body real estate that is readily visible to the user is quite limited (in general, limited to the forearms and hands) and even more dramatically limited when the user is engaged in a simultaneous task. This limits effective wearable display to those displays that can be mounted close to the eyes: eyewear and head-mounted displays. In the case of auditory display, an auditory display that does not rely on earphones is likely to be socially problematic.

It should be noted that visual display as perceived by individuals *other* than the wearer is another domain entirely. This topic will be discussed in Chapter 8 under the heading "Clothing for Sensory Perception."

Tactile display is a viable and underexplored communication modality that has interesting potential for many application areas, and especially for clothing. One significant reason that tactile display is not common in personal devices is that nonwearable devices do not often make contact with enough sensory receptors to provide detailed information. A mobile phone, for example, has a vibrate function that allows information to be transferred through the tactile modality. However, because the phone provides only one large point of contact, it can only communicate a very limited amount of information (generally through vibrating patterns). Clothing, on the other hand, makes contact with a large surface area close to the body. Thus, it holds the potential for a far greater amount of information to be communicated.

Because the tactile modality is not commonly used for displaying information, it also presents a cognitive advantage. Different information presented simultaneously in different modalities (e.g., looking at a picture and hearing a spoken instruction) can be more easily understood than information presented in one modality such as vision alone (e.g., being shown a picture and text at the same time). Therefore, if an individual is engaged in a physical and visual task such as flying a plane, information presented in the tactile modality is more easily understood while concurrently engaged in the physical/visual task than information presented in one of the occupied modalities (e.g., vision). Finally, tactile display is also more invisible than other modalities and can be used in situations where visual or auditory display would be socially inappropriate or otherwise undesirable.

Systems that are designed to facilitate or promote tactile sensing are often called **haptic** systems, materials, or devices, meaning that they pertain to the sense of touch.

Basics of Tactile Perception

Most of the body's sense of touch takes place through the skin. Touch, pressure, and pain are also perceived in the muscles and organs, but this information is used more to sense the position and movement of the body, or to sense pain. The skin senses a wide variety of tactile impulses through specialized mechanoreceptors, which translate mechanical stimuli into electrical signals carried by the nerves to the brain.

The sensory organs in the skin detect a variety of forms of tactile impulse (stroking, pressure, vibration, and others) as well as temperature, itch, and pain. Sensing these impulses is accomplished by a variety of mechanoreceptors and by free nerve endings in the skin. The types, names, and functions of the various mechanoreceptors in the skin are described in Table 4.1 and illustrated in Figure 4.11.

Most of the skin's sensory organs are located in the **dermis**, the layer of skin that lies below the **epidermis** (the outermost layer of the body). The right-hand side of Figure 4.11 shows hairy skin, the most common type of skin on the body. Most of the body, except the palms of the hands, soles of the feet, and areas like the lips and insides of the mouth is covered with hairy skin (even if the hairs may be very fine). The palms of the hands, soles of the feet, and some surfaces of the genitals are covered with **glabrous** skin (Figure 4.11 left), which has no hairs and is much more sensitive to touch.

Mechanoreceptors each respond to a specific type of stimulus by transforming that stimulus into an electrical signal, which is carried by the attached sensory nerve to the brain. Mechanoreceptors are classified as either slowly adapting (SA) or rapidly adapting (RA), depending on the length of time it takes the electrical signal generated by the receptor to decay and return to a resting state in the presence of a constant stimulus. For example, the Merkel discs, which sense pressure, are slowly adapting mechanoreceptors. It takes a long time (from 10 to 100 seconds) for these

TABLE 4.1 Mechanoreceptors and Their Functions

RECEPTOR TYPE	SENSATION	ADAPTATION
Meissner corpuscle	Stroking, fluttering	Rapidly adapting
Merkel disc	Pressure, texture	Slowly adapting
Pacinian corpuscle	Vibration	Rapidly adapting
Ruffini ending	Skin stretch	Slowly adapting
Hair follicles	Stroking, fluttering	Rapidly adapting
Free nerve endings	Temperature, pain, itch	Both rapidly and slowly adapting

FIGURE 4.11 Mechanoreceptors in hairy skin and glabrous skin.

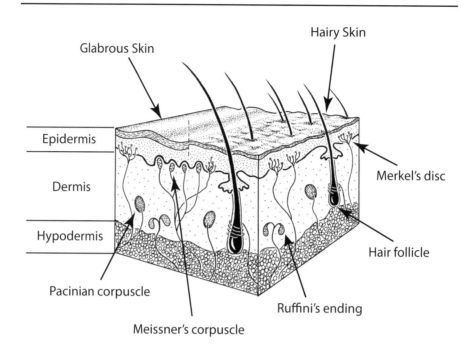

mechanoreceptors to stop generating an electrical signal if the pressure applied to the skin is constant. Rapidly adapting mechanoreceptors stop generating an electrical signal within as little as 0.1 seconds if the stimulus remains constant.

This adaptation of mechanoreceptors is the reason that a constant tactile stimulus like the pressure applied by a ring or watch stops being noticed as long as it does not change. Not only does the brain become accustomed to the body's physical condition, but the sensory receptors themselves also adapt and stop sending the brain signals about tactile stimuli. However, as soon as the tactile stimulus changes, the receptor will once again begin firing electrical impulses to the brain.

Psychophysics of Tactile Perception
In any sensory modality, there is a difference between the properties of the stimulus itself (the *physics* of the stimulus) and the way the stimulus is interpreted by the person's brain (the *psychology* of perception). This relationship between what actually happened and what was felt is called the **psychophysics** of perception. The perception of tactile sensation is described in a variety of ways. One of the most common is the **two-point threshold**, the distance at which two points of tactile stimulus (two pins or pencil points, for example) are perceived as two rather than as one single point. The two-point tactile threshold is a measure of the resolution of the skin. It indicates how fine-grained the sense of touch is on various parts of the body. The fingertips and tongue are amongst the most sensitive parts of the body for tactile perception, in two-point threshold as well as other measures. Fine textures that are easily perceived with the fingertips may be completely invisible to the upper arm, for example.

Sensitivity to pressure over the body surface can be measured using calibrated hairs of specific stiffness. The skin is stimulated using one hair at a time, increasing in stiffness with each trial. The point at which the touch of a hair is perceived is the tactile threshold, and the stiffness of the hair can be used to determine the amount of pressure applied. However, this method measures the *perception* threshold. Also of use in designing functional clothing is the *pain* threshold, the point at which pressure becomes uncomfortable. Sensitivity to vibration also varies over the body surface, both in frequency of the vibration and amplitude of the vibration, the latter being much more closely linked to the sensitivity to pressure.

Electrical and Electromechanical Actuators

There are two ways in which tactile sensation is commonly generated on the skin: by using a small motor or moving part (an *electromechanical actuator*) to make physical contact with the skin or by using an electrical current to stimulate the sensory neurons in the skin and evoke the sensation of a tactile stimulus (an *electrotactile stimulus*).

Electromechanical actuators use electricity to generate a mechanical movement. Motors are common electromechanical actuators, and vibrating motors are commonly used to generate tactile signals. For example, the vibrating motor in a mobile phone alerts the user to an incoming call using a tactile vibration signal. A pressure sensor on the outside of a protective garment could be used to trigger a vibrating motor inside the garment, letting the wearer know that they have come close to or in into contact with something on the outside surface. Arrays of vibrating motors can be used to map external tactile stimuli directly to the body underneath. Tiny vibrating motors attached to pins can be used to create a pixelated display that can translate finer textures from outside a glove to the fingertips, for example.

Shape-memory alloys, piezoelectric materials, and electroactive polymers are fiber- and film-shaped electromechanical actuators that can contract or bend when an electrical signal is applied. When used to move a surface, they can also create the feeling of movement or touch on the skin.

An electrotactile stimulus creates the feeling of touch without actually applying a touch. It does so by activating the mechanoreceptors directly through a small electrical current applied to the skin. For an electrotactile stimulus, rather than applying a force to the skin that would then be transformed into an electrical signal in the mechanoreceptor, the electrical signal itself is generated by the stimulator and subsequently transmitted to the brain by the nerves in the skin.

Because different types of mechanoreceptors are generally found at different depths in the skin, it is possible to activate receptors individually by controlling the depth of the electrical stimulus that passes through the skin. Whereas mechanical stimulation like vibration or pressure always feels like vibration or pressure, selectively stimulating mechanoreceptors makes it possible to produce the full range of tactile sensations in the skin. One approach uses selective stimulation of mechanoreceptors to mix and blend tactile responses like primary colors in order to produce the full range of tactile perception through electrical stimulation (Kajimoto et al. 2004).

Designing Technology for the Wearable Environment

The marriage between clothing and electronic technology is not always a seamless junction. It involves the blending of at least four distinct disciplines: textiles, clothing design, electronics, and information systems. Each of these has bearing on the other three, and developing a successful smart garment requires taking into account the strengths and weaknesses of each, as well as the trade-offs involved in each decision in the design process.

The following sections address the relationship between these disciplines and the design variables that are unique to designing technology for the wearable environment.

GARMENT- AND TEXTILE-INTEGRATION OF SENSORS AND ELECTRONIC COMPONENTS

One of the most evident differences between the fields of apparel and electronic systems is in physical properties: Apparel prioritizes the physical comfort of fabrics and garments, often emphasizing softness, breathability, and conforming to the body. Electronic systems prioritize stabilizing and protecting the device, often emphasizing rigidity, impermeability, and flat surfaces. Electronic components have been around for much longer than smart clothing has, and the standards and conventions of electronic parts were designed for rigid devices, not for integration into textiles. For the designer, it is important to understand the conventions of electronic components, and the ways in which circuits can be formed in textile structures.

While some forms of wearable technology can be condensed into a single unit and located in a comfortable accessory such as an armband or belt using the manufacturing techniques common to electronic devices, body sensors often need to be distributed around the body to effectively detect signals where they occur. For example, an ECG electrode may need to be placed near the heart, or a motion sensor detecting hand position may need to be worn on the hand. This often means that all of the components of a system that involves

body sensors (the sensors, as well as the central processor, battery, and other components) cannot be located in one spot. Further, sensors commonly need to be connected electrically to a central processor in order to send signals to the system. These electrical connections can make it challenging to design wearable sensing systems that are as comfortable and wearable as traditional textiles.

Some sensors, such as the stretch sensors discussed earlier in this chapter, can be created using traditional textile and apparel processes, and connected via conductive stitching or woven conductors to a processing unit. Other sensor components, like accelerometers, are commonly available in the standard packages that have been developed for use in traditional electronic devices. Some common electronic packages are depicted in Figure 4.12. They differ by size and by the shape and arrangement of their leads, or points of electrical connection. Radial or axial packages usually contain only one discrete component, such as a resistor or a single LED. Radial leads are arranged around the edge of the component body, usually all in one direction, and axial leads are arranged along the axis of the component body, usually one on either side. In-line packages have leads that are designed to be soldered through holes in a rigid circuit board. Even though axial and radial components are also soldered through holes in a circuit board, in-line packages have leads arranged in standard numbers and spacing. Finally, tiny surface-mount components minimize the physical size of the component and have exposed metal pads rather than extended legs or leads. These flat leads are soldered to exposed pads on the surface of a circuit board.

These packages have been designed to make standard printed circuit boards (PCBs) easy to manufacture. PCBs are fabricated using soldering

FIGURE 4.12 Common package types for electronic components. (A) Radial and axial packages; (B) in-line packages; (C) surface-mount packages.

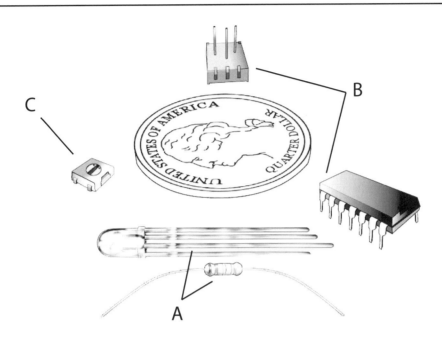

processes, which melt metal to join the metallic leads of the component package to the metal connections (called *traces*) on the PCB. Soldering processes and standard component packages are not always well-suited to the materials and methods used to make textile-integrated circuits, as the following sections will describe.

E-textile Materials

E-textiles, or electronic textiles, are materials that contain electrical circuits or make connections between electrical circuits. Most current e-textile materials connect standard PCBs and component packages to textiles in some way. However, many of the components (e.g., sensors, actuators, processors) described earlier in this chapter and other electronic components (e.g., solar cells or batteries) can also be made in the form of a fiber.

Components made in the form of fibers can then be woven or knitted into textile structures, or stitched/applied to the surface of a textile or garment.

E-textile materials generally fall into one of two categories: materials that act as conductors, connecting parts of a circuit, or materials that actually contain components of a circuit such as power sources, sensors, processors, or actuators.

E-textile Conductors

An important part of any electronic circuit is the *conductor* or conductive material that forms connections between electronic components in the same way that metallic traces form the connections on a PCB. In smart clothing, components of a circuit may need to be distributed over the surface of the body but powered by a central power source. The electrical connection between these components can be one of the most significant influences on both the comfort of the garment and the durability of the system.

The ability to conduct electricity using a textile is usually achieved by weaving, knitting, laminating, printing, or stitching conductive material into or onto the textile structure. Conductive materials can be created by spinning yarns out of conductive filaments, such as very thin filaments of metal or other conductive materials like carbon. Often conductive materials are brittle, and therefore may not be strong enough for the intended application. To add strength and resiliency, conductive filaments or staple fibers can be blended with nonconducting fibers. In blended yarns made of staple fibers, conduction relies on the short conductive fibers coming into contact with each other. Therefore, the amount of resistance of the yarn depends on a few variables: the conductivity of the staple fibers, the ratio of conductive to nonconductive fibers, and the tightness of the twist of the yarn (which holds the staple fibers together).

Another approach is to wrap a nonconductive core yarn in a layer of metallic foil. This allows the core to absorb most of the forces experienced by the textile while the foil wrapping expands and contracts like a coil as the core bends and stretches. Nonconducting yarns can also be coated with a conductive coating, such as a layer of silver or gold. For many applications, this coating can be as thin as a few molecules thick to be effective.

When metallic and nonconducting materials are blended, however, it can result in a yarn that is not solderable. Soldering temperatures often exceed the melt or burn point of standard fibers. Adding stretch to a conductive material can also be a challenge. Approaches like core-spun yarns (see Figure 3.20) can be used with conductive wrapping to create stretch. However, many conductive

materials are not perfectly conductive. They have some amount of resistance that usually increases with length. When a resistive conductor is wrapped or zigzagged to incorporate some slack in the nonstretch portion, this slack can produce undesirable consequences for the whole system. For example, it could allow the loops of conductive material to come into contact, creating a short circuit path (Figure 4.13). Because resistance depends on length, the shorter path has much less resistance. However, when the fiber is stretched and the loops or turns of the wrapping move away from each other, the current in the circuit must take a longer path. This longer path has a higher resistance, and thus the electrical properties of the whole circuit are changed. This problem can be minimized by using a very conductive material or by wrapping in a manner that minimizes or prevents the conductive material from coming into contact with itself in the relaxed position.

Conductive fabrics can be made by weaving or knitting a fabric entirely out of conductive yarns, by weaving or knitting insulated or noninsulated conductors into a standard fabric, or by stitching conductors onto the surface of a fabric. Many

FIGURE 4.13 Adding stretch to a nonstretch conductive yarn through looped stitches. (A) Loops in contact lower the overall resistance. (B) If loops separate when stretched, resistance increases. Preventing contact in the relaxed position minimizes the resistance change during stretch.

A   B

conductive yarns have properties very similar to standard yarns, so it is generally possible to use standard equipment to weave or knit the textile. One of the challenges of creating a textile-integrated circuit is making conductive pathways that can connect components in different places on the textile. Standard textile structures such as weaves or knits usually allow conductors to be integrated in a horizontal or vertical direction (or both), which creates a grid of conductors once textiles are made into garments. These conductors must be isolated in some parts and connected in others to create the desired path.

In addition, connections must be made between conductors where parts are joined with seams. For example, if during the construction of a shirt, a sleeve must be sewn to a bodice, there must be a way for conductive pathways to form good electrical connections across that seam to connect sleeve components to bodice components.

Another challenge is that integrated conductors need to be electrically isolated from each other in order to prevent short circuits or unintended pathways. Because garments are flexible, a smart garment with many noninsulated conductors may form many short circuits if the garment is folded or the sleeves are rolled up, for example.

Stitching a conductor to the surface of a textile allows for the pathway to be laid out in a more free-form fashion: The yarns can travel wherever needed over the textile surface. Many conductive yarns are too fragile to survive the many trips through the take-up mechanism of the needle thread of a sewing machine and must be used as bobbin threads. (Some manufacturers report that thread passes as many as 70 times through the needle before being embedded into the garment!) Stitching a conductive pathway on the surface of a textile also requires that the pathway be electrically isolated in places

where conductors cross each other and sometimes also be insulated from the outside so that the circuit is not affected by external moisture, for example. It is also important that conductors not come into contact when the garment is folded, and so that the wearer is protected from any electrical shocks. Adjusting the tension on a lockstitch machine can allow the conductive yarn to float on one side of the fabric without passing through to the other side during each needle pass. This will allow conductors to cross each other without coming into contact by traveling on opposite sides of the fabric. Stitched conductors can also be insulated after sewing by laminating a protective fabric, film, or coating over the stitching.

Conductive pathways can also be added to a textile by printing or surface treatment. Most conductive inks, paints, and adhesives are made by mixing conductive particles (like carbon or metal dust) into a binder or base liquid. Because there needs to be enough conductive material to bring the particles close enough to each other for energy to flow, these materials are generally more difficult to work with than traditional inks, paints, and adhesives and can also be less durable.

Finally, a stable, durable electrical connection must be made between the integrated conductive pathway and an electronic component or PCB. This can be done by stitching through a perforation in the component lead or PCB, but the leads of most standard component packages (as seen in Figure 4.12) do not have perforations, and therefore cannot be sewn. PCBs can be designed with holes that are plated in metal and connected to traces on the PCB, making a sewable board. The connection between the board and the conductive thread is a weak point in the circuit and must be reinforced in order for it to withstand the forces of everyday wear (and, in some cases, washing).

Fiber and Textile Electronics

E-textile materials often transform traditional electronic components into fiber or textile form. Fiber transistors, for example, are created using various methods that translate the semiconductor structure into a fiber scale. Like some fibers and yarns, fiber-form electronic components usually require the combination of several different types of material to form the component. However, unlike traditional blended or multicomponent yarns, it is often necessary to form electrical connections to the ends of a fiber. It may even be necessary to form multiple electrical connections to individual component materials along the length of a fiber or at specific intersections between fibers. Because of this, it is necessary for the materials to be arranged in specific, structured ways.

There are many strategies for meeting these requirements for smart fibers. One common approach is to create a concentric structure where the component materials are coated over each other or extruded together into a layered fiber. An example of this approach is shown in Figure 4.14, which illustrates the construction of a *photovoltaic* (solar cell) fiber. The solar cell requires two conductors (an anode and a cathode), separated by a light-sensitive material that allows current to flow when its electrons are excited by light energy. In traditional photovoltaic panels, these materials are usually laid flat like a sandwich. In the photovoltaic fiber, each layer is coated on top of the one before, and the center of the fiber is made out of a traditional textile material, which gives the whole structure strength and flexibility. However, in order to gather the electrical energy from the fiber and use it to do work, a circuit or battery must be connected to the two conducting layers of the fiber, usually at one or both ends of the fiber.

FIGURE 4.14 Concentric structure of a solar cell fiber.

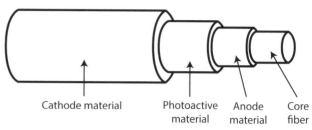

Cathode material   Photoactive material   Anode material   Core fiber

In a photovoltaic fiber, the entire length of the fiber can act as one long solar cell. However, some components need to be laid side by side along the length of the fiber and connected to adjacent components or to crossing fibers. Often this takes the form of tiny electronic components attached to or embedded in a fiber. Electrical contact points along the length of the fiber can be exposed selectively by insulating some parts of the fiber and leaving other parts exposed so that electrical connections can be made between fibers. Similarly, once components are attached to these connection points, they can be insulated for protection or left exposed. An example of this is illustrated in Figure 4.15.

Electrical connections can be made within a woven textile by melting or soldering fibers

FIGURE 4.15 A woven circuit with connections made between crossing fibers/yarns.

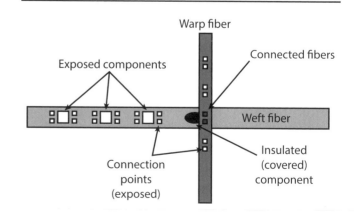

Warp fiber

Connected fibers

Exposed components

Weft fiber

Connection points (exposed)

Insulated (covered) component

together at appropriate locations, in much the same way that mechanical connections can be made by melting fibers together.

COMFORT AND ACCURACY

Effective integration of electronics into a textile structure should aim to preserve both the physical comfort and function of the user and the functionality of the electronics. The trade-off between user comfort and the function of electronics in clothing is most evident in the case of body sensing, where the sensor may be most accurate under conditions that compromise comfort for the wearer.

For example, sensing techniques like ECG which rely on placing conductive electrodes directly against the skin often require that the skin be moist, and that the electrode be held firmly in place with no movement. This may involve wetting the electrode and applying a force against the electrode and skin (using an adhesive or a tight strap) to keep the electrode from moving. The system needs for variables like moisture management and skin pressure are directly at odds with user needs for the same variables: the user would like to be dry and loosely fitted, while the system would like the user's skin wet and tightly fitted.

In some situations, a compromise can be reached. For example, it may be possible to still detect a usable heart rate signal with a dry (or more dry) electrode in a tightly fitted garment. It may also be possible to achieve both comfort and accuracy through clever design. For example, the designer may use a second sensor that specifically detects movement or physical proximity on top of another type of sensor, to detect when the target sensor has moved. This information can then be used to select good parts of the sensor signal and discard bad parts, or perhaps to filter or adapt the signal from the sensor to correct for the error introduced by movement.

Another approach is to use many sensors in place of one sensor, under the assumption that the average of the sensor signals (or a few signals selected out of the many) are more likely to be accurate than one individual sensor.

Finally, depending on the end use of the sensor information, a lower degree of accuracy may be acceptable. For example, a single acceleration sensor attached to a mobile device casually placed in the pocket is enough to detect acceleration during many basic activities, despite the error and inaccuracy that may be present in the sensor signal.

However, most sensors have fundamental needs. For example, an electrode must be in contact with the skin to pick up any signal at all, which limits how loose a garment that contains electrodes can be. Two major variables for which user comfort needs and sensor accuracy needs are often directly in conflict are the need for skin contact and the need for *mechanical coupling* (tight physical connection between the sensor and the body, such that the sensor stays in place and does not slip around during movement). It is important that designers understand these sensor requirements in order to understand constraints that might be placed on potential design solutions.

Table 4.2 illustrates the levels of skin contact and mechanical coupling required for various sensor types. To help manage the trade-off between sensor needs and human comfort, the choice of sensor material can take into account user needs for operating force, flexibility, and breathability. A designer can also explore possible locations and shapes of rigid processing or communications hardware so that they conform ergonomically to the body (either in a closely fitting or loosely fitting configuration, depending on the design context). In addition, textile solutions to thermal balance and moisture management can be employed to increase comfort.

TABLE 4.2 Requirements for Skin Contact and Mechanical Coupling in Wearable Sensors

SENSOR TYPE	SKIN CONTACT REQUIREMENT	MECHANICAL COUPLING REQUIREMENT
Electro-dermal	High	High
Temperature	Moderate (some applications)	Low
Infra-red or Light	Moderate to High	Moderate to High
Bend and Stretch	Moderate (some applications)	Moderate
Inertial	Low (cardio-ballistics = high)	Moderate to High
Acoustic	Moderate to High	Moderate to High

DATA, COGNITION, AND CONTEXT AWARENESS

Interacting with information can affect user comfort in much the same way as interacting with physical structures like garments. However, in the case of information, the comfort is mental, rather than physical. A well-designed information system preserves the user's cognitive and psychological comfort in the same way that a well-designed garment system preserves the wearer's physical comfort. For apparel designers, designing for a user to effectively communicate with a device and process information can be a new challenge. The following sections address design principles that guide the design of interfaces, and the challenge of helping a user to find meaning in a large amount of available data.

Interacting with Wearable Interfaces

The field of human-computer interaction (HCI) has devoted considerable time to studying the way that humans interact with systems through interfaces. In wearable technology, the garment may have an interface that resembles the interface of a computer, mobile device, or other piece of electronic technology; it may have an interface that resembles a fastener such as a snap or zipper; or it may have an interface that takes an almost invisible form,

by responding to gestures and body signals. The principles and processes of HCI are very useful in understanding the way in which a user may perceive and understand a garment system.

Principles and processes that are especially useful for functional clothing design include helping the user to build an accurate mental model of the interface, promoting discoverability in the interface, presenting information through multiple sensory modalities simultaneously, ensuring that display elements are effectively perceived in the use context, and placing information in the world to the extent possible (rather than relying on the user's memory).

When a user encounters a new smart garment or wearable device, he or she immediately begins to build a mental model of how it should be operated. Often, this is based on previous experiences. Depending on the expected functionality, the user may be expecting commonly used icons and functions like power, select, back, or home. Referencing commonly used icons, functions, and physical configurations is an effective way to minimize the time and effort of building a mental model.

Mental models are easier to build if interface elements are discoverable—if it is easy for the user to notice and understand what the garment or device does and how it does those things. Donald Norman (1998) describes the qualities of the object or interface that communicate to a user what actions can be performed as the "affordances" of the object or interface. For example, a raised bump or set of bumps on a garment surface may afford button pressing, as they visually evoke keypads and buttons seen on other devices. Gesture-based interfaces in electronic devices pose a problem of affordances: interfaces based on buttons and menus can use graphics and words to explain functions, but gestures (like stamping a foot or bending an elbow to activate a function) are difficult to label. Designers may need to rely on an emerging "vocabulary" of common gestures or on other feedback techniques to communicate functions to users.

Another way to minimize the time spent building a mental model is to provide feedback to the user as the interface is explored. This also helps build trust in the system. If a light lights up after the user has pressed a button, the user knows that an action has happened. However, if the user is not provided feedback indicating that the button has been pressed, it may result in multiple button presses (which could cause errors in operating the system) or in the user pressing much harder than needed on the button (which can cause discomfort or pain, particularly in a flexible, body-mounted interface where users are actually pressing hard on their own bodies, or damage the functionality of button itself).

For these sensory signals to be perceived reliably, however, the designer must take into account the context of use. A visual signal will not be helpful in the dark nor will an auditory signal be effective in a loud environment. Because garments are often worn in more than one context, redundancy in presenting information (through multiple modalities) is usually necessary.

It is also important to take into account the user's limitations while wearing the garment—both in terms of limitations imposed by the task (e.g., not having a free hand to push a button) and in terms of the limitations of reach and visibility (See Chapter 9 for a further discussion of this topic). A visual interface or graphic placed on the upper chest would be very difficult for the user to read, for instance. Space suits are a good example of a use context where the user's range of vision is very limited because the rigid neck-ring of the helmet prevents any visibility of the chest. However, chest-mounted interfaces are necessary due to the large number of controls needed for the suit and the limited amount of stable real estate on the body surface. Designers solved this problem by mounting a mirror on the astronaut's wrist and printing interface labels backwards on the chest of the suit, as shown in Figure 4.16. The astronaut can then use the mirror to view labels and visual elements as the interface is operated.

FIGURE 4.16 Interacting with chest-mounted controls in the space suit.

Another benefit to incorporating perceptible feedback into interface elements is that it minimizes the need for the user to remember how to use the garment. Information that the user must remember can be a source of error, especially in situations where there is a lot to remember and where the user interacts infrequently with the garment. Putting information in the world by using labels, icons, and sensory feedback in the interface can limit the amount that the user has to learn about the garment system.

For on-body interfaces located outside of the field of view or used in contexts where the user is attending to other visual stimuli (as when driving), tactile navigation is especially important. It is often necessary that the system be designed so that groping for the interface cannot cause accidental activation. Some systems have used a trigger button or interface that must first be activated before any other interface elements can be activated to control for this problem. The system in Figure 4.17 shows a textile interface integrated into the strap of a messenger bag, that uses touch-sensitive

embroidered buttons. The user slides a hand down the strap until the raised embroidery can be felt. The thumb is then rested on the first button to activate the interface so that the desired button can then be chosen and touched.

Context Awareness

One of the most interesting aspects of wearable technology is its ability to be omnipresent, collecting information over long periods of time in many different situations. However, the flip side of this potential is the immense amount of information that then must be processed in some way in order to make sense or utilize it. How does the system know what information is the most important? What aspects of the collected information are useful and interesting? How is this information captured and communicated?

The answer to these questions often depends on the specific design problem. However, one approach that can help make information more useful is to present not only what happened, but in what context it happened. For example, if a patient is being monitored for a heart condition, it is very important to know if the patient's heart rate is increasing while they climb stairs or while they are sitting on the couch. For the designer of functional apparel, this means that it may be important to include sensors that are not strictly related to the most important parameter, but are able to capture context.

The use of smart systems often relies on the system's ability to detect changes in the wearer's behavior or in environmental parameters and respond appropriately. This ability in a smart system is often described as **context awareness**. For example, a traditional winter coat without any ability to be context-aware cannot detect when the wearer's core temperature has changed or when the wearer has gone inside. Therefore, if wearers would like to change body temperature, they must

FIGURE 4.17. A gropable touch-sensitive interface. *(Komor et al. 2009)*

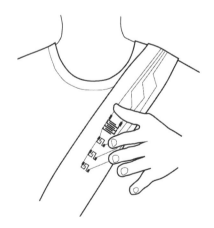

unzip it or remove it. A smart winter coat with a context-aware sensing and actuating system could turn on or off an electrical heater when it detected changes in core temperature or environmental temperature.

It is vitally important that a system be designed to gather contextual information in a way that is effective for the user in a specific context. Because of this, the apparel designer's role in designing a smart system may extend to designing the flow of information in and out of the wearable system.

The two major methods of gathering context information are the same ways in which a user can interact with a wearable system: *implicitly*, by detecting changes in the wearer or environment and using them to deduce the wearer's needs, and *explicitly*, by asking the wearer to provide information about their needs.

Smart Clothing Design

It is possible to make many technological functions wearable, but it is not always a good idea. For example, it is very possible to integrate the remote control for a TV into a shirt. This solution might prevent things like losing the remote in the couch cushions, but it would also require that the users remember to wear their "TV shirts" whenever they needed the remote and that they also be willing to wear the remote to the grocery store. The "shirt-ulator" depicted in Figure 4.18 is an example of an unhappy marriage of technology and clothing. Both t-shirt and calculator performed their respective functions well in their original form, but both work less well when integrated together. The user cannot read the display or buttons when they are upside down, the calculator adds weight and stiffness to the shirt, and the device is located in an awkward body area for others to interact with.

FIGURE 4.18 A shirt-ulator. *(Design: Jeremy Fischer)*

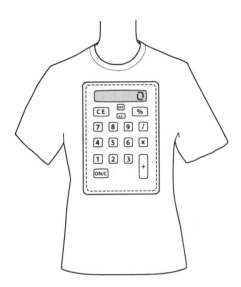

By contrast, there are other technological functions that are vastly improved by integration into a garment. For example, a patient with a heart condition that requires constant monitoring may find a bra with an integrated heart monitor to be a significant improvement over having to stick electrodes all over her chest.

Clothing has three key properties that benefit the design of electronic systems: clothing is physically proximal (close to the body), is socially ubiquitous (worn almost all of the time, in almost all situations), and has a large surface area. For technology, these properties mean that a device can know more about the user, in more situations, than ever before. Similarly, the augmentation effects of technology that extend the user's knowledge base and ability to communicate can be integrated more seamlessly into everyday or job-related activities.

For clothing, electronics offer one significant advantage—the ability to make a change, either on demand (activated by the user) or in response to a change in the user or the environment. Traditional clothing typically has a predefined function, which is performed continuously whether it is needed or not. For example, a garment that provides a barrier between the wearer and a hazard in the environment provides that barrier whether or not the hazard is present. A smart barrier garment may be able to detect that hazard and present the barrier only when it is needed.

One area in which the intersection of clothing and technology produces a particularly effective result is in sensory substitution systems. Sensory substitution systems are those that allow a non-impaired sense to make up for an impaired sense. The impaired sense may be permanently impaired (as in blindness), situationally impaired (as in the dark), or cognitively impaired (as in a situation where there are too many things to watch at once). Because clothing is physically proximal, it can provide stimulation to another sensory modality without occupying the wearer's hands. Because it is socially ubiquitous, the wearer does not have to remember to bring another special device. Because it has a large surface area, it can allow technology to be placed close to sensory organs and can gather contextual information about the condition and position of the wearer's body, as well as about the environment. Similarly, because technology brings dynamic functionality to the system, it can be activated only when needed and can be designed to be imperceptible otherwise.

Sensory Substitution for Position and Orientation

The vestibular sense detects the position and orientation of the body relative to gravity. The kinesthetic sense allows the brain to keep track of changes in the orientation and position of limbs in space. (Both senses are discussed in more depth in Chapter 2.) Because these senses are strongly influenced by the sense of touch, tactile stimulation can often be used to substitute for or augment kinesthetic and vestibular senses.

The kinesthetic sense relies highly on vision and touch to provide landmarks for determining the exact position. Over time, the brain can train the body to assume precise positions (exactly the learning process that takes place as a dancer or athlete or artisan trains), but often it is difficult to close the loop and provide feedback to the brain about the position of the body while the activity is happening. A dancer may accomplish this by looking in the mirror, but a swimmer may need to rely on verbal feedback from a coach to make immediate changes to a body position. Tactile signals can provide quick, intuitive feedback to help the individual know when the right position has been assumed. In this way, the tactile feedback can stand in for visual feedback when it is not possible to see one's own body.

Many medical conditions can cause impairment of the vestibular sense, including injury, inflammation, or infection of the ear, as well as the natural aging process. When the inner ear is not providing feedback about the position of the body relative to gravity, it becomes very difficult to maintain balance during everyday activities like standing and walking. A tactile stimulus that provides feedback about the position and movement of the center of gravity is very effective in compensating for the impaired inner ear. The stimulus can be effective when applied to almost any part of the body—the feet, waist, torso, and legs are common choices. Further, in cases where peripheral sensory nerves (such as those in the feet) are also impaired, remapping tactile sensory perception to a different body part (e.g., moving the missing tactile sensing from the feet to the calf) is also a very quick and effective method for restoring balance and ability. Even without training, patients can often resume normal standing and walking patterns immediately upon donning tactile feedback garment or device.

Figure 4.19 shows a wearable device that uses pressure sensors embedded in an insole to detect changes in weight distribution and balance, and a band of vibrating motors worn around the calf to provide feedback. When the wearer starts to shift off balance, the device activates a vibrating motor on the side the wearer is leaning too far toward to nudge them back in the other direction.

The U.S. Navy's Tactile Situational Awareness System (TSAS) is a good example of the power of tactile processing in overcoming a bottleneck of attention and visual processing and augmenting the body's vestibular sense. It was designed to help U.S. Navy pilots who may need to fly complex and fast-paced maneuvers over water. On a cloudy day, the sky and the surface of the water can be visually very similar, and difficult to distinguish. Complex flight patterns may include 360° turns and rolls, which can disorient the pilot. When the pilot's internal vestibular sense is confused, he or she may consult the plane's altitude indicator, which depicts the orientation of the plane relative to the horizon. However, in a situation that requires a quick decision, this indicator can be difficult to read and process; and misunderstanding the plane's orientation can cause the pilot to fly into the water instead of into the sky. Further, weather conditions can make it very difficult to perform maneuvers without visual cues.

The TSAS vest (illustrated in Figure 4.20) uses an array of tactile actuators to provide stimuli to the torso, mapping the orientation of the aircraft relative to gravity onto the body. Pilots wearing this vest were much more quickly able to determine their orientation when their internal vestibular sense was augmented with tactile feedback than when they needed to rely on a complex visual processing task (McGrath et al. 2004).

FIGURE 4.19 Tactile feedback for balance. *(Oddsson and Meyer 2014)*

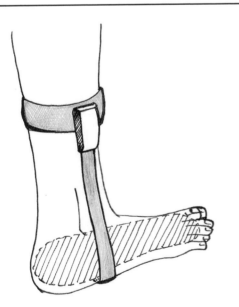

FIGURE 4.20 U.S. Navy Tactile Situational Awareness System. *(McGrath et al. 2004)*

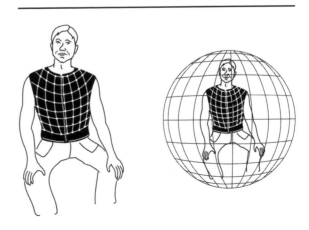

The kinesthetic sense provides feedback to the brain about the position of limbs and body segments in space. However, remember that the brain is better at sensing changes than absolute positions. Augmentation of the kinesthetic sense using tactile feedback systems can help overcome this limitation in sensing absolute positions. For instance, a tactile feedback system can use sensors to detect joint positions and activate a tactile stimulus when a joint reaches the extent of its healthy range. Or it can remind the wearer to keep a joint in a specific position. A posture-sensing garment, such as the one illustrated in Figure 4.21, could use tactile feedback to remind the wearer to sit up when they have been sitting in an unhealthy position for too long. A bend sensor held in the channel on the vest's back (the dotted lines in Figure 4.21) senses the position of the wearer's back and generates a virtual tap on the shoulder by activating a vibrating

motor when the wearer has been in an unhealthy position for too long.

Sensory Substitution for Vision and Hearing

Whether vision impairment is temporary or permanent, tactile display can be effective in substituting for or augmenting reduced vision. The glove in Figure 4.22 was designed for use by firefighters in dark or smoky environments. It uses an ultrasonic distance sensor on the back of the hand to detect the distance between the hand and an obstacle. This distance is then mapped to the intensity of vibration provided by a vibrating motor also located on the back of the hand. In this way, firefighters can scan a room as they would visually, when visibility is reduced.

A similar technique can be used to help a fully sighted person navigate in a foreign environment. In a situation like navigating an unfamiliar city, there are many reasons why cognitive overload may make map reading difficult. For example, while cycling there may be too many other things to keep track of visually (cars, pedestrians, obstacles), and it may be too noisy to rely on audio commands. While walking, reading a map may

FIGURE 4.21 A posture-sensing garment.

FIGURE 4.22 Vibrotactile distance-sensing gloves for firefighters.

have negative social consequences (marking the individual as a tourist, which can be dangerous). Tactile displays can provide silent, intuitive instruction guiding wearers to their destinations. The belt in Figure 4.23 has vibrating motors spaced at intervals around the waist. In communication with position sensors such as GPS and map applications, the system can guide wearers to their destinations by showing through tactile vibrations on the waist the direction in which they should travel.

Finally, vibrotactile augmentation or substitution can also be effective in overcoming impaired hearing. The vest in Figure 4.24 maps bands of audio frequency to individual vibrating motors. This way, the wearer can feel the frequency spectrum of surrounding noises. When used in parallel with lip reading, this can be particularly effective in compensating for impaired hearing.

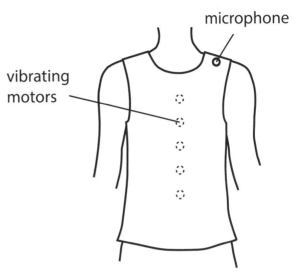

FIGURE 4.24 A vest that translates sound frequencies into tactile vibration.

Conclusion

This chapter introduced the basic principles of electricity and electrical systems that underlie wearable technology and discussed the role of information in smart systems and the unique challenges of designing technology for the wearable environment. It is important to note, however, that there are far more body signals, sensing techniques, input methods, and display technologies available and emerging. Subsequent chapters will discuss the technologies and techniques that pertain to smart systems that address a particular functional goal. However, there remain concepts and methodologies that will not be covered in depth. Many of these have not yet achieved the kind of stability or development necessary to make them practical solutions either for garment-integration or for use in the wearable environment. Similarly, there are many alternative approaches to sensing a given aspect of the body or environment,

FIGURE 4.23 A wearable tactile navigation belt.

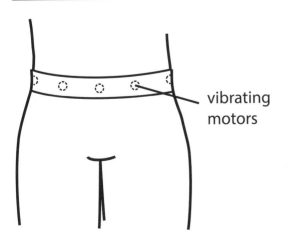

as seen in the many methods discussed that sense heart activity, for example.

Although electronic technology may not be the first domain of apparel designers, the more fluency and understanding designers have in electronics and information systems, the more effective their design solutions can be. Electronics are as much a tool for functional apparel as textiles are, and both are means to a functional end. Selecting and adapting the right technology to the needs of the user and the environment is crucial to a successful solution.

5 Thermal Protection

This chapter focuses on how clothing keeps the body in *thermal balance* (i.e., at a temperature that is within the bounds of safety). It covers the ways in which the body responds thermally to its environment; the role of textiles and other materials in providing warmth or cooling; and the effect of clothing design, modes of wearing, and combinations of clothing items on modifying heat loss and heat gain from the environment.

Thermal Balance and the Human Body

The human body adjusts to temperature changes by producing or releasing heat in specific ways. Heat can also be transferred from the environment to the body by various means. To see how body processes of heat production and dissipation are called into play, it is important to understand the basic ways in which heat can be transferred from one object to another.

MECHANISMS OF HEAT TRANSFER

Heat is the transfer of energy from one object to another as a result of a temperature difference between them. Objects cannot actually be said to contain heat—objects contain something called *internal energy*. When heat has been transferred to an object, it becomes part of its internal energy (i.e., the grand total of all energies) in the object. There are four general mechanisms by which heat transfer occurs in the environment, whether from the surroundings to the body or from one inanimate object to another. These are conduction, convection, radiation, and evaporation.

FIGURE 5.1 Heat is lost or gained by (A) conduction; (B) convection in air; (C) convection and conduction in water; (D) radiation; (E) evaporation.

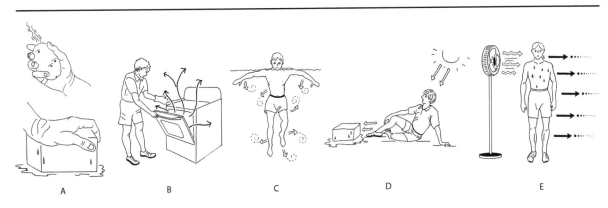

A   B   C   D   E

Conduction of heat occurs when the surfaces of two objects touch. (See Figure 5.1A.) The surfaces of objects often act as conduits for heat exchange for the whole object, with heat flowing from the warmer object into the cooler object until both are at equal temperatures. Objects may have surfaces that serve as barriers so that only the heat from their outermost surfaces is conducted while the inner portions of the object remain at their original temperatures. The healthy body has a surface capable of reacting either as a conduit or barrier to heat conduction.

Most people have experienced the shock of conduction that occurs between a doctor's cold metal stethoscope and the warm surface of the body. Each time the stethoscope contacts the body again, however, heat flows from the skin surface into the metal surface so that by the end of a physician's exam, it has warmed to a tolerable temperature. An important characteristic of conduction is that no exchange of materials occurs in this process. In other words, the skin surface does not actually become part of the stethoscope surface. A hand gains heat by holding a hot potato, and heat flows from the hand into a block of ice (Figure 5.1A), but neither object mixes with the hand. The two surfaces merely contact at their outermost layers. Although conduction generally occurs between solids, it can also take place between fluids, providing no mixture of molecules occurs. An example would be the heat exchange between hot oil and cold water carefully placed together in a container. Although the liquids do not mix, the hot surface of the oil can conduct heat to the cold surface of the water it touches.

It is important to recognize that heat flows from hotter areas to colder ones. A hot object will transfer heat to a cooler one, losing heat in the process.

The more temperature difference there is between the two objects, the faster this process takes place. So the body will lose heat rapidly if it is warm and leans back against a very cold bathtub, or will gain heat rapidly if a heating pad is laid against it.

If conduction occurs because of contact, then it is logical to assume that the more contact there is, the more conduction can take place. That is why two surfaces can be at the same temperature and yet feel very different to the touch. When one puts on a smooth satin-lined sleeve of a jacket that has been stored in a cold room, it initially feels very cold against the skin, whereas a textured fleece garment stored in the same room will not feel as cold. Although both surfaces are at the same temperature, not as much of the surface of the fleece lies in direct contact with the skin surface, so there are not as many points at which conduction can take place.

Convection relies on some sort of fluid medium, either a gas or a liquid, for heat transfer. Unlike conduction, convection involves material transfer, which occurs when liquids or gases mix, and heat exchange occurs as warm and cold particles integrate. (See Figures 5.1B and C.) Forced hot air heating systems rely on convection as warm air streams out of vents to mix with the cooler air in a house. Convection occurs when cold water is added to a tub of hot water to bring the tub water down to the desired temperature. When the body is submerged in water, both conduction and convection may be at work with a warm skin surface losing heat to cold water at the points where they touch, and the water warmed by that contact with the body mixing with colder water and convecting heat away (Figure 5.1C). Again, the greater the temperature difference between the two liquids or gases being mixed, the more rapid the heat exchange.

Radiation involves the transfer of heat by **electromagnetic energy**. As discussed in Energy Basics 5.1, electromagnetic energy travels in waves. Whereas conduction, convection, and evaporation rely on molecules touching, vibrating, mixing, and breaking bonds, radiation can travel through space where there are no molecules. The body gains heat from the sun and other warm items in the environment and radiates it to colder things surrounding it (Figure 5.1D).

Two types of radiant energy are important to the study of thermal balance. One is the short

---

Energy Basics 5.1: Electromagnetic Energy: Thermal Radiation

Most forms of energy rely on manipulating molecules and atoms through collisions between atoms or through passage of electrons from atom to atom. So how is energy transmitted when there are no atoms, such as in space? How does the energy from the sun get to the Earth?

Energy travels through space in the form of *electromagnetic radiation*. This is an interesting form of energy that has both wave-like and particle-like behavior. Electromagnetic waves are formed because of the interaction between an electric field and a magnetic field as they move through space. There are a number of types of electromagnetic waves, which differ from each other in *frequency* and *wavelength*. Figure A shows the types of electromagnetic waves and their relative frequencies. The frequency of a wave is its number of vibrations or oscillations per unit of time. A wavelength is the distance from crest to crest of oscillation. The more frequent the vibrations, the shorter the wavelength of radiation. Radio waves have the lowest frequency and the longest wavelength while gamma rays have the highest frequency and the shortest wavelength.

Visible light makes up an extremely small segment of the electromagnetic spectrum. Light is made up of separate packets of energy called photons. These have no mass, but they exhibit both particle-like and wave-like behavior. With the proper equipment, it is possible to see light's wave-like travel and observe its particle-like behavior when photons release electrons as they move along. Probably the most well-known electromagnetic waves are those responsible for the *color* components of light. These waves form the intermediate portion of the electromagnetic spectrum—the portion that is visible. The longer waves, which are just beyond the red end of the visible spectrum but are shorter than radio and microwaves, are called **infrared** rays. These are noted for their penetrating heating effect. The waves that are just beyond the violet end of the visible spectrum are called **ultraviolet** rays. Sunlight is an example of this form of radiant energy.

All objects radiate electromagnetic waves in proportion to their temperatures. In the higher temperature ranges, radiation is visible in the form of light. At lower temperatures such as those of the human body and of most objects that surround it, radiation is in the non-visible, infrared portion of the spectrum.

FIGURE A The electromagnetic spectrum.

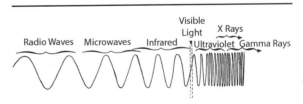

wavelength radiation emitted by objects such as the sun, and the other is the long wavelength or infrared radiation given off by the body and other objects in its surroundings.

It may be helpful to recognize that it is radiant *energy*, not heat, that is being transmitted by electromagnetic waves. The heat of the sun, for example travels through space as radiant energy; it is reconverted into heat when it strikes an object. Radiant heat transfer does not require air or atmosphere to operate, as convection does—the electromagnetic waves transfer energy across space. Nor does radiation require any sort of matter for its transfer, as does conduction. In fact, the presence of matter may block the transfer of radiant energy.

Surfaces differ in their ability to transform radiant energy into heat and make it available to other objects around it. Some surfaces are good reflectors, and some are good absorbers. The radiant energy produced by a fire or a radiator may bounce off skin, clothing, and other surfaces in the environment or it may pass through them without being absorbed or reflected. Thus, the structure of clothing materials can have a lot to do with how much available radiant energy can be used to heat the body. As with the other methods of heat transfer, heat flows from warmer surfaces toward cooler surfaces, and it flows more quickly if a greater temperature difference exists between two objects. Therefore, when environmental temperatures are higher than the skin surface temperature, the body cannot dissipate heat by radiation (unless there are cooler objects in the environment). The environment instead radiates heat toward the body, and it does so more rapidly when temperatures are higher.

Evaporation is an extremely effective means of heat transfer that occurs when a liquid changes into a gas. This change of state requires a great deal of heat, as is evidenced in the boiling of water. A teakettle and the water in it absorb enough heat from the burner to convert the liquid water into gaseous steam. The evaporative heat exchange between the human body and the environment involves much lower temperatures than does the boiling of water; nevertheless, the vaporization of liquid provides substantial heat transfer (Figure 5.1E).

A good example of evaporative cooling can be seen in the way hikers use a canteen. Most canteens are light metal containers covered by cloth. A hiker will fill the canteen with water and then dip it in a stream so that the cloth is saturated. As he or she hikes along, the cloth is continually drying out (vaporizing the water it has absorbed) by drawing heat both from the environment and from the water inside the canteen. By the end of the hike, if enough drying out has taken place, the water inside the canteen may even be colder than it was when the hike began. Because it requires so much heat to change the water absorbed by the cloth cover into vapor, the heat needed for evaporation is drawn from all available sources. Any heat in the water in the canteen is readily conducted by the metal of the container to provide a source of heat for this process. If you think of the canteen as the skin surface and its cloth cover as clothing, you will find this situation paralleled by many examples of protective clothing as you learn more about how body coverings affect thermal balance. As with the other methods of heat transfer, evaporation takes place more rapidly when temperature differences are greater. In addition, humidity affects the process in that more evaporation can take place under low humidity conditions.

BODY RESPONSES TO THE THERMAL ENVIRONMENT

As warm-blooded creatures, humans share with other mammals and birds the ability to produce enough heat, within certain environmental limits, to maintain thermal balance. The rather complex physiological mechanisms for thermal regulation in the body all work to balance the heat equation (i.e., heat produced equals heat lost). If more heat is produced than is dissipated, then the body must struggle to get rid of the excess before body temperatures become too high and illness results. If there are more debits or heat lost than credits or heat produced, then the body must find some way to increase heat production or preserve the heat already produced in order not to risk body damage from the cold.

There are only two ways the body can *produce* heat: by absorption of heat from the environment or by the body's chemical processes. The ways that heat can be transferred from the environment to the body have already been discussed. Standing in front of a fire, lying on a heating pad, or sitting in a sauna, the body could absorb heat through radiation, conduction, and convection, respectively. The additional heat source—the one that enables the human body to attain thermal balance—is its *metabolism*. The term metabolism includes all of the chemical and physical reactions that occur within the body. When food is digested, the burning or oxidation of that food provides energy in the form of mechanical energy (which appears as body activity or work), stored energy (as that in fat deposits), and heat. The **basal metabolic rate (BMR)** is the metabolic cost of living or the amount of energy expended to keep the body processes going.

Metabolism is affected by many things. The ingestion of food has already been mentioned. Activity is another extremely important factor. The metabolism is stimulated by exercise. Age, sex, emotional state, height-weight ratio, disease, and many other factors also play a part in determining the metabolic rate of an individual. The body uses

its metabolism to keep the heat equation balanced. If eating habits and physical activity do not produce enough heat for a specific environment, the body can activate other chemical activities. It triggers glandular secretions and some other involuntary actions to stimulate the metabolism.

Heat production in an individual is generally expressed in terms of calories or kilocalories per hour. A **calorie** is a unit of energy. It is the amount of heat required to raise the temperature of 1 gram (g) of water 1°C. The International System of Units uses joules rather than calories. One calorie equals approximately 4.2 joules. Calories or joules may be used to express the heat content of energy absorbed or produced by the body or sources of energy in the environment.

Most people associate the word calorie with weight gain. This is because the term calorie is used as an expression of the energy produced by the metabolism of specific foods by the body. Each food item contains energy that is used by the body in a variety of ways. Some is metabolized to produce heat; some is stored as energy in the form of fat. It is important to note that the radiant energy absorbed from a source such as the sun does not enter the digestive system and thus does not become part of the metabolic process. It is a transfer of energy from the sun to the skin surface that simply adds heat to the body. This is why, despite the calories of heat absorbed, one does not gain weight from lying in the sun. (Unless that is the only form of activity one gets!)

Studies of humans in specific environmental temperatures might state that the body in a hot, humid climate absorbed a certain number of calories. Others may detail the number of calories *produced* by the body during certain types of exercise. It is important to understand these expressions of heat production and absorption since they provide an indication of what the body heat loss mechanisms and clothing must do together to bring an individual into thermal balance with the environment.

One *kilocalorie* (kcal) equals 1,000 calories and is sometimes distinguished from a calorie by adding a capital C (1 kcal = 1 Calorie). The term *Btu (British thermal unit)* is also used as an expression of heat production. One Btu is the amount of heat required to change the temperature of 1 lb of water 1°F. One BTU is approximately equivalent to 1055 joules in the International System of Units. The calories assigned to foods are actually kilocalories. The convention of adding the capital C is not followed.

The response of the body to extremes of hot or cold is similar to the thermostat-furnace connection in a home. The body's central thermostat is the *hypothalamus*, a small region near the underside of the brain. The hypothalamus is like a switchboard, taking in information that affects metabolism, growth, and other functions and sending appropriate signals to the parts of the body most equipped to respond. If the body does not produce enough heat to cope with outside temperatures, the hypothalamus may tell it to shiver. This involuntary increase in body activity produces three to four times more heat than the basal metabolic rate. If this is still not sufficient, the hypothalamus may trigger emergency changes in glandular secretions such as those produced by the thyroid and adrenal glands. These secretions have a powerful effect on energy production in most body tissues. The body may also react by producing goose flesh or goose pimples. During this reaction, nerves in the skin surface at each pore cause body hair to stand on end. This reaction is very effective for animals since it causes their layer of fur to, in essence, become thicker. However, it has less value for most people today who have considerably less hairy bodies. Most

of the processes mentioned so far are emergency measures. The body accomplishes regular minute-to-minute adjustments in body temperature using some rather fascinating processes in the circulatory system.

Blood Flow and Temperature

The vehicle that carries heat throughout the body is blood. Blood carries heat from the deeper body tissues to the surface tissues, where it can be released to the environment. Changes in body temperature occur when something happens to bring greater or lesser amounts of blood near the skin surface. This can be accomplished in several ways: the *rate* of blood flow may be increased or decreased; the *volume* of blood may be increased or decreased; or the *access* of blood to the outer body surfaces may be opened up or blocked in some way.

A typical response of the body on a warm day proceeds like this: the hypothalamus sends messages to the pituitary gland and to the nervous system to open up or dilate the blood vessels near the surface of the skin. This allows the blood, which carries heat from the deeper recesses of the body, to reach the body's outer surface where radiation, conduction, and convection can operate to carry that heat away. As long as body heat is kept deep in the body, it is insulated by fat layers and other body tissues and cannot be carried off easily.

Once surface vessel expansion or **vasodilation** takes place, other mechanisms work to increase the rate at which heat reaches the body surface. The hypothalamus may trigger an increase in blood volume. Approximately seventy percent of the body is made up of fluid, some within specific channels such as the blood vessels and others flowing as interstitial fluids between and around the cells. The walls of the smallest blood vessels, the capillaries, are extremely thin and allow these interstitial fluids to pass in and out of the blood stream. With the increased blood volume, there are more vehicles available to carry heat. The rate of circulation may also be stepped up so that more blood reaches the surface faster.

When it gets cold, the opposite occurs. Surface blood vessels constrict. This **vasoconstriction** forces blood away from the body surface. The pores of the skin constrict, too, closing over fat layers and muscles that insulate the vital inner body organs. Blood volume and blood flow are decreased.

Figure 5.2 shows the effect that vasoconstriction and vasodilation have on maintaining appropriate heat losses from the skin surface. When the environmental temperature drops (Figure 5.2A), in this case from 74°F (23.3°C) to 58°F (14.4°C), the body responds by vasoconstricting and lowering skin temperature. If vasoconstriction did not occur and the skin remained at 86°F (30°C), there would be a 32°F (0°C) difference between the skin and the environment. By vasoconstricting, the skin temperature is lowered to 73°F (22.8°C), so that there is only a 15°F (9.4°C) difference between the skin and the environment. Because there is less of a temperature difference, the rate of heat flow away from the body is decreased.

Figure 5.2B shows the effects of vasodilation. As outside temperatures rise, vasodilation *increases* the temperature difference between the skin and the environment so that the body is able to throw off heat faster.

The purpose of all these circulatory processes is to protect the body's *core*. Figure 5.3 shows an outline of the portion of the body known as the core. This is the interior portion of the body that houses the vital organs and that must be kept at a relatively uniform temperature. The body works to maintain blood supply to the core at all times, even if it must sacrifice blood supply to the extremities. So each individual's vital heat-balance equation represents the body's attempts to protect its core— that is, to keep it within the temperature range in which it can continue to function.

One of the interesting things about the core is that it includes the head, a part of the body that has a relatively thin insulating layer. Some studies show the head accounting for up to 50 percent of heat loss in the body, but this number is strongly affected by the amount of insulation covering the rest of the body. A study showed that when the whole body was exposed, the head was only responsible for ten percent of total body heat loss (Pretorius et al. 2006). The face, neck, and upper torso are very sensitive to changes in temperature. One study found that cooling the face results in a reduction of blood flow in other body locations like the fingertip (Collins et al. 1996), and another showed that cooling the head caused a disproportionate decrease in body core temperature (Pretorius et al. 2006).

FIGURE 5.2 The effects of (A) vasoconstriction and (B) vasodilation.

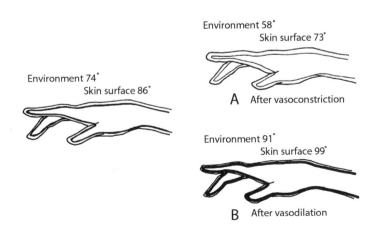

Environment 74°
Skin surface 86°

Environment 58°
Skin surface 73°

A After vasoconstriction

Environment 91°
Skin surface 99°

B After vasodilation

FIGURE 5.3 The body core.

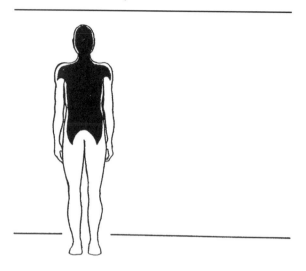

Local Changes in Circulation

While vasoconstriction and vasodilation help the hypothalamus control overall body temperature, temperature changes that occur on isolated areas of the skin surface can also trigger local responses without communicating with the hypothalamus. For example, when a hand picks up an ice cube, blood vessels in the palm constrict due to local exposure to cold before cooler blood can reach the hypothalamus and trigger whole-body vasoconstriction.

However, over time, information the hypothalamus has about the thermal balance of the body may override this local reaction and force the local blood vessels to dilate. For example, if the person holding the ice has a high core temperature following exercise, vasoconstriction will continue if the body core temperature is only slightly elevated. However, once the core begins to experience heat stress, the hypothalamus will override the local reaction and trigger vasodilation in the blood vessels of the iced hand.

Perspiration and Evaporation

In hot weather, as environmental temperatures approach body core temperature, it becomes impossible for heat exchange to work to the body's benefit. Since heat flows from hotter surfaces to cooler ones, when the temperature rises to 100°F (37.7°C), heat flows from the environment toward the body. When temperatures become so high that radiation, conduction, and convection can no longer carry off enough body heat, the body must call upon evaporative cooling.

The body experiences evaporative cooling by means of two processes: insensible perspiration and sweating, which may be called simply perspiration. **Insensible perspiration** is the continual drying out of the skin or of moisture that seeps into the skin surface from the environment. Insensible perspiration is not something an individual controls. It is simply an interaction between the body surface and the environment, similar to the drying out of morning dew from a lawn as the day progresses. The combined insensible moisture loss from the skin surface and in the breath exhaled from the lungs varies widely for individuals but is generally considered to be in the range of 1.5 to 2 pints per day (0.7 L to 0.95L). (This is separate from the additional liquid lost due to sweating and does not include liquid lost in the urine and feces.) Although the *rate* of evaporation may be affected by humidity, this drying out of the skin surface occurs almost constantly in most environmental conditions. This uncontrollable loss of fluid is one of the reasons why humans may not be able to survive for very long periods without water.

Sweating is a body-controlled process that is activated by the hypothalamus when the blood temperature rises. Sweat glands in the skin are stimulated, and droplets of sweat flow through tiny ducts to the skin surface. Once there, the droplets draw heat from the skin surface and evaporate (i.e., change from liquid to vapor). This warm vapor can then be carried off by convection (Figure 5.1E). This is similar to the process mentioned earlier where a teakettle draws heat from the surface of a stove and water changes from liquid to steam. The heat needed to evaporate the moisture is called the **latent heat of vaporization**. Because sweating involves not only the loss of heat from the droplet of sweat leaving the body but also the loss of inner body heat drawn to the skin surface to cause this evaporation, it is an extremely efficient means of dissipating body heat. Some dissipation can also occur when an individual does not really need to lose body heat, as when someone breaks out into a cold sweat. In that case, the sweat glands are activated by fight-or-flight hormones released by the adrenal glands. Nevertheless, this emotion-triggered response can still result in cooling.

Individuals may also use food to trigger the sweating response and thus provide evaporative cooling. Research studies have confirmed the so-called *gustatory sweating* (Clark and Edholm 1985, 59) that occurs after eating spicy meals containing chilies or curry. The response of the body to hot and cold drinks has also been studied using **thermography** (Clark et al. 1977). This is a process that uses a special camera to look at body heat by making infrared radiation visible. Thermography can also be used to assess the protection provided by various clothing items. (See Figure 5.4.)

Sweat production is not evenly distributed over the body surface. Havenith et al. studied the sweat patterns of male and female athletes during intense exercise, and mapped the differences in sweating rates (2008). As seen in Figure 5.5, women in general sweat less than men. While both men and women sweat most around the upper back and spine, women also have an area of concentrated sweating under the bust.

FIGURE 5.4 A thermograph making visible the heat emitted by a clothed body. Lighter areas show where there is greater heat emitted by the body or clothing items.

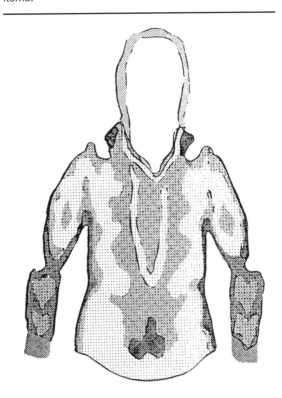

Evaporation takes place at a more rapid rate if the environment is relatively dry. On a day when the humidity and temperature are both very high, sweat may drip off the body because the humidity is too high for evaporation to take place. Since no latent heat of vaporization is lost when this happens, the body is not cooled as much as it would be if the sweat could evaporate from the skin surface. This may be one of the main reasons why humidity is critical to thermal comfort and even to survival at high temperatures. When the air is completely dry, survival is possible at an air temperature of 266°F (130°C) for 20 minutes or longer. In very moist air, a temperature of 115°F (46.1°C) may not be bearable for more than a few minutes (Vander et al. 1998, 629).

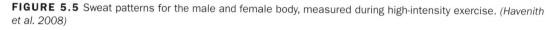

FIGURE 5.5 Sweat patterns for the male and female body, measured during high-intensity exercise. *(Havenith et al. 2008)*

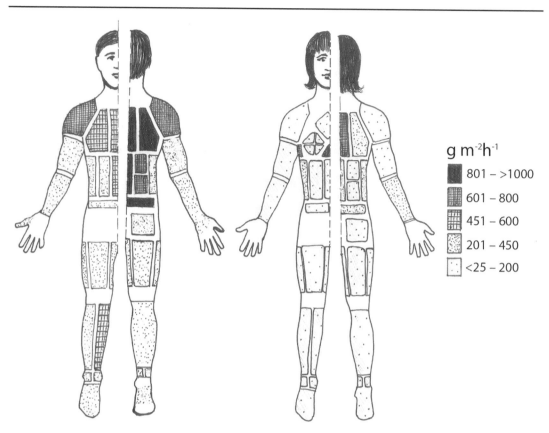

g m^{-2}h^{-1}
- 801 – >1000
- 601 – 800
- 451 – 600
- 201 – 450
- <25 – 200

Even though evaporative cooling takes place in cold environments, relative humidity does not appear to play a part in the response of the body at lower temperatures. A number of studies have found no evidence that individuals exposed to damp cold actually suffer more heat loss than those exposed to dry cold, as long as their skin surface is not wet. It is true, however, that they may feel colder when it is damp (Renbourn and Rees 1972, 217). This is because thermal receptors are buried fairly deeply in the skin. As humidity increases, the skin becomes damper and thus more conductive. This increase in conductivity essentially allows the sensation of cold to be more readily perceived and fed to the brain. Thus, the individual may *feel* a greater sensation of cold in damp weather, whereas the actual physical heat loss to the environment may be no different than it is in dry weather.

Wind, Water, and Temperature Extremes

Wind and water are tremendously important factors in heat dissipation. Wind can quickly move warm air surrounding the body away. It can also work to evaporate sweat and carry off the resulting warm vapor. Wind is so important to thermal balance that temperatures are often quoted along with a **wind chill factor**. This factor represents an equivalent temperature under no wind conditions. For example, the wind chill chart (Table 5.1)

TABLE 5.1 Wind Chill Chart

WIND (MPH)	OUTDOOR TEMPERATURE					
	30	20	10	0	−10	−20
10	16	2	−9	−22	−31	−45
15	11	−6	−18	−33	−45	−60
20	3	−9	−24	−40	−52	−68
25	0	−15	−29	−45	−58	−75
30	−2	−18	−33	−49	−63	−78
35	−4	−20	−35	−52	−67	−83

indicates that if the current outdoor temperature is 0°F (17.7°C) and there is a 20 mph (32.2 km/hr) wind in motion, in terms of the cooling power of the environment, it has the same effect as a windless temperature of −40°F (−40°C). Since wind affects the rate of both convection and evaporation, it is an extremely important factor to consider in designing clothing.

Water is a far more effective conductor of heat than air, absorbing it up to 25 times faster. Nowhere is this fact made clearer than in the sport of scuba diving, where an unprotected diver can chill rapidly at temperatures that would be uncomfortably warm in air (Figure 5.6). In a water-filled tank just larger than a diver, the body would continually produce heat to replace that lost to the water until the water temperature and the diver's skin temperature reached equilibrium. In the larger expanse of the ocean, body heat is continually lost. Water conducts body heat so much more rapidly than air that a diver might experience serious injury in 65°F (18.3°C) water in a matter of hours, whereas the diver may be relatively comfortable in 65°F (18.3°C) air. Goldman et al. (1966) state that an individual without a thermally protective diving suit who was submerged in 35.6°–53.6°F (2°–12°C) water would probably die of hypothermia within 53 to 105 minutes.

The opposite temperature extreme of water also poses safety problems. Since water conducts heat so rapidly, hot water may burn the skin while wood and even metal surfaces heated to the same temperature may not cause skin damage. Newburgh, in his classic study of thermal regulation states:

> If a piece of wood 5 mm on a side and 2 mm thick is heated dry to the temperature of boiling water, a finger placed upon it would feel warm or even hot but would not burn. The total heat transferred to the skin would be 1 to 2 small calories. The same thing done with a piece of metal of equal size would produce a sharp feeling of heat, but the amount of injury done to the tissue would be minimal. The number of calories transferred in spite of the greater weight of the metal

FIGURE 5.6 The effects of water temperature on a diver. (U.S. Navy)

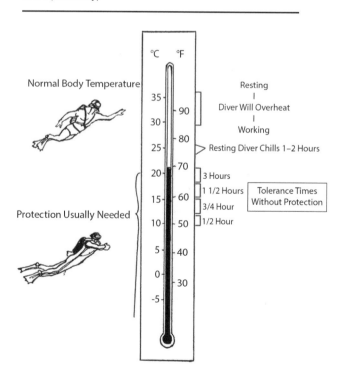

would probably be under 1. If water of this volume and temperature were placed on the skin about 3 to 4 calories would be transferred and a slight burn would probably result. (1949, 321)

Heat transfer by vaporized water (i.e., steam) can be of critical importance to protective clothing designers. Because heat is *released* when steam condenses to a liquid, burns from steam are common in firefighting, for example. Newburgh, continuing his previous discussion, states: "the same weight of water in the form of steam would release about 29 calories on condensation plus approximately 3 calories delivered while the condensed water cooled to body temperature. The result would be a most unpleasant burn" (1949, 322).

It seems obvious that the critical factor in heat transfer by wind, water, and water vapor is the *rate* at which the transfer takes place. Heat transfer or *heat flux* through any medium is generally expressed in calories per surface area per time period. One common expression of heat flux is calories per square centimeter per second. Heat flux becomes particularly important at temperature extremes. For example, although the temperature at which skin tissue is damaged can be documented (approximately 111.2°F or 44°C), a more important factor to examine in order to provide protection from burns is the heat flux that the skin can tolerate.

In the late 1950s and early 1960s, Alice Stoll and Maria Chianta conducted burn tests on volunteers at the U.S. Naval Air Development Center. This resulted in what is known as the *Stoll curve*, which quantifies the level of heat and length of time needed to develop a second-degree burn on human skin. In one test, Stoll and Chianti established that 0.06 cal/cm^2/sec was the heat flux the

skin can tolerate (1969, 1234). In terms of protective clothing design, this means that the body requires a clothing system that will control the rate at which high-temperature air, liquid, or vapor reaches the body surface so that it does not exceed 0.06 cal/cm^2/sec. When condensation occurs, a clothing system for environments where high heat and moisture are present must insulate the wearer from the point at which condensation takes place.

Individual Responses to Cold and Hot Environments

While the basics of heat transfer rely on physical principles that do not change, in any field that deals with human beings, it is inevitable that these principles will apply in different ways to different individuals. It is important for designers to realize that different people will have different experiences wearing the same designs and to assess the characteristics of the possible clients for specific garments before beginning to design.

Individuals differ greatly in their ability to tolerate and adjust to environmental temperatures. Differences have been found between the sexes, for the same individual at various stages of the life cycle, between races and for individuals who have acclimated by living and working in climate extremes. Some of these differences are the result of years of evolution, and others may be attained through long- and short-term exposure to environmental conditions.

Individuals adapt more easily to temperature extremes because they either have greater capacity for heat production and/or absorption, or they dissipate heat more or less readily in comparison to others. Among the most critical factors that appear to influence individual responses to heat and cold are surface area to weight ratio, percent of body fat, hormones, a variety of circulatory system functions, sweating patterns, and fitness. In addition, individuals have different tolerances for heat and cold and may feel hot or cold when others in the same conditions are quite comfortable.

There is voluminous research on each of these topics, and researchers continue to explore how different individuals respond to different thermal conditions. A brief review of some of the major factors will be presented here, and the findings of research papers will be listed with the hope that readers will explore some of these references and use the keywords in them to look for additional up-to-date research in this area. It is important for designers to be aware of these differences when using human subjects to test the success of their designs.

Body Size, Shape, and Fat Deposition

Body size, shape, and fat deposition all play a role in both generating and conserving heat in the body. Additionally, age, gender, and race may all influence these factors.

Researchers have posed different theories about the reasons for differences between the sexes. Lewis et al. (1986) state that, as a group, since women tend to have a less lean body than men, they have a smaller active mass to produce heat. Graham et al. (1989) found that men exposed to a cold environment increased their metabolism in 10 minutes while it took 20 minutes for normally menstruating women to increase their metabolism. It should be noted that in this particular study, both men and normally menstruating women achieved the same metabolic rate after 30 minutes.

In terms of conservation of heat, women generally have a higher percentage of body fat, and this should help them conserve core heat. However, Stephenson and Kolka state that "Since heat is lost from the body proportionally to surface area/mass, and smaller individuals have a smaller thermal

mass and larger surface area to mass, smaller individuals (i.e., women) are less resistant to cold stress than larger individuals" (1993, 242). Lewis et al. (1986) believe that this difference is particularly a problem for women's extremities, which are geometrically thinner than males. It should be noted that these effects may be caused largely by anatomical differences that exist in the general population of men and women. Haymes (1984) found that when men and women are matched for percentage of body fat, many differences in response to heat stress between the two groups disappear.

In a study of individual thermal profiles, Koscheyev et al., using all male subjects, found that the subjects were similar in the heat transfer that occurred in high dense tissue areas (such as the head, hands, and feet, which are composed largely of bone and connective tissue such as ligaments). Muscles transmit more than three times as much heat as fat, and bones transmit more than four times as much heat as fat. Bony areas like the head and hands transmit heat faster than areas covered by fat or muscle, but bony areas are also proportionally smaller than muscular areas. However, in the body areas where there was a greater amount of fat and muscular tissue, there was less similarity between subjects. These findings suggest that it may be the difference in tissue composition (the proportion of fat on the body) rather than the sex or age of an individual that is responsible for individual differences in heat transfer (2002, 1201).

Infants, who have a large head in relation to their body size can lose heat extremely rapidly, especially because the head is part of the core, and thus continually supplied with heat. This, coupled with an infant's still developing circulatory system, is why newborns are covered with hats even on the warmest summer day. At the other end of the life cycle, the loss of subcutaneous fat in old age is part of the reason why the elderly frequently complain of being cold.

The anthropologist, Carleton Coon (1968), explored evolutionary factors that have produced differences between the races with regard to fat deposition. Figure 5.7 shows the typical fat deposition patterns he observed for three races. Note the heavy deposition of fat in the cheeks of the Eskimo. Since the adaptation of Eskimos to the cold is largely accomplished with clothing, the cheeks are virtually the only exposed portions of the body. Europeans have fairly evenly deposited fat as do the Bushmen, but this latter group, existing in the hotter climate of Southern Africa, have far less fat deposition.

Lambert et al. observed that long-term adaptations to environmental temperatures may be accommodated by evolutionary changes in size and shape, with smaller individuals usually found in warm climates and larger individuals in colder ones (2008, 105).

Circulatory Patterns and Sweat Rates

The efficiency of each individual's circulatory system plays a large role in establishing individual differences in heat conservation. There is evidence that some responses of an individual's circulatory system are established during infancy. Vigotti et al., in a study on heat tolerance and mortality, state that "Results suggest that mortality risks differ by birthplace, regardless of the place of residence; namely heat tolerance in adult life could be modulated by outdoor temperature experienced early in life" (2006, 335). In other words, an infant of Eskimo heritage raised in the tropics might have quite a different tolerance to cold than an infant of Eskimo heritage raised in Alaska.

A number of researchers have demonstrated that women have a greater delay in the onset of sweating and a slower sweat rate than men (Grucza et al. 1987; Baker 1987). Others have related the differences in the efficiency of the sweating response to fitness and general capacity of the body for efficient exercise. Havenith et al. stated that "the effects of individual characteristics on human response to heat stress cannot be interpreted without taking into consideration both the heat transfer properties of the environment and the metabolic heat production resulting from the exercise type and intensity chosen" (1998, 233).

FIGURE 5.7 Fat deposition patterns. *(Coon 1968)*

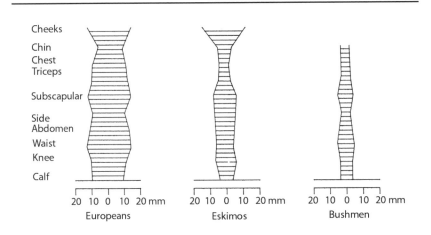

Acclimatization may involve changes in metabolic, circulatory, and sweating systems. Lambert found that for a person acclimatized to high heat, sweating may begin much sooner and be more copious. Thus, core temperature may rise much more slowly and a worker may be able to perform well for longer periods of time (2008, 107).

Many studies have focused on the effects of acclimation on more localized aspects of circulation. The circulation patterns of Arctic animals and some races that typically live in extremely cold climates appear to be different than those who live in more temperate climates. This is often ascribed to a process known as *countercurrent heat exchange*, a body response that occurs in the arms and legs during exposure to extreme cold. The alignment of blood vessels in the extremities allows outgoing arterial blood, which is warmed by the core to pass its heat to closely aligned veins as they carry blood back to the core. Less heat is delivered to the extremities, and, thus, less heat is lost from them (Brown 2010, 209). This is why acclimated Arctic fishermen may be able to work in frigid waters without protective gloves. Coon identified similar vascular patterns in a number of cultures living in extremely cold climates (1968, 247).

Metabolic Heat Production and Hormones

Although metabolism of food is a major component of heat production, a factor that causes metabolic differences between individuals is the amount and kinds of various hormones in the bloodstream. Thus, teens and pregnant women are noted to have high heat production, and post-menopausal women and the elderly tend to have less heat production. Hormones also affect heart rate and sweat rate and thus affect skin temperature.

Several studies have indicated that there are differences between women's responses in the follicular phase of the menstrual cycle (days 1–7) and the luteal phase (days 18–22). Stephenson and Kolka state that women in the luteal phase have a higher core temperature and "altered control of heat loss mechanisms" (1993, 890). They also found that women in the luteal phase sensed skin cooling more quickly than they did in the follicular phase. Haslag and Hertzman found an even a greater delay in the onset of sweating during the luteal phase (1965). These findings indicate why it is important to note the cycle phase of women subjects in any thermal study.

Wagner and Horvath (1985) conducted several studies that included both age and gender differences in its subjects. They found that older women had the most rapid increase in metabolism of any group (eight times as fast as either young women or older men). Older men appeared to be most at risk of declining core and skin temperature during cold exposure. Younger men clearly showed a better maintenance of body temperature in the cold than any other group.

Research on increasing tolerance for cold has identified the factor of rate of supply of metabolic fuels as the "critical bottleneck that limits the rate of heat production" (Wang 1986, 85). Wang likens the situation to keeping a house warm in the winter: One needs a good furnace, good air (oxygen), and a good fuel supply (natural gas, etc.). It appears that the ability to produce heat is limited primarily because of the rate at which humans can break down fuel (food) and convert it into the simple forms needed for heat production. Experiments have shown that the injection of humans with chemicals that boost fuel conversion rates do have an effect on metabolic heat production (Wang 1986, 86).

Skin Color, Hair, and Other Factors

Individuals may differ in the amount of heat they gain through absorption of radiant energy from the environment. For example, black skin reflects only 16 percent of the radiant energy of sunlight, whereas white skin reflects approximately 30–40 percent (Clark and Edholm 1985, 108). However, the effect of this difference is somewhat muted by the fact that dark skin allows less depth of penetration of solar radiation. This appears to be due to the filtration effects of the pigment in black skin.

Hair, which serves as an insulator, may also play a big part in the ability to lose heat to the environment. The texture of hair, wool, and other natural fibers discussed in Chapter 3, may affect the amount of insulation provided.

Finally, it is impossible to ignore the potential effect of the mind on the reactions of individuals to thermal conditions. Through biofeedback, meditation, yoga, and other techniques, it is possible to change heart rate, increase the flow of blood to specific body areas, and affect various body systems in ways that can dramatically affect thermal balance.

It is important to examine individual differences in response to heat gain and loss in light of all possible means of heat transfer. For example, a person with a greater amount of insulation in the form of fat may also have an increased surface area that leads to more heat loss by radiation and convection. Another individual with less body fat may experience a greater heat loss not only because of the lower amount of insulation but also because of a delayed onset of sweating, and thus less heat loss due to evaporation. The complex combinations of anatomical and physiological characteristics that clothing must accommodate are part of the challenge of designing protective clothing.

Individual Perceptions of Thermal Balance

Individuals may gather impressions of their overall thermal balance based on the temperature of specific body areas. For example, having cold hands or feet often leads some people to an overall feeling of being cold, even if the rest of their bodies are warm. Koscheyev et al. (2005) found that finger temperature was a better indicator of overall *perceived* thermal comfort than core temperature. A 1962 study by Veghte showed that subjects had greater cold tolerance when insulation was added to the extremities than when the same level of insulation was added to the torso. Goldman states that because of these findings, the focus on warmth in Arctic conditions shifted in the early 1960s to protecting the extremities (Goldman and Kampmann 2007, 1–4).

Other external influences on physiology and circulation may also change the individual's perception of thermal balance. For example, consuming alcohol increases circulation (including to the extremities), which can create the sensation of being warm while the core temperature continues to drop. More significantly, however, alcohol inhibits the body's shivering reflex, which prevents it from generating heat through muscle activity (Freund et al., 1994). A person consuming too much alcohol in a cold environment might feel very comfortable, but be at risk of hypothermia or other cold-related illness.

Thermal Illness

A number of debilitating conditions can occur when the body is exposed to extremes of heat and cold. *Hypothermia* is a condition in which the body's core temperature drops below 95°F (35°C). When this occurs, normal metabolism and normal body functions cannot take place. Hypothermia is especially prevalent when water and wind greatly magnify heat loss, as, for example, during boating in cold water or under windy conditions when clothing is soaked. It may also occur when the body is so exhausted that it cannot produce sufficient heat. Elderly people or those impaired by alcohol, drug addiction, and the like can suffer hypothermia after prolonged exposure to air temperatures as high as 65°F (18.3°C). Some of the signs are violent shivering, drowsiness, speech impairment, and loss of coordination and ability to reason.

One might think that *fever* is a result of an abnormal production of heat by the body, but it is actually triggered by a resetting of the body thermostat. Unlike hypothermia, normal heat production and dissipation mechanisms continue during a fever, but they operate in response to a higher level set by the hypothalamus. This is why fever may begin with a feeling of chill. The body is responding to its temperature, which is below the new higher temperature goal, and it is beginning the intense heat production that will be felt as fever. Many things cause the hypothalamus to reset the body's temperature goals, from chemicals produced during infections to glandular secretions. Fever is considered to be an important factor in the body's defense against infection, since most organisms that cause infection thrive best at 98.6°F (37°C).

Heat stroke or heat exhaustion may result when the environment adds so much heat to the body that it cannot deal with it effectively. This could happen in a factory where workers are exposed to the high radiant heat of furnaces; in the jungle, where high environmental temperatures and humidity make convective and evaporative heat loss difficult; or in total barrier clothing such as chemical/biological protective garments, which produce a climate within a suit that prevents heat dissipation. A *heat stroke* results when environmental conditions cause body temperature to rise so high (above 104°F (40°C)) that it puts the hypothalamus out of commission. Thus, the body's heat regulating mechanisms, including sweating, can no longer function, and the body core rises to dangerous temperature levels. If it is prolonged,

organ damage can occur. A condition called exertional heat stroke may also result from strenuous exercise.

In *heat exhaustion*, the body's heat-dissipating mechanisms are working so hard that an individual becomes exhausted. Body temperature is low during heat exhaustion because the vasodilation and sweating processes have been carried to extremes. However, the loss of body fluids and of the minerals they contain, plus the demands on the circulatory system, can cause a state of collapse. Although clothing cannot affect the onset of fever, it can help to prevent heat stroke and heat exhaustion. Because clothing is the body's immediate environment, it must be planned to set the conditions under which thermal illness will not occur.

Frostbite occurs when there is freezing of deep body tissues. It can occur on any body part, but tends to occur more on exposed areas such as the face and on the extremities, which have a high surface area to mass ratio and are also more often exposed to conductive heat loss. Most skiers and others who are active in cold environments are more familiar with *frostnip*, a freezing of the skin and its immediately adjacent tissues that appears as a blanching of the skin. Frostnip rarely results in any permanent tissue damage if the skin is returned to its normal state through warming of the tissues. With frostbite, however, the freezing extends more deeply and may result in permanent damage to skin, blood vessels, nerves, muscles, and even bones. Treatment of frostbite includes removal of any wet garments and rapid rewarming of the affected body parts after all danger of exposure to the cold is past.

EXPLORING THERMAL NEEDS IN A SPECIFIC SITUATION

It is important to recognize that the thermal balance of the body with the environment depends on the net heat gain and heat loss by each of the mechanisms discussed. Every interaction between an individual and the environment is different. In some situations, the body may be losing heat through all four methods of heat transfer. In others, one may, for example, be losing heat through conduction and gaining it through radiation, as is often the case when swimming in cool water on a sunny day. It is possible to lose heat from one part of the body through conduction at the same time another part of the body is gaining it through the same method. Design Strategies 5.1 summarizes some of the thermal principles covered thus far. It is always necessary for designers to explore all possible methods of heat gain and loss before proposing a solution that will bring an individual into thermal balance with a specific environment.

Materials for Thermal Protection

The materials used in a garment affect the thermal balance of the system in several ways: by resisting conduction of heat; by helping to preserve still air in a garment system; by dealing with moisture so that it promotes desired heating or cooling; and by having a surface that handles radiant energy in an effective way.

THERMAL CONDUCTIVITY

The ability of a material to conduct heat is called its **thermal conductivity**; its insulative value is called its **thermal resistance**. Materials vary greatly in their rate of thermal conductivity and thermal resistance. The flow of heat through metals, for example, is approximately 1,000 times greater than the flow of heat through an equal thickness of a textile fiber (Hatch 1993, 30). For glass, the conductivity is five times greater than most textile fibers. Even though fibers have a

relatively narrow range of values in terms of thermal conductivity, there are differences between them, with cotton being the most thermally conductive fiber and polypropylene being the least conductive.

The choice of a relatively nonconductive fiber forms the base on which a thermally insulative fabric can be built. For example, their ability to resist heat conduction is part of the reason why silk and polypropylene are often chosen for thermal underwear.

AIR AS INSULATION

Materials insulate because they are largely composed of air. A knitted blanket contains approximately 90 percent air and 10 percent fiber. Even a thin, woven windproof parka contains about 50 percent air and 50 percent fiber. Fourt and Hollies describe this characteristic of fabric in an interesting way: "We need to think of fabrics as mixtures of air and fiber in which fiber dominates by weight and visibility but air dominates by volume" (1969, 37). In other words, you cannot see the part of a fabric that provides thermal insulation. The fiber you do see, however, is vital to the system because of its ability to trap air.

There is a very thin layer of air surrounding every object that is relatively resistant to movement. This is called the **boundary air layer** or sometimes the **aerodynamic layer** (Renbourn and Rees 1972, 180). Fibers represent a surface to which boundary air can cling. The best insulators provide many surfaces to which air can cling or trap air in and around their surfaces in small pockets so that it will remain protected and still.

A number of studies have supported the idea that air, not fiber type, is the most important factor in thermal insulation (Mazzuchetti et al. 2007; Onofrei et al. 2011). Rees cites one in which very fine steel wool was compared to sheep's wool at

Design Strategies 5.1: Principles of Thermal Protection

As you use this text, you will need to take the principles it explains and apply them to analyze each design situation. The basic thermal principles covered thus far include the following:

1. The body gains heat by generating it through its metabolic processes or absorbing it from the environment. Heat is transferred toward or away from the body by radiation, conduction, and convection. Evaporation of moisture from the skin surface provides an additional means of heat loss.

2. Heat travels from hot to cold, and it travels faster when the temperature difference is greater.

3. Vasodilation and sweating are keys to heat loss; vasoconstriction is a key to heat conservation.

4. The primary goal of the body's thermoregulatory processes is to protect the core during heat stress and cold stress. Larger amounts of heat loss from the head, neck, and torso will result in vasoconstriction at the skin surface and the extremities.

5. Local heating or cooling will induce an immediate local response, which can be overridden by a central response that takes the body's overall status into account.

6. The more surface area a body contains, the greater is the area available for heat loss.

7. Conduction occurs more rapidly between two smooth surfaces.

8. Wet and windy conditions hasten heat transfer. Wind carries heat away from the skin surface and hastens evaporation of moisture on the skin. Water conducts heat far more rapidly than air.

9. Individual differences in metabolism, body tissue composition, and circulatory system function may change the rate or distribution of heat exchange. (There are exceptions to every rule.)

Although this chapter has thus far only explored the interaction between the body and the environment, you should already have some ideas about applying these principles to the choice of appropriate clothing for various thermal conditions. In cold environments, clothing should

1. Absorb radiant energy from the environment;

2. Be nonconductive (so that body heat is not conducted readily to the environment);

3. Not allow air or water to circulate freely near the body surface where it can carry off body heat;

4. Allow freedom of movement (so that circulation is not impaired);

5. Keep the core, especially the head, warm; and

6. Allow adjustable protection (so that overheating, which causes sweating, can be prevented).

In hot environments, clothing should

1. Reflect radiant energy from the environment;

2. Be nonconductive (so that environmental heat is not readily conducted to the body);

3. Allow air to circulate as freely as possible over the skin surface (to aid convective cooling and evaporation of sweat);

4. Allow freedom of movement (to prevent any extra physical effort that would increase metabolism); and

5. Provide minimum coverage or maximum ventilation for the body core.

Note that some of these recommendations are the same for both warm and cold environments, whereas others are direct opposites. For example, nonconductive materials are recommended for both hot and cold environments because the objective of a protective system is to form a barrier between the body and environmental temperatures. You will see how these principles of thermal balance can be applied to choices in materials and forms for clothing as this chapter proceeds.

the same fiber thickness and density (Renbourn and Rees 1972, 137). To visualize this experiment, think of a vest in which the left side has a layer of sheep's wool sandwiched between the lining and a windproof outer fabric, and the right side has a layer of steel wool as this middle layer. The steel wool fibers would need to be the same diameter as the sheep's wool fibers and each half of the vest would need to have precisely the same number of fibers of the same dimensions. Although the steel wool used in the study was about 100 times more conductive than sheep's wool, the steel wool provided only about 12 percent less insulation. A vest lined with steel wool might not be comfortable, but it could clearly provide thermal insulation. The study in no way suggests that fibers are insignificant in thermal protection. It simply points to still air as the key factor in warmth.

The fibers used to form a fabric can help increase its proportion of still air in a variety of ways. Those with hollow cores (See Figure 3.5)

contain protected still air. Others provide irregular textures or projections on their surfaces so that they cannot lie flat against one another in a weave or knit. Chapter 3 contains many examples of fibers with irregular surfaces and projections such as textured manufactured fibers (Figure 3.7) and fibers with unusual cross sections (Figure 3.4). The scales of wool and its twists (Figure 5.8A) make it particularly good at incorporating still air. Obviously, filaments of the smooth manufactured fiber can lie more closely packed together in a fabric than yarns of the wool fiber or textured fibers.

Down, the fluffy covering of ducks or geese that is located just beneath their outer feathers, is another material that traps a lot of air. (See Figure 5.8B.) It occurs in pods rather than in single fibers, and these pods are generally stuffed into channels in garments rather than being formed into a fabric. A single ounce of goose down may contain more than two million interwoven fluffy filaments or extensions that are available to trap air. Down

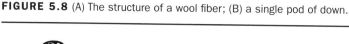

FIGURE 5.8 (A) The structure of a wool fiber; (B) a single pod of down.

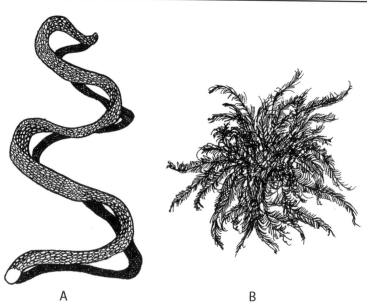

A   B

is highly prized for its ability to provide warmth without weight. Backpackers also value it because its compressibility allows a lot of thermal protection to be stored in a small space.

Conventional wisdom about dressing warmly often links thickness to warmth. Although thickness does make an appreciable difference in the insulative value of a fabric, it is the way in which fibers, yarns, and fabric structure form that thickness that is really important. A ½ inch (1.278 cm) thick fabric *will* probably be warmer than a ¼ inch (0.6 cm) fabric of the same structure since more air is incorporated in the ½ inch (1.278 cm) thickness. However, it is really the thickness of protected air that is referred to in the phrase "thickness equals warmth."

Bulk density values are often used to express the amount of thickness in a fabric that is due to air and the amount that is due to fiber. The bulk density of a textile material is its weight per volume of fabric. A fabric of a specific length and width can be weighed and its thickness measured. Then it can be described in pounds per cubic foot (grams per cubic centimeter). If a fabric has a low bulk density, or a low number of pounds per cubic foot, it is generally a good insulator. (Presumably, the weight is low because there is less fiber and more air.) Aerogels (discussed in Chapter 3) are among the least-dense materials on Earth, with only a tiny amount of solid per unit volume. The bulk density of a material often provides a good indication of its insulative value, but there are limits to the usefulness of the value. The important factor—that of how well the air is *protected* from invasion by wind and water—is more or less ignored in the bulk density calculation.

It should be noted here that the weight of a fabric is not the same thing as its bulk density. The term, weight is a fabric descriptor that allows garment manufacturers to identify one of the qualities of fabrics they are selecting. It is used to express the weight of a specific *area* of a fabric and is generally stated in ounces per square yard (grams per square meter). A garment manufacturer might choose a 5 oz (141.7 g) version of a weave for one design and a 7 oz (198.4 g) fabric for another. Bulk density is the weight per *unit volume* of a specific fabric.

RESILIENCE

It is not sufficient enough that fibers used in thermally protective clothing have the capacity to entrap air when they are formed into a fabric. They must be able to *retain* that capacity when a garment is being worn. For this reason, the *resilience* of a fiber—its ability to return to its original shape when distorted—is extremely important. This resilience must remain through all of the conditions that affect end use. If it is affected by extreme heat or cold, rain, sunlight, chemicals, or any one of a host of hazards in the environment, the material may become compromised when it is most needed for protection.

One of the best examples of how resilience can affect the thermal conductivity of clothing is shown in Figure 5.9. It shows what happens to down-filled pads when they become wet. Down-filled clothing and sleeping bags can be extremely warm, but since rain is a likely part of life in the outdoors, the fact that down pods absorb water and collapse when wet shows how a change in resilience can be critical to thermal protection. It is left to the designer, then, to choose a more appropriate fiber (i.e., one that does not collapse when wet) *or* to protect down from water. In other words, in order to build the most thermally protective clothing, designers need to find a way to build a barrier between fibers and fabrics and the conditions that make them less effective.

FIGURE 5.9 (A) Two 6 inch (15.24 cm) stacks of pads of down (left) and fiberfill (right) after being soaked with water; (B) thickness of stacks after 10 minutes of tumble drying at 160°F (71.1°C); (C) and (D) after 1 hour and 3 hours of tumble drying, respectively. *(E. I. DuPont de Nemours and Company)*

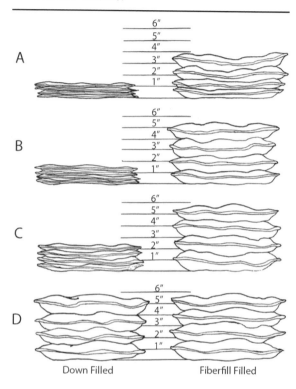

Down Filled   Fiberfill Filled

REACTIONS TO LIQUIDS

Water and other liquids play a significant role in heat loss, because they can not only destroy the effectiveness of insulations such as down and make them more conductive but also create the conditions needed for evaporative heat loss and rapid conduction of heat away from the body.

Different fibers, however, can create additional thermal effects with regard to liquids and moisture vapor. Wool provides an interesting example because it is often touted as being "warm while wet." Early bathing suits were made of wool because although they absorbed water readily, upon emerging from the water, wool suits released that water very slowly. Because wool held the water in its structure, it was not immediately evaporated from the suit surface and this prevented chilling.

There is another phenomenon that occurs with wool when humid conditions exist whether that humidity is inside clothing or in the environment. Although the exterior of wool fibers is **hydrophobic** (water repellent), their interior is **hygroscopic**, that is, wool has the ability to pick up large quantities of moisture from the humidity in the air. A number of researchers have noted something called the *heat sorption phenomenon* (sometimes called the heat of sorption of wool) that accounts for its ability to feel warm while wet (Renbourn 1971, 19; Gibson 2008, 2). When dry wool absorbs moisture vapor and that vapor reaches a low enough temperature to condense, heat is liberated. If you have trouble understanding this concept, think of it as the opposite of the phase change that occurs when sweat evaporates. Evaporation—the change from liquid to vapor—requires (absorbs) heat. Heat sorption involves a change from vapor to a liquid (i.e., condensation), which releases heat. Renbourn found the resulting heat to be negligible; however, Gibson's research showed that temperature changes due to the heat created by absorption of water vapor content in wool "can be as much as 15°C (~27° F.)" (2008, 3). This sorption phenomenon may contribute to the reason manufacturers have experimented with adding wool fibers into polyester knits and fleece fabrics for cold weather garments.

TREATMENTS FOR FIBERS AND FABRICS

Many of the ways that fibers and fabrics can be treated so that they incorporate more still air are covered in Chapter 3. The contributions of textured fibers, hollow core fibers, and those with a different cross-sectional shape have already been discussed. Surface treatments such as brushing and napping can help incorporate more stagnant air in materials. Microfibers can lead to a tremendous increase in the available surface area to which boundary air can cling. Manufacturers of microfiber insulation claim that equal warmth can be obtained with considerably thinner layers of microfibers than is true for traditional insulation fibers. Coatings and laminates that add waterproof, water-resistant, and permselective capacity to materials are of critical importance to many items of thermally protective clothing.

The surface texture and color of a fabric may greatly affect the degree to which all four methods of heat transfer can operate. Much of the ability of fleeced materials to protect still air, for example, lies in the way in which surface fibers extend from the fabric surface or are entangled. In materials such as synthetic fleece, more surface fibers are pulled out of the fabric and entangled, so that the fabric mimics the air-holding capabilities of animal fur. If one examines lamb's wool, part of its ability to prevent heat loss is due to the fact that its individual hairs, although initially growing out perpendicular to the hide, eventually bend and curl, intertwining to form many protected air pockets which are difficult to disrupt (Figure 5.10). By contrast, a pile fabric such as velvet, which has straight fibers that extend from its woven base, may have its air spaces invaded fairly easily by even a light wind. Many of the synthetic versions of natural materials such as lamb's wool use the basic model of curly, intertwined fibers to form a material that incorporates a great volume of still air.

Fabric Surfaces and Radiant Energy

Both color and texture are particularly important to the heat gain and loss through the transmission

FIGURE 5.10 The structure of lamb's wool is such that the curly fibers bend and intertwine in ways that preserve natural air spaces.

of radiant energy. When radiant energy strikes a fabric, some of it will probably be *reflected* or bounced back out toward the environment (Figure 5.11). Some will be *absorbed* by the fabric and subsequently *emitted* (radiated out from) the fabric either toward the body or out toward the environment. Some of the energy will miss the fibers altogether and be *transmitted* directly through the fabric interstices to whatever lies beneath. Once absorbed, it may be emitted through either face of the fabric.

FIGURE 5.11 Radiant energy can be (A) reflected; (B) absorbed; or (C) transmitted directly through the interstices between the yarns of a fabric. (D) Once absorbed, it may be emitted through either face of the fabric.

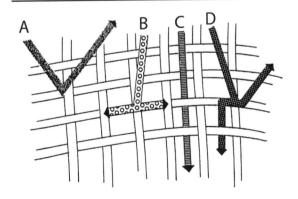

Fabrics that absorb radiant energy need to be good emitters if they are to pass it toward the body efficiently and poor emitters if they are to keep the heat from adding to the warmth of the body. An object's ability to emit heat is called its **emissivity**. The different temperature settings suggested for baking in glass or metal pans provides a good example of emissivity. Because glass has a higher emissivity, the temperatures given for baking a cake in glass pans are generally about 25°F (14°C) lower than those for the same cake baked in a metal pan. Even though metal would conduct heat more rapidly toward a cake and convected heat would reach the surface of cakes in either pan equally, the fact that the radiant energy reaching the pans are emitted so much more fully toward the cake by glass than by metal means that a lower oven temperature is needed for glass pans. This is another example of the importance of looking at the transmission of heat by all four methods in analyzing the thermal balance of any situation.

The beginning of this chapter included an introduction to short-wavelength (ultraviolet) radiation and long-wavelength (infrared) radiation. (See Energy Basics 5.1 Figure A) Each interacts with textile fabrics differently. For short-wavelength radiation, color is a critical factor. In general, black or darker colors absorb the shorter wavelengths of radiant energy and white or lighter colors reflect them. So, when one is standing in the sunlight, wearing white or lighter colors could help reflect radiant energy and keep one cooler. However, in the case of textiles, texture is as important as color. The effect of color may not be as great or as precise for textiles as it is, for example, for rigid housing materials. Since textiles are flexible and textured, they create their own contours and shadows when they are worn. Although a smooth, light-colored roof on a house or automobile may reflect radiant energy directly back to the environment, a light-colored drapable fabric may reflect light rays in a number of directions, including adjacent folds on the fabric surface.

Although certain dyes and chemical finishes may block the transmission of infrared rays, color itself does *not* contribute to heat transfer through long-wavelength or infrared radiation. Since infrared radiation is emitted by objects at lower temperatures that are outside the wavelength range needed to produce visible light, the transfer of infrared radiation takes place whether an object is in a light or dark environment. There needs only to be one surface warmer or colder than any other. The warmest object(s) will send infrared rays toward all colder objects in a system until they are of equal temperature.

Aluminized Fabrics

The basics of adding coatings to fabrics are covered in Chapter 3. Coating a fabric with a metallic finish increases its ability to reflect both short- *and* long-wavelength radiant energy. A variety of metals may be used as coatings, but because aluminum is frequently used for high-heat protective clothing, it is the focus of this section.

It is important to remember that while aluminizing a material greatly increases its ability to reflect radiant energy, heat transfer by conduction may greatly increase because of metal's higher conductivity. Many aluminized coatings are placed on nonconductive fabric or film bases to prevent conduction from occurring. For example, the so-called space blankets used by campers are composite fabric structures that have an aluminized face and a plastic face. The aluminized face is placed toward the body when cold, so that the radiant energy emitted by the body is reflected back toward the skin surface. In warm weather, the aluminized face is placed away from the body in order to reflect environmental heat away from the skin surface. In both cases, the plastic face prevents heat from being conducted through to the other side of the material. Some nonconductive materials are coated with aluminum on both sides so that exchange of radiant energy given off by either source is minimized.

Because of its conductivity, there is less value in having aluminized materials lie directly on the skin surface. Generally, they are separated from the body and from each other by **spacers**. Spacers create an insulative air layer, which inhibits conduction. The density of a spacer between reflective materials is critical. Breckenridge and Goldman found that interspersing reflective layers with layers of low-density batts—what they called look-through spacers—could raise the insulative value of a clothing system by as much as 50 percent (1977, 197–198). Since radiant heat exchange cannot occur through dense fabrics, interspersing aluminized layers with layers of dense fabric has little or no effect on the system's ability to protect the wearer against radiant heat loss.

Aluminized materials have several drawbacks that, for many years, limited their use in cold weather clothing. First, some are extremely noisy. While they can be extremely effective in the cold weather experienced by winter hunters, for example, any movement in clothing made of some aluminized materials could be heard from some distance and thus would alert their prey.

Second, since the most effective aluminized materials are those that involve a film or a solid coating of some sort, the impermeability of aluminized materials often leads to the buildup of body moisture within a clothing system. This is one reason why these types of aluminized materials have not been prevalent in everyday clothing. Instead, they tend to be used in specialized industrial or fire-fighting garments worn for protection against extreme levels of heat. Newer technologies have resulted in processes that allow aluminized materials to be quieter and have more porosity than had been possible in the past. For example, aluminized Mylar may be quilted to thin layers of fiberfill or sheets of aluminized materials may be perforated by another means before being put in a fabric layering system (Figure 5.12). The stitch holes and perforations allow the material to be both porous to moisture and more flexible. Processes that allow the deposit of aluminum on fibers and leave fabric interstices open have also been developed. These also allow aluminized finishes to be less stiff and less of a barrier to vapor transport. In addition, aluminum coated yarns may be knitted or woven into fabrics and these leave interstices between the yarns.

Another approach to aluminizing fabrics was developed by Columbia Sportswear®. They designed a lining composed of aluminized reflective dots covering 35 percent of the fabric surface with the rest of the fabric surface available to breathe. This fabric is very drapable and soft and can be used in a variety of garments and accessories such as gloves and boots to reflect body heat back toward the wearer.

FIGURE 5.12 An aluminized material quilted with spacers to add still air and prevent conduction between layers. Stitch holes perforate the aluminized films so that air and water vapor can pass through.

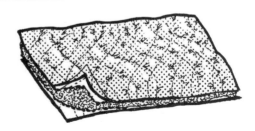

The texture of aluminized materials is still of concern with regard to their reflective abilities. As was mentioned with regard to color, the more textured a surface is, the less it can perfectly reflect radiant energy. In this regard, an aluminum film or foil laminated to a base fabric will probably be a better reflector of radiant energy than a fabric woven with aluminum-coated yarns. This is of particular importance for short-wavelength radiation (i.e., that in the visible range). In addition, dirt and oils may affect the reflective capacity of aluminized materials.

Clothing Systems for Thermal Protection

It is relatively straightforward to keep an inanimate object at a constant temperature. However, the human body is constantly changing in its level of heat production and varying its metabolic rate. The environment also changes constantly in temperature, humidity, amount of sunlight and precipitation, and so on. These factors and the ways in which individuals combine clothing items and wear them all interact to create a constantly changing thermal balance. Fourt and Hollies provide an excellent description of some of these interactions:

> It is important to realize that the clothing is not just a passive cover for the skin, but that it interacts with and modifies the heat regulating function of the skin and has effects which are modified by body movement. Some of this interaction is automatic, derived from the physical properties of the clothing materials and their spacing around the body; the larger scale interactions, however, arise from conscious choice of amount and kind of clothing, and mode of wearing, especially how the clothing is closed up or left open and loose. (1969, 37)

Another way of stating this is to say that clothing forms the most immediate environment of the body. To successfully design this environment, one must take into account the constant changes that occur in the body and the outer environment as clothing attempts to provide a buffer between them.

To choose a thermally protective clothing ensemble for a particular situation, it may be helpful to think about the manner in which each method of heat transfer operates in the larger environment. For example, if one looks at the function of radiant heat transfer in the desert and tropics, one finds two very different environmental conditions even when both are at similar air temperatures and the sun may be shining in both. In the desert, there is virtually no natural protection from the sun, so radiant heat gain is significant. The vegetation in the tropics often prevents the radiant energy of sunlight from reaching the skin surface, so it is less of a factor there. Radiation is not the only form of heat transfer, however. If one looks at the effects of evaporation on each of these environments, it is clear that the extremely humid air in the tropics prevents evaporation from being very effective, while the dry air of the desert can allow significant heat loss by evaporation. Because the sources of heat gain and heat loss are different in each situation, the clothing ensembles worn in the desert and the tropics may be quite different. In the desert, it is best to have materials and designs that provide maximum coverage for protection from radiation yet allow air to flow through the system for maximum evaporative cooling. In the tropics, where direct heat gain from solar radiation is not as much of a factor, it is better to have minimum coverage to allow maximum heat loss directly from the skin through both radiation and evaporation.

The manner of heat transfer becomes even more critical in decisions about clothing design for unusual environments such as outer space. On Earth, a great proportion of heat exchange between an individual and the environment is due to convection. Because there is no air or atmosphere through which convection can take place in space, radiation and conduction become the major sources of heat transfer. Without atmosphere to filter the effects of radiation, radiant heat gain and loss are considerably more significant than on Earth. For this reason, most garments for activities outside a spacecraft include many layers of aluminized materials. Conduction is particularly critical for the parts of the body that may touch metal objects in the space environment; thus, special heat protection is often needed for the hands and feet. Gloves may contain nonflammable and nonconductive materials on the palmar surface and boots make use of nonconductive materials and spacers. The factors that determine how heat is gained and lost in any environment are critical for a designer to understand in order to develop basic design criteria for protective clothing.

KEEPING WARM

The following sections offer practical suggestions for using clothing to adjust to cold environments. They are based on the processes of heat transfer in the environment, the thermal functions of the body and the thermal resistance of materials. What has been covered thus far about materials for thermal protection can be linked to the basics of textiles in Chapter 3 to provide ideas about the kinds of fibers and fabrics that incorporate many tiny protective spaces for air: wool, down, textured manufactured fibers, pile fabrics such as furs and terry cloth, brushed ones such as fleece, foams, fiberfills, and so on. Often, a thick, lightweight (low bulk density) fabric is an excellent insulator because it is primarily air. The air in all of these materials, however, must be in relatively small pockets where it is

protected from movement. A large air-filled pocket can be subject to convective currents that could actually promote heat loss.

Among the most important concepts to remember when designing an ensemble to keep warm are (1) building up layers of protected air spaces, (2) protecting air spaces in insulation from wind and water, (3) insulating the body core, and (4) providing ventilation features to avoid overheating.

Layering Garments

Layering garments is a sensible approach to dressing for warmth for several reasons. First, it allows the opportunity to put on and shed layers of clothing as thermal balance changes due to temperature changes of the body or the environment. Second, it allows a more effective buildup of air spaces in the clothing system. Building up several thin layers may be more effective than wearing a single thick layer because of the air spaces between the fabric layers (i.e., the boundary air that clings to each surface of a fabric). One caution is that the layers must be large enough to fit over one another so that the insulation offered by the lower layers is not compressed. If a sweater is squeezed into the sleeve of a down jacket, for example, air spaces in both may be squeezed out. In this case, layering may destroy more insulation than it creates. People often make this mistake with socks, squeezing thick socks into fitted boots. This makes the entire system more conductive and also may make the foot colder because the tightness tends to cut off circulation.

Layering also allows garments with different functions to be used in combination. When wind and water threaten to upset the thermal balance of an ensemble, a windproof or waterproof cover can be donned. The number of layers needed and the thickness of each will vary a great deal with the physical activity of an individual and the body's basal metabolic rate. A jogger might be quite comfortable running in a t-shirt and shorts in 30°F (−1.1°C) weather, whereas someone else might not be comfortable sitting in the same outfit unless the outside temperature was about 80°F (26.7°C).

When putting together an ensemble for cold weather, it is important to look for every area where there are gaps between the edges of the layers or places where thickness is decreased because these are potential sources of heat loss. Several solutions to maintaining thickness in insulated clothing can be found in the methods used to manufacture quilted sleeping bags. Figure 5.13A shows a cross section of a quilted, down-filled item with its resulting decrease in insulation (and thus, a cold spot) that occurs at each stitching line. The same types of cold spots occur at seam lines of garments if quilting is done before garment construction. Figure 5.13B–E show several methods of eliminating the cold spots created by quilting. A two-layer jacket can have quilting lines sewn in alternating positions on the outer jacket and lining (5.13B). The methods shown in 5.13C–E use baffles created by sewing fabric strips between the outer layer and the lining so that no thin areas occur. These techniques are common in sleeping bags but in clothing are reserved for items that will be worn in extremely cold weather because their construction is expensive and they almost completely insulate an individual from the environment. Because most insulated garments are subjected to stress and strain as the body moves, it is easy for insulation materials to be deformed or displaced, resulting in cold spots where the insulation material is no longer creating an air space. For this reason, the resilience of insulation—the ability of what fills these spaces provided by the quilting technique to retain its loft—is, of course,

also critical. Design Solutions 5.1 illustrates another approach: inflation as a method of keeping spaces open.

Protecting Layers from Wind and Water

There are two basic ways to protect the air spaces in insulation within a garment from being invaded by wind and water. One is to develop a waterproof but breathable system; the other is to block all

FIGURE 5.13 Quilting methods that prevent cold spots. (A) a cross section of a quilted material showing cold spots; (B) offsetting quilting in a lining and an outer layer; (C) straight box-tube quilting; (D) box-tube quilting filled (example at right shows how this method maintains its thickness even when slanted); (E) slanted box-tube quilting.

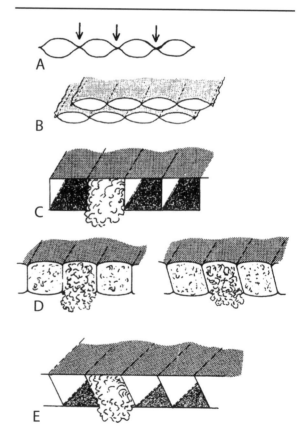

Design Solutions 5.1: Inflation: Varying the Depth of the Air Layer

Inflation technology has the potential to vary the air spaces in clothing layers as environmental conditions change. In addition to its potential for infinite variability in depth of insulation, it can greatly reduce bulk and weight for people in situations where both are critical factors: backpacking, motorcycling, traveling in space, or even when simply packing a vacation suitcase with items that need to span a variety of climatic conditions.

Figure A shows a sleeping bag that makes use of inflation as a means of providing a variable amount of still air in a down-filled product. It is a structure that can be inflated by hand or with a foot pump to any one of a variety of thicknesses. The lower (mattress) portion is inflated to provide a comfortable, cushioned surface that is insulated from the ground. The upper (blanket) portion is inflated to provide the desired amount of thermal protection from the environment. The compressibility of down makes it possible for the blanket to protect the occupant from a wide range of temperatures. A flat blanket (no inflation, with the

FIGURE B Inflatable hiking jacket. A hollow heel in the hiking boot contains an air chamber that opens and closes with each step, pumping air into or out of the jacket. *(Design: Robert Todd O'Neal)*

down fully compressed) might be used for a 70°F (21.1°C) environment while fully inflating it will fluff the down to incorporate air spaces that, combined with the waterproof, air-tight cover, will protect the occupant to –40°F (–40°C).

Figure B shows a hiking jacket based on a similar concept. This inflatable jacket is attached to a plenum in the hollow heel of a hiking boot by a tube that runs from the pocket of the jacket, down the pant leg, and into the boot. As the hiker climbs up a mountain and the air becomes cooler, each step pumps a little more air into the jacket, increasing the air spaces within it. When hiking down the mountain or into warmer weather, a deflation valve on the boot can be activated so that each step pumps air *out* of the jacket. The result is decreased air spaces and a thinner, less insulative jacket.

FIGURE A Inflatable down-filled sleeping bag. Inflating and deflating the bag allows thermal comfort at a wide variety of temperatures. *(Design: Richard Malcolm)*

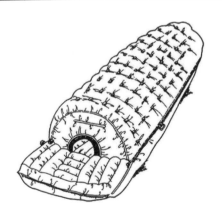

airflow and liquid transport with the use of waterproof materials. Each method is used in specific environmental conditions and may need to be chosen according to individual needs and activities under those conditions. Waterproof and water-resistant finishes, coatings, and laminates were discussed in Chapter 3. These may have a significant influence on the thermal protection offered by a clothing ensemble.

Water may get into insulation from the outside or the inside face of a garment. Although a waterproof cover could be added to the outside of a garment to prevent rain from soaking through to the insulation, it would introduce another problem: Because the body is constantly liberating insensible perspiration, an escape route for that moisture is blocked when a waterproof layer is added to an ensemble. If the body becomes overheated and sweats, that moisture is also prevented from escaping. Once sweat migrates into clothing layers and moisture starts to fill the air spaces in insulation, the garment will no longer provide thermal protection. The entire structure will become much more conductive and in many cases, less resilient.

Breathable Systems

There are several ways to develop a breathable system that deters rain or other environmental moisture from entering a garment. One is to use a water-repellent rather than a waterproof fabric. Since most water rolls off the surface of a water-repellent fabric, unless a heavy downpour occurs, the water is not likely to enter the insulation layer beyond. At the same time, water-repellent fabrics breathe so that any water vapor on the skin surface can pass outward toward the environment.

Another solution is to use two layers of moderately wind-resistant/water-resistant material with a thin spacer between them rather than one layer of totally impenetrable material. The theory behind this system is that the first layer will cut down on the force of wind or water to such an extent that it will not possess the energy needed to pass through the second layer.

A third solution is to use a microporous material that is waterproof yet allows air and vapor to pass through. Any of the microporous treatments discussed in Chapter 3 could provide a breathable, waterproof cover for a system of insulation. It is important to remember that microporous materials only allow moist *vapor* to pass through. Breathable systems that include them need provisions for ventilation so that *drops* of moisture do not enter the system or accumulate from within the system (e.g., through excessive sweating) because these will not pass through the micropores.

The choice of some form of protection from liquids for the outer layer of a garment solves only half the problem. It is important that the inner layers support vapor transport outward from the skin. Materials that wick moisture provide an excellent beginning for this. (See Chapter 3, "Fiber Interactions with Moisture.")

Sometimes waterproof materials are part of garments used for flotation rather than simply to exclude rain and other forms of moisture. Design Solutions 5.2 discusses a unique design planned to maintain breathability in a flotation garment.

Vapor Barrier Systems

Vapor barrier systems (often referred to as vapor barrier insulation or VBI) do not make the same attempt to move moisture through the clothing system. They completely surround insulation with a waterproof and windproof cover. This means that moisture cannot enter the insulation from the outside or the inside of the garment. A good example of a vapor barrier system is the one used by many mothers as they cover their children's feet with plastic bags before putting them into fleece-lined

Design Solutions 5.2: A Survival Suit for Pilots

Individuals often need to be dressed to prepare for emergencies while remaining comfortable during regular activities. Figure A and B illustrates an inflatable thermal barrier designed as part of a survival system for U.S. Navy pilots who may have to eject from a plane over water. Since there is usually not enough time for a pilot to don an emergency suit before ejecting, the situation calls for a garment that can be worn at all times. Therefore, the suit must allow ventilation in the aircraft, which can become quite warm, yet be highly insulative if a pilot must enter the water. The thermal barrier shown is made of two layers of nylon fused together to form a **bladder** (a form that holds air or water.) The entire garment is perforated with large ventilation holes, and the circumference of each hole is firmly fused so that no air can escape from the bladder itself. That is, when the pilot inflates the suit, it inflates in the spaces around the holes, but the holes are cut through the sealed portions of the suit like doughnut holes, so that they always remain open for airflow (Figure B). This barrier is part of a clothing system and is worn under several other items. The layer directly over it is a waterproof, microporous suit with rubberized cuffs and neckband. This suit keeps water out of the inner layers while the wearer is in the water, but is breathable when the pilot is in the air. While in the cockpit, the thermal barrier is not inflated, and it provides ventilation through many large air holes in its surface. When the thermal barrier is inflated, it increases the thickness of the whole system. In

addition, inflation causes it to hug the body, preventing air from flowing next to the skin surface. The inflated suit also provides some buoyancy.

FIGURES A AND B (A) Inflatable thermal barrier placed under a waterproof, breathable layer in a survival system for navy pilots; (B) detail of construction of holes in the suit.

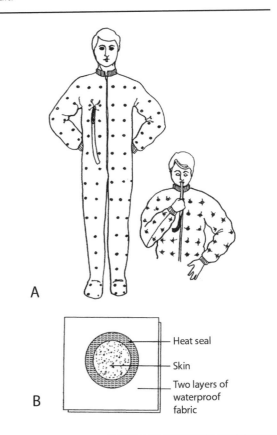

Heat seal

Skin

Two layers of waterproof fabric

A

B

rubber boots on a snowy day. The plastic on the inside prevents perspiration from the foot from reaching the fleece, and the waterproof cover (i.e., the rubber on the outside of the boot) prevents environmental moisture from reaching the fleece.

A vapor barrier not only protects insulation but solves the problem of heat loss resulting from the evaporation of insensible perspiration as well. The body only produces insensible perspiration to keep the skin moist. Once the skin reaches the proper humidity level, production shuts down. In fact, the skin is capable of reabsorbing excess moisture from insensible perspiration when the body is enclosed in a vapor barrier system. This means that a vapor barrier garment should not feel uncomfortably wet against the skin unless sweating begins. If the body begins to overheat, an individual should open zippers, remove clothing layers, or employ other techniques for ventilating the garment so that sweating does not take place.

A person's preference for breathable or vapor barrier insulation will depend on the temperature, the level of activity, the body part being protected, and the degree of ventilation or variability of insulation that can be achieved in a particular ensemble. Vapor barrier systems are not generally recommended for temperatures above 40°F (4.4°C.) and they are more frequently used by people who are less active. Duck hunters, for example, who sit motionless for hours in water-filled bogs in cold weather often prefer vapor barrier systems. If an individual is very active and likely to build up a sweat, a breathable system may be a better choice. Vapor barrier clothing would probably be warmer, but unless clothing is ventilated well, it may become uncomfortably wet. As discussed in the next section, in some diving ensembles, where being wet is part of the activity, water is actually used as part of the system for thermal balance.

Regardless of the choice made, that choice must be followed through in the selection of *all* fabric layers that cover a particular body part. It is not possible to create a combination system; a garment that includes a vapor barrier somewhere in its layering system is not breathable. Placing a microporous fabric inside two layers of vapor barrier to allow a system to breathe is useless because no air or water vapor can get to it through the vapor barriers. It *is* possible, however, to vary systems within an *ensemble* (e.g., to combine a breathable jacket and pants with vapor barrier gloves and boots). Individuals who have poor circulation in the extremities, for example, may choose to use vapor barrier gloves and boots even though they choose a breathable system for the rest of the body.

Diving Suits

Diving suits provide an excellent example of the ways in which clothing can prevent body heat from escaping when the body is surrounded by water. As mentioned earlier in this chapter, the convective heat loss in water is far greater than that in air because of the conductivity of water. It *is* possible to use the conductivity of water to one's advantage for protection from the cold. Recreational divers generally wear something called a **wetsuit** for thermal protection (Figure 5.14). Wetsuits are made of closed-cell foam, usually made of a synthetic

FIGURE 5.14 A typical scuba diving wetsuit made of closed-cell neoprene.

rubber called neoprene. They allow a thin layer of water to flow in between the inside of the suit and the skin as the diver submerges in the water. Heat from the diver's body soon heats this thin layer of water and the closed-cell foam of the suit protects that heat from escaping.

In order for the water inside the suit to continue to conduct heat back toward the skin surface, the suit must be extremely form fitted and not allow additional water to enter and circulate. Many measurements are taken for custom suits so that they fit every curve of the body closely. Overlaps on garment parts are planned so that water streams past, not into, the opening as the diver swims forward (e.g., the jacket is lapped over the pants). A custom-made suit may have padding that fills in body indentations (such as the one created by the spine) so that water cannot flow easily into the suit and begin to circulate.

Researchers at the U.S. Army Soldier Systems Center have experimented with a so-called adaptable skin—a composite material that incorporates a gel that can absorb water (U.S. Army SBCCOM "Adaptable Skin"). The gel in this skin is thermally sensitive, so the material is added to a neoprene wetsuit in areas where it can expand to block water flow when the diver's body temperatures drop below a certain level. When the diver's body heats up, the gel contracts and allows freer water flow through the suit.

Wetsuits come in a variety of thicknesses, sold for different water temperatures. Typical suits for temperate climates are sold in ¼ inch or 6 mm versions although suits as thin as 1 mm (.04 in) may be sold for diving in the tropics or 80°F (26.7°C) and above water. Suits and accessories (boots, gloves, etc.) for extreme cold water diving can be as thick as ⅝ inch (15.88 mm).

Drysuits are more typically used for extreme cold water diving. As their name indicates, they do not allow the entry of water for warmth. Instead, they completely exclude water in order to prevent convection from carrying off body heat. Most are made of neoprene or natural rubber, which may be either in the form of a film or a closed-cell foam. Neoprene foam suits often have a layer of knit nylon bonded to their inner and outer surfaces to provide abrasion resistance and ease of donning. To maintain a complete exclusion of water, the pieces of these suits are fused or glued together and then stitched, usually with a blind stitch that only penetrates the nylon on the surface of the material. Suits may also be made of nylon coated with a waterproof backing, such as urethane, or laminated suits of butyl rubber coated on both sides with nylon. Suits of these materials may often be heat sealed (see Chapter 9). Because some of these materials may not have a lot of stretch, these suits may be cut more generously to allow movement.

Figure 5.15 shows several examples of drysuits. The diver generally wears a layer of thermal underwear under the suit. Foam neoprene suits incorporate a lot of air, and are thus rather buoyant and warm at the surface but air spaces in the foam are flattened at lower depths. Air may be blown in to prevent the suit from squeezing the skin and to provide additional insulation as the diver descends and pressure increases.

All of the openings and edges are designed to be impermeable so that no water can enter and destroy the insulating air spaces of a drysuit. Waterproof zippers are used. (See "Impermeability" in Chapter 9.) Boots may be permanently sealed to the suit or attached with seals at the ankle. Neck and wrist seals are most commonly made of latex rubber and designed to stretch relatively tightly around the neck and wrists. If wrist seals are damaged, it is possible to replace them using a rigid ring similar to

FIGURE 5.15 Drysuits for scuba diving. (A) A neoprene suit with a waterproof entry zipper that zips from center back between the legs to mid-center front; (B) a natural rubber suit with entry through a vertical zipper that extends over the head; (C) a natural rubber suit with access provided by a long horizontal zipper in the shoulder blade area. *(B and C based on suits formerly produced for Viking USA.)*

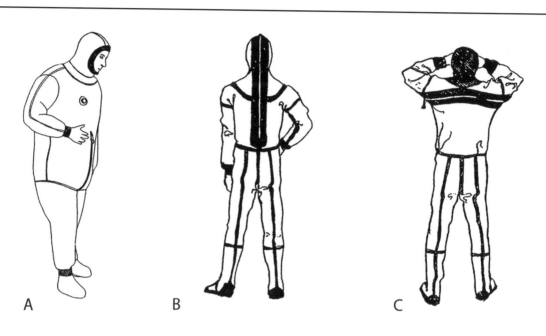

A   B   C

those used on chemical/biological (C/B) protective suits. (See Figure 7.15.)

Figure 5.15 shows three configurations of openings for suit entry. There are also suits that have diagonal zippers that provide a long opening across the suit front much like the C/B suit in Figure 7.16A. The bulk of some drysuits is such that some divers are more comfortable supporting the lower half with interior suspenders and tethering suits at the ankles with ankle straps.

Protecting the Core

Because blood flow to the body core is relatively constant regardless of core temperature, it is even more important that the core be well insulated in cold conditions to prevent excess heat loss. Adding a layer of insulation to a clothing ensemble in the area of the body core (the head, neck, and torso) can significantly decrease the amount of heat lost from the core. A hat, scarf, t-shirt, or even a thin camisole can add considerable warmth. If core warmth can be increased to the point where the body has excess heat, this can override peripheral vasoconstriction and warm the extremities even in cold temperatures. Insulating the core to the point where excess heat builds up and triggers vasodilation in the extremities can allow the designer to minimize insulation where more mobility is needed (Figure 5.16). This is the origin of the adage, "If your feet are cold, put on your hat." It is important to note here that individual conditions, such as circulation impairments, hormonal imbalances, and countercurrent heat exchange, can play

FIGURE 5.16 An ensemble that provides extra protection for the body core.

protection for the core. The beavertail feature is still popular today, and many protective items for those working in and around cold water have been based on the concepts in the U-Vic jacket.

Functional Distribution of Insulation

Many designs for cold weather are based on the principle of *functional distribution of insulation*. This principle involves two concepts: Focus on placing insulation over areas where the greatest heat transfer to the environment could occur, and, whenever possible, place thick insulation so that it does not interfere with movement. Designs such as those shown in Figures 5.16 and 5.17 and

FIGURE 5.17 The U-Vic Thermofloat®.

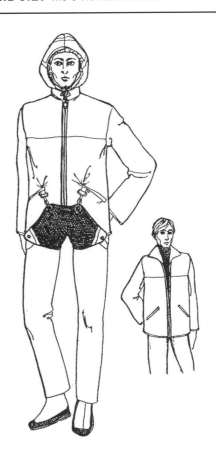

a large role in determining the degree to which the extremities benefit from warming the core.

Flotation vests and other protective garments for many sports activities cover major portions of the core. This can be a benefit in cold weather and a curse in hot weather. Figure 5.17 shows a jacket designed to conserve the body heat of individuals exposed to water. The Mustang Survival U-Vic Thermofloat® life jacket was developed by scientists from the University of Victoria. Since they found the groin to be a major area of heat loss from the core, they designed a hidden rear flap, sometimes called a beavertail, of closed-cell foam that can be released and wrapped through the legs to the front, where it is attached by hooks to form protective shorts. When not in use, the beavertail could be fastened to the inside of the back of the jacket. This convertible feature provided extra thermal protection for the trunk and upper leg regions, areas of high heat loss during cold stress. The jacket hood and the flotation materials around the torso provide additional in Anatomy and Design 5.1 are examples of this principle. Insulation is placed over the core (which stores a lot of heat) or over large blood vessels close to the skin surface. Areas around the joints have lighter coverage to allow more freedom of movement.

This idea of distributing insulation in areas where it will have the greatest effect may also be used in designing coverings for individual body parts. For example, more insulation may be placed over the major veins on the hands and feet so that less heat can be carried away from the skin surface of the extremities. (See Anatomy and Design 5.1.) Adding extra insulation in these areas on a glove can allow fingers to be covered more lightly and thus be freer to move.

The concepts behind functional distribution of insulation may also be considered when planning auxiliary heating and cooling. If it is practical, placing heated wires or cooling tubing over major vascular networks near the skin surface may allow designers to concentrate the placement of these items rather than having to distribute them over the whole body. The composition of body tissues is a partner with blood flow when it comes to heat loss. Koscheyev et al., believe that large muscular areas that have more complex vascular networks with high circulation and a high capacity for heat storage, such as the torso, thighs, and calves, are optimal locations for heat transfer (2006, 480).

Providing Ventilation

While it may seem contradictory, keeping cool is sometimes a critical part of keeping warm. Features in clothing that can be opened to provide airflow are critical to ensembles for keeping warm because they allow excess body heat to pass off into the environment and thus keep the sweating cycle from beginning.

Effective ventilation of excess body heat depends on allowing access to the skin surface or the inner layers of clothing so that heat can be radiated, convected, or conducted away. In extreme cold, however, it is not always wise to expose the skin surface directly to the environment, especially if the skin surface is moist. The loss of heat can be too rapid, and cold injury, including frostbite, can occur. Cooling may be more safely achieved by exposing one of the inner layers of clothing to the environment so that the inner environment of the ensemble is cooled and the body can dissipate heat more gradually.

Keep in mind the fact that heat rises. For the upper body, this means that if an individual begins to feel warm, the head should be partially uncovered first; then the neck area and upper front or back opening of a garment should be loosened. This will provide a space for the **chimney effect** (the rising of warm air) to take place. Loosening the wrist areas of sleeves, even though they are not uppermost, may help ventilate the arms because the pumping motion of the arms during walking or running can force the air to move out of the sleeve. Cunningham (1972, 12) suggests that although loosening the cuffs of pants can provide the same kind of ventilation for the legs this is not always a practical solution. When hiking in deep snow, for example, this could compromise the insulation of the whole system by allowing water to enter insulation at the cuffs and wick its way up the inside of the garment. He discusses a method whereby ventilating zippers are placed on the side seams of the pants so that they open from just below the waist downward. This allows a hiker to open the zippers downward to ventilate large areas above the snow depth. If pants with suspenders or loose-waisted overalls are worn, they can even provide ventilation for the entire torso by allowing cool air to enter low and pass upward through a loosened neckline. The method of ventilation Cunningham describes emphasizes again the importance of

Anatomy and Design 5.1: The Vascular System and Glove Design

The hands and feet can be sources of great heat loss because they have such large surface areas, are composed of relatively dense tissues with blood vessels close to the surface and, in the case of the hands, are the most likely body areas to be exposed to conduction through direct contact with the environment. The latter factor also makes them extremely vulnerable to injury from heat gain in high heat environments.

Since blood flow is the key to heat transfer, it is important to know where the major blood vessels occur in any body part in order to design clothing that either insulates effectively or allows maximum heat loss. If one examines the major blood vessels of the hand, for example, it is easy to see that the largest arteries—the vessels that carry warm blood out from the core to the extremities—occur on the back of the hand. The radial and ulnar arteries come down the arm along the bones of the same names and form two loops just below the wrist (Figure A). One loop is near the surface of the hand and the other runs more deeply into the palm. These are the *superficial palmar arch* and the *deep palmar arch*. Additional arteries, the *palmar digital arteries*, run from the superficial palmar arch along each of the metacarpals branching out to run down the sides of each of the phalanges (Figure A). (See Sidebar 2.1 in Chapter 2 for a discussion of the bones of the hand.)

The location of these large veins is of great importance for glove design. Insulating the areas of the hand where these major heat radiators are located keeps heat from being released and lightly covering them or opening them up allows heat to pass off into the environment. The two items of handwear shown in Figures B and C illustrate the way in which this knowledge of the body's vascular system can be used. Figures B shows a three-finger mitten developed by the U.S. Army for soldiers in the Arctic. It has an extra layer of thick fur directly over the metacarpals where the arteries are closest to the skin surface. In addition, three of the fingers have been placed in one compartment so that heat is not lost where the arteries lie along the inside of these three phalanges. The index finger has been left

separate to allow more dexterity for some tasks.

Figure C shows a racing glove with a good deal of the glove cut away in the very area where the fur occurs in the Arctic mitten. This racing glove is worn in a warm environment primarily for grip on a steering wheel or bicycle handles, not for warmth. Leaving the open area over the large vessels in the region of the metacarpals allows body heat brought to the skin surface to be radiated and convected away. It allows cooling to occur directly from the skin surface.

Learning more about the vascular system in the body areas for which designs are intended is an important early step in helping designers to set design criteria.

FIGURES A, B, AND C Functional distribution of insulation. (A) Anterior view of the vascular system of the lower arm and hand; (B) arctic glove with thick insulating fur over major vessels on the back of the hand; (C) racing glove with the major heat radiating surface on the back of the hand open.

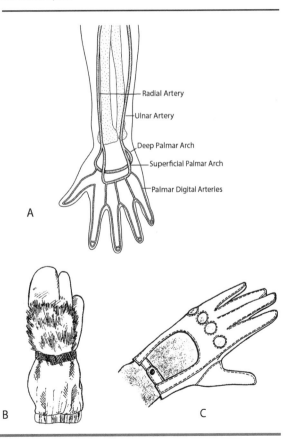

A

B

C

evaluating each environment and activity to see how one can make best practical use of thermal theory.

One method of ventilating the body is to provide a spacer between the skin and the first layer of clothing. The ventilating net underwear shown in Figure 5.18A provides a ⅛ inch (0.32 cm) space in which body heat and water vapor can travel upward to pass out of a garment opening such as a neckline. The *ladder* **net** fabric shown in Figure 5.18B is structured to increase the ease of airflow. Vertical channels are created in the ladder net by thick vertical ribs in the fabric structure, and these are placed so that they will lie vertically on the body. If, while wearing either of these types of net underwear in an ensemble, an individual begins to feel warm, venting areas (cuffs, necklines, waistlines of jackets, etc.) can be opened, and heat and water vapor from the skin surface have a space through which they can travel and pass off into the environment. This action will prevent overheating with its subsequent sweating and wetting of insulation. Ventilation is aided if the layers of clothing placed over the net

underwear are relatively loose so that the bellows action of clothing can circulate air freely as the body moves. If an individual becomes cold, the venting areas can be closed off so that the netting will help provide protected pockets of still air for insulation.

In thinking about moving air through a garment, it may be useful to consider the concept of lines of nonextension discussed in Chapter 2 (see Figure 2.26). The lines of nonextension mapped by Langer and Iberall show in which direction skin does *not* stretch during movement. Langer and Iberall both showed that extension or stretching is experienced in directions other than along these lines, with the greatest extension being found perpendicular to the lines of nonextension. When planning garment features that can be unzipped or opened in some way to provide ventilation, it makes sense to place them along the lines of nonextension so that movement will pull them open.

Two factors are critical to an understanding of ventilation:

1. Remember that heat travels from hot to cold regions. If allowed an opening to do so, heat will flow from the skin surface to the colder environment, taking with it any water vapor in the system as well. Body heat is the pump that moves vapor outward toward the environment. Conversely, if the environment is hotter than the body, the environment will send heat and moist vapor back through the system toward the body.

2. Ventilation requires both an ingress and egress for the air and often needs a stimulus to cause airflow through a garment. It is important that the openings that allow air to flow in and out of a garment are well placed so that body movement, activities, or the environment can be used to promote airflow.

FIGURE 5.18 (A) Ventilating net underwear; (B) ladder-net underwear fabric.

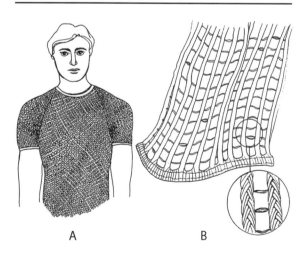

A   B

Ventilation may involve the **bellows effect** (air forced in or out of a garment by the pumping of the arms during movement) or positioning openings that will allow air movement created by both the body and activities such as cycling to be effectively used by a garment. Examples of ventilation techniques for specific end uses can be found throughout the text, for example, in Chapter 6 under "Keeping Cool in Impact-Protective Garments" or Chapter 7 under "Clean Room Clothing Design."

KEEPING COOL

The principles involved in keeping warm should have already provided some ideas about keeping cool. Some of the most important concepts to remember when dressing for hot weather include (1) choosing thin garments, (2) uncovering the core and the skin surface, (3) blocking radiant heat flow toward the body from the environment, (4) wearing loose clothing so that air can circulate around the body, and (5) in many situations, using nonconductive materials.

Wearing Thin Garments

In hot weather, it is important to wear thin garments for several reasons. Thin garments generally incorporate fewer insulative air spaces. They also tend to allow air and water vapor to pass more easily through the fabric structure. The thinness of its fabrics is probably the most important characteristic of a garment for hot weather. Any fabric, even mosquito netting, will have some effect on air movement, and thus on vapor transport as well. If wind is available to carry off warm air near the body surface, even the openness of a fabric's weave does not seem to make as much difference as its thinness, unless, of course, a fabric has been windproofed. Thin fabrics are particularly important for evaporative cooling. Even in the tropics,

where evaporative cooling is difficult to achieve because of the high humidity, thin garments of open-weave fabrics are recommended to allow the limited amount of evaporation possible to take place.

Since fabrics that trap air are favored in cold weather, those that do not trap air are favored in warm weather. Terry cloth, for example, though sold for beachwear because of its absorbency, is not a cool fabric. Most garments made of this fabric are intended for situations in which an individual wants to warm up (as after a swim). The material removes moisture from the skin surface and the loops in its pile surface trap a lot of air and create quite a good insulation.

A thin garment means just that. A thin fabric is only one aspect of a thin garment. Any area where fabric layers are built up—as they are at the collar, buttonhole plackets, pockets, and so on—has added thickness, and so it is logical to examine these areas in any clothing to be worn in warm weather. In work situations, tools and equipment carried on the body not only increase the thickness of the ensemble but also are impermeable. If it is possible, some sort of spacer should be placed under them, so they are lifted off the surface of the body.

Uncovering the Core and Skin Surface

In hot environments, it is important to uncover as much of the core and the skin surface as practical. This suggestion has practical limits not only because of modesty, but also because of other factors in the environment. For example, if the temperature is very hot and the sun is shining, it is possible to experience more radiant heat gain through bare skin than convective and evaporative heat loss through the skin surface. In high-temperature work environments, such as in firefighting or smelting, the danger of burns far outweighs the benefit of open areas over the core. There are other occupational hazards: workers who mix pesticides and athletes who need protective equipment may not find it safe to uncover the body core. However, whenever it is practical to incorporate large open spaces in a garment, this creates the potential for radiant, convective, and evaporative heat loss if the environment is cooler and drier than the skin surface.

Because heat rises, it is particularly important that the head remain uncovered or, at the very least, that head protection is lifted off the skin surface with a spacer. Many sports and industrial helmets utilize an inner suspension system that only touches the head in the hatband area. (See Figure 6.31.) The band lifts the helmet off the surface of the head so that air can flow around the head while the protection of the helmet shell stays in position.

Functional distribution of insulation also applies to individual garments for hot weather. Leaving necklines of garments open is important to dissipate heat not only because of the chimney effect but also because large blood vessels lie close to the surface there. Whenever possible, uncover the portions of individual body parts where large blood vessels are closest to the skin surface. The leather racing glove shown in Anatomy and Design 5.1 Figure C provides another example of how this idea applies to heat dissipation for individual body parts.

Blocking Radiant Heat Gain

On warm days when the sun is out in full force, an individual may actually find it cooler to wear clothing, if the right kind is worn, than to go without it. In a study of soldiers in the desert, where the sun is intense and its radiant energy unblocked by vegetation, it was found that nude men at rest absorbed 110–140 cal/hr more than clothed men (Newburgh 1949, 332). For desert clothing, extra

layers of fabric may be recommended for head coverings and the tops of the shoulders and feet, the body surfaces most directly exposed to the sun. Adding layers may seem to be in direct contradiction to the first two recommendations for keeping cool; however, in this situation, the extreme heat gain from radiation outweighs the possible heat loss from convection from these body areas. Since the entire desert terrain reflects radiant energy from the sun, most desert dwellers cover their bodies with loose, full-length garments to provide maximum protection from heat gain from radiation. This also helps avoid heat gain by convection when the environment is at a considerably higher temperature than the skin surface.

It is important to choose clothing that reflects radiant energy from any source away from the body. As discussed earlier in this chapter, when in the sun or another source of *visible* radiant energy, white or light-colored clothing tends to do this more effectively than dark-colored clothing. Also remember the difference between light and dark clothing may also be cut down considerably by wind. Although dark clothing may absorb radiant energy, if a wind is blowing, it is possible that the heat in the fabric may be convected away by the wind before it can be transferred from the outer surface of a garment to the body. Therefore, on a warm, sunny day, if a wind is blowing, it makes less difference whether light or dark clothing is worn.

It is particularly important to block radiant heat flow when extremes of temperature, such as those found in firefighting or some high-heat industrial jobs, are present. These situations generally require full body coverage, not only to prevent heat gain but also to prevent burns to the skin. Often the heat is so dangerous that thick, many-layered garments must be used to block heat flow toward the body.

For these environments, a flame-resistant fabric such as an aramid is generally used as the outside layer of a multilayer system. Outer fabrics may be aluminized to increase their ability to reflect radiant energy. (See examples in Figures 5.36 and 5.37.)

The space suit layers shown in Figure 5.19 illustrate another approach to solving the problems presented by extremes of radiant heat gain. The layers illustrated represent those used in the suit for the first moon landing. On the moon, temperatures range from –250°F (–122.1°C) to 330°F (165°C). As was mentioned earlier in this chapter, because there is no air or atmosphere on the moon's surface to filter the effects of the sun's rays, protection

from radiant heat transfer is of critical importance. The temperature variation of almost 600°F is due to the presence or absence of radiant energy. These differences in temperature may be experienced instantly as an astronaut steps out of the shade of the spacecraft into the sun. Many of the fabrics used in the outer garment of the Apollo moon suit (the Integrated Thermal Micrometeoroid Garment) were aluminized to provide protection from radiant heat gain and loss. There were five layers of aluminized Mylar film each separated by a thin, nonwoven Dacron® and two layers of aluminized Kapton® film that were laminated to Beta-Fiberglas® mesh. The aluminized Mylar® film layers were separated by the nonwoven Dacron so that heat would not be conducted between them. In addition, the Dacron layers inhibited the transfer of heat through any gases that might be trapped within the layers as the astronaut stepped out of the spacecraft. A Teflon®-coated Beta-Fiberglas fabric was used as the outermost layer. Fiberglas is non-flammable, and the Teflon coating gave the Fiberglas more abrasion resistance and flexibility. All of the fabrics were chosen for their ability to perform well in temperature extremes.

As designers learned more about what was needed to protect the body from the effects of outer space, subsequent versions of the so-called soft space suits contained fewer layers. The Shuttle Program suit, for example, had only seven layers in the thermal micrometeoroid garment. Until hard suits replaced them, layering systems continued to rely on the principle of multiple layers of aluminized materials separated by thin, nonconductive spacers and an outermost layer of a nonflammable material (Young 2009).

Wearing Loose Garments

Loose clothing allows air to circulate across the body surface. If there are sufficient loose openings,

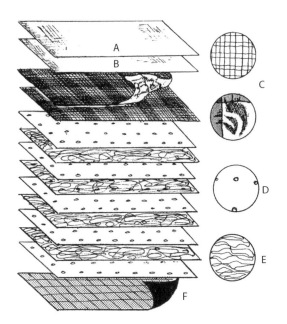

FIGURE 5.19 The fourteen-layer fabric system used for the Apollo II Integrated Thermal Micrometeoroid Garment (moon suit). (A) Teflon coating for patches; (B) Beta-Fiberglas; (C) aluminized Kapton film laminated to Beta-Fiberglas marquisette mesh; (D) perforated aluminized Mylar film; (E) nonwoven Dacron; (F) rubberized ripstop nylon. *(de Monchaux 2011, 320)*

the pumping action of the arms and other body movements cause clothing to pump warm air and vapor inside of garments out to the environment. Free air circulation also allows evaporation to take place on the skin surface, where it can provide the most effective cooling.

As was discussed previously with regard to ventilating the core, rigid wearable items, such as helmets, often have an inner suspension system that provides a *standoff* (i.e., an open area between the head surface and the outer surface of the helmet). Standoffs and spacers hold clothing off the skin surface so that air can pass through as one walks along.

Loose clothing however, allows easier body movement. If the body has to work against clothing as it moves, a lot of heat is generated, and the metabolic rate is increased. This effect is highly undesirable on a hot day.

Using Nonconductive Materials

The use of nonconductive materials was also suggested for protection from *cold* weather. Clothing that is to protect the body from temperature extremes essentially forms a barrier between the body and the environment. Regardless of whether the temperature is extremely low or extremely high, clothing is there to prevent heat flow when temperatures are above or below normal body temperatures. Since heat flows from hot to cold, the heat from a hot object or from high-temperature environmental air will flow *toward* the body and cause it to become warmer. Therefore, it makes sense to use nonconductive materials to reduce conduction of heat toward the body, just as one uses aluminized materials to reduce radiant heat transfer toward the body.

Because still air spaces in clothing help provide a barrier to heat flow, it is also possible that thick clothing may be used to keep cool as well as to keep warm. The thick, high-temperature protective clothing shown in Figures 5.36 and 5.37 are examples of this. Firefighters and others who work in environments where temperatures reach hazardous levels wear thick clothing made of fire-resistant materials that are often aluminized. The aluminization reflects radiant energy, whereas the thick, nonconductive layers underneath prevent heat from being conducted through the aluminum to the skin surface.

One caution must be given with this recommendation. Since the body is constantly producing heat, unless some provision is made to avoid the buildup of heat within the nonconductive garment system, heat illness can occur. In the case of the desert dweller, it was suggested that loose clothing be used so that the warm air that builds up inside a garment can be pumped out by body motion. In the case of the firefighter or astronaut, who may need to be cut off entirely from the environment, some auxiliary, powered method of cooling may need to be added to the ensemble.

Nonconductive substances other than textiles may be used to provide still air pockets and form protective insulation. Figure 5.20 shows a unique protective suit for a racecar driver. The basic shell of the suit, which was made of two layers of flame-resistant aramid fabric, already offered 20 seconds of protection against heat conduction when used alone. However, this particular shell was fitted inside with a network of tubing. If a crash occurred, the driver could activate a mechanism that would emit foam through the tubing, where it formed a thick insulative layer filled with air between the suit and the body. Since the foam was heat resistant and stable for approximately 5 minutes, it added significant protection to the system.

FIGURE 5.20 Protective clothing for racecar drivers. *(ILC Dover)*

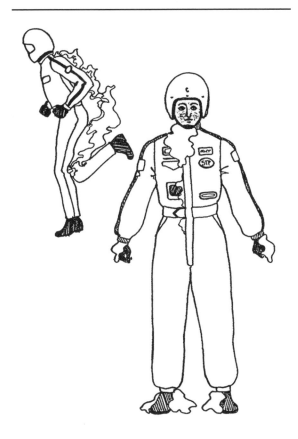

KEEPING DRY

It seems appropriate to insert a few comments about keeping dry at this point because dryness affects the success of garments designed for both hot and cold environments. Water may play a major role in heat loss or heat gain as was discussed earlier in this chapter. When it fills the air spaces of insulation, it promotes heat conduction, whether toward or away from the body; when it evaporates from the skin surface or from a clothing layer, it can provide a significant loss of heat by evaporation. When it condenses, as it can when steam in a firefighting environment touches a cooler skin surface, it can cause a burn.

Water often plays another role, however, and that is to cause discomfort. Many people feel that being wet is worse than being too cold or too hot. Some even perceive themselves as being too hot or too cold when they are wet, even if their skin temperature is measurably in a normal range. What this means to the designer is that it is not enough to simply keep a wearer warm or cool. Even if water in the system is handled in a way that maintains thermal balance, individuals are often not satisfied unless an ensemble is dry as well.

There are a number of methods of handling moisture in a garment system. Several of these have been mentioned in the last two sections of this chapter. For cold weather clothing, a designer must determine ways to protect insulation from wind and water and provide ventilation features in clothing so that excess body heat and moist vapor can pass off into the environment and sweating can be avoided. In hot weather, the important factors for keeping dry are to wear thin garments that provide fewer insulative air spaces and allow air and water vapor to pass through the garment structure and to wear loose clothing that allows air to circulate across the body surface.

In addition to these, two other concepts are important to keeping dry. In cold environments, in a breathable clothing system, one needs to use a wicking layer next to the skin surface to move water away from the body toward the environment. In hot environments, when out of direct sunlight or a source of high radiant heat such as a furnace or fire, it is important to uncover as much of the skin surface as possible so that evaporative cooling can take place directly from the skin surface. In enclosed environments, it may be necessary to control body temperature precisely with auxiliary devices to prevent sweating from taking place.

One solution for keeping warm and dry is to provide an ensemble that can be varied depending on weather conditions. Figure 5.21 shows a glove for cold weather based on a modular system. It features two separate gloves that zip together at the wrist. The outer water-resistant shell is lined with a microfiber insulation and contains a waterproof, breathable insert. The zip-in liner is made of polypropylene pile. The two are used together for maximum warmth, but the liner can also be worn alone when wind and rain are not factors or the shell can be used alone on milder days. This design was created so that alternative liners could also be zipped in. Among those available are an aluminized, heat-reflective liner and an electrically heated liner. The outer glove can be removed if heat and moisture begin to build up in the hand and replaced again if the hand begins to chill.

DESCRIBING THERMAL INSULATION

A number of descriptive units have been developed to express the thermal resistance of clothing

FIGURE 5.21 (A) Insulated glove with removable liner; (B) the two are zipped together at the wrist and each can be worn alone in different weather conditions. *(Based on a design formerly produced by Grandoe)*

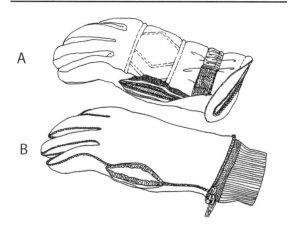

ensembles or systems. Specifying a level of insulation for all the garment layers in a clothing system is quite a challenge, since the body, clothing, and the environment constantly interact. In addition, thermal balance may be achieved by using totally different thicknesses of fabrics on the head, hands, and torso.

The **clo** is a unit of thermal insulation that has achieved widespread use because it clearly conveys to the layperson the warming power of an ensemble. Although it does have a precise physical definition (Goldman 2007, 1–3), one clo is commonly described as "the thermal insulation of a business suit as worn in Philadelphia, New Haven or Toronto."

The clo was intended to express the insulation provided by a total clothing ensemble, not a single item. For example, to achieve thermal comfort under the conditions listed in the definition, several layers would probably be worn around the torso (underwear, shirt, jacket, etc.) and perhaps only one or two around each arm and leg. Therefore, strictly speaking, it is not reasonable to talk about the clo value of a sweater, for example. However, since the clo is expressed in physical terms, it is possible to calculate a clo value for each garment in an ensemble. Because thermal insulation largely depends on the air that lies between layers, and because most clothing items cover only one part of the body, the sum of these individual clo values will not add up to the same value calculated for the whole ensemble. Nevertheless, a number of studies have been undertaken to develop formulas to determine the clo of a clothing system from an assemblage of garments or to estimate the insulation provided by ensembles by other means.

The other unit frequently used to express thermal insulation is the *tog*. Even though the tog also has a precise physical definition (Renbourn and Rees 1972, 114), it is described as the approximate insulation of light summer clothing. It was formulated to express the thermal resistance of fabric layers, not a clothing ensemble. This definition may become clearer if one thinks of a heat source, such as an iron, with layers of fabrics to be used in an ensemble lying on top of it. The tog value represents the amount of heat the iron must put out (or the number of watts it takes to heat the iron) to produce a certain temperature on the outermost fabric. Since this is a measure of resistance to heat flow, a high tog value means that heat cannot flow as easily through a fabric system. Therefore, layers of fabrics that have a high tog value provide good insulation. The tog has a smaller insulative value than a clo; 1 clo equals 1.55 togs (Goldman & Kampmann, 2007, Appendix p. 13). Since the test method used to determine the tog value uses flat fabrics rather than garments in which shaping and design features contribute to total insulation, the tog represents something slightly different from the clo.

Havenith et al. adapted the Universal Thermal Climate Index (UTCI) to include clothing as the interface between the body and the environment. They considered the following in developing their *UTCI-Clothing Index*:

(1) typical dressing behaviour in different temperatures, as observed in the field, resulting in a model of the distribution of clothing over the different body segments in relation to the ambient temperature, (2) the changes in clothing insulation and vapour resistance caused by wind and body movement, and (3) the change in wind speed in relation to the height above ground. (2012, 1)

THERMAL TESTING OF CLOTHING

Although fabric testing may yield a great deal of information about the protection a garment may offer, the interaction between the environment, clothing, and the body is so complex that the most detailed information must come from testing the garment as it is worn.

There are a number of approaches to thermal testing of clothing. Some involve subjective testing, and others, objective testing. Some methods are used in a controlled laboratory setting, and others are used in the natural environment. A simple subjective method is to survey individuals who are wearing specific clothing items in a specific environment in order to find out how they feel. Another is to assess the work output of an individual who is dressed in a particular clothing assembly. In this case, the researcher is assuming that if an individual is too hot, sweating and fatigue will occur and less work will be accomplished. On the other hand, if an individual is too cold, a decrease in dexterity or loss of muscle control will be experienced, which will also affect productivity. It is possible to weigh clothing before and after use for a specific activity to determine the amount of sweat (an indicator of overheating) that has been picked up by the clothing system. Skin temperature can be determined by attaching thermocouples to the body in various areas.

Thermography provides another method for detecting heat loss from clothing. (See Figure 5.4.) A series of photographs can be used, or the images can be displayed on a television screen so that changes can be monitored and the effects of body movement can be observed. Thermography enables a designer to determine specific areas of heat loss such as seams, quilting lines, and garment openings, and to make adjustment in insulation or construction techniques accordingly.

One objective method of measuring the thermal protection offered by clothing is to use manikins. The copper man, shown in Figure 5.22 was developed in the 1940s and updated models are still in use in research labs today. The model shown is a hollow manikin the size of an average army infantryman. Inside the manikin is a complex system of heating wires, thermocouples, and a thermostat.

FIGURE 5.22 The copper man, a device used to measure thermal insulating (clo) values of clothing assemblies.

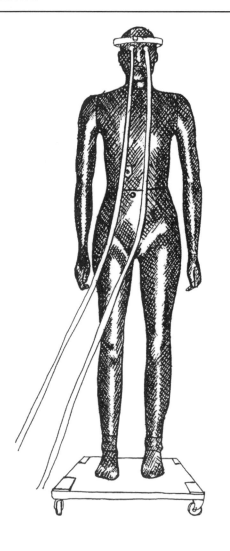

The thermocouples measure the skin temperature at 19 locations on the manikin. The thermostat controls the power delivered to the heating wires so that a constant skin temperature is maintained. Thus, the manikin has parts that correspond to the hypothalamus (thermostat), the nervous system (thermocouples), and the circulatory system (heating wires). The amount of power required to keep the manikin's skin at a constant temperature parallels the amount of heat the body must produce through its metabolism to keep the skin temperature constant. Therefore, the number of watts needed by the copper man to maintain a constant surface temperature in a specific garment is a good indication of that garment's insulative value. If the garment is an effective insulator, it will conserve the heat produced by the manikin, and the power can be shut off. If it does not insulate properly, heat will be lost and will have to be produced repeatedly by the manikin.

Modern copper manikins exist at a number of universities and independent testing laboratories. They incorporate increasingly sophisticated features. Some have segmented, movable features to test garment function in a variety of body positions. Manikins such as Coppelius® can be both sweat- and heat-producing and are computer controlled to simulate specific activities. Sweating manikins are programmed to produce varying degrees of perspiration from various body areas. Their sweating capacity adds the factor of evaporative cooling to the analysis. Nonsweating manikins are often covered with a wet absorbent skin. Clothing is placed on a sweating manikin and the amount of evaporative cooling that takes place is measured and expressed in a *moisture permeability index* (im) (Goldman 2007, 1–5). Fan and Chen added the capacity for walking and a fabric, breathable skin to their sweating manikin, "Walter"

(2002). Smaller manikins such as a thermal hand manikin developed by Measurement Technology West and thermal evaporative manikins for the hands, feet, and head developed by UCS (Universal Customization System) have been used to test individual clothing items such as gloves, footwear, and head coverings.

Other manikins have been developed to withstand flames. DuPont developed its THERMO-MAN® system to test protective clothing ensembles under realistic flash fire conditions. The THERMO-MAN is an instrumented, 6-foot, 1-inch (1.85 meters) tall, high-temperature mannequin system with 122 heat sensors that record flame temperatures and the duration of burn. The manikin is dressed in complete protective gear and then engulfed in flames for specific periods of time so that the extent of thermal protection can be both observed and measured. Copper manikins are able to provide valuable information in the design stages before expensive, time-consuming, and potentially dangerous field studies are attempted.

USING AUXILIARY HEATING AND COOLING SYSTEMS

There are limits to what insulation can accomplish. Continuing to layer garments on top of one another to meet the challenge of extreme heat or cold results in interference with mobility and flattened insulation. Complete isolation from the environment such as the system found in a space suit is not always practical either. Adding auxiliary heating or cooling systems to clothing is sometimes the most practical method of solving a variety of thermal balance problems. Auxiliary heating and cooling can allow a garment to provide adaptive protection from heat or cold. For example, a winter coat functions in much the same way as the insulation in the walls of a building, but an auxiliary heating/ cooling system functions like the building's heating and air-conditioning systems.

Auxiliary heating and cooling are often applied to specific areas of the body rather than to the body as a whole. They may be used for the extremities because the lack of circulation to those areas during vasoconstriction makes them particularly susceptible to frostbite. In addition, the small cylinders of the fingers are difficult to insulate without interfering with mobility. Both auxiliary heating and cooling may be applied to the core because of its effect on the thermal balance of the body.

Considerable research must be undertaken to establish the needs of an individual for auxiliary heating or cooling. Environmental conditions, the insulation provided by protective clothing worn, and the metabolic heat generated by specific activities must be known in order to calculate the heat that needs to be added to or removed from an individual in order to reach thermal balance.

Auxiliary heating and cooling systems use electrical or chemical energy to transmit or absorb thermal energy. Because they are often powered or triggered on-demand, they can be switched on as needed (similar to using a space heater or fan). Many heating and cooling systems can also be designed so that they are activated or deactivated automatically, as a designer and/or a user specifies (similar to setting the thermostat in a building).

Auxiliary systems contain three main components: a *mechanism* of active heat transfer such as a compressor, a chemical reaction, or a heat-exchanging device; a *medium*, such as air or water through which the heat or cold is delivered; and a *garment system* that distributes the medium and keeps it close to the body parts that need to be heated or cooled. Powered systems also contain a power source such as a battery or solar cell.

This section will explore mechanisms of auxiliary cooling and auxiliary heating, and the media used to distribute heat or cooling throughout a garment system.

Active Cooling

There are four major physical processes that can be controlled by a power source to create a cooling system: convection, phase change, thermoelectric energy transfer, and endothermic chemical reactions.

Air-Cooling Systems

Powered convective systems are perhaps the simplest forms of auxiliary cooling. These methods use fans to move air through a garment or ensemble, and therefore they are often referred to as air-cooling systems. Air cooling has a number of advantages over other methods of supplementary cooling. For one thing, the medium is lighter in weight than any other. For another, very little power is needed to run a device that circulates air. Even ambient air temperatures can provide cooling if air can be delivered to the skin surface to provide evaporative cooling, and moist air near the skin surface is then provided an exit from the garment. However, it is important to remember that these systems are most effective when they work with the body's natural systems of thermal balance and transfer. For example, they are very effective when they support the evaporative cooling process, but not if the evaporated sweat cannot be moved away from the skin. If a fan simply stirs the air, it will quickly become heated and saturated with moisture, and no cooling will occur.

Figure 5.23 shows one very logical application of an air-cooled system: an inflated character costume. Costumed characters at an amusement park or promotional event typically experience a great deal of discomfort because the body is completely enclosed in thick or impermeable materials that allow virtually no heat escape by any of the four methods of heat transfer. This means that one can wear the costumes for only very short periods of time (generally 30 minutes is an absolute maximum even in the lightest weight garment without a cooling system), and even then, wearers report that they are drenched with sweat when they emerge. The system shown in Figure 5.23 provides a large costume without the added bulk of padding by inflating the costume with air. The fans in the costume run continuously to keep the costume inflated so fresh air is always being provided to the system. At the same time, air continuously exits the system

FIGURE 5.23 An air-cooled inflatable costume. *(Based on design formerly produced by Entertainment Research Group, Inc.)*

fan

through mesh panels located toward the top of the costume. (The specific placement of exits differs for each design.) Thus, the air used for inflation provides convective and evaporative heat loss as well.

Note the location of the fans in this costume. This not only is a logical arrangement in terms of the chimney effect but also places the fans far from the head where even a quiet hum might interfere with hearing. These fans are powered by a rechargeable battery that will last from 2 to 4 hours. Many inflatable costumes use fans that can be powered by two AA batteries. The manufacturers of this costume stated that wearers could spend an average of 1.5 hours in their costumes without discomfort. The lightness of weight of this system also minimizes the metabolic costs of wearing the garment.

The military has played a large role in the development of air-cooled systems, but fan noise and the heat signature of the fan have proven to be a camouflage and detection issue for soldiers. In addition, outside of a controlled lab or industrial setting, environmental factors present problems. Sand and loose dirt can clog intake valves and get into motors, disabling them.

The basics of an air-cooled system can be illustrated by examining an early air-cooled system developed for the soldier. Figure 5.24A shows a system developed for military applications. It was based on a *desiccant* (drying agent) system in which both environmental air entering the system and the air currently circulating in the suit were continually brought back to a unit that scrubbed it of moisture, cooled it and then directed it back into the suit. The delivery system in this case was a cooling vest with cooling focused on the core. Figure 5.24B shows an interior view of the vest. The interior surface of the vest was covered with a mesh that allowed air to exit throughout the entire vest surface. The filtration/cooling system was worn as a backpack. An alternate model contained a renewable desiccant in which the moisture scrubbed from the system was heated and sent out

FIGURE 5.24 An air-cooled system for soldiers. (A) Basic air-cooling vest; (B) interior view of vest; (C) filtration/cooling system with renewable desiccant; (D) regenerable desiccant system mounted over a soldier's backpack. *(U.S. Army Natick Research, Development and Engineering Center)*

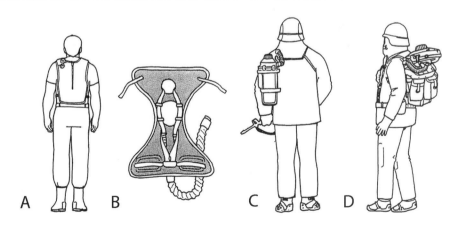

to the environment. This system not only had the advantage of not needing desiccant replacement but also had an advantage for the wearer in that the weight of liquid scrubbed from the system was dumped rather than being carried by the body until the desiccant could be replaced.

One consideration in the design of air-cooled systems is that the air is most effective if it is delivered directly to the skin surface. This means that often some sort of spacer or suspension system needs to be used in order to provide a channel for airflow. The bush helmet shown in Figure 5.25 provides a good example of this. The hat is suspended away from the head surface by an interior band. A solar-powered fan at the top of the brim directs air over the head surface. The manufacturer of this helmet also noted that the leather suspension band included a foam pad that could be dampened to add extra evaporative cooling.

It should be noted that air-cooled systems can be simpler if the wearer is located near to a power source and can be tethered to an air supply. With a tether, often called an *umbilical* cord, air-cooled garments can be linked to power sources in vehicles or buildings. Pilots or laboratory technicians,

for example, generally need a limited range of movement away from the power source. An umbilical system also allows the weight and bulk of a power source to be eliminated from clothing. (See Figures 7.12 and 7.13.)

Liquid-Cooling Systems

Many systems use liquid rather than air as the transfer medium. Liquid can be contained inside of tubing and delivered to precisely controlled body locations. Liquid cooling involves both conduction and convection. Heat from the body is conducted to a garment that contains liquid, and a power unit pumps that liquid through the garment to a cooling unit. As the body-warmed water circulates through or over the cooling unit, it is cooled by convection and the cooled water is then circulated through the garment again. Liquid-cooled garments are frequently used in high-heat environments, such as the smelting industries, to draw off excess heat radiated to the body by the surroundings. However, they may also be used when the body must be heavily insulated as is true for many traditional, heavy costumes worn at amusement parks. A number of medical conditions have been treated with liquid cooling. People born without sweat glands, cancer patients, individuals with multiple sclerosis, and quadriplegics are among those who have benefited from the use of liquid-cooled garments.

Intuitively, it may seem that the colder the liquid used to provide conductive cooling is, the faster it will cool the body. Indeed, the larger the temperature difference between two substances, the faster the transfer of thermal energy will be. However, Koscheyev and colleagues found that extremely cold liquid actually slowed the heat transfer from the body. They believe that this was due to the body's local vasoconstriction response, which causes vasoconstriction in the surface blood vessels when the skin senses extreme cold. This

FIGURE 5.25 A helmet with a solar-operated fan for head cooling.

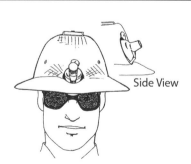

Side View

vasoconstriction prevents blood from flowing close to the surface, where the most heat transfer can take place. They recommend using slightly warmer (18°–20°C or 64°–68°F) liquid to cool the body.

Figure 5.26 shows several models of portable liquid-cooled garments. These garments house a tubing or channel system that distributes water close to the body surface; a power pack that provides for circulation of the water; a cooling unit that holds crushed ice and water; and, in some cases, an outer cover garment that insulates the system from environmental air. Many systems do not contain this last protective element, relying instead on the basic protective clothing worn for the end use to provide that function. For example, no cover layer would be used for firefighters because the firefighting garment already provides insulation from the high-heat environment. The system shown in Figure 5.26A shows a vest and head cover that each contains a plastic layer into which channels have been sealed (Figure 5.26B). This layer is then attached to a vest on which the power pack and cooling unit are mounted. Figure 5.26C shows another model in which channels

FIGURE 5.26 Liquid-cooled garments. *(A, B, C and D based on designs by ILC Dover; E based on MSA design)*

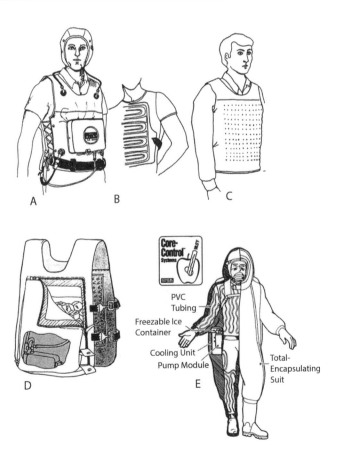

have been heat-sealed directly into the nylon vest on which the power and cooling units have been mounted. Figure 5.26D shows how an ice pack through which the water flows is mounted on a vest. Figure 5.26E shows a stretch cooling garment onto which plastic tubes have been sewn. Instead of depending on ice packs, some suits can also be connected to an external power or water source through an umbilical cord with the use of quick-connect hose fittings.

When individuals are seated, as are pilots or soldiers in a tank, oil or other heavier liquids can be used. Often, these systems are hooked up to power sources in vehicles to provide the power for circulation.

One of the most interesting power sources proposed for liquid cooling garments is an ergonomic one (Knapp 1988). In it, the energy needed to propel liquid around the body would be provided by body motion. Using mechanical energy such as that provided by a foot pump or systems developed to capitalize on arm or elbow movements, enough energy could be produced to circulate liquids during periods of activity. Some supplementary power source would, however, be needed for rest periods.

Another interesting proposal for liquid cooled garments is the use of vapor-permeable tubing or channel walls (Knapp 1988). These would allow vaporized sweat to enter the liquid flow stream where it could be filtered out and evaporated to the environment. This would not only relieve the discomfort of sweat that built up inside the system (either from an overload to the liquid cooled system or anxiety) but also add the element of evaporation as a method of cooling the liquid in the system.

Phase Change

Phase-change materials use energy exchange to either warm or cool a system, depending on the needs of a wearer. They work on much the same principle as the body's sweat mechanism (which cools the body as liquid sweat becomes gas) or like ice packs that melt (changing phase from solid to liquid) as they absorb heat from the body. The substances in phase change materials absorb and release heat when they change from gaseous to liquid phase or from liquid to solid phase. Different materials change phase at higher or lower temperatures so they can be very useful for temperature control in apparel.

For example, the vest shown in Figure 5.27 contains a series of cooling packs that are inserted throughout it. Each pack contains a phase-change substance that is engineered to remain at 65°F (18.3°C). When the skin surface rises to a temperature that is above 65°F (18.3°C), the material absorbs the excess heat. When all of the material has changed phase due to the body heat it

FIGURE 5.27 A vest with channels for inserting phase change cooling packs (one shown at A). *(Based on a design by Mainstream Engineering Corporation)*

has absorbed, the packs must be replaced and/or recharged. One of the advantages of using phase-change chemicals is that recharging does not usually require freezing. Because the packs in the illustrated vest change phase well above freezing, packs can be prepared for reuse by placing them in portable coolers or refrigerators. In addition, unlike ice packs or ice-cooled vests, the temperature of the packs is closer to normal skin temperature and thus can be worn directly on the skin without discomfort. The efficacy of encapsulated phase-change materials is limited to the amount of heat they can absorb before all of the encapsulated material has changed phase.

To significantly increase the temperature difference and speed cooling, it is usually necessary to place a substance under pressure and use a powered compressor to force it to change phase. The compressor applies pressure to the substance, such as a gas, which is contained in a chamber. Under pressure, it changes phase from a gas to a liquid. Refrigerators and air conditioners use compressed gases such as ammonia, carbon dioxide, or fluorocarbons as the phase change substance because they have very low boiling points (the temperature at which their liquid phase becomes gas). The compression process generates heat as the gas becomes liquid, and the heat generated is dissipated into the surrounding air or into a heat sink. This is why the back of an air conditioner or refrigerator is usually hot. When these liquids are then released and depressurized, they change back to their original gaseous phase. As they do this, they immediately evaporate. Since evaporation requires the heat needed to achieve a phase change, that heat is drawn from the cooling chamber, thus reducing its temperature.

In outer space there is no need for a compressor to change a gas into a liquid. The low-pressure environment outside of the space suit causes substances that are liquid in Earth gravity to quickly evaporate. The liquid cooling base layer of a space suit transfers some liquid outside of the pressurized capsule of the suit to create evaporative cooling without the need for a powered compressor. The evaporation of the liquid into the vacuum of space cools the remaining liquid in the suit, and this is then pumped around the body to cool the astronaut.

Lower-power cooling systems known as swamp coolers are common in dry climates where evaporation happens quickly and easily into the surrounding air. Swamp coolers pump small amounts of water into a pad or distribution system, and a fan passes the warm environmental air over or through this system. The water absorbs heat from the nearest heat source (the body, or perhaps the air around the body) and uses that heat to power the evaporation of the water from the wet pad into the dry air. Tying a wet cloth around the head or neck when outside in a dry environment is an effective way to cool down, and water-carrying pads can be integrated into clothing to achieve the same result.

Thermoelectric Transfer

Electrically activated devices can also make use of the *Peltier effect*, which allows some materials to transform electricity into a change in temperature. This is known as *thermoelectric energy transfer*. Peltier junctions place a semiconducting material (usually bismuth) between two conductors (usually copper). When current is passed through, one bismuth-copper junction heats up and the other cools down. Peltier junctions can create a temperature drop of about 40°F below ambient temperatures. Peltier junctions do require a means to draw the excess heat away from the hot side of the module, which can be achieved with a fan or circulating liquid from a chiller. This effect is commonly used to cool the processor of personal computers and mobile devices. Although not currently used for clothing, it has the potential to be useful in smart clothing.

Endothermic Chemical Reactions

Endothermic (heat-absorbing) chemical reactions can also be used to remove heat energy from the body or the environment around the body. Endothermic reactions steal heat from their surroundings to power a chemical reaction. Chemical cold packs operate on this principle. Usually they are made of water with an encapsulated chemical agent floating inside. Bending or squishing the pack punctures the tube or bag inside the pack, which releases water-activated chemicals into the water-filled outer bag. When the reagent mixes with the water, an endothermic chemical reaction takes place. This reaction uses energy from the water and the area around the pack to crystalize the mixture. The environment around the pack gets colder because of the thermal energy absorbed to fuel the crystallization.

A number of items for rehabilitation and sports injuries involve the use of chemicals for local heating or cooling. In some, the reaction is provided when the barrier in a two-part packet is broken so that the chemicals can be mixed.

Active Heating

It should be noted that many of the mechanisms and components involved in auxiliary cooling systems may be used to produce heated clothing. This has already been shown in the discussion of phase change materials. If the air or liquid circulating through the system is heated rather than cooled, it can be used to heat the body in cold surroundings. Mechanisms like Peltier junctions move heat from one side to the other, so they can be used to heat or cool depending on their orientation. However, there are a few additional mechanisms that can be used to transform chemical or electrical energy into thermal energy in order to provide auxiliary heating.

Electrically Heated Systems

One of the most common methods of providing auxiliary heat to a garment system is to convert electrical current into heat. As was discussed in Chapter 4, as electrical current flows through a material, electrons frequently collide with atoms of the material itself. The more resistive the material, the more frequent these collisions are. Each collision produces a tiny bit of thermal energy, and when there are a lot of electrons and a lot of collisions, it can result in a perceptible increase in temperature. Electrically heated garments usually use very thin wires or conductive fibers to conduct electricity through the garment. Increasing the current running through the garment results in an increase in temperature.

Because the temperature change is caused by a high current running through the system, electrically heated systems generally consume a lot more power than most electronic systems. For battery-powered systems, the size of the battery limits the amount of current that can be supplied, and the length of time that the current can be supplied. Because of this, the most significant problem connected with electrically heated garments is the weight and bulk of a power source. When an individual is seated in an aircraft, working in a relatively stationary position or within a building, power can be provided without weight by simply plugging the garment into an AC (wall) power source or a power source within a vehicle. A variety of approaches have been used to both capitalize on and avoid this problem with electrically heated garments.

Figure 5.28 shows an electrically heated motorcycle suit built much like a shaped electric blanket.

FIGURE 5.28 A heated motorcycle suit that can be plugged into a motorcycle battery. *(Based on a design formerly produced by Gerbings Heated Apparel)*

FIGURE 5.28 A heated motorcycle suit that can be plugged into a motorcycle battery. *(Based on a design formerly produced by Gerbings Heated Apparel)*

Thin, flexible metal wires insulated with plastic are distributed throughout the garment and can be interconnected to items such as gloves or boot liners. This type of garment can be plugged directly into a power source—the cycle's battery. Similar suits can be developed for any seated individual who is near a power source: pilots; tank crewmen, or individuals in hospital beds. It should be noted that these types of systems are by no means new. Similar garments were in use in Europe during the Second World War when there was limited fuel for heating homes and businesses (Watkins 1986).

A hybrid middle ground between plugged-in heated garments and fully self-contained heated garments has also been proposed, in the form of portable fashion garments that could be plugged intermittently into stationary power sources (Watkins 1986). These garments would rely on a combination of auxiliary heat, body-generated heat, and insulation, with the garment adding heat to the body for short periods of time, and the combination of body heat and the insulation maintaining sufficient heat until the next power source is available. The design shown in Figure 5.29 relies on the availability of plug-in power sources along the exterior of buildings, or at places where people stand and wait, such as bus stops or ski lifts. An individual wearing this garment could plug into metered power sources similar to parking meters at each point where they had to wait. One could also plug in a coat to prewarm it shortly before going outside. This approach has the benefit of eliminating the need to carry a bulky power source, but it has the limitation of relying on availability of power from the surrounding infrastructure.

Because of the high amount of current needed to produce heat, self-contained systems often need larger batteries than other electrically powered smart garments. Therefore, commonly available heated garments are most often small items such as vests, gloves, socks, and boots. Figure 5.30 shows two typical items, each of which operates on a single battery.

FIGURE 5.29 An electrically heated jacket that can be plugged into outlets at emergency stations, bus stops, ski lifts, and so on. *(Watkins 1986)*

FIGURE 5.30 Electrically heated garments for the extremities. Dotted lines indicate the location of heating wiring.

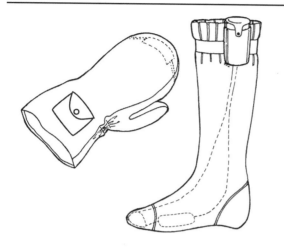

Exothermic Chemical Reactions

Just as endothermic chemical reactions remove thermal energy from the environment to fuel the chemical reaction, exothermic (heat-releasing) reactions release energy as heat when bonds are formed between atoms and molecules. A controlled exothermic reaction can be used to heat a garment system. One of the simplest of these is a small packet of iron powder that releases heat when it is exposed to oxygen. These packets are sold commercially in sealed plastic wrappers. When the user wants to slip one in a glove or boot, the plastic wrapper is opened and the iron powder immediately begins to be activated by exposure to air. Since the iron powder is enclosed in a nonwoven cover that moderates the flow of heat, the packet can be placed directly against the skin surface without danger of burns.

Some garments have special pockets in which these heated packets can be placed. The closer to the skin surface they are in a clothing system, the greater warming power they have. Figure 5.31 shows the elements in a system that serves as a distributor for heat given off by an iron powder heat pack. It includes a hand-shaped bladder (A) that has been partially filled with mineral oil. This is placed directly under a thin lining on the palm of the hand. As the wearer's hand moves, the oil circulates throughout the bladder, coming into close contact with a heat pack that lays in a pocket (B) against the wrist area of the bladder. The heat from the heat pack is then circulated throughout the bladder, covering the entire palm surface. Although this would seem to interfere with dexterity, in fact, the mineral oil is pushed out of the way when the hand grips items and the circulation was found to be much greater in the palm than in a corresponding position on the back of the hand.

FIGURE 5.31 (A) An oil-filled bladder serves as a distribution system for (B) a disposable heat pack placed in the pocket of a glove liner. *(Design: Dixie Rhinehart)*

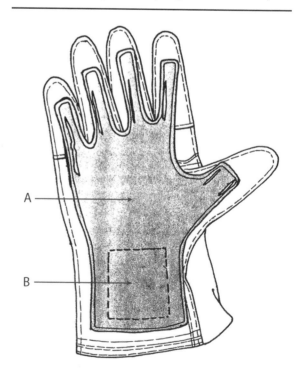

Combustion Heating

Chemical reactions that are endothermic or exothermic result in the rearrangement of atoms into new molecules. When there are many bonds broken between atoms in the reaction, it becomes endothermic (breaking bonds requires energy). When there are many bonds made between atoms, the reaction is exothermic (making bonds releases energy).

Combustion, or burning of a substance or fuel, is similar to these chemical reactions, with the important difference that combustion is the reaction of a fuel substance with oxygen. In many cases, this reaction must be triggered by energy introduced into the system, but in some cases exposure to oxygen without any trigger is enough to start the reaction (these reactions are often called spontaneous combustion). A combustion reaction will generally continue until all of the fuel and/or oxygen in the reaction has been broken up and/or reformed into new molecules. Combustion is always an exothermic reaction.

The Norwegian military developed a combustion-based form of auxiliary heating for extreme cold involving the use of charcoal as a heat source (Rustad, 1984). A charcoal fuel element is placed in a small combustion chamber and lit (Figure 5.32). The chamber is then sealed tightly closed and a battery-operated fan distributes the heat produced through tubing or other distribution elements. The distribution system may target one body area or be set up to heat the entire body, utilizing a hot air delivery tube down each arm and leg as well as one or more on the torso.

FIGURE 5.32 A charcoal personal heater. A charcoal fuel element (inset) is lit and placed in the combustion chamber.

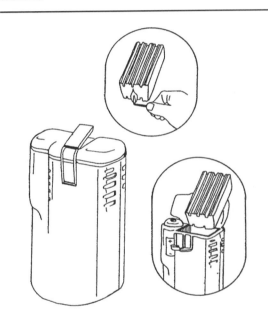

215

CASE STUDY 5.1 Keeping Cool: Ensembles for Firefighting

There are three types of ensembles worn for fighting fires: **turnout gear**, worn for regular firefighting duties; **proximity suits**, designed for work close to flame; and **entry suits**, designed to be worn in and around flames, including high-temperature flames produced by airplane fuels.

Turnout Gear

Turnout gear is intended to be worn at structural fires when firefighters operate hoses and other equipment at some distance from the burning structure. Figure A shows one typical model of turnout gear. It consists of a jacket (usually called a *turnout coat*), pants (generally called *bunker pants*), boots, gloves, a helmet, an SCBA (self-contained breathing apparatus) facemask, a hood, and a backpack with an oxygen tank mounted on it.

User Needs

Structural firefighters face a wide variety of hazards. Potential injuries due to their work include burns, heat exhaustion, inhalation of toxic gases, cuts, heart attacks due to stress and overexertion, sprains, and strains. As changes in building materials and structures have evolved and concerns about terrorism attacks have grown, the risks to all service personnel from known and unknown hazardous substances have also increased. Manufacturers of turnout gear constantly search for new materials and develop designs that will minimize injuries to firefighters.

Materials and Layering Systems for Heat and Burn Protection

Regardless of whether a fire is being fought in the cold of winter or the heat of summer, firefighters need a great deal of insulation in order to be protected from direct burns and the high heat of the fire. Materials need not only to retain their structure when exposed to flames and intense heat but also need to prevent conduction of that heat through to the body. In the past, nonflammable and flame-resistant materials such as neoprene and natural rubber were used as the outer layer of turnout coats. Then flame-retardant cottons were used. Today, coats are typically made of one of the polyaramids—Nomex or Kevlar—or PBI. (Additional information on high-temperature and flame-resistant materials can be found in Chapter 3 under, "Flameproof and Flame-Resistant Fibers.")

In order to minimize burns, turnout gear needs to include protection from radiated,

FIGURE A Turnout gear for structural firefighting. *(Globe Firesuits®)*

conducted, and convected heat. It also needs to provide protection from the steam that results from the constant spray of hoses and the intense heat of the fire. As discussed at the beginning of this chapter, condensation of steam releases a tremendous amount of heat, so it is important to prevent this condensation from taking place on the skin or in a layer of the garment too close to the skin surface.

In most commercial firefighting garments, protection from steam burns is accomplished by placing either a vapor barrier or a material that slows down the rate of vapor transmission somewhere in the fabric system. In the older rubber or neoprene coats, the outer material was waterproof and served as a vapor barrier. In the newer fabric coats such as those made of one of polyaramids, flame-retardant cotton or PBI, a moisture barrier is generally either bonded to the underside of the outer coat material or is the outermost layer of the lining. Regardless of where the moisture barrier is located, there must always be some insulation material between it and the skin surface. Because condensation of steam can occur on a moisture barrier, the barrier itself may become quite hot, and the skin must be protected from heat conducted through it. The moisture barrier is so critical to protection that a number of manufacturers have permanently attached it to the outer collar so that those in charge of a fire scene can immediately tell if a firefighter is *not* wearing a moisture barrier.

Firefighters exert a great deal of energy in their work, and with the insulation needed to protect them from the fire environment, they build up quite a bit of heat inside turnout gear. In order to keep them in thermal balance, designers need to provide possibilities for ventilation or some other form of cooling. Because of the dangerous nature of the fire setting, it may only be possible to open firefighting garments to provide ventilation once a firefighter has stepped back from the fire scene. One method of preventing moisture from building up inside the ensemble is to incorporate a microporous material in the system instead of a waterproof barrier. Although the micropores will eventually allow steam to penetrate the system (just as vaporized sweat may pass outward into a cooler environment), the steam will *gradually* move through the fabrics so that the skin is acclimated rather than causing the threshold of pain to be reached (Watkins et al. 1978, 38).

The manufacturer of the turnout gear shown in Figure A offers the design in a variety of materials and material configurations. All include an outermost layer of a woven fabric made of aramid, PBI, or other similar fibers and chosen for its resistance to flame and heat conduction as well as for its strength and durability. Directly beneath that is a moisture barrier made of a Gore-tex membrane bonded to a Nomex aramid woven fabric for strength. Directly below the moisture barrier is a thermal barrier. It is offered in a variety of fabrics as well, but all consist of some sort of batting sandwiched between layers of flame-resistant, heat-resistant face fabrics. Battings are often made of spun aramid fiber but sometimes include fibers such as wool or modacrylic. Face fabrics for the thermal liners are generally made of a lightweight aramid woven cloth such as a lightweight Nomex or a fire-retardant rayon. Because there are high-compression areas on the coat, such as the elbows, knees, and the areas where the backpack straps lie, the coat has additional thermal layers in those areas.

Turnout Gear Mobility

One of the key criteria for the design of turnout gear is to preserve as much freedom of movement as possible. Chapter 2 includes a number of principles that can be used to design more mobile garments for any end use. Of particular importance to firefighting are methods to increase the ease of movement at the joints, particularly at the shoulders, hips and knees; ways to decrease the weight of an ensemble or shift weight to areas where it is best supported by the body and does not interfere with movement; and ways to place accessories on the body so that they do not block movement features.

The jacket shown in Figure A has a unique shoulder pleat that allows a firefighter to reach forward and upward, movements needed in a variety of tasks, such as climbing a ladder (Figure B). There are two things that need to be pointed out about this feature. First, it falls outside the area of the straps that support the backpack that holds the firefighter's breathing system. This allows the expansion to take place even when the breathing apparatus is in place. Second, the liners contain features that also expand in the same area. It is important that any movement features take place in all layers of a protective system. Sleeves are also contoured in a forward position with an elbow curve, so that the shoulder and elbow can move and bend without strain. The pants are also contoured with a shape that allows extra length over the back of the hip and the front of the knees. This allows room for climbing and for crawling without restriction.

It is difficult to provide freedom of movement without producing gaps between the turnout garments and accessories such as gloves and boots. When one reaches forward in everyday clothes, the sleeves ride up the arm leaving a gap between glove and sleeve. When one sits down, pant legs ride up above the ankle leaving a gap between socks and pants. In the intense conditions of firefighting, gaps between items of protective gear mean increased injuries. So there are generally wide overlaps between pants and jacket, boots and pants, and so on, and fasteners are used to pull cuffs and other closures close to the body so that no open areas are exposed to high heat.

FIGURES B-E Features of a turnout coat. (B) An action sleeve with pleat at back of jacket and contouring over the elbow; (C) a telescoping sleeve well that prevents water from entering sleeve once a glove is in place; (D) free-hanging throat tab; (E) zipper with storm flap. *(Illustrations courtesy of Globe Firesuits)*

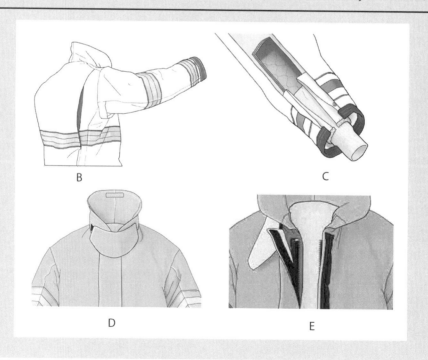

B

C

D

E

In some cases, however, an overlap is not sufficient. For example, a simple overlap between glove and sleeve would not prevent water from running into the sleeve when a firefighter's arm was raised, as it might be when aiming a hose or climbing a ladder. Water in the system would destroy insulation and create more potential for steam burns. Figure C shows a telescoping sleeve well that allows the arm to reach forward without creating a gap between the sleeve and glove. The gauntlet of any glove fits over a knit cuff on the coat and extends into a deep pleat that prevents water from entering the sleeve. The pleat allows the extra length needed to reach forward without stress on the body or sleeve.

Because of the range of movement of the head on the neck, the interface between the helmet and coat is probably the most difficult to achieve without getting in the way of free motion. Most firefighters wear a Nomex or PBI knit hood to protect the ears, neck, and lower face. It is a nonconductive accessory that bridges the gaps between the helmet, the facemask, and the coat and is flexible enough to allow neck movement. The collar can also be worn turned up to help bridge the gap between helmet and coat. Figure D shows a free-hanging throat tab that helps secure the front neckline of the coat and the collar over the knit hood.

Fitting is of primary concern to providing free movement. The ensemble shown in Figure A has a number of features that help fit the garments to individual bodies. First, the manufacturer has a component system of cutting and assembly that allows custom fitting for each firefighter. (See Design Strategies 2.3, "Mass Customization and Sizing.") The pants are worn with suspenders, which allow length adjustability, and they also include an adjustable feature for the waistline.

Other Turnout Gear Features

There are a variety of other concerns when designing protective clothing for firefighting. One of the most important is that *all* outer materials need to be able to withstand the high heat of the fire. This means that any trims and fasteners (including seams) must be flame resistant and that they must not heat up and cause burns to the hands when being operated. In addition, it is important that donning and doffing fasteners neither melt and fuse together nor ice up and trap an injured firefighter in the garment.

Regular fasteners such as zippers and Velcro®, regular seam stitching and many trims can allow water to pass through them, so they need to be incorporated into the design in a way that retains the waterproofing of the outer garment. The turnout coat shown in Figure A uses a high-temperature-resistant zipper that is covered with a storm flap (Figure E) that incorporates a microporous membrane. The storm flap is closed with flame-resistant Velcro®. This same Velcro is used to secure the free-hanging throat tab and as a front closure for the pants. Fasteners such as these should be able to be operated with a gloved hand.

High-visibility trim is used on turnout gear so that injured firefighters who may be trapped in the low-visibility fire environment can be more easily located by other firefighters. Since it is on the outermost layer of the garment, it must also be able to withstand the high heat of a fire. In addition, it is helpful if the surface of the trim can be easily cleaned, since a buildup of dirt can destroy its reflective capacity. Additional information on high-visibility materials and their placement can be found in Chapter 8 under "Visibility."

As is true for a number of activities, firefighting requires a number of tools and accessories, and it is often helpful if they can be carried on the body. Pockets for these items must be placed where they can be opened while the backpack straps are in place. There are cargo pockets on both the coat and pants shown in Figure A. Individual pockets for those handling radios, etc., can be added as needed.

The turnout coat shown in Figure A has an additional safety feature—a rescue strap. This strap, shown in Figure F, is hidden between the inner and outer jacket and extends around the shoulders and under the arms. The end loop of the strap emerges from the jacket through a flap at the base of the collar. If a firefighter is for some reason unable to escape from a fire, he or she can be dragged to safety using this strap.

Proximity and Entry Suits

Since proximity suits are worn in situations where the firefighter is close to flames, the outer layer of the suit needs to be able to reflect high radiant heat. Often a proximity suit has the same design as regular firefighting gear, but the outer fabric has an aluminized surface. Some models are one-piece, and many contain room to house a breathing apparatus inside the suit so that it is also protected from high heat. Figures G and H show two models of proximity suits.

FIGURE F Rescue strap in lining of turnout coat shown in Figures B-E. *(Illustrations courtesy of Globe Firesuits)*

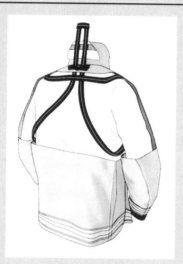

FIGURES G AND H Proximity suits for protection from high radiant heat environments. (G) A proximity suit with integrated hood and boots (the back extension in the suit covers breathing apparatus); (H) a suit with separate hood, boots, and gloves. Wide overlap areas are important to this type of suit.

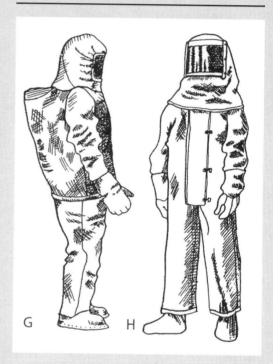

Newtex® has developed a five-layer composite for their proximity garments, Z-Flex®, that contains (1) an outer aluminized film, (2) a high-temperature resistant nonconductive barrier film, (3) another layer of the aluminized film like the outer layer to increase the radiant reflectivity, (4) a thermoset polymer layer that bonds the layers while resisting degradation by heat, and (5) a "Mock Knit"™—an innovative weave of PBI and aramid that is woven for strength, but has the flexibility and hand of a knit.

FIGURE I An entry suit for emergency personnel. *(Newtex Industries)*

Firefighters in entry suits (See Figure I) actually walk into flames, so entry suits must be made with a fireproof outer layer and contain a lot of nonconductive insulation. Some inorganic materials such as Zetex® glass fabrics used for the outer layer of an entry suit may be used without a finish, but most often the outermost material of an entry suit is aluminized to add extra protection from radiant heat.

Every interface in an entry suit must be carefully designed to ensure that heat and flames do not enter the system at any point. Often, pant legs extend into boot covers that can be adjusted to fit different boot sizes. Double storm flaps and inner drapes and cinches are employed to keep any gaps in protection from occurring. Both the system used to provide breathing air and the facemask are housed within the suit. Hoods may be held close to the jacket using underarm straps. Often, cooling vests that provide air circulation or vests housing cold gel packs are used under entry suits.

CASE STUDY 5.2 Full-Cycle Research: The Cyberia Suit

The Cyberia project provides an outstanding example of full-cycle design research, where designers study user needs, search for and/or develop materials and test them, produce prototypes, test them on users, evaluate their effectiveness and redesign as necessary.

The Cyberia Suit (Figure A) was designed for experienced snowmobilers (Rantanen et al. 2000). Its purpose was to prevent accidents and to help ensure survival if an accident occurred. The researchers involved wanted to integrate information technology, electronics, and advanced materials to develop smart clothing. They hoped that prototypes developed through their work would also benefit a variety of other people whose activities were performed in extreme cold.

User Needs

In developing the Cyberia suit, the designer-researchers concentrated on three areas: the design of the clothing, the design of the technology, and the relationship between these two areas and users' needs. An essential aspect of these interrelated areas was on the trade-off that exists between *being* wired and *looking* wired. Much of the resistance of many individuals to smart clothing lies in the fact that they would like the features provided by technology, but want to look normal. Some designers refer to *seamless* design when they talk about products that work without any visible hint to the consumer as to why they perform well or feel so good.

One of the primary goals for this ensemble was to be able to provide information about the location and movements of the wearer. The researchers wanted the user to be able to send emergency messages and wanted the suit to be able to send automatic alarm messages if sensor data was abnormal and the user did not respond to cancel them. The aim was then to have the suit automatically inform various emergency services in the event of an accident using phone numbers preprogrammed into the system. In addition to asking for emergency assistance, the designers wanted the user to be able to ask the location of another suit.

As discussed earlier in this chapter, one of the limiting factors in adding powered devices to clothing is the weight and bulk they add to the clothing ensemble. The developers of the Cyberia suit were aided in this by the fact that the wearer is seated most of the time. Still, they focused on additions to the suit that were small in size and low in weight and used a limited amount of power. Their aim was not to add more than 1 kg (2.2 lb) of weight to the typical snowmobile suit.

A study of user needs helped set a variety of other criteria for the suit. Among the final criteria were the following:

1. Users would be wearing gloves, so the interface with any control device needed to be able to be operated with gloves on and be able to be used by both right- and left-handed users.
2. From a safety standpoint, the power source used needed to operate for at least 24 hours without recharging.

FIGURE A The Cyberia survival suit. *(Rantanen et al. 2000)*

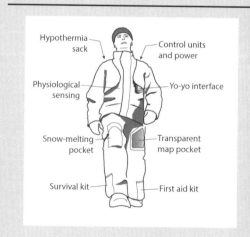

3. If components were woven or knitted into a textile structure, they needed to be able to be machine washable. If not, they needed to be easily detached before washing.

4. The electronic components needed either to be soft, or any hard edges would need to be cushioned so that they were comfortable on the body.

5. The electronic components of the system needed to be separated into smaller units and distributed around the body, keeping in mind the areas of the body that were most capable of supporting weight without strain and avoiding placing rigid or bulky components over the joint areas to prevent loss of movement. It also was important to consider the possible effect of body heat and perspiration on the components.

6. The electronic components needed to operate in temperatures from $-4°F$ ($-20°$ C) to $122°F$ ($50°C$). Therefore, the suit needed to provide insulation so that the temperature of the devices did not dip below $-4°F$, yet provide some method of cooling them if the combination of heat from the device and heat from the body was so insulated that it created a microclimate that reached $122°F$.

Designing a Prototype

The prototype suit developed consisted of five pieces: an undershirt and underpants, a support vest, and a snowmobile jacket and pants. The underwear contained Outlast phase-change materials and electronically heated conductive woven heat pads at both wrists. Cables ran from both heating pads for the wrists along the underside of the sleeves to a central processing unit (CPU) at the lower back. The underwear also contained electrodes to monitor pulse rate.

Between the jacket lining and the outer jacket was a vest that was closely fitted to the body so that it could support the electronic units. The vest was attached through two interior loops on the shoulders and zipped to the lining at the front opening. This arrangement allowed two things to happen. First, the vest could be form-fitted to the body without changing the shape and drape of the outer garment. Second, this allowed the unit to be easily removed so the suit could be washed. The vest contained the CPU, which housed acceleration sensors.

The jacket and pants were made of a PTFE-laminated polyamide fabric. Sensors were spread out in the jacket shell and connected to the support vest by a cylindrical connector plug. A digital temperature sensor was positioned inside the jacket's outer fabric and also inside the support vest in order to measure microclimate temperatures. Sensors at waist height were intended to detect when the suit had fallen into water. A loudspeaker in the jacket collar and an LED white light in the sleeve of the jacket provided audio and visual alerts to the user that emergency messages were being automatically sent by the suit. This would allow a user to take measures to cancel them if they were being sent erroneously.

The jacket and pants contained a variety of other unique features: a disposable pocket made of aramid fibers on one thigh for melting snow, a transparent map pocket on the other thigh, a waterproof pocket for matches, ice spikes integrated into the sleeves (for helping the user get out of a hole in the ice), a mobile phone pocket, and an impermeable bag that could serve as a shelter to protect the user from hypothermia. To allow the user to interact with the communications and information functions of the suit while wearing bulky gloves, the designers created a Yo-Yo interface consisting of a retractable cord that allowed the user to scroll through menu options. Squeezing the device allowed the user to select an option. The Yo-Yo retracted back into a dock beneath a flap on the front of the jacket. The dock for the Yo-Yo was made of a sturdy foam to both protect the device and to cushion the wearer from impact as it retracted.

All of the materials for these features and others were thoroughly tested before being chosen for the prototype. The jacket and trouser fabric was tested for abrasion resistance and bursting strength. Its windproofness, waterproofness, and breathability were tested. Snow melted in the snow-melting pocket was analyzed to be certain it was drinkable. The clear plastic of the map pocket was washed and tested in freezing temperatures, and its transparency was unchanged. A reflective finish used on the outer suit material was put through both washing and abrasion tests. Its reflectivity was maintained after abrasion, but diminished a bit after ten washings.

Washing and dry cleaning tests were conducted for any sensors, circuit boards and other electronics that were not removable, and they remained functional. These components were also given perspiration and seawater durability tests. Some circuit boards experienced operational breaks during these tests, but functioned normally after drying.

The function of all of the electronic modules was tested indoors, both individually and collectively before being tested in Arctic conditions.

Evaluation of the Design

The testing was done with individuals who were driving a snowmobile, skiing, or walking with snowshoes. A variety of emergencies were simulated. The tests showed that the alarm systems were operational and that the suit appearance and comfort was acceptable. The distribution of the electronic components on the body achieved a comfortable weight balance.

There were some minor problems with some of the connections between components and the cables made the suit a bit stiffer than a regular suit, especially for movements that required stretching. The designers recommended that succeeding models be attempted with wireless short-range communication devices rather than serial cables. Some of the electronic components were not well suited for the temperature range experienced, so alternatives will need to be found. Battery life and weight are always a problem, and even though those used in this suit achieved the designers' goals, it was recommended that newer battery technologies such as those using lithium polymer be explored. The Yo-Yo was difficult to use with gloves in place, and the display slowed down in very cold temperatures. The snow-melting pocket leaked a bit when placed on a campfire, so the sealing processes used needed to be reconsidered.

In general, the very thorough evaluation provided designers with much helpful information with which they could improve the suit. The designers' next step was to apply this comprehensive research plan and the many lessons learned in this research to other professions, such as firefighting, and to groups such as elderly and disabled people.

Conclusion

Thermal balance is a factor in the design of every item of clothing. As more complex functional designs are discussed in succeeding chapters, especially those in Chapters 6 and 7 that involve impermeable materials and full body coverage, the principles in this chapter will need to be applied in creative ways.

6 Impact Protection

Impact protection is not generally thought to be a primary function of clothing, although a great number of clothing items for military, sports, industrial, and service activities are used for this purpose.

When impact-protective clothing is mentioned, one may immediately think of a historic suit of armor such as the one shown in Figure 6.1A. You need only look at the changes in its modern equivalent—the "bulletproof" (ballistics) vest—to see the effects of technology on impact protection

over the years. Rigid materials have been replaced by flexible ones (Figure 6.1B), and flexible forms have been given fashion appeal (Figure 6.1C). To understand how flexible and rigid materials both provide impact protection and how clothing items can protect the body during collisions, it is important first to briefly review the physical principles involved in impact. In physics, these principles usually fall under the heading of *mechanics*. Mechanical principles are the tools that designers have at their disposal in selecting

FIGURE 6.1 (A) A medieval suit of armor; (B) a ballistics vest for police officers made of a flexible textile fabric; (C) a sport jacket with layers of ballistics material in its lining.

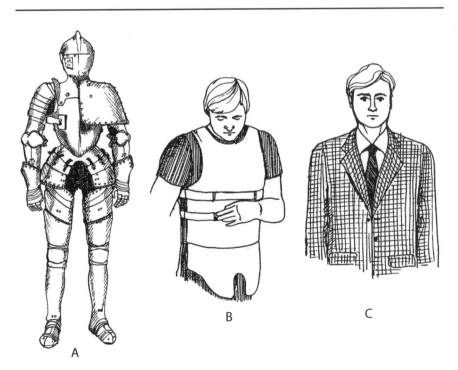

A

B

C

materials and designing impact-protective clothing.

A number of physics terms are introduced in this chapter to help designers understand why impact-protective garments work. In particular, it is important to understand the terms **pressure**, mass, **acceleration**, **deceleration**, momentum, and **elasticity**, and the concepts of **energy exchange** and **energy conservation**. Additional terms are used to help define these concepts and to give the reader enough of the language of physics to consult literature on impact protection. In this text, the focus is not on mathematical calculations, so these terms should be easily understood even without a math or physics background. Try to understand the concepts rather than simply memorizing specific definitions. Keep examples of familiar impacts in mind as the chapter progresses. It may help to observe contact sports or other activities that involve impact and practice using the terms and concepts in this chapter to explain why the results of an impact occur as they do.

Impact

Dictionary definitions of impact use the phrases, "*a striking together*" or "*violent contact*." The word *collision* is often used as a synonym. These definitions refer to only one type of impact—one due to compressive forces. Actually, three actions result from the application of forces on impact: tension, shear, and compression. Each application of force places different stresses on an object. Figure 6.2 shows what happens when force is applied to the opposite ends of a body made of a pliable material. This action increases the length of the body or pulls it entirely apart and is called **tensile stress** or tension. In most materials, there is a corresponding thinning of the cross section when a material is under tension, and the amount of thinning in one direction is related to the expansion in length of the material. There is tension in a rope used by a mountain climber as it supports the climber's weight. **Tensile impact** is abrupt tensile stress. For example, a parachute cord is subject to tensile impact when the parachute becomes fully inflated and the cords are suddenly snapped taut by the weight of the skydiver below.

When a pair of opposite forces act on a material so that adjacent parts slide over one another, this is termed **shearing stress** or shear. If a person brushes past a wall and the inside surface of a sweater sticks to the skin while the outside

FIGURE 6.2 Tensile, shearing, and compressive forces.

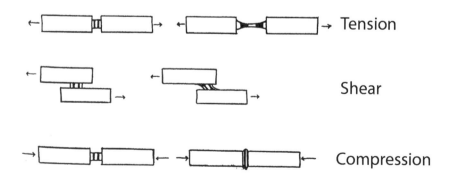

Tension

Shear

Compression

sticks to the wall, shearing stress develops on the sweater fabric. The outside fibers of the fabric are forced in the opposite direction from the inside fibers. The advent of artificial turf brought about the use of arm and leg covers for football players as they tried to prevent the shearing stress between their skin surfaces and the turf resulting in an abrasion, with the outer layer of skin separating from the inner skin layers.

When forces acting on the ends of a material decrease its length, this is termed compressive stress or **compression**. In most materials, one can note a corresponding thickening of the cross section of the material when compression is applied. **Compressive impact** is distinguished from compression in much the same way that tensile impact is distinguished from tension. Compressive impact begins and ends rapidly. There is a high level of force involved. The dents in automobiles that result from high-speed collisions provide visible evidence that compressive impact has taken place. Broken bones and bruises provide visible evidence that the body has received a compressive impact beyond its tolerance.

At some level, all three types of stresses may be involved in the collisions discussed in this chapter. For example, although a bullet initially compresses a protective vest and the body behind it, eventually, the threads in the material of the vest elongate with the tensile stress placed on them as the bullet attempts to break through them. If the bullet glances off the fabric of the vest, it may place shearing stress on the yarns as it moves past them. Although tensile and shearing impacts affect textiles to some extent in many collisions, most of the collisions between the body and foreign objects of many kinds—whether the objects are sports equipment, bullets, or environmental hazards—involve compressive

impacts. Therefore, much of this chapter is devoted to studying ways to design protective equipment and clothing that reduce the effects of compressive impact on the body.

PRINCIPLES GOVERNING THE EFFECTS OF IMPACT

Some alternatives for preventing impact from harming the body can be illustrated with the following example. Imagine that a woman is standing beside a building as bricks from the roof begin to fall toward her. To prevent the bricks from injuring her, she can change something about herself; change something about the bricks; or alter the relationship between the bricks and her body.

The best way to prevent damage to a body is to prevent a collision from occurring at all. That is, she should move, or, ideally, the bricks might not fall far enough to be a threat. As an alternative, the impacting object, the bricks, could be padded or made of nondamaging materials such as foam rubber. Since there are situations in which neither of the preceding measures could logically be taken, a third alternative—wearing protective clothing (e.g., a hard hat and/or a padded jacket)—would seem to be the most effective solution.

All three approaches to protection have merits under specific conditions. For example, automobile crash testing has shown the clear superiority of restraint systems (seat belts) that prevent an individual from colliding with the car interior. In other situations, padding on the interior surfaces may be best. Parents have long used bumper cushions on crib interiors as an effective method of protecting a baby's body from contact with the hard surface of the crib. Padding or restraining the baby would seem to be far less appealing solutions to this problem. There are other instances in which body padding provides the best solution. In sports such as football, where contact is an essential part of the game, restraint is not possible. In ice hockey, where the composition and surfaces of the ice, puck, and stick are essential to the game, padding of some of the impacting objects would completely change the game and make play impossible. As a result, protective body coverings are the only feasible choice for many sports as well as a variety of industrial and service occupations.

In order to design protective body coverings, it is important to understand the factors related to impact on the human body that may lead to injury. There are a number of interesting cases in literature that can serve as case studies to explore these factors. During the 1930s, De Haven investigated the conditions of a number of individuals who had fallen from great heights (Sells and Berry 1961, 285). He recorded that one man fell spread eagle (supine) 55 ft (16.8 m) into a flower bed that had been freshly spaded, left a 4 in (10.16 cm) depression, and emerged relatively unharmed. Another fell spread eagle (supine) from an elevation of 93 ft (28.35 m) into soft earth, left a 6 in (15.24 cm) depression, and also survived relatively unharmed. Physics concepts related to these falls can provide insight to designers about how to develop impact-protective clothing. Pressure, mass, acceleration, gradual deceleration, momentum, and elasticity will be explored here.

Pressure

Pressure is the force per unit area of contact (Pressure = force/area). As this formula indicates, to decrease the pressure of an impact on the body, it is essential to spread the force of that impact over the widest area. To do this, the body can either be oriented so that it contacts the greatest amount of surface of an impacting object or the impacting object can be changed so that its surface is extended or is more capable of contacting a larger area of the body.

One of the effects of pressure can be seen in the stiletto or spiked heels that have been in and out of fashion over the years. The very small contact area of these heels when a step is taken in them can result in flooring surfaces being covered with many indentations. It would be unusual for the heel of a flat shoe, like a man's loafer, to make such indentations because the force of these wide flat heels is spread out over a much larger surface. In a spiked heel, all of the weight of the wearer is placed on an area of about $1/16$ in^2 (0.4 cm^2), and the pressure exerted on the floor is considerably greater in that small area. For example, a 110 lb (50 kg) woman landing on one such heel would exert almost a ton of force per square inch (0.17 metric tons/cm^2).

In the De Haven examples discussed earlier, the body orientation of both men was a major factor in the outcome of the collisions since it allowed the force of the impact to be spread out over the entire body. Had either man landed feet first or head first, a much smaller area of the body would have hit the ground, and considerably greater injury might have occurred to the impacting areas.

With regard to pressure, the rationale for freely flowing liquids is not the same as it is for solids. For example, even though it is important to contact the greatest area of a solid, the opposite is generally true for liquids. Fluids do not compress but can only be displaced. A skilled diver takes advantage of this by presenting the smallest portion of the body to the water and entering in a way that parts it gradually. In contrast, a belly flop presents the maximum body surface to the water surface and results in an audible and visible collision.

When protective clothing and equipment act as a barrier between the body and an impacting object, it is important to remember that the contact area for an impact to the *body* is the interface between the body and the equipment. For example, it is possible for there to be *no* difference in impact to a woman's *foot* in the example of the stiletto versus the man's wider heeled shoe. Even though the pressure between the two sizes of heels and the floor may result in quite different impacts to the *floor*, the woman's foot contacts only the interior surface of the shoe. If the interior surfaces of both shoes were composed of the same materials and both met the full surface of the woman's heel, there should be no difference in impact to the *foot* due to pressure. The force of the floor pushing back on the shoe is transferred through the sole material and spread over a larger area of the individual's heel. This body/equipment interface is one of the most critical factors to keep in mind when designing impact-protective equipment.

A familiar example of pressure and impact in daily life can be found in the design of restraint systems in automobiles. If, for example, a driver is properly restrained by seat belts and a car comes to a sudden stop, the body is thrown forward so that the first impact it feels is with the seat belt. Although this collision is infinitely preferable to colliding with the dashboard and windshield or being thrown from the car, people who have experienced this type of collision are well aware of the extremes of pressure placed on the body by the narrow band of the seat belt. Because it is the interface that is critical, variations in anatomy, such as those that occur during pregnancy or for infants and young children, may change the design requirements for restraint systems. (See Design Solutions 6.1.)

Designers of sports equipment and industrial protective items make use of the concept of pressure in developing rigid forms that contact wide

areas of the body, spreading the force of a blow rather than allowing an impacting object to hit a small contact area. (See Figure 6.3.)

Newton's Second Law

One of the most fundamental principles of mechanics is expressed in Newton's Second Law of Motion: Force = mass × acceleration ($F = ma$). In order to alter the force placed on a body by an impacting object, one of the factors on the other side of the equation—either the mass or the acceleration—of the impacting object needs to be altered. It is important to begin, then, with a definition of those two terms.

Mass is the amount of matter in a body. It is expressed in kilograms (kg) in the International System of Units (SI). Mass is perhaps best explained in terms of the concept of **inertia**, the quality of a body that makes it continue to do whatever it is doing. If a ball is lying still, its inertia will make it resistant to movement. If it is rolling, its inertia will cause it to continue to roll until some force stops it. A 2 kg ball has more mass and more resistance to a change in its state of motion than does a 1 kg ball.

Mass is often confused with weight, but the two are not the same. Weight is the force that gravity exerts on a body. It is expressed in pounds in the English system and Newtons (N) in the International System of Units. Mass, in contrast, is not affected by gravity. The difference between the two becomes clearer in outer space where, for example, on the surface of the moon, one-sixth gravity conditions exist. Because the moon's gravity is only one-sixth as strong as that on Earth, a rock weighing 6 lb (26.9 N) on the Earth would only weigh 1 lb (5.5 N) on the moon. However, its mass would remain the same in both locations. This means that although it would be considerably easier to hold the rock, it would not be easier

Design Solutions 6.1: Car Seats for Infants and Children

The potential effects of the seat belt/body collision on infants and children have resulted in considerable research and development by the auto industry. Since the growth centers in a child's bones are composed of softer tissues than the firm bones of an adult, the pressure placed on their bodies by the narrow band of a seat belt could cause substantial damage. In addition, a child's head is much larger and heavier in proportion to its body than is the head of an adult. Because of this, the forces delivered to a child's head during an auto collision can place an enormous stress on the neck. Child restraint systems, particularly those for infants and younger children, must take both of these factors into account.

Since many collisions occur to the front end of a car and the impact throws a body forward, one of the ways infants' bodies are protected is with rearward facing seats. Figure A shows this kind of infant restraint. In the event of a sudden stop or an impact to the front of the car, the entire back of an infant's body is thrown forward and contacts the surface of the infant seat. Thus, the impact is spread over the entire length of the body, and chances of injury due to localized pressure are reduced. A rearward facing seat is so effective in reducing injuries that the U.S. National Highway Traffic and Safety Administration has recommended keeping young children in this kind of seat as long as possible.

Figure B shows a car seat for an older child that has restraints over both shoulders and a lap restraint that surrounds both thighs. Figure C shows a seat that increases the area of contact of the restraint system. Instead of a harness that contacts a relatively small portion of the body surface, a molded, padded surface is placed in front of the child's torso, particularly in front of the face. In a crash, the same force would be spread over a larger body area in model C than in model B, and less pressure would be applied to any specific area of the child's body. This seat offers the additional benefit of limiting the forward motion of the head, and thus reduces strain on the neck and spinal cord. Car seats for both infants and children have increasingly added protection from side impact as well by significantly extending the sides of the seat in the area of the head and adding extra cushioning there.

FIGURES A–C Three models of child-restraint systems. (A) A rear-facing seat for an infant; (B) a model for a child; (C) a model for a toddler.

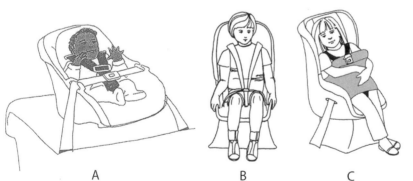

A B C

to throw it. The rock would continue to resist a change in its state of motion because it would still have the same mass even though it weighed less (Figure 6.4). An object's mass, not its weight, is the important factor for a designer to consider in developing body protection for a collision.

Since something large is often said to be massive, mass also tends to be confused with volume.

FIGURE 6.3 Shin guard for ice hockey. The long, rigid plate that extends the length of the shin spreads the force of an impacting object such as the puck over a much wider area.

FIGURE 6.4 In zero gravity in outer space, an astronaut finds a rock easy to hold motionless (it has no weight) but just as hard to shake from side to side as on Earth (its mass resists a change in state of motion).

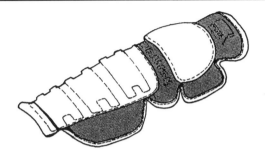

Volume and mass are not the same. Mass refers to the quantity of matter in an object, not the total size of an object. Although one can change the volume of a foam sponge by squeezing it, the amount of matter in it—its mass—remains the same.

Acceleration is the rate at which velocity increases. **Deceleration** is the rate at which velocity decreases. A key factor in the injury a body sustains in a collision is the degree to which acceleration or deceleration can be changed *gradually*. A body falling toward the ground accelerates because of gravity (i.e., it increases in velocity 32 ft/sec (9.75 m/sec) for every second of the fall). When a moving object is involved in a collision, the rate of acceleration may often drop to zero within a few milliseconds.

Because the men in the De Haven study cited earlier fell into freshly spaded earth rather than hitting a rigid surface, they experienced a more gradual deceleration. Had they fallen on a concrete walk, deceleration would have occurred instantly. As it was, the earth offered some resistance to their fall, but the force of their bodies eventually fully compacted the soil in the areas of contact. During this compacting process, the rate of acceleration changed gradually rather than instantly. In both

instances (hitting concrete versus hitting soft soil), the men would have been moving at the same speed when they hit the ground. However, because the soil allowed more *time* to bring their bodies to a rest, the rate of deceleration was lower (i.e., the "a" in F = ma is smaller), so the force experienced by their bodies would also be smaller.

One of the most familiar examples of gradual deceleration can be found in the airbag restraint system used in automobiles. Airbags (Figure 6.5)

FIGURE 6.5 An automobile airbag.

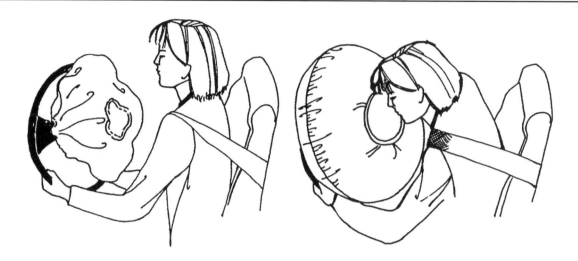

inflate fully in the milliseconds that follow a crash, pinning passengers back against the seat before they can be thrown forward. However, air begins to be released from the bags very gradually almost immediately after they are fully inflated, either through venting at the rear of the bag or through uncoated fabrics that are engineered to have a controlled porosity to the inflation gas (Ashley 1994). Therefore, the body begins to "ride the bag down" (i.e., the force of a body being thrown forward begins to compress the bag and air is slowly forced out of it). A minute or so after a crash, a seat-belted body may end up in much the same position with or without an airbag. However, with the airbag, the body eases forward gradually instead of jack-knifing forward abruptly. This avoids tensile impact on the tissues of the body as well as the compressive impact that might occur with items such as the dashboard and steering wheel.

Velocity involves both speed and direction; it is the distance traveled per time period in a specific direction. In order to achieve a gradual deceleration, one may change either speed or direction

or both. This idea is used to great advantage by athletes and designers of sports equipment. For example, a well-trained athlete may be able to roll with the punches, changing direction and thus the velocity with which the body enters and leaves a collision. Instead of coming completely to a stop, the athlete keeps moving but moves in a different direction. This allows the impacted area to decelerate over a longer period of time. Thinking back to the F = ma equation, the more time it takes for a body to decelerate (the lower the rate of change of velocity or a), the lower the force (F) on the other side of the equation. (See Figure 6.6.) This generally means less chance of injury.

Protective materials and the shapes and surface textures of protective equipment may also affect the rate of deceleration following impact. (See Figure 6.7.) For example, a rounded football helmet for American football may slide off another rounded helmet immediately after contact so that the heads of both players need not decelerate abruptly. Because the direction in which the players' heads are traveling changes slightly, their

FIGURE 6.6 (A) A boxer moving toward the glove shortens the time during which momentum is changed and so increases the force of a punch; (B) a boxer moving away extends the time over which momentum is changed, and thus decreases the force.

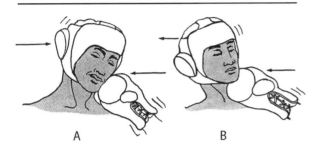

A   B

speed decreases much more gradually than if the helmets locked together at impact. The resulting gradual deceleration helps decrease the injurious effects of the collision. Designers can build the potential for this gradual deceleration into items of protective equipment by looking at potential contact areas and avoiding shapes and textures that

might stick to one another or to impacting items in the environment.

The terms, **momentum** (the quantity of motion in a body) and **impulse** (the time period over which momentum is changed) may also be used to describe collisions. Momentum is the product of mass and velocity (momentum = mass × velocity). Something with a small mass (such as a bullet) traveling at a high speed in a forward direction could have the same momentum as a large mass (such as a truck) that is traveling forward very slowly. If both bodies in a collision are susceptible to equal deformity, the one with the least momentum will be deformed the most. (See Energy Basics 6.1.)

Although the discussion thus far has centered on changing the velocity rather than the mass part of the equation, it must be noted that it is possible to effect a change in momentum by changing the masses of the bodies involved. When the human body is involved, mass can be more easily increased than decreased. In addition, *where* the mass is added may make a huge difference. (See Anatomy and Design 6.1.) When someone picks up a hammer and swings it at a nail, that person is, in effect, adding mass to the arm. A football player who puts on heavy protective gear is adding mass to several segments of the body and increasing mass increases the force he brings to an impact. One professional American football player who was asked for suggestions as to how to reduce injuries on the football field jokingly proposed a system of "designated tacklers" who would prohibit players with more mass than his own from tackling him. It is imperative for a designer to consider the mass added to the body by an item of protective equipment,

FIGURE 6.7 In fencing, the combination of the concave shape of an armpit, a pointed weapon, a textile with interstices, and the forward lunge of a fencer concentrating efforts on a target area all make the underarm an area with great potential for injury.

Energy Basics 6.1: Impulse and Injury

It is important not to make the mistake of thinking that the force of the impact is associated with the length of time two objects are pressed together during impact. The time of contact between two bodies is *not* the critical factor that determines the force an impact delivers. What is important is the length of time during which the *momentum* of the two bodies is changed, (i.e., its impulse). Several adventure movies have shown an engine being sent to rescue a train whose engine has lost its brakes while descending a mountain. The rescuing engine enters the track somewhere down the mountain and, just before the runaway train approaches behind it, accelerates so that it is traveling the same speed as the runaway. There is no collision upon contact because the trains are traveling in the same direction at almost the same speed. The rescue train then applies its brakes and gradually slows down both trains until they come to a halt just short of a grateful community. In this example, the contact time is extremely long and so is the time over which momentum is changed.

Similar effects may be experienced when two cars collide while traveling in the same direction at similar speeds. When cars crash head on, they may also stay in contact for a long period of time, but the momentum of the cars would be stopped at the instant of impact.

However, consider what would happen if an automobile traveling north at 50 mph (80 km/hr) collided with a truck traveling south at 50 mph (80 km/hr). Because of its greater mass, the truck would be likely to change the velocity of the automobile in a matter of milliseconds. At the crash, the automobile would probably deform around the front of the truck and be pushed backward by it for some period of time. Although the automobile would remain in contact with the truck for a fairly long period, the time over which its momentum was changed would be very short (the instant of impact). The instant change in the momentum of the automobile, which would be due primarily to force, would cause a great deal of damage.

---

particularly if the item is worn or carried quite far from the center of the body.

Elasticity

The final variable discussed here as a major factor in the outcome of a collision is the elasticity of the colliding bodies. **Elasticity** is the ability of a material to temporarily change shape when a force acts on it, but return to its original shape when that force is removed. If a material deforms permanently as a result of a collision, it is said to be **inelastic**.

Materials have **elastic limits**. We can feel this ourselves when the force of an impact exceeds the elasticity of our body tissues and a strain or sprain

occurs. Obviously, it is preferable for the human body to return to its original shape following a collision rather than sustain a deformation. Its ability to do this depends not only on the pressure, deceleration, and the force of the colliding objects but also on the elastic properties of both the body and the objects colliding with it. In order to understand how elasticity affects a collision, designers need to have some understanding of the concept of energy conservation. (See Energy Basics 6.2.)

Elasticity and Impact Injury

At first thought, if you had a choice between being in an elastic or inelastic collision, you might think you would prefer to be in an elastic one. After all,

Energy Basics 6.2: Energy Exchange and Impact Protection

At its most basic level, impact protection involves exchanging one form of energy for another. The law of conservation of energy (see Energy Basics 3.2) governs energy exchange. Because energy is always conserved and cannot be created or destroyed, the energy in a hurtling rock cannot be eliminated. However, that energy can be changed into a form less harmful to the object it contacts.

Many of the different forms that energy can take have already been presented in Energy Basics 3.2. In any impact, the kinetic energy of the impact is converted into one of these other forms. For example, a book on the edge of a table has mechanical potential energy by virtue of its position. As it falls toward the floor, it loses potential energy and gains kinetic energy. Since the total energy in a system always remains the same, once the book hits the floor, it has lost both its potential and kinetic mechanical energy, so they must have been converted into other forms—in this case to both heat energy (as molecules in the floor and book are stimulated by the collision) and sound energy (as the book hits the floor, mechanical energy is transferred to the surrounding air, which is compressed, forming a sound wave).

The book, depending upon the elasticity of its materials and its orientation when it hit the floor, was probably not damaged. However, inelastic collisions frequently result in deformation of one or both of the impacting objects. If, instead of the book, a ball of dough were dropped from the table, the dough would probably change shape as it hit the floor. A feather pillow would do the same. In both cases, the objects would cease moving shortly after impact so that the mechanical energy would not be conserved. However, if a rubber ball fell from the table surface, it probably would have a largely elastic collision with the floor. That is, its elasticity—its particular arrangement of molecules and their bonding mechanisms in rubber—would result in an elastic composition that caused it to retain much of its kinetic energy shortly after impact. It would hit the floor and compress, converting a small portion of its kinetic energy to sound and heat as well as potential energy. However, its elasticity would cause it to rebound (i.e., to convert its remaining potential energy to kinetic energy and continue to move), this time, traveling upward.

in the collision described in Energy Basics 6.2, a rubber ball is not permanently deformed in an elastic collision with the floor, but a ball of dough in its inelastic collision was. However, the human body is not a rubber ball. The rebound involved in some elastic collisions can be highly undesirable. It might be far preferable to be the nondeforming object in an inelastic collision (e.g., the floor in the dough/floor collision). If some item in a collision—either a protective device for the body *or* the impacting object itself—can be made crushable, rebound will not occur, and the uneven

acceleration of various body parts will be a less serious problem.

Many impact-protective garments provide the conditions under which an inelastic collision can take place. They become the deformable element in the collision. If an object such as a brick were to strike a protectively clothed body, the objective of that clothing should be to suffer the deformation so that the body did not feel the effects of the collision. If an individual were moving and struck the sidewalk after falling off a bicycle, for example, protective foam could deform, allowing the body

Anatomy and Design 6.1: Body Segments and Whole Body Impact

Another very important factor that relates to mass is that objects are often made up of segments that contain different masses. The mass of the human body, for example, is distributed over a series of articulated segments that each contains very different amounts of mass. Therefore, the response of each body part to the same collision may differ. Figures A and B show a type of restraint system for pilots that takes this into account. Because the arms and legs may flail uncontrollably when the pilot impacts the air mass during an emergency ejection, a strapping system has been built into the pilot's clothing to pull the limbs into position against the body. In this position, the strapping removes the articulating points of the shoulders, elbows, hips, and knees, and the limbs become part of the total body mass. Therefore, they are not free to be subjected to a different change in momentum from the rest of the body.

The effects of adding an item of equipment to a body segment must be considered because the extra mass may result in more stress on joints and further increase the potential for injury. For example, when a chest-to-chest collision occurs and an item such as a heavy helmet is worn, the momentum of the head can be greater than that of the rest of the body and lead to tremendous potential for neck injury.

FIGURES A AND B A restraint system for emergency escape for pilots. (A) A strapping system built into clothing with tension lines that loop through an ejection seat. (B) Tension lines are drawn tight as the pilot ejects, pulling the limbs close to the body so they cannot be flailed about by the inertia of ejection. *(Bohlin 1963)*

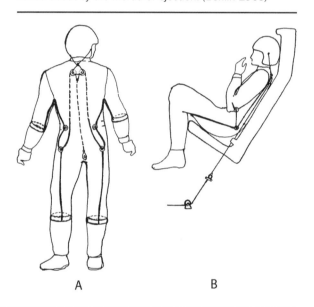

A   B

to sink into it and avoid injury. In both cases, if the protective clothing is well designed for a collision, energy exchange occurs within the clothing rather than on the surface of the body. The ability of impact-protective garments to provide this energy exchange depends on the composition of materials and the ways in which they are combined and shaped into designs.

IMPACT THEORY AND CLOTHING DESIGN

The interactions of many factors related to a specific impact situation need to be explored—from the physical characteristics of the individuals involved to their tasks to conditions in the environment to materials available for use in a design.

An incident with regard to American football helmet design provides a good example of why the relationship of all of the variables in an impact situation needs to be examined before making design decisions. A number of years ago, physicians and trainers working with football players realized that the helmet (See Figure 6.38A) had become so efficient at protecting the head that it was itself being used as a weapon and was the source of many injuries. Hoping to cut down on injuries, attempts were made both to change the rules about head-butting and to produce and develop a helmet with padding on its outer surface. This padding would presumably cushion the blows inflicted on opposing players. (Of course, it would be imperative for the opposing team to wear them as well, or they would continue to be able to inflict injury with their helmets!) When the padded helmets were put into use, however, those who proposed the idea put an immediate stop to their use. The padding materials used to coat the helmet compressed on impact, so opposing helmets tended to stick together when players collided. Instead of sliding off one another and allowing gradual deceleration as the smooth, rigid helmets did, the padded helmets stuck together and the momentum of the two impacting bodies decreased almost instantly. This allowed a tremendous amount of force to be delivered to the neck and thus there was a greatly increased potential for paralyzing injuries. Exploring all of the factors involved in a collision might have better informed the designers before putting players in danger with these helmets.

BODY TOLERANCE TO IMPACT

Since the objective of protective equipment is to change dangerous impacts into forces that are tolerable for the body, it is important to understand the ways in which the body can be injured.

The most basic objective for an item of protective equipment is to prevent *penetration* of the body by an impacting object. If an impacting object is sharp, for example, even impacts with very low levels of force may penetrate the skin and cause injury. In some impact situations, the objective may be to protect specific body parts not only from penetration but also from any *indentation* of the apparel and the body surface behind it. Still others may have the objective of completely absorbing impact forces so that the momentum of the impacting object never reaches the body at all.

You will see evidence of these objectives in the materials and designs used for most items of protective equipment.

Designers also need to be aware that impacts to certain body areas may cause more serious, life-threatening injuries than they do to others. For example, if the two men in the De Haven study discussed earlier in this chapter had fallen feet first, they would have suffered badly broken legs but they probably would have survived. Had they fallen head first, however, the damage might have proved fatal. In many occupations where impact protection is needed, it is provided first for the areas vital to life—the head and chest. Then, if it can be accomplished with reasonable comfort and freedom of movement, and for a reasonable cost, protection for other areas may be provided, too.

It is important to understand as thoroughly as possible the body part that needs to be protected. There may be a considerable difference between an impact to a fat-padded body part and one where the bone is relatively exposed. Sometimes, a fleshy body part can provide cushioning that absorbs part of the impact, whereas a blow to a bony, relatively unpadded area translates directly to the framework of the body. For other body areas, impact to a well-padded body part might result in a critical injury. Body tissues and the connections between them are so varied that a blow to one area may cause an entirely different type of injury than the same blow to an area a short distance away.

Much of the information about how well the body can tolerate various impacts has come from the automotive industry, which uses cadavers, animals, or laboratory-simulated body parts to gather its data. Experiments below the injury threshold may even use human volunteers. One difficulty in establishing tolerance levels for impact is defining a *tolerable* injury. Many researchers consider injury to be tolerable if it is reversible, that is, if it can be repaired or cured. However, this may vary depending on the individuals involved and the nature of the injury situation. What may be tolerable in one situation is often not tolerable in another. The danger of the situation, its injury potential, and the conditions surrounding the impact may have a strong bearing on what might be considered acceptable injury. Therefore, a different definition of injury tolerance may have to be established at the outset of every project on protective equipment.

Even if a specific level of injury could be established as tolerable, the same impact would probably not produce the same injury to two different people. The age, sex, size, general health, and physical and psychological condition of an individual all affect body tolerance to a specific injury. In one study of skull fracture, researchers found that "variations in the shape and thickness of the skull and scalp produced a 100 percent variation in the amount of energy required for fracture" (Damon et al.1966, 276). Even for one person, the propensity for injury to body parts varies, particularly if there is a past history of injury or illness.

In addition to differences in anatomical structure in the area being hit, some people in excellent physical condition are more able to roll with the punches, avoiding many of the effects of impact with their swift reactions. Consequently, any maximum levels of force that are set as tolerance levels tend to be a compromise. The impact conditions they define would produce serious but nonfatal injuries for the weakest person and no injuries for the strongest person or the one in the best physical and psychological condition.

Many types of injuries may be produced by impact. They are often classified in the categories of soft tissue damage, bone damage, and internal organ damage. Each has distinct repercussions that depend largely on the severity of the injury and

the function of the body part that was damaged. As mentioned previously, because of potential fatality, head and upper torso injuries that involve the function of body parts vital to life are considered the most dangerous body injuries. Injury to the soft tissue and organs in this area may be the result of either a direct blow or the rapid acceleration or deceleration involved in impact. These actions can generate forces that exceed the tensile strength of various body tissues. Even if there is no outward evidence of injury, rapid acceleration may cause body fluids to be displaced so rapidly that blood vessels may not be able to keep blood circulating. More information on the effects of acceleration, including a discussion of design of protective apparel for this type of injury is provided in Chapter 8 under "Acceleration."

Although a complete review of impact injury must be left to anatomy and physiology texts, a brief introduction to the terms used to describe them can be found in Table 6.1. These definitions provide a summary of the range of injuries for which impact protection may be needed.

The information presented here about the basics of impact—the importance of mass, force, deceleration, elasticity, and other factors involved in impact—can help designers understand the nature of an impact hazard. Studying the structure and function of a particular body part that needs to be protected will add knowledge about its ability to withstand impact. An understanding of protective materials and design configurations discussed next will help designers learn how to bridge the gap between the forces of an impact and the forces the human body can tolerate.

Impact-Protective Materials

The impact theory discussed thus far in this chapter establishes several criteria for the materials used

TABLE 6.1 Impact Injury Terminology

Abrasion	A scraping of the skin, often called a brush burn
Laceration	A cut or tear of the skin, or, subsequently, the underlying tissues
Contusion	A bruise; an injury where no broken skin is present, but the damaged tissue, including broken blood vessels underneath, cause a characteristic discoloration
Hematoma	A severe bruise; a swelling filled with blood
Hemorrhage	Bleeding, especially severe bleeding
Damage to a bursa	Swelling of one of the fluid-filled sacs that act as shock absorbers at a number of the body joints
Sprain	A twisting or pulling of a ligament, the elastic tissue that holds bones together
Strain	A twisting or pulling of a tendon, the connective tissue that joins a muscle to a bone
Dislocation	The movement of a bone out of its normal position in a joint causing strain on surrounding tissues, but not complete separation
Sublaxation	Incomplete dislocation; bones slide slightly out of position causing strain on surrounding tissues, but never complete separation
Fracture	A crack or break in a bone

for impact-protective clothing and items of personal protective equipment. An impact-protective material should

1. Prevent a colliding object from breaking the skin surface or entering the body;
2. Prevent an impacting object from focusing all of its pressure on one small area of the body (i.e., it should spread out the force of an impact);
3. Allow the impacting object *or* the body to decelerate gradually upon impact;
4. Help prevent an abrupt change in momentum at the moment of collision or immediately after it collides with an impacting object; and
5. Change the kinetic energy of an impacting object into a form of energy less harmful to the body.

Although certain materials can protect in all five of these ways, most materials perform only one or two of these functions effectively. Therefore, many impact-protective garments contain combinations of protective materials to provide full protection. The most commonly used materials for impact-protective clothing and equipment can be divided into three groups: flexible foams, rigid materials, and textiles.

FOAMS AS IMPACT PROTECTORS

Foams are the most widely used materials for absorbing the energy of an impact (i.e., converting the kinetic energy of an impacting object to heat, sound, potential, and other forms of energy less harmful to the body).

Information on the structure and formation of foams can be found in Chapter 3. (See Chapter 3, "Open- and Closed-Cell Foams" for a discussion of the manufacturing processes for foams.) Most of the foams used for impact protection are *elastic solid foams*. Elastic foams have one potential disadvantage for protective clothing: a return to their original shape poses the risk of rebound for the body. For many types of sports and recreational protective equipment, the most effective foam is one that is elastic but returns to its original shape slowly so that an impacting body does not rebound from its surface. This slow return characteristic is critical to the performance of impact-protective equipment. This is why many items of impact-protective equipment are made of closed-cell rather than open-cell foam.

Remember that a finished piece of closed-cell foam contains cells filled with gases at partial pressure. This allows the cells to give the foam the capacity to slowly compress. In the process of compression, closed-cell foams convert kinetic energy to potential energy. As the molecules of gas are moving in and out of a compressed state and the elastic solid is distorted, the friction involved also converts a portion of the kinetic energy to heat, which is then dissipated to the environment. Closed-cell foams are thus referred to as *energy absorbing*. At the same time, the presence of these gas-filled cells in a closed-cell foam means that it can never fully collapse, so an impacting object cannot make intimate contact with the body behind it.

It is interesting to observe energy conservation at work in closed-cell foam. Although the heat generated in most collisions involving closed-cell foams can be measured, it probably cannot be felt. However, the effects of the conversion of kinetic to potential energy are easily noted. When an object strikes closed-cell foam, the compression of the foam can be seen as the gases in each cell are forced to squeeze into the now smaller cell spaces. When the impacting object is removed, an indentation remains momentarily on the foam's surface. Then it slowly disappears as the gases pushing out on the cell walls gradually return the cells to their original size. One of the keys to a closed-cell foam's ability to provide impact protection

appropriate for protective clothing and equipment for the body is this ability to slowly compress and slowly return to shape.

Although some open-cell foams may be used as impact protectors, their formation does not naturally lend itself to effective energy absorption. The interconnections between the cells allow air to be squeezed out rapidly; consequently, an impact could flatten an open-cell foam to a thin layer of its base material. A 1/2 in (1.27 cm) sheet of open-cell foam could be compressed to about the thickness of a rubber glove if an object with sufficient force struck it. So, a protective garment made of open-cell foam could leave its wearer in rather intimate contact with a colliding object. At the same time, the flexibility of open-cell foam allows it to move readily with the body, compressing and expanding as needed during body movement. An ideal protective material would retain this ability for free movement with sufficient energy-absorbing qualities.

Open-cell foams *can* be made to provide better impact protection in several ways. A denser base material may be chosen to reduce the collapsibility of the total structure. The thickness of the cell walls of the foamed structure may be increased, thus increasing the proportion of material to gas. Or the thickness of the foam used in the final protective item may be increased. Each of these alternatives poses some type of compromise. An increased base material to gas cell ratio, for example, increases foam weight and decreases its flexibility. The bulk of thicker foam may interfere with body movement. Therefore, open-cell foam is generally used in combination with other materials so that its open-cell structure can lend positive qualities to the system while other materials compensate for its collapsibility.

Inelastic foams such as Styrofoam™ may also be energy absorbing. However, instead of compressing and then expanding, they provide effective impact protection by crushing or deforming permanently upon impact. The kinetic energy in this type of collision is converted primarily to heat and sound. Inelastic foams are not often used for clothing items for athletes because their inflexibility tends to restrict movement and decrease comfort and because they become dysfunctional after one impact. If a shoulder pad for football were made of inelastic foam, for example, one impact would flatten it, and the player would have to leave the game to change before the next play. However, because they are generally harder to compress, many inelastic foams have the capacity to absorb great amounts of energy with less thickness. This makes them useful in items where either a slim profile is required or high forces are involved in impacts. Helmets for motorcyclists and construction workers, for example, often incorporate rigid, inelastic foams in energy-absorbing liners, or they may be made completely of rigid inelastic foam.

There are many brands of impact-protective foams on the market. Manufacturers may use different base materials or different blowing agents and finishing processes to form foams. The resulting materials have different weights and different types of protective capacities.

Impact-protective foams can be made from a variety of materials including natural rubber, synthetic rubber (such as neoprene), polyurethane, polyethylene, polyvinyl chloride, and polystyrene. Both the base material and the process used to manufacture it determine whether a foam is elastic or inelastic and whether it is easy or difficult to compress. Other substances used in the manufacturing process, the treatment of the foam during and after formation and the placement of a foam in an impact-protective item all help to determine its behavior upon impact.

Foams and Energy Absorption

The response of a foam to impact consists of two phases: first, the gases in the cells are compressed or released, and then the material surrounding the cells is compressed. In open-cell foams, the first compression phase may squeeze all air out of the cells; in closed-cell foams, the cells are squeezed and flattened until the gases inside cannot be further compressed or the cells rupture.

Foams absorb energy most effectively during the first phase. Once the cells of a foam are flattened to the point where the solid rubber or plastic matrix material begins to be compressed, the kinetic energy of the impact is far more likely to be transmitted through the foam to the body. The most effective protective foam is one that makes the fullest use of the first phase, that of cell compression. If the foam is too stiff, its cells may not be fully compressed, and the kinetic energy of the impacting object is not likely to be fully converted. If the foam is too soft or too easily compressed, the energy is not fully absorbed during cell compression, and material compression will begin to take place. This is why open-cell foams are in general less effective as impact protectors than closed-cell foams. If easily compressible foams are to be used for impact protection, they need to be used in much greater thicknesses so that there are more cells available for energy absorption.

It is important for designers to understand these aspects of how and why foams absorb energy in order to develop new forms of impact protection. This knowledge is also is critical for understanding why some designs contain no closed-cell foam, yet are able to provide the same type of protection as closed-cell foam would. For example, the early model of protective liners for football helmets shown in Figure 6.8A serves as an inspiration for another approach. It works on the principle of restricted fluid flow between cells in the liner. This liner contains a series of polyethylene pockets or cells that are interconnected by tiny channels. Inside the liner are air and a certain amount of fluid, generally water and ethylene glycol, the latter added to prevent the water from freezing in cold temperatures. When the rigid helmet shell is contacted, the cells in the liner directly underneath are compressed and the fluid in them is forced toward the other cells in the system. Because of the limited size of the channels, however, the flow of the liquid takes place very slowly. This slow compression allows the impact to be absorbed by the system. Similar systems could be created with larger, less restrictive channels if more viscous fluids such as mineral oil or fluids that have been partially gelled were used instead of water and air. (In general, these are

less likely candidates because of their weight and, for some viscous substances, their toxicity.) The sensation of being in a fluid-filled liner of this type is somewhat similar to sinking into an automobile airbag or sitting down quickly on the cushions of a vinyl-covered couch. Since the vinyl does not breathe, the couch cushion is like one large closed cell. Like an automobile airbag, most vinyl couch cushions have tiny vents so that air can escape slowly and the body can sink down into the cushion gradually.

Figure 6.8B shows an air-filled helmet liner used for American football. This liner is made of flexible plastic and filled with air. Two of these structures are placed over one another with their spokes slightly offset. Each liner acts as a single closed cell and the combination of resistance to

FIGURE 6.8 Helmet liners. (A) The Hydra-flo® helmet liner. Tiny channels between the cells restrict the flow of air and fluid in the system; (B) two air-filled liners nested inside each other as an impact-protective liner in a helmet. (C) replaceable foam padding in a helmet. *(Design (A) formerly produced by Bike Athletic Company)*

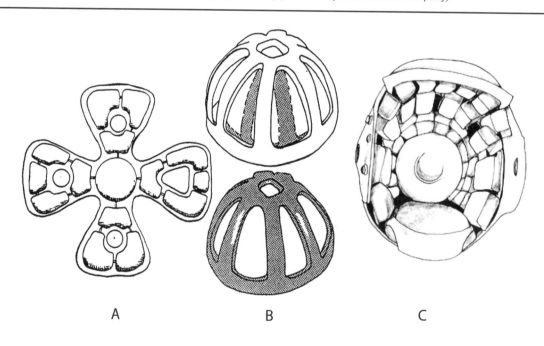

A   B   C

compression by the plastic and resistance to compression of the trapped air inside aids in absorption of energy. These liners have an additional feature in that air can be added through the top of each liner with an air pump to vary the fit of a helmet. This gives some additional resistance to compression to this impact-protective system.

The amount of stiffness or softness needed in protective foam depends on both the amount of force involved in an impact and the object being protected. Manufacturers often refer to stiffer foams as *shock absorbing* and softer foams as cushioning. Shock-absorbing foams are needed when high forces are involved; cushioning foams are needed when delicate materials are being protected. For example, before seatbelts and airbags kept occupants from colliding with an automobile dashboard during a crash, many dashboards contained a combination of a relatively soft foam backed by a rigid, compressible structure much like stiffened corrugated cardboard underneath the vinyl cover. The purpose of the rigid structure was to deform and allow the body a space in which to decelerate. If only the stiffer structure were used, delicate tissues such as those on the face would be more likely to bruise during minor collisions with the dashboard. If only the softer structure were used, it was likely that not enough energy would be absorbed to prevent serious injury in a more major collision. Similar combinations may be found in various types of protective equipment, with the stiffer layer being a closed-cell foam used to gradually decelerate the impacting object and a softer, easily compressible foam next to the skin surface to provide comfort and cushioning for the skin.

Other Characteristics of Foams

Characteristics such as flame resistance, durability, and puncture resistance may be required of protective foams for specific end uses. One thing to keep in mind for foams used in items such as protective sports equipment is that they be able to be coated so that the surfaces of pads made from them can be easily cleaned. Most closed-cell pads for sports uses are dipped in a vinyl bath and cured to form a durable, waterproof finish. Open-cell foams cannot be similarly dipped because the open cells soak up the vinyl, destroying its impact-protective capacities and making the pads very heavy. When open-cell foams are used in pads, attention needs to be paid both to protection from moisture and to cleanability of the surface. Some pads are heat-sealed or sewn into a fabric cover or *envelope*—a much more costly process than vinyl dipping. When thermoplastic materials are used, a hot iron or sealer may be placed lightly on the outer surface of the envelope fabric so that the uppermost surface of the foam is melted to the under surface of the fabric. This helps stabilize the pad in the envelope.

Another way to provide a finish for open-cell foam pads is to use **integral-skin foams**, also known as *self-skinned* foams. These are formed with a higher-density surface on a lower-density foam interior. Integral-skin foams eliminate the need to coat a foam pad and can add considerable durability and abrasion resistance to the pad.

A foam needs to retain its characteristics during all conditions of use. One characteristic it is extremely important to assess is how extreme temperatures affect a foam's behavior. Extreme cold in particular may stiffen many of the synthetic materials used to create foams, and this can affect both its impact-protective behavior and a wearer's ability to move in an item made of the material. High temperatures may melt or soften foam and likewise change its protective characteristics.

Another condition that may affect foams is pressure. The closed-cell foam used in a wetsuit for scuba diving reacts to extremes of increased pressure under the sea by compressing and becoming thinner. This can affect its ability to provide thermal protection and change the buoyancy of a diver. It would also affect the ability of foam to provide impact protection. In outer space, where foams are subjected to decreased atmospheric pressure, the opposite effect takes place. Gases in cells expand and foams increase in size. In foam-lined helmets, for example, pilots may feel an uncomfortable tightening of the helmet.

A number of innovative approaches to developing foams for these end uses have been attempted. In underwater diving, for example, the Navy has experimented with the development of an open-cell foam diving suit that is sandwiched between two waterproof skins. The suit, in essence, acts like one closed cell with separate but interconnected chambers inside. When pressure causes the foam to collapse, air can be pumped in to reinflate the foam so that both the thermal and buoyancy characteristics of the suit are retained. This would affect its impact-protective capacity as well.

Smith and Dye (1954) developed a different approach to decreasing the pressures caused by foams used in high altitudes or outer space. They suggested that a grit-like substance be incorporated in the base material before it was foamed. Then, when pressure changes occurred and gases expanded, the foam would develop tiny ruptures wherever the grit-like substance was present, allowing enough alleviation of the pressure buildup to prevent injury and discomfort. This in some ways was a rather shortsighted solution, since the foam could no longer function as effectively for impact protection during the return to Earth's atmosphere—the portion of the flight where it might be most needed. A more accommodating solution to the problem of pressure and the changing thickness of foam layers is to use a combination of open-cell and closed-cell foams. For example, a helmet liner might contain a closed-cell foam directly beneath the outer helmet shell to absorb energy, and an open-cell layer next to the head. The open-cell layer would easily compress to allow the closed-cell impact-protective layer room for expansion without any squeezing of the pilot's head. Its elasticity could then allow it to return to its original size during the return to the Earth's atmosphere. This type of technique is also used to achieve a comfortable fit on a variety of sizes and shapes of heads.

Another property of foam that is important in many end uses is its ability to be heat-set. Heat-settable foam can conform precisely to body contours and thus can be used as a fitting feature or a support in an item such as a splint or cast where precise contact with the body surface is essential. Figure 6.9 shows a polyethylene foam with a heat-setting capacity being cut, molded on a fractured arm, and formed into a cast.

One important consideration for moldable foams is whether their ability to absorb energy is changed when padding is shaped to line a curved surface rather than allowed to lie flat. Although data on this subject is limited, a few studies have shown that as some closed-cell foams take on a greater curve, their ability to absorb impacts decreases, possibly because some compression of cells occurs as the foam bends.

Tests for Impact-Protective Foams

Impact testing can provide many types of information about foams. Of particular importance is the amount of energy the foam absorbs during impact. One standard test method for testing energy absorption involves dropping a solid weight with a specific amount of force onto an impact-absorbing foam that has been laid on a platen below (ASTM "Standard Test Method for Dynamic"). This test

FIGURE 6.9 Heat-set, moldable closed-cell foam. (A) A sheet of foam is placed in an oven and heated; (B) the sheet is then molded around the arm and cooled; (C) the foam set in the contour of the arm; (D) the foam placed on the arm and wrapped in place with an ace bandage. *(Cramer Products, Inc.)*

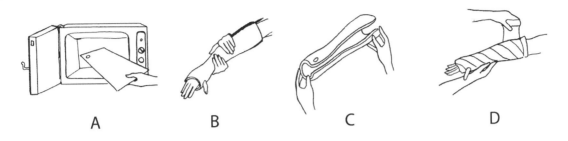

A   B   C   D

measures the amount of shock transmitted through the foam to the platen.

Similar tests have attempted to determine energy absorption during actual impact conditions by mounting materials on simulated body parts and placing them in the position in which they would be in a finished protective item. For example, football helmets are placed on a simulated head form that has force-recording devices mounted on it. The head form, which has a specified weight, is dropped from a specified height onto a platform below such as the steel anvil shown in Figure 6.10. The force transmitted through the helmet to the surface of the head form indicates how protective the helmet-foam combination will be. This test can be repeated with different foams and helmet shells so that the effectiveness of the helmets can be compared. Standard tests for football helmet safety involve multiple tests where the head form is oriented at various angles so that a protective item can be tested for energy absorption as it is impacted from front, top, and sides. The weight of the head form and the height of the drop are both designed to simulate the type of impact forces a player would receive in a game.

The tests just described are termed *dynamic* tests because they involve the action of a moving

FIGURE 6.10 A typical drop test used to study the impact protection offered by a football helmet.

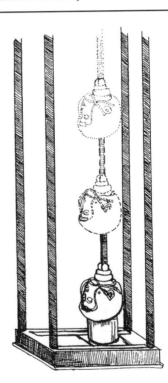

force on the material. However, manufacturers' specifications for foams report mainly the results of *static* tests, or tests that examine nonimpact forces. The effectiveness of foams is generally described in terms of its *compression strength*, often expressed as Indentation Load Deflection (ILD). A company citing the properties of one of its protective foams might say that it had an ILD of 4 lb/in² (0.28 kg/cm²). This is the amount of pressure required to compress the foam by 25 percent of its original thickness. Foams with a low ILD are cushioning foams, whereas those with higher ILDs are generally used for support or shock absorbance. Compression strength often varies with environmental temperature, pressure, and humidity, so a designer needs to consider these factors in evaluating true compression strength, particularly when it is known that the foam is to be used in extreme environmental conditions.

Compression strength is only one aspect of a foam's behavior that should be tested. It is just as critical to know how foam *recovers* from compression. If recovery is too fast, undesirable rebound occurs. If the foam does not recover at all, it may have lost its value as an impact protector. A foam's recovery rate may be measured with ball rebound tests. These are expressed in percentage of rebound, with foams with less than 20 percent rebound typically described as a slow-recovery foam. Other testing procedures for compression recovery are static and involve measuring recovery from specific conditions of compression over a certain period of time. The amounts of each vary depending on the intended end use of the foam. Smith and Dye (1954, 9), in their early work with closed-cell foam, determined that the important aspect of rebound was not the time required for full recovery but rather the amount of recovery that took place the instant after impact. Although tests have been developed to measure instantaneous recovery, this information is often not found on specification sheets that manufacturers use to describe their products. Occasionally,

manufacturers cite tests that detail "rebound velocity" or "percentage of rebound" but in general, most specifications show only "compression set" or "permanent set," which tells how much a foam remains compressed after it has relaxed for a certain period of time following compression (ASTM "Standard Test Methods for Rubber"). Although the compression set of a specific foam does not seem to have any bearing on rebound, it does reveal important information about the foam because recovery is related to a foam's capacity for energy absorption.

RIGID MATERIALS AS IMPACT PROTECTORS

While foams are referred to as *cushions* of protective padding, rigid materials are usually called armor plates. Effective rigid armor performs three types of protective functions. First, it spreads the impact over a larger surface area. The resulting decrease in localized pressure can be a significant factor in injury prevention. Second, rigid armor may prevent a protective item from being indented or penetrated by any object that is sharp or has a high momentum. Third, it absorbs some energy, although in general foams or other flexible materials are much more effective at energy absorption.

Information on three types of materials that are used in rigid armor plates can be found in Chapter 3 under "Rigid Materials." *Metals* have been used in clothing since the days of knights in armor. Some commonly used metals for rigid protectors are steel, aluminum, and titanium. (See Figure 6.11A.) *Ceramics* such as aluminum oxide or boron carbide have been used in protection from **ballistics** (i.e., high-speed impact by projectiles such as bullets). (See Figure 6.11B.) *Plastics*, especially *fiber-reinforced resins* have become more popular in recent years because of their lightness in

FIGURE 6.11 Rigid materials used for impact protection. (A) A ballistics vest with a portion of the back cut away to reveal overlapping titanium (metal) plates; (B) a nylon military ballistics vest with pockets that hold ceramic-fiberglass composite plates; (C) a molded hard hat made of various materials, from polycarbonates to fiberglass. *(A and B: U.S. Army)*

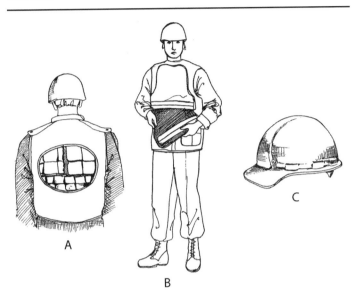

weight, durability, resistance to electrical conduction, low cost, and the ease with which they can be molded into complex forms. (See Figure 6.11C.) All three materials may be used in conjunction with cushioning materials, but plastics in particular are frequently found as part of combination protectors used in applications such as sports equipment.

Metals

Metals may be used as the backbones of impact protectors, particularly for ballistics protection. The qualities of metals used in apparel were discussed in Chapter 3. The ductility and toughness of a metal are critical for a designer to know when choosing an appropriate metal for a specific type of protection. If the elastic limit of a brittle metal is even slightly exceeded, protection may shatter, propelling fragments of metal from the impact site. And although a ductile metal may completely resist fracture, it may indent so much in order to absorb the energy of the impacting object that the body underneath it may be damaged. When choosing an appropriate metal and deciding on the form of a metal protector, it is critical to observe the behavior of metals after impact under different conditions of temperature and humidity. The geometry of the craters left in ductile metals by specific projectiles may be photographed or cast in plaster or wax for study. Gauges can also be placed on metal samples to record stress waves passing through the material during impact.

Ceramics and Impact Protection

The most common use of rigid ceramic plates for clothing is in ballistics garments worn by military personnel for protection against extremely high-energy metal projectiles. Ceramics are very brittle and much harder to compress than metals. They defeat projectiles first by resisting compression (a metal projectile is more likely to compress in a collision with a ceramic) and then by fracturing or shattering as the energy of the impact is transmitted throughout the ceramic plate. The kinetic energy of the projectile is thus transferred both into heat (presumably in the deformation of the metal projectile) and the kinetic energy of many fragments of ceramic or **spall**, as it flies away from the impact site.

Although the kinetic energy in each ceramic fragment after an impact is just a fraction of the energy possessed by the original object and many fragments are traveling away from the impact site, the wearer still has to be protected against fragment impact when ceramic material is worn. One combination used to solve this problem in bal-listics vests is shown in Figure 6.12. The energy-absorbing ceramic layer is backed by an equal thickness of aluminum. Since aluminum is consid-erably lighter than ceramic, this composite material is much lighter than a vest of this thickness com-posed totally of ceramic. When a metal projectile impacts the ceramic, the projectile, which is gen-erally more easily compressed than the ceramic, is first flattened, causing its kinetic energy to be partially converted to heat. If enough energy remains in the projectile to fracture the ceramic, the fracture occurs in a cone-shaped pattern that spreads out from the point of impact and thus causes the force of the impact to the aluminum to be spread over a larger area. In addition, aluminum is a ductile metal that extends rather than fractur-ing when it is hit. This prevents injury from spall. It holds the cone-shaped piece in place, yet can be deflected just enough to lengthen the time involved in the change of momentum of the bullet. If the

combination of materials is successful, the energy involved in the fracture of the ceramic and the dis-tortion of the aluminum will equal or exceed the energy possessed by the projectile.

As was mentioned in Chapter 3, thick, solid panels of ceramics capable of protecting from machine gun fire are most often used in items worn by seated individuals because they do not have to carry the weight of the material. The vest shown in Figure 6.11B, for example can weigh up to 30 lb (13.6 kg), and similar models for air crew weigh up to 40 lb (18.1 kg). Most often ceramics are used in removable panels or additional vests that can be donned and doffed in an emergency (Figure 6.13). Silicon carbide, boron carbide, and alumina are probably the most commonly used ballistics ceramics. Metal backings for ceramic plates have also been replaced by lighter plastics, which are discussed next.

Plastics as Impact Protectors

Plastics are found in many types of protective equipment such as the hard hat shown in Figure 6.11C or as the armor plate in items of sports equipment such as the shin protector shown in Figure 6.3. The plastics used in these rigid forms are fairly tough, but because they have a rather low elastic limit, they may become permanently indented when a projectile strikes them. If a rigid protective form worn close to the body indents on impact, the protector itself may cause injury. This is one reason why fiber-reinforced resins (see Chapter 3) are often used in protective apparel. Fibers such as Kevlar® aramid have a very high tensile strength, and they help to prevent indenta-tion or penetration of the basic resin. They also help transfer the stress caused by the impact over a larger area of the form. The resin not only gives an item its shape but also provides some energy absorption.

FIGURE 6.12 An aluminum-ceramic composite material showing a bullet (right) impacting the ceramic layer (middle) and its flattened surface fracturing the ceramic in a cone-shaped form (dotted lines); the wide end of the cone impacts the aluminum layer (left) which deflects enough to absorb the energy but keeps the fractured ceramic and bullet from passing through.

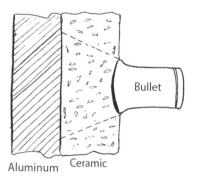

Aluminum Ceramic

FIGURE 6.13 Tactical armor containing ceramic plates to provide protection against higher level ballistics. *(American Body Armor and Equipment)*

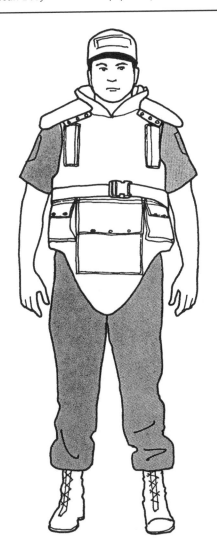

TEXTILES IN BALLISTICS PROTECTION

Textiles are used to protect military personnel, police, controversial political candidates, and others from bullets and fragments (spall). If they can provide sufficient protection, textiles are preferred for ballistics protection because they are inconspicuous and because they allow more freedom of movement than does equivalent protection in a rigid form. A political figure can wear "bulletproof" undergarments at all times in public appearances without appearing unduly nervous. An undercover policeman can wear a fitted ballistics undershirt under a regular uniform or don a trench coat with a ballistics liner without a significant change in apparent body size or shape or difficulty in movement.

Most people find it impossible to understand how a thin, flexible textile fabric could be "bulletproof." In point of fact, a single layer of textile fabric is *not* bulletproof. It is more accurate to say that textiles can be used in garments that provide protection from projectiles, but that they must be used in multiple layers to do so. Each layer successively attenuates a portion of the energy of a bullet so that it can be stopped before passing through to the body (Figure 6.14).

Ballistic-protective textiles most commonly provide a specific type of protection from projectiles—they help prevent penetration. They do not prevent indentation; they merely stop the projectile from entering the body where it could lodge in the spine or a vital organ such as the heart. A bullet might bounce off the surface of a rigid protector without changing its shape, but it will definitely indent the flexible protector and the body behind it. Although it does absorb some of the energy of the bullet, enough is transmitted through to the body that it can cause severe disruption of tissues and bruising that is known as *blunt trauma*. Despite this fact, its ability to prevent penetration and be comfortable enough to be constantly worn makes it a life saver.

Fiber Properties

Three properties of a fiber are of utmost concern for high-energy impact protection: tensile strength, modulus, and breaking elongation. Each

FIGURE 6.14 The effects of a bullet on ballistics nylon. (Top row) View perpendicular to the fabric: layers one, four, six, and nine; (bottom row) side view of the same layers. The bullet was stopped at the ninth layer. *(Susich et al. 1958, 376)*

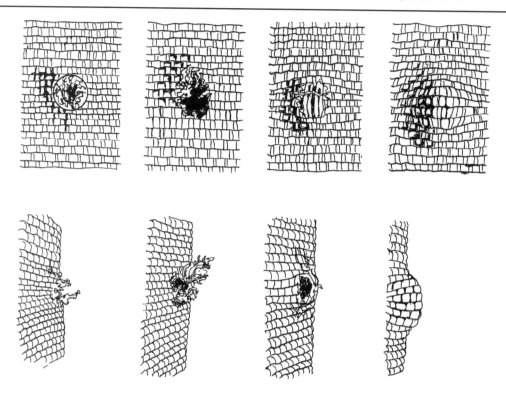

contributes to the behavior of an impact-protective fabric in a slightly different way.

First, if the fibers chosen (and the yarns and fabrics into which they are made) have a *high tensile strength* (i.e., they resist being broken), it becomes more difficult for a bullet to penetrate a protective garment made of them. In other words, if the energy possessed by a bullet does not equal the energy needed to rupture a material, then the bullet will be defeated.

Second, if a fiber (and fabric made of it) has a *high breaking elongation* (i.e., can experience a high degree of extension before it breaks), it will be difficult for a bullet to penetrate it. It will simply continue to elongate until the bullet's kinetic energy

is converted to heat or potential energy and it stops moving.

Third, if a fiber has a *high modulus* (i.e., it is hard to extend), it takes more energy to stretch the fibers and, thus, more kinetic energy can be converted to potential energy in the period of time before breakage occurs.

It is important to understand how each of these properties contributes to the behavior of a material and its ability to provide protection. When a bullet strikes a material, as each fiber breaks, the kinetic energy of the bullet is converted to heat as a result of the disruption of the bonds holding the fiber together. The more resistance to breakage, the greater the energy needed to break these bonds,

FIGURE 6.15 A .38 caliber bullet before (top) and after (bottom) impact with Kevlar fabrics.

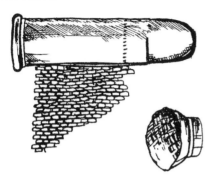

and, thus, the greater will be the conversion from kinetic energy to heat. The heat from a high-speed missile like a bullet may actually be observed, as fibers close to the impact site are melted or charred.

When a fiber elongates, the bullet's kinetic energy is converted to the potential energy of the stretched fiber. After the impact, fibers that were not stretched to their breaking points may begin to recover, turning the potential energy they possess back into kinetic energy. Others may exhibit the effects of energy conversion as they are permanently melted and deformed by the heat generated by friction between the molecules of the fiber as it stretched and between the surface of the bullet and the fiber/fabric surface. Evidence of the heat generated may also be seen on the surface of the bullet, which may be softened enough by heat to allow the fabric's weave to be imprinted on it (Figure 6.15).

Tests for Ballistics Materials

Ballistics materials are typically tested on a firing range. Both penetration resistance and the energy transmitted through the vest may be measured. Either the weapons the vest has been designed to defeat are used or a firing mechanism is set up for the test. Tests may be done on layers of fabrics or finished vests. Panels of fabric or finished vests may be hung freely, mounted in a frame, or placed on a simulated body form. Much research has taken place to develop clays and gels that respond in the same way body tissues would respond to impact. When used, these substances are placed directly behind the surface of the fabrics being tested and the depth of the indentations are measured.

The term, **V50 ballistics limit** is commonly used to report ballistics penetration. This term refers to the velocity at which 50 percent of the impacts given to a test material will result in complete penetration. So, a description of a protective garment or a material might contain the statement that its V50 is 600 m/s (656.2 yd/sec). This means that it will stop bullets or fragments traveling 600 m/sec (656.2 yd/sec) 50 percent of the time. A V_0 limit (no penetration, 100 percent of the time) may also be used.

A diagram of a typical test range is shown in Figure 6.16. A bullet is fired and passes through two separate frames (B and C) containing photoelectric cells. Since the screens are a specified distance apart, the velocity of a bullet can be calculated by comparing the times at which it passes by each of the screens. The bullet then strikes the test panel containing the ballistics fabric layers. The velocity of the bullet is changed upward or downward until the fabric being tested is penetrated in 50 percent of the tests, that is, until the V50 ballistics limit is reached. High-speed photography and high-speed electron microscopes are often used to gather additional information about the behavior of a yarn or fabric when it is impacted. High-speed electron microscopic views of ballistics materials have also provided a wealth

FIGURE 6.16 A ballistics test range. A bullet is fired from a test mechanism (A), it passes between two screens (B and C), its speed is determined photo-electrically by recording the time it takes to pass from B to C.

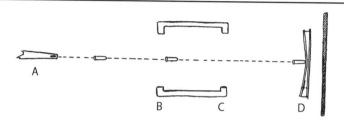

of information about the behavior of ballistics materials following impact.

Dilatant Materials

Pairing flexible materials with rigid ones to avoid blunt trauma from an impact involves a trade-off between movement and protection. The class of materials known as **dilatant** materials offers a solution to this trade-off. Dilatant materials (see Chapter 3, "Responding to Movement and Force") act like liquids when at rest or experiencing weak forces but instantly stiffen and act like solids when exposed to sudden forces. Such materials can be used to coat high-tensile-strength textiles and protective foams. A dilatant-coated textile is flexible to wear, but when exposed to projectile impact, the textile stiffens into a solid capable of spreading force over a larger area. The hybrid of high-tensile-strength textile and dilatant coating brings the best of each category to the solution.

Impact-Sensing Materials and Methods

It is often desirable to determine how well impact-protective materials are performing in place. For example, in football, players are often subjected to severe impacts from the ground and from other players. Designers need to be aware of the levels of force and acceleration involved in those impacts for each body part as players experience them. Equipment that contains impact-protective materials with a sensing capacity can provide feedback to designers to help them develop more effective protective equipment.

There are a number of ways materials can be formed, finished, and combined so that they can serve as part of a smart system that senses impact. Impact-sensing systems can respond directly by measuring the pressure applied to a body part, or indirectly by detecting other characteristics of the impact such as strain, bend, or acceleration.

MATERIALS WITH SWITCH-LIKE PROPERTIES

A simple method of detecting or measuring impact is to create a switch or opening in an electrical circuit, which is held open by a piece of compressible foam. As Figure 6.17 shows, two conductive layers on either side of the foam are separated when the foam is uncompressed, but they come into contact (closing the switch) through a hole in the foam when the foam is flattened. Calibrating the strength of the foam and the size of the perforation can allow forces of different magnitudes to be

FIGURE 6.17 The structure of a soft switch.

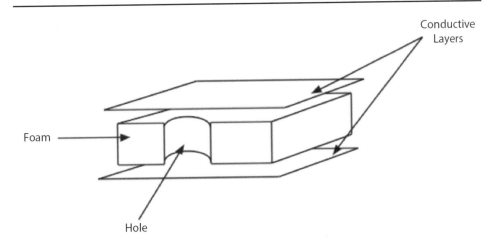

detected. However, each switch can only indicate when its specific force level has been exceeded. They cannot measure variable amounts of force.

PRESSURE-SENSITIVE FOAMS

Coating an impact-protective foam with an electro-active polymer that responds to being flexed can make it possible to calculate the force needed to compress a foam. When this type of polymer-coated foam is compressed, it results in a change in its electrical resistance. Controlling the properties of a coated foam such as its strength or stiffness, then, makes it possible to calibrate the electrical response and calculate the amount of force experienced by the foam. This in turn makes it possible to detect the amount of force transferred to the body.

For example, the stiffer the foam, the more force will be required to indent it. An electro-active coating may respond to a given amount of flex with a specific resistance change. Mapping the relationship between stiffness and flex can allow the resistance response to be used to determine exactly how much force the foam experienced.

SENSING STRAIN, BEND, AND ACCELERATION

In addition to measuring the force directly applied to the body, there are several indirect ways of measuring an impact. Impacts often produce strain or stretch in the skin or in a joint. They may result in bending of body parts or involve an abrupt change in acceleration. All of these conditions can be sensed and used to help understand the characteristics and magnitude of the impact.

In many cases, an impact results in an elongation of a body area, such as in pushing in the skin or in stretching out an arm or leg. The approaches to sensing stretch described in Chapter 4 (Figure 4.9) can also be used to detect impacts, as can the approach to sensing strain described in Chapter 4 (Figure 4.3).

The changes in acceleration during an impact can be an important indicator of how severe the impact is. **Accelerometers** detect acceleration in many ways. Some involve measuring movement, such as the displacement of a tiny ball within a chamber or the distance between a fixed plate and a suspended plate. Some accelerometers use piezoelectric materials (force or bend sensors), by deducing acceleration from the rate of change of the force experienced by the sensor. Accelerometers are capable of measuring the specific amount of acceleration at each time instant. Many accelerometers are only capable of detecting accelerations in two directions (x and y planes) because the sensing mechanism is flat and is more easily oriented to detect two dimensions. In order to detect accelerations on the third (z) axis, it is often necessary to use a second accelerometer, oriented perpendicular to the first sensor.

Design of Impact-Protective Clothing

If impact protection were the only concern of designers, they would have no difficulty creating protective garments from the array of materials on the market. If people were inanimate, unfeeling objects, they could simply be packaged like eggs or china vases, in protective cartons. The real challenge for designers is to create impact-protective clothing that allows people to work and play effectively.

People functioning under hazardous conditions must be able to move freely and sense hazards in the environment, whether to dodge a bullet or to avoid a tackle. In many activities, such as sports, movement is so critical to performance that some athletes prefer to play without protection in order to gain an edge in performance. For example, for years, professional hockey players played without helmets because they claimed that helmets were too hot and interfered with vision and hearing. Athletes may also reject protective items if they think wearing them signals weakness to the opposition or makes them less physically attractive. There are limits to what many individuals will wear even if injury prevention is at stake.

A garment cannot provide protection if it lies on a shelf. The designer's most difficult job is to design *acceptable* protective forms. The perfect protective garment would involve no trade-offs—it would meet an individual's physical *and* psychological needs. This ideal is often impossible to reach, so designers must work to maximize the degree to which each need can be met. This challenge is what makes designing protective clothing both fascinating and frustrating.

DESIGN CRITERIA FOR IMPACT PROTECTION

Determining the locations and levels for the impact protection needed in a specific design setting is difficult because impact often involves the unexpected. Chapter 1 contains a number of techniques that can be used for gathering information

FIGURE 6.18 (A) The Fem-Gard® breast protector. The rigid cups made of polyethylene are flared at the edge to prevent cups from digging into the flesh; the cups are inserted into a special bra. (B) The Hip-Guard® protector. *(Designs formerly produced by Fem-Gard, Inc.)*

A   B

about specific impact situations. When planning impact studies that involve direct observation, remember that protective equipment itself often influences the way in which wearers move and perform various activities. Equipment may make ideal motion impossible and some items of equipment may be so protective that they may themselves be used as weapons. Also be aware that athletes, coaches, and industry managers, among others, may not discuss information about injuries and potential hazards in interviews because they could reveal team weaknesses or open companies to lawsuits. If limited information about body injury is available, a designer may need to assess the need for protective equipment by observing the *potential* for objects in the environment to pose life-threatening or debilitating injury and noting the body parts most likely to be struck.

PADDING FOR SPORTS AND INDUSTRIAL PROTECTION

Any of the impact-protective materials described earlier in this chapter may be used alone in providing body protection. For example, the breast and hip protectors shown in Figure 6.18A and B are composed entirely of rigid polyethylene and

entirely of flexible foam, respectively. Many ballistics vests are made entirely of flexible textiles. (See Figure 6.1.) Most items of impact protection are, however, made up of a combination of materials, most frequently, a rigid armor plate covered on one or both sides by an energy absorbing foam.

Combination Pads

A typical combination pad used in sports equipment is shown in Figure 6.19. In this pad, a ⅛ in (0.3 cm) armor plate is sandwiched between two layers of closed-cell foam. The outer layer of foam absorbs part of the energy of the impact. The rigid plate spreads the force of a localized impact over the entire pad surface, prevents penetration or indentation of the pad by a sharp object, and gives a body-related shape to the pad. The inner layer of foam absorbs as much of the remaining energy as possible, cushions the rigid pad so that it is more comfortable against the skin, and may also help somewhat to fit the pad more closely to the contours of the body. Sometimes, this inner layer is composed of open-cell foam because it is softer and conforms more readily to the body contours.

A number of items of very effective combination padding have been designed using open-cell foam as the primary energy-absorbing component.

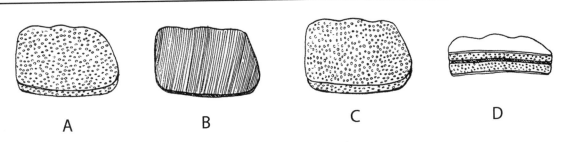

FIGURE 6.19 A typical combination pad for impact protection. (A) A 1/4 in (0.6 cm) closed-cell foam; (B) a 1/8 in (0.3 cm) rigid plate; (C) a 3/8 in (0.95 cm) closed-cell foam; (D) a cross section of the three layers bonded together and dipped in a vinyl bath.

A   B   C   D

Open-cell foam is able to accomplish this function if its cell structure or the nature of the matrix material makes it sufficiently resistant to compression and if it is placed *behind* a rigid armor plate. When the impacting object strikes the armor plate, the force of the impact is spread over the whole surface of the open-cell foam. The resulting force in any one area is not sufficient to fully collapse the open-cell foam. It should be noted that the reverse configuration, with the open-cell foam on the outside and the armor plate closest to the body, would add only slightly more protection than that provided by the armor plate alone.

Whether a single material or a combination of materials is used to form an impact-protective item, its final form will depend to a great extent on the movement needs of the wearer. There are a wide variety of ways that impact-protective materials may be formed into items of protective equipment. The approaches discussed next are not meant to be mutually exclusive. Many share characteristics with each other, and several can generally be found in any one item of protective equipment. Each approach should provide a designer of protective equipment with an alternative method of reaching the goal of effective impact protection for the body.

Segmented Pads

One method of helping pads to move with the body is to simply segment protective materials so that they can bend more easily. Even a flexible material such as a foam can be helped to conform to the body more effectively using segmenting techniques. Segmenting can involve processes as simple as machine quilting or as complicated as the insertion of separate foam inserts in channels in a protector. Perhaps the simplest method of segmenting is to *score* (i.e., to cut part way through a protective material leaving a thin layer at its base to hold the material together). The technique is much like that used in making garlic bread when a cut is made *to* but not *through* the bottom of the bread so that the entire loaf remains connected.

FIGURE 6.20 A segmented knee/shin protector with provision for continuous protection from impact. *(Design: Suzanne Horvath Reeps)*

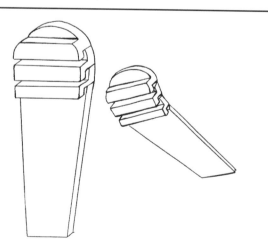

FIGURE 6.21 Segmented body padding. (A) A women's softball chest protector segmented vertically on top to conform to the female anatomy and horizontally below to accommodate the crouched position of the catcher behind the plate; (B) a typical catcher's chest protector for men.

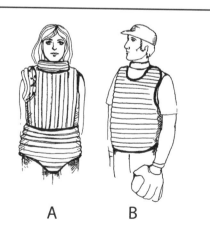

A   B

An example of rather complex scoring of protective equipment can be seen in the segmented pad shown in Figure 6.20. The cuts in this closed-cell foam knee and shin protector allow it to present a full thickness of protection to an impacting object, while the thin joint provided at the base results in a foam that is much easier for the knee to bend. If a protective material is not strong enough to hold together when cut this thinly, another strong, thin material may be affixed to the back of a protector as a hinge to support the segments. These segments do not provide for the increase in length that occurs over the front of the leg when the knee is bent, but they do allow contouring of the pad around a curved body part.

One example of the advantage of segmenting can be found in the catcher's chest protectors for baseball shown in Figure 6.21. They consist of a 5/8 in (1.59 cm) layer of closed-cell foam covered on both sides with vinyl fabric. The three layers are quilted together at intervals with stitching. In essence, this means that the foam has been thinned at each stitching line so that it is less difficult to bend. The horizontal segments in the protectors allow them to lie closely along the concave contours of the lower body when the catcher is crouching behind the plate. In the two-part protector for women (Figure 6.21A), the vertical segments in the upper portion allow it to bend more easily around the curves of the chest. The separate sections over the arm and neck provide protection for these areas while the quilting lines allow natural movement of the body.

Another method of achieving a type of segmentation is to imbed rigid protectors within flexible materials. Figure 6.22 illustrates several garments for which this has been done. The goalie's chest protector for lacrosse shown in Figure 6.22A is made of closed-cell foam. Imbedded in its center is a rigid protector that covers the area at the base of the sternum. This is to protect the goalie from experiencing a solar plexus knockout (i.e., having the wind knocked out). The rigid forms spread force of an impacting object out over a wider area of the chest protector in order to decrease its effects on the sternum but leave the rest of the protector flexible. The hockey padding shown in Figure 6.22B provides a similar function over a wider body area. The entire lower torso is protected from injury by a large double-layered closed-cell

FIGURE 6.22 (A) Lacrosse chest protector with embedded rigid plate over the base of the sternum; (B) a closed-cell foam liner for hockey pants with embedded rigid plates over vulnerable body areas; (C) soft body armor with pocket for a rigid shock plate. *(Design (C) formerly produced by American Body Armor)*

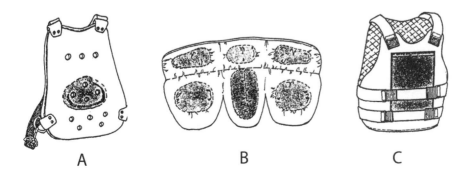

A   B   C

foam pant liner, while areas in particular danger (e.g., the crest of the hip and the tailbone) have rigid armor plates sewn between the foam layers. Because the foam is flexible, the areas between the rigid plates allow the protector to take on the curve needed to surround a body. Figure 6.22C shows a flexible fabric ballistics vest that has been fitted with a pocket so that a rigid protector can be added when higher powered gunfire is expected. This vest is molded into a curved shape, but when the armor plate is in place, the edges of the plate form a sort of segmentation line that still allows the vest to curve around the sides of the body.

The most effective protection is offered when the method of segmenting allows continuous protection of an area while bending is taking place. Often this is done by creating separate pads such as those shown on the hockey glove illustrated in Figure 6.23. These thick, rounded pads are raised from the surface of a leather glove. The innermost leather layer acts as a hinge for these segments. Even when the hand is in a fully bent position, the shape and closeness of the pads makes it impossible for a puck, stick, or elbow to maneuver past them to the base of the glove.

It should be mentioned again that segmenting only allows an item to bend more easily; it does

not provide for the change in length unless both the material and the design configuration are stretchable. If the length of a body segment changes significantly when a joint is flexed, segmenting may need to be combined with other design features to allow full mobility.

Shingled Padding

Shingling is closely related to segmenting. It involves the overlapping of protective materials so that they appear much like the shingles on a roof. With protective equipment, however, the isolated shingles are connected not to a solid surface like a roof but to a strong *flexible* material that allows the segments of the equipment to bend with the body. Suits of armor (see Figure 6.1) were made using a shingling technique with leather, or sometimes, even velvet, forming the hinge between the overlapping armor plates.

The bulletproof vest shown in Figure 6.11A is made of titanium (metal) plates that are joined using a shingling technique. This approach can also be used with other rigid materials like ceramics. One of the advantages of using this design method is that there is no gap in coverage during movement yet almost unlimited flexion is allowed between the plates. Another is that when rigid materials form the plates that are shingled, the force of an impact to any single plate is spread to each plate it touches and then is passed on again to every plate that second layer of plates touch, and so on. The result, then, is much the same in terms of spreading of force (and thus alleviating the effects of pressure in any one area) as if a solid armor plate had been used, yet the protector's capacity for movement is considerably improved.

Shingled padding can be used over any joint, but the most common item in which it is seen in sports equipment is the shoulder pad. The overlapping of several rigid pads on the shoulder pad for

FIGURE 6.23 A protective glove for ice hockey.

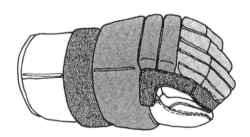

American football linemen shown in Figure 6.24 and the impingement of these shoulder protectors on rigid chest and back panels allow a blow to the top of the shoulder to be transferred over the whole shoulder and upper chest and back areas. The shingled design allows free mobility of the shoulder and arm while providing extensive protection for the top of the shoulder, the area most likely to be hit.

Shingle techniques are most frequently used for rigid materials (Figure 6.25A), but they also have advantages for flexible ones. The inner lining for an Army ballistics vest shown in Figure 6.25A is made of layers of titanium plates mounted on overlapping sections of an aramid material. The same technique can be used for a vest made totally out of fabric. Since the materials used for these vests are relatively stiff and many layers are used, shingling can make a considerable difference in mobility.

Another type of shingling is illustrated by the ballistics vest shown in Figure 6.25B. It has a

FIGURE 6.24 A football shoulder pad with rigid epaulets that help distribute blows over a wider area of the pad.

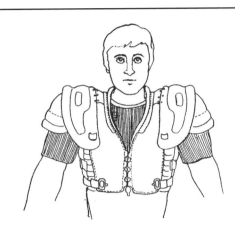

separate overlapped shoulder section joined to the body of the vest only at the neck edge and by an elastic strap at the front and back armscye edges. The overlapping of this panel allows upward movement of the arm when needed without the soldier having to lift the weight of the entire vest.

FIGURE 6.25 Ballistics vests for the military. (A) Overlapping interior rigid plates and fabric panels contribute to mobility; (B) a model with a pivoting shoulder section. *(U.S. Army Natick Research, Development, and Engineering Center)*

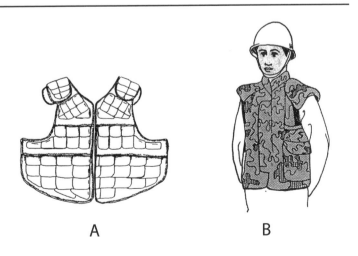

A　　　　　　B

A unique variation of shingling can be seen in the protective undergarment for bobsledders shown in Figure 6.26. Bobsledders typically wear a stiff, nonstretch aramid garment on the torso and upper arms to protect them from burns due to the shearing impact with the ice in the event there is an accident and the bobsled turns over. The shirt shown in Figure 6.26 is composed of two layers of a stretch material to which patches of thick aramid fabric have been sewn. Together, the patches in the two layers cover the whole upper torso and arms. The top layer covers all the areas left free to stretch on the lining layer and vice versa. The aramid patches on the two layers overlap just enough so that when the bobsledder fully reaches forward, the entire surface of the back is still protected. The stretch materials in this garment allow full movement, while the unique, two-layer system with alternating aramid patches accomplishes full protection. Similar forms could be developed for protective pads.

Cantilevered Pads

Cantilevering is a method of suspending a pad over a body part so that impact with the body is completely avoided. In architecture, a cantilever refers to a horizontal structural member fixed only on one end, or a member that extends/overhangs

beyond its supports, in much the same way that a diving board is extended over a swimming pool. Similar structures in protective equipment, like the uppermost rigid cap of the shoulder pad in Figure 6.24, are referred to as cantilevers. The shoulder cap in this pad is held in place by a leather or vinyl hinge that allows the cap to move upward to permit shoulder movement but resists downward movement, thus protecting the shoulder from impact. Neck protectors that are suspended from facemasks for a variety of activities from fencing to baseball umpiring often use this same sort of cantilevering technique.

In protective equipment, another form of cantilevering may be used. It involves building an arch over the body part to be protected and cantilevering each end of the arch from different sections of padding. Figure 6.27 shows how a cantilever of this sort works on a football shoulder pad. A rigid spring steel arch is built so that it lies well above the shoulder surface, just under the top shoulder cap pad. The arch is held in place by fitting the shoulder pad snugly to the chest and back of the player. When a blow is taken to the top of the shoulder, the arch is flattened slightly, changing some of the kinetic energy of the hit to potential energy. If the pad is firmly fitted to the torso, the

FIGURE 6.26 The outer layer and lining of a stretch undergarment for bobsledders. Patches of aramid fabric (darker areas) have been applied in alternating areas. These two layers are sewn together so that both full protection and maximum mobility are achieved.

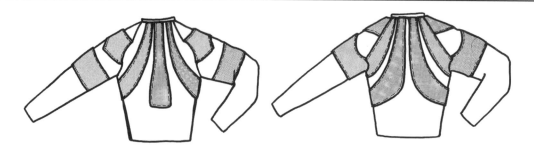

FIGURE 6.27 A cantilevered pad. (A) A side view of a shoulder pad for football. The cantilever arch rises above the shoulder (B). The dotted area marked "C" shows the position of the cantilever arch under the front of the shoulder pad. *(Bike Athletic Company)*

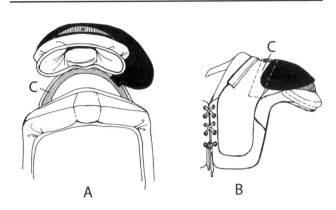

A   B

blow should be dissipated over the entire chest and back area. The shoulder joint itself should lie well beneath the arch and thus even the interior of the padding may not come into contact with the top of the shoulder. Although this technique is used primarily for shoulder pads, it has the potential to provide protection for a variety of body areas.

Upward suspension of items has many similarities to cantilevering. For example, the padding illustrated in Figure 6.28 has an upward extension at the back and sides of the neckline that helps to stabilize the position of an American football helmet. Since today's helmets are so heavy, the sort of whiplash that can occur in many contacts experienced in the game of football poses a tremendous injury hazard for the neck. The illustrated pad performs a function similar to a neck roll but provides more protection. This pad is worn under a shoulder pad, and the helmet nestles down into the extended neck pad so that the pad (rather than the player's neck)

takes the stresses of helmet movement. Tying it down to the precise position needed can vary the position of the neck pad.

Cupping or Bridging Techniques

Many of the rigid plates used in segmented, shingled, and cantilevered protectors are shaped to cup or bridge over a body part in order to transfer impact forces to less sensitive body areas as well as spread force over a larger area. The breast cup shown in Figure 6.18A, for example, surrounds the soft tissue of the breast. The edges of each cup lie against the rib cage so that a blow to any area of the cup will not be felt at all by the breast tissue, but will be dissipated over a wider area on the rib cage. Because of its own flexibility, the rib cage acts like a springboard to absorb the energy of the impact. Similar cupping techniques with rigid materials are employed for the protection of male genitals in contact sports.

Areas where bones are relatively unprotected by muscle tissues and fat (e.g., the point of the elbow, the crest of the hipbone, the ankle) are also easily injured by a focused blow. Often, protectors for those areas are shaped to stand away from the exposed bony areas and rest on wider adjacent

FIGURE 6.28 Equipment to prevent neck injury in American football. This pad, worn under regular shoulder pads, stabilizes the position of the helmet so that neck injuries are prevented. *(Design: Dale Strauf and Bernie DePalma)*

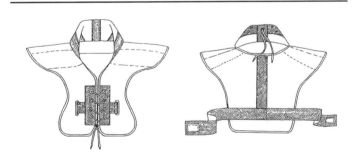

areas that have more natural body padding. Bridging is an extremely important method to use when an injury such as an abrasion, a bone bruise, or blistering has occurred. If a bridged pad is well designed, it can prevent any pressure at all from being placed on an injured body part. The hip protector shown in Figure 6.29, for example, not only has a shaped rigid form that bridges the hip crest but also contains a removable foam section at its center. The hollowed out pad can be used in the event that injury to the hipbone prevents a player from tolerating any pressure at all on the hip. The pad is placed in the pocket of a hip girdle or other body-hugging garment so that the foam on either side of that hollowed out section lies against broad areas of the abdomen and torso surrounding the hip crest.

The elbow presents a particularly difficult area for bridging because there are no areas around the protruding bones where the edges of a bridge

can safely lie. Pressure on either side of the elbow can injure blood vessels and nerves that are near the surface, consequently affecting lower arm and hand function. Because of mobility considerations, a separate item generally accomplishes elbow protection. Two examples of protectors are shown in Figure 6.30. The protector in Figure 6.30A uses a rigid form cantilevered from the forearm area. It involves a cupped shape in the working position that sits well off the elbow. The protector in Figure 6.30B uses a buildup of protective foam with a hollowed out center. The point of the elbow, then, sinks into the padded hole, while padding cushions the areas around it.

Suspension with Slings or Webbing

Many items of rigid protective equipment are held away from the body surface by a suspension system. The most common suspension system is probably the webbing inside a helmet (Figure 6.31A). The purpose of this webbing is to provide a **standoff** or space between the rigid protector and the body. The standoff keeps the helmet shell from colliding with the head surface when an impact occurs. Similar web systems can be used in many other types of protective equipment. (See Figure 6.31B.)

Webbings are typically made of strong, durable materials that stretch only slightly under force. When an object strikes a rigid outer helmet shell, the helmet descends toward the head, and the force is distributed over the entire area of contact between the webbing and the head. If the force is great enough, the webbing stretches slightly, allowing the head and webbing to sink just slightly into the shell. This stretching action can play a small

FIGURE 6.29 Hip protector. (A) This pad protects the crest of the hipbone. For prior injuries, the foam center of the pad can be removed so that there is no pressure at all on the crest of the hipbone. (B) The position of pad in a hip girdle. *(Design: Byron Donzis)*

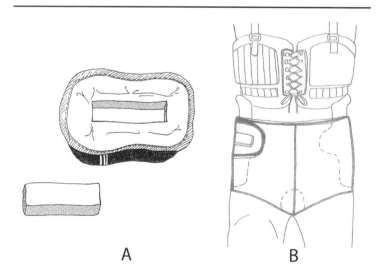

A   B

FIGURE 6.30 Elbow protectors. (A) A rigid pad bridges over the back of the elbow joint; (B) a relatively flat model showing padding inside, with a cut-out area for the point of the elbow to sink into during impact. *(Design (A) formerly produced by Volvo of America, Jofa Hockey Products)*

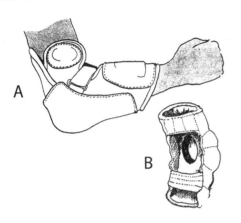

should it be possible for the outer shell to contact the head.

Many suspension systems in helmets today would hardly be called *webbing* based on their physical appearance, but they serve many of the same functions. The air-filled and fluid-filled helmet liners shown at the beginning of this chapter (Figure 6.8) all provide a standoff from the helmet shell that does not fully collapse under impact but provides a slow deceleration of the head into the standoff area.

When a solid panel of material is used in suspension, it may be referred to as a **sling**. Figure 6.31C shows a sling liner that has been used in a hockey shin guard. Fabric slings generally have less of a curve than the outer rigid shell of a protector. This allows the rigid shell to stand away from the surface of the body. They are flexible so they can conform to the entire length of a body surface yet be quite comfortable. Their ability to conform allows them to provide an even greater contact area and thus spreads the force of an

part in the energy dissipation of the helmet system. It is critical that the standoff that the webbing provides from the shell is sufficient to allow for the stretching of the liner. Under no circumstances

FIGURE 6.31 (A) Webbing inside a military helmet; (B) a webbing-like suspension system in a hockey shin guard; (C) a fabric sling in a hockey shin guard.

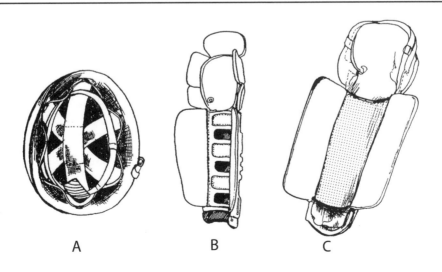

A B C

impact out over the entire body area covered by the sling. The standoff between a breathable sling and a rigid protector often is designed to provide for dissipation of heat as well.

Protection of the Body from Padding

Poorly designed padding can itself injure the body. In addition to being properly placed and designed for the body part being protected, there are several precautions that need to be taken to protect the body from padding.

The edges of rigid padding must be designed so that they do not dig into the body and injure body tissue, damage nerves, or cut off blood supply. Figure 6.32 shows an example of the precautions taken to keep a shin guard for ice hockey from

FIGURE 6.32 A shin protector for ice hockey with a close-up of the curved edge, an extra cube of padding, and several layers of padded vinyl on the portion that contacts the foot.

digging into the top of the foot. The lower edge of the pad is flared so that it extends slightly out on the foot. This curved edge is padded with foam and then covered with foam-backed vinyl so that the foot is padded if the protector collides with it. Another example of the treatment of an edge on a rigid protector can be seen in Figure 6.18A. The edge of each breast cup has been thinned and curved outward so that a flexible, rounded surface contacts the body.

The silhouette of a pad is also important for prevention of injury to the body. Figure 6.33, for example, shows how a thigh pad is contoured to the body so that the leg can be bent at the hip without the thigh pad digging into the abdomen. At every joint area, care must be taken to shape the outer edge of pads so that movement can take place without injury. The shape of pads is also critical to movement when separate pads are worn in close proximity. They must be designed in a

FIGURE 6.33 A left thigh pad. (A) The outside view showing the shaped upper edge that allows a wearer to flex at the hip comfortably; (B) the smooth, contoured inner surface that contacts the thigh along its entire length; (C) placement of pads.

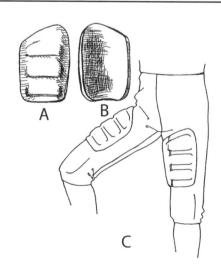

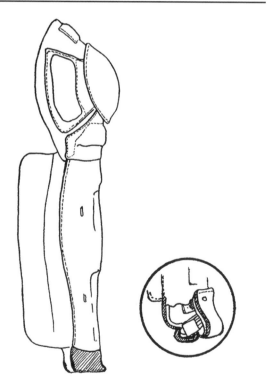

way that allows movement without their impinging on one another.

Fit and Adjustability

Most manufacturers of impact-protective equipment would probably agree that proper fit is the most critical factor that determines whether padding will provide adequate protection or not. Obviously, the most effective helmet sized for an adult would be useless for a child. In fact, it would probably cause injury. Although this is an extreme example, the effect is similar to that of a small shoulder pad placed on a medium-sized body or a slightly large elbow protector that slides off the elbow. A protective pad must lie directly over a body part at the moment of impact in order to protect it. Although this criterion could be met if protective pads were custom-made, this solution is often not economically feasible for most people. The designer's task, then, is to find ways to make protective items adjustable so that they fit a variety of body sizes and shapes and allow a variety of body movements.

One means of achieving fit is to choose materials wisely, perhaps incorporating the use of heat-set, moldable foams in the design. For isolated pads, the key to proper fit lies in an effective method of suspension and proper choice of fastening systems. (These two topics are covered in more detail in Chapter 9.) A few examples of successful methods for adjusting pads to fit individual bodies are presented here to help illustrate some of the many possibilities in this area.

By far the most common method of adjusting width is to rely on the nature of the padding itself. If isolated pads rather than a solid shield are used, the pads can be strategically placed on the most exposed or most vulnerable areas of the body. Elastic material or straps surround the rest of the body expanse to provide a close fit for a wide range of body types and sizes. Boxing head guards and fencing helmets (Figure 6.34) both protect the front portion of the head, which is the area vulnerable to a blow during a match. Elastic bands provide adjustability for different head shapes and sizes on the boxing headgear, and a malleable, fabric-covered metal piece extends and molds over the center back of the head to hold the fencing mask in place.

The idea of providing straps or elasticized bands in areas where the body is least vulnerable has been used in a wide variety of protective clothing and equipment. The football shoulder pad shown in Figure 6.24 is open under the arms and is adjusted to different torso widths by means of elastic straps. Some ballistics vests (see Figure 6.1B) use this same method. It is interesting to note that the open area in these cases is one where body heat is most easily dissipated—an important factor wherever the buildup of body heat tends to be a problem. Some width adjustment between the shoulders of a rigid pad may also be provided by means of lacing at the center front, although selecting properly sized pads generally provides the width here.

Shin guards and elbow guards for many sports and recreational activities such as skateboarding

FIGURE 6.34 Fitting protective equipment. (A) Boxing headgear with adjustable elastic straps at the back of the head; (B) a fencing mask with a malleable metal clamp at the back of the head.

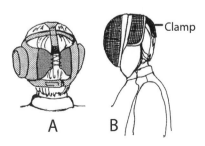

protect the more vulnerable bony areas (the shin and the point of the elbow), while stretchy fabrics or straps hold the guards in place over the fleshier areas of the calf and inner arm. Since the relatively unprotected bony areas of the knees and elbows are also points of contact during a fall, it is doubly important that they be covered by padding. It is more difficult to protect the wearer from blows around the full circumference of a body part, or on the interior fleshy portions of the limbs, especially if mobility is needed. The only solution in this case is to overlap (shingle) protective padding or to provide slits or spaces between protective pads that will allow mobility and adjustability but will be too small for a weapon or hazard to penetrate. For example, the pockets on girdle pads such as the one shown in Figure 6.35 might need to be sewn more closely together so that when the pads were inserted, they rested against one another, and

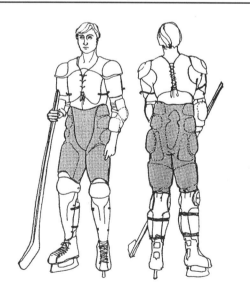

FIGURE 6.35 The Cooperall® stretch garment holding a number of lower body protective pads used in ice hockey. *(Design formerly produced by Cooper Canada)*

a weapon could not pass between them. (This, of course, would limit the stretchability of the girdle and affect fit.) The weapons in any activity must be thoroughly investigated before separation distances or openings can be planned. Obviously, separations would not be appropriate for most areas of ballistics protection, but closely placed pads could be effective in excluding a blow from a baseball or the shoulder of an opposing player, for example.

Length adjustments are more difficult to provide. Although only part of the body circumference may be involved in an impact, the entire length of that part is usually in need of protection. When a skater falls off a skateboard, for example, the calf may not be affected but the entire length of the shin may contact the sidewalk. When an athlete wears a protector that is too short, it simply means that less body area is protected. The need for length adjustment can be met to some extent by the use of separate pads that are sized in proportioned lengths. They can be held in place with fasteners or can be placed in pockets of a stretchable garment such as the body suit in Figure 6.35. Modular units may also be used. For example, a long forearm pad might be fastened to a short upper arm pad to fit a specific body. Chapter 9 presents more details on the various methods of keeping these pads in place once they have been correctly fitted to the body. In addition, many of the principles presented in Chapter 2 can be used to develop new methods of providing mobility in protective equipment.

KEEPING COOL IN IMPACT-PROTECTIVE GARMENTS

Next to lack of mobility, perhaps the greatest complaint of people who must wear impact-protective equipment is how hot it is to wear. Both the thickness and the nonporous nature of the materials used for impact protection prevent body heat from being conducted, convected, or radiated away, and they provide little or no opportunity for the perspiration resulting from this buildup of heat to be evaporated.

When rigid materials or closed-cell foams are used in protective equipment, cooling can be achieved in a number of ways. First, as mentioned previously, the materials can be used in isolated pads, leaving large areas of the body uncovered. Obviously, this solution is more effective in some situations than in others. Although the head, which is a primary radiator of excess body heat, may need maximum coverage in a work environment, the sides of the torso might be able to be uncovered, allowing for dissipation of body heat there.

Nonporous materials may also be perforated or fabricated in an open mesh to allow ventilation. (See Figure 6.36A.) Since holes tend to weaken a structure, perforations are generally kept to a minimum as they are in the hockey goalie mask shown in Figure 6.36A. It is difficult to place enough perforations in a rigid protector to achieve significant ventilation and yet maintain protection, but the skeleton construction of the field hockey shin

protector in Figure 6.36B has met these criteria. It provides protection with ventilation. The openings must be small enough to prevent a weapon (in this case, the ball or stick) from passing through. A skeleton network may also be used when open areas are needed for vision, as in a football facemask (Figure 6.36C). The wire-mesh facemask for fencing provides another example of a porous rigid structure that provides protection, visibility, and some ventilation (see Figure 6.34).

The most practical cooling devices in most sports and industrial equipment involve either spacer material or a sling construction. Net underwear (see Figure 5.18) is a typical spacer. Other semirigid structures—such as those used in the space industry and the military for ventilation channels—may also be adaptable for this purpose.

Sling constructions are generally made of porous materials. If it is not too easily stretchable, ventilating netting can also serve as an effective sling material. Figure 6.37 shows a proposal for a lacrosse chest protector to which netting has been applied tightly across the inside to serve as a sling. The shaped foam shell is lined with a nonstretch netting that is pulled taut across the inside of the protector and does not quite take the curve of the foam. When the protector is placed on the body, a channel is formed between the foam and the netting, and air can pass through it to cool the body.

Most powered, supplementary cooling units worn in industry and in outer space are not really feasible for sports or occupations such as police work because of their weight and size. However, they can be used under the heavy ballistics protectors worn by helicopter pilots or others who are in a seated position and close to a power source. They may also be needed with

FIGURE 6.36 Ventilated, rigid protectors. (A) Ice hockey goalie mask; (B) field hockey shin protector; (C) American football facemasks.

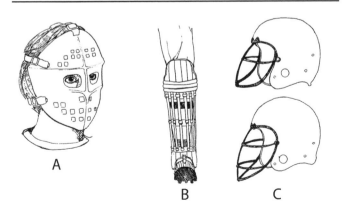

A   B   C

FIGURE 6.37 (A) A ventilated chest protector for lacrosse; (B) inside view showing the net liner. *(Design: Carol Fitzgerald)*

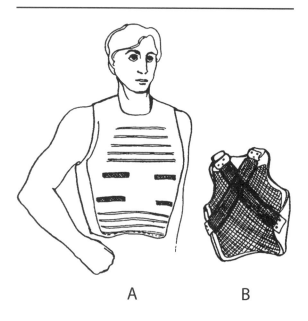

A   B

items such as the ordnance disposal suit shown in Figure 6.39 because of the extreme coverage and the stresses imposed by the work. Options for supplementary cooling units such as these can be found in Chapter 5.

It is important to consider how a provision for cooling may affect impact protection, particularly for an item like a ballistics vest for which added materials can alter energy dissipation. Although the woven materials used in ballistics clothing might appear to overcome the heat buildup problems created by the nonporous materials used in sports equipment, they actually do not. Since moisture affects the ability of some ballistics materials to absorb impact, many protectors are encased in a nonporous waterproof cover before they are worn. Ventilation is usually provided in one of two ways: Ventilating net underwear may be worn beneath the vest, or a vest model may be designed with open areas at the sides of the body to allow heat to dissipate there.

CASE STUDY 6.1 Protective Equipment for American Football

Protective equipment for football provides an excellent example of many of the principles and design techniques covered in this chapter. The ensemble shown in Figures A–D consists of a helmet; a neck roll; shoulder pads; rib pads; arm, hand, and elbow protectors; a girdle pad that incorporates hip and tailbone padding; pants that incorporate knee padding; and shoes. Players may also wear items such as knee braces and ankle protectors if the latter are not built into the shoes. They also wear a mouthpiece, which is not shown.

The helmet is the most important item of football equipment. It consists of two parts: a hard outer shell and a liner. Older liners contained a series of straps or webbing such as those shown in Figure 6.31. More current helmet liners use a variety of types of foam padding or air-filled cushions or a combination of

the two. (See Figure 6.8.) The purpose of the rigid shell is to spread the force of the impact; the purpose of the liner is to absorb energy and provide a standoff (i.e., not allow the rigid shell to collide with the head). The liner may also be used as part of a sizing system. The helmet should fit as snugly on the head as possible to prevent injury. There are several methods used to fit a helmet more closely to various head shapes, among them: adding extra inflation to the liners shown in Figure 6.8B, adding thicker foam padding to the liner, and tightening or repositioning the chin strap.

Figure A shows the features of a typical helmet. The chinstrap with its chin cup keeps the helmet firmly located on the head. The nose bumper and similar padding at the back of the neck prevent injury to the bridge of the nose and the back of the neck should the helmet be knocked forward or backward on the head. The cheek pads come in different thicknesses and may be involved in fitting. Other pads in the helmet may snap in place or adhere to the shell with hook-and-loop tape. If a helmet is too loose, a thicker pad can be snapped in place.

Face guards protect the eyes, nose, mouth, and jaw from accidental and intentional contact from opposing players. The type of face guard worn varies with the position being played. (See also Figure 6.36.) More bars provide increased protection, but also add to interference with vision. Because they need an unrestricted field of vision to set up plays and see the ball clearly, quarterbacks and receivers tend to wear face guards with fewer bars. However, some players who have had previous injuries or simply want more face protection may have more extensive custom guards made or use clear plastic face shields. Face guards may be made of rubber-covered metal or plastic. Metal guards were sometimes preferred in cold climates in the past because

some plastics became brittle and shattered in the cold. However, improvements in technology have virtually eliminated this concern and plastics can offer advantages in terms of lighter weight.

Because of the serious injuries that can occur with improper head protection, there are standards regulating helmet performance. Every helmet used in officially sanctioned college and high school football games in the United States must meet the safety standards of the National Operating Committee on Standards for Athletic Equipment (NOCSAE). Helmets are tested at designated test centers (see Figure 6.10 for an example of one type of test performed) and stamped with a seal that certifies that it meets those standards (Figure B).

Shoulder pads provide the primary protection for the shoulders and upper torso. The pad shown in Figure C is called a cantilever pad because it rests on the chest and back to form a bridge above the shoulder surface. (See also Figure 6.27.) This provides extra

FIGURES A–D Protective equipment for American football: (A, B) the helmet; (C) shoulder pads; (D) other body padding. *(McLean and Watkins 1985)*

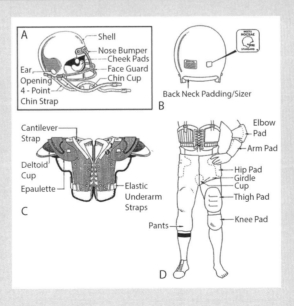

protection for the top of the shoulder. The shaded areas on Figure C indicate the placement of rigid shock plates. Note also the shingling or overlapping of pads, with the epaulette distributing the force of a blow onto the chest, back, and deltoid (shoulder cap) pads.

Energy absorption is accomplished with a lining of foam. Some padding systems contain a special inch-thick open-cell foam, while others contain a half-inch of closed-cell foam as a base for all of the rigid plates. Many shoulder pads have an extra layer of cushioning foam directly over the end of the shoulder. (See the solid black area under deltoid cup on Figure C.) Edges of rigid plates are usually covered with foam and a vinyl or leather strip so that they do not dig into the body when players are hit. The shoulder pad alone provides an example of the use of many techniques for providing impact protection: combination pads with rigid plates and energy-absorbing foam; shingling; bridging; cantilevering; and contouring of the outer edge of the pad.

Other body padding is shown in Figure D. Rib protectors are generally made of foam covered with a fairly hard-to-compress plastic. Sometimes these pads are partially filled with air. Vertical channels or segments of foam allow the pad to curve around the rib area. Some rib pads are designed to be attached to the shoulder pads; others contain their own shoulder straps and are donned under the shoulder pads.

Because of the use of artificial turf in many stadiums, arm and elbow pads are increasingly in use. These are worn primarily to prevent abrasions caused by sliding on the turf, but they also provide protection from contusions. Hand pads in the form of fingerless padded gloves may be worn as well.

The jersey (not shown) with its identifying colors and symbols, is generally thought to merely provide decoration. However, it has the important function of holding all upper body padding close to the body and keeping it in place.

Lower-body padding is put on in layers beginning with a rigid cup protector and a girdle. The girdle is made of a stretch material and contains pockets that house pads that protect the hips and spine. These generally are combination pads that contain shaped rigid plates that bridge the crest of the hip and the spinal column and curve under the tailbone. Most pants are also made of a stretch material, generally nylon or a nylon/spandex blend. Some pants contain a very high modulus stretch in the main body of the pant with an easy stretch panel in the crotch that makes separate leg movement easier. A combination pad is inserted in an inner pocket of the pants to protect the front of the thigh. A foam pad is generally used over the knee because of the flexibility for movement needed in that area. Note that the hip pads contained in the girdle extend above the waistline of the pants. This portion of the hip protector contains no rigid plate so that it is possible for the player to bend easily to the side. At the same time, however, the pad remains firmly upwardly suspended over the kidney/lower rib area.

Fit and adjustment are provided for each of the items (e.g., the laced opening of the shoulder and rib pads; the stretch fabric of the girdle pad, pants, and jersey; the elastic straps that hold the shoulder pads around the torso and the separate padding structure of the ensemble). Each pad must be planned to work with pads adjacent to it regardless of the size of the wearer. Although fabrics have been planned to allow ventilation and evaporation of sweat, in general, the critical importance of impact protection for the head and chest and the impermeable materials needed to achieve protection often allow less than optimal thermal comfort.

There are many different brands and models of each item of football equipment. While the examples provided here are typical of high school and college level football equipment, youth and professional equipment may use different approaches. By examining other items of protective equipment for football and other sports, designers can find many different applications of the concepts in this chapter.

CASE STUDY 6.2 Protective Ensembles for Ordnance Disposal

Explosive ordnance disposal (EOD) personnel dismantle bombs or move explosive devices to a location where they can be safely detonated. Protecting them requires extensive body protection that must be highly functional. EOD workers face four major threats: impact from solid material flying away from the bomb site, puncture and cuts from high velocity fragments, radiant heat and flame, and shock waves (i.e., sudden blasts of pressurized air).

Figures A–D illustrates a typical EOD suit, which consists of multiple garments, each with multiple layers. There are three types of materials used in EOD suits. The outermost layer, or one near the outermost surface of the ensemble, is a rigid armor layer designed to deflect fragments flying away from the bombsite and to bounce shock waves away from the wearer. It is typically made of a solid, hardened material—usually a composite of aramids. These form a structure that is both strong and high heat resistant and, unlike many metal or ceramic counterparts, relatively lightweight.

While this first line of defense resists the blast of a shock wave, it is impossible for it to deflect all of it. Some of the pressure involved will pass through the rigid protector and needs to be absorbed by the layers underneath. Many suits have a flexible energy-absorbing layer of foam directly under the rigid layer, and this helps to attenuate some of the shock wave. Beneath the energy-absorbing layer is soft body armor made much like a police vest, with many layers of aramid textiles. If fragments from the blast manage to penetrate the rigid layer, this layer helps keep them from entering the body.

FIGURES A–D (A) Protective ensemble for explosive ordnance disposal; (B) pants and protective leggings; (C) helmet; (D) back view showing cummerbund attachment. *(Design formerly produced by American Body Armor)*

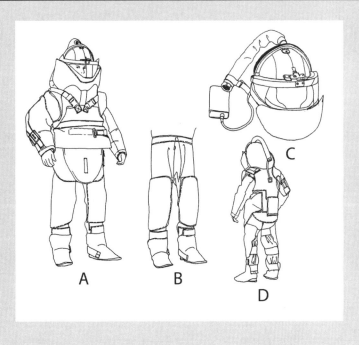

The basic protective items of the ensemble shown in Figures A–D include trousers; leggings; a jacket with an upward, extended collar and chest protector; arm protection; a groin cup; a helmet; and a cummerbund. The rigid layer of an EOD suit may be strapped on over the suit or carried in a high-heat-resistant cover.

Each of these items contains ballistics panels composed of woven Kevlar and may include as many as 20 layers of this fabric. The outside cover of the suit is made of a fire-resistant material such as Nome®. Any inner face that lies next to the body is made of a heavy-duty nylon with a waterproof, urethane backing to prevent body moisture from entering the Kevlar panels.

The pants, shown in Figure B have an expansion panel in the center, which extends from the front waist through the crotch and up to the back waistline. This allows them to fit a wide range of sizes. Ballistics leggings are strapped over them. They are designed to offer 270° of coverage on the front and sides of the legs. In order to achieve maximum movement, the arm protectors are separate from the sleeveless jacket but designed in a way that prohibits a gap in protection from forming between the armscye of the jacket and the sleeve cap area. The jacket contains an additional chest protector and a groin protector. Both of these protectors have a ballistic steel plate insert to dissipate the shock of an initial blast and protect from fragments. The jacket also contains a wide shaped collar that stands up to provide extra neck and lower face protection and bridge any gap between the jacket and helmet. The helmet, shown in Figure C, contains a wraparound ballistics visor and built-in ventilation and communications systems. These latter features are specially engineered to protect the wearer's hearing from the effects of sudden pressure. A cummerbund is strapped on over the jacket to provide additional protection at the center front area. It attaches with hook-and-loop tape to panels at the side back of the jacket. (See Case Study 6.1 Figure D.) Protective gloves and boots are also worn as part of the ensemble.

The EOD suit represents one of the most difficult design tasks in protective clothing because it requires extremes of protection with a high need for flexibility and dexterity. The use of flexible textiles with inserts of rigid materials in the areas of maximum need, the use of separate components and overlapping techniques to achieve better mobility with maximum protection, and the contouring of each of the components to work successfully with the others all contribute to the success of its design.

Conclusion

This chapter has dealt primarily with protection from what are essentially large-scale impacts. The human body is subjected every day to smaller-scale impacts such as those from particles of dust, aerosol chemicals, and radiation. As you read about these hazards in the next chapter, you will see how many of the principles used to explain impact in this chapter also apply to smaller scale impacts.

7 Living and Working in Hazardous Environments

This chapter involves protecting human beings who enter environments that contain hazards such as radiation, chemical or biological contamination, and electric shock. Because many of the same principles are involved in protecting people and products *from* human contamination, it also includes a discussion of clothing for personnel who work in medical facilities or cleanrooms.

The Nature of Hazards in the Environment

Four significant types of environmental threats from which individuals in a variety of work and life situations need to be protected are chemical, biological, radiological, and nuclear hazards, generally referred to as **CBRN**. While these hazards can occur in any of the three states of matter (solid, liquid, or gas), some of the most hazardous to humans often occur in a combination of those states as aerosols. **Aerosols** are tiny particles of solids or liquids suspended in a gas. They include dusts, sprays, smoke, and mists. Because they are airborne, they can lead to more widespread transmission of hazards than, for example, a solid, which would need to be contacted by each individual. Dusts, often referred to as *suspended particulate matter*, can distribute fibers such as asbestos; chemical hazards such as oily chemical agents and pesticides; and radioactive material or biohazards such as molds and spores over a relatively large area.

The size of particles in the environment or suspended in aerosols can be of major concern to protective clothing designers as they choose appropriate materials and configure designs. The way in which particles behave is also a factor. Since particles are often irregularly shaped, the term **aerodynamic diameter** is used to describe particle size. Aerodynamic diameter is the equivalent diameter of a sphere with a specific density that would move at the same rate as the particle being described. Most aerosols contain particles of many different sizes, so specifications for protection often include the maximum number of particles of each size that is acceptable for protection to be considered sufficient.

Examples of chemical substances from which humans need protection include pesticides, industrial byproducts, or chemical warfare agents. Because many of these hazards involve not only solids, liquids, and gases but also mixed phases such as aerosols, they thus require attention to their solid, liquid, and gaseous components for proper protection. Many substances in this category are grouped together under what are labeled **toxic industrial chemicals (TICs)**. The U.S. Occupational Safety and Health Administration (OSHA) states that TICs "can be chemical hazards (e.g., carcinogens, reproductive hazards, corrosives, or agents that affect the lungs or blood) or physical hazards (e.g., flammable, combustible, explosive, or reactive)" (OSHA, "Toxic Industrial").

Of primary importance is that materials used for protection must not be damaged or defeated by the chemicals involved.

Biological hazards involve living organisms that can reproduce in supportive environments. These include bacteria, viruses, and infectious wastes of many kinds. They are particularly dangerous because even minute amounts can debilitate a community once they have entered just one "host" and subsequently been passed to others while they continue to grow. In the face of epidemics, as the public becomes increasingly concerned about contagious diseases such as hepatitis, Ebola, or various forms of flu, clothing that provides protection from biological hazards has been of special interest in health care fields.

Radiation hazards may result from the accidental release of radioactive material from a nuclear power plant or the explosion of an atomic bomb. Some of the substances in this category, such as the radioactive materials in a so-called "dirty bomb", are among the hazards referred to as *toxic industrial materials (TIMs)*. Radiation hazards in the workplace may involve either ionizing or non-ionizing radiation. (See Energy Basics 7.2.)

Nuclear hazards involve damage from blasts, intense heat, and blinding light as well as the nuclear radiation that results from the explosion of nuclear weapons.

In addition to CBRN hazards, many work situations contain dangers from electric shock or potential fire hazards from static electricity. Static electricity generated by personnel, and especially by the clothing they wear, also can damage products being manufactured.

Designers need to be aware of the ways in which each of these hazards is propelled toward the body and protective clothing. It is also important to understand the pathways by which these hazards reach the body and how they affect human health. These two topics will be discussed next. The remainder of the chapter is organized around the basics of each of these hazards: the effect of each hazard on the human body, the types of materials used for protection, and the factors that are important for clothing designers to consider in designing protection.

THE MECHANISMS OF HAZARD MOVEMENT

The danger of intrusion of a substance begins when some force attracts or moves hazardous substances toward the body or the surface of a protective garment. Thus, one of the keys to protection lies in eliminating the attraction of hazards to the area being protected and increasing their acceleration away from the area.

Airflow provides much of the impetus required to move substances toward, away from, or around the body and protective clothing. For example, when a surgeon bends an elbow in a surgical gown, that movement pushes air in the sleeve toward a localized area and may force bacteria or blood through interstices in a gown made of woven fabric. Movement in clothing may also create the kind of bellows effect discussed in Chapter 5. It propels organisms from the inside of a garment through the nearest garment openings into the air outside. Other movements, as well as inhalation can create a negative pressure that draws organisms into garments or into the respiratory tract.

The kinetic energy of moving air is often utilized in protective clothing. People who work with nerve gas or unknown disease-bearing agents generally wear a **positive pressure** (inflated) garment. (See Figure 7.1 and also Case Study 2.1 in Chapter 2.) Air fed into the suit is vented outward so that if a leak should occur, the air flowing out would propel dangerous substances away from the body.

FIGURE 7.1 A positive pressure suit for a child born with no natural immunities. *(NASA)*

Isolation clothing and transport equipment for people with infectious diseases use **negative pressure** to protect people *around* the wearer. (See Figure 7.2.) Thus, if a break occurs in an isolation garment, any organisms would be pulled into the

FIGURE 7.2 A negative pressure stretcher isolator designed for transporting individuals who have been radiologically contaminated. Air that is constantly drawn into the isolator is purified before being vented; portholes in the sides end in rubber gloves for use by medical personnel. *(Formerly produced by Defense Apparel)*

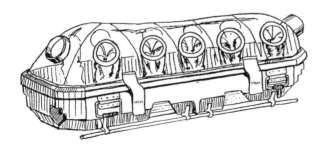

garment rather than pushed out toward a noninfected person.

Air-flow techniques may be designed into the circulation systems in rooms to direct the flow of particles in the environment and thus reduce the need for protective clothing. In an operating room, for example, a surgeon may stand on the downwind side of the operating table so that any infectious particles are accelerated away from the patient. Airflow techniques are also used to direct radioactive gases and particles away from workers in uranium mines.

Airflow alone may not be effective in directing particle movement if some other attractive force is present. Static electricity, for example, may cause electrically charged particles to accelerate rapidly toward an area having an opposite charge, even opposing airflow. That is why antistatic finishes are so important in many medical and industrial garments. If particles are accelerating toward a protective garment, then the size, shape, and elasticity of the particle become critical considerations in determining the types of protective materials needed. All of the factors that affect larger-scale impacts discussed in Chapter 6 also affect these smaller-scale interactions. In addition to mass and velocity, compressibility and surface roughness of the particles need to be considered. If protection from a specific particle is to be provided, not only will these factors need to be determined, but the ways in which particles may be changed after the initial collision must also be anticipated.

PATHWAYS INTO THE HUMAN BODY

Hazardous substances may reach and eventually harm the body by four different routes. The first is by *direct contact.* The substance can be touched or spilled on the skin. Substances that enter the body in this manner are termed **percutaneous** (through the skin) threats. A droplet of moisture containing the organism of a disease, for example, may be propelled through the air toward a healthy individual by means of a sneeze or cough, or it may be left on items that the infected individual has touched. Direct contact may also occur through an open wound or exposed mucous membranes, such as those surrounding the eye.

Various areas of the body may be affected by contact with the same chemical, biological, or radioactive substance in different ways. Figure 7.3 shows, for example, the degree to which different areas of the body can absorb the pesticide, parathion. While the palm of the hand absorbs only about 2 percent of the parathion that contacts it, the scrotum may absorb as much as 100 percent. Biological organisms in particular may be very system-specific in terms of their route into the body and the way in which they harm the body. The military has developed a model called the *Body Region Hazard Analysis (BRHA)* that is used to convert measures of exposure at 20 different locations on the body into a value that indicates the relative

FIGURE 7.3 The percent absorption of the pesticide, parathion, on various body areas it contacts. *(Maibach et al. 1971)*

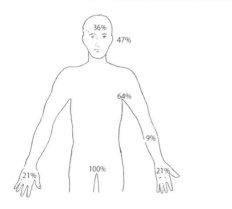

protection offered by items of chemical protective clothing (Standing Committee, 1997). This analysis takes into account both the exposure to chemical/biological hazards and the relative sensitivity of each body area.

Second, damage may result from *breathing in* hazardous substances that are vaporized or suspended in the air. Hazards like pesticides, coal dust, or disease-bearing microorganisms may destroy the lining of the lungs or may move through the lungs into the bloodstream or the central nervous system where they can effect changes. Air containing radioactive particles may be breathed in and cause cell damage throughout the body. OSHA states that if TICs enter the body through the lungs, poisoning occurs more quickly "because of the ability of the agent to rapidly diffuse throughout the body" (OSHA "Toxic Industrial Chemicals").

Third, hazardous substances may be *ingested* either directly or by ingesting contaminated food, drink, or drugs. As with airborne hazards, these may affect the digestive system directly or move through it to the circulatory or nervous system.

Fourth, a hazardous substance may be *injected* into the body. The substance may be a hazardous chemical or a biological organism deposited on a contaminated needle, or a toxin may be injected through the bite of an animal or insect.

Much of the protective clothing on the market today has been designed to cope with the first two pathways into the body and these will be the focus of this chapter. However, it is worth noting that although clothing and respirators are primarily designed to prevent hazards from touching the skin or being inhaled, many CBRN protective ensembles must totally enclose the body in order to be effective. Therefore, such activities as safe eating and drinking must be provided for in the design of the ensemble. In addition, because even minute amounts of toxins can be lethal, CBRN protective ensembles must be designed to avoid any puncture.

It should also be noted that since radiation is a form of electromagnetic energy that travels through space without the involvement of physical matter, radioactively contaminated material and other forms of radiation in the environment may affect body cells without actually entering the body via any of the routes discussed above.

Protection from Chemical/ Biological Hazards

Although chemical and biological hazards involve different substances, the ensembles used to protect the body from them are similar, and thus many clothing ensembles are designated as providing *chemical/biological* (**CB**) protection.

MATERIALS AND PRODUCTION METHODS FOR CB GARMENTS

The materials used for CB protection fall into three types: impermeable, permeable (most of which are microporous), and selectively permeable membranes.

Impermeable materials appropriate for protection from CB hazards are generally films or sheets. (See Chapter 3.) They share many of the qualities of waterproof materials discussed in Chapter 3, but they must also have the characteristic of being non-reactive chemically with the hazardous substances in a specific environment. Films or sheets of poly-vinyl chloride (PVC) polypropylene, polyurethane, polyethylene, and natural rubber are among those that provide CB protection. These differ in density (which eventually affects the weight of a garment), resistance to cracking, flexibility, tensile strength, and performance in extremes of temperatures. The relative cost of these materials may influence a

designer's choice of a material for a specific garment, particularly for a disposable item. In cases where films are not thought to have sufficient tensile strength, they may be bonded or laminated to a strong, thin fabric such as woven nylon. It is important for both designers and users to understand diffusion, which is a major concern for impermeable materials. (See Energy Basics 7.1.) To defeat a wider range of chemicals, several layers of different films may be laminated together into a single thin film.

Woven fabrics may also be made impermeable with coatings. One material that is frequently used for chemical protection is butyl-coated nylon. "Butyl" refers to butyl rubber, a synthetic rubber that resists a variety of chemicals and is impenetrable to gases. Because butyl rubber is highly elastic, has excellent elastic recovery, and resists sunlight, ozone, and other factors that accelerate aging, butyl-coated nylon does not suffer the amount of cracking and leakage commonly associated with coated fabrics. In addition, the nylon backing increases the strength and puncture resistance of the system. Neoprene and other synthetic rubbers may also be used in some industrial situations.

It is important that the materials chosen for CB garments have relatively smooth surfaces. This characteristic is essential if particles or drops of moisture are to be prevented from lodging in the fabric surface and making decontamination difficult.

In addition to a fabric's resistance to toxic substances, one of the most important characteristics of an impermeable material for CB protection is the ease with which it can be made into clothing. Because stitching creates holes in clothing, garment parts must be joined by means of heat-sealing methods. (These methods are discussed in Chapter 9.) Some manufacturers sew garments in the normal fashion and then fuse a strip of thermoplastic suit material over each seam to fill in the needle holes (Figure 7.4). Barrier zippers such as those shown in Figures 9.25 and 9.26 may be

FIGURE 7.4 A taped and sealed seam. The seam is stitched (left); then a thermoplastic strip slightly wider than the seam area is placed over it (middle) and sealed in place. The wide textured area on the right is the imprint left by the heated sealing tool and represents the finished appearance of the seam.

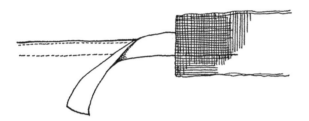

used, or if a suit is disposable, a heat-sealing process may be used to close a suit once it is donned, and the suit is then merely slashed to allow exit. (See Figure 9.47.)

The characteristic resistance to chemicals of many of these materials makes them resistant to many adhesives and some may be resistant to specific heat sealing techniques as well. Therefore, it is extremely important that the possibilities for construction processes be explored as fabrics are being evaluated for their resistance to particular hazardous substances.

Selectively permeable membranes (SPMs) used for CB garments need to be carefully chosen so that protection is provided for all of the hazards in

Energy Basics 7.1: Diffusion

Even though it is easy to think of an impermeable material as a total barrier, in fact, it is possible for molecules of a hazardous substance to work their way through an impermeable film. They do so through the process of *diffusion*, which was briefly introduced in Chapter 3. Diffusion that results in the permeation of a film, for example, is achieved because the molecules of a substance pass through the spaces between molecules in the film.

Raheel describes the process of permeation by diffusion as having three steps: (1) absorption of individual molecules of the chemical into the exposed surface of the material, (2) molecular diffusion through the material matrix along a concentration gradient, and (3) desorption of the chemical from the inside surface (1994, 53). So, even if an impermeable protective material is used, many chemicals may eventually permeate them. The rate at which this permeation takes place (i.e., the *breakthrough time*) must be sufficient to provide adequate protection. It is critical to know the breakthrough time for a material so that clothing can be changed before a hazardous substance

reaches the inside face of a protective garment. Schwope et al. (1983, 5) state that no one material will be a barrier to all chemicals and that for certain chemicals, there is no commercially available glove or clothing that will provide more than an hour's protection. There are, however, multilayer laminates that combine several different materials into one layer to provide multichemical protection. Material thickness is a factor in breakthrough time. Schwope et al. (1983, 11) state that permeation is inversely proportional to thickness (i.e., doubling thickness will double breakthrough time).

It is also important to note that decontaminating the outer face of an impermeable material may not be sufficient to protect a worker against a chemical hazard. Once permeation has begun, some chemicals continue to permeate protective materials while they are in storage so that when a worker dons a garment with a cleaned outer surface the following day, the chemicals may actually have worked their way through to lie on the inner face, next to the skin (Schwope et al. 1983, 7).

the environment. Information on the structure and function of SPMs can be found in Chapter 3 under "Permselective Treatments."

Permeable materials may be worn for emergency or splash protection to provide a more comfortable, breathable garment for constant wear that can be removed quickly before chemicals completely penetrate the material. Sometimes material thickness is used to add to the necessary breakthrough time, or water-repellency may be used to discourage moisture that contains bacteria or other particles from being wicked through clothing. A surgeon's gown, for example, may be made water repellent or waterproof in the areas most likely to come into contact with moisture. Thus, the gown in Figure 7.5 has a fluid-resistant section from midchest to knees and from wrist to elbow to prevent a fabric soaked with fluid (from the surgeon's perspiration or the patient's blood) from transferring bacteria through the garment to the sterile operating field.

Although one might think that tight weaves of cotton or of synthetic fibers (which do not absorb much moisture) might provide a good barrier to liquids, it has been shown that they may actually increase the penetration of liquids and sprays (Marer 2000, 165). This is particularly true with synthetics because the long, smooth, tightly packed fibers promote wicking and this capillary action encourages the rapid transport of liquids, especially those in droplet or aerosol form, from one face of a fabric to the other. Other studies have found that as the temperature of some liquids rise, their permeability rate increases, with some liquids being more significantly affected than others (Cao 2007).

GARMENT DESIGN FOR CB PROTECTION

The type of clothing needed to protect the body from CB hazards depends upon the hazards in the

FIGURE 7.5 A reusable surgeon's gown with liquid-repellent fabric from midchest to upper thigh and from the wrist to just below the elbow, the areas most likely to come in contact with the sterile operating field.

environment and the activity of the wearer. Sufficient protection may be provided by a face mask and rubber gloves or may require a totally encapsulating suit with a positive pressure backup system. Some of the most difficult problems for clothing designers arise in trying to isolate the body totally from CB hazards. Thus, many CB-protective garments are among the most innovative functional clothing designs.

In addition to providing basic protection, CB garments must meet many of the same criteria as everyday clothing. Ideally, they should (1) not interfere with the movement needed to do a specific job; (2) allow the wearer the maximum possible use of the senses of touch, hearing, and sight; (3) allow or provide for adequate relief from heat stress; and (4) if reusable, be easily cleanable. Both reusable and disposable garments need to be designed in a way that allows wearers to doff them without risking contamination. Because many items of CB protection are expensive, companies may own only a limited number of items. This means that adjustability may be a prime consideration in garment design since one suit may have to fit people of a variety of sizes and shapes.

If separate items (e.g., a jacket, pants, and hood) are being designed, the interfaces between them are particularly critical. Attention needs to be paid to providing wide overlaps so the pieces do not separate during movement. Garment edges need to be kept close to the body. For example, to keep a jacket hem close to the pants, some jackets have a strap that passes from back to front between the legs that can be secured at the front and adjusted to pull the jacket hem against the pants. Other jackets may have an inner elasticized "skirt" to hug the jacket to the pants below the waist. Restraint straps that pass under the arms may also be used to keep the lower edge of separate hoods close to the jacket. If equipment, such as that containing air supply, is to be worn *over* the garment, the location of garment overlaps may need to be planned so that the equipment helps secure garment edges but does not interfere with movement.

If protection is needed for a liquid hazard, once the proper liquid-protective material has been selected, a designer needs to develop garment features that will prevent liquids that run off the garment surface from penetrating the garment. This is usually done by paying close attention to overlaps and relating them to typical body positions for the worker. For example, the ensemble shown for a greenhouse worker spraying pesticides in Figure 7.6 has overlaps planned to accommodate the direction of liquid flow. Since the hands are generally up holding the hose, gloves overlap the sleeves to minimize liquid flow that might occur into the sleeve cuff if the gloves were tucked in. The neckline opening is lapped from front to back because of the direction in which the spray would be striking the body. The jacket provides a wide overlap and runoff area over the pants as do the pants over the boots. If the hands were held

FIGURE 7.6 A protective garment for pesticide spraying made of tightly woven cotton. Note the minimal seams and the direction of the closure and overlaps. *(Design: Ellen Conti)*

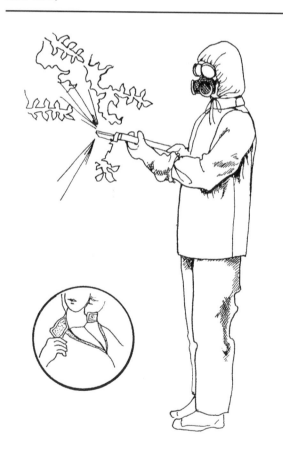

down at the sides, and water was being sprayed from above the body, it would make more sense to place the sleeve of the garment *over* the glove or to develop a secure connection that prevented penetration from any direction.

Exhaust valves or crack valves are usually placed in positive pressure suits to avoid an accidental bursting or blowout. **Crack valves** open when a predetermined level of pressure builds up, allowing a one-way escape of air from the suit. Exhaust valves or other openings of this type are often protected under some sort of *splash cover* (Figure 7.7) to prevent liquid from running down into vents and being accidentally propelled through them. Note that the opening of the splash cover is placed at the bottom so that gravity can assist in keeping liquids from entering the area.

In addition to understanding the user, activity, and environment before beginning to design CB clothing, designers need to be aware of government regulations in this area. For most activities in which hazards are present, there are recommendations or even mandates regulating what people in those situations must wear. Even if clothing is not mandated to be worn, many items of protective clothing must pass certain regulations in order to be manufactured or imported into specific countries. Having a thorough knowledge of these regulations is critical before beginning design work.

Levels of CB Protection

A number of groups and government agencies have researched hazards and the health risks with exposure to CB agents and proposed systems for classifying the levels of CB protection needed. Two types of classification systems for CB protective clothing will be discussed here—one for industry and one for the military.

The U.S. Environmental Protection Agency (EPA) has developed recommendations for

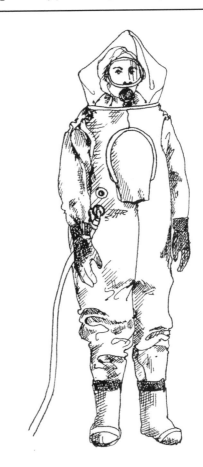

FIGURE 7.7 A disposable chemical-protective suit with exhaust valve protected by a splash cover on the chest. *(Design formerly produced by ILC Dover)*

personal protective equipment (PPE) for pesticide application. (EPA, "Personal Protective"). The International Organization for Standardization (ISO) and the American Society for Testing and Materials (ASTM) are also currently developing performance standards for pesticide applicators that will designate categories of protective clothing for three different levels of risk (NASDA "PPE for Pesticide"). There are also regulations for exposure to biological hazards such as bloodborne pathogens (OSHA "Occupational Exposure").

The Occupational Safety and Health Administration has designated levels of personal protective equipment needed for work involving hazardous waste and for first responders who are at risk (OSHA "General Description"). These are used as guidelines for people who work in agriculture with pesticides as well as for those who work with chemicals in industrial situations. An example of a suit that could be worn for Level A protection can be found in Figure 7.11. It is to be used when the highest level of respiratory, skin, and eye protection is needed. It involves complete coverage with a totally encapsulating suit, a self-contained breathing apparatus (SCBA), and chemically resistant gloves and boots. A disposable protective suit may be worn over this ensemble to help with decontamination.

Level B is to be used when the highest level of respiratory protection is required but a lesser degree of skin coverage is needed. It involves the use of hooded, chemically resistant clothing for the areas in which the chemical hazards are most likely to contact the body (e.g., coveralls or an apron); a positive pressure, full-facepiece SCBA; chemically resistant gloves and boots; and a hard hat (Figure 7.8). A face shield is optional.

Level C guidelines are to be followed when specifics about respiratory hazards are known and criteria for protection with respirators can be set at a level lower than for Level B. The criteria for skin protection is similar to that for Level B. Level C protection typically involves the use of a filtered breathing system such as a gas mask with a sorbent canister, chemically resistant clothing that covers the most likely areas of contact with the chemical, and chemically resistant gloves and boots (see Figure 7.8C). A face shield is optional.

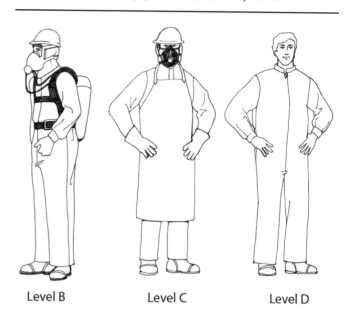

FIGURE 7.8 Examples of garments used for three of the levels of personal protective equipment established by OSHA.

Level B   Level C   Level D

Level D protection is basically a work uniform with no respiratory or skin protection for what OSHA terms "nuisance contamination only." It involves the use of coveralls and chemically resistant steel toe and shank boots (see Figure 7.8D). Items such as safety glasses or goggles, gloves, face shields, and hard hats are optional.

Military groups categorize degrees of CB protection using MOPP (Mission Oriented Protective Posture) levels. Each level is planned for a specific situation, from readiness when there is the threat of a chemical/biological warfare attack to the levels needed during and postattack. Figure 7.9 illustrates the gear worn by the U.S. Army for each of the MOPP levels. The protective gear includes a CB overgarment that is designed to be worn over the regular uniform, CB protective overboots and gloves, and a mask that filters out CB agents. The mask is accompanied by a hood that is either separate or part of the overgarment. The overgarment

FIGURE 7.9 Mission Oriented Protective Posture levels of protection used by the military.

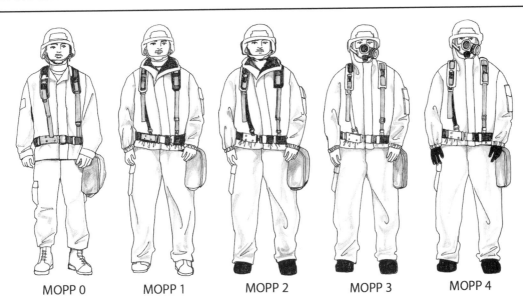

MOPP 0   MOPP 1   MOPP 2   MOPP 3   MOPP 4

is breathable and employs carbon to filter toxins so that they do not reach the suit interior. (See the discussion of selectively permeable treatments in Chapter 3.) The overboots and gloves are impermeable and typically made of natural rubber or neoprene.

For each level, there is a prescribed set of items to be accessible within a certain period of time, a set of items to be carried, and a set of items to be worn. In MOPP 0, a protective mask is carried and a suit, gloves, and overboots need to be readily available. In MOPP 1, a CB attack is considered possible. For this level, a CB protective overgarment is worn over the regular uniform and a protective mask, overboots, and gloves are carried. In MOPP 2, an attack is likely. For this level, the overgarment and overboots are worn, and the mask and gloves are carried. In MOPP 3, there is an airborne threat but no percutaneous threat, so the overgarment is worn completely closed; the boots,

mask, and hood are worn; and the gloves are carried. MOPP 4 is used for the highest level of threat, and all items are worn.

FULLY ENCAPSULATED CB PROTECTION

Probably the most familiar full-enclosure suits are the **hazmat** (hazardous material) suits seen on workers cleaning up toxic spills or contaminated facilities. These are impermeable garments worn with some sort of breathing apparatus so that the wearer is completely isolated from the environment. Impermeable suits are generally used when there is a need for the additional protection of positive pressure and/or when air for suit inflation can be provided without a significant energy cost to the wearer.

For some situations, fully encapsulating suits may also be made of selectively permeable membranes. Most chemical warfare garments worn by soldiers in the field, for example, use SPMs because of the heat stress that would be caused by wearing a totally enclosed impermeable system for long periods of time. SPM systems have also been designed for first responders who might need to be prepared for the threat of chemical spills or "dirty bombs." Full-enclosure systems all require some sort of respirator for the provision of breathable air. Impermeable suits also need some way to cool the body as heat builds up inside the suit. This is often provided by circulating air. In positive pressure suits, the air used to inflate the suit may also be circulated and used to remove built-up heat and moisture.

Care must also be taken to consider features that allow safe donning and doffing. Often, the outer face of a garment cannot be touched during doffing. Managing this may involve adding features to both clothing *and* dressing facilities. Special benches may be provided or hooks hanging from ceilings and loops on an upper garment aid in keeping one-piece garments from dragging on the floor during donning and doffing. It is important for a designer to understand the decontamination procedures used for a specific situation because this may determine the order in which garments can be doffed and the features needed to ensure safe doffing.

Supplying Air for Breathing and Temperature Regulation

There are two basic situations for which fully encapsulating suits are designed. In the first, individuals cannot be hooked up to clean air for breathing and cooling, so a self-contained system for those functions must be worn on the body. Some suits used with self-contained systems are designed to be worn *under* a backpack that contains the breathing/cooling system, whereas others

FIGURE 7.10 A CB suit with a backpack containing a breathing system worn over the suit.

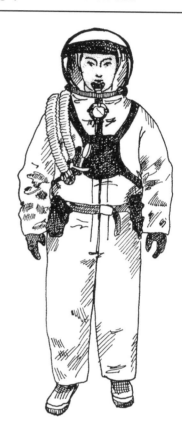

FIGURE 7.11 A CB suit designed to be worn over a breathing/cooling system.

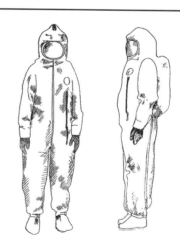

are designed to be worn *over* the system. The multilayered impermeable garment in Figure 7.10 is worn with an exterior backpack that provides breathing and ventilating air. The suit in Figure 7.11 was designed to be worn *over* a specific type of air-supply backpack so that the breathing system is protected as well. It is important to know and understand the specifications for the breathing/cooling system that will be in use before beginning to design. It is also critical to know if the suit has to be designed to interface with several types or different brands of equipment, each of which may have different shapes and different features.

The other situation for which CB suits are designed is for a laboratory or for working near a facility where there is a life-support system to which the wearer can be attached by way of an umbilical cord (Figures 7.12 and 7.13). Air for breathing as well as cooling or warming may be fed into the suit as shown in Figure 7.12. This constant air supply also gives the suit positive pressure, lifting it off the body so air can circulate close to the skin surface.

The features of a suit and a breathing device must be designed to work together. Breathing systems should be carefully designed and placed so that they do not create stress points or cause suit puncture. In addition, the suit must allow access to air supply devices in emergencies, and users need to be able to monitor air supply and leave an area before air runs out. Figure 7.11 shows a zipper to the side of the center front for emergency access and a clear vinyl window above it over the air supply gauge. It should be noted that many systems use audible alarms to indicate this since in some environments, vision may be obscured by smoke, and the like.

Backpack straps or other additional equipment worn over many full-enclosure suits may crush air

FIGURE 7.12 A CB suit with an umbilical cord for use in a lab where infectious diseases or chemical agents are studied.

spaces needed for both ventilation and the protective benefits of positive pressure. Therefore, many full-enclosure systems contain spacers as part of an air-cooled undergarment system. These keep the suit materials from collapsing and shutting off airflow. A schematic diagram of a typical undergarment system is shown in Figure 7.14.

If an umbilical cord is not used, there are two types of air delivery systems worn with CB suits: self-contained units or filter systems. Self-contained units either circulate breathing air or

FIGURE 7.13 A CB suit with an umbilical cord that supplies breathing and cooling air and provides the suit with positive pressure. This suit has a special belt across the waist area to cinch it in and prevent ballooning.

FIGURE 7.14 The airflow pattern in an air-cooled underwear system designed for use with the suit shown in Figure 7.10. Both the outer suit layers and the underwear layers are shown in this diagram. *(U.S. Army Natick Research, Development and Engineering Center)*

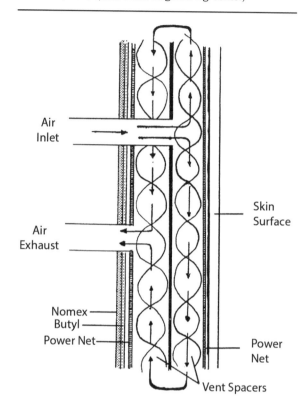

provide oxygen on a demand basis (the wearer draws in oxygen with each inhalation in a closely fitted mask). Filter systems merely detoxify air in the environment to make it breathable. Self-contained units are heavy because of the weight of the pressurized tanks needed to carry oxygen. However, the lighter filter systems may not provide sufficient breathing air in some toxic or flame environments where an oxygen deficiency exists.

Various methods are used to direct and circulate air around a CB suit for ventilation. Some suits are fitted with a network of plastic tubing that is laced through keepers or loops on the inner suit surface. These deliver ventilation throughout the garment to areas where airflow may be cut off as the body moves. This is especially important for the extremities. In some places, the tubes feed air into

baffles that prevent air from blowing directly on the eyes or other sensitive areas. For example, the ventilation system of the suit shown in Figure 7.12 has a nylon coil sole in the boot that directs air to the underside of the foot, an area normally cut off from airflow, but does not allow the air to blow out directly and tickle the foot.

Maintaining Vision

Both the clarity and range of vision are important for many activities for which full-enclosure suits are worn. The suits shown in Figures 7.10, 7.12, and 7.16B, in particular, have totally clear head coverings that allow a full range of side-to-side vision. The clear rigid helmet in Figure 7.16B can be rotated so that if scratches interfere with vision, a clean visual area can be moved into place. Often, clear helmets and hoods will be made of specially treated materials that do not fog up when the wearer breathes. Some of the air supplied to the suit may also be directed onto the face shield to provide fresh air for breathing and to prevent the wearer's breath from fogging the viewing area. Air flowing into a hood or helmet for vision provides the additional function of moving the carbon dioxide exhaled by the wearer away so that it does not cause ill effects when continually rebreathed. It should also be noted that since airflow within a head covering often creates a fairly high level of noise, various methods of baffling sound from this air supply may need to be incorporated into the system.

The relationship between hoods and respirators is a particularly important part of designing full-enclosure garments. Clear panels for vision need to be kept in front of the face as a wearer moves. Because many respirators are considerably heavier in front, they are generally fitted with tight, rubberized straps that hug the head to hold the facepiece in place. If respirators are worn *over* the hood, the tight straps of the respirator hold the facepiece of a hood in place. If respirators are worn *under* the suit, the suit design needs to be carefully examined in the hood area to be certain that the hood accommodates them and that any facepiece on the respirator lines up with the facepiece on the hood, particularly when the head turns. The type of clear plastic hoods or helmets shown in Figures 7.10, 7.12, and 7.16B go a long way toward solving visibility problems. Better visibility may also be achieved by tethering the hood in some fashion to the facepiece or support straps on the respirator.

Maintaining Continuous Coverage

Providing continuous coverage between head and face covers, gloves, and boots and the main body of the suit poses particularly difficult problems for designers. The gaps between these body segments have been handled in a variety of ways. Head coverings and bootie-type foot coverings are generally sealed permanently to the suit or, in some cases, may be cut in one continuous piece with the suit. Although this keeps coverage continuous, it may create problems with durability and sizing. Because of the great amount of wear on the soles of the feet and the possibility of stepping on something that might puncture the suit, steel toe and shank boots are usually worn over bootie extensions of the suit. These outer boots also help control ballooning in the leg area of positive pressure suits and provide a sizing feature by restricting the excess length and width of the suit leg so that it does not trip the wearer or interfere with movement. (See Figure 7.16A.)

Even though gloves may occasionally be permanently sealed to a suit, the stiffness of suit materials, the importance of individual glove sizing, and the wear on gloves make it more likely that they will be joined to each suit with some airtight mechanism. Two different systems for sealing a glove to the sleeve are shown in Figure 7.15. Figure 7.15A shows the sleeve of a suit with rigid **wrist rings** permanently attached at the sleeve cuff. These have a *bead* or ridge on each edge. Rubber gloves are stretched over each wrist ring, and then a rubber ring, much like a garter or a thick rubber band, is placed over the top of the assembly to form an airtight seal. This same sealing mechanism can also be used for boots.

FIGURE 7.15 Wrist rings. (A) A rubber glove is stretched over the rigid wrist ring at the end of a sleeve and a thick rubber band is pulled over it for extra security. (B) A bayonet lock type of system where rigid male and female connectors are connected to the sleeve and glove, respectively, and snapped together. *(Source for (B): Trelleborg Viking)*

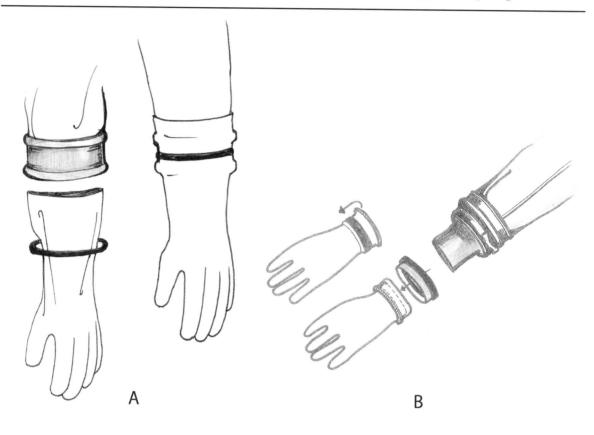

A   B

Figure 7.15B shows a so-called *bayonet system* that employs rigid rings on both sleeve and glove. The two are joined together by inserting one into the other and twisting until it snaps in place, in much the same manner as a bayonet is attached to a rifle, or a special lens is attached to a camera. The rigid ring that is the male portion of the connector may be permanently glued to the sleeve or force-fit with a ring inside the sleeve. Because gloves generally have a shorter life, the rigid connector on the glove is generally clamped onto the glove rather than permanently attached. Some similar systems employ more cone-shaped rigid

connectors rather than rings. Others may snap into one another with a force fit rather than twisting in place.

The connection of a helmet or hood to the rest of a full-enclosure garment is a difficult one to achieve. In items such as a space suit, the connection with separate segments of the suit can be made with locking rings. (See Figure 9.27.) In lower-tech and disposable suits, such as hazmat suits, head coverings are generally permanently sealed to the suit. One challenge, then, is to develop a fastening system that allows access into the suit, since a seam that runs directly up the center front and over the face area would interfere with vision. Some suits use a rear entry design; others use long, diagonal closures. (See Figure 7.16A.) Another approach is shown in Figure 7.16B, with a zipper that runs over the shoulders on either side of the helmet, looping around below the helmet in back. Regardless of the garment opening, if a rigid helmet is sealed to the suit, the neck opening of the helmet must be large enough for the head as well as any respirator or communication equipment

being worn to pass through, and the opening must be long enough to allow the suit to be pulled up and over the head.

Other Design Considerations for Full-Enclosure Suits

Often, suits designed for work in an outdoor environment must have additional protection from extreme thermal conditions or other environmental hazards. The ability to rescue an injured worker may also be important. The suit shown in Figure 7.13 has special safety loops near the wrist area to allow the attachment of lifelines for rescue in an emergency.

Much attention must be paid to durability issues for full-enclosure suits. It might be more accurate to say that CB suits that totally enclose the body are engineered rather than designed. Designers and engineers must work together, since each applied stress on a particular garment area can affect multiple areas of the garment and must be considered with all other stresses in the course of design decisions. The stresses on both fabrics and garment forms become considerably more complex for a total-enclosure suit with positive pressure. Although the optimal internal air pressure can be calculated for a static geometric form made of any given material, it is not so easily calculated for a garment. Movement may change suit volume or cause localized increases in pressure. For example, when a worker bends at the waist in a positive pressure CB suit, air inside the suit is pushed down toward the crotch, and the pressure there is increased. Unfortunately, this is also an area where several seams come together so it may already be a weak seam location. Reinforcements in areas such as this, where pressure builds up, can help ensure that the suit will not burst as the wearer moves.

FIGURE 7.16 Two models of total-enclosure suits with permanently attached head coverings: (A) Entry achieved through a diagonal zipper. Note the way the overboots control the suit inflation and suit leg length. (B) A design with a zipper that runs up the sides of the suit front and around beneath the helmet in back.

A   B

Since larger sizes of the same design involve increased volume and thus increased pressures, a specific design cannot be merely graded up to a larger size. Mathematical calculations have to be made to determine the specific stresses for this larger volume and the suit must be redesigned or additional reinforcements must be built in to accommodate them.

There are also practical and psychological considerations for those wearing total-enclosure suits for long periods of time. It is a time-consuming and sometimes costly process to don and doff suits, so once a suit is donned, it is advantageous to keep an individual in it as long as possible. One of the major issues that needs to be considered for long-term wearing of full-enclosure suits is toileting (i.e., waste removal). A unique system of waste management was developed in a design research study using MOPP gear (Cardello et al. 1991). The designers for that project placed a zippered expansion panel in the underarm seam of a one-piece MOPP 4 garment in the torso and upper arm areas and another in the crotch area. These functioned in much the same way as an expansion panel on a suitcase. When the zippers were open, they revealed panels of CB protective material so there was no break in protection. The extra width allowed a wearer to retract his or her arms from the sleeves and into the suit. With the panel at the crotch also open, this allowed the operation of a waste removal system for both urine and fecal matter. A two-way air lock pocket system then was used to pass the bags of waste out of the suit. The excess material in the panels could then be zipped closed so that excess suit bulk would not interfere with mobility. In combination with a safe nutrient delivery system, this suit allowed soldiers in the study to remain encapsulated for 54.5 hours, more than doubling the previous duration record.

Protection of Workers from Radiation Hazards

Potential radiation hazards are present in many different situations in daily life and in work settings. Radiation is used for the inspection of goods; the sterilization of food; the production of plastics and rubbers; and the elimination of static electricity in the film, printing, and textile industries. It is present in the paint used for luminous dials and in research equipment such as electron microscopes. It exists in uranium mines as well as nuclear power plants and X-ray facilities.

In general, the major radiation hazards that occur in industry are controlled by shielding the radiation source with lead or concrete rather than by clothing the worker. Inspection of products is often carried out by remote control in an isolated room shielded by lead walls. Warning devices are used to indicate leakage of radiation into a work area. When workers must move in and out of a potentially radioactive area, each may wear a **dosimeter**, which measures the amount of radiation to which the wearer has been exposed. These devices range from clip-on badges to rings to wristwatches to devices that can be plugged into a smartphone. When a worker approaches the maximum allowable dose, he or she is simply removed from an area where radiation is present for a specific period of time.

In order to develop radiation protective clothing, designers must first understand the hazard and the type of exposure each work situation presents and be aware of the role clothing can play in protection. For example, nuclear reactors require a concrete wall approximately 10 feet (3.05 m) thick to prevent the escape of some of the high-speed particles that may be emitted. It is inconceivable that any material suitable for clothing could provide this protection. Clothing can, however, protect workers from other forms of radiation and from radioactive substances carried in dust, oil, and grease in areas where repair and maintenance jobs have to be carried out. Clothing and respirators keep these substances from being deposited on the skin surface or carried into the body through the lungs.

RADIATION

There are a variety of radiation hazards in the environment, some of which are present in daily life and some that occur in special situations or in specific work environments. Energy Basics 3.1 provided a basic discussion of atoms, protons,

neutrons, electrons, and nuclear energy. Chapter 5 presented some basics of radiation from the standpoint of heat. (See Energy Basics 5.1 for a basic discussion of radiation.) Although radiant thermal energy in moderate amounts does not pose a threat to the body, other forms of radiation can be more hazardous. This chapter will discuss methods of protecting the body from the potential hazards of ionizing and nonionizing forms of radiation (Energy Basics 7.2), including information about radioactivity, X-rays, and microwaves. Understanding the basics of ionizing radiation will provide a foundation for developing protective garments for people such as nuclear power plant workers and for hospital workers and patients

Energy Basics 7.2: Ionizing and Nonionizing Radiation

When radiation causes electrons to be released from an atom, it becomes electrically charged and is said to be *ionized*. **Ionizing radiation** has the potential to damage the human body by breaking the chemical bonds that hold the cells of the body together. Naturally occurring ionizing radiation, at low levels, is common in the everyday environment. It occurs mostly from cosmic rays and from naturally occurring radioactive elements. X-rays are a form of ionizing radiation as is the radiation released by the explosion of an atomic bomb. The term, *radioactive fallout* refers to ionized particles in the air or water following their accidental release from a nuclear power plant or the explosion of an atomic bomb. Some of these elements in the air fall to Earth, whereas others drift in the wind or water, gradually experiencing radioactive decay and releasing radioactive rays miles from the site of the explosion.

Radiation that does *not* have the potential to change the structure of atoms or produce ions is called **nonionizing radiation**. Heat, light, sound, radio-frequency (RF) waves, and microwaves are all examples of nonionizing radiation. The critical difference between ionizing and nonionizing radiation for clothing designers is the fact that ionizing radiation, because of its ability to disrupt atoms, has been thought to have a significantly more profound effect on the body. However, it should be noted that some electronic devices such as televisions, RF heat-sealing equipment, and microwave ovens, while they are nonionizing, do have the capability of adding energy (heat) to living tissues. (See more on the effects of nonionizing radiation in "Shielding from Microwaves and Other Electromagnetic Radiation" later in this chapter.)

exposed to X-rays. Understanding the basics of nonionizing radiation will help designers decide on the necessity of providing protective clothing for many modern day objects such as microwave ovens and cell phones.

Radioactivity

When an atom contains more than 83 protons in its nucleus, its neutrons have difficulty holding the nucleus together. The nuclei of these so-called *heavier atoms* may begin to come apart or *decay*, releasing kinetic or electromagnetic energy in the process (Energy Basics 7.3). Atoms that spontaneously emit particles from their nuclei are termed **radioactive**. When the nucleus of a radioactive atom comes apart, the resulting nuclei each have only a portion of the protons of the original nucleus. Each lighter nucleus is electrically charged and picks up electrons to form atoms of new, lighter elements. Eventually these atoms may disintegrate to the point that their nuclei contain less than 83 protons and lose their radioactivity.

Energy Basics 7.3: The Results of Radioactive Decay

During radioactive decay, materials emit four kinds of radiation. **Alpha rays** are composed of two protons and two neutrons. Although alpha rays travel at great speeds, about 20,000 mi/sec (32,180 km/s), they are slowed down so greatly by collisions with atoms in the air that they can travel only several inches before losing their energy. Even a thin sheet of paper can stop an alpha ray because the positively charged particles of the ray collide and interact with the atomic particles of the paper.

Beta rays are streams of electrons. Even though electrons have considerably less mass than protons or neutrons, beta rays travel considerably faster than alpha rays and therefore possess considerably more momentum and are far more penetrating than are alpha rays. The energy a beta particle possesses depends on its source material and the nature of the radioactive decay that produces it. Some can penetrate several layers of living tissue but because of the collision of the negatively charged rays with other atoms, a thin sheet of metal or thin layers of plastic can stop most. Some of those with lower energy levels may even decay due to collisions with particles in the air. Whether alpha and beta rays penetrate a surface depends upon the energy they possess at the time of impact and the composition of the surfaces with which they collide.

As alpha or beta particles leave an atom, the remaining particles in a nucleus rearrange themselves and gamma rays may be given off. **Gamma rays** are waves of electromagnetic radiation, which, like X-rays, do not consist of particles. They have a very short wavelength, are extremely powerful, and can pass easily through most materials. They need to be shielded by a heavy metal, such as lead, or by thick concrete walls.

Neutron radiation consists of free neutrons that are released from atoms in the process of a nuclear reaction or radioactive decay. Neutrons are more penetrating than alpha or beta rays. They also have the ability to induce radioactivity in other substances with which they collide, including the human body. In facilities like nuclear power plants, neutrons are shielded by water and contained within the reactor so that they are not considered a daily threat from which workers need to be protected. For situations in which neutron and gamma radiation are factors, workers generally use remote handling tools and robotics and work at a distance behind heavily shielded partitions.

X-radiation

X-radiation is a type of ionizing radiation that has an extremely short wavelength. It can pass through materials that would ordinarily reflect or absorb visible light. X-radiation is one of the more commonly experienced radiation hazards.

The most widely known X-rays are those that are used in hospitals and doctors' offices. The images (commonly called *X-rays*, but more properly called *radiographs*) that subsequently appear on the film show the degree to which various body parts absorb or reflect X-radiation. Lighter areas show body tissues that are denser or have more electrons (a higher atomic number) and that therefore scatter and absorb more X-rays. Darker areas are less dense body tissues that allow X-rays to pass through. Thicker tissue masses scatter and absorb X-rays more than thinner ones, and diseased tissues often absorb X-rays differently than normal tissues do. Consequently, radiographs may be used to make visible any breaks in bones or cancerous masses inside the body.

In the laboratory, X-rays are produced by bombarding a metal target with a stream of high-speed electrons (Figure 7.17). As they impact the metal, the electrons are stopped and their kinetic energy is transformed into heat and X-rays. The more rapidly the electrons are moving when they hit the target, the shorter the wavelength and the more penetrating the X-radiation that is produced. Planning for appropriate protection therefore requires precise knowledge of the wavelength of X-rays emitted by equipment.

A complicating factor in controlling X-rays is that they do not continue in a forward path indefinitely. As they strike atoms in various materials, they may scatter in different directions (Figure 7.18). In order to prevent this, the X-ray beam may be made narrower or a material with a high atomic number, such as lead, may be placed

FIGURE 7.18 The path of X-rays. (A) The dotted lines show the path of radiation, which is scattered as it bounces off an object being X-rayed and the metal plate behind it; (B) when a diaphragm is placed over the ray, the beam narrows and radiation is scattered over a narrower range.

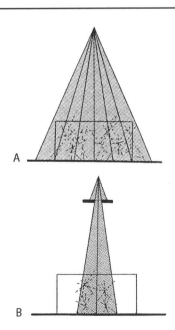

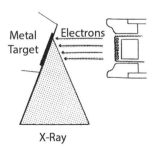

FIGURE 7.17 An X-ray tube emitting streams of electrons. When electrons hit a positively charged metal target, they are repelled and form a cone of X-rays.

behind the item being X-rayed, so that the rays that pass through are absorbed rather than scattered back through the item.

THE EFFECTS OF RADIATION ON THE HUMAN BODY

Establishing guidelines for body tolerance to radiation is a complex task because radiation not only takes many forms (light, X-rays, microwaves, and so on), but it is also measured and described in many ways. Human exposure to radiation is usually expressed by the unit, the *rem* (roentgen-equivalent-mammal) or the millirem (1/1000th of a rem). The rem takes into account both the dose of radiation received and its relative biological effectiveness.

Radiation is everywhere in the environment. The U.S. Nuclear Regulatory Commission (USNRC) states that the average annual radiation dose per person in the United States is 620 millirem (USNRC "Doses in Our"). A typical chest X-ray subjects the body to between 0.05 and 0.3 rem. The USNRC has established limits on the amount of ionizing radiation exposure permitted for workers in facilities licensed by them. It sets limits for whole body exposure, with special limits for the lens of the eye and higher limits for the skin of the extremities (USNRC "Occupational"). Special limits have been set for the entire gestation period for pregnant workers (USNRC "Dose Equivalent"). It should be noted that focused rays used for localized exposure, as is done with radiation therapy for cancer, may greatly exceed the dosage limits for workers with no fatal effects. Researchers have found that shielding the head, the spinal column, and the blood-forming organs increases tolerance for the presumed fatal doses of radiation.

The tremendous increase in the use of electronic equipment such as cell phones in everyday life has prompted much debate about the safety needs of workers exposed to nonionizing radiation such as RF energy and other radiation in the microwave frequency range. It is clear that microwaves can warm living tissues, and that heat alone can sometimes present a hazard. Thus at higher levels, such as in its use in a microwave oven, the heat could clearly present health problems. However, at the lower levels required for the use of a cell phone, most scientists do not believe the heat generated by nonionizing radiation will produce particularly hazardous effects on the body. It should be noted that this varies with the area of the body being heated—the scrotum and the eyes are particularly vulnerable to RF heat.

Scientists do not always agree whether both high- and low-level RF energy produces nonthermal effects as well. There have been many reports of serious medical problems experienced by military personnel who work with radar equipment and people in communities in the path of power lines or radio transmitters often claim that they have a higher than average incidence of cancer. One of the difficulties of drawing conclusions about health hazards posed by electronic items that emit nonionizing radiation is that there are so many variables that need to be explored. The National Cancer Institute states that although cell phones emit radio-frequency (nonionizing) energy that can be absorbed in body tissues closest to where they are being held, the amount absorbed depends on the time of use, the location of the antenna and its distance from the user, the technology used by the phone and the distance of the user from cell phone towers. They state that "Studies thus far have not shown a consistent link between cellphone use and cancers of the brain, nerves, or other tissues of the head or neck. More research is needed because cell phone technology and how people use cell phones have been changing rapidly" (National Cancer Institute "Cell Phones").

One early and very fascinating account of the long-range effects of microwaves is contained in a study of the U.S. Embassy in Moscow (U.S. Senate Committee 1979) in which medical tests on the personnel and their families living in the embassy are detailed. These studies were conducted following an extended period during which it was determined that a low-level beam of microwave radiation was being directed at the building, presumably as part of an effort to spy.

CLOTHING DESIGN FOR RADIATION HAZARDS

Because radiation takes so many forms and is present in many aspects of individuals' personal and work lives, clothing that protects from radiation takes many forms. Three types will be explored here: garments for nuclear power plant workers; X-ray-protective garments, and protection for people exposed to microwaves.

Clothing for Nuclear Power Plant Workers

Three factors that are reviewed when determining measures to take for personal protection of workers in nuclear power plants are time, distance, and shielding. As the *time of exposure* to sources of radiation increases, a greater number of particles will strike the body. The *distance* of the body from a source of radiation affects the intensity with which the particles strike as well as the number of particles that impact a body. *Shielding* the individual from radiation involves the isolation of the radiation source *or* the individual with appropriate materials and enclosures.

The purpose of most protective gear for nuclear power plant workers is to keep radioactively contaminated particles from being deposited on

clothing or the body. Ensembles generally take the form of a respirator and a fully encapsulating coverall with integrated or overlapping gloves, boots and hood. Figure 7.19 shows two typical ensembles. *Anticontamination* suits such as those shown are made of various materials—from impermeable vinyl to bonded paper-like materials such as Tyvek® to closely woven materials made of cotton. Most of these garments are baggy, relatively nonfitted designs that provide complete coverage while allowing as much mobility and safe movement as possible for many different figure types. Elastic at the wrists, ankles, and sometimes the waist keep garment segments in place. Necklines are often elasticized under overlapping hoods so that they will be close to the body. Great care is taken to ensure that no skin is exposed between garment parts. Rubber gloves are usually worn overlapping wristbands or wrist elastic. Foot

FIGURE 7.19 Two typical anticontamination suits for nuclear power plant workers. (A) A model with integrated foot covers to be worn with an external air supply hose; (B) a suit with a Velcro hood attachment to be worn with a respirator face mask.

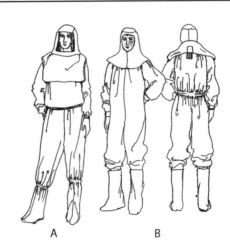

A   B

protection may be integrated into the coverall or separate shoe covers may be worn. Because of the hard wear on fabric shoe soles, rubber or vinyl boots are usually worn over booties or shoe covers.

A separate hood may be used to allow freer movement of the head from side to side. Hoods that are designed to be used with an external respirator have a closely fitted face opening. Suits that have an air supply provision or an interior respirator can have a less closely fitted hood with a clear vinyl head or face area. The hood design in Figure 7.20 allows 360° visibility.

Any reusable protective clothing that is worn around radiation hazards must go through rigorous decontamination and laundering to ensure that radioactive particles have been totally removed before the garment is worn again. Therefore, the garments chosen for power plant workers are often disposable. While they present the problem of contaminated waste, disposable materials reduce

the cost and difficulty of laundering contaminated garments and creating contaminated wash water. Whether disposable or reusable, the fabrics in these garments serve as a type of filter, presenting a barrier to prevent dust, grease, and other substances in the environment that contain radioactive particles from settling on workers' clothing. Where liquids are present in the work area, these materials may have waterproof or water-resistant finishes or be composed of laminates of several thin layers of materials.

Figure 7.21 shows a method used by many workers who wear disposable coveralls to fit them

FIGURE 7.21 Disposable coveralls are often purchased in one size (extra large) and fitted by wrapping tape around a suited worker. *(Design formerly produced by Defense Apparel)*

FIGURE 7.20 This air-supplied hood for use with an anticontamination suit provides complete coverage from head to shoulder. *(Design formerly produced by Defense Apparel)*

closely to the body. To save on cost and inventory, some companies buy suits in one or two larger sizes, and workers do their own custom fitting in the dressing room by wrapping out extra length and width with tape.

Clothing for X-Ray Hazards

The protection required by workers exposed to X-rays is quite different from that required by nuclear power plant workers. X-ray equipment is shielded as much as possible. Technicians often stand outside the X-ray room or behind a lead shield as they work. However, in some situations such as with infants, where technicians may need to help locate the body parts to be X-rayed, or fluoroscopy (where continuous X-ray images are made visible on a screen as the patient moves), a technician may have to work near the X-ray source, and in those instances clothing provides a logical answer to protection. The person being X-rayed may also need to have body parts other than those being X-rayed shielded, and many of those shielding items involve clothing.

Elements that provide a shield from X-rays are high-density ones such as lead, antimony, and tungsten. The material that has been most commonly used in X-ray protective clothing is lead-impregnated vinyl. This material is generally made of lead powder mixed with vinyl and extruded and formed into sheeting. Leaded glass may also be used for visibility when protection is needed for the eyes. Raheel discusses the use of melt spun fibers of lead metal for shielding mats and reports that they are flexible and easy to cut and sew. "Thus, it is suitable for making work clothing (vests) for nuclear power station workers or x-ray shielding aprons" (1994, 3). It is also possible to provide equal protection from X-rays using antimony rather than lead in protective materials. Antimony is considerably lighter than lead but about four times as costly, so its

use in clothing has not been as widespread. Because of concerns about possible health hazards of lead, several tungsten-filled high-density thermoplastic composites have also been developed for X-ray protection. Polymer compounds have also been used for radiation protection, often fused with several layers of other kinds of protective materials (e.g., those for chemical threats) in a composite fabric.

The protection offered by many radiation protective materials is expressed in millimeters of **lead equivalency**. This is the amount of protection that would be offered by a specific thickness of lead if it were substituted for the fabric. For example, many materials used in garments are designated as offering "0.5 mm protection." This means that they provide the same protection as a sheet of lead 0.5 mm thick. The millimeter equivalency protection needed in a particular setting depends on the particular hazard and the state laws in effect. The specific requirements for a setting must be determined by a physicist or an environmental health and safety specialist. Materials may need to be tested to determine that their lead equivalency protection is *maintained*. Manufacturers caution that garment protection levels can be affected, for example, if a garment is folded or draped over corners. Many provide a special hanger with each garment they sell.

Many states still require lead aprons with specific lead equivalencies to be placed on dental patients prior to X-rays, although the scattering of rays is increasingly less likely with modern dental X-ray equipment. Most X-ray bibs cover the chest and torso area. The model shown in Figure 7.22 also covers the throat and neck since exposure of the thyroid gland to X-rays is of major concern. The weight of the leaded material and a Velcro attachment at the neckline keep the bib in place on the body. Some models are backed by a textured

FIGURE 7.22 A leaded bib for a dental X-ray patient. *(Shielding, International)*

these items allow some of the weight of the leaded protection normally carried by the shoulders to be transferred to the hips.

When the need for protection occurs primarily on the front of the body, the imbalance of weight has been handled in a number of ways. One manufacturer has developed a stretch back panel from waist to shoulder blades to help increase conformity of their full aprons to the back of the body. Other aprons contain wide straps that wrap around the body and secure with hook-and-loop fasteners so that size and contour can be greatly varied.

Other strap designs are used to secure the open-back type of apron shown in Figure 7.25. Since

material such as an open-cell foam between the bib and the body so that friction helps hold it in place. When X-rays are taken, for example, of a broken bone, some type of leaded garment or blanket may be placed over the rest of the body, particularly over the reproductive organs. Such a covering prevents any rays that might scatter from the X-ray site from reaching specific areas of the body.

The major problems in designing X-ray protective garments are due to the heavy weight of leaded materials and, often, their imbalance on the body. Coverage that provides maximum protection with minimum material is the ideal. X-ray technicians generally wear a leaded apron that protects the front chest and torso, the areas most directly exposed to the X-rays that may scatter from the equipment (Figure 7.23). Although front-closure as well as front-wrap aprons are available, they tend to gape along the front opening and have the extra weight of a full back piece and the front overlap areas (Figure 7.24A). Separate wrap skirts and vests are available (Figure 7.24B) and while the total weight of these is greater than an apron,

FIGURE 7.23 A leaded apron protecting the front chest and torso of an X-ray technician. *(Shielding, International)*

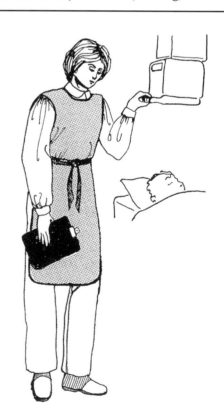

FIGURE 7.24 Two models of lead-impregnated clothing worn by X-ray technicians. (A) A front-wrap apron; (B) a separate wrap skirt and vest. *(Shielding, International)*

A   B

FIGURE 7.25 Two methods of securing a heavy leaded vinyl apron to the body. (A) Strong reinforced straps riveted through an apron serve as attachment points for adjustable straps; (B) a fabric cover integrated into the entire back of the garment is extended to form straps that are wrapped around the body. *(Shielding, International)*

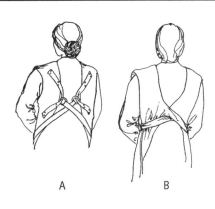

A   B

any backstraps must counterbalance a considerable amount of weight from the front of the garment, they must not only be strong but also be attached to the garment in such a way that they do not tear away from it under the strain. Figure 7.25A shows strong, reinforced straps that are riveted through the apron back at several points. Adjustable straps can then be looped through them. Figure 7.25B shows an apron that has been placed in a fabric cover that extends to form the back of the garment as well. The back portion of the cover extends into straps, which are wrapped around and tied for proper fit in the front. Because the straps are part of the back—there are no seams or attachment points for them—this design helps keep the straps from separating from the garment.

There is great concern for eye and thyroid protection for both X-ray technicians and patients. Although collars and other head-protective devices may succeed in protecting the thyroid gland, they may fail to protect the eyes. Leaded eyeglasses are available as are leaded acrylic face shields.

Since X-rays can scatter, the rule of thumb used for protecting openings in a garment is that each opening must be backed with a protective piece one and a half times the width of the opening. This means that if there is an air space at the waistline 1/8 inch (0.32 cm) deep between the skirt and the hem of the vest shown in Figure 7.24B, a minimum of 3/16 inch (0.487cm) overlap would be required to remain at all times to provide protection from scattering rays. Because many areas of the body expand during movement, the overlap in many areas would actually need to be much wider to be certain protection was maintained.

Leaded vinyl garments are extremely hot. Although X-rays are generally taken during a brief period of time, the technician may wear an apron continuously because the intervals between patients are too brief to disrobe. The design in Figure 7.26 was developed to deal with this problem. The front flap, which is fastened with Velcro, can be dropped to provide momentary ventilation and then quickly returned to place when needed. The neckline of this design also provides extra protection for the thyroid gland.

Because of the many X-ray procedures used, a wide variety of accessories are available both for the technician and for the patient. Figure 7.27 shows some of these items: gloves, diapers, gonad shields, collars, and apronettes. Many of these items are now being incorporated in garments such as panties or bras that make donning the leaded panels easier and keep them in place more effectively.

Basic shielding materials are often coated or enclosed in other materials to make them more attractive in clothing. The many colors and textures as well as the printed materials seen in X-ray protective clothing are the result of either enveloping the leaded apron in a decorative outer fabric covering or coating them with vinyls or similar

waterproof coatings that can be easily sponge-cleaned and thus used by many people.

Shielding from Microwaves and Other Electromagnetic Radiation

Microwave protection has existed in industry and for the military for some time and a number of companies have begun to produce fashion items to shield the body from microwaves in the home or office. Originally marketed for pregnant women, these consumer garments are now available for both sexes, particularly for individuals who spend long hours at a computer. Garments may be made using a fine stainless steel mesh or knitted metal-coated yarns, among the most prevalent being nylon coated with silver.

Garments that shield from electromagnetic radiation can also be used for security. Some credit cards, garment security tags, and other devices use Radio Frequency Identification (RFID) chips to store information so that it can be read back by a reader without requiring power. RFID technologies rely on radio waves as both communication and power: the reader sends out a radio signal, which the chip uses as power to return a short communication to the reader. Because some chips will respond to any reader, it is possible in some cases to lift information from RFID chips a person may be wearing or carrying by putting a reader in proximity to the chip. However, radio waves can be reflected, as can many other forms of radiation. The same metallic layer in a garment that can shield the body from microwaves or other forms of electromagnetic radiation can also shield an RFID chip from the radio waves produced by a reader.

Protection from Solid Particles

There are many situations in which clothing is used as a filter to keep hazardous particles in

FIGURE 7.26 An X ray-protective apron with a center front panel that can be dropped between X-rays to provide a technician with ventilation in the upper chest and neck area. *(Designer: Martha Sill)*

FIGURE 7.27 Accessories for X-ray technicians or for protection of specific body areas of patients being X-rayed. (A, B) Protective shields and cups for the genitals; (C) a diaper; (D) an apronette; (E) a collar; (F) gloves. *(Shielding, International)*

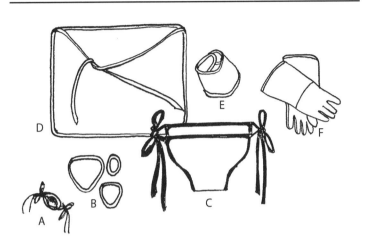

the air, in dust, or in liquid and oily substances away from the body. In other situations, it may be important to keep oils, skin particles, and hair from dropping off the body and contaminating the *environment*. Before choosing filtration materials, it is important to understand the nature of the particles a garment needs to exclude. A filter may be as simple as mosquito netting or as complex as a chemically protective fabric for workers cleaning up a toxic waste spill. This next section looks at the structure of filters and discusses two examples of the ways in which they can provide protection for or from people.

FILTERS

Although solid films or coated materials offer protection from small particles, they may not always provide the most satisfactory clothing solution. In many situations, garments made of these impermeable materials are too hot and cumbersome and really provide more protection than is needed.

Therefore, a good number of materials used in protective clothing and equipment serve as *filters* to strain out hazardous particles, yet allow air or water to pass through.

Filters for face masks or respirators are made of webs of many types of materials, depending on the end use. A typical surgeon's mask such as the one shown in Figure 7.28 may be made of several layers of tightly woven cotton and polyester or of disposable filtration materials. Some of the most commonly used filtration materials for solid particles as well as liquids and gases are disposable webs such as Tyvek.

Disposable webs are commonly used for full garments as well. Because of the problem of decontaminating and laundering garments that have been exposed to bacteria, chemicals, pesticides, or radioactive particles, disposable protective clothing has become popular in many fields. At the same time, concerns about the

FIGURE 7.28 A disposable surgeon's mask.

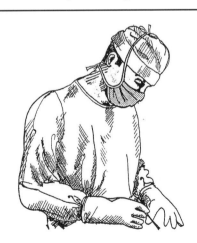

disposal methods for these materials and the condition of landfills has raised concerns about their safe and efficient disposal.

A more sophisticated filter structure must be used in the presence of sprays or vaporized liquids. A respirator for a spray painter, for example (Figure 7.29), may contain a filter composed of fibers such as glass or a nonreactive plastic material. Much attention has been given to the health hazards introduced by the filtration materials themselves. It is important to know that materials used as filters will not degrade or decompose into hazardous particles that can irritate or injure the skin surface or enter the body by being inhaled.

All of the materials just described are part of what are termed **mechanical filters** that trap particles by having interstices that are too small for particles to pass through. **Chemical filters** work like the SPMs discussed earlier in this chapter and in Chapter 3. They bind toxic gases and other substances chemically. Specially treated (activated) carbon, for example, is able to **adsorb** gas molecules into its open sites or pores.

The effectiveness of a filter depends not only on choosing appropriate materials (See Design Strategies 7.1) but also on how well those materials are used in a design. Tight areas in garments may create pressure points that can force particles through a filtration material. Loose areas in masks or respirators may create large gaps that allow particles to pass around filtration materials. Thus, the most reliable tests for the efficiency of filters come after filtration materials have been incorporated into garments and equipment that meet specific needs of workers.

PROTECTIVE CLOTHING DESIGN FOR ASBESTOS ABATEMENT

Although asbestos has been used since prehistoric times and health problems due to its use have been

FIGURE 7.29 A respirator for workers exposed to spray paints or other vaporized liquids.

suspected for centuries (Ashdown 1989), the Environmental Protection Agency first banned its use in the United States in 1978. By that time, because of the wide use of asbestos as an insulation material for construction of buildings and ships since the 1930s, hundreds of thousands of public and commercial buildings contained asbestos that needed to be removed for public safety. This spawned an expanding industry of workers trained in *asbestos abatement* (the reduction or removal of asbestos from existing structures).

Asbestos causes disease primarily because its fibers are inhaled and subsequently lodge in the lungs. Once there, since they cannot be expelled or absorbed, they trigger a reaction that causes chronic scarring of the lung tissue known as asbestosis. This reduces the ability of the lungs to use oxygen and results in a reduced life expectancy. Although the vast majority of asbestos-related disease is due to inhaled fibers with no evidence that the fibers can travel through the skin, asbestos abatement workers must wear *both* a respirator and protective clothing. This is because regular work clothing might attract fibers that could be carried

Design Strategies 7.1: Determining Filter Efficiency

Descriptions of filter effectiveness detail the particles they exclude. For microscopic particles, these descriptions are usually given in micrometers (microns). One micrometer (μm) equals 1/25,000 of an inch (1/1,000 of a mm). A commonly used example is that 1,000 μm would span the head of a pin. Some biological particles are so small that they are measured in angstroms rather than micrometers. An angstrom (Å) equals 1/10,000 of a μm or 1/25,000,000 of an inch (1/1,000,000 of a mm). The size of viruses, which range from 0.2 to 0.02 μm, is usually expressed in angstroms.

A typical statement of a material's effectiveness as a filter gives the percentage of penetration of a specific kind, size, or concentration of particle. For example, a manufacturer may state that a protective fabric allowed only 3 percent of asbestos fibers measuring 10 μm or less to penetrate it. Often, the rate of flow or number of particles per unit of air is stated.

Similar statements may be made about materials that protect from specific types of bacteria, which average 1–2 μm in diameter, or for substances containing radioactive particles or lead dust. In medicine, as well as in some industrial situations, the effectiveness of a material may only be expressed in terms of its ability to filter out a specific hazard. Therefore, a manufacturer may simply state that a filter excludes 99 percent of all viruses and bacteria or 95 percent of all dust.

The effectiveness of a filter is generally tested by exposing it to a specific hazardous substance. Often, the filter being evaluated is used to cover a sterile chamber. Then, the hazardous substance is introduced and may be pressed against the filter to simulate body movement. Some test chambers rotate to allow particles in the air to impact them. After a specified time period, the number of particles that have passed through the filter into the chamber are counted electronically.

away from the work site and later inhaled when the worker is not wearing a respirator, or carried into the family laundry to provide hazards to others.

Asbestos abatement takes place in a sealed area. Workers totally isolate themselves and the asbestos-containing area by sealing it off with double layers of heavy plastic and providing a single entrance/exit through a series of airlocks. The airlocks serve as areas to don protective clothing on the way in and shed contaminated clothing to become progressively cleaner as a worker moves outward. Air is constantly pumped out of the work area through a high-efficiency particulate air (HEPA) filter. This collects fibers so that only clean air emerges and creates a negative pressure

so that no fibers are accidentally propelled to the outer environment. The HEPA filter and all materials used in the work area, including contaminated protective clothing, are surrounded by plastic and either disposed of as hazardous waste or kept totally contained until they can be placed within the next sealed work area.

The basic ensemble worn by an asbestos abatement worker includes a respirator, a coverall with a hood and foot coverings (both preferably attached to the coverall), rubber gloves, and boots. Because of the difficulty and cost of decontamination, most coveralls used for work with asbestos are disposable and closely resemble the ensemble shown in Figure 7.19 for nuclear power plant workers.

The process of asbestos removal creates specific clothing needs. Because asbestos is generally located in the ceilings or the wrapping of overhead pipes, workers need great range of movement. They need to be free to reach overhead, climb ladders, and bend or kneel down to shovel up removed debris that has fallen to the floor during the process. Because many types of asbestos are wet down with a surfactant to facilitate removal, the environment and the worker are often wet and this places additional demands on a protective garment. The enclosed nature of the removal site and the totally encompassing ensemble both create a very warm environment. When added to the physical effort the job requires, the worker will sweat profusely. The wetting of disposable garment materials from both sides and the strain placed on garments by movement extremes leads to a situation in which protective clothing is easily torn. Snagging on equipment and other items in the work area adds to the incidence of coverall tears. For these reasons, the basic disposable material needs to be strong and water resistant. The materials used are usually a spunbonded polyethylene or polypropylene and the basic material is sometimes coated with a breathable, waterproof finish.

Several options have been posed for improving the design of coveralls for asbestos abatement. Ashdown (1989) proposed contouring of the pattern for disposable coveralls so that they more closely mimic the working position of the abatement worker and adding a cut-on underarm gusset to facilitate arm movement. These changes are discussed in Chapter 2 and a diagram of suggested pattern changes is shown in Figure 2.43. Developments continue to be made in the area of materials that have sufficient strength, especially when wet.

PROTECTIVE CLOTHING DESIGN FOR CLEANROOMS

A **cleanroom** is defined by the International Standards Organization as a "room in which the concentration of airborne particles is controlled and which is constructed and used in a manner to minimize the introduction, generation, and retention of particles inside the room and in which other relevant parameters, e.g., temperature, humidity, and pressure, are controlled as necessary" (Whyte 2010, 1). Typical contaminants that are controlled within a cleanroom include dust, human skin particles, hair, lint, bacteria, cigarette smoke, and dirt. Cleanrooms are used to manufacture items such as sterile supplies, pharmaceutical products, microchips, and precision instruments. Although there are many similarities between the types of protection needed for asbestos abatement and work in a cleanroom, they involve opposite problems. In asbestos removal, the focus is on protecting the wearer from hazards. In the cleanroom, the focus is on protecting the items being produced from human contamination. The situation is similar to that in the operating room, where surgical gowns and gloves protect a patient from any contamination from medical personnel. However, some cleanrooms actually exceed the cleanliness of operating rooms.

Establishment of a Cleanroom

Cleanrooms are designated in terms of *classes* that are determined by the maximum number of a specific size of particle that will be allowed in the room. Both the U.S. government and the International Standards Organization have cleanroom classification standards.

Assuring a contamination-free room generally involves five steps. First, air entering the room is filtered to remove contaminants. This is accomplished with the HEPA filter described for asbestos removal, except that in this case it filters air *entering* the room. Second, particles that enter the room on workers (e.g., lint from clothing) or are generated in the manufacturing process need to be removed from the room through a constant process of air exchange. The placement of entrance and exit air grills establishes a pattern of airflow. Most cleanrooms use what is called **laminar airflow** in which air moves in layers (i.e., at a uniform velocity along parallel flow lines), either from an entrance point in the ceiling to a removal grid in the floor or from one wall of the cleanroom to the opposite wall (Austin and Timmerman 1965).

Third, every precaution must be taken to limit the production of particles within the room. Nonlinting fabrics and nonchipping wall and floor surfaces should be used. Even pencils and paper are prohibited because of the particles that might be produced during their use. Static-generating materials may cause particles to cling to surfaces where they can be knocked off into the production area.

Fourth, the products need to be protected from the settling of particles. Workstations and people interrupt airflow and serve as areas of deposit for particles. Laminar flow helps maintain airflow and cleanrooms are generally set up so that production moves from the area nearest the air exit to the cleanest areas that are nearest the air inlet.

Fifth, personnel and materials brought into the room need to be thoroughly cleaned. Austin and Timmerman state that personnel are the "single greatest cause of contamination. They leave a trail of particulate and gaseous contamination behind them" (1965, 77). To minimize this trail, workers must don garments that cover every body area but the eyes, wear no makeup or skin lotions that might contaminate the cleanroom, and enter the room through a series of airlocks that contain air

showers. Many cleanrooms use a tacky mat at the entrance to the last airlock to clean any remaining particles off of the shoes before donning cleanroom shoe covers.

Cleanroom Clothing Design

The preceding review of the principles of cleanrooms should net the designer a list of criteria for cleanroom clothing. An ensemble must provide total containment to prevent contamination of the room from skin particles, hair, and other contaminants from the body. The fabrics used for the ensemble must either be impermeable or serve as filters that maintain the class level of the cleanroom. All materials and fastening devices must be lint-free and they should not generate static electricity. Design forms must be as simple and flat as possible. Any details such as gathers, stitching ridges, etc. provide areas for particles to lodge.

Figure 7.30 illustrates two typical cleanroom ensembles. The ensemble shown in Figure 7.30A consists of a one-piece loosely fitted coverall, a hood, a snap-in mask, gloves, and booties. The ensemble shown in Figure 7.30B is comprised of separate pants and coat, short booties and gloves. Both disposable and launderable materials are used for these types of designs. When disposable materials are used, they are sometimes combined with a microporous film that provides waterproofing with breathability. Reusable clothing is more practical in this situation than it is for asbestos removal because there are no hazardous particles involved, so decontamination is not an environmental or health issue. Reusable clothing is generally made of polyester continuous filament fibers, often with the addition of an antistatic treatment or the incorporation of a grid or stripes of metallic or other electrically conducting threads. These ensure that there is no static buildup on the garment that might

FIGURE 7.30 Cleanroom ensembles. (A) A one-piece coverall, a hood with a snap-in mask, high boots and gloves; (B) a two-piece ensemble with pants, a lab coat, short booties, and gloves. A mask would also be worn with this ensemble.

A   B

attract particles, which could then be brushed onto a work surface. Fabrics are woven rather than knitted to control pore size and reduce surface texture. All seams in the garment must be either heat sealed (see Chapter 9) or flat felled (i.e., double stitched like jeans so that all raw edges—even those *inside* the suit—are completely covered). Zippers with a covering flap are used at the front of coveralls for donning. Fitting adjustments are usually made with gripper snaps because hook-and-loop tape, buttons and buttonholes, and other types of fasteners often have too much potential to generate and collect particles.

The coverall designs in Figure 7.30 illustrate the emphasis placed on simplicity in design features. Belts, pockets, flaps, and other design features are discouraged, and in some cleanroom classes, prohibited. In some classes of cleanrooms, it may be permissible to have limited gathers, belting, and other design features, on the *back* of the garment where it is less likely to be knocked off onto the production area during work.

The ensembles shown in Figure 7.30 contain several potential problems for containment. The primary area of concern is the face. The hood often does not fit properly around the face. Employees are also able to remove the face mask and tend to do so even though it is not allowed because the mask and hood are so hot and uncomfortable. This exposes the area most problematic for contamination. A number of cleanroom professionals have expressed the belief that the one-piece coverall may also contribute to contamination because the only exit route for air inside the suit is through the neckline. Some firms select long coats and pants because the pumping action of the arms during work moved air to the point of least resistance, the hem of the coat, and toward the air outlet grille in the floor. By contrast, movement that forces air out of the neckline of a coverall would dump contaminants on the work area. This is but one example of the many situations that call for a designer to carefully examine both the nature of airflow in the environment and the activity of workers to determine the best design solution.

Restrictions on design features limit methods that can be used to achieve fit and this often results in restrictions of mobility. Thermal comfort can also be a problem, particularly in the hood area, although it may be minimized by the fact that cleanroom temperatures can be lowered to accommodate workers and often is lowered for the sake of products being manufactured.

Donning and doffing are considerations as well. Both ensembles shown in Figure 7.30 are easy to don and doff, but the coverall has the potential to be contaminated during donning because the whole upper garment drags on the floor as the lower garment is donned.

Aesthetics presents an additional problem. Ashdown found that, in part because asbestos abatement workers were almost exclusively male and worked completely hidden from view by others, they had no concerns about the visual appearance of their clothing. Loker found quite the opposite in her survey of cleanroom personnel. They *did* complain about the lack of visual appeal of their garments, from their overall "bunny suit" silhouette to the lack of versatility and opportunity for individual expression. Because of the restrictions on design features, it is difficult to introduce individual details and more body-conforming designs. A range of colors of cleanroom materials are available, however, and have potential for introducing more visual interest than the traditional white.

Electricity

The basics of electricity were covered in Chapter 4. (See especially Energy Basics 4.1.) Three concepts are important to an understanding of electrically protective clothing: current, voltage, and resistance. Electrical current is expressed in amperes (the rate at which an electrical charge moves through a circuit). Current cannot travel through an electric circuit unless there is enough voltage (the difference in electrical potential from one end of a conducting wire to the other). Chapter 5 noted that heat flows from hot to cold and that the rate of flow of heat depends on the difference in temperature between two objects. Electricity behaves in much the same way. When there is a highly negative charge on one end of a wire and a highly positive charge on the other end, there is

a greater difference in potential (voltage) and thus a greater rate of flow of electricity. As was discussed in Energy Basics 4.1, some materials offer more resistance (measured in ohms) to this flow of electricity than others. In addition, temperature may affect the resistance of a specific material.

The combination of a strong current and a high resistance may produce great amounts of heat. This makes sense if you think of this action as an inelastic collision in which free electrons often bump into fixed particles, increasing their rate of vibration. This heat is put to good use in toasters, irons, or electric heaters. In items such as clothing, however, excess heat can cause burns to skin or textile materials. Heat-producing components must be appropriately insulated from the body. Electric wires and cords are designed to have a specific amount of resistance, handle a specific potential difference, and carry a specific load of current. If these limits are exceeded, the heat and electrical current could destroy the insulation surrounding the cord (by melting it or by forcing loose the electrons of the material) and could cause both fire and electric shock.

ELECTRIC SHOCK

Electric shock occurs when too much electric current passes through the body and stimulates the body's electrons to excessive vibration. Since current only flows through a closed circuit, it is clear that electric shock occurs when the body completes a circuit. A difference in electrical potential between one area of the body and another come about when a hand, for example, touches a high-voltage wire while the feet are touching the ground, which has low electrical potential. Current then flows from the hand through the body to the feet and the ground.

Electric current passing through the body affects the nervous system. If the current is great enough to affect the nerves that control breathing and the heartbeat, electric shock may lead to electrocution. An AC current as low as 0.05 amperes or a DC current of 0.5 amperes can be fatal. These levels may sound very small, but it is important to bear in mind that the body acts as a significant resistor in an electrical circuit. The amount of resistance introduced by the body depends on a number of factors, such as what part of the body is in contact, whether the skin is dry or wet with sweat (and thus high in salt content and highly conductive) or whether it is immersed in water, which readily conducts the current. It also depends on whether the point of contact of the body has been insulated with an electrically resistant garment such as a rubber glove.

CLOTHING DESIGN FOR ELECTRICAL UTILITY WORKERS

Workers who repair electrical lines or work around electric shock hazards make good use of both equipment and clothing to prevent body injury. The power lines near electrical lineworkers are generally draped with insulating blankets to reduce potential sources of shock (Figure 7.31). Workers wear insulating garments on body areas most likely to contact shock hazards. In addition, they may use nonconductive tools called hot sticks to work on potentially dangerous electrical lines. Safety belts and other equipment that connect them to the work area are made of nonconductive materials such as filament nylon.

The material most commonly used for protective clothing is thick rubber. Rubber and many other materials used for protection from electrical hazards are termed **dielectric**. Dielectric materials are insulators that work by storing energy rather

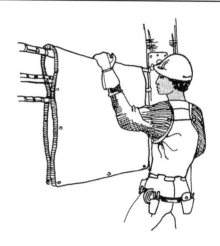

FIGURE 7.31 Protective clothing and equipment for electrical workers. A rubber blanket drapes the area surrounding the worker.

than blocking its flow. The protection provided by a rubber garment depends on the weight, thickness, and purity of the rubber used. Electrical lineworkers wear thick, insulating rubber gloves and sleeves over their work clothing (Figure 7.32). They may also wear thick-soled rubber boots so that the other end of the circuit, the feet, can be insulated from low electrical potential areas such as the ground. This is so that electric current will not be drawn through the body so readily. This approach to electric shock prevention is particularly useful when the environment is wet, since water increases the ease of electrical conduction. Dielectric hard hats made of plastics such as polyethylene are also worn.

Glove design is critical to both protection and a worker's ability to do a job. In the United States, the Occupational Safety and Health Administration defines classes of gloves that provide safe protection for various levels of voltage (OSHA, "Personal Protective"). Gloves carry a color-coded

FIGURE 7.32 A typical electrical worker's protective rubber glove and the leather protector worn over it to keep the rubber from snagging or tearing during use.

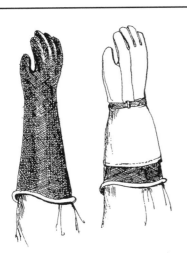

tag for each classification level. Lower classes might be used for someone working with electric meters; higher ones would be used for work on utility poles. For example, Class 0 gloves must provide protection for up to about 1,500 volts; Class 4 gloves must provide protection for up to 54,000 volts. OSHA regulations also specify tests that gloves must pass before, and every six months after, first use. It is also recommended that rubber gloves be inflated to inspect them for leakage after each wearing to ensure that they can still be counted on for maximum protection.

To aid in visual inspection, gloves are generally made in two colors. A base layer of protection is laid down in one color of rubber and then the glove is dipped in successive layers of another color. When the base color can be seen through outer surface, it indicates that protection is compromised and the glove needs to be replaced. Manufacturers give precise care and storage instructions, cautioning users not to fold protective items to prevent even the smallest crack from developing and destroying insulation.

Gloves worn by electrical workers are formed in the working position and should be fire-resistant if, in the jobs workers perform, they are at risk of being exposed to electric arc or other fire hazards. Many gloves are also treated so that they are protected from damage by ozone or ultraviolet rays. Liners may be worn under the gloves to absorb sweat in hotter weather or to provide additional insulation from colder weather. Because of the ease with which rubber is snagged or cut by wood or metal in the work area, protective gloves made of leather are often worn over them (Figure 7.32).

Sleeves made of the same rubber extend from the wrists up over the shoulders to provide additional protection (Figure 7.33). The sleeves attach to one another across the front chest and back shoulder blade area. (See also Figure 7.31.) Many are molded into a working position. Workers are cautioned to wear clothing that is closely fitted with no loose edges that might catch on the work environment. This clothing should be made of inherently flame-resistant fibers such as Nomex®, modacrylic, or carbon or of a cotton treated with a flame resistant (FR) finish because of the danger of sparks that might ignite synthetic materials and cause them to melt to the skin. These cautions also extend to fasteners and trim on garments as well as rain or cold weather gear worn over work clothing.

Many utility workers wear regular work boots because contact with electric current occurs normally in the hand, arm, and shoulder area. However, firefighters, emergency personnel, and others who may work around fallen high-voltage lines in wet conditions generally wear heavy rubber boots that have been tested to protect the wearer from electrical hazards (OSHA "Foot Protection").

FIGURE 7.33 Rubber protective sleeves for an electrical worker.

STATIC ELECTRICITY

Static electricity occurs when an object has excess electrons or excess protons. Electrons jump from a negatively charged object (one that has extra electrons) to a positively charged object (one that lacks electrons). Static electricity can be the result of friction, that is, the rubbing off of electrons from the surface of a material that has relatively loosely attached electrons. Thus, it may be experienced by shuffling across a thick carpet in rubber-soled shoes. Since electrons are easily knocked off the carpet (especially if it is made of wool or nylon) but not easily knocked off the rubber, extra electrons build up on the shoes, giving them a negative charge. This type of contact charge through friction is called the **triboelectric effect**. If the body then touches a good conductor such as a metal surface or even a seated person who has not built up as negative a charge, these extra electrons jump from the body and create an electric spark that is experienced as a mild shock. The *triboelectric series* is a list of materials in order of the polarity of their charge. Materials nearer each other on the list are less likely to exchange a static charge when they touch.

Static electricity creates problems in a variety of workplaces. First, the sparks created when static electricity is transferred may initiate a fire or explosion, especially in environments where fuel is plentiful. Therefore, in a spacecraft or in hospital areas where the oxygen content in the air is high, in operating rooms where anesthetic gases are present, or in mines where combustible gases may be released during the mining process, care is taken to avoid static electricity in all aspects of the environment, including clothing.

Second, even small amounts of static electricity built up on the surface of a fabric may cause it to attract dust or other particles in the environment. In operating rooms, bacteria must be kept from the sterile field of the operating table. Static electricity on a surgeon's gown could attract nonsterile particles from the rest of the room, and these particles could inadvertently be knocked onto the patient. In nuclear power plants, static buildup on workers' clothing may cause the clothing to attract radioactive dust, grease, or other particles in the plant and make decontamination difficult. Static electricity has become an expensive problem in a number of industries, most notably those involving microchips. A worker who releases a slight static charge—even one not perceived by the worker—in the process of touching a microchip, can erase the entire contents of the microchip.

CLOTHING DESIGN FOR PROBLEMS WITH STATIC ELECTRICITY

There are several methods of dealing with problems created by static electricity. First, it is possible to reduce the potential for static buildup by introducing humidity into the air of the environment. This approach can also be applied to fibers and fabrics (i.e., they can be given finishes that help them attract any moisture in the air). This helps a fabric avoid the buildup of static charge on its surface.

Another approach is to incorporate highly conductive fibers in fabrics. These fabrics are made by incorporating a conductive material such as carbon, silver, or stainless steel (1) within a polymer such as polyester as part of the dope forming an extruded fiber; (2) as part of a bicomponent fiber; (3) in a core-spun yarn; (4) as particles integrated into the surface of a base fiber; or (5) as a fiber or fabric coating (Alluniforms, 'Clean room fabric'; Kirsten, 2013). A typical material for cleanroom clothing, for example, consists of a polyester fabric with a grid or stripes of carbon/polyester fibers. One blend for static protection where volatile fuels are present combines Nomex and carbon (Euclid Vidaro "Cleanroom").

Garments made with conductive fibers are often called ESD (electrostatic discharge) garments. Their purpose is to shield sensitive devices by helping electrons transfer easily from a garment surface to the atmosphere or move through a grounding strap on the wrist that is connected to the work table (Figure 7.34). This approach of incorporating conductive fibers in garments may be a more long-lasting and effective one because of the lack of durability of some antistatic finishes.

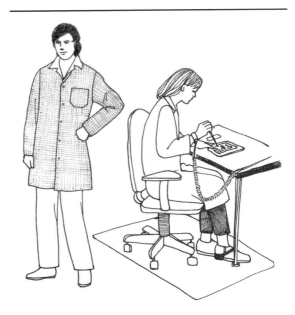

FIGURE 7.34 ESD protection for industry.

Static-dissipating garments such as the lab coats shown in Figure 7.34 have features such as an extended coattail and long sleeves. These garment features ensure contact with the grounded chair and work table, respectively, so that any static charge that might build up can be conducted away from the work surface. Workers may also wear static-dissipating shoe covers or straps.

Protection from Cuts and Punctures

A number of occupations and recreational activities require protection from blades, sharp tools, or punctures due to a variety of hazards (e.g., animal teeth). In general, the materials used to protect the body from these hazards are similar to those described in Chapter 6 for ballistics protection. Aramids (e.g., Kevlar), steel-reinforced fibers, ultra-high molecular weight polyethylene, and stainless steel meshes are perhaps the most widely used materials for cut resistance. For protection from cuts and punctures, however, these base materials have been formed in rather innovative ways to create unique fabrics that are specifically engineered to meet the needs of end users such as loggers, meat packers, and recreational divers.

Materials used solely for cut resistance differ from ballistics materials in that they generally do not have to provide impact protection; they simply need to resist being cut. Therefore, knit structures can be used, resulting in items such as functional, mobile gloves for meat cutters, who need protection primarily on the hands and lower arms. (See Figure 7.35A.) Similar gloves may be used under a surgeon's rubber glove to provide cut protection from the scalpel. A unique application of high-strength fibers can be seen in the development of loggers' chaps, which are used to protect legs from accidental contact with a chain-saw. (See Design Solutions 3.1.)

Another structure for cut protection is a chain link material made of stainless steel. Figure 7.35B shows a meat cutter's glove made of this material. Figure 7.35C shows a unique application of the material in these chain link gloves to a puncture-resistant end use. The material was made into a full length suit to protect divers from sharks. The chain link is worn over a 1/4 inch (0.64 cm) thick neoprene foam diving suit. The nature of sharks' teeth, which have sharp points but quickly widen, allows them to sink only slightly into the mesh before the small diameter of the metal link prevents their penetration. Because the foam suit provides a stand-off from the diver's skin surface, damage to the diver is prevented. While the material is relatively heavy, this is not an issue for the diver underwater, especially with the buoyancy of the foam suit. The use of this rigid material in this flexible fabric formation is uniquely suited to meet the user's needs in this particular situation. The provision of standoff may be a critical factor in other situations where protection from punctures

FIGURE 7.35 (A) Knitted gloves for meat cutters made of a high-strength fiber; (B) stainless steel chain link gloves designed for meat cutters; (C) the same material applied to the design of a full suit for protection from sharks.

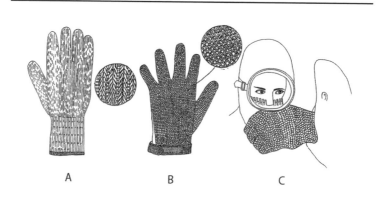

A   B   C

is needed. Mosquito netting and the meshes used on items such as beekeeping hats contain openings that are small enough to exclude the creatures but not necessarily their stingers. These materials must be used in a way that provides space between them and the skin surface.

Cut resistance is far more easily provided than protection from punctures. Metal chain link fabric such as that used in meat cutters' gloves could be used as a flexible layer in a ballistics vest that would add protection from knife penetration but not necessarily from ice picks. SuperFabric® is a composite material made of a cut-resistant fabric substrate with tiny "armor plates" applied to the surface. The armor plates are made from a hard resin, and are shaped in a geometric pattern like hexagonal tile (Figure 7.36). The resin is not flexible and would create a rigid (but very durable) shell if coated continuously onto the fabric. However, printed as tiny dots, the resin can resist cuts and abrasions while allowing the material to flex and breathe. Because none of the spaces between dots line up, even a knife edge will rest on top of the dots rather than cutting into the fabric.

Needles, nails, and other thin, sharp pointed objects such as ice picks, however, are more problematic. In the past, the only way to prevent punctures was with the incorporation of a solid, rigid plate. Many solid shields are seen in accessory items, for example, the solid steel soles and

toe caps in boots for firefighters that protect their feet from puncture by nails, glass, and other sharp objects. Puncture-resistant plates in clothing are generally inserted into pockets in clothing items over body areas most exposed to threats or most vital to life.

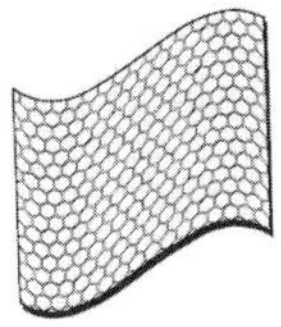

In recent years, a number of composite materials and puncture-resistant coatings have been developed and applied to items such as gloves. Often, a puncture-resistant composite material is applied only to the palm of a knit glove, protecting the area most likely to come into contact with, for example, an AIDS-contaminated needle, while leaving the rest of the glove freely mobile.

Clothing Design for Flame and Molten Metal Hazards

Situations where flame or hot materials or surfaces are present pose several types of hazards. First, much of the danger to individuals comes as a result of exposure to the radiant energy produced by the heat source. Air temperature, although a lesser hazard, also poses a threat in some fire situations that can degrade many materials. In addition, in industrial work where molten metal may fall on clothing or in firefighting where a flaming portion of a building structure may fall on a firefighter, protection from conduction and ignition is critical. The fabrics planned specifically for fire and flame hazards, then, must be both flame and ignition resistant (i.e., they should remain intact—not tear, shrink, or melt—when confronted with flame and should not support combustion). They should also be nonconductive and able to reflect radiant energy.

The ability of a fabric to resist heat conduction is as important as its ability to resist flames. Anyone who has baked a potato knows that although

FIGURE 7.36 SuperFabric®.

the foil does not burn, it still conducts sufficient heat to bake the potato. Nomex aramid, PBI, and novaloid all provide significant resistance to conduction of heat. Conduction of heat is also prevented in many ensembles by the use of thick, nonconductive, air-filled layers. (See, for example, Figure 5.37.) The heat protection provided by a series of fabric layers can be tested using a standard test method in which a flame is placed below the outermost layer and a heat sensor above the innermost layer of a system. The rating of each system is expressed as its *thermal protective performance (TPP)* (NFPA, "NFPA 1971: Standard").

One of the most difficult problems facing designers of clothing for molten metal hazards is that more heat-resistant fibers are less likely to degrade and, thus, less likely to shed the molten metal. When the metal sticks to a garment, there is more potential for the heat of the metal splashed onto the suit to eventually work its way through to the skin layer of the worker, even if the fabric does not degrade. Thus, some manufacturers favor flame-resistant fibers that are engineered to shed molten metal over aramids and aluminized leathers and the like, to which molten metal tends to stick.

Molten metal protective clothing presents an excellent example of how the material in several chapters of this book need to be read and understood to solve a specific clothing design problem. As with other protective clothing situations, using the techniques in Chapter 1 to gain an understanding the precise nature of the hazard, the worker's environment and activity and the needs and wants of the user will aid greatly in making appropriate design decisions. Information about flame-resistance and flameproofing has already been presented in Chapter 3. (See "Flameproof and Flame-Resistant Fibers" and "Coatings.")

The theory on which high heat resistant materials are based has also been covered in Chapter 5. (See "Fabric Surfaces and Radiant Energy," "Blocking Radiant Heat Gain," and the case study "Keeping Cool: Ensembles for Firefighting.") Protection from radiant energy at very high temperatures (such as those found in front of furnaces in many industrial situations or in airport fires where high-temperature flames are produced as airplane fuels burn) is best provided by aluminized materials. These are discussed in Chapter 5 under the heading of "Aluminized Fabrics." In addition, since condensation of steam releases a tremendous amount of heat, in some situations it will be important to prevent this condensation from taking place on the skin or in a layer of the garment too close to the skin surface. (See Chapter 5, "Wind, Water, and Temperature Extremes.")

The situations that involve flame and molten metal are so varied that a different approach may be needed for each. In some situations, a protective apron and long gloves may be sufficient. In others, a full suit such as the fire entry suit shown in Figure 5.37 must be worn. Design details that may provide places for molten metal to lodge must be eliminated in some situations; flame-resistant fasteners and thread may be a necessity in others.

Because of the bulk of materials and the full body coverage needed, many of the provisions for mobility discussed in Chapter 2 will apply to the design of clothing for molten metals. Of particular importance is the designer's attention to other equipment, such as breathing apparatus that must be worn with these ensembles. Some of the provisions needed for these are discussed earlier in this chapter under the heading of "Fully Encapsulated CB Protection."

Conclusion

While each of the hazards in this chapter has been discussed separately, most industrial, military, first-responder, and medical environments will probably contain combinations of several of these hazards. In addition, most activities that require protective clothing will demand that designers have a thorough understanding of mobility, thermal balance, and many additional factors discussed in other chapters. Integrating all of these issues effectively poses some of the greatest challenges to clothing designers.

8 Enhancing and Augmenting Body Functions

This chapter explores ways to enhance the body's abilities to perceive and be perceived, particularly in challenging environments. It covers aspects of sensory perception such as visibility and camouflage. It also focuses on adding functions to the body that have either been impaired or need to be increased due to the demands of specific tasks. Included among these topics on augmenting body functions are buoyancy, body power and speed enhancement, and conditions of weightlessness and acceleration.

Clothing for Sensory Perception

A garment is perceived by both its wearer and others. The quality of this perception—whether the garment is comfortable or uncomfortable, attention grabbing or unnoticeable—depends on designers' choices with respect to the design elements that stimulate the senses.

Effective design for sensory perception relies on understanding the mechanisms of perception, some of which were discussed in Chapters 2 and 4. The visual and tactile senses are perhaps the most widely used in apparel. Clothing can be used to make up for sensory deficiencies, such as reduced visual perception in dark environments or the muffled sense of touch when wearing a thick garment.

The sense of touch was discussed in depth as it relates to communicating information through electronic tactile display systems in Chapter 4. However, it is also possible to augment tactile perception using nonelectronic materials. Many approaches to augmenting tactile perception focus on translating tactile stimuli through a bulky protective garment using an array of protruding stiff elements embedded in a flexible textile. The examples shown in Figure 8.1 use rigid materials in the fingertips of a glove to help pressures applied to the outer surface of the glove to be translated through to the fingertips inside. Figure 8.1A shows a series of rigid, round beads on the outer surface of a glove. When the outside of the glove is pushed against an object, the pressure of an object is translated through the glove by the beads. Figure 8.1B shows a matrix of stiff plastic monofilament 'whiskers' that protrude through the liner of a glove. When the outside of the glove is pushed against an

FIGURE 8.1 (A) Glove liner with rigid beads embedded in the glove liner that translate tactile surface details from the surface of the glove to the hand; (B) a similar approach using a matrix of monofilament "whiskers." *(Mayer 2003)*

A   B

object, the pressure of the object is translated more precisely through the glove by the matrix of whiskers (Mayer 2003). Since additional approaches to augmenting tactile perception have been discussed in depth in Chapter 4, this section will focus on vision and visibility.

VISIBILITY

The importance of high-visibility clothing for many occupations should not be underestimated. A large percentage of injuries to road workers, traffic officers, and utility workers occur because the drivers of moving vehicles do not see these individuals. The low-visibility conditions often present in occupations such as mineworking or firefighting jeopardize the safety of workers and hinder attempts to rescue them when they are injured. Visibility is important to many recreational endeavors as well. Joggers, hunters, and others may need to be visible to be safe.

Clothing can be made more visible in a variety of ways. To understand the method needed for each situation, it is helpful to have a basic understanding of light, color, and the physiological processes involved in vision.

Light

Light is a visible form of radiant energy. Although it travels in waves like other forms of radiant energy, light waves are not continuous. They consist of tiny packets of electromagnetic energy called *photons*. At times, the wave-like character of light predominates, and at other times, the particle-like character does.

Light travels in a straight line called a *ray*. The direction of a ray of light is changed when it comes into contact with a surface. If the surface is transparent, the ray is slowed down and undergoes **refraction** or bending. (Figure 8.2A). It passes

FIGURE 8.2. (A) Refraction; (B) reflection. In refraction, a light ray striking a transparent surface is bent as it enters and leaves; in reflection, a light ray striking an opaque surface bounces off the surface at the same angle as it strikes the surface.

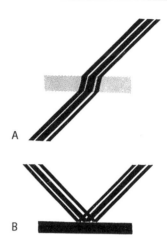

obliquely from one medium to the other. If the surface is opaque, light is *reflected*. When a light ray strikes an opaque surface, it bounces off at an equal but opposite angle. Figure 8.2B shows the law of reflection. The **incidence angle** (sometimes stated as as angle of incidence or approach) always equals the angle of reflection or departure. When a surface is translucent, a combination of reflection and refraction occur. Translucency can vary greatly, and the behavior of light as it strikes a translucent surface varies accordingly.

Visual light is an extremely small portion of the electromagnetic spectrum (see Figure S5.1), but within that visible portion are a variety of wave frequencies that result in different colors. The range of colors humans perceive varies from the longest visible light frequency (red) to the shortest visible light frequency (violet).

Emitted Light

Much of an object's visibility depends on the light it gives off in relation to the light given off by its surroundings. Objects give off light in two ways: by emission or by reflection. Objects that produce light may emit it; those that do not produce light merely reflect it. There are two types of light emission: incandescence and luminescence. **Incandescent light** is produced by heating a conductive material until it glows with intense heat. The amount of light an incandescent substance emits is proportional to its temperature. A typical light bulb is supplied with energy until its filament is hot enough to glow to the desired brightness. Thus, it is hot to the touch when it emits incandescent light.

Luminescent light or "cool light" is produced through electrical stimulation or absorption of radiant energy. Luminescence does not require heat for light emission; it only requires radiant or electrical energy. This energy, used to excite the atoms of a material or begin a flow of electrical current, is transformed into light."

Luminescent light sources emit light through **fluourescence**, phosphorescence, or electroluminescence. **Fluorescent** substances are composed of atoms that can be excited and rearranged by high-frequency radiation such as ultraviolet light. Part of the energy of this excitation of the atom is released as a photon of light (Hewitt 1989, 548). When the energy source is removed, the electrons of fluorescent substances return to their original state very quickly. Fluorescent materials, then, are constantly emitting light when exposed to sunlight because radiant energy stimulates a constant rearrangement of electrons. When this emitted light is added to the basic light rays reflected from the surface of an object, the result is an unusually bright appearance. The so-called DayGlo® colors and other fluorescent substances only maintain this high visibility during the period in which sunlight strikes them. Because of the immediate return of electrons to their original state, light emission does not occur when sunlight is removed. Therefore, fluorescent materials do not appear unusually bright under artificial light or at night.

Phosphorescent substances are those composed of atoms that can be excited or rearranged by any form of visible light or electricity. Unlike fluorescent materials, however, the atoms of a phosphorescent material do not return to their original state the minute light is removed. They get stuck in their excited state and return to their original position very slowly, giving off light over a longer period of time. Glow-in-the-dark items are made of phosphorescent materials. The amount of light emitted is very low and varies in accordance with exposure to light and the type of phosphorescent material. The brighter the light or the greater the radiant energy supplied to a phosphorescent material, the brighter the glow for the same time period of exposure. The length of time various materials glow can vary widely, too. Some early phosphorescent materials glowed continually in the dark because they contained a radioactive material such as radium that continually supplied energy to the atoms of the phosphorescent material. These are no longer in use because of the potential danger radioactive materials present to the consumer. Electroluminescence is most commonly observed in LEDs, discussed in Chapter 4 under "Actuators."

Reflected Light

Materials that do not emit light are only visible when they reflect light from another source. There are many factors that influence what is seen when light is reflected off of a material. First, the strength of the light source determines how much light is available. This is known as the *luminous flux* (Figure 8.3) of the source and is measured in *lumens*. Second, the distance between the source and the material determines how much of the emitted light hits the material. The amount of light that reaches a material is known as the *illuminance* of the material. Third, the properties of the material dictate how much of the illuminance is reflected by the material and how much is absorbed. The amount that is reflected is known as the *reflectance* of the material, measured as the amount of light reflected by the material compared to the amount of light that struck the material. Finally, the *luminance* of the material is the amount of light that gets back to the viewer.

The relationship between the direction that light hits a surface and the direction in which it is reflected from the surface defines the type of reflective property of the surface. There are three types of light reflection: mirror, diffuse, and retro. *Mirror reflection* occurs when light strikes

a surface that is microscopically smooth. Light bounces off a smooth surface according to the law of reflection: at an equal but opposite angle (Figures 8.2B and 8.4A). The headlights of an automobile use a smooth, mirrored surface behind the headlamps, but the surface is a concave dome shape, so that all the light that bounces off the surface focuses forward onto the road.

Diffuse reflection occurs when light strikes a surface that is microscopically rough. Light rays are diffusely reflected, that is, scattered in all directions (Figure 8.4B). The law of reflection is still in operation for diffuse reflection, but because a rough object presents so many different surfaces for light to strike, the reflected rays depart from the object in many directions. Skin, cloth, painted surfaces, and so on, are more difficult to see when a single light source strikes them because, no matter where the eye is, very little light is reflected directly back toward it. Rough objects are particularly difficult to see at night, when a car headlight or a flashlight might be the only light source

FIGURE 8.3 Relationships among luminous flux, illuminance, reflectance, and luminance.

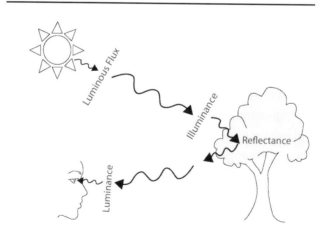

FIGURE 8.4 Three types of reflection. (A) Mirror reflection due to a microscopically smooth surface (inset); (B) diffuse reflection due to a rough surface (inset); (C) retroreflection due to a transparent surface having reflective elements (inset) below it.

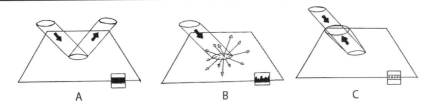

A   B   C

projected at an object, because a relatively small amount of light from the source is scattered in the direction of the viewer.

With **retroreflection**, light rays striking an object are sent directly back toward the light source (Figure 8.4C). In retroreflective materials, reflective elements are placed under a transparent surface. The elements can have any one of a variety of shapes but are generally spheres or prisms. Light is refracted by the transparent surface, passes through it to strike the reflective element, is reflected and then refracted again as it passes through the transparent surface again, so that it travels back along the same path as it entered. When an individual is directly behind a single light source such as a flashlight, retroreflective materials appear brightest of all, since all of the reflected light rays are sent directly back toward the light source and the eye behind it.

The visibility of an object, then, depends on its material, its surface characteristics, the type of light source, the direction in which the rays from the light source travel, and the location of the eye in relation to both the object and the light source. In addition, color and movement become important factors in many situations.

Vision

Vision is the result of the complex interaction of light, the eye, and the brain. Figure 8.5 shows the general structure of the eye. Light enters through the *cornea*, a transparent membrane at the front of the eye. The cornea helps to bend light rays together and sends an image of what an individual is looking at through the pupil, the hole in the center of the iris. The *iris* acts like the diaphragm of a camera, opening and closing to admit more or less light as needed. The admitted light then passes

FIGURE 8.5 The human eye.

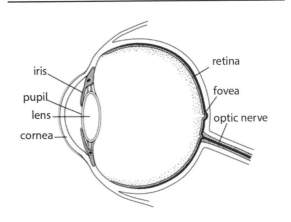

through the *lens*, which focuses it on the *retina*, the back interior wall of the eye.

The retina contains millions of light-sensitive cells called cones and rods. Light striking them creates electrical impulses that are sent to the brain through the optic nerve. The *cones* are concentrated in the center of the retina in the area where vision is most sharp, the *fovea*. They are responsible for daytime vision and for color perception. Most vision involves light rays bouncing off objects and entering the eye. Since the most acute images are formed on the fovea, visibility is clearer in daylight or strong light, where there are no environmental factors such as smog or smoke to dull the reflection, and when objects are directly in the line of vision.

The *rods*, which are most sensitive to light, are located primarily outside the fovea. They cannot detect color, but they can detect very low light and very small changes in light levels and thus are responsible for nighttime vision. One of the reasons nighttime vision is less clear is that rods are located on the periphery of the retina, outside the fovea. In addition, their lack of ability to detect color and the wide area of the retina from which information needs to be gathered means that less information is sent to the brain and it is sent more slowly. Rods are very sensitive to movement (making it possible to notice things "out of the corner of the eye"). However, they are less flexible in responding to large changes in light level. When rods that have adapted to very dim light are exposed to a very bright light, they adapt to the higher threshold quickly, but can take up to 30 minutes to readapt to low light.

Whether in the dark or light, the ability to define a visual image depends on *contrast*. An object can be made more visible by separating it from other objects in its background through color, shape, size, or motion.

Color

In daylight, color may be particularly important in helping to visually separate an object from its background. The hues that appear brightest to the eye are yellowish greens, greenish yellows, and yellows. These colors provide the greatest stimulation to the retina. The longest and shortest wavelength colors—red and violet, respectively—are the least bright to the eye.

Color visibility research has led to emergency vehicles and clothing gradually turning away from the traditional low-visibility reds. More often, yellowish greens are used for these items in order to add greater visibility. It is important to state again, however, that visibility depends largely on contrast. If a yellowish green fire truck were totally surrounded by early spring foliage, its visibility might not be as great as that of a red truck. However, since yellowish green does provide contrast with most backgrounds in addition to its being most bright to the eye, it is becoming the most widely used high visibility color for daytime. At night, when the color-perceiving cones are not in operation and the background is black, white or silver offers the greatest contrast and is thus most visible.

MATERIALS FOR HIGH VISIBILITY

Reflective and fluorescent materials are readily available commercially in fabrics and in fabric tapes that can be sewn or ironed onto the garment as a trim. Most of the reflective materials on the market are the retroreflective type. Because retroreflection sends light directly back to the source, these materials appear a normal color in daylight and are not highly visible at night unless the viewer is positioned directly behind the light source. Retroreflective materials can be produced in a full spectrum of colors—including black, brown, and navy. The fact that they glow brilliantly under a concentrated light at night yet appear normal in daylight makes them ideal for fashion items, particularly for pedestrians and cyclists. Clothing can even be trimmed in matching tape so that it does not appear to be treated specially in any way.

Fluorescent fabrics and tapes are generally used to protect construction workers and service personnel whose work proceeds during daylight hours. Since there has been a general misconception that fluorescent materials are the most highly visible materials under all conditions, pedestrians and even traffic policemen have erroneously used them at night. Since the eye does not perceive color readily at night and fluorescent materials are not activated by artificial light, although day-glow orange provides some contrast, it does not provide nearly as much as white or silver does to low light levels at night.

Individuals in hazardous professions are increasingly using tapes that combine retroreflective and fluorescent properties for maximum day and night protection. These materials appear a bright fluorescent color in the daytime and glow silver or white at night. They can reflect more than 100 times the amount of light reflected by a white nonretroreflective material.

Since many reflective materials used for tapes are too stiff to be used for whole garments, some more flexible reflective fabric finishes have also been developed. Some are made by adhering millions of microscopic glass beads or prisms to the surface of a base fabric. These reflective elements are translucent, but coated with an opaque reflective material on the back of the structure, the side that faces the base fabric. Light that passes into the

structure reflects off of the reflective material and is redirected back to the light source by the shape of the bead or prism. They appear a normal color and texture in daylight and general artificial light but glow a bright white when struck by a single light source, as they might be at night. The flexibility and drape of these materials depend on a number of variables, among them, the flexibility of the base material, the size and number of the reflective elements, and the flexibility of the adhesive used to attach the reflective elements to the fabric. Some manufacturers have attempted to create more flexible reflective materials by weaving or knitting single retroreflective yarns into a fabric at intervals to form a striped or plaid material. Others silkscreen logos or other patterns on selected areas of a garment. These methods allow reflectivity in critical areas of a garment while greatly decreasing the overall stiffness that would be present in a garment covered completely with reflective elements or made totally of reflective yarn.

Keeping reflective materials clean is essential, since dirt or grease may dull reflection, affect color contrast, or change the refractive qualities of a retroreflective material. One of the biggest problems with reflective materials is their loss of reflective properties after repeated cleanings. Although hand washing is generally tolerated well, repeated machine washing often destroys reflectivity. Since hand washing company-provided uniforms would be too costly, many industries, such as mine working, have to limit reflective trim to nonwashable helmets, boots, or removable vests, which can be rinsed or sponged off after use. Some reflective tapes use enclosed optics (i.e., a clear finish over the reflective surface so that optical elements—the beads or prisms—cannot collect dirt). Many plastic tapes of this type are in use in firefighting clothing because of the tremendous decrease in reflectivity caused to exposed, beaded surfaces by soot in the firefighting environment. Plastic tapes can easily be wiped clean. Some, however, may be less heat resistant than some tapes made with glass beads on the surface.

CLOTHING DESIGNED FOR HIGH VISIBILITY

There are two basic reasons to make clothing highly visible. One is to avoid an accident by alerting people, such as motorists or hunters, that other individuals are in the area. The other is to help teams of workers find each other or rescue personnel find an injured person. The key factors a designer needs to understand about either of these design situations are the sources of light and the ways in which contrast with the environment can help enhance visibility.

Light Sources

The sources of available light determine the kinds of high-visibility materials that need to be applied to clothing. Fluorescent materials can be used for activities such as hunting, which normally take place during the day. They can also make highway construction workers more visible during the day. Since fluorescent materials are not especially bright at night, police, firefighters, and those who may work in both daylight and dark conditions need garments made of, or trimmed with, both fluorescent and retroreflective materials.

For retroreflective materials to be effective, the sources of light striking them need to be near the eyes of viewers. This is the case when drivers are behind auto headlights, miners are wearing headlamps, or rescue personnel are carrying searchlights. The closer to eye level the light, the brighter the retroreflective material will appear. It is important to explore two factors with regard to

a retroreflective material for a specific end use: its angle of incidence and its angle of divergence. The **incidence angle** of a material is the angle at which the light source strikes the reflective material. The **divergence angle** is the angle at which the viewer can perceive that reflection.

Figure 8.6 shows how incidence and divergence angles are measured. The angle of incidence is measured by drawing a line from the light source (a car head lamp) to the object (a pedestrian) and another perpendicular to the object (pedestrian). The angle between them is the incidence angle. A reflective material should have an incidence angle of about 75°. This wide incidence angle is important for items like clothing for joggers because it means that a high-visibility material can reflect the light from auto headlamps even if a jogger is at some distance to the side of the road or may be approaching from a crossroad. The incidence angle is particularly critical for clothing since reflective materials are not usually held flat or perpendicular to the light source, as a rigid or fixed object such as a highway sign would be. As the diagrams in

FIGURE 8.6 (A) The angle of incidence, with the preferred angle for visibility on the far right; (B) the angle of divergence of reflected light with the preferred incidence angle on the left.

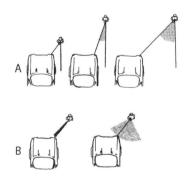

Figure 8.6A show, angle of incidence needed will depend on a combination of how far to the side and how far to the front the reflective material is from the light source.

Divergence angles (Figure 8.6B) are measured by drawing a line along one side of the cone of *reflected* light and measuring the angle it forms with the light beam that strikes the object. If a single light source is involved, as is typical at night, reflected light needs to be returned in a concentrated beam close to its point of origin to be highly visible. Therefore, the most effective reflective materials can seldom have a divergence angle of more than 1° to 2°. If the reflected light beam is scattered over a wide area, as it is in diffuse reflection, so little of the light is reflected directly back toward the eye that the object may be barely visible. At the same time, the reflective brilliance of a nighttime high-visibility material—that is, one with a small divergence angle—can only be appreciated when the eye is very close to the light source, as it would be when a flashlight is held up at eye level.

Contrast

Human vision is fundamentally sensitive to contrast, from birth. Strong differences in hue, brilliance, shape, size, or movement help in capturing attention. Therefore, the primary way clothing can be made more visible is by making it contrast in some way with its environment. The most common ways to achieve contrast are to use a hue or a saturation of color for garments that is very different from the colors in the environment or to incorporate materials in the design that are specially developed to reflect or emit light.

The relationships between daylight and incandescent light and various types of high-visibility materials have been discussed earlier in this chapter, as have the colors of materials most easily visible in daylight and at night. Once the appropriate materials have been selected, their placement, in other words, *where* contrast occurs on clothing, is extremely important (Sayer and Mefford 2004). The possibility of motion as one factor that may provide contrast was mentioned earlier. Placing high-visibility materials on the most highly mobile parts of the body—the arms and legs—may help alert a motorist to the fact that a pedestrian is near the roadway.

One critical aspect of motion is that the human eye is particularly sensitive to movement that seems life-like—what is called **biomotion**. Highlighting parts of the body such as the limbs in such a way as to show human-like movements or outlining a human-like shape can be an effective way of differentiating a human worker from other reflective or brightly colored objects, such as road signs, that are also in the environment.

It is important that high-visibility clothing be designed so that it can be seen regardless of the orientation of the body (3M 2012, 8–12). Even though pedestrians and joggers may typically be seen head-on or directly from the rear, highway or construction workers may be in a variety of positions with regard to motorists.

For rescue operations, it is often helpful to be able to determine the position of a body. Watkins et al. (1978) have suggested that reflective trims for firefighting garments be placed on moving body parts but also in configurations that allow a rescue team to identify the body position of an injured or trapped worker. Figure 8.7 shows one of the suggested trim placements. The configurations of trim are different when the firefighter is seen from the front, back, or side. Reflective trim is also placed under the arch of the boot. All of the placements allow coworkers to know where their coworkers

FIGURE 8.7 Reflective tape placement for firefighting garments. *(Design: Laurie Rosen Cohen and Mary Valla Ippolito)*

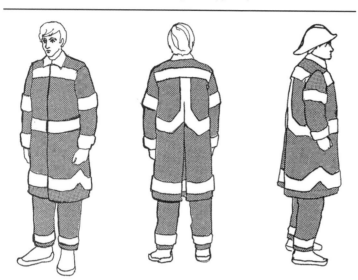

are while crawling or climbing through a dimly lit burning structure but also allow rescuers to identify the position of an injured firefighter quickly so that they can decide on the best rescue procedure.

Standards for High-Visibility Clothing

In 2008, a U.S. federal regulation established mandates for the use of high-visibility garments for all highway construction maintenance and utility workers and emergency responders who are exposed to traffic on the roadways or work vehicles such as construction equipment (3M 2010, 1). This regulation requires workers to wear garments in one of three classes that meet ANSI/ISEA—107 standards (Ibid.). Surveys provided by the U.S. Federal Highway Administration help users determine the risks in specific situations so that the appropriate class of high-visibility garments can be selected. The standard for each class specifies the minimum amount of background (fluorescent)

materials as well as the amount, minimum widths, and placement of retroreflective trim that needs to be worn. In addition, the standard specifies brightness and durability requirements for all classes.

CAMOUFLAGE

For some activities, such as warfare and hunting, it is important that visibility be decreased. When camouflage is desired, the criteria for visibility are simply reversed: the clothing worn must closely match the color, size, shape, and motion of its background.

The jungle camouflage patterns seen in military, camping, hunting, and even fashion items represent camouflage for only one type of background. There are dozens of different camouflage patterns, each representing the random shapes, shadows, and color distributions found in a particular setting. Figure 8.8A–D shows a variety of camouflage patterns for the military (woodlands, desert, Arctic) and hunting (marsh, treebark). Figure 8.8E shows an example of a pattern called MultiCam, developed by the U.S. Army for use in many different environments. The pattern contains elements of woodland, desert, and jungle camouflage. When a soldier is in the desert, for example, the desert motifs are spaced in such a way that the eyes and brain fill in the spaces between them to present an all desert camouflage pattern to the viewer (MultiCam "How MultiCam"). Digital patterns, consisting of carefully planned squares of color, have also been developed by the military.

Nighttime espionage activities may be conducted in black clothing so that individuals blend in with the background at night. Again, avoiding contrast with the background is critical. Black figures against a white wall even slightly illuminated by moonlight would probably be considerably more visible than figures dressed in lighter colors.

In addition to trying to match the colors and shapes of an environment, the leaf patterns on some woodland fabrics for hunters have die-cut free edges that flutter with the breeze in the same manner as the surrounding trees, so that their motion matches the environment as well. When colors and patterns closely match the surroundings, motion becomes a much more critical factor for detection. Both the military and hunters have used *ghillie suits* (Figure 8.9), which strongly resemble heavy foliage. These suits are made up of loose strips of fabric, twine, and other materials and generally contain mesh or straps through which foliage and twigs, etc., from the surrounding area can be

entwined. They help break up a more linear outline of the human body and so that it can blend in with the environment. Other camouflage patterns may be planned with the capacities of specific viewers in mind. (See Design Strategies 8.1.)

Camouflage from Specific Detection Mechanisms

One of the most important factors in visibility is the detection mechanism involved. For the military, technology in the field of detection has advanced so greatly that soldiers need to be protected from much more than simply being seen by the naked eye. Light-enhancing devices, the so-called starlight scopes, make objects visible using even minute amounts of light. Infrared detection devices provide a picture of the long wavelength radiation emitted by objects. Because the human

FIGURE 8.8 Camouflage patterns. (A) Woodland; (B) desert; (C) Arctic; (D) marsh; (E) MultiCam *(A, B, C, and E, U.S. Army; D, Columbia Sportswear.)*

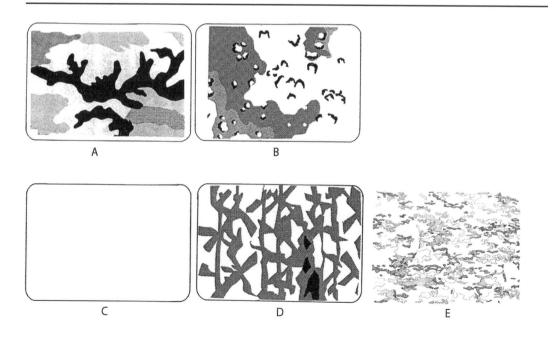

A

B

C

D

E

FIGURE 8.9 A ghillie suit.

body is constantly producing heat and thus emits infrared radiation, a soldier dressed in a visual camouflage pattern suitable for the environment would still show up clearly on an infrared screen.

Infrared camouflage patterns for fabric depend largely on the differences in reflectivity between dyes (Renbourn 1972, 125). Two fabrics dyed the same color with different dyes may appear the same to the naked eye, but their infrared reflection capacities may differ greatly. Therefore, fabrics for infrared camouflage are dyed with methods that produce an infrared reflectance as close to the surrounding environment as possible. Because most colors can be achieved using a wide variety of different dyes, this makes possible fabrics that provide both visual *and* infrared camouflage.

Dynamic Camouflage

Static camouflage that changes the visual appearance of the object may help the object blend into its surroundings; however, dynamic camouflage can allow the object to more effectively disappear. Two important features of dynamic camouflage are its ability to replace the surface of the object with the exact appearance of the background, and its ability to compensate for light blocked by the object (referred to as *counterillumination*).

Dynamic camouflage can present the appearance of the background on the surface of the object in several ways: by projecting a picture of the background onto the object surface using an external projector; by using powered electronic display technologies to display the background on the surface; or by using nonpowered, light-bending technologies like fiber optics to move light from one side of the object to another. (For some examples of color-changing technologies that could be used to create a dynamic image on the object surface, see "Addition of Color to Textile Materials" in Chapter 3 and "Actuators" in Chapter 4).

Approaches that use color-changing fabrics or materials to change the appearance of a surface can be linked to imaging technologies (cameras or light detectors) to help match the surface to the background. Alternatively, some less-complex approaches use planned camouflage patterns and thermochromic inks to change the color palette of the camouflage pattern according to ambient temperature. For example, a hunter with one set of gear may need a richly-colored camouflage pattern in the early fall, but a dull brown palette in the late fall/early winter, and a white and grey pattern in the winter. A textile with a light neutral background can be printed with thermochromic inks of

Design Strategies 8.1: Meeting Conflicting Criteria: Visibility for Hunters

One of the most interesting applications of the principles of visibility is clothing for hunters. Many hunters want to be completely invisible to their prey. At the same time, to avoid being accidentally injured, they want to remain visible to other hunters. Some states now require hunters to wear a minimum amount of fluorescent orange when they hunt. There are many similar situations in protective clothing design—where opposite criteria need to be met for the same activity depending on changing circumstances or the participants in an activity.

Most hunting clothing is sold in a wide variety of patterns to match the environments in which hunters will be seen. (See Figure 8.8A and D.) In response to concerns about the high visibility of solid fluorescent

vests worn for safety, new hybrid hunting materials were developed. These took advantage of the difference between the vision of animals from which hunters wish to be *hidden* and the vision of other human hunters, by which they wish to be *seen*. Proponents of fluorescent or "blaze" orange clothing for hunters have long argued that many animals, such as deer, do not detect color (Jacobs 1983). Therefore, bright colors can be used to alert other hunters while not alerting deer. Still, the lack of pattern in solid protective vests broke up the effectiveness of the camouflage pattern, so some manufacturers integrated blaze orange into camouflage patterns for hunting. These materials lend visibility to other hunters, but provide the shapes and textures of the background for colorblind animals.

---

brighter colors, which can be calibrated to change from colored to translucent when the temperature drops.

Counterillumination approaches are important in situations where the camouflaged object is often seen against a more brightly lit background, such as in the air or in the sea. A surface that can generate a small amount of light colored to match the background lighting conditions can conceal an object better than an opaque surface.

Clothing for Diving and Water Safety

Staying afloat is important for many work and recreational activities. Life preservers and other flotation devices are used in a wide range of sports, from pleasure boating to waterskiing and fishing.

Flotation devices are used to assist children or people with handicaps as they learn to swim. They are used in several phases of scuba diving. Emergency flotation clothing has been used in aircraft by pilots whose flight pattern takes them over water and by fishermen, oil riggers, and others who work on the sea. In order to understand how flotation materials work and why they must be carefully positioned on the body, it is important to understand the basic principles of buoyancy.

THE PRINCIPLES OF BUOYANCY

An object floats if it is less dense than the fluid that surrounds it. Many people have experienced how easy it is to float in saltwater. Because saltwater is denser than freshwater, the human body is less dense in relation to saltwater than it is in relation to freshwater. Most women, who have a higher proportion of body fat, float more easily than men. This is because fatty tissue is less dense than muscle or bone, and density is critical to buoyancy. Even materials more dense than water, however, can be made to float with the right design. A solid block of aluminum would probably sink in a pool of water, whereas that same quantity of aluminum rolled thin and shaped into a pan would probably float. The design of objects that float is based in part on obtaining the greatest volume per unit weight. The more fluid an object displaces when it is placed on that fluid's surface, the better. The volume of water displaced must be great enough to balance the weight of the object in order for the object to float.

The first step in understanding the principles behind buoyancy is to think of a fluid, such as water, exerting pressure on all sides of a submerged cube. In still water, the pressure on the four side faces of the cube will be equal because they are all at relatively the same depth. The only real difference in pressure will be between the top and bottom faces of the cube. Since the bottom of the cube is at a greater depth than the top, the upward pressure of water is greater than its downward pressure. This upward or *buoyant* force can be calculated by measuring the volume of a submerged object and calculating the weight of the equivalent volume of the fluid that it displaced when it was submerged. For example, water weighs 62.4 lb/cu ft (1 g/cm^3), so a 1 cu ft (0.028 m^3) block that is submerged in water will be buoyed up by a force equal to the weight of the water it displaces—62.4 lb (28.3 kg). The buoyant force on a submerged object remains the same regardless of the depth of its position in the water because it is the result of the *difference* in the pressure water places on an object from above and below. Since

pressure increases both above and below as an object is more deeply submerged, that difference, and thus, the buoyant force, remains the same.

In order for an object to float, the upward pressure of the buoyant force must exceed the downward pressure (the weight per unit area) of the object itself. This is why a dense object sinks whereas one with the same weight distributed over a larger area floats. In a sense, more area is provided on which the buoyant force can act.

Because individuals cannot do a great deal to effectively change the density of their bodies at the instant they need to be more buoyant, flotation devices do this for them by changing the apparent body size without adding much to body weight. When someone puts on a life preserver, it becomes, in effect, a part of the body, adding substantial volume to it. At the same time, because it generally contains a large volume of air, it adds very little to that person's weight. Therefore, overall, the individual's density is decreased.

DESIGNING LIFE PRESERVERS

Floating a human body is more complicated than floating a cube of metal. For one thing, buoyant forces act through the center of gravity (the center of weight distribution) of an object. Every individual has a different body build and distribution of weight, so the center of gravity of each body may differ. In addition, it is not enough merely to keep a human body afloat. Many flotation devices must keep the face out of water, so that if a person is unconscious, he or she will not drown. This means that the maximum volume must be concentrated high on the body and placed in greater proportions on the chest than on the back. If large flotation devices were placed only on the feet, the feet could conceivably rise to the surface leaving the rest of the body to dangle submerged in the water. If low-density materials were strapped only down the back, they would continually try to rise to the surface and would turn the body so that it was face down in the water.

Most flotation devices use air in some way to achieve buoyancy, either by incorporating materials that have a high proportion of air to solid material or by using waterproof chambers that can be inflated with air. Flotation devices used to be made of cork. Today, most life jackets are filled with closed-cell foams. Unlike inflated vests, these have the advantage of maintaining their buoyancy even when punctured. Because of buoyant forces, an average adult weighs only about 10–12 lb (4.5–5.4 kg) in the water. This means that buoyant materials must increase buoyancy by only slightly more than that amount to keep a body afloat. Unfortunately, body weight alone does not determine buoyancy. Size and shape (i.e., the way the weight is distributed on the body) is of major importance. Therefore, each individual needs to experiment with flotation devices to determine how much his or her particular body needs.

There are a number of ISO standards and federal regulations for flotation devices. In the United States, for example, U.S. Coast Guard regulations must be followed for the design of every *personal flotation device* (**PFD**) used for recreational boating. The U.S. Coast Guard has designated five types of PFDs and specifies the type that must be carried on board each type of craft for each person aboard. The five types vary in the amount of buoyancy they provide and the degree to which they turn an individual face up in the water (U.S. Coast Guard "PFD Selection"). Each type may be made with inherently buoyant materials, be inflatable, or be a combination of the two approaches to buoyancy.

Type I has the greatest buoyancy and is designed to turn even an unconscious person to a vertical and slightly backward position. This type of protector, which is made with inherently buoyant materials, has a positive buoyant force of 22 lb (9.99 kg) and is sometimes referred to as an *offshore life jacket*. Type II is made of inherently buoyant materials, has a positive buoyant force of 15.5 lb (7 kg), and has a less pronounced turning action on the body. It is less bulky and less expensive and is sometimes referred to as a *near shore buoyant vest*. It will still turn most individuals from a face down to a slightly back-resting position. Type III also has a buoyant force of 15.5 lb (7 kg) but no turning force. It is sometimes referred to as a *flotation aid*. The wearer can take a vertical, slightly backward position, and the vest will hold the body in that position, but it would probably not turn a body from face down to face up. Type IV is a throwable cushion for rescue, and Type V is a specialized work vest approved only for use under specific work conditions. In general, the greater the buoyancy, the more bulky is the PFD. Since greater bulk means greater thermal insulation as well, the type of PFD chosen depends on the type of emergency situation expected. For boating in cold or rough water, or in an isolated area where immediate rescue would not be expected, Type I protection would probably be needed. For fishing or water skiing in an area where the water is relatively warm and many other people are around to effect a rescue, the less bulky Types II or III would probably be sufficient and more comfortable.

Life preservers vary in form, but most take the shape of a horseshoe-collar vest or jacket vest (Figure 8.10 A and B). In many models, flotation materials are sewn or stuffed into waterproof coverings. Solid blocks of closed-cell foam are generally used

FIGURE 8.10 Life preservers. (A) A horseshoe-collar Type II vest; (B) a Type I vest; (C) a foam-filled segmented vest.

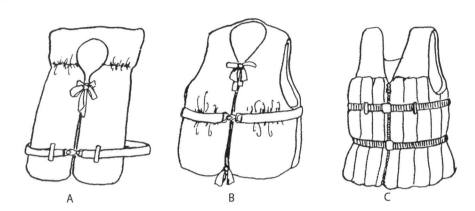

A   B   C

(Figure 8.10B), but smaller blocks sewn into a segmented cover may be used to make a more flexible and comfortable PFD (Figure 8.10C). Some vests used for water skiing may be vinyl-dipped blocks of foam attached at the sides with straps.

Because only a properly fitted vest will keep the wearer afloat and U.S. Coast Guard regulations prohibit alteration of PFDs, variable adjustment features are critical. Although some PFDs are sold by chest size, those that can be adjusted to fit many sizes are important for both pleasure boating and commercial boating where the size of the eventual user cannot always be predicted. Many of the techniques for creating adjustable garments discussed in Chapter 9 also apply to the design of PFDs. Vests may be zipped or tied shut. Often, metal D-rings or plastic clasps are sewn to firm, durable adjustable webbing straps to close a PFD at the center front. The use of noncorrosive metals and other materials not affected by water or salt is critical in choosing appropriate fasteners. Special attention must be paid to the design of life preservers for children and infants. (See Design Solutions 8.1.)

Many special features may be added to PFDs for specific activities. Fishing vests with emergency flotation provisions may have pockets for fishing gear (Figure 8.11). The survival jacket shown in Figure 5.17 provides thermal protection as well as some flotation. The armholes of some vests are lower cut for ease of movement in canoeing and kayaking. Other vests contain special provisions for attaching safety lines for support or rescue. It may also be important to provide thermal protection as well as flotation for certain situations.

A number of emergency devices for military equipment and learn-to-swim items are inflatable. Since one puncture could render an inflatable item totally useless, the situations in which they are used must be noncritical, or special protective provisions must be made. The materials used for them must be extremely strong and durable, or the air-filled channels must be separate so that a puncture will affect only a small portion of the positive

Design Solutions 8.1: Children's Life Preservers

Children's life preservers require additional care in design. Because children may not know how to swim and may panic easily in the water, they need a PFD with a strong face-up turning ability.

A child's body proportions and distribution of weight are different from that of an adult. Children's heads are larger in proportion to the rest of the body than are adults' heads, and, thus, more flotation is needed around the head. The life vest shown in Figure A was designed for infants. Note the large amount of flotation material around the head. This ensures that not only will the head be supported but also the face will be held above the water level. Another style of infant flotation device is shown in Figure B. It is a cocoon shape that also has a large foam-filled section around the head to keep the face supported out of the water.

FIGURES A AND B (A) Infant life vest with large foam pads around head; (B) cocoon-style infant life vest. *(Design: Connelly)*

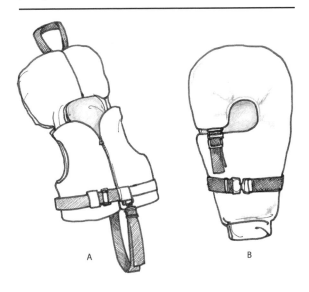

A   B

FIGURE 8.11 A flotation vest with pockets for fishing gear. *(Design formerly produced by Stearns Manufacturing Company)*

buoyant force. One advantage of inflatable buoyancy devices is that they can be relatively flat and thin when they are not in use. In addition, if the devices are to be worn constantly rather than being thrown on at the point of emergency, their thinness makes them both less conspicuous and cooler. (See Figure S5.4.) Some devices are inflated by mouth, whereas others rely on an easily triggered carbon dioxide cartridge (Figure 8.12). One tug on a rope pull or toggle causes a pin to puncture the end of the cartridge and the pressurized carbon dioxide (CO_2) gas then rapidly escapes into the chambers of the buoyancy device and inflates it. One advantage of a CO_2 cartridge is that the wearer, who may presumably be frightened and out of breath, does not have to attempt the difficult task of blowing up

FIGURE 8.12 A carbon dioxide cartridge for inflation of flotation devices. (A) The rope pull; (B) the pin; (C) the pin puncturing the cartridge.

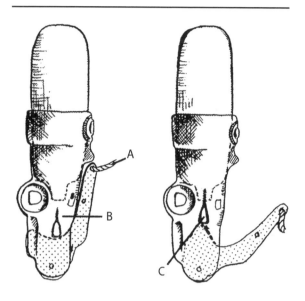

a device while fighting to stay afloat. If air must be blown into a device by mouth, the valve must be easily accessible, protected from water entry, and near the face.

BUOYANCY AND DIVING

The design of wetsuits and drysuits for diving were discussed and illustrated in Chapter 5. In addition to providing thermal insulation, the closed-cell foam used in wetsuits and the volume of air inside many drysuits causes divers to float on the surface of the water. They must exert a great deal of effort to descend. Once a certain amount of descent has been achieved, the increased water pressure at lower depths compresses the cells of a closed-cell foam or the air within the material of a wetsuit. Consequently, the diver and suit together become more "dense" and eventually reach a point that is called **neutral buoyancy**. A neutrally buoyant diver neither floats nor sinks but remains

suspended as if weightless. At this point, all of a diver's efforts can be used to swim or work rather than to stay down or rise up.

Obviously, not all of a diver's interests may lie at the neutrally buoyant point. Therefore, several devices are used to help a diver descend and ascend quickly and without great effort. In order to descend easily, divers wear a weight belt, which is made of metal weights mounted on a stretchable belt (Figure 8.13). The amount of weight added to the belt depends on the type and thickness of the suit and the body composition of the wearer but, in general, 1 lb (0.45 kg) of lead weights is added for every 10 lb (4.54 kg) of body weight. With the weights in place, a diver descends easily until a new point of neutral buoyancy is achieved, or in shallower water, until the bottom is reached.

FIGURE 8.13 A scuba suit with a weight belt.

Although the addition of a weight belt helps a diver stay submerged, it does not really solve the problem of the narrow range of neutral buoyancy. Furthermore, the weight belt might allow easy descent, but it hampers the diver's ascent. Although a weight belt could be dropped from the body for emergency ascent, this would be a costly way of solving the problem. Thus, buoyancy compensators are used.

A **buoyancy compensator** is a variable volume item that is inflated or deflated depending on whether a diver wants to become more buoyant (ascend) or less buoyant (descend). Buoyancy compensators can take a number of forms. The most common designs are the vest and the horse-collar styles (Figure 8.14). A diver wearing a compensator

FIGURE 8.14 A buoyancy compensator.

eventually reaches a depth at which the combination of weights and the decreased buoyancy of the suit (caused by compression of the foam cells in a wetsuit) causes neutral buoyancy to be overcome. If the diver does not want to descend further, he or she can add air to the buoyancy compensator until neutral buoyancy is reached. The ability to make an instantaneous change in buoyancy also allows a diver to easily ascend with a load of treasure or a companion in tow.

Buoyancy compensators can be filled with air directly from the scuba tank, from cartridges attached to the compensator, or directly by mouth. They also contain a pressure relief valve to prevent them from overinflating and rupturing. In some models, weights are carried on the compensator rather than on the diver's waist belt. Others achieve compensation automatically rather than demanding continuous attention from the diver.

Because of the air within drysuits, their buoyancy can be varied without the use of a separate compensator vest. The closed-cell foam drysuit shown in Figure 5.15A, for example, has been inflated to provide increased buoyancy and insulation. This particular type of drysuit features a pushbutton valve (shown on the upper chest) through which air from the tank can be added to the suit to increase buoyancy. Other equipment such as the breathing mask and tank also affect buoyancy. A diver's buoyancy, then, is affected by a number of things, some of them constantly changing: the composition and compression of the diver's body tissues; the type of suit and the amount of air incorporated in it; weights and other accessories; equipment such as the air tank; the amount of air in the tank; the amount of air in the buoyancy compensator, and so on.

An additional aspect of diving that is of importance to designers is the fact that the body takes a position when floating that is similar to the weightless position in outer space. (See Figure 8.18.) Figure 2.39 shows a diving suit that has been shaped in the *working position* with contours that reflect this neutral position.

SPEED ENHANCEMENT

There are two basic approaches to enhancing speed with clothing without adding powered devices to the body. One is to modify the body's surface to reduce the drag and friction between it and the environment. The other is to *increase* the friction or drag on the body while training so that the body builds strength in ways that will allow it to be faster once that drag is removed.

Both the materials used and the way that they enclose the body may be part of the first approach. Drag, or resistance, may be created by the shape of the body and clothing or by friction with the air or water that surrounds it. Power stretch and a close fit may change body shapes and fabric surface texture can be used to reduce friction.

During movement, the air or water that the body displaces is pushed out and around the body. As this happens, drag is generated based on two factors: the amount of turbulence created as the flow passes over the surface and the amount of turbulence created behind the body as the flow comes back together. The amount of surface turbulence depends on the smoothness of the surface. The amount of turbulence behind the body depends on how broad the front of the body part is and what happens to the flow as it passes over and behind the body part. A tapered object like an airplane wing has a very narrow front that widens slowly and tapers at the end. This airfoil shape only displaces the flow a little bit as it moves. Because of this, surface drag is the most important factor. However, for a broader object like the body, there

is a much greater force generated by turbulent flow behind the body. In some cases, very smooth surfaces can encourage flow to separate even more behind the body, creating a larger area of turbulence and increasing drag further. A slightly bumpy surface, while it increases surface turbulence, can also encourage flow to stick to the surface more closely as it passes the body. The overall result is a decrease in the drag behind the body, which can mean an overall decrease in the total amount of drag. (This is why the surface of a golf ball is dimpled.) Some speed-skating uniforms, for example, use tiny bumps on key body areas to promote turbulence and reduce drag.

The shape of the body determines how much turbulence is experienced behind it. A more streamlined shape reduces the amount of drag generated by this turbulence. Streamlining the shape of the body requires a power stretch material with as few seams and bulky edges and other production features that might interrupt the flow of air or water. Compression garments can be used to decrease the overall circumference of the body uniformly, or can be used to alter the shape of the body to improve its aerodynamics or hydrodynamics so that air or water flows more easily over the body. One of the problems with using too much power stretch is that it needs to be carefully placed on the body to avoid restriction of movement. A number of studies have identified the body areas where maximum drag occurs for each athletic activity. Once this is known, a combination of low-friction fabrics and compression (power stretch) materials can be carefully placed in clothing to minimize drag.

In some cases, reducing drag can also be viewed as less desirable for speed. A suit developed as a training tool for Olympic speed skating athletes serves as a good example of both understanding how drag affects a specific sport *and* the idea of increasing drag during training (Demarest et al. "Article of Apparel"). The suit was developed by placing a highly textured surface on various areas of the body. Each section of the suit had ridges aligned in a way that restricted the predominant airflow for each body segment as it would occur while in a speed-skating position. (See Figure 8.15.) This so-called turbulence-generating fabric created a far more realistic pattern of drag than whole-body solutions such as having the skaters wear weights or pull parachutes behind them. The principles involved in this suit design lend inspiration to the design of body coverings for training in any "fluid" environment such as in water sports.

It is also possible in water sports, such as swimming, to increase buoyancy by trapping air inside the materials of a suit. This allows all of the effort of a swimmer to be exerted in moving forward. Modifications to clothing like this one may be prohibited by some governing bodies for athletic competitions. Some clothing and equipment innovations are referred to as "technology doping" and banned from use because they are believed to give an unfair advantage to athletes. Before beginning to design, it is important for designers to be aware of any design constraints imposed on specific sports by these types of restrictions.

Clothing for Physical Strength Enhancement

In addition to improving the body's own ability to use energy as efficiently as possible in a given

FIGURE 8.15 (A) Stripes indicate direction of turbulence-generating texture in material placed on a training suit for speed skating; (B) the speed-skating position. *(Demarest et al. "Article of Apparel")*

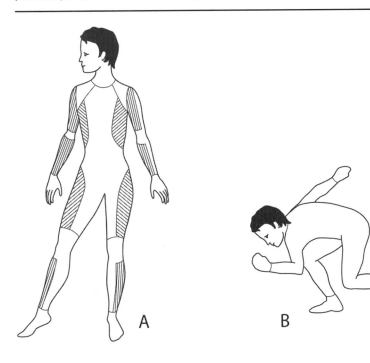

A   B

environment, augmentation systems can add to the energy normally produced by the body to increase its strength and power. Systems that augment the body's ability to do work can do so through two primary mechanisms. First, body energy can be captured and reused in another way, increasing the efficiency of the system but not adding any additional energy. Second, external power can be added to the system, either in addition to or in place of muscle power.

IMPROVING BODY EFFICIENCY

When the body moves, some of the energy used to create that movement is absorbed by other materials, such as clothing items or the surfaces that the body is pushing against. As discussed in Chapter 6, materials with *elastic* properties have the ability to return some of this force to the body. In a shoe that has springs in the heel, for instance, the springs are compressed when body weight pushes against them, but they return this force to the heel when the body's weight is moved. An *inelastic* material, such as a corrugated cardboard box, would absorb all of the body's force as it deformed and not return any force to the body. Elasticity can be used to improve the efficiency of body movements in direct ways (like springs in a shoe's heel) or in less direct ways, where the force is saved and returned to the body in another way. For example, in some individuals who have experienced a stroke or disease affecting the muscles of the legs and feet, foot drop, or difficulty keeping the ankle flexed during walking, is a common problem that interferes with walking. An insole or shoe fitted with an air chamber could use the force generated by compressing the air within that chamber (as the person steps down) to move a locking mechanism, which applies a force to hold the foot in a flexed position during the rest of the step (when the leg swings freely).

Energy-harvesting materials convert the energy of body movements or even the body's thermal energy into electrical energy, which can be stored in a battery. One method of harvesting body movements is to use the body movement to drive a small generator, which produces electricity. Another method is to use piezoactive materials, such as those discussed in Chapter 4, which produce a small electrical current when they are deformed. The body's thermal energy can be transformed into electrical energy through materials like the Peltier junction discussed in Chapter 5, provided there is a difference in temperature between the body and the surrounding environment.

It is also possible to extend the body's ability to generate power by controlling the internal thermal environment. One of the enzymes that muscles use to generate energy is sensitive to temperature. If the muscle gets too hot, this enzyme is deactivated, and the muscle begins to tire quickly. However, if the muscle can be cooled, the effect is canceled and the muscle's endurance is dramatically increased. Wearing cooling garments that can control muscle temperature during exercise has been shown to increase endurance.

Finally, garments that minimize the amount of nonproductive muscle activity that takes place during exercise can also help improve the efficiency of the body. Although findings are not conclusive, some studies show that using compression garments during high-impact exercise (such as running) can help improve the efficiency of the muscles by minimizing the amount of vibration and reverberation in the muscles during impact.

AUGMENTING BODY POWER

Energy collected from the body or generated through an external source can replace or be added to body energy to help the wearer perform movements. Systems that augment body power range from small targeted devices that assist the movement of a specific muscle or joint to whole-body exoskeletons that magnify body power hundreds of times. The following sections discuss two types of wearable devices that augment body power: devices that use mechanical actuators to generate forces and devices that use electrical power to activate existing muscle and joint structures.

Powered Orthoses and Exoskeletons

Powered orthoses are braces that contain mechanical joints that assist the movement of a specific body joint, such as the knee or hip. These devices can be designed to function in a specific rhythm (e.g., to help the wearer to walk), on demand to perform a specific action (e.g., to help the user sit down or stand up at the push of a button), or in response to muscle signals (e.g., to sense a small muscle movement and use that signal to trigger a larger response from the powered orthosis).

Movements of the powered device can be achieved in many ways. The most common methods are through motors, pneumatic tubes, and electromechanical materials. Motors usually produce a rotational movement (which can be translated or redirected using gears, levers, and other mechanical devices). Pneumatic tubes act like long skinny balloons. When inflated, they create a strong straightening force and can be very rigid when fully pressurized. (See Figure 8.16.) (Imagine trying to bend a half-filled long balloon, as compared to a very full long balloon.) Pneumatic tubes could also be used in a configuration in which the force of the body flexing a limb or taking a step pushed a plunger into an air-filled tube (the soft-closing door hinge is an example of this). If the tube had a slow leak, it would resist the plunger being forced into the tube but would eventually allow it to happen. This could be useful in designing soft landings for impact-protective clothing. If the tube did not have a leak, it would cause the air to be compressed within the tube, and would return the force like a spring when released. A small pneumatic tube could be used like the spring in a running shoe to help return force to the body.

Electromechanical materials, as discussed in Chapter 4, operate in two ways. Some electromechanical materials contract when exposed to an electrical current, shortening their length. Others are trained into a specific shape (such as a spring). When there is no electrical current, they act like thin, flexible wires. When exposed to a current,

FIGURE 8.16 The Orthowalk®, a device with inflatable tubes that straighten the lower body of a paraplegic when inflated and can be slowly deflated to allow bending to sit. *(Formerly produced by ILC Dover)*

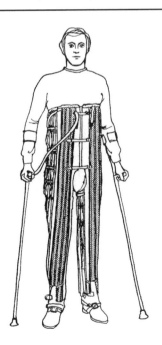

they assume the trained shape, which can be used to create a movement or contraction.

Single-joint assistance is very helpful in performing targeted tasks or in replacing the ability of an impaired muscle or joint. More complex systems can provide movement assistance or replacement for multiple joints, and the most complex (often full-body) systems are called **powered exoskeletons** (Figure 8.17).

Power is supplied to a powered exoskeleton from a battery pack, a small engine, or a fuel cell. Because an exoskeleton is usually required to perform more work than the human body is capable of, it often demands large amounts of power. Powering the exoskeleton for long periods of time is a challenge for system design. However, unlike other kinds of wearable devices, the mass of the exoskeleton is not necessarily a problem for the wearer. As long as the exoskeleton can carry itself, it is not relying on the wearer to support its weight.

FIGURE 8.17 An assisted movement exoskeleton.

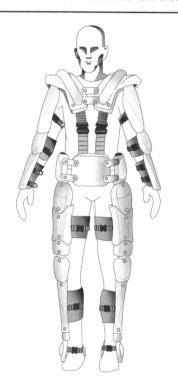

Functional Electrical Stimulation

Another approach to generating body movements is to activate existing human muscles. This can be accomplished using electrical currents of specific frequencies. Functional Electrical Stimulation (FES, also known as Neuromuscular Electrical Stimulation, NMES) is similar in many ways to electrotactile stimulation (discussed in Chapter 4). Electrotactile stimulation uses electrical current to stimulate the sensory neurons in the skin and produces the sensation of touch. FES uses a similar approach but different electrical current frequencies. These frequencies stimulate the motor neurons rather than the sensory neurons and cause the muscles that these neurons innervate to contract. Functional electrical stimulation is used in exercise (to strengthen muscles) and can also be used to augment an impaired muscle. For example, in the case of an individual with a neurological injury or disorder that prevents messages from the brain from getting to the motor neurons in the leg, an FES device can activate those neurons either on demand when a button is pressed or automatically by sensing other contextual information like where the body is in a gait cycle and activating specific muscles at appropriate times. A common use of FES is to overcome the foot-drop tendency mentioned earlier that often follows a stroke. Stroke patients often have difficulty flexing their ankles as they walk. If the ankle is not flexed enough as the foot leaves the ground, the toes drag on the ground as the leg swings forward, which often leads to falls. An FES sock or ankle device can activate flexor muscles in the ankle at the appropriate time, lifting the foot for the patient.

Clothing for Flight and Outer Space

Many aspects of space suits and other garments for flight and outer space have been covered in previous chapters. Chapter 5 discussed the thermal aspects of garments. (See especially Figures 5.19 and S5.4 and information on auxiliary heating and cooling.) Chapter 2 discussed mobility issues related to space suits and other positive pressure garments. (See especially Figures 2.11–2.13 and the surrounding text on movement notation and Case Study 2.1.) This chapter will focus on two additional problems that face designers in designing for flight and outer space: gravity and acceleration.

WEIGHTLESSNESS

Weight is the pull of gravity on an object. Every planet has an area around it that pulls objects toward its surface, but the force of gravity is not the same for each planet. The moon, for example, exerts only one-sixth of the pull of the Earth's gravity. A person who weighs 120 lb (54.4 kg) on Earth would weigh only 20 lb (9.1 kg) on the moon. When astronauts defy the Earth's gravity and travel into outer space, they become almost weightless until their spacecraft begins to be pulled into the gravitational field of another planet.

Everyone has probably experienced a few seconds of weightlessness in an elevator or a plane, where rapid descent leaves at least part of the body's weight suspended above the surface on which they are standing or sitting. Gravity cannot be shielded as X-rays or other forces can, so scientists on Earth can cause apparent weightlessness for only 20 seconds or so. Weightless experiments on Earth are generally accomplished by sending a plane on a parabolic flight pattern. As the plane begins to descend, the weight of the passengers disappears for about 20 seconds and they float around the craft.

One of the longest opportunities for studying living in weightless conditions occurred on the Skylab Space Station. The astronauts on the three Skylab missions spent a total of 171 days in outer space. Because of the size of the space station and the fact that astronauts were free to move around inside a craft to a degree never before possible in space, clothing became an important factor in the weightless environment (Cooper 1976; ILC Space Systems 1984).

The human body is designed to function under the conditions of the Earth's gravity. The circulatory system, for example, is designed to pump blood against gravity. When gravity is almost completely removed, in what are called zero-g conditions (or more appropriately **microgravity** or micro-g, since gravity never completely loses its influence), the body continues to push fluids upward. The Skylab astronauts discovered this when they developed flushed, bloated faces and upper bodies, while their legs and hips became thinner. Their pants became too large while their shirts became noticeably snug. Without gravity pulling on their upper body weight, they became 1–2 inches (2.54–5.08 cm) taller. The spaces between the vertebrae in their spinal cords elongated, making their bodies longer in much the same way that people on Earth become taller each morning after relaxing their spinal cords by lying in bed for 8 hours or so each night. In moving from Earth to a microgravity environment, then, some consideration must be given for fitting adjustments in clothing. Many of the mechanisms discussed in Chapters 2 and 9 to add mobility or use fasteners for adjustment were applied to clothing for Skylab and Shuttle crews. Figure 2.33, for example, showed a garment designed for Space Shuttle IVA (intravehicular activity). Note the expansion pleats that work, not only to add mobility but also to provide for the increasing width of the upper body in microgravity. Expansion features on the waistline of pants also increased their adjustability.

With no need to oppose gravity, the body takes the somewhat relaxed position shown in Figure 8.18. Arms rise and float, the head drops, the body bends slightly at the hips and knees and the feet drop slightly. Clothing designed for maximum comfort in weightlessness should consider the shape of the body in Figure 8.18 in the same way designers use the upright, standing body as the basic form for most fashion items. Based on complaints about earlier IVA garments for weightless environments, later versions of IVA clothing took this into account. For example, the 15 percent shift in line of sight, with the head tilted downward, caused the Skylab astronauts to complain about the front of the collar digging into the chin (ILC Space Systems 1984). Later versions, then, eliminated turtlenecks and other higher necklines and replaced them with more open collar styles. Pants

were lengthened at the back waist and shortened in front. The back shoulder area and sleeve were redesigned to accommodate the upward float of the arms and shoulders.

Clothing itself reacts to the weightless environment and must be designed accordingly. Without the weight of gravity, loose edges float free. IVA garments for the Shuttle program contained several features designed to hold the garments close to the body, not only so that they would provide body coverage, but also so that they did not snag on the interior of the spacecraft as the astronaut floated by. Elastic straps on the jacket hem were snapped to the pants to keep the edge of the jacket from floating up. In addition, most pants had some kind of stirrup or strap to keep them from migrating up the leg. Stand-up collars were placed on a lowered neckline so that typical collar edges could not float upward into the face. Since tools and personal use items also float weightless in the micro-g environment, many pockets were placed on the legs and arms of the garments (Figure 8.19). These were planned for individual item storage so that tools and other items stored in the pockets could be taken out one at a time and would not float away from the astronaut.

The process of getting dressed can be much more difficult when gravity is not present. When an individual bends over to tie a shoe on Earth, gravity helps lower the upper body and hold it in a bent position. On Skylab, astronauts had to use their stomach muscles to bend at the waist and had to hold the muscles taut until they were finished tying. Obviously, there are advantages to clothing that requires little bending, has large openings, and has easily and quickly closed fasteners.

Staying in place in micro-g also has its challenges. The astronauts had to be wrapped in sleep bags at night to keep them from floating away and

FIGURE 8.18 The position of the body in micro-gravity. *(NASA)*

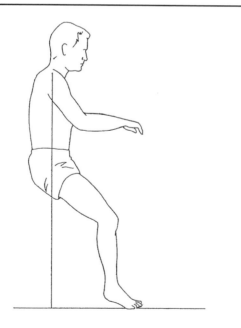

FIGURE 8.19 IVA clothing for Skylab astronauts. *(NASA)*

FIGURE 8.20 Skylab's sleepbag. *(NASA)*

FIGURE 8.21 Footwear for staying in position in micro-gravity. (A) Boot with a triangular cleat; (B) bottom view of the cleat; (C) the flooring grid of the spacecraft; (D) magnetic cleats applied to astronauts' shoes. *(NASA)*

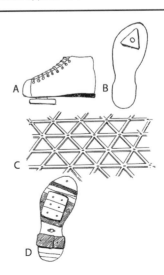

bumping into things as they slept (Figure 8.20). A number of different features were used to help astronauts stand in place at a workstation. The shoes shown in Figures 8.21A and B had triangular cleats that matched a gridding in the floor of the station. These were raised slightly off the surface of the shoe sole. When an astronaut wished to stay in one location, he would push the shoe cleat through the floor grid and give it a quarter turn, so that the points of the cleat locked under the sides of the triangles in the floor grid. A mushroom-shaped cleat that could be slipped in and out of the grid more easily was also used (Cooper 1976, 38). Many other ways of holding shoes in place on the floor of a space vehicle have been attempted—from magnetic cleats to suction cups.

Acceleration

Acceleration and deceleration have already been discussed in Chapter 6 as factors in the design of impact protective clothing. As noted there, acceleration, the rate of change of velocity, is directly proportional to the amount of force that is applied to a body. On Earth, acceleration due simply to gravitational forces (free falling) is expressed by using the symbol g, and equals 32 ft/sec^2 (981 cm/s^2). This means that if an object simply dropped off the top of a building without being thrown or pushed, gravity would cause it in theory to fall 32 feet (9.75 meters) in the first second, 64 feet (19.5 meters) in the second second, and so on. A greatly magnified acceleration is present when jet propulsion and other accelerative forces act on aircraft during flight, especially in high-performance aircraft. These forces are expressed by comparing them to the gravitational forces on Earth and stating them as multiples of g. One g, then, expresses the gravitational force on Earth, whereas a rocket might be said to experience forces of 4 or 9 g as it is propelled away from Earth at an acceleration four times that of gravity or nine times that of gravity, respectively.

Since acceleration is the result of force acting on a body in a specific direction, it is difficult to describe acceleration during space flight using only the g-forces. On Earth, direction can be specified in terms of the Earth's surface. However, there are no such reference points in space. The addition of a pilot or astronaut creates further difficulties because of the elasticity of the human body. When a human body is accelerated, the internal organs and blood may accelerate in different directions relative to the skeleton. The difficulty this presents

to basic descriptions can be illustrated by visualizing a man sitting in a car. At rest, the heart is pulled slightly down in the chest by gravity. On forward acceleration, the heart is thrust backward, toward the spine, while the skeleton is moving forward. The inertial forces of the skeleton are overcome because the auto seat moves the skeleton along, but the more elastic internal organs try to remain at rest and are, thus, displaced relative to the skeleton.

Figure 8.22 shows the terminology used to describe the directional aspects of acceleration on the body in flight. The basic figure is seated, as it would be in an aircraft seat. Three basic axes are used, each representing a direction the organs would be displaced with respect to the skeleton. Each of the positive and negative accelerations along each axis are then given vernacular terms in relation to the displacement of the eyeballs during this movement. A capital G, the gravitational constant, is used to express these movements. Acceleration forward occurs on the x-axis and is termed Gx (eyeballs in); acceleration backward on the x-axis is termed Gx (eyeballs out) and so on.

The terminology illustrated in Figure 8.22 is all used to describe *linear acceleration* or acceleration that occurs in a straight line. Tactical maneuvers in aircraft often result in *radial acceleration*, or acceleration produced by centrifugal force. In radial acceleration, a point on the aircraft is at the center of rotation, so that the pilot experiences the effects as if he or she were placed on the end of a long line of skaters holding hands and circling around a skater at the center of the ice. When the pilot is at the axis of rotation, this is termed *angular rotation*. A gymnast doing a back flip experiences angular rotation. A pilot may also experience *oscillatory rotation*, where alternating forces move

FIGURE 8.22 Linear acceleration and its physiological effects. *(Biotechnology, Inc. 1968)*

Pictoral Description	Descriptive Term	Symbol	Heart Displacement
	Forward acceleration or forward acting force.	$+G_x$	Moves toward the back.
	Backward acceleration or backward acting force.	$-G_x$	Moves toward the front.
	Rightward acceleration or rightward acting force.	$+G_y$	Moves toward the left.
	Leftward acceleration or leftward acting force.	$-G_y$	Moves toward the right.
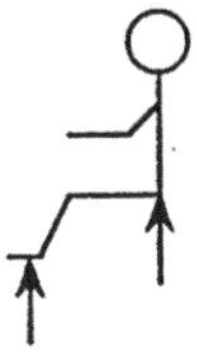	Headward acceleration or headward acting force	$+G_z$	Moves toward feet.
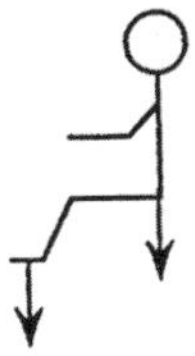	Tailward acceleration or tailward acting force.	$-G_z$	Moves toward head.

the body back and forth rapidly in motions much like a pendulum.

One of the practical results of increased acceleration is, in effect, to increase the weight of the body. If a pilot weighs 200 lb (90.8 kg) on Earth, an acceleration of 4 g will exert a pull on the body that would cause it to weigh in at 1,000 lb (454 kg). Since this effective weight increase is present on every portion of the body, simple movements are much more difficult to perform. Arm muscles must move an arm that is four times as heavy and neck muscles must lift a head that is four times its normal weight. In addition, the direction of the force created by acceleration is not constant (i.e., it may move quickly from linear acceleration to radial acceleration outward to oscillatory acceleration to radial acceleration inward, etc., as the pilot is executing a tactical maneuver).

The various types of acceleration affect the internal organs and blood flow in a similar fashion. When a pilot is subjected to positive linear acceleration, the blood has an effectively increased weight and is pulled down into the lower extremities and abdomen. This pooling of blood in the lower body causes the blood supply to the brain to be diminished. Since the brain depends on blood flow and the oxygen contained in the blood for normal functioning, lack of blood to the brain for even a few seconds can cause a blackout or temporary unconsciousness. Even if forces are below those that will cause blackout, concentration, judgment, and memory are all affected by a decrease of oxygen to the brain.

A number of methods have been used to decrease the effects of acceleration on the body. One is to find a position for the pilot in which blood will not be drained from the head. If an astronaut were prone and feet first in a space capsule, blood would be sent toward, not away from, the head in upward linear acceleration. Pilots also perform what are termed straining maneuvers, closing the glottis and pushing the breath against it, to improve their tolerance to G forces.

Clothing can also assist in this process by pushing blood upward in the body. Pilots have used antigravity suits for many years. Coverage in the early years was only on the legs, but this quickly extended to the abdominal area (Figure 8.23). The traditional suit is composed of air-filled bladders that inflate automatically when rapid ascent causes

FIGURE 8.23 An antigravity suit worn by pilots.

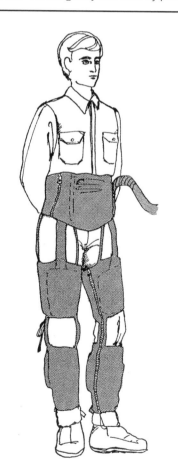

the g-forces to be greater than four times the acceleration of gravity. This inflation places pressure on the legs and abdomen, squeezing blood upward so that it does not suddenly drain from the brain and cause unconsciousness. Today, anti-g suits include vests and other more extensive body covers.

Coverage of the torso increased so much over the years that pilots began to experience severe arm pain from pooling of the blood in the arms (Sokolowski 1996, 2). Figure 8.24 shows gel-filled wraps designed to place pressure on the forearm and upper arm in order to alleviate this pain. They are composed of thin closed-cell foam that has been laminated to a nylon knit on each side. This fabric stretches to place pressure on the arm. In addition, each wrap has a gel-filled bladder inside. The viscosity of the gel and the pressure of the wrap keeps the gel fairly evenly distributed along the arm during normal conditions. However, because the gel used is slightly heavier than the fluids and tissues of the arm, it migrates more quickly when G forces

are applied to it. This means that gel would react first, filling the lower portions of both wraps and applying more pressure on the areas where blood would pool.

Designs for Special Populations

Any enhancement or augmentation of body functions occurs relative to the baseline ability of the body. In situations where a specific body function is limited in some way, clothing and wearable systems can help in augmenting body function to overcome limitations and help individuals achieve a so-called normal level of activity. Some activities and occupations may require or expect "superhuman" function from the body and, again, clothing often holds the key to enhancing body abilities to achieve that function.

This text contains chapters that each focus on specific aspects of the way clothing functions.

FIGURE 8.24 Gel-filled wraps for the arms used as part of a pilot's antigravity suit. *(Design: Susan Sokolowski)*

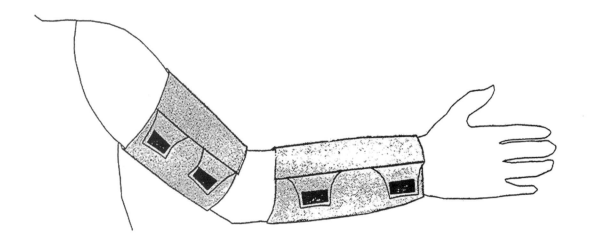

Although designers would probably prefer to have precise formulas to solve problems for each user population, the specific needs of people engaged in any activity are so varied that it would take many volumes to do this. Three groups for whom protective clothing is critical are discussed in the following sections: people with medical conditions and physical handicaps; athletes; and military personnel. Each group contains individuals who may have many different design requirements. The sections that follow will include suggestions for finding information in this text that is pertinent to different medical conditions, activities, and environments of group members.

DESIGNING CLOTHING FOR PEOPLE WITH MEDICAL CONDITIONS AND PHYSICAL HANDICAPS

The terms disabilities, infirmities, and impairments cover such a broad range of conditions that it is difficult to develop any one line of clothing that will meet the needs of multiple situations. However, even though each individual may have a different combination of medical or age-related conditions, there are a number of problem areas faced by many. These include paralysis or weakness that necessitates carrying out activities of daily living (ADL) in a wheelchair; weakness or stiffness of limbs and decreased dexterity that make ADL, particularly dressing, difficult or require the use of braces or supports; missing body parts; loss of one or more of the senses, particularly vision; incontinence; osteoporosis or other conditions for which falling presents a risk; and difficulty regulating thermal balance.

It is critical for designers to understand and explore the specific problems of clients with physical conditions and look for alternative ways to deal with each of them separately before beginning to develop clothing designs. This text can provide resources to inspire design solutions to many of the problems listed earlier. For example, if a client has trouble dressing, Chapter 9 contains an extensive section on fastening systems for self-donning and doffing with many suggestions for adapting and designing clothing for those with limited reach, dexterity, and vision. It also contains a section on accommodating braces and other medical devices that need to be worn on the body. Chapter 2 contains information on fitting and contouring garments to different body shapes, including the position of the body when seated. (See especially Figure 2.31.) Information on analyzing wrinkles in that chapter can be used to assess where garments are binding over braces or are too restrictive to allow self-dressing. Much of the section of Chapter 2 on increasing mobility in clothing through the choice of materials and designs can be used to make movement for weakened individuals easier. This chapter (Chapter 8) contains a section on enhancing physical strength. The ideas there could be applied to those with weakness or paralysis.

Chapter 9 also contains an analysis of suspension systems (i.e., how clothing stays in place on the body). Using this as a guide, designers can pose alternative ways to develop clothing that can be anchored to the body when there are amputated body parts. Many older individuals have a loss of subcutaneous fat or circulatory impairment that makes it difficult for them to stay warm. Chapter 5 contains a thorough analysis of ways both materials and designs can assist with thermal balance. Chapter 6 contains information on impact protection that could be used to develop protective items for those who cannot risk injury from falling. Chapter 3 contains information on moisture transport in materials, and this can be very useful in understanding how to design clothing items to handle incontinence and keep moisture off the skin surface to help prevent bedsores. Finally, the material in Chapter 4 on smart fabrics and clothing may hold the keys to innovative new ways of dealing with many medical conditions.

Whenever there is a group that contains individuals with vastly different physical needs, one of the most significant problems is finding a way for designs to reach people who need them. The size and wealth of the groups that need specialized clothing are often not perceived to be great enough to invest in design development or mass production and distribution. The distribution aspect is particularly problematic because many of these individuals cannot easily shop in retail establishments and often are reluctant to order items they are not certain will work with the prospect of having to arrange their return. In addition to focusing on ways to make clothing items adjust to and work for a variety of physical conditions, designers need also to turn their attention to creative methods of production and distribution for their designs.

DESIGNING CLOTHING FOR ATHLETES

As is true for medical conditions, the wide variety of sports make it difficult to design an item for one sport that works well for another. For example, the athletes in both football and ice hockey wear shoulder pads, but they need to be designed quite differently. This is because the types of impact and the sources of impact athletes receive in each of these sports are quite different. Even within the sport of football, shoulder pads for linemen are quite different from those for quarterbacks because their activities and stances are so different.

As has been said repeatedly in this text for other design situations, the most critical activity that needs to take place to design clothing for athletes is to assess their needs. If impact is a factor, Chapter 6 is devoted to developing impact-protective equipment and clothing and is largely aimed at sports equipment. If keeping cool (running) or keeping warm (skiing) is of major concern, Chapter 5 contains a wealth of information on ways to achieve those ends. Because of the extreme exertion that occurs in sports, the information in Chapter 5 on the ways in which moisture in a clothing system can be handled may be of particular interest.

Mobility is always of great concern to athletes, and Chapter 2 provides a number of ways to use materials and the cut of clothing to achieve ease of motion in clothing. In addition, because clothing can only protect if it is fitted over body parts that need protection, techniques to adjust clothing fit are also covered in Chapter 2. This, combined with information from Chapter 9 about alternative ways to suspend equipment from the body and fasten it so that it adjusts to varying body shapes should be quite helpful to the design process. In addition, since many of the materials used in sports equipment may be unfamiliar to clothing designers, it may be important to consult Chapter 3 for information on materials and Chapter 9 for information on alternative production methods.

DESIGNING CLOTHING FOR THE MILITARY

The environment of military personnel comprises one of the most complex combinations of threats presented to an apparel designer. Figure 8.25 illustrates some of them. Designing for the various branches of the military requires information from every chapter in this text: mobility and fit in Chapter 2; material choices for different threats and multifunction materials in Chapter 3; the potential for the use of smart materials and systems

FIGURE 8.25 Among the threats to military personnel are (clockwise from the sun) weather; disease; bullets and fragments; directed energy weapons; biting animals; puncture; CBRN agents; detection by the enemy; sonic boom; and impact

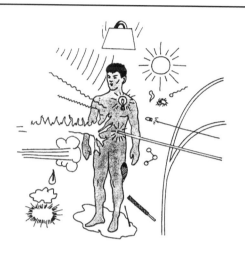

in Chapter 4; thermal balance in Chapter 5; both physical impacts and ballistics threats in Chapter 6; CBRN threats in Chapter 7; visibility, camouflage, flotation, and acceleration in Chapter 8; and ways to mount the wide variety of protection needed on the body using fastening and suspension systems discussed in Chapter 9.

One of a designer's primary functions when designing for the armed forces is to determine the rank and weight of threats in a particular situation order to decide how to proceed. (See Chapter 1, especially "Resolving Conflicts.") As technological developments provide increasingly sophisticated equipment and approaches to protecting military personnel, it may also provide increasingly sophisticated weapons. Thus, future military clothing will need to accommodate new hazards as well as take advantage of new materials and equipment.

Conclusion

The topics covered in this chapter represent only the tip of the iceberg in terms of developments in enhancing and augmenting body functions using functional clothing. New technologies and new designs emerge daily. Exploring them using all of the principles covered in this and previous chapters should provide a rich source of inspiration for functional designers.

9 Commercial Product Development and Production

One of the most basic decisions a designer needs to make is how to put material together to give shape to a garment. There are many ways to do this: simple stitching; the application of a wide range of fasteners and fastening systems; or a variety of more permanent production methods, such as heat sealing and molding. As with every subject covered in this book, a thorough understanding of the user, the activity, and the nature of hazards in the environment is the key to choosing an appropriate way to turn a protective material into a garment that continues to provide that protection.

Garment Production Methods

Even though most consumers tend to assume all garments are stitched together, many items of protective clothing cannot be stitched. They must be formed using a variety of types of heat sealing or molding processes because the holes left by the stitching reduce their effectiveness. When stitching *is* used to form protective clothing, there are additional considerations that need to be made to ensure that the particular stitch type, stitch length, thread, and other factors are appropriate for the garment being produced.

This section will cover a variety of aspects of stitching; heat sealing processes such as ultrasonics, radio frequency sealing, and laser welding; and molding and heat shaping. Some of these processes will be appropriate for joining some materials and not others. Some processes will maintain the protection offered by the materials chosen for a garment and others will not. Designers need to understand the advantages and disadvantages of each production method in order to choose those that offer the best protection. It is important to understand the behavior of any hazard facing a user so that the proper material joining technique can be chosen for a specific end use.

STITCHING

The most familiar method of giving shape to clothing is to sew its parts together with stitching. This production process is so prevalent in the apparel industry that it may be largely taken for granted. However, the extreme demands placed on many items of protective clothing make many details of the stitching process critical for a designer to specify. Some of the factors that can be varied to change the effectiveness of a stitched seam are the seam type; the thread fiber and size; the needle size and type; and the number of stitches per inch. Because each manufacturer has different production equipment, final decisions on many of these issues are generally made by production personnel in consultation with the designer. At a minimum, however, the designer must be aware of the variations of the stitching process as one of the many factors that can literally make or break a garment.

Three aspects of a seam that are particularly important for protective clothing are its durability, its extensibility, and its permeability. Designers need to critically assess each design situation—the nature of the environment in which the garment will be used, the type of material used for the garment, and the stresses on seams during a typical user's movements—so that factors that could affect seam durability can be identified and addressed.

For example, seams in firefighting garments made of the aramid fiber, Nomex must be sewn with Nomex or another flame-resistant thread or the thread could burn away and the whole garment could come apart. A garment that will be subjected to great amounts of stress typically requires a strong fabric that will need to be sewn with a strong seam (i.e., using a strong thread, a durable seam type, and a sufficient number of stitches per inch to hold fabrics together without perforating them so that they tear too readily). A garment made of spandex and nylon stretch material will need to be sewn with a stretch stitch and thread that allows the seam to stretch to the same degree as the fabric. A strong, nonstretch seam might provide a durable joint for a stretch leotard, but without stretch in the seam, part of the garment is unable to function to allow full movement. In addition, when the fabric in a seam is stretchable and extends during movement, choosing a nonstretch seam type generally means that the seam will break during movement. To ignore the durability of the seams while carefully planning for the durability and function of the fabric and other features of the garment is to risk its failure.

National and international standards can be used to specify the type of stitch and seams used for a particular application. For example, Figure 9.1 shows one type of U.S. Federal Stitch Method and one Federal Seam Type. One criterion often used

FIGURE 9.1 (A) U.S. Federal Stitch Method 301; (B) U.S. Federal Seam Type LSc-2.

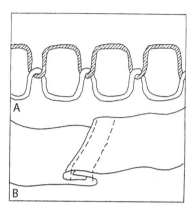

to assess the appropriateness of a method of seaming is to determine the point at which it fails. For most garments, stitching should break at levels of stress just slightly below those at which the material of the garment will tear. If the stitching breaks too easily, the garment will not be as durable as it could be. If, however, stitching is too strong, the fabric of the garment will tear before the stitching breaks, and the result will be a much more difficult and, in some cases, impossible, repair.

The same type of consideration is needed for permeability. It is important to use impermeable seams when impermeable fabrics are needed for protection. For less life-threatening situations, as in the case of rainwear, garments may be stitched and then an adhesive or thermoplastic tape can be laid over the areas that contain the needle holes and adhered or fused in place. This process is called a strapped seam stay (e.g., as for tuxedo pants or Adidas stripes placed on top of the side seam). A liquid seam sealer may also be used to fill in needle holes. Where any minute opening in a garment could prove hazardous to the wearer, an alternative production method called heat sealing is generally used.

HEAT SEALING

Heat sealing is the process of fusing two pieces of material together using heat to melt them and pressure to force the melted areas to combine and form a seal. Because the basic process depends on melting, there must be at least some thermoplastic element in the joint area. This element may be a plastic film like those used in raincoats or chemical/biological protective garments, or it may be a woven or knitted textile that contains a sufficient amount of thermoplastic manufactured fibers. Most sources recommend at least 60 percent thermoplastic fiber content, such as a 60 percent polyester/40 percent cotton-blend shirting, although fabrics with as little as 50 percent thermoplastic content have been joined with some heat-sealing processes. Sometimes, the thermoplastic element is simply a finish applied to the materials to be joined or a thermoplastic interfacing used between two layers of a natural fiber fabric.

There are a number of reasons why heat sealing has long been a mainstay of production in many functional clothing industries. First, heat sealing is an extremely strong method of joining materials such as films. Traditional sewing methods perforate films; in heat-sealing, the molecules of two films being joined melt and mingle into one unit, resulting in a seal that can be even stronger than the materials themselves.

Second, heat sealing is an extremely quick and simple method of production that requires minimal operator training. While the initial investment in heat-sealing equipment can be high, the gains in production efficiency can be enormous.

Third, heat sealing offers a unique advantage to many protective garments—the absence of needle holes. For garments that protect from toxic gases or suits used for the exploration of outer space, even the minute openings created by stitch holes would pose a serious threat to life. Heat sealing provides the safest and most secure, puncture-free joining method. This is critical for the development of inflatable garments and fluid-filled items found in medicine, sports, and recreation. Surgeons' gowns and facemasks that protect medical personnel from blood-borne pathogens are often heat-sealed. Heat sealing also forms leak-free seams that keep water and air out of many types of camping gear and rainwear.

Heat sealing can provide designers with exciting new potential for designs, but it also can force a change in the production process, and thus in the way designers proceed with their work. For example, most chemical/biological heat-sealed garments made of PVC film are *not* joined by laying right sides of garment pieces together as they are when seams are stitched. The most common seam type is a **pinch seam**, where two layers are laid wrong sides together and the seam is sealed so that the fabric edges (seam allowances) are on the *outside* of the garment (Figure 9.2A). Patterns for heat-sealed items generally include narrow seam allowances determined largely by the width of the seal and little if any width of fabric extends beyond the finished sealed area. With films, there is no raveling, so no seam finish is needed.

Having the seam allowances turned toward the outside rather than the inside as is generally done with fashion garments also makes the garments more comfortable against the skin. With the materials that are used for many protective garments, however, these seams may be stiff and present a

FIGURE 9.2 (A) A pinch seam; (B) a lapped seam.

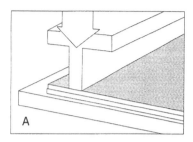

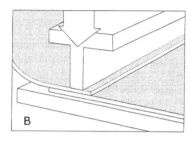

ridge on the outer surface of the garment. Therefore, some attention may need to be paid to where the seams lie so that they don't interfere with other items worn with the garment. For example, the width of pinch seals used to form a bootie on a chemical/biological suit must be considered as a factor in the wearer's ease of donning a protective overboot. Thus, designers of items like these may not only need to consider location but also to pay attention to how much excess material is needed to form a seam.

The other type of seam frequently used in heat sealing is the **lapped seam** (Figure 9.2B). Lapped seams are formed when the edges of the garment sections to be joined are laid over one another with one raw edge on the outside and one on the inside of the garment. This produces a flatter seam area and reduces the possibility that the seam will peel open when stress is placed on it as can be true for a pinch seam. Lapped seams may be more difficult

to achieve for some configurations, but in others, they may make the joining process considerably simpler. Some heat-sealing operations cut and edge-seal garment parts as well. Pinch and lapped seams, especially when they are accompanied by cutting and edge sealing, can produce mass-manufactured forms that would be prohibitive with traditional cutting, stitching, trimming, turning, and pressing methods.

A common problem for a designer of heat-sealed garments is that it is difficult to seal more than two layers of a material together. This makes sense if one considers the difficulty of directing the same amount of energy to multiple thicknesses and interfaces at once. However, what this means for the designer is that details such as darts, tucks, pleats, gathers, and easing must, in most cases, be eliminated from designs. This adds to the difficulty of developing garments that will conform to the human body, especially when it is in motion. When more than two layers of material come together, as they may at the crotch, or the neck seam at the shoulder when a hood is joined to a suit, one solution for chemical/biological protective garments has been to place a reinforcement patch over the point where seams meet (Figure 9.3).

Designers must constantly explore the production machinery available to be certain that the details of a proposed design can be executed. Both ease of production and the security of the joint achieved in the final product need to be considered. Curved seams, for example, are harder to execute unless both pieces being joined contain identical curves that can be laid over one another and joined with a pinch seam. Tight curves or angles that add major amounts of shaping to a garment may be impossible to achieve if lapped seam techniques are being used.

FIGURE 9.3 A reinforcement patch sealed to an area where more than two seams come together.

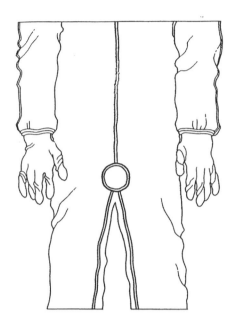

Another factor that is critical to the end user, and thus designers must keep in mind, is that heat-sealed garments cannot be altered. There are no seam allowances, and once a seam is sealed, the physical structure of the joined materials is changed. They cannot simply be separated. This often means that sizing and fitting details on garments must be carefully considered.

Despite the limitations placed on designers by the technology itself, a number of unique design features are made possible by heat sealing. For example, heat sealing allows waterproof areas to be directly applied to impermeable clothing, not just for protection from inclement weather, but for a variety of functional reasons (see Figure 5.38 (map pocket) and Figure 8.24). Electronic components, battery-operated lights, medical monitoring equipment, and other items can be sealed into

impermeable patches on clothing. Emergency rations and medical supplies can be sealed into survival clothing where they will be protected from water. Gels and other impact-protective materials can be sealed directly into washable form-fitted protective clothing. There is endless potential for creative approaches to development of heat-sealed apparel. (See Figure 9.4.)

Because materials respond in different ways to heat, there are a number of types of heat sealing. In general, they are identified according to the way in which heat is generated and directed toward the materials to be joined.

Thermal Welding

In **thermal welding** (sometimes called contact heating), a heated tool is lowered onto the materials to be joined. Industrial thermal welding takes only a short time, generally from one to four seconds. Iron-on interfacings and fabric repair patches used by home sewers are thermally welded

FIGURE 9.4 A collar made of live plants. Heat sealing makes possible the enclosure of liquids in garments. This collar contains a series of vinyl vases that support the growth of a living garment.

to garments using an iron. Retailers of custom t-shirts use small thermal welding systems to add designs to shirts while the customer waits. Many manufacturers attach labels to their garments using thermal welding. Often, small thermal welders that fit in the hand (Figure 9.5) are used as a form of *basting*—to tack layers of thermoplastic materials together to prepare them for production.

A variation of thermal welding is **hot air welding**. Heat is delivered to fabrics with a blast of hot air. Both heated tools and hot air welders are available in a variety of sizes and shapes. In the apparel industry, larger thermal welders use devices such as rollers to apply heat and pressure. Teflon conveyor belts are used to carry multiple garment parts along so that welding can occur continuously.

Radio-Frequency Sealing

Thermal welding is not always a successful means for joining many of the thermoplastics used in apparel because so many of these materials do not conduct heat. In thicker, more protective and durable fabrics and films, the materials themselves actually function to insulate the seal area. Thermal welding may cause some melting on the outer surface; however, the interface, where melting is really needed, isn't affected at all. Therefore, most heat-sealed garments are manufactured using radio-frequency waves or ultrasonics. The goal for both of these types of sealing is to effect melting of the materials where they interface. Figure 9.6 shows what happens when either of these sealing methods is applied to materials. The energy directed at the seam produces heat at the interface, melting the interface surfaces. Pressure on the melted material then forces them to merge, creating a seal.

FIGURE 9.5 A hand-held thermal welder.

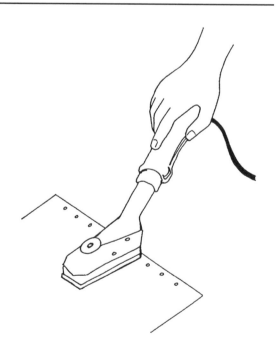

FIGURE 9.6 Heat sealing. When heat is directed toward materials to seal them, the interface of the material melts together so that the resulting joint is permanent. (A) Tool directing energy to seal; (B) two layers of fabric to be sealed (C) heat sealed area or 'seam'; (D) base of heat sealer or platen.

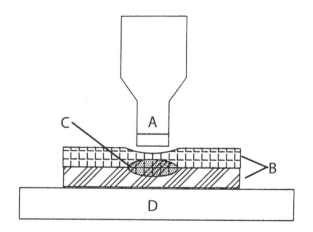

Radio-frequency (RF) sealing, sometimes called *dielectric sealing*, is frequently used in the manufacturing of protective apparel because it provides the most effective stimulus for many impermeable materials such as polyvinyl chloride that are used for a variety of protective garments.

The RF sealing process begins with radio waves being directed toward the materials to be joined through a pair of electrodes: a live electrode (a **die** or metal bar in the shape of the desired seal) and a ground electrode (generally a flat plate called a platen or bed). Most RF sealers place these two electrodes in a hydraulic or pneumatic press that uses a **plunge welding** technique (Figure 9.7). The garment sections to be joined are laid on the bed, and the press lowers the metal die down onto the garment. As the press plunges the die down onto the garment, the live electrode is activated, and in a single stroke the seal is made. The press then lifts again to be ready for the next weld.

The total area that can be sealed is dependent on the capacity and size of the press. Unlike a sewing machine, which rolls continuously over an area to be joined, a plunge-welding press seals only in the area of the die. On a long seam, once each seal is completed, the operator must then move the garment into position to seal the next portion of the seam. Dies are made in many shapes, each made to achieve a specific seal (Figure 9.8). Sometimes, dies are a part of the press and sometimes they are separate structures. Mounted dies are almost always used in assembly lines for rectilinear products such as notebook covers and product packaging. Both mounted and separate dies are used for the production of apparel, depending on the seal needed. Separate dies are used when several different shapes of seals are needed in sequence or where the seal needs to be precisely placed on a complex shape (Figure 9.9). For example, if one

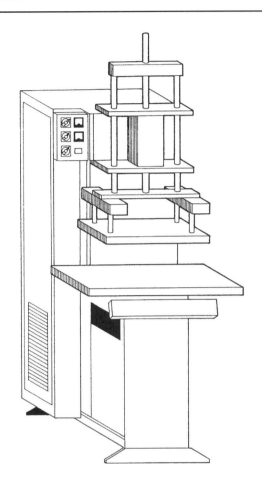

FIGURE 9.7 A radio-frequency (RF) press or plunge welder.

seam requires a combination of both straight and curved lines, it may be simpler for one operator to place a straight die on a garment, seal that area, and then move the garment into position for sealing with the curved die, rather than passing the garment on to another operator or changing a die mounted on the machine. Typical dies range from about ½ to 2 inches (1.3 to 5.1 cm) or so in depth. This depth is primarily for ease of use by the press operator. The depth of the die is sometimes planned to allow room for the fingers to hold a die

FIGURE 9.8 Dies for an RF sealer.

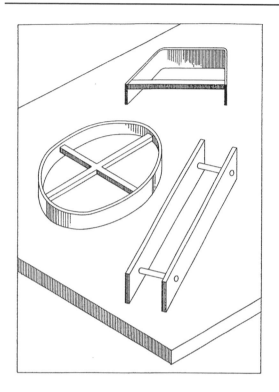

To a great extent, manufacturers judge the quality of a seal by examining the appearance of the **bead**—the melted plastic that flows away from the die on either side of the seal (Figure 9.10). On a machine where a shaped die and a flat bed are used, the bead appears only on the top surface. Except on the thinnest of materials, all heat-sealed products should contain a well-formed bead. Too little beading may indicate that not enough energy and/or pressure were used and therefore not enough of the molecules in each layer have mingled to create an effective seal. Excessive beading can indicate that too much pressure and/or energy was used, and that so much material has melted and flowed away from the die that it has created a thin, weak area or a burn. The combination of energy, pressure, and time needed to form an effective seal may need to be determined for each material for each size and configuration of die. In

FIGURE 9.9 An RF press with a separate die.

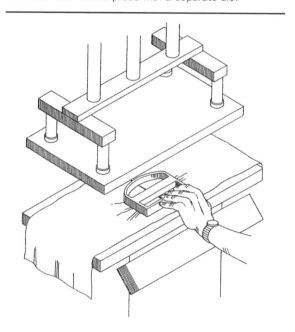

into place while the press is slowly lowered down toward it before the RF energy is applied.

The quality of an RF seal depends on three things: the amount of RF *energy* delivered to the die, the *pressure* used, and the *time* period over which the energy and pressure are applied. These three factors are generally programmed into a press and must be in good balance for an effective, stable seal. In most cases, manufacturers want to keep the time needed for a seal as short as possible to speed up production, so they may want an operator to work at top power and pressure so that the time needed for the seal can be short. However, the critical decision-making factor is the condition under which the most secure and durable seal can be made.

FIGURE 9.10 A cross section of a bead (b) formed during heat sealing. (A) Die; (B) two layers of materials to be sealed; (C) platen.

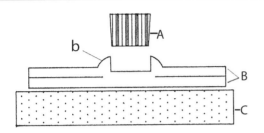

addition to subjective evaluations of the appearance of the seal, traditional methods for testing the tensile strength of materials are used to test the strength of the seal. Final garments are also tested, especially those used for hazardous environments. Items such as impermeable chemical/biological protective suits, for example, are fully inflated over an extended period of time so that any air leaks or other weaknesses in the seals can be detected.

Ultrasonics

Another method of supplying heat to a seal area is with ultrasonics. **Ultrasonics** are vibrations that are beyond humans' normal hearing range. In ultrasonic welding, these high-frequency vibrations are used to cause fabrics to melt and fuse together.

Figure 9.11 shows the essential components of ultrasonic welding equipment. Basically, electrical energy is converted into mechanical energy that results in vibrations at ultrasound frequencies. These vibrations are then modified and focused on the specific parts being joined by what is called

a **horn**. The tip of the horn is placed on the surface of the top fabric to be joined, and the bottom fabric lies against an anvil, much like the platen or bed of the RF sealer. The vibrations cause heat to be generated at the *interface* of the two materials—their surfaces melt and form a permanent molecular bond. (See Figure 9.6.) All of this may occur in less than one second. As is true for any type of sealing, fabrics that contain primarily thermoplastic fibers are used, and the balance of the amount of energy, the length of time for the seal, and the amount of pressure are all critical to the success of a seal.

Most ultrasonic seals are not even attempted when thermoplastic fibers constitute less than 50 percent of the material. Even though manufacturers claim good success when fabrics have about 65 percent or more thermoplastic fibers, the most effective ultrasonic bonds tend to occur with materials containing greater than 65 percent thermoplastic components. If the equipment is set properly for the specific material being sealed, the ultrasonic seals achieved are generally considered to be from 75 to 80 percent as

FIGURE 9.11 The components of an ultrasonic sealer. Electrical energy is fed through (A) a power supply into a (B) converter, which converts electrical energy into the mechanical energy of vibrations at ultrasound frequencies. These vibrations then pass through a (C) booster that modifies the vibration to the proper amplitude before they reach the (D) horn. The horn then increases the amplitude of the vibrations and focuses them on the materials to be joined.

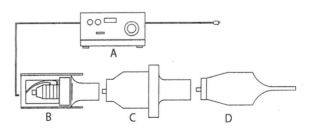

strong as the materials being sealed. If nonthermoplastic materials are used, they must first be coated with an adhesive that can be stimulated by ultrasonics or a separate strip of adhesive material may be laid between the two fabrics. A thermoplastic interfacing placed between two layers of cotton, for example, may serve as the sealing surface. The key to the success of these efforts lies in the ability of the added material to adhere firmly to both materials being joined and to resist degradation itself.

An ultrasonic sealer is often smaller than an RF sealer. However, the sealing process may appear quite similar, with a plunge welding press that completes a seal in a single plunge of the horn. When garment seams are formed with ultrasonics, they are generally lap seams or pinch seams (see Figure 9.2) with little or no seam allowance. For fashion garments, several horns are often lined up next to one another over a single bed so that details such as buttonholes on a shirt placket can all be made at once (Figure 9.12). Ultrasonics can also be used to seal the outer edges of complex curves such as those found on pocket flaps and cuffs or achieve a smooth, bulk-free slit on a neckline or sleeve placket (Figure 9.13). This eliminates the need for cutting, sewing, trimming, turning, and pressing. The elimination of thread from the joining process, the time saved in construction processes like these, the lack of sewing skill needed, and the lack of bulk with the elimination of seam allowances are all benefits of using ultrasonics.

Some ultrasonic sealers have a rotary die in the bed of the machine, so that sealing takes place not in just a single stamp or 'plunge' but more in the manner of a sewing machine (Figure 9.14). These rotary dies are called **stitching wheels**. They allow continuous sealing in the same pattern so that one

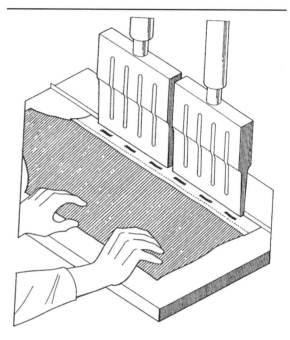

FIGURE 9.12 Multiple horns can be set up so that a series of operations can take place in one plunge weld. This operation is forming six buttonholes in a single plunge.

long seam can be sealed by running it through the machine. A single stitching wheel contains a pattern that is repeated over and over again, but the patterns may differ from wheel to wheel (Figure 9.15). For example, the width of the seal and the number of seals per wheel may vary. The seals may progress at intervals or appear in different shapes such as zigzagging. Wheels may contain intricate patterns that appear as embossing on a variety of items from fashion apparel to blanket bindings.

Widths of fabrics such as those used for bedspreads or quilted garments are often quilted together using a rolling stitching wheel called a

FIGURE 9.13 An ultrasonic plunge welder. (A) Sealing a facing to a slit at the bodice front; (B) the completed seal (shown on the inside of the garment) cuts and finishes the edge and is more durable at the point than most sewn seams.

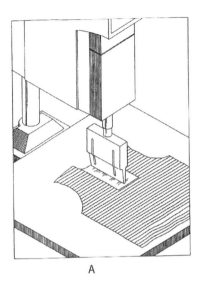

A

B

FIGURE 9.14 The dotted lines show the position of a stitching wheel or rotary die in the base of an ultrasonic sealer.

FIGURE 9.15 Stitching wheels.

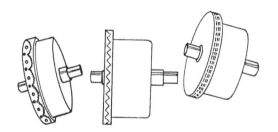

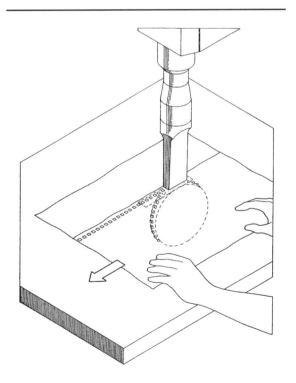

drum. Figure 9.16 shows one example of this type of operation. In this procedure, several horns are lined up next to one another over the drum. Each of the raised pins on the drum serves as a contact points for a horn. Whole bolts of fabrics, then, run continuously through this in an extremely quick, secure joining process.

Ultrasonics may also be used to slit or cut wide fabrics into narrower ones. A braid or a single layer

FIGURE 9.16 Multiple horns in position over a rolling drum to produce ultrasonically quilted material for items such as coats, mattress pads, and bedspreads.

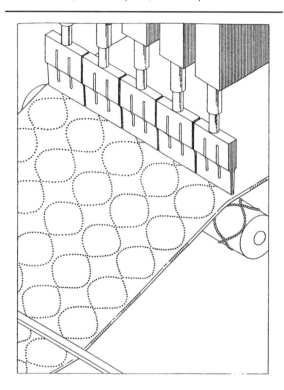

of fabric made of a thermoplastic fiber runs past single or multiple rolling anvils that cut and seal the raw edges of the resulting narrower strips or ribbons.

Many waterproof products that are sewn have their seams taped with an impermeable film that is heat sealed directly over the stitching line. Tape sealers look much like a sewing machine that is set up with a roll of tape rather than a spool of thread. Energy on these machines is directed to the seam area by means of a roller, which also provides pressure, forcing the melting tape material into the stitch holes in the sewn seam. Tape may also be used to reinforce the seams in heat-sealed garments.

For example, parts of soft space suit sections were heat-sealed and then that seal was doubly reinforced by heat sealing an impermeable tape over each seam.

Laser Welding

Fabrics may also be joined using lasers. Laser welding involves a noncontact heating process in which a laser beam is directed at the materials being joined. One of the advantages of lasers is that they can focus energy very precisely, melting thermoplastic materials in specific areas.

Although dies are not used, much of the process used for laser welding is similar to ultrasonic welding: Fabrics must contain a certain amount of thermoplastic material. Pinch and lapped seams are used, and fabrics pass under the laser beam in a sewing machine that uses a rotary system similar to the one in Figure 9.14. Like other forms of heat sealing, it is problematic to use features such as pleats or gathers or join more than two layers.

The transmission of the laser beam through to the lower layer of fabric is critical. The color of fabrics and any additives or finishes, particularly on the upper fabric layer closest to the laser is a factor in whether or not materials can be joined with laser welding. Materials must first be prepared by applying an infrared absorber to them. These substances are either dispersed throughout the lower layer of the two fabrics to be joined or applied at the interface between two materials. Even though black substances would absorb infrared beams most readily, because of aesthetics, a clear substance has been developed for use with clothing materials. In order to achieve a seal while the materials are melted, the fabric layers must either be clamped together or placed on a vacuum table.

In addition to welding, lasers are frequently used in decorative applications, burning out holes to make eyelet patterns or fusing fibers to created textured effects.

MOLDING AND HEAT SHAPING

Molding is a production process that can form garments with little or no seaming. It is essentially the process of changing the shape of a plastic material by softening it with heat; forcing it into, under, or around a mold; cooling it until it is no longer at a moldable temperature and removing it in its heat-shaped form from the mold (Figure 9.17).

Molding is used to make many rigid items of protective clothing such as helmets and the rigid portions of protective padding. It may be used for flexible materials like the nylon, knit-covered closed-cell foam of the chest protector shown in Figure 9.18 or in rubber gloves and boots. It is also used to form permanent shapes in sections of fashion items such as seamless bra cups or shaped heels in stockings.

There are many different molding processes, among them: **blow molding**, where air pressure is used to expand a tube of plastic into a shape such as a milk container and **injection** or **compression molding** (Figure 9.17), where material is pushed by a shaped die into a heated mold and pressure is applied. Many fabrics and films are molded using **vacuum forming**, a molding process that involves drawing a heated, softened film onto the surface of a perforated mold using the force of a vacuum behind the mold. When porous fabrics are used, a nonporous film may be placed over the fabric being molded in order to seal the system against loss of vacuum.

When thermoplastic textile fabrics are heated, formed and then cooled (i.e., heat-set), into various shapes, they are often referred to as heat molded

FIGURE 9.17 Compression molding. (A) the plastic (p) to be formed is placed in or on one part of the mold and heated; (B) male and female sections of the mold are pressed together and the liquid plastic flows into the space between them to create the finished shape (S).

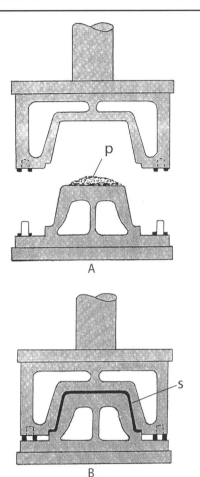

or **heat shaped** (Clarke and O'Mahoney 2005, 79–83). Heat shaping may also be used to give three-dimensional surface texture to garments and decorative effects to fabrics (Haar 2011).

The simplest method of molding would be to spray material right on the body (Figure 9.19). Indeed, since the 1970s, there have been a number of projects aimed at developing processes for spraying fibers directly onto manikins or directly onto human bodies and heat setting them to form molded garments (Fabrican "What Is Fabrican?").

The biggest advantage of molded products is also their biggest drawback—they retain their shape. If that shape is not the wearer's shape, little can be done. Because they have no seams, molded products cannot be altered unless they are remolded. In terms of wearing apparel, this means that loose garments incorporating gentle curves tend to be more successful than those that are tightly shaped and fitted to the body, unless the garments can be custom molded. However, this ability to take on and retain shape holds some extremely exciting possibilities for complex garment configurations that could not be achieved with traditional stitched seams. It also has the potential to reduce seaming in protective garments and thus reduce both production costs and the risk of garment penetration.

Efforts to put molded garments on the market began as far back as the 1950s. Early attempts were somewhat hampered by sophistication of the molding technology and consumer attitudes toward thermoplastic fibers, which pass in and out of favor. In a number of European countries, men's pants shaped by molding have been relatively common at times. Tubes of knitted fabric are pulled over a pants molding form, hip curves and leg shape are set in the fabric and the crotch seams, fasteners, and waistband are completed with traditional sewing techniques. In the early 1990s, Stern developed a molding process that could create a t-shirt in under 30 seconds

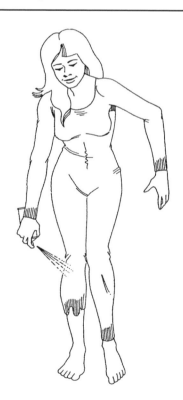

FIGURE 9.19 Forming a garment by spraying fibers directly on the body.

FIGURE 9.18 A molded chest protector. Stretch fabric containing Lycra® is sealed to closed-cell foam as it is being molded in the form of the protector so that no sewing is needed to form the segments on the protector.

including the time needed to pull materials into the mold and release it. In this type of process, bust and shoulder curves could be put into the mold, and any necessary seams could be sealed with heat at the same time as the molding took place (Figure 9.20). The molding of complete garments using either a thermoplastic dope or fibers eliminates the production tasks of spreading fabric, cutting, bundling, sewing, finishing of raw edges and pressing. Despite these advantages for the manufacturer, relatively very few molded garments are on the market. Custom molded garments could become more prevalent if molding devices were linked to body scanners or computer programs containing individual body contours as well as measurements. As molding technologies are refined, they offer unlimited possibilities for unique protective clothing.

Another method of creating a three-dimensional shape from a polymer material is by 3-D printing. The most common type of 3-D printing works much like squeezing glue out of a glue gun. The printer lays down successive layers of a tiny bead of polymer to build up a 3-D shape. For complex shapes, a temporary material may also be used to support fine details or protrusions as the shape is being developed. This material is then removed after the shape is complete.

Three-dimensional printing is most commonly used to prototype objects that would later be manufactured by processes such as injection molding, because it doesn't require the creation of expensive molds. However, 3-D printing can also be used to build complex structures, such as interlinked rings or chain mail (made of polymers), which would otherwise be difficult or complex to create.

FIGURE 9.20 A machine for molding a blouse. (A) A dress form is heated and fabric is rolled up on either side of it; (B) inflated bags push the fabric toward the form and hold it in place until molding is achieved; (C) after edges are cut and sealed, shoulder and side seams are sealed with a heat sealer, the blouse is ready to be peeled off the form and worn. *(Concept: Joann Boles)*

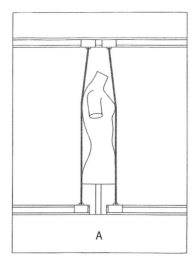
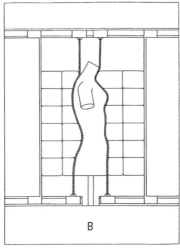

Garment Assembly Processes

The decisions a designer makes about materials and methods used to produce a garment affect the production process in significant ways. Each production method discussed in the previous section has different requirements in terms of how materials are manipulated and fastened together to form a 3-D garment. Within the requirements imposed by a particular production method, the designer's decisions about the order in which operations occur and the specific operations performed have distinct effects on the quality, aesthetics, and functionality of the resulting garment. The integration of other systems, many of which are non-textile (such as tubing or electronic circuits), may also require the production process to be adapted to meet the requirements of these additional systems.

It is important to note that assembly processes in larger-scale production are often different than those used in the production of a single garment or developmental prototype. Similarly, processes and strategies used in home sewing or crafting are often dramatically different than the requirements of mass production. For example, a home sewer often produces a garment by first assembling the major pieces (the body) and then finishing and embellishing the resulting garment by adding hems, pockets, surface embellishments, and trims. In mass production, this process is often reversed: embellishments and even hems are often sewn before body pieces are assembled into a full garment.

CUT-AND-SEWN PROCESSES

Cutting shaped pieces from a rectangular length of textile and sewing them together is the most basic definition of *cut-and-sewn*. However, the particulars of this approach apply to most types of seaming, not just seams made by stitching. The processes described earlier in this chapter such as thermal welding or adhesive seaming can also be used to attach pieces in a cut-and-sewn process.

Cut-and-sewn assembly requires strategic planning for two reasons: first, because some processes must take place before other processes and, second, because it is important to increase the efficiency of the assembly process to reduce labor costs. Because most apparel assembly is still done manually by skilled workers, labor costs are a significant portion of the finished product price.

Before a textile is cut, it is typically spread on a cutting table, many plies deep. A *marker*, or piece layout, is laid on top of the multi-ply fabric, and pieces are cut using a knife, die, or laser. During cutting, placement markings for internal embellishments are marked onto the cut pieces. This is usually done by drilling through the plies to make a small hole or by marking each piece with chalk (if a drill hole would compromise the integrity of the finished garment). Pieces are then bundled and sent to the sewing operator to begin the sewing process.

Assembly process planning follows a few basic rules. Trims and embellishments that are attached to only one piece and do not cross any seams are attached first, before the piece is sewn to other pieces. These might typically include things like patch pockets and embroidery details but in functional garments may also be things like ports for attaching hardware. The order of operations is arranged to preserve a flat position of the piece or garment as long as possible. For example, a shirt sleeve may be hemmed and sewn to the body of the garment before the garment side seam and sleeve underarm seam are sewn. In that way, both the sleeve and the garment body stay flat as long as possible. Flat pieces are easier to manipulate and are less prone to being wrinkled or distorted when they are piled. Subassemblies, such as collars or cuffs, may be completed in a parallel process (which also follows the principles of attaching single-piece embellishments first and preserving the flat position as long as possible) and attached to the body of the garment at the appropriate time. Finally, embellishments that must cross seams are integrated into the production process at the most optimal time, again adhering to the principle of maintaining piece flatness. In some cases, embellishments are applied to a fully assembled garment, especially in cases where the embellishment must cross many seams. Processes for surface treatments like embroidery and screen printing are common enough that they can be completed using machinery optimized for fully assembled garments but often are limited to very specific garment shapes and locations.

Preserving flatness is very important to the efficiency of garment production: An awkward process that requires an operator to apply a difficult embellishment to a finished garment can easily double the cost of production. However, many functional garments require that an auxiliary system cross seams or be applied to a fully assembled garment. For example, a smart garment that requires an embedded inertial sensor at the wrist to be connected to a processing and power unit at the waist may require two or more seam crossings. It is often not possible to stitch a conductive thread or adhere a cable on the surface of a closed (3-D, tubular) sleeve. Therefore, the conductor and inertial sensor must be applied before the sleeve underarm seam is sewn or be woven into or attached to the fabric before any seams are sewn. If the latter approach is taken, the two parts of the conductor must make an electrical connection across the seam. Strategic design of both the system and the process can allow these conflicting needs to be balanced.

FULL-FASHIONED PROCESSES

The term "full-fashioned" is used to describe garment pieces knitted in their final shape with all edges finished rather than being cut in a length of knit material. Full-fashioned pieces, often found in hosiery or sweaters, can be assembled more easily since there is less danger of runs or raveling edges during production. Full-fashioning reduces waste by forming only the material that is needed.

Most full-fashioned garments are made by knitting, with a machine programed to add and remove stitches from subsequent rows of the developing piece as a human knitter would do. In contrast to the traditional flat full-fashioned pieces, modern technologies can produce full 3-D garments without the need for cutting and sewing. These technologies expand on the circular knitting machine by allowing stitches to be inserted and removed from successive rows of a circular knit as the knit is formed. Technologies like 3-D printing or sprayable fabrics (see Figure 9.19) also allow garments to be fully formed in three dimensions with little waste.

Another advantage to full-fashioned processes is the ability to lay in additional (often nontextile) components as the garment is formed. For example, a 3-D printer can form conduits or surface textures as the garment is produced, eliminating the need to add in tubing or apply a finish. A 3-D knitted garment production process can insert electrical pathways as the garment is knitted. This eliminates the need to plan for seam crossings in the finished garment.

Fastening Systems

Because a number of elements usually work together in the joining of garment parts, it is more logical to think of garments as being joined by a *fastening system* rather than simply by a *fastener*. A fastening system in apparel is a group of functionally related elements that work together to join parts of a garment. A fastener, then, is a single part of that system, such as a zipper, a button and buttonhole, or a safety pin.

Three of the most basic purposes of fastening systems are

1. To form a closure or an enclosure, whether its purpose is to secure a garment around the body, to close a garment feature such as a pocket, or to close an accessory or attach it to a garment.
2. To change the shape of a garment or adjust it to fit multiple sizes.
3. To change a garment's configuration (to rearrange the position of garment segments)

The choice of a fastening system for a garment is one of the most significant choices a designer has to make. The success of a design can be influenced to a great extent by the attention given to fastening systems when a design is in its *early* conceptual stages. A simple change in a fastening system can turn an unimaginative design into a truly innovative one. Fasteners are often the critical elements that determine whether or not a garment functions. They not only control how well a garment works but also affect a garment's shape and appearance. If a fastener fails, a garment is often, at least temporarily, unusable.

A fastening system is often the part of a garment the wearer most directly manipulates. Other aspects of the garment such as its cut or textile components are more likely to remain in the state or configuration that the designer specifies, but the wearer interacts with the fastening system. This direct interaction introduces new design variables: Will the wearer understand how to use the fastening system? Will the wearer don the garment or need assistance? Are there areas of the garment where openings need to be avoided? Will physical impairments or the bulk and stiffness of the garment limit a wearer's ability to reach and operate fasteners? Does the user have limited dexterity or vision or need to manipulate fasteners while wearing gloves or a facemask? Is the speed of donning and doffing critical?

These questions reinforce the idea that, as with the design of any aspect of a garment, it is important to start by identifying and understanding users. This guide to fastening systems, however, is not organized by users but by a series of fundamental variables that underlie the fastening system. Some of the most unique and well-planned fastening systems are developed, not by applying typical solutions for one user but by reaching across fields to look for similar problems and applying design concepts from one field to another. For example, those planning an adjustable fastening system for a total enclosure suit, where thick gloves are often worn, can find many applicable concepts by looking at solutions that have been developed for those with limited dexterity, such as those for people with disabilities or infirmities.

FASTENING SYSTEM VARIABLES

The process of gathering information about the user, the environment, and the activities in which the user is engaged while exploring the preceding questions uncovers a number of variables with which designers need to familiarize themselves. Among these are

- the dexterity, reach and handedness of the user;
- the force a user is able to exert to operate fasteners in a variety of locations and orientations in terms of both the user's capabilities and the interaction of the body and the garments worn; and
- the strength, security, and permeability or impermeability required of fasteners in the environment and for the activities of the wearer.

With these in mind, designers then need to explore options for the following:

- the location of openings;
- the length of openings;
- fasteners that meet the needs of the user, the environment, and the activity; and
- operating procedures for fastening systems that can be easily perceived and understood by the wearer (or an aide assisting the wearer) in the context of use.

In most cases, the decisions that need to be made about each of these variables are so interdependent that it is difficult to make them separately or plan the order in which they will be made. It is useful to explore as many options for each of these decisions as possible and then use some of the idea development techniques discussed in Chapter 1 to generate alternative ways to combine ideas.

FASTENER OPTIONS

Even though most people think of zippers or buttons when they hear the word *fastener*, there are literally hundreds of fasteners. For each of these, there may be hundreds if not thousands of variations. Some fasteners rely on mechanical forces; others rely on adhesion. Fasteners may achieve a permanent joint or a temporary one. Traditional fasteners such as zippers and buttons may provide the best fastening solution in some situations, while more unique fasteners such as those involving magnetism or biological elements (e.g., clothes that grow together) may provide the key to an innovative design for another situation.

Table 9.1 lists some of the characteristics that may be needed in a fastener, and Table 9.2 provides a list of some of the basic fasteners that can be part of a fastening system. These lists are not meant to be all-inclusive but only to provide a base for the exploration of fasteners and the purposes they serve.

TABLE 9.1 Functional Characteristics of Fasteners

abrasiveness	flexibility
adjustability	heat/cold resistance
appearance	launderability
bulk	noise created by operation
chemical resistance	permanence
comfort	quickness of operation
cost	resistance to pressure
durability	resistance to snagging
ease of application to garment	sealability to air/water
ease of operation	strength
ease of repair in field	water/dirt/corrosion resistance
flammability	weight

TABLE 9.2 Examples of Fasteners

adhesives	lacing
buckles	magnets
buttons/buttonholes	none (design without)
buttons/loops	pins
clips	rigid bearing rings
cord lock devices	rivets
D-rings	rubber rings
extruded zippers	slide fasteners (zippers)
fusion	snaps
garters	staples
hook-and-loop tape	stitching
hooks and eyes	ties
hooks and rings	toggles

Each of the fasteners in Table 9.2 may be produced in many different materials. For example, hook-and-loop tape might be produced in lightweight, flexible nylon, metal, or rigid plastic. It may be backed with an adhesive or produced on a tape to be sewn in place. It may contain standard hooks or mushroom-shaped projections that alter both the strength and the sound of opening and closing the fastener (3M "3M™ Dual Lock™"). It may be sewn flat around all edges of a tape or on one edge or down the center. (See Figure 9.21.) One variation contains both hooks and loops on the same tape so that the tape can be looped through a D-ring and joined to itself.

In addition to being offered in a variety of materials, each fastener may be offered in slight design variations that can better meet the needs of users. The shirt button shown in Figure 9.22 was made with an indentation designed to hold a headphone cable in place. The separating zipper shown in Figure 9.23 was made with a small extension at the end of the insertion tab. This little projection was designed to help keep the tab from sliding out of

FIGURE 9.22 A shirt button designed with an indentation that holds a headphone cord. *(Shapeways)*

place as the zipper was being started. This would be helpful for anyone, but is particularly useful for individuals attempting to close a separating zipper with one hand.

Designers often become so accustomed to a specific fastener that they may not even consider others that might better solve a design problem. Designers can test their tendency to rely primarily on one or two basic fasteners by trying a brief experiment. Once a design problem is identified, several atypical fasteners can be chosen from the list in Table 9.2, and solutions that incorporate each of those fasteners can be sketched. Each may require a different garment formation or a different location and length of opening to be successful. Some may require additional fasteners to be used

FIGURE 9.21 Applying a hook-and-loop tape by sewing it down the center rather than around its edges as a way of allowing it to take more stress before opening.

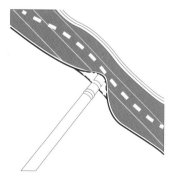

FIGURE 9.23 A separating zipper with a locking tab developed for one-handed operation. *(Talon, Inc.)*

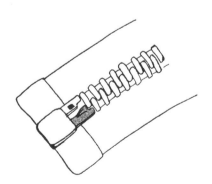

in combination with them. Experimenting with new fastener combinations often uncovers a solution that can change the entire approach to a design problem leading to a far more successful end product.

Many fastener choices for protective clothing will be covered as the process of creating fastening systems is discussed. Three characteristics of fasteners that are often of key importance to protective clothing are the force needed to operate a fastener, fastener strength, and the impermeability of fasteners and fastening systems.

Operating Force

The amount of force needed to open and close a fastener has a great impact on how easy or difficult the closure will be to operate. This force, however, must be explored in the context of use. There is a lot of variability in the amount of operating force required by various fasteners. For example, think of the difference between opening a pocket with a magnetic flap closure and the same pocket with a heavy snap closure. However, there can also be a lot of variability in the required operating force between fasteners of the same type (e.g., both magnets and snaps come in a wide variety of strengths).

Some of the forces influencing the operation of a fastener are:

- The frictional forces between the hand or device operating the closure and the closure itself (using a textured zipper tab to make grasping the zipper pull easier);
- The direction of the force applied and its relationship to the anatomy of the body (closing a snap at the wrist vs. closing a snap on the shoulder blade);
- The availability of opposing forces to keep a garment in place while force is applied to the fastener (zipping up a loose fitting coat with one hand versus zipping a jumpsuit, where the restriction at the crotch exerts an opposing pull); and
- The mechanical, magnetic, or adhesive forces between the components of a fastener (is a buttonhole large enough so the button can slide in easily or small enough so that it cannot slide out easily?).

In some cases, the operating force required to separate fasteners can be vastly different depending on design choices, such as the way they are placed on a garment. For example, hook-and-loop fasteners are much stronger when force is applied perpendicular to the joining surface than when they are 'peeled' apart. (See Figure 9.21.) Understanding where forces are present in the garment and orienting the fastener in the most appropriate direction can help ensure a good fastening system design.

Strength and Security

For many occupations, fail-safe fasteners are critical. It is important to understand the conditions under which a fastener will be used and then choose one that is sufficiently strong and unaffected chemically and physically by those conditions. A break in a fastener may be due to weakness in the material that forms the fastener itself or because it is weakened by specific hazards in the environment.

A fastener can fail at its own closure or at the joint between the fastener and the garment. It is especially important to consider the strength of the joint between a fastener and a material that must be heat sealed. These fasteners must be able to be heat sealed to a garment by the same method and at the same level of power as the material of the garment. Both the conditions of use and the processes needed for cleaning need to be considered. Even in fashion garments, it is important to know, for example, that fasteners chosen for a garment that is machine washed and dried can themselves survive those cleaning procedures.

Most fasteners are available in a wide range of strengths. Zipper teeth, snaps, and hook-and-loop fasteners can be made from metal or various plastics in a wide range of strengths and thicknesses. Buttons can be sewn on with a variety of strengths of thread—from light polyester to thick button and carpet repair thread. Or they can be attached by machine with a plastic fastener. Just as seam strength should be just slightly less than the strength of the fabric the seam joins, it is important that the attachment of a fastener be just slightly less strong than the garment to which it is attached. If a fastener breaks away from a garment, it can be put back on; if part of a garment tears off when the fastener attachment is stressed, it results in a more difficult and costly repair. Often, it is possible to reinforce the garment in the area of fastener attachment. For example, the thread attaching a button can pass through the holes of a second button sewn on the inside of a garment. This way, when the button is pulled, the most localized strain is on the

inside button rather than the fabric of the garment (Figure 9.24) .Interfacing or other strong materials are often added to garment openings so that they can bear some of the stress placed on fasteners.

Impermeability

One of the most difficult problems in designing clothing for hazardous environments is providing a means of getting in and out of an impermeable protective garment. Designers of clothing for hazardous environments must be aware of the characteristics of fasteners as well as alternative fastening systems for these complex garments.

One of the simplest ways to deal with this problem is to avoid fasteners altogether by sealing a wearer into a suit after it is donned and cutting them out of the suit when it is ready to be doffed. (See Figure 9.47) Sealing or taping people into garments, however, is a process used primarily for disposable suits. Many impermeable items are simply too expensive to be disposed of after one use.

There are three types of fasteners that are most frequently used for impermeable garments: waterproof, airtight zippers; extruded zippers; and rigid locking rings. Airtight zippers (Figure 9.25) are generally composed of metal teeth set in a rubber

FIGURE 9.24 Methods of attaching buttons.

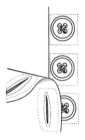
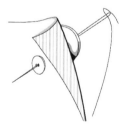

FIGURE 9.25 Sealing out liquids and gases. (A) An O.E.B.® (Omni-Environment Barrier) slide fastener with metal teeth that clamp rubber sealing surfaces together; (B) a cross section of the zipper-sealing mechanism. *(Talon, Inc.)*

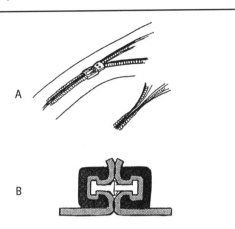

tape with the tape forming a type of gasket that extends up between the teeth. When the zipper is closed, the teeth press the sides of the rubber gasket together in a tight seal. These zippers are usually produced with two closed ends to be set in an opening in a garment. They are difficult to incorporate into a separating style because of the opening at the insertion end of the tab that would result. It should be noted that for less critical situations, there are waterproof zippers made with zipper tape that is impermeable and zipper teeth that tightly lock together. These keep water droplets out but do not necessarily exclude air.

Extruded zippers (Figure 9.26) are similar to the closures found on sealable plastic sandwich bags. Those used for protective garments are considerably thicker and contain deeper tracks and thus are stiffer than those in sandwich bags. They come with a variety of numbers of sealing tracks. These

FIGURE 9.26 (A) A plastic extruded zipper; (B) zipper elements meeting and forming a seal; (C) a double track extruded zipper; (D) an opening in a chemical suit with an extruded zipper set over a regular zipper so that the system is impermeable.

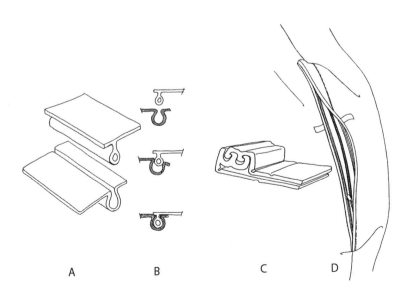

A   B   C   D

tracks may be found close together so that they are sealed in one pressing movement or in separate groupings, so that a set of primary closure tracks is closed first and another series is closed second to provide backup protection.

Extruded zippers suffer one of the same drawbacks as hook-and-loop fasteners in that long lengths of them are difficult to align and seal properly. While containers and waterproof covers that use extruded zippers may be sealed with a zipper tab permanently attached, tabs present the danger of having a tiny opening at the end of the track. In some situations, even one molecule penetrating that space would threaten survival. A number of separate sliding devices have been developed for insertion in the extruded zipper track to seal a long zipper more quickly and easily, but the devices must be removed at the top of the zipper and an area roughly the width of the device must then be pressed closed by hand.

Extruded tracks may be set into their backings in a number of different ways. The configuration shown in Figure 9.26C and D allows pressure to be applied on both sides of the zipper rather than the traditional configuration in which the body provides the backup surface against which pressure is applied to close the zipper.

Garments may also achieve airtight closures by being joined by rigid rings. Two types of rings are typically used in protective clothing. Metal locking rings are used for items such as space suits. (See Figure 9.27.) Impermeable materials are permanently sealed to the rings or clamped together between sections of the ring so that the joint remains impermeable. Rigid plastic rings may be used in areas such as the sleeve cuff area of chemical/biological suits. Rubber gloves are stretched over these cuffs and often an additional elastic band is then donned over the wrist area of

FIGURE 9.27 A space suit with rigid locking rings.

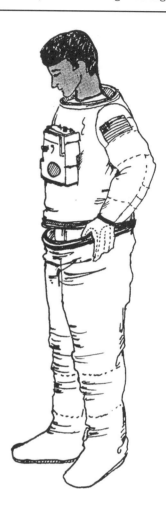

the glove to keep it in place. (See Figure 7.15.) This allows an airtight seal between the sleeve and glove of a chemical suit with ease of changing the glove between wearings.

One unique concept for an airtight closure developed by the U.S. Army involved using a four-way waterproof/airtight zipper on a full MOPP 4 chemical ensemble (See Chapter 7, "Levels of CB Protection") with a matching zipper on a positive pressure rest shelter. The zipper on the suit ran from one shoulder diagonally to the opposite knee

(Figure 9.28A). When needing a break from work in a toxic environment, a soldier could walk up to the tent, open the covering flap on the zipper and attach the suit zipper into a matching zipper on the tent (Figure 9.28B). Zipping the tent and suit together created a seal (the left side of suit zipper joined to the left side of tent zipper, etc.). As the suit and tent zippers joined, the space between the left and right sides of both zippers opened and the suit became part of the tent wall. The soldier could then step out of the suit directly into the tent with no contamination (Figure 9.28C). The suit remained on the outside of the tent ready for donning when work resumed (Figure 9.28D) (Symington 1986, 273).

SUSPENSION SYSTEMS

Since enclosing the body in clothing is one of the main purposes of fastening systems, it is important, early in the design process, to explore *suspension systems* (i.e., the ways in which clothing is fastened to or suspended from the body). The ways in which suspension systems work are based on some of the same physical mechanisms on which fastener operation is based: resistance (opposing forces), gravity, applied pressure, friction, and adhesion. Most clothing items are suspended by combinations of these mechanisms.

Gravity and *resistance* work hand in hand. In order for gravity to work, there must be a horizontal body surface or a body indentation to resist it.

FIGURE 9.28 (A) Chemical suit with a four-way zipper; (B) soldier in sealed suit joins suit zipper to matching zipper on positive pressure, contamination-free tent; (C) slipping out of outer suit through impermeable opening created by zipping suit to tent; (D) suit now forms part of tent wall and is suspended on outside of tent ready for soldier to back into it and detach from tent.

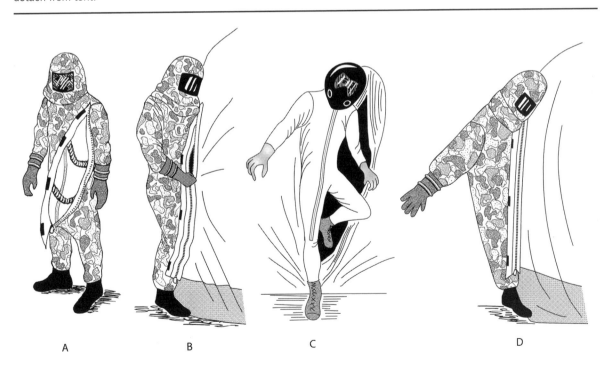

A   B   C   D

Glasses, for example, while pulled downward by gravity, depend on the resistance provided by the ears and the bridge of the nose in order to stay in place. Shoulder pads rest on the horizontal body surface provided by the top of the shoulders. Horizontal body surfaces, body indentations such as the neck and waistline, and areas such as the crotch and underarm, where vertical body surfaces meet horizontal ones, provide anchoring points where gravity and resistance work together to suspend clothing.

Designers should be aware of the wide range of potential body areas that can be used to provide resistance. Although the waistline provides an obvious indentation from which a skirt can be suspended on many people, the bridge of the nose is not as frequently considered as an indentation from which other items could be suspended. The armscye area is often used to suspend items such as backpacks, whereas the junctures between the fingers and the hand are less likely to be used. Unique approaches to design problems can often evolve from consideration of a wider variety of areas from which clothing can be suspended or supported.

Varying body shapes, degrees of muscular development, and changes in position and environments (such as zero gravity conditions or deep in the ocean) make it important to consider resistance points each time a new design problem is presented. The importance of the resistance of a body part becomes clear when amputation or deformities remove a potential point of resistance. When a woman has a mastectomy, for example, the indentation below the breast is no longer available as a point of resistance against the upward movement of a bra. Even though an artificial breast form can be placed in her bra and weighted to simulate the natural breast, there is little to prevent the bra cup with the form in it from migrating upward as a shoulder is raised. Women who have had double mastectomies have the side resistance point on both sides removed and thus have problems anchoring a bra to prevent both upward and side-to-side movement. Resistance must be transferred to another body area, in this case, often the crotch. A strap sewn to the base of the bra may be attached to the panties or the waistline of pants or a skirt so that the pull from both the shoulder and crotch is equalized. The design considerations for a bra might be very different for a trapeze artist who hangs upside down for a good deal of the time or a female astronaut, where gravity does not cause the breasts to fall down into bra cups. Ways to incorporate resistance in these cases need to be reconceptualized.

Changing body positions may actually provide new horizontal surfaces from which suspension may be accomplished. People who are wheelchair-bound can often use the thighs (or the seat of the wheelchair) as a point of resistance. The same is true for seated individuals such as pilots. In addition, when rigid items of clothing are worn, as is the case with many impact-protective clothing items, resistance can be used for upward suspension of an item as well. Figure 9.29 shows a baseball umpire's chest protector that contains a thin rigid plate. Because the umpire is in a crouched position behind the catcher, the protector can rest on the knees and its rigidity will allow it to be suspended upward over the chest regions. When the umpire is standing, the protector hangs from a strap around the neck and/or straps that encircle the armscye area.

Upward suspension of rigid items can also be accomplished by using a body indentation. Figure 9.30 shows a unique suspension system for body armor. The suspension of the thick, heavy bulletproof plates is accomplished by the use of a

FIGURE 9.29 Upward suspension of a rigid item.

stiffened waist belt that has a strong vertical strap at each side. The belt is put on first. Then, a vest that carries chest and back protection is donned. When the straps on the waist belt are brought below the waistline edge of the vest, wrapped around it, and lifted, the weight of the vest is transferred from the shoulders to the waist and hip area. The straps are then held in place on the vest with Velcro.

Another version of this technique has been used in the Improved Outer Tactical Vest (IOTV), body armor used by the U.S. Army. This vest has a wide elastic belt threaded through channels (wide belt loops) only inside the back of the vest and joined at the center front of the soldier by large Velcro patches. This waistband allows part of the weight of the vest to be supported by the waist rather than the shoulders. Since it is not attached to the front of the vest, this support system frees the front half of the vest so that it can be lifted away for medical treatment and the like. This same approach to redistributing load from the shoulders to the waist is used in large backpacks with waist straps.

Often, clothing items are used to provide resistance to keep body-related items in place. Padding and other rigid items that are carried on the body may be placed in garment pockets or may be strapped, clipped, or laced through garment openings. One well-known suspension system used

FIGURE 9.30 Upward suspension. (A) A heavy ballistics vest designed to be suspended from the waist rather than the shoulders. (B) A stiffened waist belt is donned first; then the vest is put in place. (C) Straps are wrapped around the lower edge of the vest and pulled upward and secured with Velcro, transferring the weight of the vest from shoulders to waistline. *(U.S. Army Natick Research, Development and Engineering Center)*

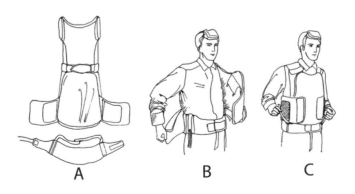

A   B   C

by military personnel is the Modular Lightweight Load-carrying Equipment (MOLLE). It involves a system of heavy-duty webbing applied to items such as ballistics vests and backpacks, and a series of compatible storage pouches. The attachable pouches have similar webbing on their undersides as well as attachment straps. The attachment strap or straps are woven between the webbing on the garment and the webbing on the pouch and then snapped or clipped in place so that they are securely attached. A MOLLE system is shown on the ballistics vest in Figure 9.31. This system can be applied to a variety of functional garments for outdoor activities and to fashion garments as well.

Applied pressure is often used to force a clothing or accessory item close to the body surface. A clip earring, an elasticized waist, and a stretchable watchband all use a mechanical form of applied pressure to accomplish suspension. Items of easily moldable metals also use applied pressure for suspension. Wide-band bracelets and adjustable rings use this mechanism. Thin wire as well as elastic can be inserted into garment edges to help them conform to the body shape or stand away from it.

Pneumatic pressure, i.e., air pressure, is also used for suspension. Figure 9.32 shows an inflatable splint that is held in place by means of pneumatically applied pressure. Although not widely used, negative air pressure or suction may also help secure items to the body. Some similarly shaped braces are filled with Styrofoam beads and vacuum fitted. Once secured in place, air is pumped out of the brace so that the beads form a rigid mass around a body part.

Hydraulic (fluid) pressure provides a possible means of suspension but is not used frequently because of the weight that fluids add to the system. In some protective sports equipment,

FIGURE 9.31 A military vest with a MOLLE system.

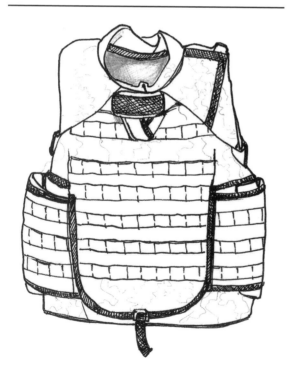

FIGURE 9.32 Suspension by pneumatic pressure: an air splint.

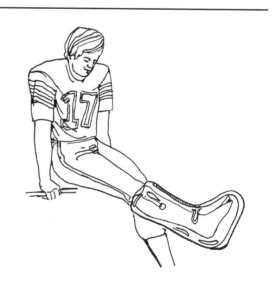

a combination of pneumatic pressure and fluids is used to add both impact protection and precise fitting to an item of equipment. Both are also found in a variety of medical uses. For example, pneumatic pressure is used in garments for burn patients because of the improved skin surface that occurs during healing when constant pressure is applied to a severely burned skin surface. Braces and rehabilitative devices of many kinds rely on mechanically applied pressure, not only for suspension, but for healing purposes as well.

Friction and *adhesion* are often relied upon when body resistance points are not available or convenient to use. In most cases, they are used in combination with applied pressure. For example, an elastic knee support stays in place on the knee because of applied pressure. In most cases, people would probably balk at the appearance and discomfort of a knee support suspended from the waistline. However, because the leg narrows increasingly from the hip to the ankle, an elasticized form tends to slide down the leg in an effort to reach the narrowest area. If friction is added to the applied pressure of the elastic, or if the brace is taped or otherwise adhered in place, more secure suspension can be expected.

Frictional resistance can be accomplished by adding a variety of textures to fabrics, but by far the most successful examples can be found in synthetic and natural rubbers or rubber-coated fabrics. Waistbands in men's pants often have rubberized surfaces to help keep shirts from sliding out. Thigh-top nylons for women have a similar surface—which often looks as though rows of small rubber bands have been woven into it—to keep nylons from sliding down the leg. Rubberization may help keep straps from sliding out of place or may help garment parts stay in position more easily in relation to one another.

Many items of functional clothing use all five methods of suspension methods to stay in place. Figure 9.33 shows a protective ensemble for ice hockey that uses several different suspension methods to support rigid body padding. Suspension is accomplished by a stretch bodysuit that is closely fitted to a player's body. Hook-and-loop fasteners are used to attach shoulder, upper chest, and arm padding on the precise areas of the upper bodysuit where they are needed. A belt laced to the inner face of a shaped hip and rib pad is laced also through buttonholes on the outside of the bodysuit. This allows the pad to be precisely placed on an individual player, and the single suspension line allows the lower edge of the pad to move freely up and down the side of the leg so that abduction and adduction are not restricted. Thigh padding is inserted in pockets on the outer face of the bodysuit. Shin padding rests on the top of the foot and is held in place under the stretchy leg of the bodysuit.

Sometimes, it is necessary to discard the common methods of suspending a specific item in order to solve a design problem. For example, most eyeglasses depend on the resistance of both the ears and the bridge of the nose. The glasses in Figure 9.34 rest on neither. Instead of gravity and resistance, the primary suspension method is applied pressure. A thin, flexible band, from which the lenses are hung, encircles the head. Because the band contacts much of the head circumference, it does not feel tight and does not place undue pressure on any one area. (Remember that the body adjusts to constant pressure, not sensing it after a period of time.) Gravity plays a part in that the ends of the band are weighted to counterbalance the weight of the lenses so that the glasses stay level on the head and the bridge of the nose is not needed for support. This counterbalancing of

FIGURE 9.33 A protective system for ice hockey. (A) Thigh and shin padding are contained in a stretchable bodysuit; (B) padding for the ribs and hips is belted onto the bodysuit through buttonholes placed at intervals around the midsection, and shoulder-arm protection is attached to the bodysuit in various positions with wide patches of Velcro; (C) the outer suit is simply a shell that retains the traditional appearance of a hockey uniform.

FIGURE 9.34 Using applied pressure for suspension. Glasses ride above the ears and the bridge of the nose and a circular, flexible band applies light pressure all the way around the head to hold the glasses in place. *(Design formerly produced by Space Age Optics)*

weight is often needed in clothing. For example, the most successful hooded garments have some sort of weight on the front of the garment to counterbalance the weight of the hood when it is down so that the front of the garment doesn't ride up and strangle the front of the neck. Often this is provided by the weight of toggles or other adjustors on the ends of the drawstrings that cinch the face edge of the hood. Innovative clothing and accessory design is often the result of discarding traditional methods of suspension for items such as these glasses and exploring entirely new means of securing them to the body.

LOCATION OF GARMENT CLOSURES FOR SELF-DONNING AND DOFFING

The goal for most garments is for individuals to be able to get in and out of clothing by themselves. One of the first choices a designer will probably need to make is *where* the closures involved in donning and doffing garments will be located. The choice of location for self-donning depends on several things, among them

- the ease that most users will have in reaching and manipulating closures,
- the presence of any environmental conditions or physical hazards (such as items that could snag on openings or fasteners) that affect the user, and
- the presence of accessories worn as part of a protective ensemble.

Self-donning is often easiest if the fastening system is located on the front of the garment and fasteners either start low enough so that they can be seen or are chosen for their ability to be manipulated easily without being seen. For people who are standing while getting dressed and undressed, the location of fastening systems should be planned to be operated easily given the carrying angle of the arm. (See Anatomy and Design 9.1.) For people who are seated in bed or in wheelchairs, the area most easily accessed is generally from midchest to lap in the center front.

Often the choice of a location for a fastening system cannot be made without looking at ways of putting together new approaches to all of the factors involved in planning a fastening system: location, length, combinations of fasteners, and the overall design of a garment.

Even though most people are used to lengthwise openings for donning clothing, it is important for

designers of functional clothing to recognize that sometimes crosswise openings may present the best solution for donning. This is particularly true when accessories such as face masks or monitoring devices need to be worn over or covered by garments. A number of full-body coverage garments, such as those for outer space, diving, and chemical/biological protection provide excellent examples of this approach. Figure 9.27 shown earlier in this chapter is an example of this. Each segment of the space suit is connected to the next by rigid locking rings. Each ring needs to be large enough for the widest dimension of a body part to pass through. (The head needs to pass through the neck opening of both the torso covering and the base of the helmet.) The rings for this particular suit have the added feature of containing ball-bearing (sliding) joints so that the upper torso can rotate freely at the waist, the head can rotate the helmet without turning the torso, and hands can rotate the gloves at the wrist without turning the sleeve.

Reach

Understanding the anatomy of the human body is critical for locating closures in a way that they can be easily reached. Anatomy and Design 9.1 illustrates the carrying angle of the arm and includes a basic map of the areas of the body that can be easily reached with each hand.

One of the factors that can affect the ease with which fasteners can be manipulated is handedness. Planning designs for hemiplegics (those who have paralysis of one side of the body) requires that fasteners not only be placed within reach, but also that they be placed so that the functioning (or dominant) hand can exert the greatest force. Figure 9.35 shows a fastener planned to adjust the width of a long-line bra in the rib cage area. This adjustment device has been placed on the paralyzed side so

Anatomy and Design 9.1: **The Carrying Angle of the Arm**

In Chapter 2, there were a number of examples of garments designed for the *working position* of the body. The design of the human body—its anatomical structure—to a large extent determines the base from which a working position begins. It makes sense, then for designers to explore the anatomy of the arm and hand when designing a closure system, both in terms of the way the body's joints are structured and the way that muscles are designed to work, because the hands manipulate the vast majority of openings and fasteners.

One of the major factors in the ease of operation of a closure is how well it is related to the carrying angle of the arm. If you look at the shape of the arm in the anatomical position (Figure A–C), you can see that the lower arm bones do not continue in a straight line from the humerus (the upper arm bone). They actually angle away from the body at the elbow. This influences the position of the hand when the arm is bent at the elbow and extended across the body. The hand moves in an arc across the torso, most of the time lying most comfortably, *not* straight up and down, but at an angle to the length of the body. If the arm is abducted at the shoulder, the arc changes at each position of abduction. When closures are located along an arc that the hand can reach quickly and without an extreme amount of abduction, operating the closure is considerably easier.

The effect of the carrying angle of the arm can also be seen in the natural hand position when the hands are placed on the hips with the elbow bent and the arm is forming a triangular shape at the side of the body. This hand position is reflected in the shape of pockets on many jackets and pants. Figure D shows a map of upper body areas that are easily accessible with one hand.

One of the most interesting examples of considering the environment, the activity, and the capacity for reach by the human body in planning a design can be found in the intravehicular (IVA) garments for Skylab

FIGURES A–C The carrying angle of the arm (A) influences the position of the arm and hand as it reaches to manipulate fasteners. To avoid extreme wrist positions, the arm abducts and adducts to comfortably reach fasteners in different positions (B) and (C).

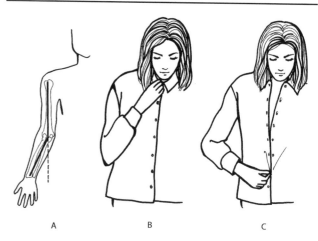

A   B   C

astronauts. Part of the rationale for the pocket design for these garments was based on the environment, in which gravity was not a factor. Using pockets as a place to rest hands was not important since the arms and hands float without gravity to pull them down. In addition, not having to plan vertical pockets in which items carried would nestle at the bottom allowed designers to plan primarily for ease of reach and for the astronauts' ability to see pocket contents.

The pockets in the Skylab IVA garments opened along the center front zipper and the pockets themselves extended (inside the garment) horizontally out toward the side seam so that the astronaut's right hand could reach across into the left pocket and vice versa. (See Figure E.) This horizontal position is actually a convenient one for the hand to reach into (think of hugging oneself). The main reason for this position, however, was because pocket contents in zero gravity scatter everywhere when pulled out. Since items are not affected by gravity, they are propelled by inertia and continue in the direction the user pulls them out. With this pocket position, the zippered opening can be

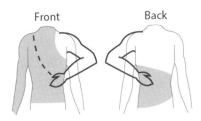

FIGURE D Torso areas reachable with one hand.

FIGURE E An IVA jacket for a space shuttle flight with zippered pocket openings on either side of the center front zipper. *(ILC Space Systems 1984)*

seen, and the contents empty right at the center front of the body where they can be more easily corralled. If items were pulled out of a side pocket, they would continue out to the side and back of the body where it would be hard to find them.

FIGURE 9.35 A bra for a hemiplegic woman. It can be adjusted to the proper size with Velcro straps that are easily reached and pulled in the direction of the nonparalyzed arm. *(Concept based on a design by the Disabled Living Foundation 1974)*

that the functioning arm can reach across and exert the greatest leverage on the strap. Many unique, alternative fastening systems for limited reach can be found by exploring solutions that have been created for people who have physical disabilities or infirmities. Attention to these factors these can make dressing easier for anyone.

Dexterity and Ease of Manipulating Fasteners

There are many situations in which it is important to choose fasteners that are easy to manipulate. People with arthritis or workers wearing thick gloves may have difficulty manipulating fasteners that require precision. People with failing vision or workers wearing bulky clothing or face masks may need to manipulate fasteners without being able to see them.

Two significant factors that increase the operability of fasteners are size and roughness of the fastener. A small, slippery fastener requires significantly more force to grip and operate than a large,

Fastening Systems

rough fastener. In addition to operating force, small or slippery fasteners are harder to detect by touch (especially when the sense of touch is impaired), since they exert less force on the skin.

A third factor, adding a protrusion to the fastener, can allow force to be applied in a different way (e.g., by hooking a finger through the fastener rather than squeezing it between the fingers) and can allow the user to use stronger muscles to operate the fastener.

When dealing with garments on the lower body, it is often important to choose fasteners that are easy to manipulate without being seen. However, if the whole fastening system is considered rather than just the fastener, it is also possible to alter the way in which typical fasteners are placed in a garment so that they become easier to use. Figure 9.36 illustrates two techniques that have been developed for individuals with lower body weakness who cannot step into clothing or slide easily into the typical tubular forms many garments take. Wrap-around garments provide one solution, but when they are tight, it is difficult to manipulate the fasteners needed to close them around the body. While the solutions in Figure 9.36 were developed

for a corset, they could be applied to any brace or tight garment that encircles the body. The garment shown in Figure 9.36A has been adapted by inserting two zippers: a separating zipper that runs down the entire length of one side and a shorter zipper that closes in the opposite direction. The separating zipper allows the girdle to be wrapped around rather than pulled on. When *starting* the separating zipper, the shorter zipper is opened so that tension is relieved when the greatest dexterity is needed. Once the separating zipper has been closed, a downward pull on the shorter zipper serves to tighten the lower girdle area and close it completely.

The garment shown in Figure 9.36B uses a slightly different approach. Here the zipper extends well past the lower edge of the garment. This achieves two things: It allows the insertion area for the zipper tab of the separating zipper to be lifted up where it can be seen and more easily started. It also allows the zipper to be started while it is not under tension.

Human Interface: Finding and Understanding Fastening Systems

Another challenge of fastening systems for the designer is communicating to a user how to operate the system. Challenges like this can take the form of something as simple as "Which is the front?" in a garment such as a hospital gown. In many cases, text-based instructions for how to use a garment are not a reasonable solution.

The human interface systems discussed in Chapter 4 provide a good foundation for designing fastening systems. The fastening system and donning/doffing process can be considered as the interface of a traditional garment. As discussed in Chapter 4, there are five key design principles of interface design that also apply to fastening systems. These principles include helping the user to

FIGURE 9.36 Two zippers alter a tubular garment for ease of dressing. *(Concept based on a design by the Disabled Living Foundation)*

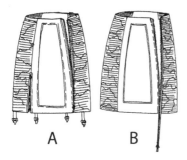

build an accurate mental model of the fastening system, promoting discoverability in the fastening system, presenting information through multiple sensory modalities such as sight *and* touch simultaneously, ensuring that elements of the fastening system can be easily seen or felt in the user's environment, and placing information in the world to the extent possible rather than relying on the user's memory.

As with technological interfaces, the user's mental model of a new fastening system is usually initially based on previous experience: If it looks like a shirt, the user will expect that it opens down the front or pulls over the head and has a place for arms and neck. A shirt with no arm openings might be more likely to be compared to the mental model of a pillowcase than a shirt. Although the systems in Figure 9.37 have identical functionality, a user donning the harness (A) may have more difficulty because it is less similar to an existing mental model than the shirt (B).

Good discoverability in the fastening system promotes easy mental model building. One example of poor discoverability in a fastening system is the common consumer misunderstanding of pockets

that are sewn shut during production. In most cases, this is done to make garment assembly easier and to keep the pockets from getting misshapen or collecting debris during the manufacturing and shipping processes. However, many consumers incorrectly assume that they have purchased a garment with fake pockets. The operation of these pockets is therefore not effectively discoverable for the user.

Providing feedback to the user helps build trust in the model and in the fastening system. For example, a snap that provides an audible and tactile click when fully fastened is more easily trusted (and, therefore, operated) than one that does not. Providing feedback in more than one sensory modality helps the user trust the feedback and also speeds up the mental processing time to understand whether or not the interaction has been successful. Fasteners can provide feedback through visual signals (graphics elements such as color coding, dots, or lines that show when a fastener is properly aligned, which direction to turn/push/pull a fastener or which fastener components attach to which other components), tactile signals (a click or pop, the feeling of a securely seated fastener), or auditory signals (the sound of the fastener seating securely).

As with interfaces to smart systems, a fastening system must also be easily perceived by the user in the context of use. In a dimly lit environment, graphics and visual cues may not be effective. In a loud environment, an audible click may not be helpful, but a tactile click may compensate for the audible component. Similarly, if the fastening system is located on a part of the body that is difficult to see, tactile cues may be more effective. Making fastening systems "gropable" (and taking into account whether one or two hands are available to locate and operate the system) is important as well.

FIGURE 9.37 Systems with identical functionality may be more (A) or less (B) conducive to mental model-building depending on their physical form.

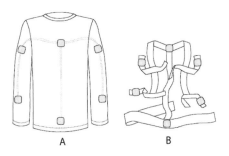

A   B

Finally, a complicated fastening system may require that the designer provide reminders or instructions in the form of graphics or (in some cases) text as a permanent part of the garment. This allows the knowledge of how to operate the system to be placed in the world rather than needing to be held in the user's memory.

LOCATION OF CLOSURES FOR ASSISTED DONNING AND DOFFING

In situations where it makes more sense for a caregiver or co-worker to help with donning and doffing, fasteners need to be located where assistants can most easily manipulate them. One of the simplest examples of this is the bib worn by infants, toddlers, patients, nursing home residents, and others for whom self-feeding poses difficulties. For years, most bibs closed at the center back, with fasteners in the position most difficult for a caregiver to see, reach, and manipulate when an infant was sitting in a high chair or a patient was lying back in bed. Many bibs now have straps that slide around the back of the neck and snap or Velcro near the shoulder on the front of the bib, an area much more easily seen and accessed by someone other than the wearer. (See Figure 9.38.)

On the other hand, if a patient is seated in a wheelchair and needs assistance with closures, it may be easiest for aides to reach fasteners at the back of the neck, or anywhere on the upper back, above the level of the back of the wheelchair.

The length of an opening is as critical for assisted donning and doffing as location. It is important to note that in order to accommodate longer openings, designers need to think beyond just placing openings in seams or placing seams in traditional locations. Many mothers know how important the extended length of an opening on a one-piece garment sleeper is to the ease of getting an infant in and out of a garment. Two of the many approaches to extending the opening of an infant sleeper are shown in Figure 9.39.

The length of an opening is also a critical consideration for people with stiffness, weakness, or absence of body parts or those who wear supports or braces. The length of opening needed will depend on the amount an arm or leg can be raised or the dimensions of bracing or other devices a garment part has to pass over. For example, someone with stiff shoulders or limited shoulder movement may find it difficult to dress in a pullover shirt or a suit jacket. Figure 9.40 shows a top to

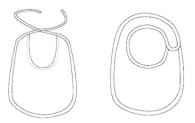

FIGURE 9.38 (Left) Infant bib with traditional ties and center back closure; (right) bib with hook-and-loop closure moved to the side front neckline for easier access.

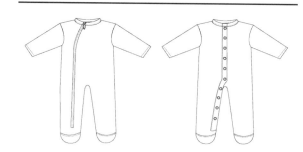

FIGURE 9.39 Two placements of fasteners on a one-piece sleeper for infants that extend the length of the opening to allow easy donning.

FIGURE 9.40 An easy-on blouse with zippered openings down the top of each sleeve, designed for someone with stiff or fixed shoulder. *(Based on a concept by the Disabled Living Foundation)*

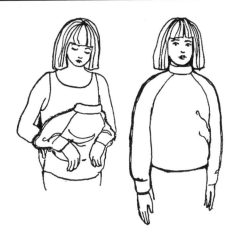

FIGURE 9.41 (A) A jacket with a zipper inserted at the underarm to allow ease of donning. (B) A jacket with a hook-and-loop closure added to the center back seam for ease of donning. *(Concepts based on designs by the Disabled Living Foundation.)*

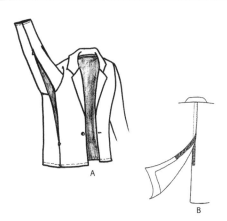

which zippers have been added from wrist to neckline over the top of the shoulders. The entire top can be dropped over the head to waist level; the arms can be inserted into wrist openings, and the top can then be pulled upward and zipped in place.

Figure 9.41 illustrates two methods of adapting a suit jacket for someone with limited arm and shoulder movement (Disabled Living Foundation 1974). Figure 9.41A shows a zipper inserted in the underarm seam of a jacket. This releases some of the tension across the back and chest so that the jacket can be more easily donned. Figure 9.41B shows a jacket with its center back seam opened and hook-and-loop fasteners inserted. This closure allows an aide to spread out each side of the garment separately so that an individual can place each arm in its sleeve with limited lifting of the arms. Using wrinkle analysis (see Chapter 2) to observe lines of strain on a garment during the dressing process can help a designer determine which seams or areas of a garment need to be opened to release tightness for ease of dressing.

Figure 9.42 shows how both the location and length of a fastening system can be varied to adapt a riding boot for a patient who has multiple handicaps. One altered boot opens down the center back so that a contracted, spasmodic foot can slide forward into the boot rather than having to experience the painful contortions needed to slip the foot

FIGURE 9.42 Two methods of adapting a riding boot for easier donning.

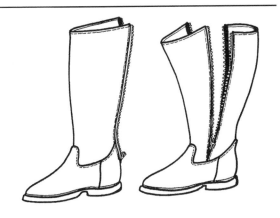

down through the narrow, fitted calf area. Another has two side openings so the foot can be laid into the foot bed.

Wrap-around garments such as the one shown in Figure 9.43 often provide a good solution for people who find the dressing process difficult. While wrap-around skirts are common, it is possible to wrap garments around any body segment. The dress in Figure 9.43 was developed for a nursing home patient who had lower body paralysis and limited shoulder and arm movement. It can be opened and laid flat on a bed, and the wearer can be lowered or rolled onto it so that a caregiver can complete the dressing operation without any movement by the wearer. This garment uses a combination of lengthwise and crosswise openings to wrap the garment. The slipper shown in Figure 9.44 has separate wraps around the top of the foot and the ankle, making it easy to both don and fit.

CREATION OF MODULES

Another alternative to lengthening the openings needed for ease of donning is to create modules so that garments can be built around the body. Garment units that can be placed on separate body segments and quickly fastened around an individual

FIGURE 9.43 A wrap-around dress for a woman with limited mobility.

FIGURE 9.44 The FlexiShoe® wrap-around slipper.

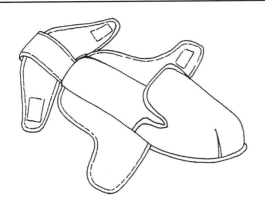

Modular garments have the added advantage of being able to link different sizes and lengths of segments to fit any body configuration. Space suit components are made in different lengths to accommodate the different arm, leg, and torso measurements of individual astronauts, for example. Mass-production techniques can be used to make custom-fitted clothing by joining different lengths of segments based on individual customers' measurements. (See the example of firefighting clothing production in Chapter 2, under "Design Strategies 2.3 Mass Customization and Sizing.")

An ultramodular approach can also be taken using very small modules to build a garment piece by piece. The example shown in Figure 9.46 uses small modules made of nonfray materials (e.g., leather or felt), which have protrusions that can be inserted through perforations in other modules for a nonsew attachment method. Using these modules, a wide variety of garment shapes and sizes can be built up and customized for the wearer. Although more time-intensive to customize, this approach offers a great deal of versatility.

without painful or difficult movement can solve dressing problems for many people with disabilities. For example, the shirt in Figure 9.45A has been completely cut apart at the center back and a hook-and-loop closure added so that each half of the shirt can be slid onto the body separately. The jumper in Figure 9.45B wraps around the body and is closed by a caregiver, or even sometimes by the wearer, with several large, easy-to-manipulate buttons.

FIGURE 9.45 (A) A shirt with an extra opening at the center back. This allows the shirt to separate into right and left halves for easier donning; (B) a modular jumper. Front and back sections are buttoned together with a single large buttons at each shoulder and each side of the waist.

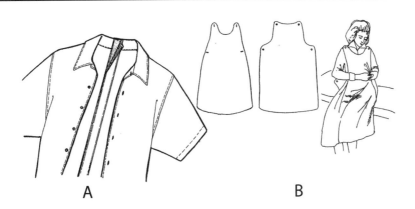

A   B

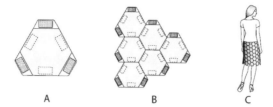

ACCOMMODATION OF ACCESSORIES AND BRACES

There are many rigid accessories and items of equipment that are worn on the body—from braces to breathing apparatus to medical monitoring devices. Many of these need to be donned first and covered by garments. This necessitates a change in garment design, of course, but it often also means that fastening systems for donning and doffing need to be creatively placed.

For example, many chemical/biological suits are shaped in the front head and neck area to accommodate a breathing mask worn under the suit. (See Figure 7.7.) Locating closures on the front of these items often poses difficulties because designers need to work around a face-mask and breathing apparatus. Closures in the front neck area can create bulk that will interfere with vision. Getting a worker's head through the neckline into the hood area is much more easily achieved from the back of a positive pressure suit, where there is a long, flatter area for fastener placement. Therefore, some suits are closed by a coworker who can see the fastening system regardless of where it is located. Instead of using a separate fastener, the chemical suit shown in Figure 9.47, is simply cut open down the back and heat sealed shut by a coworker after it has been donned. This completely eliminates the

problem of finding an impermeable fastening system. Workers are then decontaminated after they finish their shift and the suit is slashed open.

Some items worn on the body may require that garments have added length or width. Accessories such as braces or monitors may fit under regular clothing, but may require a change in openings either for ease of donning or so that items can be quickly accessed for readings or adjustment. The pant leg shown in Figure 9.48 has had a zipper added so that a leg brace can fit through the knee area more easily when the pants are being donned. This opening also allows access to the

FIGURE 9.47 A heat-sealed closure for a disposable chemical-biological protective suit.

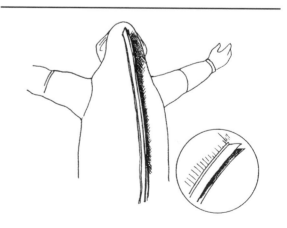

FIGURE 9.48 Pants that have been altered to include a zipper for ease of dressing with lower leg bracing. *(Concept based on a design by the Disabled Living Foundation)*

brace if it needs to be adjusted. The garment areas that lie over braces may need to be reinforced so the edges of the brace do not wear through garment materials. Similar openings may be planned for medical monitoring devices. Again, keep in mind that openings do not necessarily need to be in seams, although this is the easiest place to put them to adapt ready-to-wear garments. Designs can also be created so that seaming passes directly through the areas that need openings.

FASTENING SYSTEMS FOR FITTING AND ADJUSTMENT

One of the main reasons fastening systems are so critical to the success of a garment is that they can provide adjustment for fitting a wide variety of types and sizes of bodies. Often combinations of fasteners are used.

The helmet shown in Figure 9.49 has removable interior padding. This allows the placement of different sizes and thicknesses of pads in the helmet for fitting as well as removal for cleaning or replacement when specific areas are damaged.

Another example of using a combination of fasteners can be found in the fitting system used for pressure suits for pilots. Lacing, although it can be extremely time-consuming, is a fastener that provides very precise fitting possibilities. Figure 9.50A shows an adjustment panel on a pilot's inflatable pressure suit. The lacing is used to fit the suit precisely to each pilot once, and then an elasticized, expandable cover is closed over the lacing, generally with a zipper. (This cover prevents the laces from getting caught on items in the aircraft interior.) The suit is then donned using a quicker fastening system such as a zipper. Lacing techniques in protective clothing often make use of **loop tape** (Figure 9.50B), a woven tape that contains continuous, strong loops. This tape can

FIGURE 9.49 Fasteners for ease of replacement and sizing. Helmet pads can be individually cleaned, repaired, or replaced. Thicker pads may be added to better size the helmet to individual heads.

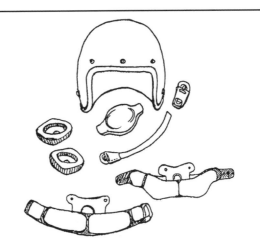

FIGURE 9.50 (A) Lacing used as a precise fitting adjustment for a pressure suit for pilots; (B) loop tape.

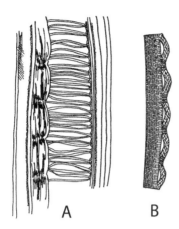

by bulky equipment that often must be worn with them. Because the ability to provide protection for any size of combat boot with a single item is very cost-effective for the military in terms of both production and distribution, the basic overboot shown in Figure 9.51 has been widely used despite its difficulty of use. Because of the danger of exposure

FIGURE 9.51 A one-size-fits-all chemical boot with closed-loop lacing and a cord-lock fastener that snug the wide boot around the foot. (A) and (B) insets show alternate fasteners and (C) illustrates an added gripping surface for the lacing. *(U.S. Army overboot; fastening system design: S. Watkins)*

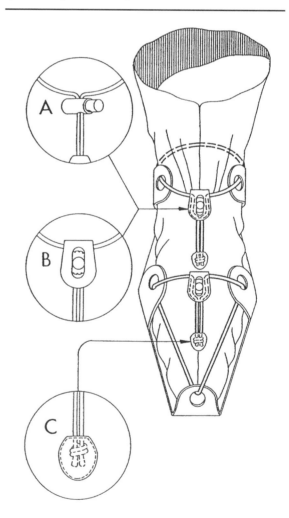

be sewn in like a zipper, reducing the production time that would be needed to form loops or insert eyelets for lacing.

A similar fastener system can be found on many winter boots, with lacing at the center front and a zipper at the side. The lacing is used for precise fitting for the foot, ankles, and lower leg, and the zipper is used for quick donning and doffing. The lacing does not have to be opened and adjusted each time, but it is available for adjustment if, for example, thicker socks are worn.

FASTENING SYSTEMS FOR QUICK DONNING AND DOFFING

Reconceptualizing fastening systems can often provide the key to improving the ease of use of an apparel item and the quickness with which it can be donned and doffed. One example of this can be seen in the overboot that is worn over a combat boot to protect it from chemical contamination.

Donning garments for a chemically contaminated environment is complicated both by the size and weight of the garments themselves and to lethal toxins, the overboot must be donned and doffed while the wearer is fully clothed (i.e., wearing a suit, mask, hood and gloves). For years, this boot has been distributed with an open cord that needed to be looped through the eyelets on the edge and tied in the manner of shoelaces. The loss in dexterity due to a two-layer glove system worn and the vision obstruction caused by a facemask makes it extremely difficult for a wearer to thread the laces through the eyelets and almost impossible to tie the laces. The fastening system shown in this figure proposes one solution to simplify donning in this situation: a closed-loop system. The cord completes a full loop around the boot with no free ends. The laces do not need to be threaded in the holes each time. Instead a single upward pull

on the loop completes the fitting and a cord-lock device is used to secure the ties, eliminating the need for fine dexterity (Secrist et al. 1987).

In other situations, fasteners that allow a clothing system to be quickly doffed may be extremely important. For example, the aircrew armor system shown in Figure 9.52 is heavy, bulletproof protection planned for seated helicopter pilots. If a pilot must escape from the helicopter quickly in an emergency, the weight and bulk of this protector would greatly inhibit mobility and thus hamper quick escape. Therefore, the protector incorporates a quick release feature. Even though hook-and-loop fasteners hold well against shearing stresses and thus suspend the protector in place on the body, these fasteners are relatively easy to *peel*

FIGURE 9.52 A quick-release ballistics vest. *(U.S. Army Natick Research, Development and Engineering Center)*

open. Pulling on the release strap in front of the armor peels off the hook-and-loop strips that join the front and back vest sections at the shoulder and waistline and the vest drops off of the body in an instant. In designs such as this one, it is important to protect the release strap so that it does not peel accidentally. The current U.S. Army ballistics vest (IOTV) has its quick-release strap enclosed in a pocket near the center front neckline of the vest.

RECONFIGURATION OF GARMENTS WITH FASTENING SYSTEMS

One of the most fascinating purposes of fasteners is to allow the conversion of one garment form into another. This reconfiguration may be done to modify its degree of protection or allow a garment to serve totally different purposes. Often garments are changed to respond to changing conditions in the environment. The MOLLE system shown in Figure 9.31 is one example of a system that individuals use to reconfigure a protective garment.

Figure 9.53 shows a pilot's hand protection system that can be converted from normal in-flight use to emergency cold protection if the pilot has to eject from the plane into a cold environment.

Figure 9.54 shows a lightweight nylon enclosure that emerges from a hat brim to serve as a tent-like shelter that can be used like a cabana at the beach. Clothing placed in headgear is unique in that it can quickly be released to provide full-body coverage. Designs similar to the one in Figure 9.54 were prevalent in the United States in the 1940s and 1950s when people were concerned about having easily accessible total body protection—a sort of portable bomb shelter—for radiation protection from atomic explosions.

The sport shoe shown in Figure 9.55 has a replaceable sole that can be changed to allow for

FIGURE 9.53 Handwear for pilots. This flight glove has an insulated "bear paw" overlay mounted on the sleeve that can be pulled down over the basic glove to add protection to the hand in extremely cold environments. *(Design: Arthur D. Little)*

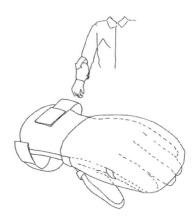

FIGURE 9.54 A hat that converts to a tent. (A) Snapped straps under a hat brim hold the rolled-up shelter in place; (B) snaps release a lightweight nylon shelter; (C) a drawstring can be pulled to form a completely enclosing structure. *(Design: Heidi Specht)*

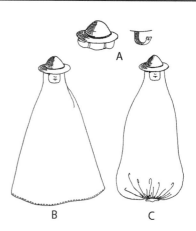

FIGURE 9.55 Convertible athletic shoes. Hook-and-loop surfaces on the basic shoe sole and replaceable soles allow the basic shoe to be converted to a golf, tennis, or basketball shoe or to have different soles applied for changing weather conditions. *(Design: Carl Dilg)*

FIGURE 9.56 A child's garment that converts from a bunting to a snowsuit using zippers.

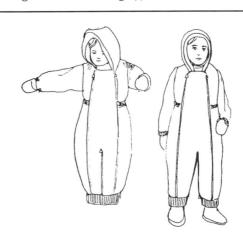

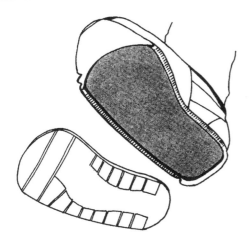

different surfaces. This feature also allows simple replacement of the sole when it is worn out rather than the replacement of the entire shoe.

Fastening systems also allow garments to convert from one size or body type to another or to form shapes that better relate to other garments worn in an ensemble. Figure 9.56 shows a baby bunting that can be converted from a sack-like form to a garment with separate legs by connecting its zippers so that they join the garment halves from front to back instead of from right to left. This allows the garment to be converted from a bunting appropriate for an infant to a snowsuit appropriate for a toddler. Note also that the length of the zippers allows the entire front of the snowsuit to be opened for ease of getting a toddler, who is often uncooperative, inside! A similar conversion principle is used for the apron shown in Figure 9.57, which can be used over both skirts and slacks.

FIGURE 9.57 A protective apron that converts for use with pants using snaps. *(Design: Marsha Cohen)*

ADAPTATIONS AND COMBINATIONS OF FASTENERS FOR SPECIFIC END USES

It is also important to recognize that fastening *systems* can be developed to take advantage of strengths of fasteners and minimize their disadvantages. The hook-and-loop storm flap closure shown in Figure 9.58 was developed for a firefighting turnout coat. Hook and loop itself is a permeable fastener, but the storm flap in this design encases the hook and loop in such a way that the *system* is waterproof.

Other fasteners may be used as backup as well. For example, as was shown earlier in this chapter in Figure 9.26, an extruded zipper on a chemical protective suit may be part of an impermeable panel that covers a regular (permeable) zipper. Or the two zippers may be in reverse positions: a protective panel that includes a regular zipper may be placed over an extruded zipper to ensure that no stress is placed on it or to prevent anything from catching on the extruded seal and accidently opening it.

Conclusion

New production methods and fastening systems are constantly being developed and each new development opens a vast number of possibilities for designers. The principles covered here and in preceding chapters can be used to analyze new design developments to determine new ways of solving design problems for specific users and for new activities, new hazards, and previously unexplored environments.

The chapters in this text cover clothing design principles that apply equally well to both function and fashion. There is no magic functional clothing formula that can be applied to mass manufactured items or fashion apparel to turn them into more functional designs. For fashion as for function, designers must take into account the needs of the user and the environment in which the garment will be used. The variables of the problem may be different, but the approach remains the same. Applying functional theory to mass-marketed clothing requires not only a thorough understanding of a single aspect of a clothing item such as how to make it warmer or more mobile but also an understanding of how those factors interact. Thus, it may require the integration of material in multiple chapters of this text.

The authors hope that the information in this text helps designers to improve the comfort and function of all types of clothing in order to enhance the health and welfare of many individuals.

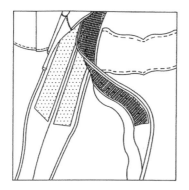

FIGURE 9.58 A storm flap encases a hook-and-loop fastener so that the front opening on a firefighter's turnout coat is resistant to water. The side of the center front opening on the right side of the diagram has loop tape on both sides. Hook tape is sewn to the jacket opening as shown on the left side of the diagram. A storm flap then covers this side with hook tape on its underside. The loop tape at the right is sandwiched between the two strips of hook tape on the left.

GLOSSARY

abduction movement away from the midline of the body.

acceleration the rate of change of velocity.

accelerometer a sensor that detects changes in velocity.

actuator the part of an electrical circuit that makes a perceptible change, such as light, heat, or movement.

adduction movement toward the midline of the body.

adsorption the adhesion of substances such as water to the surface of a fiber.

aerodynamic diameter the equivalent diameter of a sphere with a specific density that would move at the same rate as the particle being described.

aerogel a low-density solid material made by removing the liquid component of a gel, leaving only the solid component.

aerosol tiny particles of solids or liquids suspended in a gas.

alpha rays particles emitted during radioactive decay that contain two protons and two neutrons.

anatomical position a basic body position in which the individual stands in an erect position with legs straight, feet flat on the floor and the arms hanging straight down beside the body with the palms forward.

antero (prefix) toward the front of the body.

anteroposteriorly (AP) from front to back.

aramid a generic class of manufactured fibers noted for high strength and heat resistance.

armscye armhole.

auxetic a material that becomes thicker when stretched.

ball-and-socket joint a joint such as the hip or shoulder with one concave articulating surface and one ball-shaped surface.

ballistics the study of the dynamics of high-speed projectiles.

basal metabolic rate (BMR) the metabolic cost of living or the amount of energy expended to keep the body processes going.

batt or batting a loose, fluffy mat of fibers often used for insulation or quilting.

bead the melted plastic that flows away from a die on either side of a heat seal.

bellows effect air forced in or out of a garment by the pumping of the arms during movement.

beta rays streams of particles equivalent to electrons that are emitted from the nuclei of some atoms during radioactive decay.

bias the direction on a woven fabric that is at a 45° angle from its warp and weft.

bicomponent fibers fibers made of more than one polymer.

biomechanics the study of the effects of force on motion in living bodies.

biomotion movement that evokes or simulates life-like movements or outlines.

bladder a form that holds air or water.

blowing agent (foaming agent) an additive that forms bubbles during the process of making foam.

blow molding a process in which air pressure is used to expand a plastic, heat-settable tube using a vacuum.

body image an emotional representation of one's own body.

body schema the brain's unconscious representation of the size and shape of the body, its limits, movement, and the space it occupies.

bonding attaching loose fibers or separate fabrics together using adhesives or heat.

boundary air layer (aerodynamic layer) a thin layer of air on the surface of an object that is fairly resistant to movement.

brainstorming an idea-generating technique that seeks to generate large numbers of creative ideas in a short period of time.

brittle metals metals that shatter when they reach their elastic limit.

brushed fabrics fabrics with surfaces brushed with wire brushes so that fiber ends extend from the fabric surface.

bulk density the weight per volume of a specific material.

buoyancy compensator an inflatable item for diving that aids in ascent and descent.

cable a cord formed by twisting several plied yarns together.

calorie the amount of heat required to raise the temperature of 1 gram (g) of water 1°C. Calories are used to express the heat production of an individual.

cantilevering suspending a rigid, protective pad over a body part by one edge so that it rests above the area to be protected.

CB acronym meaning chemical/biological.

CBRN acronym meaning chemical/biological/radiological/nuclear.

chemical filter a material that filters out unwanted particles or gases by binding them chemically.

chimney effect the rising of warm air.

circumduction a movement that combines flexion, abduction, extension, and adduction, so that a body segment moves in a cone shape.

cleanroom an area in which an attempt is made to limit the number and size of contaminants in the air.

closed cell foam a foam structure in which each bubble of gas is enclosed by the base material of the foam.

coating a substance applied to the surface of a material in such a way as to close the interstices without permeating the material itself.

comfort stretch a material that is easily elongated.

composite fibers fibers made by embedding nanoscale fibrils of one fiber in a matrix of another fiber.

compression a force that acts on opposite sides (or ends) of a material to decrease its length.

compressive impact abrupt compressive stress.

conduction the transfer of energy that occurs when the surfaces of two objects touch.

contact angle the angle the edge of a drop of water makes with the surface of a fabric with larger angles indicating water-resistance.

context awareness the ability of a smart system to detect changes in the wearer's behavior or environment.

convection the transfer of heat through the mixing of the molecules of fluid such as air and water.

converter a manufacturer who finishes fabrics.

core-spun yarn a yarn consisting of a central core (often elastic) wrapped in fiber.

courses yarns in a weft knit that move across a fabric.

crack valve a one-way opening for air to pass out of a positive pressure suit to prevent it from overinflating.

cut (of clothing) the general shape and style of a garment based on the contour of garment segments.

deceleration the rate of decrease of velocity.

decision matrix a tool that allows options for a design element or a completed design to be comparatively evaluated.

denier unit of measure that equals the weight in grams of 9,000 meters of fiber. The smaller the denier number, the finer the fiber.

dermis the layer of skin that lies below the epidermis.

die in heat sealing, a metal bar in the shape of the desired seal.

dielectric insulating.

dilatant materials that flow easily under low force but stiffen in response to a strong force.

display a device that communicates information to a user through any sensory modality.

distal farther from the attachment point of a bone or muscle or the midline of the body.

divergence angle the angle at which light reflects or bounces off a surface it strikes.

dope the liquid phase of a polymer.

dope dyeing adding color to a thermoplastic fiber before it is formed.

dosimeter a device that indicates the amount of radiation to which a wearer has been exposed.

drysuit a diving suit that is worn in more extreme cold water conditions. Drysuits are designed to completely exclude water.

ductile metals metals that become plastic and elongate rather than fracturing when impacted.

dye (dyeing) a colored substance that is made of molecules that dissolve in water (adding color to materials using dye).

ease the space between a garment and the body wearing it.

elasticity the ability of a material to stretch or elongate.

elastic limit the elongation at which a material permanently deforms.

elastic modulus the force required to stretch a material.

elastic recovery the ability of a material to regain its original length, shape, etc.

electrocardiogram (ECG or EKG) a test that measures the electrical activity of the heart.

electrogoniometer (elgon) an electronic device that continuously measures body joint movement; an electronic goniometer.

emissivity a material's relative ability to emit energy from its surface.

endothermic a chemical reaction that results in a net absorption of thermal energy (cooling).

energy conservation the basic principle of physics that states that energy is never created nor lost but may change from one form to another.

energy exchange the process of conversion from one form of energy to another, as for example, electrical energy to heat or sound.

entry suits firefighting ensembles designed to be worn in flames, including the high-temperature flames produced by burning fuel.

epidermis the outermost layer of skin.

e-textiles textiles with conductive and/or electronic functionality.

extension straightening (of a body part).

extrapersonal space the space around the body that is outside the limits of reach.

fabric count (thread count) the number of yarns per square inch.

felt a nonwoven fabric made by laying wool fibers together and joining them by subjecting them to a combination of heat, moisture, and pressure; by needlepunching; or by bonding synthetic fibers.

fiber the smallest visual unit of a textile. Fibers have extremely long length in relation to their diameter.

fiberfill a batt of manufactured fibers, often made with polyester.

fiber-reinforced rein a rigid, molded material composed of fibers embedded in a thermoplastic resin.

fiberweb see *nonwoven*.

filling the crosswise yarns in a weave, also called weft.

film a thin, continuous sheet of material less than 0.01 in. (0.025 cm.) thick.

fireproof will not burn.

flameproof see *fireproof*.

flame resistant (flame retardant, fire resistant, or FR) igniting with difficulty and self-extinguishing when the source of the fire is removed.

flammable easy to burn; readily catches on fire. See also *inflammable*.

flexion bending.

float a missed interlacing of a yarn in which a lengthwise yarn passes over more than one crosswise yarn or vice versa.

fluorescent composed of atoms that can be excited and arranged by high-frequency radiation such as ultraviolet light. When the source of energy is removed, atoms return to their original position immediately.

foam a material made by trapping bubbles of gas inside a solid material.

fourchettes separate, shaped strips of fabric that cover the sides of the fingers in fitted gloves.

four-way stretch fabrics that elongate in both crosswise and lengthwise directions.

frameworks graphic illustrations of the most important variables of a design problem and the relationship between those variables.

frontal plane an imaginary plane that divides the body into a front and back.

g an abbreviation for acceleration due to gravity on Earth. "One-g" expresses the acceleration due to the gravitational force on Earth.

gamma rays powerful, short wavelength, electromagnetic radiation released during radioactive decay.

goniometer a two-armed tool with a pivot point at the center that is used to measure the range of motion of a joint.

gravity dependent goniometer (inclinometer) a goniometer, one end of which is placed on a body part and the other of which hangs free so that the readout is dependent upon gravity.

greige goods unfinished fabrics.

gusset a small piece of fabric, often diamond-shaped or triangular, that is added to a garment to increase ease of movement or change the overall shape of the garment.

haptic pertaining to the sense of touch.

hazmat an abbreviation meaning hazardous materials.

heat sealing the process of fusing two pieces of material together using heat to melt them and pressure to force the melted areas to combine and form a joint.

heat shaping (heat molding) the process of heating, forming and then cooling thermoplastic fabrics so that they form desired shapes.

hinge joint a joint such as the elbow that allows only flexion and extension.

horizontal abduction the movement that occurs when the arm is flexed to the shoulder level and then abducted.

horizontal adduction the movement that occurs when the arm is abducted to shoulder level and then moved horizontally to a forward flexed position.

horn (in heat sealing) the part of an ultrasonic welder that delivers ultrasonic vibrations to materials being sealed.

hot air welding heat sealing in which heat is delivered with a blast of hot air.

hydraulic pressure pressure generated by liquids.

hydrophobic water-hating.

hygroscopic able to pick up and hold moisture.

hyper (prefix) beyond the anatomical position.

ideation the idea generation process.

imbibe hold liquid between the yarns of a fabric rather than absorb it.

impulse a term used to express change in momentum.

incandescent light a form of light that is produced by heating a conductive material. It produces heat.

incidence angle the angle at which light approaches a surface or object.

indirect observation observing evidence that an activity has taken place rather than the activity itself.

inelastic unable to return to original shape after a collision; deformable.

inertia the quality of a body that makes it continue its state of motion.

inferior (position) lower on the body; closer to the feet.

inflammable readily catches on fire. See also *flammable.*

infrared light with a wavelength just longer than the longest wavelength of visible light (red).

injection or compression molding a shaping process whereby material is pushed by a shaped die into a heated mold and pressure is applied.

insensible perspiration the continual drying out of moisture that lies at the skin surface; it is not related to the actions of the sweat glands.

integral skin foams (self-skinned foams) foams that are formed with a higher-density skin on the surface of a lower-density foam interior.

interaction matrixes an ideation tool in the form of a grid structure that allows new combinations of design variables to generate new ideas.

interaction narratives short storytelling exercises that help a designer imagine how a user will interact with a design solution.

ionizing radiation a form of radiation that is electrically charged.

kinesiology the study of human movement.

kinesthetic sense the brain's perception of the body's position and movement in space.

kinetic energy a form of mechanical energy that is the energy of motion.

knit a fabric made by linking loops of yarn on needles. Types of knits include:

> **double knit** a firm fabric made on two needle beds with two inseparable sets of loops.
>
> **raschel** an open lace-like warp knit that contains extra yarns that are laid into the knit.
>
> **warp** formed by machine, with the yarn from one row of loops moving lengthwise into to the next row forming a pattern that does not run.
>
> **weft or filling** similar to hand knitting with rows of loops drawn through a previous row of loops with a yarn moving across the fabric; breaking a loop can result in a run.

laminar airflow an air management system used in cleanrooms in which air is moved at a uniform velocity along parallel flow lines.

laminate a multilayer material produced by joining two or more materials with an adhesive, or sometimes, with a foam.

lapped seam a seam formed when the edges of the garment sections to be joined are laid over one another with one raw edge on the outside and one on the inside of the garment.

latent heat of vaporization the body heat needed to raise the temperature of moisture on the skin surface so that it evaporates.

lateral toward the side.

lateral flexion bending of the head or trunk to the side.

lateral thinking an idea-generating technique developed by Edward deBono that departs from traditional thinking to explore even unlikely solutions in order to generate new approaches to solving a problem.

lead equivalency (of protective materials) the amount of protection that would be offered if a specific thickness of lead if it were substituted for the material.

ligaments strong cords of fibrous tissue that support and hold articulating surfaces together at the joints.

light-emitting diode (LED) an electronic component that emits light when exposed to electrical current.

lines of nonextension curved lines on the surface of the body along which the skin does not expand during body movement.

longitudinal axis (z axis) the line that runs perpendicular to the transverse plane.

loop tape a woven tape that contains continuous, strong loops for lacing.

low-fidelity (prototype) an unfinished form of a design prototype used to test design ideas.

luminescent light cool light produced through the absorption of radiant or electrical energy. It does not produce heat.

manufactured fiber a fiber not found in nature; created through a manufacturing process.

mass the amount of matter in a body.

mechanical filter a material that traps particles by having small interstices.

mechanoreceptor a sensory organ, nerve, or cell that converts a mechanical stimulus into an electrical signal carried by the nerves.

medial toward the center of the body.

medial axis (x axis) a line that runs perpendicular to the frontal plane.

microfibers fibers that have deniers of less than 1, with most measuring between 0.5 and 0.8 denier per filament.

microgravity (micro-g) a synonym for weightlessness or zero-gravity but indicating that a very small amount of gravity is always present, even in outer space.

microporous having openings that allow air to pass through but small enough to exclude liquids.

mind mapping a rapid idea-generation technique in which everything that is known about a problem is laid out in a branched pattern from a central idea.

molding a shaping process for thermoplastics.

momentum the quantity of motion in a body (mass × velocity).

motor neurons nerves that communicate messages from the brain to the muscles.

nap fibers that stand up from the surface of a fabric.

napped fabrics fabrics such as fleece and flannel that are brushed so that fibers extend from their surfaces.

natural fiber a material found in fibrous form in nature.

needlepunch fabric a material formed by entangling fibers together into a batt using the mechanical action of hundreds of hooked needles.

negative pressure the condition of a suit or structure in which air is pulled inward so that any hazard inside does not contaminate the environment.

neutral buoyancy the condition in which a diver remains suspended under the water as if weightless, neither floating nor sinking.

neutron radiation free neutrons that are released from atoms in the process of a nuclear reaction or radioactive decay.

nonflammable will not burn. See also *fireproof*.

nonionizing radiation a form of radiation, such as heat, light, and microwaves, that is not electrically charged.

nonwoven (web or fiberweb) textiles made without interlacing or interlooping filaments or yarns.

open cell foam cellular materials with interconnected cells.

participant observation a research technique in which the designer experiences the user's activities.

percutaneous through the skin.

peripersonal space the layer of space around the body that is within reach or grasping distance.

permselective fabrics materials that allow water vapor and air to pass through but attract and bond chemical/biological agents.

personas characters who represent users or groups of users.

PFD an acronym for a personal flotation device; life preserver.

phase a state of matter: solid, liquid, or gas.

phase change a transition between states of matter.

phosphorescent composed of atoms that can be excited and rearranged by visible light or electricity. When the source of energy is removed, atoms return to their original state very slowly, giving off light in the process.

photochromic a material that changes color when exposed to light.

piezoelectric a material that generates an electric current when exposed to an external force, and generates a force when exposed to an electric current.

pigments microscopic particles used to add color to fabric.

pinch seam a seam in which two layers are laid wrong sides together and the seam is sealed so that the material edges (seam allowances) lay to one side. In functional apparel the edges are often on the outside of the garment.

plied yarn a multifiber yarn made by twisting several yarns together.

plunge welding a heat sealing process whereby a press lowers a metal die down onto a garment.

pneumatic pressure air pressure.

polymer a large molecule made up of many similar units connected by chemical bonds.

positive pressure slightly inflating a garment or structure so that if puncture occurs, hazards outside are propelled away from its surface.

postero (prefix) toward the back.

potential energy a form of stored mechanical energy that holds the possibility of motion.

powered exeoskeleton a mechanical device worn on the body that provides assistance for movement.

power stretch a material that requires more force to expand.

pressure force per unit area of contact.

processor an electronic component capable of performing computations.

pronation medial rotation of the forearm.

proprioception the sense of the position and movement of one's body relative to itself and the surrounding environment.

proximal closer to the attachment point of a bone or muscle or the midline of the body.

proximity suit a firefighting ensemble designed for work close to flames.

psychophysics the field of study that examines the relationship between the nature of a physical stimulus and the way that stimulus is interpreted by the human brain.

radiation the transfer of heat by electromagnetic waves.

radioactive emitting ionizing radiation.

radio frequency (RF) sealing (dielectric sealing) heat sealing in which heat is generated by radio waves.

refraction bending of light rays.

resin a thick liquid made of a variety of synthetic substances that hardens into a solid.

retroreflection a type of reflection in which light is returned directly toward the source of light.

ripstop woven with stronger yarns that form a grid approximately 3/16" (4.78 mm) wide to keep tears from propagating.

rotation the movement of a body part around its own longitudinal axis.

sagittal plane a vertical plane that divides the body into right and left halves.

selectively permeable membrane (SPM) see *permselective fabrics.*

selvage the firm, non-raveling finish on both edges of a fabric.

semiconductor a material that allows electrical current to flow through it under some conditions but not under others.

sensory neurons nerves that carry stimuli from a sensory organ to the brain.

shearing stress (shear) the result of opposite forces acting on a body so that adjacent parts slide over one another.

sheets flat materials 0.01 in. (0.025 cm.) thick or greater made from liquid dope not in fibrous form.

shingling the overlapping of materials so that they appear like roofing shingles.

Shirley cloth a fabric composed of long, fine cotton fibers that swell when wet allowing it to breathe when dry but be almost waterproof when wet.

skin strain (local skin strain) the difference in measurement between points on the skin on either side of a joint when the joint is fully flexed and when it is fully extended.

sling a fabric attached to the body side of a protective pad that has less curve than the pad and thus provides a standoff.

smart (materials or systems) a material or system that affects a change in its physical properties in response to a stimulus.

spacer a low-density material used to create an air space between two material layers.

spall small fragments of materials that fly away from a site after a high-speed impact occurs.

spinneret a device that looks much like a showerhead through which liquid dope is forced to form manufactured fibers.

standoff the space between a rigid protector or garment and the body.

staple fibers relatively short natural fibers such as those in cotton and wool, or manufactured fibers that have been chopped into shorter lengths.

stitching wheels rotary dies used in a heat sealing machine.

straight of grain the direction of a fabric parallel to its warp yarns.

strain gauge a sensor that responds to deformation with a change in electrical property.

superior (position) higher on the body.

supination lateral rotation of the forearm.

surfactant (surface active agent) a chemical substance that lowers the surface tension between two liquids or a liquid and a solid. It is used in the process of making foams.

synectics an idea-generating method in which different and apparently irrelevant elements are joined together as a stimulus to generating creative problem solutions.

tendons tough, fibrous bands of tissue that join muscles to bones.

tensile impact abrupt tensile stress.

tensile stress (tension) force acting on the opposite ends of a body that increases the length of the body or pulls it apart.

textile a flexible material made of fibers and yarns. Weaves, knits and nonwoven materials are textiles; some references consider films and the products made from textile materials to be textiles.

texturing (texturizing) the process by which thermoplastic, manufactured fibers (or natural fibers coated with thermoplastics) are given a permanent crimp, loop, or curl.

thermal conductivity the ability of a material to transfer heat.

thermal resistance the ability of a material to resist the flow of heat; the insulative property of a material.

thermal welding (contact heating) a joining process in which a heated tool is lowered onto the materials to be joined.

thermochromic a material that changes color in response to a change in temperature.

thermography a technique that uses an infrared camera to detect the heat being given off by a body.

thermoplastic able to be softened or melted by heat yet become solid when cooled.

thread count the number of yarns per square inch, sometimes called fabric count.

toughness (of metals) the energy required to fracture a bar of metal.

toxic industrial chemicals (TICs) chemical hazards (e.g., carcinogens, reproductive hazards, corrosives, or agents that affect the lungs or blood) or physical hazards (e.g., flammable, combustible, explosive, or reactive agents).

transducer something that translates a stimulus (e.g., a movement, light, or sound) into an electrical signal, or vice versa.

transition temperature the temperature at which a material changes from one phase to another.

transverse axis (y axis) a line that runs perpendicular to the sagittal plane.

transverse plane an imaginary plane that divides the body into upper and lower sections.

triboelectric effect a type of contact charge caused by friction.

turnout gear protective clothing for firefighters that is designed for regular firefighting in which firefighters operate hoses and other equipment at some distance from flames.

two-point threshold the distance at which two points of tactile stimulus are perceived as two rather than as one single point.

two-way stretch fabrics that elongate in both crosswise and lengthwise directions. Some manufacturers use this term to describe materials that stretch only in the crosswise direction or only in the lengthwise direction and use the term "four-way stretch" to describe a material that stretches in both directions.

ultrasonics high-frequency vibrations used to fuse thermoplastic materials.

ultraviolet a wavelength of light just shorter than the shortest end of the visible spectrum (violet).

V50 ballistics limit the velocity at which 50% of impacts given to a test material will result in complete penetration by a bullet.

vacuum forming a molding process that involves drawing a heated, softened film onto the surface of a perforated mold using the force of a vacuum behind the mold.

vapor barrier (sometimes called VBI or vapor barrier insulation) a system of insulation in which waterproof materials form the innermost and outermost layers.

vasoconstriction contraction of the blood vessels that slows down blood flow and helps conserve body heat by bringing less blood near the skin surface.

vasodilation expansion of the blood vessels that results in increased blood flow, bringing internal body heat closer to the skin surface

velocity the rate of speed of a body in a specific direction.

vestibular sense the body's sense of orientation and balance.

wales pile lines in corduroy; lengthwise lines in weft knits.

warp yarn the lengthwise yarns in a weave. See also *knits, warp.*

waterproof able to exclude water under demanding conditions of pressure.

water repellent treated with a finish or coating that is not easily penetrated by water.

water resistant able to shed water.

weave fabric made by interlacing yarns, usually at right angles. Types of weaves include:

basket formed by weaving two or more yarns together in both warp and filling directions as if they were one yarn.

leno (gauze) an open weave in which two weft yarns form figure eights around warp yarns.

pile textiles containing extra yarns that extend upward from the textile surface.

plain formed by alternating single yarns in a one-over, one-under pattern.

rib made by weaving heavier yarns or groups of yarns in one direction.

satin made by allowing weft yarns to pass over from four to seven weft yarns, producing a material with high lustre.

triaxial made by interlacing three sets of yarns; a stable weave with no bias.

twill made by allowing each weft yarn to float over at least two warp yarns, creating a diagonal pattern

web see *nonwoven*.

weft yarn the crosswise yarns in a weave; also called filling.

weight the force that gravity exerts on a body.

wetsuit a suit for recreational divers made of closed-cell foam. A thin layer of water is allowed to enter the suit.

wicking the transport of liquids along the surface of a fiber due to capillary action.

wind chill factor an expression of the effective cooling of a specific temperature when wind is present. Temperatures are often quoted with wind chill equivalents to indicate what a temperature feels like with specific velocities of wind.

working position the shape clothing would take if it fit a user in his or her most frequently taken body pose.

wrist ring a rigid ring at the end of the sleeve of a fully encapsulating suit over which protective gloves can be stretched for an airtight connection.

X-radiation a type of ionizing radiation that has an extremely short wavelength and can pass through materials that would ordinarily reflect or absorb visible light.

yarn staple fibers, filaments, or other materials twisted together to form a strand that can be used to form a textile fabric.

BIBLIOGRAPHY

AATCC (American Association of Textile Chemists and Colorists). "AATCC Test Method 127-2008, Water Resistance: Hydrostatic Pressure Test," https://www.aatcc.org/Technical/Test_Methods/scopes/tm127.cfm. Accessed May 14, 2013.

Adams, J. 1986a. *The Care and Feeding of Ideas*. Reading, MA: Addison-Wesley Publishing Company.

———. 1986b. *Conceptual Blockbusting*, 11th ed. Reading, MA: Addison-Wesley Publishing Company.

Adams, P., and W. Keyserling. 1993. "Three Methods for Measuring Range of Motion while Wearing Protective Clothing: A Comparative Study." *International Journal of Industrial Ergonomics* 12: 177–91.

Alluniforms.com. "Clean Room Fabric Chart," http://www.alluniforms.com/crchart.htm. Accessed July 20, 2013.

Ashdown, S. 1989. "An Analysis of Task-Related Movement of Asbestos Abatement Crews as a Basis for the Design of Protective Coveralls." Master's thesis, Cornell University, Ithaca, NY.

———. 2011. "Improving Body Movement Comfort in Apparel." In *Comfort in Clothing*, edited by G. Song. Cambridge, UK: Woodhead Publishing. 278–302.

Ashdown, S., and S. Watkins. 1996. "Concurrent Engineering in the Design of Protective Clothing: Interfacing with Equipment Design." In *Performance of Protective Clothing, Fifth Volume, ASTM STP 1237*, edited by J. Johnson and S. Mansdorf. West Conshohocken, PA: American Society for Testing and Materials.

Ashley, S. 1994. "Automotive Safety is in the Bag." *Mechanical Engineering* 116: 58–64.

ASTM (American Society for Testing and Materials). 2012. *Annual Book of ASTM Standards, Section 7: Textiles, Volume 7.01*. West Conshohocken, PA: ASTM International.

———. "ASTM D3393—91(2009), Standard Specification for Coated Fabrics-Waterproofness," http://www.astm.org/Standards/D3393.htm. Accessed May 14, 2013.

———. "ASTM F1154-11 Standard Practices for Qualitatively Evaluating the Comfort, Fit, Function, and Durability of Protective Ensembles and Ensemble Components," http://www.astm.org/Standards/F1154.htm. Accessed 4/15/13.

———. "Standard Test Method for Dynamic Shock Cushioning Characteristics of Packaging Material," http://www.astm.org/Standards/D1596.htm. Accessed July 24, 2013.

———. "Standard Test Method for Rubber Property—Compression Set," http://www.astm.org/Standards/D395.htm. Accessed July 24, 2013.

Austin, P., and S. Timmerman. 1965. *Design and Operation of Clean Rooms*. Detroit: Business News Publishing Co.

Baker, M. 1987. *Sex Differences in Human Performance*. Chichester, UK: John Wiley and Sons.

Barron, E. 1975. "An Objective Methodology Developed by the Army Using the Load Profile Analyzer for Determining the Comfort, Fit, Sizing and Effect on Performance and Acceptability of Body Armor" (unpublished report). Natick, MA: U.S. Army Natick Laboratories.

Benesh, R., and J. Benesh. 1956. *An Introduction to Benesh Dance Notation*. London: A. and C. Black.

Biotechnology, Inc. 1968. *US Naval Flight Surgeon's Manual*. Washington, DC: U.S. Department of the Navy.

Body covering (Exhibit catalog). 1968. New York: Museum of Contemporary Crafts.

Bohlin, N. 1963. "Device to Protect an Occupant against Bodily Injury during Emergency Escape from Aircraft." U.S. Patent 3,074,669, filed August 28, 1959, and issued January 22, 1963.

Breckenridge, J., and R. Goldman. 1977. "Effects of Clothing on Bodily Resistance against Meteorological Stimuli." In *Progress in Biometeorology*. Amsterdam: Swets and Zeitlinger.

Brown, D. 2010. *Human Biological Diversity*. Boston: Prentice Hall.

Buzan, T. 1984. *Use Both Sides of Your Brain*. New York: Plume.

Cao, Wei. 2007. "Factors Impacting the Liquid Penetration Performance of Surgical Gown Fabric." Dissertation, Florida State University, Tallahassee.

Cardello, A., G. Darsch, C. Fitzgerald, S. Gleason, and R. Teixeira. 1991. "Nutrient, Waste Management, and Hygiene Systems for Chemical Protective Suits," *Military Medicine* 156(5): 211–15.

Clark, R., and O. Edholm. 1985. *Man and His Thermal Environment*. London: Edward Arnold.

Clark, R., M. Goff, and B. Mullan. 1977. "Skin Temperatures during Sunbathing and Some Observations on the Effect of Hot and Cold Drinks on These Temperatures." *Journal of Physiology* 267: 8–9.

Clark, S., and M. O'Mahony. 2005. *Techno Textiles 2*. London: Thames & Hudson.

Cohen, A., and I. Johnson. 2012. *J. J. Pizzuto's Fabric Science*, 10th ed. New York: Fairchild Books.

Collins, K. J., T. A. Asdel-Rahman, J. C. Easton, P. Sacco, J. Ison, and C. J. Dore. 1996. "Effects of Facial Cooling on Elderly and Young Subjects: Interactions with Breath-holding and Lower Body Negative Pressure." *Clinical Science* 90(6): 485–492.

Coon, C. 1968. *The Living Races of Man*. New York: Alfred A. Knopf.

Cooper, H. 1976. "Life in a Space Station—I." *The New Yorker*, August 30: 34.

Crockford, G. 1977. "Trawler Fishermen's Protective Clothing." In *Human Factors in Work, Design and Production*, edited by R. Sell et al. London: Taylor and Francis.

Crow, R., and M. Dewar. 1986. "Stresses in Clothing as Related to Seam Strength." *Textile Research Journal* 56: 467–73.

Cunningham, G. 1972. *How to Keep Warm*. Denver: Gerry, An Outdoor Sports Company.

Damon, A., H. Stoudt, and R. McFarland. 1966. *The Human Body in Equipment Design*. Cambridge, MA: Harvard University Press.

Daniels, G. 1952. "The 'Average Man'?" Contract AF1860030, Report # 0302010. Wright-Patterson AFB: Air Force Aerospace Medical Research Lab.

de Bono, E. 1985. *Lateral Thinking*. New York: Viking Penguin.

———. 1999. *Six Thinking Hats*. Boston: Little, Brown and Company.

de deMonchaux, N. 2011. *Spacesuit: Fashioning Apollo*. Cambridge, MA: MIT Press.

Demarest, N. 2000. "Evaluation of Inflatable Fabric Cylinders for Use in an Elbow Orthotic." Master's thesis, Cornell University, Ithaca, NY.

Demarest, N., R. MacDonald, and J. Carbo. "Article of Apparel for Resistance Training," http://www.google.com/patents?id=pxGoAAAAEBAJ&printsec=frontcover&dq=US+2008/0078008+A1&hl=en&sa=X&ei=MTexT927KqXiiAK00M3rAw&ved=0CDYQ6AEwAA. Accessed January 9, 2014.

Disabled Living Foundation. 1974. *Clothing Fastenings for the Handicapped and Disabled*. London: Disabled Living Foundation.

EPA (Environmental Protection Agency). "Personal Protective Equipment," http://www.epa.gov /oppfead1/safety/workers/equip.htm. Accessed July 17, 2013.

Euclid Vidaro Manufacturing Company. "Cleanroom Flame Resistant Garments," http://www.vidaro .com/cleanroom-flame-resistant-garments. Accessed July 20, 2013.

EWMN Center. "The Eshkol-Wachmann Movement Noatation Center," http://ewmncenter.com/. Accessed September 21, 2014.

Fabrican, Ltd. "What is Fabrican?" http://www.fabric anltd.com. Accessed May 30, 2013.

Fan, J., and Y. Chen. 2002. "Measurement of Clothing Thermal Insulation and Moisture Vapour Resistance Using a Novel Perspiring Fabric Thermal Manikin." *Measurement Science and Technology* 13(7): 1115–23.

Fourt, L., and N. Hollies. 1969. "The Comfort and Function of Clothing," Technical Report 69-74-CE. Natick, MA: U.S. Army Natick Laboratories.

Freund, B. J., C. O Brien, and A. J. Young. 1994. "Alcohol Ingestion and Temperature Regulation during Cold Exposure," *Journal of Wilderness Medicine* 5(1): 88–98.

Gemperle, F., C. Kasabach, J. Stivoric, M. Bauer, and R. Martin. 1998. "Design for Wearability." In *ISWC "98 Proceedings of the Second International Symposium on Wearable Computers*. Pittsburgh: IEEE Computer Society.

Gibson, P. 2008. "Effect of Wool Components in Pile Fabrics on Water Vapor Sorption, Heat Release and Humidity Buffering," Technical Report TR 08/-13. Natick, MA: U.S. Army Natick Soldier Systems Center.

Goldman, R., J. Breckenridge., E. Reeves, and E. Beckman. 1966. "Wet vs Dry Suit Approaches to Water Immersion Protective Clothing." *Aerospace Medicine* 37(5): 485–87.

Goldman, R., and B. Kampmann, eds. 2007. *Handbook on Clothing*, 2nd ed., http://www .environmental-ergonomics.org. Accessed September 16, 2013.

Goldschmidt, G. 1991. "The Dialectics of Sketching." *Creativity Research Journal* 4(2): 123–43.

Gordon, W. 1961. *Synectics*. New York: Harper and Row.

W. L. Gore and Associates, Inc. "Trail 3: Waterproof, Windproof, Breathable," http://www.gore-tex .com/resources/goretex/community/mountain techs/Trail_3_WaterWindBreathe.pdf. Accessed May 14, 2013.

Graham, T., M. Viswanathan, J. Van Dijk, A. Bonen, and J. George. 1989. "Thermal and Metabolic Responses to Cold by Men and Eumenorrheic and Amenorrheic Women." *Journal of Applied Physiology*, 67(1): 282–90.

Greenleaf, W. 2001. "Neuro/Orthopedic Rehabilitation and Disability Solutions Using Virtual Reality Technology." In *Information Technologies in Medicine, Volume 2, Rehabilitation and Treatment*, edited by M. Akay and A. Marsh. Hoboken, NJ: Wiley-IEEE Press.

Grucza, R., J. Lecroart, G. Carette, J. Hauser, and Y. Houdas. 1987. "Effect of Voluntary Dehydration on Thermoregulatory Responses to Heat in Men and Women." *European Journal of Applied Physiology* 56: 317–22.

Haar, S. 2011. "Studio Practices for Shaping and Heat-Setting Synthetic Fabric." *Journal of Fashion Design, Technology and Education* 4(1): 31–41.

Haslag, W. M., and A. B. Hertzman. 1965. "Temperature Regulation in Young Women." *Journal of Applied Physiology*, 20: 1283–88.

Hatch, K. 1993. *Textile Science*. Minneapolis: West Publishing Company.

Haupt, U. 1978. "Taking a New Perspective on Design." *Astronautics and Aeronautics* 16(5): 55.

Havenith, G., J. Coenen, L. Kistemaker, and W. Kenney. 1998. "Relevance of Individual Characteristics for Human Heat Stress Response Is Dependent on Exercise Intensity and Climate Type." *European Journal of Applied Physiology* 77: 231–41.

Havenith, G., D. Fiala, K. Blazejczyk, M. Richards, P. Brode, I. Holmér, H. Rintamaki, Y. Benshabat, and G. Jendritzky. 2012. "The UTCI-Clothing Model." *International Journal of Biometeorology* 56(3) 461–70.

Havenith, G., A. Fogarty, R. Bartlett, C. Smith, and V. Ventenat. 2008. "Male and Female Upper Body Sweat Distribution during Running Measured with Technical Absorbents." *European Journal of Applied Physiology* 104: 245–55.

Haymes, E. 1984. "Physiological Responses of Female Athletes to Heat Stress: A Review." *Physician Sports Medicine Journal*, 12: 45–55.

Head, H., and G. Holmes. 1912. "Researches into Sensory Disturbances from Cerebral Lesions." *The Lancet* 179(4612): 144–52.

Hewitt, P. 2009. *Conceptual Physics*, 11th ed. New York: Harper Collins.

———. 1989. *Conceptual Physics*. New York: Harper Collins.

Hutchinson, A. 1970. *Labanotation*. New York: Theatre Arts Books.

Iberall, A. 1964. "The Use of Lines of Nonextension to Improve Mobility in Full-Pressure Suits," Report AMRL-TR-64-118. Wright Patterson Air Force Base, OH: Air Force Systems Command.

ILC Space Systems Inc. 1984. "Space Station Clothing Development Study," Contract No. 9-16589. Houston, TX: National Aeronautics and Space Administration (NASA).

ISO (International Organization for Standardization). "ISO 811:1981—Determination of Resistance to Water Penetration—Hydrostatic Pressure Test," http://www.iso.org/iso/catalogue_detail. htm?csnumber=5156. Accessed May 13, 2013.

Jacobs, G. 1983. "Color Vision in Animals." *Endeavor* 7(3): 137–140.

Kadolph, S. 2010. *Textiles*. Boston: Pearson Education.

Kajimoto, H., N. Kawakami, and S. Tachi. 2003. "Psychophysical Evaluation of Receptor Selectivity in Electro-Tactile Display." *Proceedings of the 13th International Symposium on Measurement and Control in Robotics (ISMCR)* 13: 83–86.

Keegan, J,. and F. Garrett. 1948. "The Segmental Distribution of the Cutaneous Nerves in the Limbs of Man." *Anatomical Record* 102(4): 409–37.

Kirk, W., and S. Ibrahim. 1966. "Fundamental Relationship of Fabric Extensibility to Anthropometric Requirements and Garment Performance." *Textile Research Journal* 36: 37–47.

Kirstein, T., ed. 2013. *Multidisciplinary Know-How for Smart-Textiles Developers*. Philadelphia: Woodhead Publishing Limited.

Knapp, J., ed. 1988. *Integrated Protective Clothing and Equipment Concept Development Plan*. Ottawa: Canadian Forces.

Koberg, D., and J. Bagnall. 1981. *The Universal Traveler*. Los Altos, CA: Wm. Kaufmann.

———. 2003. *The Universal Traveler*. Mississauga, Ontario: Crisp Learning.

Komor, N., S. Gilliland, J. Clawson, M. Bhardwaj, M. Garg, C. Zeagler, and T. Starner. 2009. "Is It Gropable? Assessing the Impact of Mobility on Textile Interfaces." In *ISWC 2009 Proceedings of the 14th International Symposium on Wearable Computers*. 71–74. Linz, Austria: IEEE Computer Society.

Koscheyev, V., A. Coca, and G. Leon. 2006. "Overview of Physiological Principles to Support Thermal Balance and Comfort of Astronauts in Open Space and on Planetary Surfaces." *Acta Astronautica* 60: 479–87.

Koscheyev, V., A. Coca, G. Leon, and M. Dancisak. 2002. "Individual Thermal Profiles as a Basis for Comfort Improvement in Space and Other Environments." *Aviation, Space and Environmental Medicine* 73(12): 1195–202.

Koscheyev, V., G. Leon, and A. Coca. 2005. "Finger Heat Flux/Temperature as an Indicator of Thermal Imbalance with Application for Extravehicular Activity." *Acta Astronautica* 57: 713–21.

LaBat, K., and S. Sokolowski. 1999. "A Three-Stage Design Process Applied to an Industry-University Textile Product Design Project." *Clothing and Textiles Research Journal* 17(1): 11–20.

Lambert, M., T. Mann, and J. Dugas. 2008. "Ethnicity and Temperature Regulation." *Medicine and Sport Science* 53: 104–20.

Langer, K. 1861. "Zur anatomie und physiologie der haut." *Sitzungsber der Akademie der Wissenschaften in Wien* 44(19).

———. 1978. "On the Anatomy and Physiology of the Skin: I. The Cleavability of the Cutis." *British Journal of Plastic Surgery* 31(1): 3–8.

Lawson, B. 1983. *How Designers Think*. London: Butterworth Architecture.

Lewis, D., E. Kamon, and J. Hodgson, 1986. "Physiological Differences between Genders." *Sports Medicine* 3: 357–69.

Madigan, C., and A. Ellwood. 1983. *Brainstorms and Thunderbolts*. New York : Macmillan Publishing Company.

Maibach, H., R. Fieldman, T. Milby, and W. Serat. 1971. "Regional Variation in Percutaneous Penetration in Man." *Archives of Environmental Health* 20: 573–74; 654–59.

Marer, P. 2000. *The Safe and Effective Use of Pesticides*, 2nd ed. University of California: ANR Publications.

Massachusetts Institute of Technology Age Lab. "AGNES (Age Gain Now Empathy System)," http://agelab.mit.edu/agnes-age-gain-now-empathy-system. Accessed July 24, 2013.

Mayer, K. 2003. "The Relation of Insulation Type and Coverage to Dexterity and Tactility in Alpine Cold Weather Hand Gear." Master's thesis, Cornell University, Ithaca, NY.

Mazzuchetti, G., G. Lopardo, and R. Demichelis. 2007. "Influence of Nonwoven Fabrics' Physical Parameters on Thermal and Water Vapor Resistance." *Journal of Industrial Textiles* 36(3): 253–64.

McGrath, B., A. Estrada, M. Braithwaite, A. Raj, and A. Rupert. 2004. "Tactile Situation Awareness System Flight Demonstration Final Report," USAARL Report 2004-10. Pensacola, FL: US Army Aeromedical Research Lab .

McLean, J., and S. Watkins. 1985. *Selecting Sports Equipment Series*. Ithaca, NY: Cornell Cooperative Extension.

J. Mikkonen, J. Vanhala, A. Reho, and J. Impiö. 2001. "Reima Smart Shout Concept and Prototype." In *ISWC 2001 Proceedings of the 16th International Symposium on Wearable Computers*. 174–175. Zurich, Switzerland: IEEE Computer Society.

MultiCam, "How MultiCam Was Developed," http://www.multicampattern.com/about. Accessed August 13, 2013.

NFPA (National Fire Protection Association). "NFPA 1971: Standard on Protective Clothing for Structural Fire Fighting," http://www.nfpa.org/catalog/product.asp?pid=NFPA1971ARCHIV&cookie_test=1. Accessed July 20, 2013.

NASDA (National Association of State Departments of Agriculture). "PPE for Pesticide Operators: Risk Assessment, PPE Requirements and Labeling," http://www.nasda.org/File.aspx?id=17983. Accessed July 17, 2013.

National Cancer Institute. "Cell Phones and Cancer Risk," *http://www.cancer.gov/cancertopics/factsheet/Risk/cellphones.* Accessed January 27, 2013.

Neuman, M. R. 2000. "Biopotential Electrodes." In J.D. Bronzino (Ed.), *The Biomedical Engineering Handbook: Second Edition*. 48-1–48-11. Boca Raton: CRC Press LLC.

Newburgh, L., ed. 1949. *Physiology of Heat Regulation*. Philadelphia: W. B. Saunders.

Norkin, C., and D. White. 2003. *Measurement of Joint Motion: A Guide to Goniometry*. Philadelphia: F. A. Davis.

Norman, D. 1988. *The Design of Everyday Things.* New York: Basic Books.

Oddsson, L., and P. Meyer. "Sensor Prosthetic for Balance Control," https://www.google.com /patents/US20050131317?pg=PA1&dq=oddsson+ meyer&hl=en&sa=X&ei=vy_hUvibFMOCy QG2rYDoAg&ved=https://ww (aw.google.com /patents/US20050131317?pg=PA1&dq=oddsson+ meyer&hl=en&sa=X&ei=vy_hUvibFMOCyQ G2rYDoAg&ved=. Accessed January 26, 2014.

OSHA (Occupational Safety and Health Administration), U.S. Department of Labor. "Foot Protection," https://www.osha.gov/pls/oshaweb /owadisp.show_document?p_id=9786&p _table=standards. Accessed July 20, 2013.

———. "Toxic Industrial Chemicals (TICs)," http:// www.osha.gov/SLTC/emergencypreparedness /guides/chemical.html. Accessed January 29.2013.

———. "Occupational Exposure to Bloodborne Pathogens," https://www.osha.gov/pls/oshaweb /owadisp.show_document?p_id=811&p _table=PREAMBLES. Accessed November 15, 2013.

———. "Personal Protective Equipment for the Hands (Gloves)," http://www.osha.gov/dte/grant _materials/fy07/sh-16615-07/ppe_for_hands _handout.pdf. Accessed May 19, 2013.

———. "General Description and Discussion of the Levels of Protection and Protective Gear," http:// www.osha.gov/pls/oshaweb/owadisp.show _document?p_table=STANDARDS&p_id=9767. Accessed February 5, 2013.

Onofrei, A., and A. Catarino. 2011. "The Influence of Knitted Fabrics' Structure on Thermal and Moisture Management Properties." *Journal of Engineered Fibers and Fabrics* 6(4): 10–22.

Osborn, A. 1957. *Applied Imagination.* New York: Charles Scribner.

Pensotti, L., J. Berube, B. Bucher, B. Dart, P. Dunfey, and M. Turieo. 1997. "Designing the Air Warrior (AW) System for Optimized Human Performance." In *SAFE "97 Proceedings of the 35th Annual SAFE Symposium.* Phoenix, AZ: SAFE Association.

Picard, R. W. (2003), "Affective Computing: Challenges," *International Journal of Human-Computer Studies* 59 (1): 55-64.

Pretorius, T., G. K. Bristow, A. M. Steinman, and G. G. Geisbrecht. 2006. "Thermal Effects of Whole Head Submersion in Cold Water on Nonshivering Humans." *Journal of Applied Physiology*, 101(2): 669–75.

Price, A., A. Cohen, and I. Johnson. 2003. *Fabric Science*, 7th ed. New York: Fairchild Publications.

Radnofsky, M. 1967. "Space Suits." *International Science and Technology* February: 32–39.

Raheel, M. 1994. *Protective Clothing Systems and Materials.* New York: Marcel Dekker.

Rantanen, J., N. Alfthan, J. Impio, T. Karinsalo, M. Malmivaara, R. Matala, M. Makinen . . . and J. Vanhala. 2000. "Smart Clothing for the Arctic Environment." In *ISWC "00 Proceedings of the Fourth International Symposium on Wearable Computers.* 15–23. Washington, DC: IEEE Computer Society.

Raudsepp, E. 1983. "Profile of Creative Individual, Part 1." *Creative Computing* 9(8), August, 170–79.

Renbourn, E. 1971. *Physiology and Hygiene of Materials and Clothing.* Watford Herts, England: Merrow.

Renbourn, E., and W. Rees. 1972. *Materials and Clothing in Health and Disease.* London: H. K. Lewis and Co.

Research Study Group 7 on Bio-Medical Research Aspects of Military Protective Clothing. n.d., circa 1987. *Handbook on Clothing.* Natick, MA: U.S. Army Research Institute of Environmental Medicine.

Rhinehart, D. "Finger Portion for a Glove." U.S. Patent 4,654,896, filed February 27, 1985 and issued April 7, 1987.

Riddle, D., J. Rothstein, and R. Lamb. 1987. "Goniometric Reliability in a Clinical Setting: Shoulder Measurements." *Physical Therapy* 67: 668–73.

Rodriguez, F., C. Cohen, C. Ober, and L. Archer. 2003. *Principles of Polymer Systems*, 5th ed. New York: Taylor and Francis.

Roebuck, J. 1968. "A System of Notation and Measurement for Space Suit Mobility Evaluation." *Human Factors* 10(1): 79.

Rustad, S. 1984. "Cold Climate Field Heating—Final Report," FFI/Rapport-84/4006. Kjeller (Norway): Norwegian Defence Research Establishment.

Sakaomoto Model Corporation. "Hemiplegia Simulation Suit," http://sakamoto-model.co.jp /english/pdf/pdf/sakamoto-model_p29.pdf#zoom =100. Accessed September 28, 2013.

Sayer, J., and M. Mefford. 2004. "High Visibility Safety Apparel and Nighttime Conspicuity of Pedestrians In Work Zones." *Journal of Safety Research* 35: 537–46.

Schon, D. 1983. *The Reflective Practitioner*. New York: Basic Books.

Schwope, A., P. Costas, J. Jackson, and D. Weitzman. 1983. *Guidelines for the Selection of Chemical Protective Clothing*. Cincinnati: American Conference of Governmental Industrial Hygienists, Inc.

Scribano, F., M. Burns, and E. Barron. 1970. "Design Development and Fabrication of Personnel Armor Load Profile Analyzer," Technical Report 70-65-CE. Natick, MA: U.S. Army Natick Laboratories.

Secrist, G., S. Watkins, and D. Toedt. 1987. Groundcrew Individual Protective Equipment (IPE): A Human Factors Assessment. Unpublished report. San Antonio, TX: US Air Force School of Aerospace Medicine, Brooks Air Force Base.

Sells, S., and C. Berry, eds. 1961. *Human Factors in Jet and Space Travel*. New York: Ronald Press.

Shaltis, P.A., A. T. Reisner, and H. H. Asada. 2008. "Cuffless Blood Pressure Monitoring Using Hydrostatic Pressure Changes." *IEEE Transactions on Bio-Medical Engineering* 55(6): 1775–77.

Sim U Suit.Com. "Simulate Obese and Bariatric Patients with Your Manikins." http://www .simusuit.com/manikin-obesity-suits.html. Accessed September 28, 2013.

Smith, M., and E. Dye. 1954. "Evaluation of Ensolite® as a Protective Padding Material and the Development of an Improved Instrument Container," Report YB-853-D-1. Buffalo, NY: Cornell Aeronautical Laboratory.

Sokolowski, S. 1996. "Aircrew Arm Coverage Designs for the Prevention of Arm Pain in High Performance Tactical Flight Based on Pressure, Arm Mobility, Hand Dexterity, Grip Strength and Comfort Analysis." Master's thesis, Cornell University, Ithaca, NY.

Standing Committee on Program and Technical Review of the U.S. Army Chemical and Biological Defense Command, National Research Council. 1997. "Technical Assessment of the Man-In-Simulant Test (MIST) Program." Washington, DC: National Academy Press.

Stephenson, L., and M. Kolka. 1993. "Thermoregulation in Women." *Exercise and Sports Science Review* 21: 231–62.

Stoll, A., and M. Chianta. 1969. "Method and Rating System for Evaluation of Thermal Protection." *Aerospace Medicine* 40:1234.

Susich, G., M. Dogliotti, and A. Wrigley. 1958. "Microscopical Study of a Multilayer Nylon Body Armor Panel after Impact." *Textile Research Journal* 28(5): 361–77.

Symington, L. 1986. "Combat Encapsulation: Human Factors in Advanced Integrated Life Support Systems," Technical Report Natick/TR/86/050. Natick, MA: Natick Research, Development and Engineering Center.

3M™ Occupational Health and Environmental Safety Division. 2012. "3M™ Scotchlite™ Reflective Material Product and Brand Usage Standards." St. Paul, MN: 3M.

———. 2010. "ANSI/ISEA 107-2010 Made Easy." St. Paul, MN: 3M.

———. "3M™ Dual Lock™ Reclosable Fastener," http://www.3m.com/product/information/Dual-Lock-Reclosable-Fastener.html. Accessed January 8, 2014.

Teitlebaum, A., and R. Goldman. 1972. "Increased Energy Cost with Multiple Clothing Layers." *Journal of Applied Physiology* 32(6): 743.

Todd. W. 1991. "Development of a Method for Kinematic Analysis of the Doffing Process for a Specific Garment Style." Master's thesis, Virginia Polytechnic Institute and State University, Blacksburg, VA.

Tortora, P., ed. 2010. *Berg Encyclopedia of World Dress and Fashion*. New York: Berg Publishers.

Trelleborg Protective Products. "Viking Bayonet Glove System Manual," http://protective.ansell.com/Global/Protective-Products/Viking/Manuals/Manual%20Viking%20Bayonet%20Glove%20System_080530.pdf. Accessed August 9, 2013.

U.S. Army SBCCOM (Soldier and Biological Chemical Command). "Adaptable Skin," http://www.natick.army.mil/about/pao/pubs/warrior/02/mayjune/smartskin.htm. Accessed September 26, 2012.

U.S. Coast Guard. "PDF Selection, Use, Wear and Care," http://www.uscg.mil/hq/cg5/cg5214/pfdselection.asp#faq. Accessed April 15, 2013.

U.S. Environmental Protection Agency. "Radiation Doses in Perspective," http://www.epa.gov/radiation/understand/perspective.html. Accessed May 19, 2013.

USNRC (U.S. Nuclear Regulatory Commission). "Doses in Our Daily Lives," http://www.nrc.gov/about-nrc/radiation/around-us/doses-daily-lives.html. Accessed July 19, 2013.

———. "Occupational Dose Limits," http://www.nrc.gov/reading-rm/doc-collections/cfr/part020/part020-1201.html. Accessed July 19, 2013.

———. "Dose Equivalent to an Embryo/Fetus," http://www.nrc.gov/reading-rm/doc-collections/cfr/part020/part020-1208.html. Accessed July 19, 2013.

U.S. Senate Committee on Commerce, Science, and Transportation. 1979. *Microwave Irradiation of the U.S. Embassy in Moscow*. Washington, DC: U.S. Government Printing Office.

Vander, A., J. Sherman, and D. Luciano. 1998. *Human Physiology*, 7th ed. Boston: McGraw-Hill.

Veblen, T. 1899. *The Theory of the Leisure Class: An Economic Study of Institutions*. New York: The Macmillan Company.

Veghte, J. H. 1962. "Human Physiological Response to Extremity and Body Cooling." *Aerospace Medicine* 33: 1081–85.

Vigo, T., and J. Bruno. 1989. "Improvement of Various Properties of Fiber Surfaces Containing Crosslinked Polyethylene Glycols." *Journal of Applied Polymer Science* 37: 371–79.

Vigotti, M., V. Muggeo, and R. Cusimano. 2006. "The Effect of Birthplace on Heat Tolerance and Mortality in Milan, Italy, 1980–1989." *International Journal of Biometerology* 50: 335–41.

Wagner, J., and S. Horvath. 1985a. "Cardiovascular Reactions to Cold Exposures Differ with Age and Gender." *Journal of Applied Physiology* 58(1): 187–92.

———. 1985b. "Influences of Age and Gender on Human Thermoregulatory Responses to Cold Exposures." *Journal of Applied Physiology* 58(1): 180–86.

Wang, L. 1986. "Winter Safety: How to Keep Warm Physiologically." In *Winter Cities Forum '86*. Edmonton: University of Alberta.

Watkins, S. 1986. "Electrically Heated Clothing: Is Plugging in the Wave of the Future?" *Livable Winter Newsletter* 4(4). Toronto: Livable Winter City Association.

———. 1995. *Clothing: the Portable Environment*. Ames: The Iowa State University Press.

Watkins, S., M. Valla, and L. Rosen. 1978. "The Development of Two Protective Apparel Systems for Firefighting" (unpublished report). Washington, DC: National Fire Prevention and Control Administration, U.S. Department of Commerce.

Westex, Inc. "FR Fabric Technology," http://www.westex.com/fr-fabric-technology.html. Accessed April 15, 2013.

Whyte, W. 2010. *Cleanroom Technology: Fundamentals of Design, Testing and Operation.* Chichester, UK: John Wiley and Sons.

Young, A. 2009. *Space Suits.* Brooklyn, NY: powerHouse books.

Zernike, K. 2004. "Sizing up America: Signs of Expansion from Head to Toe." *The New York Times*, March 1, http://www.nytimes.com/2004/03/01/us/sizing-up-america-signs-of-expansion-from-head-to-toe.html. Accessed April 15, 2013.

INDEX